HELLENIZATION REVISITED

HELLENIZATION REVISITED

Shaping a Christian Response within the Greco-Roman World

Edited by
Wendy E. Helleman

UNIVERSITY
PRESS OF
AMERICA

Lanham • New York • London

Library of Congress Cataloging-in-Publication Data

Hellenization revisited : shaping a Christian response within the
Greco-Roman world / Wendy E. Helleman, editor.
p.   cm.
Proceedings of a conference held in summer 1991 in Toronto, Ont.,
sponsored by the Institute for Christian Studies.
Includes bibliographical references and index.
1. Gnosticism—Congresses.   2. Christianity—Early church, ca.
30–600—Congresses.   3. Judaism—History—Post-exilic period,
586 B.C.–210 A.D.—Congresses.   4. Christianity and other
religions—Greek—Congresses.   5. Christianity and culture—
Congresses.   I. Helleman, Wendy E., 1945–   .   II. Institute for
Christian Studies.
BT1390.H45   1994   273'.1—dc20   94–22988 CIP

ISBN 0–8191–9543–X (cloth : alk. paper)
ISBN 0–8191–9544–8 (pbk. : alk. paper)

 The paper used in this publication meets the minimum requirements of
American National Standard for Information Sciences—Permanence
of Paper for Printed Library Materials, ANSI Z39.48–1984.

Historical enquiry . . . sees in Gnosticism a series of undertakings, which in a certain way is analogous to the Catholic embodiment of Christianity, in doctrine, morals, and worship. The great distinction here consists essentially in the fact that the Gnostic systems represent the acute secularising or hellenising of Christianity, with rejection of the Old Testament; while the Catholic system, on the other hand, represents a gradual process of the same kind with the conservation of the Old Testament.

A. von Harnack, *The History of Dogma*, I, IV.2

. . . Put on the new self, which is being renewed in knowledge in the image of its Creator. Here there is no Greek or Jew, circumcised or uncircumcised, barbarian, Scythian, slave or free, but Christ is all, and is in all.

Colossians 3:10-11

Contents

Contributors
Abbreviations
Preface

Gnosticism, Judaism and Hellenization: Basic Positions 1
Cosmic and Meta-Cosmic Theology in Greek Philosophy 1
    and Gnosticism, *Abraham P. Bos*
Aristotle and the Jewish God (Response to A. P. Bos), 23
    William E. Arnal
Gnosticism and Early Christianity, *Edwin M. Yamauchi* 29
Yamauchi and Pre-Christian Gnosticism (Response to E. 63
    M. Yamauchi), *Michel Desjardins*
Adolf von Harnack and the Concept of Hellenization, 69
    William V. Rowe
Alexandria or Athens as the Essence of Hellenization: A 99
    Historian Responds to a Philosopher, *Barry W. Henaut*

Hellenistic Judaism 107
Creatio ex nihilo in Philo, *Albert M. Wolters* 107
Mastery of the Passions: Philo, 4 Maccabees and Earliest 125
    Christianity, *David C. Aune*
The Voice of the Serpent: Philo's Epicureanism, *A. Peter* 159
    Booth
The Plight of Woman: Philo's Blind Spot? *Dorothy Sly* 173
The "Praeparatio Evangelica" and "Spoliatio" Motifs as 189
    Patterns of Hellenistic Judaism in Philo of Alexandria,
    Daniel N. Jastram
Muddying the Water: Metaphors for Exegesis, *John H.* 205
    Corbett

Contents

Gnosticism   223

Harnack, Marcion and the Argument of Antiquity, *Daniel H. Williams*   223

The *Acts of John*: The Gnostic Transformation of a Christian Community, *Paul G. Schneider*   241

Trimorphic Protennoia and the Wisdom Tradition, *Rosemary Halford*   271

Gnosis, Theology and Historical Method, *Schuyler Brown*   279

Gnosticism and the Classical Tradition, *Scott C. Carroll*   293

Judaism and Gnosticism, *Michel Desjardins*   309

The Patristic Response   323

Nomos Empsychos in Philo and Clement of Alexandria, *John Martens*   323

Gnosticism as Heresy: The Response of Irenaeus, *Terrance Tiessen*   339

Tertullian on Athens and Jerusalem, *Wendy E. Helleman*   361

"Spoils from Egypt," Between Jews and Gnostics, *Lawrence E. Frizzell*   383

Clement of Alexandria: Instructions on How Women Should Live, *M. Eleanor Irwin*   395

Symbol and Science in Early Christian *Gnosis*, *Padraig O'Cleirigh*   409

Epilogue, *Wendy E. Helleman*   429

Bibliography   513

Index   529

Contributors

William Arnal—Centre for the Study of Religion, University of Toronto

David C. Aune—Department of Religious Studies, Brown University, Rhode Island

A. Peter Booth—Department of Classics, Acadia University, Wolfville, Nova Scotia

Abraham P. Bos—Professor of Ancient and Patristic Philosophy, Centrale Interfaculteit (Philosophy Department), Vrije Universiteit, Amsterdam; recently completed a major study on which his present contribution is based, *Cosmic and Meta-Cosmic Theology in Aristotle's Lost Dialogues* (Leiden: Brill, 1989)

Schuyler Brown—Professor of Theology at the University of St. Michael's College and the Centre for Religious Studies, University of Toronto; author of *The Origins of Christianity: A Historical Introduction to the New Testament* (Oxford University Press, 1984)

Scott T. Carroll—Department of History, Gordon College, Massachusetts

John Corbett—Division of Humanities/Classics, Scarborough Campus of the University of Toronto

Michel Desjardins—Department of Religious Studies, Wilfrid Laurier University, Waterloo, Ontario; author of *Sin in Valentinianism* (Atlanta: Scholars, 1990)

Rosemary Halford—Department of Religious Studies, University of Windsor, Ontario

Wendy E. Helleman—Division of Humanities/Classics at the Scarborough Campus, University of Toronto

Barry Henaut—Department of Religious Studies, University of Ottawa, Ontario

Lawrence Frizzell—Associate Director of the Institute of Judaeo-Christian Studies, Seton Hall University, New Jersey

Daniel N. Jastram—Division of Religion, Concordia College, St. Paul, Minnesota

John Martens—Department of Religious Studies, University of Winnipeg, Manitoba

M. Eleanor Irwin—Division of Humanities/ Classics at the Scarborough Campus, University of Toronto

Padraig O'Cleirigh—Department of Languages and Literature, University of Guelph, Ontario

William Rowe—Department of Philosophy, University of Scranton, Pennsylvania

Dorothy I. Sly—Department of Religious Studies, University of Windsor, Ontario

Paul G. Schneider—Clearwater, Florida; author of *The Mystery of the Acts of John* (Lewiston: Mellen, 1991)

Terrance L. Tiessen—Professor of Theological and Biblical Studies, Providence College and Seminary, Winnipeg, Manitoba

Daniel H. Williams—Department of Religious Studies, University of Pittsburgh

Albert Wolters—Department of Religion and Theology, Redeemer College, Ancaster, Ontario

Edwin M. Yamauchi—Professor of History, Miami University, Ohio; author of *Pre-Christian Gnosticism* (Grand Rapids: Baker, 1983)

Abbreviations

AH	Irenaeus, *Against the Heresies/ Adversus Haereses*
AJn	*The Acts of John*
ANCL	*Ante-Nicene Christian Library*, A. Roberts, J. Donaldson, eds. (Edinburgh: T. T. Clark, 1885; repr. Grand Rapids, Mich.: Wm. B. Eerdmans, 1956)
ANRW	*Aufstieg und Niedergang der römischen Welt* (Berlin: Walter de Gruyter)
Ap.John	*The Apocryphon on John*
CSEL	*Corpus Scriptorum Christianorum Ecclesiasticorum Latinorum* (Turnhout: Brepols)
CW	*The Collected Works of C.G.Jung*, 20 vols., H. Read et al., eds. (London: Routledge and K. Paul: 1957 -)
Gos.Eg.	*The Gospel of the Egyptians*
Gos.Phil.	*The Gospel of Philip*
HTR	*Harvard Theological Review*
JPS	Jewish Publication Society
JSOT	*Journal for the Study of the Old Testament*
NHC	Nag Hammadi Codex
NHL	*The Nag Hammadi Library in English*, J. Robinson, ed. (San Francisco: Harper)
LCL	Loeb Classical Library
LD	*Lehrbuch des Dogmengeschichte*, A. von Harnack, 3rd ed. (Tübingen: J.C.B. Mohr, 1894)
LSJ	*Greek-English Dictionary*, H.G. Liddell, R. Scott, H.S. Jones (Oxford: Clarendon 1945/9th ed.)
OTP	*Old Testament Pseudepigrapha*, 2 vols., J.H.Charlesworth, ed., (Garden City, NY: Doubleday, 1985)
PCG	*Pre-Christian Gnosticism*, E. Yamauchi (Grand Rapids: Baker, 1983)

PG	*Patrologia Graeca* (J.P.Migne, ed.)
RGG	*Die Religion in Geschichte und Gegenwart*, C. Colpe, 1961.
Stob.	Stobaeus, *Eclogae* (or *Florilegium*)
SVF	*Stoicorum Veterum Fragmenta*, 4 vols., L.von Arnim, ed. (Leipzig, 1903-5, 1924)
Trim.Prot.	*The Trimorphic Protennoia*
TU	Texte und Untersuchungen
TWNT	*Theologisches Wörterbuch zum Neuen Testament*, G. Kittel (Stuttgart: W. Kohlhammer, 1933)
Zost.	*Zostrianos*

Preface

Although contemporary study of Gnosticism and early Christianity acknowledges the continuing role of Judaism, Adolf von
Harnack's characterization of Gnosticism as the "acute Hellenization of Christianity" effectively captured the approach of an entire
generation of scholars at the beginning of this century. The interaction of classical Greco-Roman culture with early Christianity is even
today typically examined in terms of the question of "Hellenization."
Harnack's authoritative formulation of the problem had an enormous impact, and must receive much of the credit for the pervasive
view of Hellenic thought as a contaminant, a negative influence on
early Christianity. This approach has provided the impetus for the
present re-examination of early Christianity in its Greco-Roman
environment.

The essays presented in this collection were originally prepared
for a conference sponsored by the Institute for Christian Studies,
held in Toronto in the summer of 1991. This conference had a
predecessor, the "Christianity and the Classics" conference held at
the same place in 1984, which resulted in a book with the same title.[1]
That conference examined the history of interaction of Christianity
with the classical tradition in Western civilization as one of synthesis,
or accommodation and adaptation, and focused on the motifs by
which Christians justified their use of literature and culture of pagan
classical origin. It concluded that these could be classified according
to the patterns presented in H. R. Niebuhr's *Christ and Culture*.[2]

The 1991 conference built on that earlier discussion by exploring
further two of these motifs of interaction, those of *praeparatio
evangelica* and of *spoliatio*. In examining these motifs the significant
impact of both Judaism and Gnosticism in the early centuries of
Christianity was recognized. The title of the present collection

acknowledges the importance of Harnack's characterization of Gnosticism for contemporary study of this period.

Before giving a brief survey of the papers which make up this collection, it is useful to introduce definitions of terms crucial to understanding these papers. The presentation of definitions cannot be straightforward, however, particularly with a term like "Gnosticism," because the attempt to arrive at an acceptable definition is itself a significant issue in scholarly work on Gnosticism. The definition agreed to at the 1966 international conference on Gnosticism in Messina is notably neglected in subsequent scholarly work. Contemporary study of Judaism likewise emphasizes the diversity of religious branches represented by that term, and it is accordingly more comfortable in speaking of Judaisms. The authors represented in this volume, too, are by no means unanimous in their approach to the questions, and numerous papers reflect on the matter of definition; the epilogue attempts to bring together the various approaches and come to some conclusions.

Definition of the key term "Hellenization" is a matter of concern in a number of essays. It is discussed most thoroughly in the paper of William Rowe, and picked up again in the response of B. Henaut.[3] The epilogue also explores its meaning, whether as historical process or culturally significant concept.[4] Both Rowe and Henaut have recognized the unacceptability of Harnack's use of "Hellenization" to explain the universality of early Christianity, in contrast to Judaism as a more exclusive system.[5] The question of the relative exclusivity or universality of Judaic and Greek Hellenistic culture receives further treatment in the epilogue.[6] Fundamental characteristics of Judaism of the Hellenistic period are also discussed by Desjardins.[7]

The definition of Gnosticism presents a more complex challenge. A. P. Bos introduces his lead paper with a definition of *gnōsis* as knowledge of one's origin. In his discussion of positions of A. H. Armstrong and R. McL. Wilson, Bos elaborates by accenting the *supernatural* character of such knowledge of one's origin as it coincides with the transcendent origin of all reality.[8] The distinction between matter and transcendent immaterial being which is basic to such knowledge, Bos argues, is a distinction resulting from a process of *abstraction*, a philosophical tool which characterizes neither the Jewish nor Christian tradition as such.

Accenting the revelatory nature of *gnōsis* and its practical, soteriological concerns, W. Arnal in the response to Bos focuses on Gnosticism as a religious movement.[9] With the definition which introduces his paper, E. Yamauchi also describes Gnosticism as a religious movement seeking salvation. He would, however, agree with Bos that *gnsis* refers to knowledge of origins, and likewise accents the significance of cosmological dualism, the opposition of spiritual and material reality which in fully developed Gnosticism also affects anthropology and soteriology.[10] In his response to Yamauchi, M. Desjardins in turn accents Gnosticism as a religious movement independently worthy of attention, not just as a heretical offshoot of Christianity.[11]

A different approach characterizes the paper of S. Brown; working from a Jungian psychologizing perspective, he defines *gnōsis* as introverted religious knowledge based on the inner confidence deriving from a transformative experience like that of Paul on the Damascus road.[12] Because such knowledge is better expressed in myth and symbol, Brown is able to appreciate the poetic language of recently discovered Gnostic documents. The epilogue provides a final summarizing discussion on the association of Gnosticism with both Greek philosophy and Judaism.[13]

The papers in the introductory section of this volume present basic positions on Greek philosophy, Gnosticism and Harnack's analysis of early Christianity; the three major papers, each with a respondent, represent keynote addresses opening the discussions of the three days of the conference. From his study of the fragments of Aristotle, A. P. Bos argues that with themes like the double theology of an unknown God and the creator/demiurge, the depreciation of *logos*, and cosmo-psychology, Gnostic thought developed philosophical positions deriving from the school of Aristotle. W. Arnal, in his response, does not deny a possible (indirect) influence from Aristotle, but accents the non-philosophical, soteriological concerns of the Gnostics, and argues for a (syncretistic) Jewish background even for themes like the double theology. Taking issue with W. Bauer and the school of thought influenced by Bultmann, E. Yamauchi updates earlier arguments for the inadequacy of evidence in support of Gnosticism as a well-articulated cosmological, anthropological and soteriological dualism of the pre-Christian period. In the response Desjardins affirms the inadequacy of arguments for early Gnosticism, but parts company with Yamauchi in his desire to protect the "purity" of early Christianity.

W. Rowe's paper on Harnack argues the importance of his concept of Hellenization as the key to the history of dogma, defined as the spirit of Greek philosophy in Christianity. As a historian, Henaut also takes exception to the definition of Hellenization in terms of dogmatic, philosophical theology, particularly because it leads to further misinterpretation of Judaism and early Christianity.

Papers of the second major section explore various aspects of Judaism of the Hellenistic period, with attention focused on the influence of Greek thought on writers like Philo. With his study of Philo's account of the creation, A. Wolters concludes that use of Plato's *Timaeus* in the attempt to allegorize the Genesis passage leads to an illegitimate synthesis of two inherently incompatible ways of thinking. In his analysis of *apatheia*, as mastery of the passions through reason rightly guided by Torah, D. Aune illustrates the extensive influence of Greek philosophy on Philo and the author of 4 Maccabees. According to P. Booth, Philo is influenced by the Platonists even in his caricature of Epicureanism as the seductive voice of the serpent, the voice of pleasure, the most dangerous of the passions and arch-enemy of virtue. In her study of Philo's use of gender-distinctions D. Sly demonstrates the implications of such an understanding of the passions for his portrayal of women; association of the feminine with passion and sense as the weaker aspects of the soul, led him to accept the subordination of women to the control of the male, associated with reason as the dominant aspect.

D. Jastram takes a different approach when he demonstrates that Philo recognized inadequacies in both Hellenistic culture and Judaism, and thus argued for a new cosmopolitan ideal as the goal of an education in the *encyclia* which would allow a new humanity to transcend the limitations of either one. With the final paper in this section J. Corbett explores water symbolism for the exegetical process; recognizing that documents like the Thanksgiving hymn from Qumran show appreciation for the muddy waters of irrigation he provides a context for the elitism of Philo's appeal to the pure cold mountain stream of reason in preference to the muddied irrationality of popular thought.

The third major section focuses on Gnosticism. Papers in this section use a variety of approaches to the question of the relationship between Gnosticism and Hellenistic thought, whether through Judaism or some other tradition. Recognizing Harnack's appreciation of the purist in Marcion and his edited version of the scriptures, D. Williams argues that the *praeparatio evangelica* argument for continued use of the Old Testament as an authoritative document served Christians as an apologetic in response to the charge of novelty. In his analysis of the *Acts of John*, P. Schneider provides support for Harnack's view of gnosticism as the "acute Hellenization of Christianity," showing that interpretation of the faith in terms of immutability prepared the way for the more clearly gnosticizing portrayal of Christ which characterizes a later interpolation. R. Halford also looks at stratigraphy of the *Trimorphic Protennoia* to argue that beyond the Christianized veneer one can penetrate to the sapiential kernel, presenting Protennoia as a redeemer figure on the model of Sophia in Judaic wisdom literature. In his discussion of *gnōsis* as introverted religious knowledge based on illumination, S. Brown focuses on a positive understanding of the language of imagination characteristic of Gnostic documents, not to supplant philosophical or historical investigation but to balance the conceptual or rational expression of faith.

S. Carroll takes a different approach to the issue of Gnosticism and Platonism to repudiate the nineteenth century view of Gnostics as philosophers; analysis of Plotinus's references to Gnostics leads him to conclude that Gnostic appeal to Plato represented a ploy to gain respectability, not a serious involvement in the philosophic debates of the time. And finally in this section M. Desjardins summarizes contemporary discussion of the Judaic origin for Gnosticism, indicating his own preference for a view which allows for the simultaneous development of Gnosticism and Christianity and a three-way struggle between Jews, Gnostics and Christians.

In the fourth major section papers approach the question of interaction from the work of patristic writers like Clement and Tertullian and explore the role of the motifs in their writing. With his comparison of the *nomos empsychos* theme in Philo and Clement, J. Martens recognizes that particularly in debates with Gnostics, Clement balanced use of Philo's presentation of Moses with use of Hellenistic Pythagorean treatises to depict Christ as a "living law" and fulfilment of the written law of Moses. In his discussion of Irenaeus's response to the Gnostics, T. Tiessen approaches use of the *praeparatio evangelica* theme from a different angle when he demonstrates the importance of arguments from creation and providence against Gnostics who denied the goodness of the creator. In her examination of the oppositionist interpretation of Tertullian's disjunction of Athens and Jerusalem in the *De Praescriptionibus*, W. Helleman shows how Fredouille's analysis of "transformation" in the thought of Tertullian vindicates the approach of Harnack, yet misses the significant role of the "rule of faith" for his repudiation of heretical interpretation of scripture.

L. Frizzell explores another motif of interaction, that of *spoliatio*, comparing Gnostic and anti-Gnostic use of the basic Exodus account, and recognizing the significance of Origen's allegorical interpretation for the paradigm of judicious appropriation of non-Christian cultural goods in the service of faith. In her study of Clement's practical instructions for Christian women, Irwin illustrates how Clement implemented the theme of *praeparatio evangelica*, for he agreed with Platonists and Pythagoreans that women, like men, were capable of virtue and philosophy, yet did not approve of a complete levelling of lifestyles, rejecting the negative expectations of misogynists as well as heroic roles of ascetic and martyr for women, in an effort to protect the dignity of Christian women. And finally, P. O'Cleirigh indicates that where Gnostics typically appreciated knowledge based on illumination and expressed in symbolic language, orthodox gnostics like Origen had a more positive appreciation for rational argument together with an appreciation of the material world as a good creation; accordingly, he questions Harnack's use of one term, "Hellenization," acute or gradual, to designate the very different approaches characterizing Gnostics like Valentinus or Catholic Christians like Clement and Origen.

Papers in the major sections, thus, are grouped according to the issues raised; they nonetheless demonstrate a variety of approaches to the questions and divergence in conclusions. In the epilogue an attempt has been made to bring together a number of themes occurring repeatedly throughout the collection. The epilogue begins by reflecting on Harnack's role in formulating the issues for this century, examining in turn his understanding of "Hellenization," his philosophical and theological characterization of Gnosticism, and his exclusion of Judaism as a factor in the form of Hellenization which influenced early Christianity. Returning to basic questions of religion and culture and the motifs of interaction, the next section of the epilogue examines implications of a pluralist approach assumed in many contemporary studies on Judaism and Hellenization, and on Gnosticism as a religious phenomenon. The epilogue concludes with an appreciation of Harnack's assumption regarding the religious root of culture, and also regarding the dialectical character of the interaction of religion and contemporary cultural patterns, but appeals for redress on Harnack's repudiation of dogmatic and theological formulations as an important factor in the process of Christian self-definition.

In preparing these papers for publication we have kept in mind the needs of a general, yet educated audience, people who have an interest in early Christianity as influenced by Gnosticism and Judaism, and as it has been studied in this century, yet are not specialists in this field. This has determined both the restricted use of original languages and bibliographical references. The book is thus not in the first placed intended for scholars of this period, though it is hoped that it will make a contribution of its own also for the scholarly world.

As editor I wish to thank all those who helped to organize the 1991 conference, prepared papers for it, and offered their work for the present publication. A special word of thanks must go to Michel Desjardins, William Rowe and Albert Wolters who gave generously of their time in the planning and preparation of this conference. William Rowe prepared the summary statements for the final round table session of the conference, and thus provided the groundwork for what now appears as the epilogue. And Michel Desjardins provided invaluable help in the critical reading and editing of the papers. We are sincerely grateful for his supportive role in this project. Our thanks must also go to Robert VanderVennen of the Institute for Christian Studies for his patient reworking of a set of papers which presented numerous unexpected challenges, and to Willem Hart for his competent assistance in the preparation of the manuscript for publication.

Notes

1. W. E. Helleman, ed., *Christianity and the Classics: The Acceptance of a Heritage* (Lanham MD: University Press of America, 1990).
2. H. R. Niebuhr, *Christ and Culture* (New York: Harper and Row, 1951)
3. W. Rowe, "Adolf von Harnack," in this volume, passim, and particularly 70-72; B. Henaut, "Alexandria or Athens," in this volume, 99-100.
4. The "Epilogue" in this volume, 430, 432-37, 442-54.
5. W. Rowe, op. cit., 72-74; B. Henaut, op. cit., 101-102.
6. In the "Epilogue," 442-47.
7. M. Desjardins, "Judaism" in this volume, 310. On the distinctive characteristics of Judaism see also the "Epilogue," 443, particularly note 62.

8. A. P. Bos, "Cosmic and Meta-Cosmic Theology," in this volume, 5-6; see particularly his note 31, in which he also presents other well-known definitions like that of the 1966 Messina conference.

9. W. Arnal, "Aristotle," in this volume, 24-26.

10. See especially note 5 of E. Yamauchi, "Gnosticism," in this volume, 48, where he develops his own definition in distinguishing it from those of K. Rudolph and H.-M. Schenke.

11. M. Desjardins, "Yamauchi," in this volume, 65-66; cf. his "Judaism," also in this volume, 312-15.

12. S. Brown, "*Gnosis*," in this volume, 279-80.

13. The "Epilogue" in this volume, 437ff.

Cosmic and Meta-cosmic Theology in Greek Philosophy and Gnosticism

Abraham P. Bos

Introduction

"All human beings by nature aspire to knowledge." With this statement Aristotle opens the *Metaphysics*.[1] But the path from ignorance
to knowledge most broadly conceived proceeds by way of an understanding of human nature itself.[2] And this, in turn, leads to the
insight that the ultimate knowledge to which human beings aspire
transcends human nature.[3] For such knowledge will be of highest
value and most divine, since it will involve knowledge concerning
God, but will also be that knowledge which God himself possesses.[4]

For Gnostics of the Hellenistic world the desire for this
knowledge, which they called *gnōsis*, permeated their entire existence. This *gnōsis* is first of all knowledge concerning one's own origin
and root; but it is also knowledge about the origin and root of all
things in the world of our experience. The historian of culture who
wishes to understand Hellenistic Gnosticism will not be satisfied
with a superficial description of the data which have been handed

down from the past, but must penetrate to a knowledge of the roots, the *Sitz im Leben*, or rather the *Sitz in der Geschichte* of that intriguing phenomenon.

Now the older theory (1) that Gnosticism represents a corruption of Christianity has long been criticized. But the alternative theory (2) that it was a wild offshoot of Greek philosophy has also received considerable attack during the past few decades. The view which is most generally supported at present, that of G. Quispel and R. M. Grant, is (3) that Gnosticism is a movement which was rooted in and inspired by the Jewish tradition. Now scholars can seldom transcend the limitations of their own orientation, and this is particularly true in the study of a phenomenon such as Gnosticism, for which a multiplicity of disciplines each provide their own contribution. Nonetheless, as a historian of philosophy, my aim in this paper will be to shed new light on Greek philosophy in order to make a reasonable case for the thesis that the ties between Gnosticism and Greek philosophy go deeper than any other.

A. J. Festugière on Greek Philosophy and Gnosticism

The relationship between Gnosticism and Greek philosophy has been discussed extensively by A. J. Festugière in his research on the Hermetic Corpus, published as the famous four-volume work *La révélation d'Hermès Trismégiste*.[5] This work presents the rise of the gnostic movement as a reaction to developments in Greek philosophy after its high point in the fourth century BCE. For Festugière the Hellenistic period is characterized by a "decline of rationalism" and stagnation in scholarly activities.[6]

After a general introduction to the entire work and discussion of the Hermetic literature which is characterized by magic and the occult (in volume I), Festugière devotes volumes II and III to an exposition of what he calls *l'hermétisme philosophique*.[7] Indeed, he does not believe that we should regard the Hermetic treatises as genuine "philosophy." Rather, they should be regarded as expressions of the religious conceptions of the Greco-Roman period.[8] But in these Hellenistic religious conceptions Festugière recognizes two contrasting tendencies, which he also observes in the Hermetic treatises. He explains these by tracing them back to two lines of thought in the work of Plato. These are (1) an optimistic line, in which the world is presented as beautiful and well-ordered, and (2) a pessimistic one, in which the world is described as evil, a place of corruption and chaos.[9] According to Festugière, the same two tendencies can be recognized in various treatises of the Hermetic Corpus, although he is aware that some intermingling of the two has also occurred.[10] But Festugière regards Plato as the common source of these two lines of thought and the father of Hellenistic religious philosophy.[11]

Thus although for Festugière these two tendencies are innately irreconcilable, he does look to one Greek thinker for the origin of both. The apparent conflict is resolved by assuming a *development* in Plato's thought, in which the dualistic, pessimistic view represents the earlier and older conception, but the positive, optimistic view derives from his final writings, notably the *Timaeus* and the *Laws*.[12]

In volumes II to IV Festugière discusses the historical development of *la philosophie religieuse* from Plato to Hermeticism. Proceeding from Plato's *Timaeus* and the *Laws*, he in turn discusses Aristotle's *De philosophia*, the Stoa, Cicero, the treatise *De mundo*, and Philo of Alexandria. In all the given stages of the positive and optimistic tradition, Festugière recognizes a "cosmic religion" (hence the title given to volume II: *Le dieu cosmique*). This cosmic religion is a "religion of the cosmic God."[13] In volumes III and IV he continues by discussing developments toward the religious-philosophical position which focused on the human soul and its desire to transcend the cosmos and be liberated from it in order to make contact with a *hypercosmic* God.[14]

According to Festugière, the rejection of the Platonic theory of Ideas resulting from Aristotle's criticism is a crucial factor in the development of the "cosmic religion."[15] For Aristotle himself, the author of *Epinomis*, and the Stoics in their admiration for the order and rationality of the celestial spheres were led to conclude that the cosmos is itself the true God.[16]

Yet it is remarkable that according to Festugière—and he follows Werner Jaeger on this point—Aristotle initially held a very pessimistic conception in his *Eudemus* and *Protrepticus*. Although tutored by Plato in the latter's final phase, Aristotle supposedly began by following the pessimistic, dualistic tendency that characterized Plato's work in his earlier period. For Festugière, as for Jaeger, that must be associated with Aristotle's initial acceptance of the theory of Ideas.[17] But after the death of Plato, with his *On philosophy*, Aristotle showed his independence and wrote consciously from an entirely new perspective.[18] A crucial element in his new view is his rejection of any form of transcendence. According to Festugière, the idea of a metaphysical Unmoved Mover would still be out of the question in the *De philosophia*.[19] Indeed, this important work of Aristotle may well have done more to disseminate the cosmic religion than Plato's *Timaeus*. For the astral theology of the *De philosophia* was adopted by the Stoa and thus marked the Hellenistic period.[20] After discussing the cosmic theology of the Stoa, Festugière proceeds with a treatment of what he calls the "eclectic dogmatism" of the first century BCE.[21] In this context he deals with Cicero, the *De mundo* treatise,[22] and Philo of Alexandria.[23]

The position developed by Festugière in this important work is attractive for its broad conception, and appears convincing because of the enormous amount of "evidence" which certainly makes an overwhelming impression on readers who first become acquainted with the subject matter through Festugière's book. Yet in the forty years since the publication of Festugière's book, research in the history of ancient philosophy and Gnosticism has made enormous strides. On a number of issues crucial to Festugière's position the views now held differ substantially from those of around 1950. So one may well ask whether Festugière's views on the philosophical background to (Hermetic) Gnosticism also need correction on the basis of the new insights.

In the present context I will only briefly list the following new developments: (1) the interest in Plato's "unwritten doctrine" thanks to the work of H. J. Krämer and K. Gaiser;[24] (2) the much more positive assessment of Philo of Alexandria;[25] (3) the much earlier dating of the *De mundo* after the commentary of G. Reale, which vigorously defends the authorship of Aristotle;[26] and (4) with respect to Aristotle's lost writings, *Eudemus* and *Protrepticus* are no longer regarded as pointless repetitions of Plato's *Phaedo*, but show critical interaction with Plato. The *De philosophia*, too, is now thought to defend a transcendent theology of an Unmoved Mover.

The Views of A. H. Armstrong
In a Festschrift for Hans Jonas, A. H. Armstrong, who is well-known for his work on Plotinus, has also developed his view on the relationship of Gnosticism to the Greek philosophical tradition.[27] With A. J. Festugière he distinguishes between an optimistic tendency in Gnosticism which values the visible cosmos positively, and a much broader, pessimistic and negative line of thought. Armstrong is convinced that the optimistic approach has been determined entirely by Greek philosophy. The appropriate treatises for the most part contain popular Greek philosophy. Armstrong recognizes this line in the pagan Gnosticism of part of the Hermetic tradition.[28] But he believes that matters are more complicated for the other tradition within Gnosticism, which is characterized by alienation from, and rebellion against the cosmos and its Maker.[29] He does not accept Festugière's view that Plato, in the different phases of his philosophical career, must be seen as the spiritual father of both tendencies. According to Armstrong, the pessimistic tradition showed the continued effect of non-Greek influences, including that of "Iranian dualism."[30]

Generally Acknowledged Elements of the Gnostic Conception
In the past few decades there have been many attempts to reach a consensus on the central ideas of the gnostic systems. A large number of formulations have been proposed. In his book *Gnōsis and the New Testament* R. McL. Wilson in 1968 described these basic elements as follows:

(1) a distinction between the unknown and transcendent true God on the one hand and the demiurge or creator of this world on the other, the latter being commonly identified with the God of the Old Testament;

(2) the belief that humanity in its true nature is essentially akin to the divine, a spark of the heavenly light imprisoned in a material body and subjected in this world to the dominance of the demiurge and his powers;

(3) a myth narrating some kind of pre-mundane fall, to account for humanity's present state and its yearning for deliverance;

(4) the means, the saving *gnōsis*, by which that deliverance is effected and human beings are awakened to the consciousness of their own true nature and heavenly origin. This deliverance, and the eventual return of the imprisoned sparks of light to their heavenly abode, means in time the return of this world to its primordial chaos, and is strenuously opposed at all points by the hostile powers.[31]

An Alternative Approach to the Philosophical Background of Gnosticism
In contrast to the positions given by the authors discussed above, A. J. Festugière and A. H. Armstrong, I would propose the development of a different approach. In this discussion I will begin by briefly outlining the consequences of this alternative approach, before indicating the grounds on which it rests.

Thesis 1
No attempt to understand the relationship between Greek philosophy and Gnosticism has done sufficient justice to the role of Aristotle's lost works, the content and significance of which require

an assessment wholly different from that of W. Jaeger and the authors following him (including Festugière).

Thesis 2
The double theology of Gnosticism, with its distinction between a meta-cosmic supreme God who has no connection with matter, and a subordinate world-creating demiurge, cannot be explained from Platonic or Middle Platonic theology, nor as a deformation of Jewish monotheism. It can, however, be explained from Aristotle's double theology, which was accepted by Middle Platonism.

Thesis 3
The (cosmo-)psychology of Gnosticism is not that of Platonism, but that which Aristotle posited over against Platonizing psychology, and was adopted by Middle Platonism in the doctrine of the "sleeping World-soul." The differences within Gnosticism between extremely pessimistic, and less pessimistic to positive lines of thought regarding the visible cosmos are associated with the ambivalence of that soul which characterized Aristotle's (cosmo-)psychology.

Thesis 4
The devaluation of the *ratio* or *logos* in Gnosticism is not the result of influences coming from non-Greek traditions. Devaluation of the *logos* was introduced into Greek philosophy by Aristotle in his distinction between discursive reasoning and intuition. That distinction is basic to his distinction between physics (as secondary philosophy) and "first philosophy," and influences the distinction between knowledge which is scientific, discursive and apodictic and knowledge of ultimate principles.[32]

My proposal for a new approach to the phenomenon of Gnosticism and its background is the result of a new view of Aristotle's philosophy which I have developed in the past few years.[33] This view relates specifically to the philosophy which Aristotle expounded in his lost writings and involves a radical rejection of Jaeger's position, which has dominated Aristotelian scholarship for more than fifty years after 1923,[34] and was also virtually accepted as a matter of course by Festugière, as I pointed out above.

The position of Jaeger, although widely accepted for decades by scholars (including myself), is no longer tenable. It supposed that for centuries in antiquity Aristotle was highly admired on the basis of writings which did not contain his true philosophy. Also without solid grounds it posits that halfway through his career Aristotle stopped presenting his views in a polished literary form. It is moreover suspect to the extent that it imposes on a philosopher from the fourth century BCE the scheme of development which Auguste Comte, the nineteenth century father of modern positivism, sketched for the evolution of humanity as a whole as an evolution from mythology through speculative thought to positive science.[35]

New research into the fragments of Aristotle's lost writings, freed from the Jaegerian paradigm, has led me to conclude that the Aristotelian corpus which we still have was written *not to replace* the dialogues which Aristotle himself published, *but to supplement and complete them.* In those lost dialogues Aristotle did not express an early and subsequently abandoned Platonist philosophical position, let alone a view which even Plato had already relinquished.[36]

The "Double Theology" in Gnosticism
We saw that for R. McL. Wilson the primary characteristic of the gnostic conception was "the distinction between the unknown and transcendent true God on the one hand and the demiurge or creator of the world on the other."[37] The *gnōsis* of Gnosticism is always "knowledge" about that supreme God, which humans do not possess "by nature," as "natural" creatures belonging to the visible world, but which they should possess to the highest degree.

The supreme God is an "unknown" God due to the fact that this God is metaphysical, transcendent, and purely intellectual or spiritual. Precisely as a perfectly spiritual being, this God cannot possibly have a (direct) relationship with material reality.

In sharp contrast with this supreme, transcendent God, Gnostics recognized an inferior deity who does occupy himself directly with natural reality, and is indeed directly responsible for it: the demi-urge. The seven planetary gods, in turn, are subordinate to him and dependent on him. All human beings have a natural knowledge of this hierarchy of divine beings because these *cosmic* gods, through their eternal revolutions, determine the order of events in the world of generation and decay. They organize and rule the entire sublunary sphere. And their government and control are inevitable and necessary for all those who live on earth. Mortal beings are subject to this regime as their Fate.

We have solid grounds for reformulating the problem of the origin of Gnosticism as the problem of the origin of this "double theology." Given the apparent lack of a plausible alternative, the attempts of G. Quispel, R. M. Grant and others who looked to Judaism for an origin are certainly to be appreciated. Yet, as W. C. Van Unnik has argued, crucial aspects of Judaic religion—the unity of God, Torah as a guide for life, the Messiah, the Passover, and the covenant—are absent in gnostic writings. And where *Sophia*/Wisdom is disguised as an independent hypostasis responsible for creation, no recognizable passages from Judaic writings are quoted.[38] H. Jonas and J. Daniélou also regard Gnosticism as anti-Judaic.

Thus, if we had such a credible alternative, we would gladly abandon the constructions of Quispel and others. I do believe that such an alternative can be found, namely among the Greek philosophers to whom all Christian authors from the period of the early church referred. *That alternative is Aristotle.* Specifically it is Aristotle as he was known to and as he influenced classical antiquity before the first century BCE: the Aristotle of the lost works, of the dialogues, and the *exoterikoi logoi.*

Now I would be the first to admit that this sounds improbable, for no modern scholar has argued this position. Aristotle plays no role at all in the entire modern debate on the gnostic world view.[39] However, the modern view of Aristotle has been seriously distorted, not only through the loss of all the writings which he published during his lifetime, but perhaps even more because Jaeger, who first paid extensive attention to the fragments of the lost works, at the same time underestimated them because he regarded them as evidence of a superseded Platonizing phase of Aristotle's philosophy.

In contrast, I would like to argue that all the ingredients for the gnostic conception were to be found in Aristotle's *Eudemus or On the Soul*, his *Protrepticus*, his *De philosophia*, and the (Aristotelian) treatise *De mundo*.

An important consequence of the distortion caused by the defective transmission of Aristotle's works is the central position usually given to the doctrine of Ideas in the debate between Plato and Aristotle. Yet from the fragments it is clear that the debate on theology, particularly that of the *Timaeus*, was at least as important. The main issue in that debate was Aristotle's view that the highest God, the perfect Intellect, or *Nous*, could *not* be the creator of the world as Plato had argued in the *Timaeus*. The same position was no doubt upheld also with regard to the government of the world and divine providence. Against the theory of Plato's *Politicus*, Aristotle would have argued that the divine supreme *Nous* cannot (directly) be the *Archon* of the cosmos. Plato's dialectical theology was attacked by Aristotle on the basis of teachings regarding God's self-sufficiency and absolute unchangeability. This led Aristotle to distinguish between the divine supreme principle, the pure transcendent *Nous*, who in perfect self-sufficiency is alone the ultimate goal or *causa finalis* of all nature, and an inferior divine level that is (directly) responsible for the generation and decay of transient beings, and for the government of the world.

In a famous reference Cicero explicitly tells us that in the third book of the *De philosophia* Aristotle ". . . at one time ascribes all divinity to mind, . . . and again places another god in control of the world and ascribes to him the role of ruling and preserving the movement of the world by a sort of *replicatio*."[40] I would certainly not claim that this text is free from difficulties. But I do wish to argue that with this passage Cicero informs us that Aristotle in the *De philosophia* recognized both a divine *Nous* and another divine entity which held particular responsibility for controlling the movements of the cosmos.

I would like to point out that the important sixth chapter of the *De mundo* also presents this fundamental distinction between one transcendent God and the many cosmic gods, using the image of the Persian sovereign, majestically enthroned in his royal citadel in Susa, delegating the administration of the provinces of his realm to his generals and satraps.

Aristotle is known to have criticized Plato's ideal of the philosopher-king. According to Aristotle, a philosophizing king could not be a good king. His ideal was the situation in which the king had sound (philosopher) advisers, and also took their advice seriously.[41] Again, he compared the relationship between the king and his advisers with that between the supreme divine Intellect which is not itself engaged in action, production, or world government, and the heavenly gods who accomplish the cosmic plan.[42] It was Aristotle who conceived of the heavenly gods as *causae efficientes* of all movement and change in nature and who expressly reproached Plato for neglecting the *causa efficiens* in cosmic events.[43]

Because Aristotle argued this theological position, the supreme God became an entity much more "remote" from earthly mortals, as is testified by countless doxographical references in pagan and Christian authors. These inform us that Aristotle confined divine providence to the celestial spheres and excluded the sublunary from (direct) participation in it.[44]

In my opinion, therefore, Aristotle obviously drew the logical conclusion from Plato's doctrine that an intellect cannot be joined to a body except through the mediation of a soul.[45] For Aristotle, who had replaced the Platonic theory of the (world) soul by the theory of the eternal, divine fifth element, this meant that one could assume an interaction between the supreme divine Intellect and the divine cosmic beings, comparable to the relationship of pure *nous* to the soul (*psyche*) of an intellectually gifted being, but that no direct interaction could be assumed with the sublunary sphere.

The Sleeping World Soul

In a study of Aristotelian theology I have argued that Aristotle elaborated the relationship between *nous* and *psyche* in a myth about the *dreaming God Kronos*. This myth which was used in the *Eudemus* may well have been narrated by the daemon Silenus.[46] In this argument I follow J. H. Waszink, who explained Tertullian's reference to a "dreaming Kronos" in Aristotle by means of the myth which occurs in Plutarch's *De facie in orbe lunae*, and presents Kronos as a dream-oracle, fettered by the bonds of sleep.[47] I believe we can establish these links between Plutarch, Tertullian and Aristotle on the basis of a large number of details from the fragments of Aristotle's lost works. But we can also argue from Aristotle's repeated use of the metaphor of waking and sleeping to illustrate the relationship between the potential possession of science and the actual practice of that science.[48]

We must also recognize that the only production (*poiesis*) which Aristotle assigns to the transcendent Intellect is the actualization of the potential intellect in a soul.[49] Here the *Nous* itself is a *causa efficiens*; however, it is not an entity that effects and produces material matters, but one that produces "images" in the *phantasia* of the soul. Any products of the *Nous* are therefore typically "intellectual," psychically characterized products.

The "dreaming Kronos" as a symbol of the world-soul is, according to the myth told in Plutarch's *De facie*, "imprisoned" in a Cave which glitters like gold; this must be explained to mean that the soul is always related to physical and somatic reality, and that it is directly responsible for all phenomena of action and production in plant and animal life, as well as in society.

Plato's allegory of the cave was adopted by Aristotle (and Xenocrates),[50] but also radicalized. For Aristotle all nature represented a "cave" and "prison" when regarded from the level of the transcendent, perfectly free *Nous*.[51]

Human nature is in many respects not free, as Aristotle taught us in the *Metaphysics*.[52] True liberation can only be provided by the knowledge which God possesses and which is also knowledge about God: *sophia*.[53] But such knowledge lies beyond the human condition and nature.[54]

How then did Aristotle explain the reason for human "bondage" and "lack of freedom?" We find nothing on this subject in the *De anima*. But the dialogue *Eudemus or On the Soul* apparently focused on the theme of "imprisonment and liberation."[55] In this regard it certainly corresponds to Plato's *Phaedo*. And Proclus also says emphatically that in the *De anima* Aristotle only spoke about the soul as a philosopher of nature (*physikōs*), and hence did not talk about the "descent" of the soul and its "coverings." However, according to Proclus, Aristotle in his dialogues did give a very explicit and basic exposition on this theme.[56] If we then note that the *Eudemus* features the daemon Silenus who offers King Midas a "revelation" regarding the misery of mortals, and if we observe that Aristotle did speak on some occasions regarding the dreaming god Kronos, then we must conclude that Silenus would have recounted a myth in the Orphic style and tradition, according to which the "sleep of the soul" and the "death of the bodily condition" would be linked to the atrocious crimes of the Titans.

This means that, even in a work from the older Greek philosophical tradition, we may well have already encountered the concept of a double theology. For Aristotle presents both visible cosmic gods and a transcendent, meta-cosmic god who is unknown to human beings in their natural condition. And this is given in combination with the concept of the human need for liberation from the bonds of that natural condition and the limitations of natural reason, all within the framework of a revelation by a supra-human being.

Thus we conclude that when early Christians objected to the basic tenets of Gnosticism while presenting them as an offshoot of pagan Greek philosophy, they were far more correct in so doing than has been recognized by many contemporary historians of philosophy.

Notes

1. Aristotle, *Metaphysics* A 1, 980a20: πάντες ἄνθρωποι τοῦ εἰδέναι ὀρέγονται φύσει.
2. Cf. Aristotle, *Metaphysics* A 2, 982b29-30: πολλαχῇ γὰρ ἡ φύσις δούλη τῶν ἀνθρώπων ἐστιν.
3. Aristotle, *Metaphysics* A 2, 982b28-29: διὸ καὶ δικαίως ἂν οὐκ ἀνθρωπίνη νομίζοιτο αὐτῆς ἡ κτῆσις.
4. Cf. Aristotle, *Metaphysics* A 2, 983a5-10. Cf. J. H. Königshausen, *Ursprung und Thema von erster Wissenschaft. Die aristotelische Entwicklung des Problems* (Amsterdam: Rodopi, 1989), 56-88.
5. A. J. Festugière, *La révélation d'Hermès Trismégiste*, 4 vols. (Paris: J. Gabalda, 1949-1954).
6. A. J. Festugière, op. cit., vol. I, 1-18. Festugière regards neglect of experimentation as an important cause; the Greeks preferred a theoretical and deductive explanation of reality (I, 7-8). However, the anti-empirical character of Greek philosophy can more accurately be ascribed to the use of "abstraction" as the chief tool of philosophical thought, following on the Parmenidean identification of Being with Thought, and subsequent devaluation of all material reality. See n.31 below and my *In de Greep van de Titanen*, (Amsterdam: Buijten en Schipperheijn, 1991), 42-53.
7. A. J. Festugière, op. cit., vol. II, *Le Dieu cosmique*: (Paris, 1949), ix.
8. Ibid., x.
9. Ibid., x-xi.
10. Op. cit., vol. II, xi, n.1: "*Courant optimiste*: C. H. II, V, VI, VIII, IX-XII (avec des morceaux empruntés à la tendance dualiste), XIV, XVI, l'*Asclépius* dans l'ensemble, certains morceaux de St. H. XXIII, XXVI. Courant pessimiste: C. H. I, IV, VII, XIII, certains morceaux de l'*Asclépius* et le fond de St. H. XXIII (*Kore Kosmou*)." Festugière does note also, op. cit., vol. II, 52, "l'inextricable mélange des courants hermétiques . . . ; c'est là, il faut bien le dire, une source de difficultés constante dans l'hermétisme."

11. Op. cit., vol. II, xii: "La source commune de ces deux courants est Platon, qui peut bien être dit le père de la philosophie religieuse hellénistique;" cf. II, 92.

12. Op. cit., vol. II, xii.

13. Cf. op. cit., vol. II, xvi, "la religion du Dieu cosmique."

14. Cf. op. cit., vol. III, ix. It is to be noted that Hermetic *gnōsis* is knowledge of a *hypercosmic* or transcendent supreme deity whether or not a positive attitude also prevailed with respect to subordinate cosmic gods.

15. Op. cit., vol. II, 153-54.

16. Op. cit., vol. II, 154: "Et l'on peut donc affirmer que la contemplation du sage se termine au Ciel visible: ce Ciel lui-même est le vrai Dieu." Cf. p. 164.

17. Op. cit., vol. II, 173, 219.

18. Op. cit., vol. II, 221.

19. Op. cit., vol. II, 245, where Festugière follows J. Moreau, *L'âme du monde de Platon aux Stoiciens* (Hildesheim: G. Olms, 1965; photorepr. of 1939, Paris ed.), 118, on Aristotle, *De philos.* fr. Ross. Cf. n.39 below.

20. Op. cit., vol. II, 258-59.

21. Op. cit., vol. II, 341f.

22. Op. cit., vol. II, 460-518. Festugière regards the *De mundo* as a rather superficial treatise which combines Aristotelian with Stoic doctrines.

23. Op. cit., vol. II, 519-85. Characteristic of his low esteem for Philo is the remark on page 534: "On peut, hélas, lire tout Philon sans rencontrer une seule réflexion originale qui dénote quelque expérience personnelle."

24. Cf. H. J. Krämer, *Arete bei Platon und Aristoteles* (Heidelberg: C. Winter, 1959); id., *Platone e i fondamenti della metafisica* (Milan: Vitae pensiero, 1982, reprinted 1987); K. Gaiser, *Platons ungeschriebene Lehre. Studien zur systematischen und geschichtlichen Begründung der Wissenschaften in der Platonische Schule* (Stuttgart: E. Klett, 1963); G. Reale, *Per una nuova interpretazione di Platone.*

Rilettura della metafisica dei grandi dialoghi alla luce delle "Dottrine non scritte" (Milan: Vitae pensiero, 1984; tenth impression, 1990); Th. A. Szlezák, *Platon und die Schriftlichkeit der Philosophie. Interpretationen zu den frühen und mittleren Dialogen* (Berlin: W. de Gruyter, 1985). In listing these developments I do not wish to neglect mention of the 1945 discovery of the Nag Hammadi library. However, it is also important to recognize the fundamental shifts which have occurred in contemporary appreciation of well-known texts. On the Nag Hammadi finds see J. M. Robinson, ed., *The Nag Hammadi Library in English* (Leiden: Brill, 1978) and J. Doresse, *Les livres secrets des Gnostiques d'Égypte* (Paris: Plon, 1958).

25. H. A. Wolfson, *Philo. Foundations of Religious Philosophy in Judaism, Christianity and Islam,* 2 vols. (Cambridge, Mass.: Harvard Univ. Press, 1947, 3rd impression 1961), v and 269. Cf. D. T. Runia, "History of Philosophy in the Grand Manner: the Achievement of H. A. Wolfson," in *Philosophia Reformata* 49 (1984): 112-33; reprinted in id., *Exegesis and Philosophy: Studies on Philo of Alexandria* (Aldershot: Variorum, 1990), chapter X; also his article "Festugière Revisited: Aristotle in the Greek Patres" in *Vigilae Christianae* 49 (1989),:1-34.

26. *Aristotele, Trattato sul cosmo per Alessandro,* con testo greco, introd., comm. e indici di G. Reale (Naples: L. Loffredo, 1974); cf. also A. P. Bos, "Supplementary Notes on the *De Mundo,*" *Hermes* 119 (1991): 312-32; D. M. Schenkeveld, "Language and Style of the Aristotelian *De mundo* in Relation to the Question of its Inauthenticity," *Elenchos* 12 (1991): 221-55. On the *De mundo* see pages 10-12 of this essay and n.40.

27. A. H. Armstrong, "Gnosis and Greek Philosophy," in *Gnosis: Festschrift für Hans Jonas,* B. Aland, ed. (Göttingen: Vandenhoeck and Ruprecht, 1978), 87-124.

28. Loc. cit., 89: "The 'pagan Gnosticism' of the cosmically optimistic treatises of the *Hermetica* is related to Greek philosophy very simply. The content of these treatises *is* for the most part popular Greek philosophy (what Theiler well called 'proletarian Platonism,' with its important Stoic elements)."

29. Loc. cit., 90: "The relationship of Gnosticism in my second sense, the Gnosticism of alienation from and revolt against the cosmos and its maker, to the Greek philosophy of the first three centuries of our era, is a great deal more complex and interesting, and the evidence is often very difficult to interpret."

30. Loc. cit., 90, 91. Armstrong correctly observes that the Pythagorean-Orphic view which also influenced Plato never radically rejected a positive attitude to the visible heavens. However, his inclination to look to Iranian dualism as the source of the more pessimistic attitude confronts him with the problem of finding two different bases of explanation for Gnosticism, one Greek and the other non-Greek.

31. R. McL. Wilson, *Gnosis and the New Testament* (Oxford: Blackwell, 1968), 4. See also *Le origini dello Gnosticismo*, U. Bianchi, ed. (Leiden: Brill, 1967), xxvi-xxix, where the key elements of Gnosticism are summarized as given at the 1966 Messina international colloquium: (1) the idea of a divine spark in human beings, (2) deriving from the divine realm, (3) fallen into this world of fate, birth and death, and (4) in need of awakening by the divine counterpart of the self in order to be finally reintegrated. K. Rudolph, *Die Gnosis. Wesen und Geschichte einer spätantiken Religion* (Göttingen: Vandenhoeck und Ruprecht, 1977), 66f., focuses on four aspects of Gnosticism: (1) a *dualism* which sharply separates the negatively appreciated visible cosmos and its maker from the pure spiritual deity of the transcendent realm, (2) a *cosmogony* which regards the material world that is enclosed by the spheres of the seven planets and fixed stars as the product of a mistake on the part of the demiurge, (3) a *soteriology* which regards salvation for human beings as a result of acquiring *gnōsis* or revealed knowledge about their source in the realm of light, and (4) an *eschatology* which regards death as liberation from the bondage of bodily existence, one instance of the universal process of the separation of matter and spirit, darkness and light.

To clarify my own position on the phenomenon of Gnosticism, I would like to add the following comment. It is crucial that *gnōsis* be recognized as supernatural knowledge, through which human beings become aware that they too contain a supernatural principle which is identical with the transcendent Origin of all reality. This means that in its ontology Gnosticism accepts the fundamental distinction between a natural (material) reality and an (immaterial) reality which transcends it. This distinction in Greek philosophy is associated with the use of theoretical *abstraction* as an important tool for philosophical reflection, and has remained characteristic of philosophical and scientific discourse. Neither the instrument of abstraction nor the distinction between a material and a spiritual reality are essential to the Jewish, or Christian religions. They were introduced into these religions later, under the influence of the Greek tradition of thought. Despite Gnosticism's critique of the Greek philosophical tradition, it remains, as a result of this fundamental distinction, more akin to that philosophical tradition than to the Jewish religion or the Christian religion as anchored in Holy Scripture.

32. This fourth thesis will not be dealt with separately. See, however, H. Jonas, "A Retrospective View," in *Proceedings of the International Colloquium on Gnosticism* (Stockholm, 1973), 6: "I suddenly glimpsed, as in a blinding light, the possible, nay persuasive, hypothesis that what the Gnostics understood by 'Gnosis' is by no means confined to them in the environment of declining antiquity: rather, that what the later Platonists—Plotinus, Porphyry and others—had to say about the highest form of knowledge, about the union with the One, is another, more refined version of this same kind of knowledge that goes beyond the knowledge of 'logos' and of 'theory' in the Greek tradition." See also V. Kal, *On Intuition and Discursive Reasoning in Aristotle* (Leiden: Brill, 1988), and in this volume P. O'Cleirigh, "Symbol and Science in Early Christian *Gnosis*, 409-27.

33. Cf. A. P. Bos, *Cosmic and Meta-cosmic Theology in Aristotle's Lost Dialogues* (Leiden: Brill, 1989). Italian translation: *Teologia cosmica e meta-cosmica. Per una nuova interpretazione dei dialoghi perduti di Aristotele*, con una Introduzione di G. Reale (Milan: Vita e Pensiero, 1991).

34. See W. Jaeger, *Aristoteles. Grundlegung einer Geschichte seiner Entwicklung* (Berlin: Weidmann, 1923). English translation by R. Robinson, *Aristotle: Fundamentals of the History of his Development* (Oxford: Clarendon, 1934; 2nd impression 1948). See on this also D. R. Lachterman, "Did Aristotle 'develop'? Reflections on Werner Jaeger's thesis" in *Revue de philosophie ancienne* 8 (1990): 3-40. Jaeger posited three phases in the life of Aristotle, (1) a Platonic dualistic phase, (2) a more speculative metaphysical phase after the death of Plato, and (3) a period of scientific empirical research in his second residence in Athens.

35. Cf. A. P. Bos, op. cit. (n.33), 99-101.

36. Cf. A. J. Festugière, op. cit., vol. II, 168-69 and A. H. Chroust, *Aristotle: New Light on his Life and on Some of his Lost Works* (London: Routledge and K. Paul, 1973), vol. II, 53-54, 70. Cf. A. P. Bos, *Cosmic . . . theology* (n.33), 105-106. It is my conviction that numerous aspects of Aristotelian works correctly interpreted anticipate important elements of gnostic positions, particularly the philosophically colored components such as (1) the profound distinction between material and spiritual reality, (2) the important role given to the astral deities in the visible cosmos, (3) knowledge of, rather than service to, or the fear of God emphasized as the key of religion, and (4) revelation or illumination from the divine and transcendent realm as the basis of this knowledge. The philosophical nature of Gnosticism is also acknowledged by U. Bianchi in his contribution to the Festschrift for H. Jonas (n.27), 33-64.

37. See R. McL. Wilson, op. cit. (n.31), 4.

38. W. C. Van Unnik, "Gnosis und Jundentum," in *Festschrift für H. Jonas*(n.27), 84.

39. In the index of K. Rudolph, *Die Gnosis* (n.31) his name does not even appear. Hippolytus's mention of Aristotle as the *auctor intellectualis* of Basilides's system (*Refutatio* VII, 14f.) today is commonly rejected. Cf. I. Müller, "Hippolytus *retractatus*: A Discussion of Catharine Osborne, *Rethinking early Greek Philosophy*," in *Oxford Studies in Ancient Philosophy* 7 (1989): 241f.

40. Cic., *De natura deorum*, 1. 13. 33:". . . modo enim menti tribuit omnem divinitatem . . . , modo alium quendam praeficit mundo eique eas partes tribuit ut replicatione quadam mundi motum regat atque tueatur. . . ." Aristotle, *De philos.* fr. 26 Ross. Cf. on this text and the debate connected with it A. P. Bos, *Cosmic . . . theology*, ch. 14.

41. Cf. Themistius, *Or.* 107c-d = Aristotle, *De regno* fr. 2 Ross. The same idea is formulated in the *De mundo*, where Alexander is encouraged not to become a philosopher himself, but to welcome generously the best of philosophers (ch. 1, 391b5-8). This text, however, has also commonly been translated and interpreted in a different way. Cf. A. P. Bos in *Hermes*, 119 (1991): 314-15.

42. Cf. Aristotle, *Eth. Nic.* X 8, 1178b7-32; *De caelo* II 12, 292a18-b2; cf. *Metaph.* Λ 10, 1075a19-22.

43. Cf. Aristotle, *Metaphysics* A 6, 987b12-14; 988a7-12; 9, 991a11; a20-b8; 992a25-26.

44. Cf. Tatianus, *Or. adv. Graecos* 2; Athenagoras, *Legatio pro Christianis* 25; Hippolytus, *Ref.* I 20; 22; VII 14; Clemens Alex., *Protr.* V 66; *Strom.* V 14; Origenes, *Contra Celsum*, I 21; III 75; Eusebius, *Praepar. Evang.* XV 5, 1; Gregorius Naz., *Or.* XXVII 10; Epiphanius, *Adv. omnes haer.* III 2. 9; Theodoretus, *Graec. aff. cur.* IV 46; Chalcidius, *In Tim. comm.* 248. See also Ps.-Plut., *Placita* II 3; Stobaeus, *Eclogae phys.* I 21. 6. A. J. Festugière, *L'idéal religieux des Grecs et l'Évangile* (Paris, 1932), 224f. viewed the testimonies about a divine providence, be it a short-range one, in Aristotle as a mistake due to the influence of the treatise *De mundo.* Cf. id., *La révélation d'Hermès Trismégiste*, vol. II 478. See on this topic A. P. Bos,

"Clement of Alexandria on Aristotle's (cosmo-)theology. (Clem. Al., *Protr.* 5. 66. 4)," *Classical Quarterly* 43 (1993): 1-12.

45. Cf. Plato, *Timaeus* 30b; *Philebus*, 30c9.

46. A. P. Bos, *Cosmic . . . theology*, 102-105; cf. 65-96, esp. 72-75.

47. Plut., *De facie in orbe lunae* 941a ff. Cf. J. H. Waszink, "Traces of Aristotle's lost dialogues," *Vigiliae Christianae* 1 (1947): 137-49.

48. Aristotle, *De Anim.* II 1,412a25-26; *Metaph.* θ6, 1048a30-b2; *Eth. Nic.* X 8, 1178b18-20; *Magna Mor.* II 6, 1201b12-20; cf. Diog. Laertius, 5.34.

49. Aristotle, *De Anim.*, III 4-5. Cf. V. Kal (n.32) 77-90.

50. Cf. Xenocrates, fr. 20 (Heinze), fr. 219 (Isnardi Parente). Cf. P. Boyancé, *Revue des Études anciennes* 50 (1948): 218-31 and *Revue philosophique* 37 (1963): 7-11.

51. Cf. K. Gaiser, "Das Höhlengleichnis. Thema und Variationen von Platon bis Dürrenmatt," *Schweizer Monatshefte* 65 (1985): 55-65; repr. in *Die alten Sprachen im Unterricht* 32 (1985): 20-29.

52. Aristotle, *Metaphysics* A 2, 982b29-30.

53. Ibid., A 2, 983a6-10.

54. Ibid., A 2, 982b28.

55. Cf. A. P. Bos, *Cosmic . . . theology*, 74-76.

56. Proclus, *In Tim.* 338c = Arist., *Eudemus* fr. 4 Ross.

Aristotle and the Jewish God

A Response to A. P. Bos

William E. Arnal

A. P. Bos's fascinating paper argues for a strong link between Christian Gnosticism and the classical tradition. The paper is a most fitting opening for this second conference on "Christianity and the Classics." In my response to his sophisticated argument, I shall not attempt a comprehensive analysis, but only a brief indication of some points of assent and disagreement.

Reconstruction of the Aristotelian Fragments

One can certainly agree with Bos's argument that the lost dialogues of Aristotle constitute the starting-point for developments in popular philosophy which eventually shaped the theology and worldview of Gnosticism. If the reconstruction of Aristotelian ideas expressed in the *Eudemus* is correct, the affinities of the pure unknowable intellectual *Nous* with the gnostic "unknown Father" are striking and considerable. The ambivalent *archōn* of the world in his somatic bondage and creative function, now sleeping, now intellectually impressed by the meta-cosmic God, is also reminiscent of the gnostic demiurge and may account for cosmically positive and negative strains which run through the *Hermetica*. Bos has recognized the necessity of giving a more effective account of Gnosticism's dual divinities, and his reconstruction certainly offers a more reasonable source for gnostic cosmology and its dualistic conception of the divine powers than is available in Plato or Jewish sources.

Yet the soundness of this position depends upon the accuracy of his reconstruction of the lost dialogues. With respect to the hypothetical quality of his claims, it may be objected that it is rather dubious to posit a source for Gnosticism in writings which no longer exist. In my view, this is not a reasonable objection. The nature of the evidence (or the lack thereof) positively requires hypothesis. Indeed, to deny Aristotle an influence on the development of gnostic theology actually depends as much on a hypothetical construction; for it assumes the position of Jaeger, which is no longer accepted without question. Evaluation of Bos's position must proceed by exploring the extent to which it plausibly accounts for extant data, *not* the degree to which it is conjectural.

By the standard of plausibility, Bos's attempt to find a dual theology in early Aristotelian thought is superior. It is based on the debate held in the Old Academy around the mid-fourth century bce; its themes continued to be important for the Aristotle of the *Corpus Aristotelicum*; and it gives a coherent place to ancient *testimonia* to Aristotelian thought in writers like Plutarch or Tertullian,[1] while Jaeger's position assumes a radical discontinuity in Aristotelian thought.

Nonetheless, I believe that an acceptance of Bos's position should be qualified. He has not proven definitively that the postulated double theology of Aristotle is *the* fundamental and critical *causa efficiens* of the gnostic movements of late Hellenism. Developments in middle Platonism and Stoicism which, according to Bos, began with Aristotle's critique of Plato[2] may have influenced the *form*, but not necessarily the basic content, with which the Gnostics expressed their disgust with the cosmos. Rather, Bos's argument only allows us to add Aristotle to the already-long list of influences on Gnosticism.

The Philosophical Character of Gnosticism

A problem arises in the definition of Gnosticism. R. M. Grant argues that the unifying feature of gnostic systems was *gnōsis*, which he understands as salvation through self-knowledge of one's divine source,[3] while Bos, using the approach of R. McL. Wilson, focuses on the double theology of "the distinction between the unknown and transcendent true God and the Demiurge or creator of this world"[4] as the defining characteristic of Gnosticism, an approach which is by no means self-evidently valid. Indeed Gnostics had a more *practical* rather than a primarily philosophical or speculative concern with redemption from this evil world. And the mythology of dual divinities represents the *framework* in which this yearning for escape was expressed.

Bos's emphasis on the philosophical character of Gnosticism, as opposed to its practical dimension, leads him to neglect aspects which do not correspond well to Aristotelian thought. Thus, while the ambivalent image of "sleeping Kronos" as cosmic demiurge may account for some contradictory tendencies in the *Hermetica*, it does not adequately explain the thorough contempt for the world and its creator found in many gnostic writings. The gnostic treatise "On the Origin of the World" describes material reality as follows:

> As with a woman giving birth to a child—all her superfluities flow out; just so, matter came into being out of shadow and was projected apart. And it (viz., matter) did not depart from chaos.[5]

It is hard to imagine a philosophical origin for such a forceful perspective; it undoubtedly has its roots in sociological conditions reflecting a profound frustration with the cosmos.[6]

Likewise hard to recognize as Aristotelian is the gnostic view of ultimate knowledge. For Aristotle, even if such knowledge surpasses human power, its pursuit is determined by logical processes.[7] Depreciation of the *logos* in Aristotle is of a *skeptical*, not a *pessimistic* character. He doubted the human capacity for ultimate knowledge, not the efficacy of reasonable thought.[8] Nor, according to Aristotle is this knowledge salvific; it may lead to happiness,[9] but is not *necessary*.[10] Yet most gnostic systems abandon rational discourse for revelation; and knowledge thus achieved is critical for salvation and preservation of spiritual life. Note the ubiquity of a revealer/redeemer figure. It is difficult to see what role such a meta-cosmic visitation on the world of matter would have in Aristotelian thought.

Gnosticism and Jewish Wisdom Speculation

Consideration of the revealer-figure leads to a final point. The role of the gnostic redeemer corresponds to the image of hypostatized *Sophia* in late Jewish Wisdom speculation.[11] George MacRae argues cogently, however, that the gnostic *Sophia*-figure reflects both this Jewish personified Wisdom, and also the image of the fallen Eve in Genesis.[12] Both evaluations may well be correct. In its fiercely anti-cosmic stance Gnosticism was compelled to "split" hypostasized *Sophia*, as both a positive source of revelation (as the revealer), yet negatively involved in creating the world (as the sexually deviant *Sophia*).[13] A similar phenomenon may well apply to the supreme God himself, even within monotheistic Judaism, through a process facilitated by apocalyptic schematization and reflection on the first chapters of Genesis. Rejection of the world could lead to a rejection of the god responsible for such an inferior product. Yet the noble and transcendent characteristics of the Jewish deity are also retained, and used in the composition of the unknowable Father. So one *can* plausibly posit a Jewish background for Gnosticism's dual theology. Indeed, if an impulse toward separation of the Jewish God's transcendence from his creative characteristics were not already present in Judaism, no Aristotelian dual theology could possibly have influenced it. The edifice of monotheism must already have had some cracks for Gnosticism to penetrate. So, if Aristotle's theology *did* influence the theological expression of Gnosticism, it is hard to imagine it as the basic and fundamental cause.

Thus a qualified assent to Bos's position is in order. His argument for an Aristotelian dual theology in the lost dialogues is cogent. But the parallels are not significant enough to justify the claim that philosophical developments from Aristotle are the *causa efficiens* of Gnosticism. Rather this popular and variegated religious movement drew freely from the cultural currents of late Hellenism where Aristotle was a significant player who may well have influenced the gnostic perspective. Yet if we wish to acknowledge the basic inspiration of Gnosticism, the views of Robert Grant (an outgrowth of failed apocalypticism),[14] and of Kurt Rudolph (a syncretistic development of the Jewish wisdom and apocalyptic traditions)[15] provide an explanation which is to be preferred.[16]

Notes

Work on this paper was supported by the Social Sciences and Humanities Research Council of Canada in the form of a doctoral fellowship.

1. See A. P. Bos, *Cosmic and Meta-Cosmic Theology in Aristotle's Lost Dialogues* (Leiden: E. J. Brill, 1989), 83.
2. Ibid., 87.
3. This is precisely the fashion in which Robert M. Grant characterizes and defines Gnosticism, in *Gnosticism and Early Christianity*, revised edition (New York: Harper and Row, 1966), 7.
4. R. McL. Wilson, quoted by A. P. Bos, "Cosmic and Meta-Cosmic Theology in Greek Philosophy and Gnosticism," in this volume, 6.
5. "On the Origin of the World," *NHC* II, 99.12-23, cf. 99.24-100.10. Quoted from James M. Robinson, ed., *The Nag Hammadi Library*, revised edition (San Francisco: Harper and Row, 1988), 172.
6. So also Grant, op. cit. (n.3), 33-38, who locates this frustration with the failure of apocalyptic hopes.
7. See, e.g., Aristotle, *Metaphysics*, 2.982b.25-30, in *The Works of Aristotle*, W. D. Ross, trans. and ed., vol. 8, *Metaphysica* (Oxford: Clarendon, 1928).
8. Regarding this "divine science" Aristotle writes, "Such a science either God alone can have, or God above all others," *Metaphysics*, 2.983a.5-10 (n.7 above).

9. Aristotle, *Ethica Nichomachea*, X.8.1178b.5-25, in *The Works of Aristotle*, W. D. Ross, trans. and ed., vol. 9 (Oxford: Oxford University Press, 1913).

10. *Metaphysics*, 2.983a.10 (n.7 above).

11. See James M. Robinson, "*Logoi Sophōn*: On the Gattung of Q," James M. Robinson and Helmut Koester, eds., *Trajectories Through Early Christianity* (Philadelphia: Fortress Press, 1971), 72-73.

12. George W. MacRae, "The Jewish Background of the Gnostic Sophia Myth," *Novum Testamentum* 12 (1970): 86-101.

13. See Kurt Rudolph, *Gnosis: The Nature & History of Gnosticism* (San Francisco: Harper and Row, 1983), 277.

14. Grant, op. cit. (n.3), 33-38.

15. Rudolph, op. cit. (n.4), 277-86.

16. Note the conclusion of R. M. Grant, op. cit. (n.3), 38:

> I should be inclined, in view of (1) the non-philosophical nature of Gnosticism and (2) the relative rarity of this kind of dualism among Hellenistic philosophers, to claim that it originates from historical experience. To be sure, the expression of the meaning found in the historical experience may owe something to reflections of philosophy, if not to philosophical reflection; but to ascribe any large measure of philosophical thought to the Gnostics seems an unnecessary hypothesis.

Gnosticism and Early Christianity

Edwin M. Yamauchi

Introduction

The Gnostics were followers of a variety of religious movements which stressed salvation through *gnōsis* or "knowledge," that is, of one's origins.[1] As the term "Gnosticism" is a modern scholarly construct, it can be used in either a broad or a narrow sense.[2] The former encompasses writings like Philo and the *Hermetica*, rendering the definition too loose. The narrow sense would require a cosmological dualism—an opposition between the spiritual and the material worlds.

The church historian Adolf von Harnack (1851-1930) contrasted Gnosticism as "the acute Hellenization of Christianity" with the slower "chronic Hellenization" of orthodox Christianity.[3] While it is undeniably significant that a portion of Plato's *Republic* was included in the Nag Hammadi Library, and there are important elements of Greek philosophy in forms of Gnosticism such as Valentinianism,[4] it is now recognized that Harnack's characterization of Gnosticism was too simplistic.

Since the History-of-Religions School from the turn of the century used a comparative approach to understand Christianity, scholars are sharply divided on when Gnosticism began and how it relates to nascent Christianity. On the one hand, some scholars are convinced that Gnosticism was not only independent but pre-Christian in origin, and that it influenced the New Testament. These scholars tend to take a synthetic view of the texts, regarding certain words and concepts as technical terms and taking these as evidence of the developed system.[5] On the other hand, the more analytic approach sees only a rudimentary, inchoate Gnosticism at the end of the first century, and concludes that the developed system cannot be understood apart from its parasitic relationship to Christianity.[6]

Gnostic Sources

Mandaean Sources

Some scholars such as R. Reitzenstein and R. Bultmann sought to recreate a pre-Christian Gnosticism using relatively late *Manichaean* and *Mandaean* sources, which they believed preserved much earlier traditions. Reitzenstein believed that the Manichaean texts preserved a pre-Christian Iranian redeemer myth. This appeal to Iranian or Persian sources[7] has largely been abandoned with the exception, perhaps, of G. Widengren.[8] In particular, the 1970 publication of the Cologne Mani Codex by A. Henrichs and L. Koenen decisively demonstrated that Mani came out of a Jewish-Christian rather than a Mandaean background, and therefore undercut the likelihood that Manichaean Gnosticism had non-Christian roots.[9]

The Mandaean sources, once in vogue,[10] have been eclipsed by the Coptic codices of Nag Hammadi. The earliest Mandaic texts are magical bowls and lead amulets; the former date ca. 600 CE and the latter may be considerably earlier.[11] Despite the conviction of such leading scholars as E. S. Drower, R. Macuch and K. Rudolph that Mandaeism is pre-Christian in origin,[12] my own view is that the sect cannot antedate the second century CE.[13] Even Rudolph concedes that the composition of the major religious works, preserved in late eighteenth and nineteenth century manuscripts, cannot be dated earlier than the third century CE.[14] The Mandaeans, who live precariously in southern Iraq and Iran, are most noteworthy as the sole surviving Gnostic community today. It is my belief that this survival is due more to their tenacious rituals than to their Gnostic theology.[15]

The Hermetica

Other sources for Gnosticism, such as the *Hermetica*, the Syrian *Odes of Solomon* and the *Hymn of the Pearl* are problematic, both because they are not unambiguously Gnostic and because there are questions about dating these. Though Hermetic texts have been found in the Nag Hammadi Library, the *Hermetica* as a whole are not radically dualistic.[16] There is continuing debate over the character of the *Odes of Solomon*; Rudolph holds that they are Gnostic, whereas J. H. Charlesworth maintains the opposite.[17] H. J. W. Drijvers, who thinks he can detect a polemic against the Marcionites and the Manichaeans in these *Odes*, has advocated a radically late date of 275 CE for them.[18] The *Hymn of the Pearl* may be a composition inserted into the *Acts of Thomas* by the Manichaeans, according to P.-H. Poirier, but this says nothing of its original character.[19]

The Nag Hammadi Library

The most exciting new source is, of course, the Coptic Nag Hammadi Library found in upper Egypt in 1945.[20] It is clear that these texts were deposited late in the fourth century. Though many scholars have asserted that they were part of a Pachomian monastery, that view has been called into question by the examination of the cartonnage by J. C. Shelton.[21]

Though the word "Gnostic" does not occur in any of the tractates, it is quite clear that many but not all of the tractates in the Nag Hammadi codices may be characterized as Gnostic. The inclusion of three copies of *The Apocryphon of John*, mentioned by Irenaeus, indicates that at least some of these works were composed no later than the second century CE. More controversial is the claim of various scholars that some Nag Hammadi documents are even earlier and provide the non-Christian evidence of pre-Christian Gnosticism.[22]

The three Nag Hammadi tractates which have attracted the greatest attention for those who wish to maintain a pre-Christian Gnosticism are (1) *The Apocalypse of Adam* (*NHC* V,5); (2) *The*

Paraphrase of Shem (*NHC* VII,1), and (3) *The Trimorphic Protennoia* (*NHC* XIII,1).

The Apocalypse of Adam

Despite statements in the *Apocalypse of Adam* as (77, 16-18): "Then they will punish the flesh of the man upon whom the holy spirit has come," scholars like D. Parrott deny that this refers to Jesus.[23] Koester maintains, "Since this book contains no reference to specific Christian names, themes, or traditions, it should be assigned to a Jewish gnostic baptismal sect."[24] Likewise Rudolph regards this document as a "witness of early Gnosis, since it still stands very near to the Jewish apocalyptic literature and has no Christian tenor."[25]

Many other scholars disagree; they see clearly Christian references in the *Apocalypse of Adam*.[26] For example, Françoise Morard affirms that "the account of the punishment of the third illuminator presupposes the Christian account of the passion of Christ."[27] And J. E. Fossum, taking the polemic against baptism to be directed against the church's perversion of baptism, dates the work no earlier than the middle of the second century CE.[28]

Several scholars, including the original editor, A. Böhlig, have noted the allusions to Mithraic motifs in the *Apocalypse of Adam*.[29] In view of what we now know about the development of Mithraism in the Roman Empire,[30] we must date the composition of this work no earlier than the second century CE, and in my opinion, in Rome rather than in Palestine.[31]

The Paraphrase of Shem

When Frederik Wisse first wrote about the *Paraphrase of Shem*,[32] he created a stir by claiming that it presented evidence of a pre-Christian "redeemer figure." He later wrote, "I still think it is basically non-Christian though most probably not pre-Christian."[33] In the third (1988) edition of *The Nag Hammadi Library* Michel Roberge acknowledges in his introduction to this treatise that the anti-baptismal polemic   is most probably directed against the Great Church (as other scholars, including myself, have argued), and not against some pre-Christian baptismal sect.[34]

The Trimorphic Protennoia

Gesine Robinson (formerly Schenke) has forcefully stated the case for maintaining that *The Trimorphic Protennoia* contains materials which may point to the *Vorlage* (drafting) of John's Prologue.[35] She also suggests that the unusual reading *monogenēs theos* of p[66] and p[75] at John 1:18 may reflect the original Gnostic source of the Prologue. The obvious Christian elements in *The Trimorphic Protennoia* she regards as quite secondary. Nonetheless, especially in light of the striking use of the word *skēnē* (tent), which seems to reflect *eskēnosēn* of John 1:14, not a few scholars have concluded that *The Trimorphic Protennoia* is simply dependent upon the Prologue.[36]

In arguing for the priority of *The Trimorphic Protennoia*, Gesine Robinson uses the same arguments as were often used to argue for the priority of Mandaean parallels to John. To this fallacious reasoning Pétrement responds:

> It is said that because Mandeism is more systematic from certain points of view, it is likely to be earlier than Johannism, which is less so. This is a questionable idea. The opposite might even appear more likely.[37]

Gnostic Origins

The Nag Hammadi texts have not settled the question of the origin of Gnosticism, although many scholars have recognized undeniable Jewish elements: Old Testament allusions as well as midrashic interpretations in these texts. James M. Robinson in his 1981 presidential address to the Society of Biblical Literature noted: "Pre-Christian Gnosticism as such is hardly attested in a way to settle the debate once and for all."[38] In a similar fashion George W. MacRae declared, "Even if we are on solid ground in some cases in arguing that the original works represented in the [Nag Hammadi] library are much older than the extant copies, we are still unable to postulate plausibly any pre-Christian dates."[39]

Scholars who assume the pre-Christian origin of Gnosticism have failed to present even a plausible historical scenario of its

beginnings. Koester, for example, writes: "Was there an original
Gnostic religion with its original pre-Christian myth? The answer to
this question must be negative."[40] Elsewhere he admits, "The history
of Gnosticism in its early stages during the period of early Christianity cannot be identified with the history of a tangible sociological
phenomenon."[41] Schenke, who earlier attempted to pinpoint Gnostic origins, has now conceded:

> Almost two decades ago, these general considerations were my
> starting point in a special attempt to trace the majority of the
> gnostic systems back to a single system or point of origin that
> could be understood as the primitive gnostic system. Such an
> attempt now has to be abandoned.[42]

The trend for many scholars has been to seek some sphere or
situation in which Jewish elements could have been inverted, perhaps by renegade Jews. The search for such a situation in the first
century CE in Alexandria is rather problematic.[43] Philo, the leading
Jewish thinker, provides much evidence for *gnōsis* in the broad
sense, but not for Gnosticism in the narrow sense. Pearson, who
believes in the possibility of a pre-Christian Alexandrian Gnosticism,
does not find this in Philo. He concludes, "Philo cannot be described
as a 'Gnostic' in the technical sense of the word," and adds, "Philo
is not dependent upon, or influenced by, Gnosticism."[44]

G. Quispel attempted to connect the Fall of Sophia with the
Descent of Ishtar, Simon's prostitute-consort Helen, the tractate
Thunder (*NHC* VI,2) and Mandaean ideas, all to explain how this
myth developed in Alexandria.[45] A serious critique of the derivation
of the Fall of Sophia from Jewish Wisdom has now been undertaken
by G. P. Luttikhuizen, who points out irreconcilable differences
between the two traditions.[46]

Although Robert M. Grant once proposed the disappointed
apocalyptic hopes of the Jews after the destruction of the temple in
70 CE as the key factor in Jewish disillusionment leading to Gnosticism,[47] he later repudiated this idea, especially in view of continued
Jewish expectations after the First Revolt.[48] I have ventured to

suggest another scenario: disillusionment after the Second or Bar Kochba War (132-35 CE).[49] If this is considered as too late, another possibility may be suggested: disillusionment over the disastrous uprising which spread from Cyrene to Egypt under Trajan (115-17 CE).[50]

Patristic Accounts and Nag Hammadi

Until the publication of the Nag Hammadi texts, our main source of information on the Gnostics consisted of the heresiological accounts of such church fathers as Justin Martyr, Irenaeus, Hippolytus, and Epiphanius. They told of outrageously immoral and licentious activities on the part of the Gnostics, and of their addiction to magical deeds.[51] Whereas the latter has received some confirmation, scholars were rather disappointed to discover that instead of orgies of such outlandish groups as Phibionites, we had an essentially ascetic dossier of texts.

It had been widely held that with the exception of groups like the Valentinians,[52] Gnostics tended to go to extremes—either to libertinism or asceticism from their dualistic principles. With the possible exception of *Thunder* and of some Simonian elements in a few tractates,[53] there is almost nothing in the Nag Hammadi corpus to confirm the patristic accounts of libertine excess. Some scholars therefore have questioned the patristic accounts altogether.

Yet there may be legitimate reasons for the differences.[54] Desjardins comments that "the emphasis on asceticism found throughout the entire Nag Hammadi corpus could tell us as much about the predilections of fourth century monks as it does about second century Valentinianism."[55] The church fathers may have been alarmed that they were being tarred indiscriminately with accusations engendered by libertine Gnostics, and may have been most concerned with these groups.[56] They could not be harmed publicly in the same manner by ascetic Gnostics. We should note also that the immorality of some Gnostics is attested by other Gnostic texts, such as the *Pistis Sophia*.[57]

One possible text which may cast some light on Carpocratian libertinism—if it is genuine[58]—is the controversial letter ascribed to

Clement of Alexandria, which Morton Smith discovered in the Mar Saba monastery.[59] We shall not need to say much about the bizarre hypothesis of Smith explaining primitive Christianity as a homoerotic mystery conferred by Jesus himself.[60] We may note that there is very little evidence of homosexuality even among the libertine Gospels, save for one sect of the Naassenes described by Hippolytus (*Ref.* 5.7.14), and the Levites described by Epiphanius (*Panarion* 26.13.1).

Simon Magus and the Early Heresiarchs

The heresiologists were unanimous in hailing Simon Magus (Acts 8) as the fountainhead of gnostic heresies. Justin Martyr (d. ca. 165), who was from Neapolis (Nablus) in Samaria, may or may not have had access to accurate information about the Samaritans. In his *Second Apology* (15), although he writes that he despises the wicked and deceitful doctrine of Simon "of my own nation," it is clear that he was a Gentile Samaritan who was converted to Christianity rather than a Jewish Samaritan.[61]

Scholars who maintain a pre-Christian Gnosticism have tried to reconcile the patristic tradition with Luke's account in Acts 8. A prime example of this approach is presented by Gerd Lüdemann, who dismisses the depiction of Simon as a "magician," and instead focuses on the address of the people reported in vs. 10: "This is the power of God, which is called great," as an indication of a link to the patristic accounts (cf. Justin, *1 Apol.* 26.3). Then seizing upon the expression of vs. 22, "a thought (*epinoia*) in your heart," as reflecting the technical terminology for Simon's female companion, Lüdemann triumphantly declares: "In conclusion, the gnostic system of the Simonians that is witnessed with certainty in the time of Justin may now, with a high degree of probability, be dated back to the time of Luke or, indeed, to the time of the Hellenistic sources used by Luke."[62]

To Lüdemann's suggestion that Luke has demoted Simon from a Gnostic to a magician, R. McL. Wilson somewhat mischievously responds, "But were Elymas and the sons of Sceva also gnostics?"[63] As opposed to scholars like Lüdemann, E. Haenchen, and K.

Rudolph, many others hold that the account of Acts is correct and that the Fathers were mistaken in foisting upon the shoulders of poor Simon the whole weight of subsequent Gnostic heresies.[64]

Fossum suggests: "It would seem right to regard at least those tenets which are unparalleled in the heresiography of Gnostic sects as genuinely Simonian, but the question remains whether they derive from Simon himself, for our story about Simon Magus in Acts 8, the first source to mention the Samaritan heresiarch, does not represent him as proto-Gnostic."[65] Pétrement suggests that Simon was actually a schismatic, who was transformed into a heretic because of the teachings of some of his followers. In any case the Simonian system is relatively simple, lacking an ontological dualism, and thus not qualifying as Gnosticism in the developed sense of the term.

Scholars have speculated about the alleged connection between the Dositheus associated with Simon by the church fathers, the Dosithean sect of the Samaritans, and the Nag Hammadi tractate, *The Three Steles of Seth* (*NCH* VII,5), which is presented as a revelation of a Dositheus. Unfortunately the name Dositheus is a very common one, and the sources on the Dositheans are not very clear.[66] The Samaritan sources such as the *Memar Marqah* (fourth century CE), the *Malef* (fourteenth century CE) and *Asatic*, which have been used by scholars like Fossum to elucidate the Samaritan roots of Gnosticism,[67] are so late that they do not inspire much confidence.[68]

From the late first and early second century we also encounter a Cerinthus in Asia Minor.[69] Cerinthus taught that the world was not made by the first God but by a certain power who was ignorant of the God above all (*Haer.* 1.26.1). According to Pétrement, "Cerinthus may have been the first Gnostic properly speaking, since he separated the true God and the creative power and considered it a power that did not know the true God."[70] Cerinthus also asserted that the Christ descended upon the human Jesus in the form of the dove, and then withdrew from Jesus before the crucifixion, as Christ could not suffer.

Ignatius

Ignatius, the bishop of Antioch, wrote seven letters (to the Ephesians, Magnesians, Trallians, Romans, Philadelphians, Smyrnaeans, and to Polycarp, bishop of Smyrna),[71] as he was taken by Roman soldiers on his way to martyrdom in Rome late in the reign of Trajan (98-117). Ignatius is noteworthy especially for stressing the importance of the bishop's authority in the face of heresy, namely the "monepiscopacy." Scholars dispute whether he was faced with one, two, or even three heresies.[72]

What is clear is that Ignatius objected to certain Jewish or Judaizing emphases, and above all to docetic views about Christ (*Trallians* 9-10).[73] Now it is most noteworthy that Ignatius was giving these warnings about the same time that Menander and Saturninus were teaching in Antioch and Cerinthus in Asia.[74] What then was the nature of Ignatius's docetic opponents? For Koester the answer is simple: "Docetism is repeatedly rejected in no uncertain terms; these opponents denied the humanity of Jesus Christ . . . which means that they were gnostics."[75]

But as an earlier study of Virginia Corwin has argued, Ignatius does not appear to direct any explicit polemic against the doctrine of a radical dualism with a foolish creator god.[76] Her position, that Ignatius faced at most only a rudimentary form of Gnosticism, has been followed by many scholars.[77] Most compelling is the judgment of W. R. Schoedel, the leading current authority on the Ignatian corpus: "There is scant evidence that the bishop was familiar with Gnosticism in a developed form."[78] This is a crucial judgment against the belief of scholars that there was already a highly developed Gnosticism in Syria and Asia Minor in the first century or even early in the second century.

Marcion

Marcion (d. ca. 154), who hailed from Sinope in Pontus in northern Asia Minor and then came to Rome ca. 140, was successful in establishing a Marcionite church as a rival to the Catholic Christian church.[79] Marcion's canon of a truncated Gospel of Luke and ten

Pauline letters would eventually also challenge the Catholic church into drawing up its own fuller canon.[80]

Though the church fathers linked Marcion with other Gnostics, his teachings differ in many respects from typical Gnostic systems, and this has divided scholars in their characterization of him. While some, like von Harnack or (more recently) J. Hoffmann and H. Koester, have stressed his non-Gnostic side, others like H. Jonas and B. Aland have stressed his affinities with Gnosticism.[81]

Unable to reconcile the anthropomorphism of the Old Testament[82] with the philosophical concept of God, Marcion concluded that there were two gods: the inferior God of the Old Testament and the supreme God of the New Testament. He regarded the former as the Creator who, though not evil, was incompetent and ignorant. The Old Testament provided a revelation valid for Jews, but no longer for Christians. Christ was not born of a woman, but he did suffer and die. Marcion also does not present the elaborate speculation regarding aeons which characterize many Gnostic systems.

Yet the development of a more typical gnostic system characterizes Marcion's disciple Apelles.[83] According to Hoffmann, ". . . in Apelles' system, the Old Testament, which for Marcion still has the value of a distinct, historical revelation, dissolves into myth."[84] But is this not an instructive paradigm of how the progressive devaluation of the Old Testament could lead toward a denigration of the Old Testament Creator God as the gnostic demiurge? Note that in this case the transformation, which is clearly documented, took place not in the first but in the second century.[85]

Basilides
Basilides was an important Gnostic teacher who taught in Alexandria ca. 132-35 (the reign of Hadrian). According to Irenaeus (*Adversus Haereses / A. H.* 1.24.1), Basilides, like Saturninus, derived his inspiration from Menander. Pearson infers from this statement that Basilides may have come to Egypt from Antioch.[86] Two different traditions of his teaching have been preserved, a monistic one by Hippolytus, and a dualistic one by Irenaeus.

Hippolytus reports (*A. H.* 7.20-27) that for Basilides the world existed in the world-seed of the inexpressible God. Three Sonships came from the seed; the third carried the souls of humans up with it. Salvation was viewed as a kind of reincarnation. This version has been preferred by R. M. Grant and other scholars.[87]

The dualistic system is preferred by Pétrement,[88] Layton,[89] and Pearson.[90] According to Irenaeus (*A. H. 1.24.3-6), for Basilides a series including Nous* ("Mind"), *Logos, Phronesis* ("Understanding"), *Sophia,* and *Dynamis* ("Power") emanated from the transcendent God; and from these three hundred and sixty-five heavens were created. The chief of the last is the "God of the Jews."

Nous, who was Christ, came to liberate souls. He appeared as a man and worked miracles. But since he could not suffer, he escaped crucifixion by a ruse.[91] The Nag Hammadi codices have yielded two striking parallels to Basilidean docetism: *The Second Treatise (Logos) of the Great Seth NHC* VII,2), and *The Apocalypse of Peter* (*NHC* VII,3), in which we have the Savior laughing at the foolishness of the mob which mistakenly believed that they had crucified him.

Valentinus and Valentinians

The most important gnostic teacher was the brilliant Valentinus, who after his education in Alexandria, came to Rome between 136 and 140 (Irenaeus, *A. H.* 3.4.3). He was probably born ca. 100. Because of conflicts with the Catholic church in Rome, he left for Cyprus ca. 160. Valentinus left a legacy of gifted disciples including Ptolemy, Heracleon and Theodotus. According to Hippolytus the first two represented the western or Italian school and the latter the eastern or Anatolian school of Valentinianism. It is not always easy to discern the original teachings of Valentinus from those of his disciples.

From Irenaeus (*A. H.* 1.11.1) we hear that for Valentinus the original pair in the divine world, or *pleroma,* were the Ineffable and Silence. From these emanated in turn a second duality, a quartet of beings, and the first Ogdoad (group of eight). With eleven pairs of male-female aeons these gave the thirty aeons of the *pleroma.*

Sophia, the last of these aeons, was filled with base desire. Her revolt gave rise to the demiurge who created the world.

In some Valentinian systems humanity was divided into three classes: (1) the *choic* or material, (2) the *psychic*, and (3) the *pneumatic*. The heavenly Christ sent down the savior Jesus to impart to the true Gnostics the *gnōsis* of their origins. Scholars have generally held that only pneumatics were saved "by nature." Desjardins, however, has argued that the sources, correctly interpreted, indicate that Valentinians also allowed the possibility of salvation for the psychics.[92]

A number of Nag Hammadi tractates have been identified by scholars as Valentinian, though not one of the works themselves explicitly claim this.[93] These include such works as *The Tripartite Tractate* (*NHC* I,5), *The Gospel of Philip* (*NHC* II,3), *The Interpretation of Knowledge* (*NHC* XI,1), a *Valentinian Exposition* (*NHC* XI,2)), *The Second Apocalypse of James* (*NHC* V,4) and others.[94] Some have even suggested that Valentinus was the author of *The Gospel of Truth* (*NHC* I,3 and XII,2).[95]

Scholars have tended to classify non-Valentinian tractates under the rubric "Sethian," to include teachings which the heresiologists described as Barbelognostic and Ophite. The oldest version of their myth is found in *The Apocryphon of John*. However, Pétrement opposes the belief of many scholars that Sethian Gnosticism preceded Valentinian Gnosticism, arguing that Sethian Gnosticism as represented in *The Apocryphon of John* developed after Valentinus.[96]

The Valentinians were among the most successful of the Christian Gnostics. They pioneered in commenting on Scriptures.[97] Many of their ideas seem to have influenced thinkers like Clement of Alexandria.[98] Unlike the Simonians, who were soon eclipsed, Valentinians were strong enough in the third century to require the refutations of Origen and Plotinus.

The Bauer Thesis Reassessed
Walter Bauer's seminal work, first published in German in 1934,[99] and belatedly translated into English in 1971 as *Orthodoxy and*

Heresy in Earliest Christianity,[100] has had a major impact upon scholars. In opposition to the tradition set forth by Eusebius regarding an initial orthodoxy from which later heresies like Gnosticism branched off, Bauer set forth several theses: (1) that from the outset there was a variety of Christian groups, (2) that in many areas (particularly Syria, Asia and Egypt) the majority of Christians belonged to groups later branded as heretical; and (3) that it was only in the second century that Rome imposed "orthodoxy" on these areas.[101]

Bauer's thesis has been warmly embraced by Koester who has written that "Recent discoveries, especially those at Nag Hammadi in Upper Egypt, have made it even clearer that Bauer was essentially right, and that a thorough and extensive reevaluation of early Christian history is called for."[102] Elaine Pagels, who studied under Koester, is aware of criticisms levelled against Bauer;[103] nonetheless her work appears to follow Bauer's programmatic revisionism, at least to one reviewer.[104]

With respect to inner Syria at Edessa, Bauer argued from Bardesanes (154-222), who opposed the Marcionites, that Marcionism was the earliest form of Christianity there. Yet, although Bauer considered Bardesanes a Valentinian, and Ephraem considered him a heretic, H. J. W. Drijvers does not consider him a Gnostic.[105] And in a recent monographic examination of the Bauer thesis, T. A. Robinson has recognized a basic inconsistency in Bauer's use of Marcionism.[106]

Bauer reasoned that the concern which was exhibited by Ignatius and Polycarp over the authority of the bishop in the face of heresies in Antioch and in Asia implied that the majority were heretical Christians. Comparing the cities addressed by Ignatius, and the seven letters of Revelation 2-3, Bauer concluded that the cities from this list which were not addressed by Ignatius had fallen away to the heretics.

Critics such as F. W. Norris condemn Bauer's use of argument from silence. Norris comments that although Ignatius and Polycarp indicate concern about "wrong" teaching and practice, "those supporting them in the Asia Minor and western Syrian cities which their writings reflect, probably represented majorities."[107] After examining the evidence for Asia in detail, Robinson concludes that "where we have an area with extensive relevant data for the question of the orthodoxy/heresy debate (i. e., Ephesus), I contend the Bauer Thesis rings hollow."[108]

In his *Introduction to the New Testament*, Koester stresses the validity of Bauer's insight, especially for Egypt.[109] For support of this thesis Koester argues as follows:

> The two oldest manuscript finds of Christian books from Egypt point to the Gospel of John. The fragment of the Gospel of John in P52 and the *Unknown Gospel* of *Papyrus Egerton 2* were both written before the middle of II CE, possibly shortly after 100. Thus both the Gospel of John and a gospel which possibly provided some of its source material were known in Egypt at a very early date. . . . Later witnesses prove that John was a favorite book among Egyptian gnostics. It is therefore likely that Christians who not much later were called "gnostics" were the first Christian preachers to appear in Egypt.[110]

We may certainly question the premise that the *Unknown Gospel* of Papyrus Egerton 2 provided some of the source material for John. The one fragment with Johannine echoes resembles a pastiche of allusions to John rather than a source for John.[111] To conclude from the popularity of John's Gospel among the Gnostics that the Gnostics themselves brought the Gospel to Egypt is an extraordinary leap in logic.[112]

Leaving aside the question of the Gnosticism of the *Hermetica*, the fact that they are non-Christian documents from Egypt hardly proves the non-Christian origin of Gnosticism in that country. They may simply demonstrate the possibility of late non-Christian "gnostic" texts.

In opposition to the Bauer-Koester thesis, a recent study of the papyri in Egypt by Colin Roberts makes a significant point:

And once the evidence of the papyri is available, indisputably Gnostic texts are conspicuous by their rarity. Of the fourteen Christian texts that I would date before A.D. 200 there is only one, the first fragment of *The Gospel of Thomas* from Oxyrhynchus, which may reasonably be regarded as Gnostic.[113]

Analysis of Valentinian documents themselves indicates that the Valentinians also regarded themselves as a minority. Consider the *Excerpta ex Theodoto* 56.2: "Therefore many are material, but not many are psychic, and few are spiritual." Pearson writes:

However successful the Gnostic groups might have been in attracting converts to their groups, it must finally be concluded, with regard to Bauer's thesis, that (1) he was wrong on the question of the origins of Christianity in Egypt, and (2) he was also probably wrong in his assessment of the relative numerical strengths of the non-Gnostic and Gnostic Christians there.[114]

The analysis of J. F. McCue is similar.[115]

Gary T. Burke has recently utilized an anti-Christian source from the second century—the critic Celsus, whom Origen refuted—to show that Bauer's thesis is flawed. For Celsus observed of Christians, "When they were beginning they were few and were of one mind; but since they have spread to become a multitude, they are divided and rent asunder, and each wants to have his own party" (Origen, *Contra Celsum* III.10). Burke concludes that "Celsus, who is known to have been in the East, where according to Bauer Christian sects had multiple independent origins, somehow saw in a deeply divided phenomenon a common point of origin."[116]

Conclusions
In the present survey I have attempted to focus on the questions (1) when a fully developed Gnosticism with its articulated dualism, cosmology, anthropology and soteriology developed, and (2) what

was the relationship between the gnostic sects and "orthodox" Christianity.

(1) Those who have followed in the train of the History-of-Religions School[117] have sought with Hermann Gunkel "to get away from the barriers of the canon and from the ecclesiastical dogma about the Bible."[118] They have followed Rudolph Bultmann in assuming that the New Testament writers both reacted against Gnosticism and assimilated some of its ideas. This relationship is sustained in part by concurrently maintaining very late dates for some of the New Testament books and very early dates for some of the Nag Hammadi texts.

(2) As for the appeal to so-called non-Christian Nag Hammadi texts to support the case for a pre-Christian Gnosticism, even some of the advocates of such sources have qualified their claims after the first rush of enthusiasm. James Robinson is among those when he declares:

> The solution to the traditional problem of gnosticism and early Christianity has not been solved by the publication of the Nag Hammadi Codices. For the early heralding of such a gnostic text as the *Apocalypse of Adam* as "pre-Christian" proved somewhat premature, in that Alexander Böhlig has clarified his usage of that term in the *editio princeps* to mean no more than that the text was not yet under Christian influence irrespective of the century of its composition.[119]

(3) At the 1966 Messina Conference on Gnostic Origins the lone scholar who was willing to argue for the traditional view of Gnosticism as a post-Christian heresy was Simone Pétrement. More scholars are now willing to acknowledge the assumption of Christianity as an indispensable basis for a fully developed Gnosticism. They include Barbara Aland, Martin Hengel, Karl-Wolfgang Tröger, and most significantly, Ugo Bianchi, the editor of the Messina conference. Bianchi concludes:

In effect it is difficult to imagine that in a purely Jewish environment, although penetrated by Greek thought, one would have been able to arrive at that extreme which is the demonization of the God of Israel. . . . Only the perspective of a messiah conceived as a divine manifestation, as a divine incarnate person, already present in the faith of the New Testament and of the Church, but interpreted by the Gnostics on the basis of ontological presuppositions of the Greek mysteriosophic doctrine of *soma-sema* ("body"-"tomb") and of the split in the divine, could allow the development of a new Gnostic theology where the God of the Bible, the creator, became the demiurge [120] . . . .

(4) We have seen how the thesis of Walter Bauer has influenced scholars like Helmut Koester regarding the gnostic nature of the earliest Christianity in Egypt. But again, after the enthusiastic initial reception of the English translation of Bauer's work in 1971, other scholars have discerned gaps in his argumentation. Even B. Pearson, who holds to the presence of a pre-Valentinian Gnosticism in Egypt on other grounds, concedes that the Gnostics relied heavily on the non-gnostic writings of the canonical New Testament. In contrast to Koester, Pearson does not think it likely that these writings were brought to Alexandria by Gnostics.[121]

(5) Though the gnostic Christians presented an alternative which was appealing to many in the second century, and to some interpreters and readers of the twentieth century,[122] they were eventually defeated and suppressed. How did they differ and why were they defeated?

In their theology the Gnostics posited a split in the Godhead. As R. A. Norris has observed, "In their eagerness to segregate matter from spirit, evil from good, the Gnostics dissolved at once the unity of the world and the unity of God."[123] They could see no good in the natural world. By rejecting the Old Testament heritage of Christianity, Gnostics lost their moorings in history.[124] They were not interested in the healing deeds of Jesus, only in the *gnōsis* which the risen Christ imparted to an elite circle. They were apparently not willing to work compassionately with those in need,[125] or to give their lives for their faith[126]—two of the great strengths of the early church. The Gnostics were fragmented into many groups without a stable set of Scriptures or central authority. The extreme ethical positions, whether the libertinism of a few or the asceticism of the majority of Gnostics, did not bode well for the continuation of their communities. The denigration of marriage and procreation meant that there might well not be a natural increase of Gnostic followers.

(6) The efforts of the Church Fathers such as Justin Martyr, Irenaeus, Tertullian and others were not without effect.[127] As Robert M. Grant has observed:

> To sum up to this point: there are two stages here, first around the time of Irenaeus when Christians (after Justin's lead) accuse Gnostics of immorality and thus indirectly point to their anti-social stance, second in the time of Origen when Christians can look down on Gnostics whose numbers, status, and importance are well below that of the Christian church. What happened? Presumably the work of the anti-heretical fathers took effect and Gnostics, excluded from the Christian community, began to wither away.[128]

Whether this is a matter of gratification or lament is a highly personal issue, depending on one's attitude toward the Scriptures and the Savior manifested in them.[129] My own judgment is that the Gnostics fatally devalued creation, the Old Testament, the incarnation of Christ, his death, his resurrection, and ethical concerns for the community. On the other hand, orthodoxy elevated institutional hierarchy and traditions to the detriment of the spiritual lives of ordinary believers. I would hope that Christians may learn from the history of these excesses to appreciate rightly the freshness and the fullness of the Gospel.

Notes

1. See E. Yamauchi, "Gnosticism," in S. B. Ferguson and D. F. Wright, eds., *New Dictionary of Christian Theology* (Leicester: Inter-Varsity, 1988), 272-74. For my earlier extended treatment of this subject see *Pre-Christian Gnosticism* [hereafter *PCG*], rev. ed. (Grand Rapids: Baker, 1983). In this paper I shall for the most part attempt to concentrate on publications which have appeared in the last decade.

2. F. Wisse, "Prolegomena to the Study of the New Testament and *Gnosis*," in A. H. B. Logan and A. J. M. Wedderburn, eds., *The New Testament and Gnosis* (Edinburgh: T. & T. Clark, 1983), 142, even ventures that "The so-called developed, Gnostic 'systems' of the second century CE may well be the invention of the ancient and modern interpreter rather than being intended by the Gnostic authors."

3. See H. Jonas, *The Gnostic Religion* (Boston: Beacon Press, 1963), 36.

4. A. H. Armstrong, "Gnosis and Greek Philosophy," in B. Aland, ed., *Gnosis: Festschrift für Hans Jonas* (Göttingen: Vandenhoeck & Ruprecht, 1978), 87-124.

5. Scholars in this camp are well represented by K. Rudolph, *Gnosis: The Nature and History of Gnosticism* (San Francisco: Harper and Row, 1983). H.-M. Schenke, "The Problem of *Gnosis*," *The Second Century* 3 (1983): 76, defines Gnosticism as "a religious salvation movement of late antiquity in which the possibility of a negative attitude toward self and world is taken up in a special way and consolidated into a consistently world-negating world view, which expresses itself in characteristic word usage, metaphorical language, and artificial myths." The problem with such a synthetic definition arises with the subjective judgment involved in discerning what is an "unmistakable" trait of Gnosticism. A docetic approach to Christianity, for example, is certainly not confined to Gnosticism.

6. This position has now been ably articulated by S. Pétrement, *A Separate God: The Christian Origins of Gnosticism* (San Francisco:

Harper, 1984). See also G. Filoramo, *A History of Gnosticism* (Oxford: Basil Blackwell, 1990).

7. On the lateness of Persian religious sources, and the lack of anything from the crucial Parthian period (247 BCE to 224 CE) see E. Yamauchi, "Religions of the Biblical Worlds: Persia," in G. W. Bromiley, ed., *The International Standard Bible Encyclopedia* (Grand Rapids: Eerdmans, 1988), IV, 123-29; idem, *Persia and the Bible* (Grand Rapids: Baker, 1990), ch. 12, "Zoroastrianism."

8. See my review of G. Widengren, ed., *Der Mandäismus* in *Journal of the American Oriental Society* 105 (1985): 345-46.

9. See L. Koenen, "From Baptism to the Gnosis of Manichaeism," in B. Layton, ed., *The Rediscovery of Gnosticism* (Leiden: Brill, 1981), II, 734-56.

10. E. Yamauchi, "The Present Status of Mandaean Studies," *Journal of Near Eastern Studies* 25 (1966): 88-96.

11. E. Yamauchi, *Mandaic Incantation Texts* (New Haven: American Oriental Society, 1967).

12. For the latest literature, see my review of R. Macuch, K. Rudolph and E. Segelberg, *Zur Sprache und Literatur der Mandäer* in *Journal of the American Oriental Society* 100 (1980): 79-82.

13. E. Yamauchi, *Gnostic Ethics and Mandaean Origins* (Cambridge, MA: Harvard University, 1970); idem, "Mandaeism," in V. Furnish et al., eds. *Supplementary Volume, The Interpreter's Dictionary of the Bible* (Nashville: Abingdon Press, 1976), 563.

14. K. Rudolph, "Quellenprobleme zum Ursprung und Alter der Mandäer," in J. Neusner, ed., *Christianity, Judaism and Other Graeco-Roman Cults* (Leiden: Brill, 1975), IV, 112f.

15. See K. Rudolph, *Mandaeism* (Leiden: Brill, 1978); J. J. Buckley, "Why Once Is Not Enough: Mandaean Baptism . . . as an Example of a Repeated Ritual," *History of Religions* 29 (1989): 23-34.

16. E. Yamauchi, "Hermetic Literature," in Furnish (n.13), 408; G. Luck, "The Doctrine of Salvation in the Hermetic Writings," *The Second Century* 8 (1991):31-41.

17. J. H. Charlesworth, "Odes of Solomon," in J. H. Charlesworth, ed., *The Old Testament Pseudepigrapha* (Garden City, NY: Doubleday, 1985), II, 726-32.

18. H. J. W. Drijvers, "Facts and Problems in Early Syriac-Speaking Christianity," *The Second Century* 2 (1982): 166-67, 169.

19. P.-H. Poirier, *L'Hymne de la perle des Actes de Thomas* (Louvain-La-Neuve: Université Catholique de Louvain, 1981); cf. *PCG* (n.1), 95-98, 214-15.

20. For the translation of these texts see: B. Layton, ed., *The Gnostic Scriptures* (Garden City, NY: Doubleday, 1987); J. M. Robinson, ed., *The Nag Hammadi Library in English* [hereafter *NHL*], 3rd ed. (San Francisco: Harper, 1990).

21. See J. C. Shelton, "Introduction," in J. W. Barns, G. M. Browne and J. C. Shelton, eds., *Nag Hammadi Codices: Greek and Coptic Papyri from the Cartonnage of the Covers* (Leiden: Brill, 1981), 1-11. On the nature of the collection, see E. Yamauchi, "The Nag Hammadi Library," *Journal of Library History* 22 (1987): 425-41.

22. See E. Yamauchi, "Pre-Christian Gnosticism in the Nag Hammadi Texts?" *Church History* 48 (1979): 129-41.

23. D. M. Parrott in Robinson, *NHL*, 278, objects that we are not told the manner of punishment, or when it ended in death. See also his, "The 13 Kingdoms of the *Apocalypse of Adam*: Origin, Meaning and Significance," *Novum Testamentum* 31 (1989): 67-87.

24. H. Koester, *Introduction to the New Testament II: History and Literature of Early Christianity* (Philadelphia: Fortress Press, 1982), 211.

25. K. Rudolph, *Gnosis* (n.5), 135.

26. See *PCG* (n.1), 110-11, 218-19. A. Henrichs in J. M. Robinson, et al., *Jewish Gnostic Nag Hammadi Texts*, W. Wuellner, ed. (Berkeley: Center for Hermeneutical Studies, 1975), 4, comments: "To regard the AA as a document of non-Christian Gnosticism is a possible inference (the most serious obstacle to such a view would be AA 78, 18f.). But to presume that it attests the existence of pre-Christian Gnosticism seems to be unfounded speculation on the

part of those scholars who are prepared to make such a tacit assumption at any rate as a matter of principle."

27. F. Mora rd, *L'Apocalypse d'Adam* (Québec: Presses de l'Université Laval, 1985), 100.

28. J. E. Fossum, *The Name of God* (Tübingen: J. C. B. Mohr, 1985), 100.

29. See most recently A. J. Welburn, "Iranian Prophetology and the Birth of the Messiah: *The Apocalypse of Adam*," in W. Haase, ed., *Aufstieg und Niedergang der römischen Welt* [hereafter *ANRW*] II.25.6 (1988): 4752-94.

30. See E. Yamauchi, *Persia and the Bible*, (n.7), ch. 14, "Mithraism."

31. See E. Yamauchi, "*The Apocalypse of Adam*, Mithraism, and Pre-Christian Gnosticism," in J. Duchesne-Guillemin, ed., *Études mithriaques, textes et mémoires*, IV (Leiden: Brill, 1978), 537-63. M. Schwartz, an Iranologist at Berkeley, has also observed (in Wuellner [n.26] 25-26): "Depending on the chronology of the 'Thirteen Kingdoms' section, the rock-birth motif may have come to our text not from the Mithraists of Asia Minor, but rather from their Roman heirs."

32. F. Wisse, "The Redeemer Figure in the Paraphrase of Shem," *Novum Testamentum* 12 (1970): 130-40.

33. *PCG* (n.1), 220.

34. Ibid., 115-16.

35. G. Robinson, "*The Trimorphic Protennoia* and the Prologue of the Fourth Gospel," in J. E. Goehring et al., eds., *Gnosticism and the Early Christian World* (Sonoma, CA: Polebridge Press, 1990), I, 50:

> As we have seen in the case of a few examples, all the statements of *Trimorphic Protennoia* are integrated so organically into the Sethian myth that it would hardly be possible to interpret them in a Christian way and derive them from the Fourth Gospel. The Prologue, on the other hand, is not explicable on the basis of the rest of the Fourth Gospel. Thus since *Trimorphic Protennoia* is the best-attested matrix for the Logos hymn, the most obvious conclusion would seem to be

that the Prologue derives from a Wisdom tradition that has
already passed through this gnostic filter.

36. See E. Yamauchi, "Jewish Gnosticism? The Prologue of John,
Mandaean Parallels, and the *Trimorphic Protennoia,*" in R. van den
Broek and M. J. Vermaseren, eds., *Studies in Gnosticism and Hellenistic Religions* (Leiden: Brill, 1981), 467-97. In an earlier study Y.
Janssens also regarded parallels with the gospel due to New Testament reminiscences, but in recent studies she is less emphatic; see
her *La Prôtennoia Trimorphe NHL* XIII, 1) (Québec: Les Presses de
l'Université Laval, 1978), and *"The Trimorphic Protennoia* and the
Fourth Gospel," in Logan and Wedderburn (n.2), 234.
37. Pétrement, *A Separate God,* 318 (n.6).
38. J. M. Robinson, "Jesus: From Easter to Valentinus (Or to the
Apostles' Creed)," *Journal of Biblical Literature* 101 (1982): 5.
39. G. W. MacRae, "Nag Hammadi and the New Testament," in B.
Aland, ed., *Gnosis: Festschrift für Hans Jonas* (n.4), 146-47.
40. H. Koester, "The History-of-Religions School, *Gnosis,* and
Gospel of John," *Studia Theologica* 40 (1986): 131.
41. H. Koester, *Introduction to the New Testament* (n.24), 297.
42. H.-M. Schenke, "The Problem of *Gnosis,*" *The Second Century*
3 (1983): 86.
43. H. A. Green, *The Economic and Social Origins of Gnosticism*
(Atlanta: Scholars Press, 1985), has attempted to postulate a socio-
economic background for the origin of Gnosticism, in first century
(CE) Alexandria. His results are not generally regarded as con-
clusive. Cf. M. Desjardins, this volume, 315 and 321 (n.31).
44. B. A. Pearson, "Philo and Gnosticism," *ANRW* II.21.1 (1984):
340. Contrast this with the situation in Alexandria a century later,
where Clement betrays clear interaction with Gnosticism. See J. E.
Davison, "Structural Similarities and Dissimilarities in the Thought
of Clement of Alexandria and the Valentinians," *The Second Century* 3 (1983): 201-17.
45. G. Quispel, "Jewish *Gnosis* and Mandaean Gnosticism," in J.-E.
Ménard, ed., *Les textes de Nag Hammadi* (Leiden: Brill, 1975),
82-122. For my critique see E. Yamauchi, "The Descent of Ishtar,

the Fall of Sophia, and the Jewish Roots of Gnosticism," *Tyndale Bulletin* 29 (1978): 143-75.

46. G. P. Luttikhuizen, "The Jewish Factor in the Development of the Gnostic Myth of Origins: Some Observations," in T. Baarda et al., eds., *Text and Testimony* (Kampen: J. H. Kok, 1988), 152-61.

47. R. M. Grant, *Gnosticism and Early Christianity*, rev. ed. (New York: Harper and Row, 1966).

48. See B. M. Bokser, "Recent Developments in the Study of Judaism, 70-200 CE," *The Second Century* 3 (1983): 25-27.

49. E. Yamauchi, "The Descent of Ishtar," 164-68.

50. See E. Yamauchi, "Christians and the Jewish Revolts against Rome," *Fides et Historia* 23 (1991): 11-30. According to Alan F. Segal the radicalization of the "Two Powers" reflected in rabbinic texts occurred after the early second century CE; see his *Two Powers in Heaven: Early Rabbinic Reports about Christianity and Gnosticism* (Leiden: Brill, 1977), and "Judaism, Christianity and Gnosticism," ch. 8 in S. G. Wilson, ed., *Anti-Judaism in Early Christianity II: Separation and Polemic* (Waterloo: Wilfrid Laurier University, 1986).

51. G. Filoramo, *A History of Gnosticism* (n.6), 236. On the pervasive practice of magic in the ancient world, see E. Yamauchi, "Magic in the Biblical World," *Tyndale Bulletin* 34 (1983): 159-200; idem, "Magic or Miracle? Demons, Diseases and Exorcisms," in D. Wenham and C. Blomberg, eds., *Gospel Perspectives VI: The Miracles of Jesus* (Sheffield: JSOT Press, 1986), 89-183.

52. See E. Yamauchi, *Gnostic Ethics*; M. Desjardins, *Sin in Valentinianism* (Atlanta: Scholars Press, 1990).

53. Even these are doubtful. See S. Arai, "Zum 'Simonianischen' in Authlog und Bronte," in M. Krause, ed., *Gnosis and Gnosticism* (Leiden: Brill, 1981), 3-15.

54. J. Fossum, *The Name of God* (n.28), 173.

55. M. Desjardins, *Sin in Valentinianism*, 9.

56. See S. Benko, "Pagan Criticism of Christianity during the First Two Centuries A.D.," *ANRW* (1980) II 23.2: 1055-1118.

57. G. Filoramo, *A History of Gnosticism* (n.6), 186.

58. M. Smith, "Clement of Alexandria and Secret Mark: The Score at the End of the First Decade," *Harvard Theological Review* 75 (1982): 449-61, indicates that Smith has convinced most scholars of its genuineness, though there have been notable dissenters. See E. Osborn, "Clement of Alexandria: A Review of Research, 1958-1982," *The Second Century* 3 (1983): 224-25.

59. M. Smith, *Clement of Alexandria and a Secret Gospel of Mark* (Cambridge, MA: Harvard University, 1973); idem, *The Secret Gospel* (New York: Harper and Row, 1973).

60. See my review essay, "A Secret Gospel of Jesus as 'Magus'?" *Christian Scholar's Review* 4 (1975): 238-51; see also C. Smith, "Mark the Evangelist and His Relationship to Alexandrian Christianity in Biblical, Historical and Traditional Literature," unpublished M. A. thesis (Oxford: Miami University, 1992).

61. Pétrement, *A Separate God* (n.6), 245. On the important distinction between Samarians and Samaritans, see E. Yamauchi, "The Archaeological Background of Nehemiah," *Bibliotheca Sacra* 137 (1980): 307-308.

62. G. Lüdemann, "The Acts of the Apostles and the Beginnings of Simonian *Gnosis*," *New Testament Studies* 33 (1987): 425.

63. R. McL. Wilson, "Simon and the Gnostic Origins," in J. Kremer, ed., *Les Actes des Apôtres* (Leuven: Leuven University, 1979), 487, n.11.

64. See *PCG* (n.1), 57-65, 201-203; Pétrement, *A Separate God* (n.6), 240-45; Filoramo, *A History of Gnosticism* (n.6), 148-51; R. Pummer, "The Present State of Samaritan Studies II," *Journal of Semitic Studies* 22 (1977): 27-33.

65. J. Fossum, *The Name of God* (n.28), 360.

66. S. Isser, *The Dositheans: A Samaritan Sect in Late Antiquity* (Leiden: Brill, 1976).

67. J. Fossum, "The Origin of the Gnostic Concept of the Demiurge," *Ephemerides Theologicae Lovaniensis* 61 (1985): 142-52; idem, *The Name of God* (n.28), 81-83, 118.

68. See also J. Fossum, "Samaritan Sects and Movements,"in A. D. Crown, ed.; *The Samaritans* (Tübingen: J. C. B. Mohr, 1989), 293-

389. For an assessment of Simon's disciple, the Samaritan Menander, see S. Pétrement, *A Separate God*, 220. On Menander's disciple Saturninus, see R. M. Grant, ed., *Gnosticism* (New York: Harper and Bros., 1961), 31-32.

69. B. G. Wright III, "Cerinthus *apud* Hippolytus: An Inquiry into the Traditions about Cerinthus' Provenance," *The Second Century* 4 (1984):103-15, attempts to follow Hippolytus in placing Cerinthus in Egypt rather than in Asia with Irenaeus. But Irenaeus's links with Polycarp, who knew John and related his encounter with Cerinthus, should not be so readily dismissed (*A. H.* 3.3.4).

70. S. Pétrement, *A Separate God*, 300.

71. The so-called Middle Recension is accepted by the vast majority of scholars. Recent attempts by Weijenborg, Rius-Camps, and Joly to cast doubts on the authenticity of these letters are sufficiently refuted by W. R. Schoedel, "Are the Letters of Ignatius Authentic?" *Religious Studies Review* 6 (1980): 196-201.

72. See *PCG* (n.1), 65-66, 203-204; C. K. Barrett, "Jews and Judaizers in the Epistles of Ignatius," in R. Hamerton-Kelly and R. Scroggs, eds., *Jews, Greeks and Christians* (Leiden: Brill, 1976), 220-44. On the possibility of a third heresy, see C. Trevett, "Prophecy and Anti-Episcopal Activity: A Third Error Combatted by Ignatius?" *Journal of Ecclesiastical History* 34 (1983): 1-18.

73. W. R. Schoedel, *Ignatius of Antioch* (Philadelphia: Fortress, 1985), 152, gives the passage:

Be deaf, then, when someone speaks to you apart from Jesus Christ, of the family of David, of Mary, who was truly born, both ate and drank, was truly persecuted under Pontius Pilate, was truly crucified and died, as heavenly, earthly, and sub-earthly things looked on, who was also truly raised from the dead. . . . But if as some who are atheists—that is, unbelievers—say, that he suffered in appearance, whereas it is they who are (mere) appearance, why am I in bonds? Why do I pray even to fight with beasts? I die, then, in vain! Then I lie about the Lord!

74. That is, the Roman province around Ephesus. See E. Yamauchi, *New Testament Cities in Western Asia Minor* (Grand Rapids, Baker, 1980), 15-17 and ch. 7.

75. H. Koester, *Introduction to the New Testament*, 286.

76. V. Corwin, *St. Ignatius and Christianity in Antioch* (New Haven: Yale University, 1960).

77. *PCG* (n.1), 68; Pétrement, *A Separate God*, 222; R. Brown and J. P. Meier, *Antioch & Rome* (New York: Paulist Press, 1983), 74, n.167.

78. W. R. Schoedel, *Ignatius of Antioch* (n.73), 16.

79. The radical revisionist views of Hoffmann, who maintains that Marcion lived much earlier, was responsible for a letter to the Laodiceans, that he inspired the canonical Gospel of Luke, and never visited Rome, are quite incredible. See R. J. Hoffmann, *Marcion, On the Restitution of Christianity* (Chico: Scholars Press, 1984); idem, "How Then Know This Troublous Teacher?" *The Second Century* 6 (1987-88): 173-91. See the criticisms of G. May, "Ein neues Markionbild?" *Theologische Rundschau* 51 (1986): 404-13; idem, "Marcion in Contemporary Views," *The Second Century* 6 (1987-88): 129-52.

80. B. M. Metzger, *The Canon of the New Testament* (Oxford: Clarendon Press, 1987), 90-99.

81. Jonas, *The Gnostic Religion*, ch. 6; B. Aland, "Marcion: Versuch einer neuen Interpretation," *Zeitschrift für Theologie und Kirche* 70 (1973): 420-47; for the position of H. Koester see his *Introduction to the New Testament* (n.24), 330: "Marcion rejected the use of the speculative method of interpretation employed by the gnostics, as well as the gnostic formation of mythological constructs. . . ."

82. E. Yamauchi, "Anthropomorphism in Hellenism and in Judaism," *Bibliotheca Sacra* 127 (1970): 212-20.

83. G. Filoramo, *A History of Gnosticism*, 166.

84. R. J. Hoffmann, *Marcion* (n.79), 164.

85. See *PCG* (n.1), 241.

86. B. A. Pearson, *Gnosticism, Judaism, and Egyptian Christianity* (Minneapolis: Fortress Press, 1990), 202.

87. See *PCG*, 241.

88. S. Pétrement, *A Separate God* (n.6), 225.

89. B. Layton, *The Gnostic Scriptures* (n.20), 417-25.

90. B. Pearson, *Gnosticism, Judaism*, 203, n.31.

91. B. Layton, *The Gnostic Scriptures*, 423; see E. Yamauchi, "The Crucifixion and Docetic Christology," *Concordia Theological Quarterly* 46 (1982): 1-20. For the Islamic tradition, which denied the crucifixion of Jesus, see G. D. Newby, *The Making of the Last Prophet* (Columbia, SC: University of South Carolina Press, 1989), 205, 209-11; N. Robinson, *Christ in Islam and Christianity* (Albany: State University of New York Press, 1991), chs. 11-13. K.-W. Tröger, "Jesus, the Kora and Nag Hammadi," *Theology Digest* 38 (1991): 213-18.

92. M. Desjardins, *Sin in Valentinianism* (n.52), 121.

93. M. Desjardins, "The Sources for Valentinian Gnosticism: A Question of Methodology," *Vigiliae Christianae* 40 (1986): 342-47. The *Apocryphon of John* does reflect the Gnostic myth of the aeons used by Valentinus.

94. M. Desjardins, *Sin in Valentinianism*, 68-75.

95. See for example, K. Grobel, *The Gospel of Truth* (Nashville: Abingdon, 1960), 26.

96. Pétrement, *A Separate God* (n.6), 17, 227-28; cf. her "Les 'quatres illuminateurs': Sur le sens et l'origine d'un thème gnostique," *Revue des études Augustiniennes* 27 (1981): 3-23. Cf. D. J. Good, "Sophia in Valentinianism," *The Second Century* 4 (1984): 193-201. Good believes that Sophia was regarded as consort of the Supreme Being and blamed for the genesis of material creation under the influence of later Sethian/Ophite traditions.

97. See E. Pagels, *The Johannine Gospel in Gnostic Exegesis* (Nashville: Abingdon, 1973).

98. See Davison, "Structural Similarities" (n.44).

99. W. Bauer, *Rechtgläubigkeit und Ketzerei im ältesten Christentum* (Tübingen: J. C. B. Mohr, 1934).

100. R. Kraft and G. Krodel, eds., *Orthodoxy and Heresy in Earliest Christianity* (Philadelphia: Fortress Press, 1971).

101. For my earlier discussion on Bauer and his critics, see *PCG*, 87-89, 210.

102. H. Koester and J. M. Robinson, *Trajectories through Early Christianity* (Philadelphia: Fortress Press, 1971), 114.

103. E. Pagels, *The Gnostic Gospels* (New York: Random House, 1979), xxxi.

104. D. J. Harrington, "The Reception of Walter Bauer's *Orthodoxy and Heresy in Earliest Christianity* During the Last Decade," *Harvard Theological Review* 73 (1980): 297, writes, "A second important development of Bauer's thesis is Elaine Pagels' investigation of the gnostic Gospels. Written for a general audience and extraordinarily well publicized, this book represents both a resurrection of Bauer's thesis and a development of it on the basis of the discovery of the Nag Hammadi documents and research on them since 1945."

105. See H. J. W. Drijvers, *Bardaisan of Edessa* (Assen: Van Gorcum, 1966); see also *PCG* (n.1), 98-100.

106. T. A. Robinson, *The Bauer Thesis Examined: The Geography of Heresy in the Early Christian Church* (Lewiston, NY: Edwin Mellen Press, 1988), 51: "Bauer's reconstruction for Edessa fails. The two fundamental elements of that theory clash, and Bauer has not reconciled them: first, Marcionism as the original form of Christianity in Edessa; second, Marcionism as a successful form of Christianity."

107. F. W. Norris, "Ignatius, Polycarp, and I Clement: Walter Bauer Reconsidered," *Vigiliae Christianae* 30 (1976): 29.

108. Robinson, *The Bauer Thesis*, 91. Cf. M. Desjardins, "Bauer and Beyond: The Scholarly Discussion of *hairesis* in the Early Christian Era," *The Second Century* 8 (1991): 72, who comments: "Robinson's points on the whole are well-taken and well-argued; he adds another row of nails to the coffin enclosing Bauer's thesis."

109. Koester, *Introduction to the New Testament* (n.29), 220.

110. Ibid., 222. The original editors, H. I. Bell and T. C. Skeat, were more cautious in dating P. Egerton not later than "about the period A.D. 140-160." Other scholars would date both P66 and this Papyrus Egerton to the mid-second century date or even about 200. See the discussion by F. Neirynck, "The Apocryphal Gospels and the Gospel of Mark," in J.-M. Sevrin, ed., *The New Testament in Early Christianity* (Leuven: Leuven University Press, 1989), 161-62. In his more recent discussion of P. Egerton (*Ancient Christian Gospels* [Philadelphia: Trinity Press International, 1990], 206-16), Koester accepts the date of 200 for the document but still insists on its independence.

111. This is cited by Metzger, *The Canon of the New Testament*, 168: "And turning to the rulers of the people, he [Jesus] spoke this word: 'Search the Scriptures in which you think you have life—they testify on my behalf (John 5:39). Do not think that I have come to be your accuser before my Father; the one to accuse you is Moses, on whom you have set your hopes' (John 5:45). But then they said, 'Well, we know that God spoke to Moses, but we do not know where you come from' (John 4:29). Jesus answered them, 'Now your unbelief accuses you. . . .' " J. Jeremias, "An Unknown Gospel of the Synoptic Type (P. Ox. 840)," in E. Hennecke and W. Schneemelcher, eds., *New Testament Apocrypha* (Philadelphia: Westminster Press, 1963), I, 95, concluded: "The value which we assign to the text is determined by our judgment as to its relation to the canonical Gospels, especially to the Fourth. . . . The fact that the Johannine material is shot through with Synoptic phrases and the Synoptic with Johannine usage, permits the conjecture that the author knew all and every one of the canonical Gospels."

112. H. Koester, *Introduction to the New Testament* (n.24), 226, argues in a questionable fashion: "Thus, also in Egypt, a non-Christian Gnosticism preceded its Christian offspring and developed further without direct borrowings from Christianity. The writings of the *Corpus Hermeticum*, certainly native to Egypt, have already been mentioned."

113. C. H. Roberts, *Manuscript, Society, and Belief in Early Christian Egypt* (London: Oxford University, 1979), 50-51.

114. B. Pearson, *Gnosticism, Judaism* (n.86), 209.

115. J. F. McCue, "Orthodoxy and Heresy: Walter Bauer and the Valentinians," *Vigiliae Christianae* 33 (1979): 130: "I have argued that relative to Valentinianism, the older interpretation that this group was a small off-shoot from an orthodox main body would seem to be substantially correct on the basis of late second-century sources, east and west. Relative to Valentinianism, Bauer would seem to be incorrect."

116. G. T. Burke, "Walter Bauer and Celsus: The Shape of Late Second-Century Christianity," *The Second Century* 4 (1984): 6. See also M. Desjardins, "Bauer and Beyond" (n. 108), 65-82.

117. E. Yamauchi, "History-of-Religions School," in Ferguson and Wright, *New Dictionary of Christian Theology* (n.1), 308-309.

118. Cited by H. Koester, "The History-of-Religions School," (n.40)

119. Koester dates the Gospel of Luke at 125 CE, and the Acts of the Apostles to 135, while the majority of contemporary biblical scholars assign a date in the 60s; cf. C. Hemer, *The Book of Acts in the Setting of Hellenistic History* (Tübingen: J. C. B. Mohr, 1989), ch. 9. And while Koester and Robinson regard the Gospel of Thomas as early and independent, H. Clark Kee has shown that it is in fact a clear example of the adaptation of earlier traditions to portray Jesus as a gnostic revelatory figure. Cf. his article "Christology and Ecclesiology," in K. H. Richardson, ed., *Society of Biblical Literature 1982 Seminar Papers* (Chico: Scholars Press, 1982), 236.

119. J. M. Robinson, "On Bridging the Gulf from Q to the Gospel of Thomas (or Vice Versa)," in C. W. Hedrick and R. Hodgson, Jr., eds., *Nag Hammadi, Gnosticism, and Early Christianity* (Peabody, MA: Hendrickson Publishers, 1986), 133. See *PCG*, 183.

120. U. Bianchi, "Le gnosticisme et les origines du christianisme," in J. Ries, ed., *Gnosticisme et monde hellénistique* (Louvain-la-Neuve: Institut Orientaliste, 1982), 228. Cf. also U. Bianchi, "Some Reflections on the Greek Origins of Gnostic Ontology and the Christian Origin of the Gnostic Saviour," in Wedderburn, 43.

121. B. Pearson, *Gnosticism, Judaism*, 207.

122. Cf. E. Pagels, *The Gnostic Gospels* (n.103), 69, who believes that the female role was a more "positive" one in Gnosticism, and we should therefore reconsider the issue of ordination of women. For critical responses to Pagels' evaluation see K. McVey, "Gnosticism, Feminism and Elaine Pagels," *Theology Today* 37 (1981): 499; S.

Heine, *Women and Early Christianity: A Reappraisal* (Minneapolis: Augsburg Press, 1988), ch. 6; L. A. Brighton, "The Ordination of Women: A Twentieth-Century Gnostic Heresy?" *Concordia Journal* 8 (1982): 12-18; and M. J. Edwards, "New Discoveries and Gnosticism: Some Precautions," *Orientalia Christiana Periodica* 55 (1989): 257-72. See also D. Hoffman, "The Status of Women and Gnosticism in Irenaeus and Tertullian," unpublished Ph.D. dissertation, Oxford, Ohio: Miami University (accepted for publication by Edwin Mellen Press).

123. R. A. Norris, *God and World in Early Christian Theology* (New York: Seabury Press, 1965), 79.

124. E. Yamauchi, "The Gnostics and History," *Journal of the Evangelical Theological Society* 14 (1971): 29-40.

125. E. Yamauchi, "How the Early Church Responded to Social Problems," *Christianity Today* 17 (Nov. 24, 1972): 6-8.

126. E. Pagels, *The Gnostic Gospels* (n. 103), ch. iv.

127. Cf. G. Vallée, "Theological and Non-Theological Motives in Irenaeus's Refutation of the Gnostics," in E. P. Sanders, ed., *Jewish and Christian Self-Definition I: The Shaping of Christianity in the Second and Third Centuries* (Philadelphia: Fortress Press, 1980), 174-85.

128. R. M. Grant, "Early Christians and Gnostics in Graeco-Roman Society," in Logan and Wedderburn (n.2), 181. Cf. G. W. MacRae, "Why the Church Rejected Gnosticism," in Sanders, *Jewish and Christian Self-Definition*, 126-33.

129. I am indebted to Michel Desjardins for his helpful critique of my paper. I would respond that in my mind there is no obstacle to the idea of the adaptation of previous literary or religious material in Scriptures, if the priority of this can be demonstrated, as in the case of the Ugaritic antecedents of the Old Testament. For the predisposition of other scholars, see P. Henry's analysis, "Why Is Contemporary Scholarship So Enamored of Ancient Heretics?" in E. A. Livingstone, ed., *Studia Patristica* (Oxford: Pergamon Press, 1982), XVII.1, 125-26.

Yamauchi and Pre-Christian Gnosticism

Michel Desjardins

In this response I would like to address three questions that emerge from the paper of Edwin M. Yamauchi: (1) what is the argument? (2) how is the argument presented? and (3) why does Yamauchi take this particular stance? These remarks are given with a view to stimulating discussion, but also as an expression of thanks for the fine paper presented.

What is the Argument?

Yamauchi's focus is on the origin of Gnosticism as he addresses two questions: (1) when did Gnosticism arise? more particularly did it arise before or after the emergence of Christianity? and (2) what relationship did it have to nascent Christianity: did it influence the earliest Christian writers or, conversely, did it derive its impetus from these writings? Thus we have here both a reiteration and a continuation of the direction taken in his influential book, *Pre-Christian Gnosticism* (1973, revised 1983).

The argument is well-focused. According to Yamauchi, Gnosticism as a clearly defined religious movement arose in the mid-second century and derived many of its ideas from Christianity. He insists that clear evidence is lacking for pre-Christian Gnosticism, whether one looks at Mandaeism, the Nag Hammadi documents, the New Testament writings, or the early church fathers. And contrary to many of the patristic claims that Gnosticism began suddenly in the first century (with Simon Magus in particular), he insists that the movement emerged slowly, becoming fully developed only in the time of Basilides and Valentinus. In his view, one cannot call Simon Magus a Gnostic; even Marcion, for that matter, should not be considered one. Gnosticism could not begin to mingle with Christianity until the mid-second century.

How Is the Argument Presented?
From years of immersion in the issue of gnostic origins, Yamauchi seeks to persuade us in a variety of ways. Six are particularly noteworthy.

1. He focuses on one issue—did Gnosticism precede Christianity?—and he provides an overview of scholarly opinion on this question. His paper is less about Gnosticism and Christianity in the second century than about the question why one cannot speak about Gnosticism and Christianity between 30-100 CE. By noting the weaknesses and inconsistencies of others, he argues the reasonableness of his own claims.

2. He critiques and invokes the support of dozens of scholars, showing that since the publication of his *Pre-Christian Gnosticism* he has kept abreast of the literature. This is no mean feat in a field that has witnessed an explosion of studies during the last twenty years.

3. He seeks to debunk Helmut Koester's stance (most clearly expressed in his two-volume *Introduction to the New Testament*) concerning the emergence of Christianity. This is a well-chosen target, primarily because of Koester's importance on the North American scene. Many scholars now use his concept of "trajectories" and accept his endorsement of W. Bauer. I would support Yamauchi's initiative here, particularly because many of Koester's key arguments lack sufficient textual support.

4. He argues that one need not seek Gnostics "behind every bush" in the New Testament documents. This point is well-taken. For too long scholars have tended to assume that the New Testa-

ment writers were constantly countering gnostic "perversity." In fact, there is little evidence to support the claim that Gnostics were all like that; and, as Yamauchi states in this presentation, it is far from certain that Gnostics actually existed as organized groups in the first century. I would differ only in claiming that Gnostics were no more perverse or disruptive than other Christians.[1]

5. He polarizes the discussion: *either* Gnosticism was pre-Christian and influenced the New Testament, *or* it depended on Christianity. And having removed pre-Christian Gnosticism, he concludes that the New Testament is free from gnostic influence. This is rhetorically effective, but from a modern historical perspective it oversimplifies the discussion. Many scholars, like R. McL. Wilson, *Gnosis and the New Testament*, H. Jonas, *The Gnostic Religion*, and J. Doresse, *The Secret Books of the Egyptian Gnostics*, have argued for the simultaneous emergence of Christianity and Gnosticism. Gnosticism may in fact have arisen alongside Christianity. Many basic components of Gnosticism existed before the time of Paul, and could very well have played some role in the writings of the New Testament. Whether one calls this proto-Gnosticism or incipient Gnosticism is not important. In other words, the presentation of an either/or situation, to be determined neatly one way or the other, poses a false dilemma. Speaking about "Gnosticism" and "early Christianity" as though they were single entities also oversimplifies matters. Contemporary scholars have come to appreciate the great variety of Christian communities in the first two centuries, and the Nag Hammadi find has taught us that gnostic works can be equally varied. To conclude with an analogy, it appears to me that we are not comparing an apple with an orange, or even apples and oranges right before our eyes, but we are examining bushels of fruit, and from a great distance.

6. In his closing remarks Yamauchi suggests that gnostic Christians were "defeated" for good reasons. Here he clarifies what remained implicit throughout his presentation: he does not view the material with a disinterested eye. Gnosticism for him was a dangerous perversion of the Christian understanding of God, the

Bible, and Christ; humanity is better served by its absence. His appreciation for gnostic emphasis on the spiritual aspects of Christian life is but faint praise and reflects a continuing Protestant anti-Catholic polemic, as we are effectively reminded in J. Z. Smith's recent *Drudgery Divine*.

Why Does Yamauchi Take This Particular Stance?

The positions held by scholars may well be less significant than their reasons for holding them. This is particularly true for the emergence of Gnosticism, where definite answers are unattainable. It is common knowledge that Robinson and Koester hold their position on early Christianity at least in part to support Rudolph Bultmann's assumptions regarding the Gospel of John. From this paper and his earlier book on the topic, it is evident that Yamauchi's argument arises from a conservative Christian orientation. He regards Christianity as pure, true, and essentially (i. e., as expressed in the canonical works of the New Testament) unsoiled by foreign ideas. For Yamauchi, Gnosticism would be the primary foreign component. Excluding Gnosticism from the period when the New Testament was written may not be absolutely necessary to preserve the purity of the New Testament, but it does allow him to argue that at least the earliest expressions of Christianity were not polluted by Gnosticism.

He may well be correct. Yet as a historian of early forms of Christianity, I have not discovered the same pure, undiluted form of first-century Christianity, and I have no confessional reason to construct one. In my judgment the first three Christian centuries, not just the first, set the framework for subsequent centuries of orthodoxy. From this perspective it is not as significant whether Gnosticism or the types of "Christian Gnosticism" attacked by the heresiologists emerged in 50 or 150 CE.

To return to a point raised earlier, one of the trends in contemporary study of Christian origins to which I am sympathetic is an appreciative recognition of the diversity of religious expression within the first two centuries. This trend includes an examination of "christianities" and "gnosticisms," and isolates various strands within nascent forms of Christianity as it investigates a "gnostic" flavor in them.

Yamauchi's scholarly and personal preoccupations, therefore, are different from my own; yet I remain impressed by his argumentative skills, and appreciate his challenging perspective on the role of Gnosticism in Christianity's formative years. Yamauchi's voice in this debate remains clear and strong.

Notes

1. See also my article, "The Portrayal of the Dissidents in 2 Peter and Jude," *The Journal for the Study of the New Testament* 30 (1987): 89-102.

Adolf von Harnack and the Concept of Hellenization

William V. Rowe

Introduction

Although my topic is "Harnack and the Concept of Hellenization," I will begin by considering briefly a second topic concealed there, "Harnack and Hellenization," a topic we cannot ignore. This second topic concerns a possible relationship between the work of Adolf von Harnack and the process of Hellenization itself. This relationship becomes discernible once we acknowledge that the process of Hellenization is not confined to the past, and that elements traceable to the ancient Greeks are still being assimilated into our culture and into the life of the Christian church.

If this assimilation or its possibility is granted, we can ask how Harnack has sought to influence this contemporary process of Hellenization; and we can ask where his own work belongs in the history of the relationship of European Christianity with its Greek heritage.[1]

Although Harnack's involvement with Hellenization in this broadest sense is, strictly speaking, not the topic announced in my title, it is not irrelevant. In many ways the relation between Harnack and Hellenization is the key to Harnack's concept of Hellenization in early Christianity. Elaborating on this connection will substitute for any special pleading regarding the importance of our main topic. The paper will, therefore, follow a route that begins with the first, patent problem, "Harnack's Concept of Hellenization," where we ask, "How did Harnack think about Hellenization in the early church?" It will be concluded with a discussion of the second, latent topic, the question of on-going Hellenization.

What may not be clear is the extent to which this discussion of Harnack and Hellenization concerns ourselves. "Harnack's thinking" about Hellenization was not his private or personal affair, but has had immense influence, and even helped to shape our own, twentieth century understanding of early Christianity. This discussion also answers our own need to reflect upon the beginnings of Christianity. Some of the diverse and contradictory reasons inspiring this need might be: (1) to criticize more effectively and distance ourselves from foreign elements in the Christian tradition (repristination); (2) to find a model in the early church's posture toward Hellenistic culture for our own relationship to the secular West (classicism); or (3) to consider our relationship to things Greek in a way that accords with our sense of Christian identity and the meaning of the Gospel (reformation).

The Meaning of "Hellenization"
Applied to early Christianity, the term "Hellenization" captures the active, gerundive sense of the Greek term, *hellenismos*. But *hellenismos* originally bore the modest meaning of "speaking the Greek language," from the verb *hellenidzo*, "to speak Greek." *Hellenismos* in this sense is the first of the "virtues of diction" mentioned by Theophrastus, the successor of Aristotle, in his philosophy of style; it means simply the grammatical mastery of the Greek language.[2]

But even if we follow Jaeger, with many scholars, and allow the term *hellenismos* to signify the broader process of mastering or appropriating Greek culture, we have not yet focused on the meaning of "Hellenization" as this appears in Harnack's analysis of early Christianity. "Hellenization," as Jaeger uses it, may indicate nothing more than the (flawless) transfer of cultural goods from one generation of Greeks to another. Yet even if we expand this notion to include the assimilation of Hellenic culture by non-Hellenic Mediterranean and West Asian peoples after the death of Alexander the Great, we still have not grasped the process of Hellenization in early Christianity as Harnack understands it. Rather, his concern was with the Christian church's reception of the already "Hellenized" culture of the Near Eastern *oikoumēnē*, the "whole inhabited world" of Hellenism.

Harnack speaks of Hellenism as a movement that, "having its origin among a small people, became a universal spiritual power, which, severed from its original nationality, had for that very reason penetrated foreign nations."[3] Clearly "Hellenistic," then, is not the same thing as "Greek," nor is "Hellenization" simply the assimilation of Greek things, a bilateral relationship between Christianity and Greek ideas or Greek ways of life. Rather it is a complex question concerning the relationship between Christianity and a Levantine culture in which Hellenic ideas and ways of life were only one—albeit the leading—component in a dynamic culture incorporating varied motives and traditions. "Hellenism" signifies a complex whose fundamental principles did not call men, women and institutions to something Greek, but rather to a *panmixia* under the leading of something Greek.

> The nations who inhabited the eastern shore of the Mediterranean sea had, from the fourth century BCE, a common history, and therefore had similar convictions. . . . There is little meaning in calling a thing Hellenic, as that really formed an element in all the phenomena of the age.[4]

In other words, if we are tempted—that is to say, misled—into thinking of Hellenization as a process in which non-Hellenic cultures sacrificed their identities and traditions in order to take on a "Hellenic" identity and tradition, then we ought to consider how much of its indigenous character the Hellenic tradition necessarily had to sacrifice in this process. The Hellenes of the great classical *poleis*—of Athens, Sparta, Corinth, and Thebes—in the fifth centuries BCE were rather parochial peoples, and their culture somewhat intro-

verted, the protestations of their philosophers notwithstanding. In
view of this, we begin to sense what Greek culture was forced to give
up in exchange for its umbrella function in the non-Greek world
designated by the name "Hellenism." What specific meaning could
the label "Greek" possibly have in a world that is "Hellenistic"? We
might as well ask what definite conclusions could be drawn about a
person's religion or politics from their ability to live and communicate in an English speaking milieu.

According to Harnack there is nothing about the New Testament untouched in some way by "Hellenism" in this sense, but also
nothing "Hellenic" about the Gospel itself. From this it is clear that
Harnack distinguishes between the Hellenic in the parochial or
ethnic sense and ecumenical Hellenism.

> There is indeed no single writing of the New Testament which
> does not betray the influence of the mode of thought and
> general conditions of the culture of the time which resulted
> from the Hellenising of the east. . . . We may go further and say
> that the Gospel itself is historically unintelligible, so long as we
> compare it with an exclusive Judaism as yet unaffected by any
> foreign influence. . . . It is just as clear that specifically Hellenic
> ideas form the presuppositions neither for the Gospel itself, nor
> for the most important New Testament writings. It is a question
> rather as to a general spiritual atmosphere created by Hel-
> lenism.[5]

The Motives of Hellenization
We must realize that in describing the Gospel as "historically unintelligible so long as we compare it with an exclusive Judaism,"
Harnack is assuming the Old Testament religion was limited to the
horizon of the Hebrew nation.[6] By contrast he understands the New
Testament message of the Kingdom of God as universal in both
content and aim. On the assumption of such a contrast between the
particularistic and the universal rests Harnack's entire understanding of the motives of Hellenization in the early Christian
church.

Israel, no doubt, had a sacred treasure which was of greater
value than all the treasures of the Greeks—the living God; but
in what miserable vessels was this treasure preserved, and how
much inferior was all else possessed by this nation in comparison with the riches, the power, the delicacy and freedom of
the Greek spirit and its intellectual possessions. A movement
like that of Christianity, which discovered to the Jew the soul
whose dignity was not dependent on its descent from Abraham,
but on its responsibility to God, could not continue in the
framework of Judaism however expanded, but must soon
recognise in that world which the Greek spirit had discovered
and prepared, the field which belonged to it.[7]

Harnack argues that this difference fuelled a tension already
inherent in the relationship between Christianity and Judaism, eventually compelling the Christian church to look away from its Jewish
roots for more "catholic" means of expression.

The result of the preaching of Jesus . . . was not only the
illumination of the Old Testament by the Gospel and the
confirmation of the Gospel by the Old Testament, but not less
the detachment of believers from the religious community of
the Jews from the Jewish church. . . . [This detachment] was
essentially accomplished in the first two generations of
believers. The Gospel was a message for humanity even when
there was no break with Judaism; but it seemed impossible to
bring this message home to men who were not Jews in any other
way than by leaving the Jewish church. But to leave that church
was to declare it to be worthless. . . . [Hence] it was necessary
to put another in its place . . . [to wit] a communion whose
essential mark was to claim as its own the Old Testament and
the idea of being the people of God, [but] to sweep aside the
Jewish conception of the Old Testament and the Jewish church,
and thereby gain the shape and power of a community that is
capable of a mission for the world.[8]

In this situation, says Harnack, it was natural, i.e., in accordance with the very nature of the Christian religion itself, that the church should turn to Hellenistic culture in its attempt to become more universal.

> When the Gospel was rejected by the Jewish nation, and had disengaged itself from all connection with that nation, it was already settled whence it must take the material to form for itself a new body and be transformed into a church and a theology. National and particular, in the ordinary sense of the word, these forms could not be: the contents of the Gospel were too rich for that; but separated from Judaism . . . the Christian religion came in contact with the Roman world and with a culture which had already mastered the world, viz., the Greek. . . . As a consequence of the complete break with the Jewish church there followed not only the strict necessity of quarrying the stones for the building of the church from the Greco-Roman world, but also the idea that Christianity has a more positive relation to the world than to the synagogue. . . . The separation from Judaism having taken place, it was necessary that the spirit of another people should be admitted, and should also materially determine the manner of turning the Old Testament to advantage.[9]

In short, it was universality—both the religious universality of the Gospel message and the cultural universality that made Hellenism a "world"—that motivated the Hellenization of the early church.

The Active Nature of Hellenization
As a movement in the direction of universality, the "turn" toward Hellenism represented in part the reception of something from the outside. But the "turn" itself was not, in Harnack's view, the mere suffering of an influence. Rather, it was the church's opening of itself to a world wider than that of Old Testament Judaism or even of the Jewish church, an opening already rooted in the "inner necessity"[10]

of the Christian religion, namely the inherent universality of the Gospel.

Hence, in receiving Hellenistic culture into itself the Christian church was essentially active; indeed, Harnack considers this turn to Hellenism one of the most decisively *active* phases in church history. The question then is not, Was the church merely receptive in the process of Hellenization, merely a passive recipient? Was Hellenization a process the church simply underwent at a certain inevitable moment in its development? Rather, the question is, *What spirit* was active in the church's active turn toward Hellenistic culture?

> Not only did an original element evaporate in the course of the second century [i.e., the element of evangelical enthusiasm]; another was introduced. . . . But to what a much greater extent was [the youthful Christian religion] exposed to the influence of this spirit after being sharply severed from the Jewish religion and the Jewish nation. [In this severed condition the Christian religion] hovered bodiless over the earth like a being of the air; bodiless and seeking a body. The spirit, no doubt, makes to itself its own body, but it does so by assimilating what is around it. The influx of Hellenism, of the Greek spirit, and the union of the Gospel with it, form the greatest fact in the history of the church in the second century, and when the fact was once established as a foundation it continued through the following centuries.[11]

We must be careful in construing the chief metaphor of this passage: that of the relation between "spirit" and "body." In this passage both "spirit" and "body" are spirit in the proper sense of the word. The spirit of the Christian religion, like every spirit, is in need of a body—a context or definite shape—in which to express itself. Every spirit, says Harnack, is capable of making a body for itself, yet every spirit must form its body from materials that are ready to hand. That explains why, after the exodus of Christianity from the context of the Jewish church, it found itself without context, and therefore momentarily "bodiless." But it also explains why the church opened itself to the influx of the Greek spirit, a spirit which early Christianity saw as material for its new bodily form. Hence, the "influx" of Hellenism was really the church's active appropriation of Hellenistic culture, or its Hellenization of itself for the purpose of building a body for itself. Hellenization is a metempsychosis, or transmigration of one living principle from an old body into a new body which it must first create for itself.

The Radicality of Hellenization
But if the "turn" toward Hellenism was active, nevertheless it was not one act but several acts, some of which were made necessary by others of the same kind. The "turn" in fact was a series of acts in which the Christian church responded both to its own nature and to its context. The former Harnack calls the "inner necessity" of Hellenization, the latter its "outer necessity." Hellenization was, in other words, essentially a process which occurred in stages, some of which were gradual, while others were sudden. The outcome of this turn taken as a whole was the creation of what Harnack calls "the Catholic church."

The Catholic church, like the first century Jewish church, was a "spirit" with a "body." It is very tempting to think of this church as a "Christian" spirit in a "Greek" body. At first, that is what Harnack's metaphor seems to imply. But this inference does not accord with Harnack's *concept* of Hellenization. Indeed, Harnack's "Catholic church" possesses a body created and inhabited by a certain spirit. But if we recall that "spirit" and "body" in Harnack's metaphor are both spirits in his non-metaphorical sense of the term, then what at first appears to be nothing more than the transmigration of the Christian spirit to another body is really its alliance with another spirit. Hellenization suddenly seems much more dangerous than transmigration, for transmigration is a process in which we can imagine—to the extent that we can imagine transmigration—a spirit retaining its integral and personal identity while simply taking up residence at a new bodily address. What we called transmigration now looks more like the dangerous arrangement of parasitism in which one life form attaches itself to another, the latter functioning as the "host" of the former. The parasite appends itself to its host in such a way that the host becomes partly a new environment for the parasite, partly an extension of the parasite's bodily organism, and partly the very principle of the parasite's life. The parasite "lives" off its host's body; and this is closer to Harnack's concept of Hellenization.

The "Catholic church" is a "body", but one inhabited by an all-too-"bodily"spirit, that is, a spirit *radically—perhaps too deeply— influenced by its assimilation of the spiritual materials around it.* Conversely, Harnack's Catholic church is a "spirit," but one that has undergone not only a metempsychosis or transmigration, but a *metanoia* that is a conversion and inward spiritual transformation. The "Catholic church" of the second century is an institution so deeply imbued with, and steeped in, Hellenism that Harnack cites with approval another author's characterization of it as "the last great production of the Hellenic [sic!] spirit."[12]

For Harnack, as we saw, Hellenization is not a question of an active versus a passive posture in early Christianity with regard to its cultural surroundings. Rather, it is a question of *what spirit* was active in the process of Hellenization itself. In answering this question Harnack wavers somewhat, for the answer is: One spirit initiated the process of Hellenization, while another, the Hellenistic Greek spirit, completed it. Hence, Harnack not only conceives the process of Hellenization as active in nature, but as radical in its proportions.

The Two Forms of Hellenization
Harnack's analysis of Hellenization makes up the first three volumes of his *History of Dogma*. In this great mass of material there is not only a wealth of detail—perhaps greater than in any history of dogma before Harnack—but also subtlety, both in its use of sources[13] and in its judgments. We must pass over the stages of Hellenization; the question is too complicated to cover comprehensively here, and only a comprehensive treatment can satisfy us that the

boundary lines Harnack draws between periods are not still too definite and rigid.[14]

I will cite very briefly Harnack's treatment of two instances of Hellenization that are paradigmatic of the whole process as he sees it. The two I have chosen represent extremes, not of degree but of form. The first is the Logos speculation of the Apologetic movement, an example of Hellenization in its positive form; the second is the struggle against Gnosticism, which Harnack calls the threat of "acute Hellenization." The church's struggle against acute Hellenization is itself—ironically—an instance of Hellenization, but Hellenization in its negative form.

The Positive Form of Hellenization
Regarding the first of these forms Harnack says,

> Besides the Greek ethics there was also a cosmological conception which the church took over . . . and which was destined to attain a commanding position in its doctrinal system—*the Logos* . . . Greek thought had arrived at the conception of an *active central idea.* . . . This central idea represented the unity of the supreme principle of the world, of thought, and of ethics; but it also represented the divinity itself as a creative and active as distinguished from a quiescent power. The most important step that was ever taken in the domain of Christian doctrine was when the Christian apologists at the beginning of the second century drew the equation: the Logos = Jesus Christ.[15]

Harnack emphasizes that Hellenization in this instance is a matter of simple "identification," an identification of something in the Gospel with something in Greek philosophy.[16]

This "positive" form of Hellenization, in which a certain element in Hellenistic culture was *posited* as something Christian, does not draw its import merely from the fact that a certain Christian dogma was fused with a Greek idea. Nor does it derive from the fact that the idea in question is perhaps the core idea of Greek philosophy. Rather, the importance of this particular fusion, this positive form of Hellenization, derives from the fact that Christian dogma in general was thereby prepared to interpret itself as a school of philosophy in the Greek sense.[17] This does not mean that Christians were now saying the very same things the Greek philosophers said.[18] To be sure, Christians were contradicting the Greek philosophers; Harnack's point is that in order to do so they began to philosophize. In other words, with this fusion of the Christian with the Greek, Christianity was beginning to interpret New Testament faith as assent to dogma and to articulate dogma as a "philosophy of religion."[19] For Harnack, Logos speculation *is* the spirit of Greek philosophy present in the church of Jesus Christ.

> The message of religion appears here clothed in a knowledge of the world and of the ground of the world which had already been obtained without any reference to it, and therefore religion itself has here become a doctrine which has, indeed, its certainty in the Gospel, but only in part derives its contents from it, and *which can also be appropriated by such as are neither poor in spirit nor weary and heavy laden.* Now, it may of course be shown that a philosophic conception of the Christian religion is possible, and began to make its appearance from the very first, as in the case of Paul. But the Pauline *gnosis* has neither been simply identified with the Gospel by Paul himself (1 Cor. 3:2f., 12:3, Phil. 1:18) nor is it analogous to the later dogmas, not to speak of being identical with it. The characteristic of this [later sense of] dogma is that it represents itself in no sense as foolishness, but as wisdom, and at the same time desires to be regarded as the contents of revelation itself. Dogma in its conception and development is a work of the Greek spirit on the soil of the Gospel.[20]

The effects of this importing of the Greek spirit are stated by Harnack himself in the following passage:

> That which Protestants and Catholics call dogmas, are not only ecclesiastical doctrines, but they are also: (1) theses expressed

in abstract terms, forming together a unity, and fixing the contents of the Christian religion as a knowledge of God, of the world, and of the sacred history under the aspect of a proof of the truth. But (2) they have also emerged at a definite stage of the history of the Christian religion; they show in their conception as such, and in many details, the influence of that stage, viz., the Greek period, and they have preserved this character in spite of all their reconstructions and additions in later periods. . . . Dogmatic Christianity is therefore a definite stage in the history of the development of Christianity. It corresponds to the antique mode of thought, but has nevertheless continued to a very great extent in the following epochs, though subject to great transformations. Dogmatic Christianity stands between Christianity as the religion of the Gospel, presupposing a personal experience and dealing with disposition and conduct, and Christianity as a religion of cultus, sacraments, ceremonial and obedience, in short of superstition, and it can be united with either the one or the other. In itself and in spite of all its mysteries it is always intellectual Christianity, and therefore there is always the danger here that as knowledge it may supplant religious faith, or connect it with a doctrine of religion, instead of with God and a living experience.[21]

I quote at such length not only in the interest of conveying Harnack's concept of Hellenization, but also because the form of Hellenization we are discussing is the form called "dogma." This form of Hellenization is "positive" because something Greek is simply *identified* with something Christian. The subtlety of Harnack's judgment on this point should not be missed. The view of the Messiah as the Word is certainly *a* doctrine in the sense of a religious teaching conveyed by the Gospel. But the identification of the Word with the Greek Logos is something more than the identification of one doctrine with another. Rather, it is an identification of the *character* of the religious teaching of the Gospel with the *character* of Greek philosophy. This identification is the fateful genesis of the very idea of "dogma" and its reality in the Christian church. "Dogma

[is] that type of Christianity which was formed in ecclesiastical antiquity."[22] The fact that this identification occurred at such an early and impressionable stage in the life of the church explains why church history can be written as the "history of dogma."[23] The fact that the study of the history of dogma represents the life work of Harnack, and not just the title of his major work, reveals how important—perhaps ominous—this form of Hellenization was in his view.

In keeping with what we have already said about the "active" character and "inner necessity" of Hellenization in the early church, it is important to add that despite Harnack's own misgivings he considers the synthesis of the Gospel with the spirit of Greek philosophy, as it produced the notion of "dogma," not a defeat for the church, but a prelude to its victory.[24] Even if the original faith in the Gospel that characterized the first century church was stifled or nearly smothered by the philosophical spirit, nevertheless this spirit—imbibed through a positive form of Hellenization—empowered the church in its defeat of rivals—including the paganism of classical Greek philosophy—in the short run. If Harnack does not approve, at least he appreciates the labor of Hellenization for this reason.

> By comprehending in itself and giving excellent expression to the religious conceptions contained in Greek philosophy and the gospel, together with its Old Testament basis; by meeting the search for a revelation as well as the desire for a universal knowledge; by subordinating itself to the aim of the Christian religion to bring a Divine life to humanity as well as to the aim of philosophy to know the world: [Dogma] became the instrument by which the church conquered the ancient world and educated the modern nations.[25]

The Negative Form of Hellenization
I will briefly discuss the second paradigmatic case of Hellenization in order to show how this process also occurred—this time ironically and behind the scenes—through the church's negation of a move-

ment external to itself. This second form of Hellenization is visible in the church's struggle against Gnosticism. This struggle, seen by Harnack as a negative form of Hellenization, is doubly ironic because here Hellenization occurred through the church's resistance to that very "Hellenization" itself. In Harnack's view, the church thereby opposed something already very characteristic of its own life and spirit.

Harnack understands Gnosticism as an instance of the "acute Hellenization"[26] of the Gospel. The label "acute Hellenization" is best understood in the context of Harnack's description of the "philosophical reinterpretation" of Old Testament religion which began even before the preaching of the Gospel. By philosophical reinterpretation Harnack means the allegorizing treatment of Old Testament texts aimed at harmonizing them, for example, with Hellenistic conceptions of ethics which focused on the struggle of the rational part of the soul with the non-rational passions.

> This spiritualising was the result of a philosophic view of religion, and this philosophic view was the outcome of a lasting influence of Greek philosophy and of the Greek spirit generally on Judaism. . . . The history of the Old Testament was here sublimated to a history of the emancipation of reason from passion. . . . This necessary allegorical interpretation, however, brought into the communities an intellectual philosophic element, a *gnosis*, which was perfectly distinct from the Apocalyptic dreams, in which were beheld angel hosts on white horses, [etc.]. . . . The view of the Old Testament as a document of the deepest wisdom, transmitted to those who knew how to read it as such, unfettered the intellectual interest which would not rest until it had entirely transferred the new religion from the world of feelings, actions and hopes, into the world of Hellenic conceptions, and transformed it into a metaphysic.[27]

But when this transformation of biblical religion was carried out in a more consistent fashion by the philosophical-theological efforts of the Gnostics, the community of believers was finally galvanized into active opposition against this acute Hellenization. Yet in Harnack's eyes this opposition was also somehow inconsistent, for what the young church encountered in Gnosticism differed from Catholic Christianity in quantity not in quality. It differed only in the intensity and radicality of the Hellenizing process at work in it.

> The Catholic church afterwards claimed as her own those writers of the first century (60-160) who were content with turning speculation to account only as a means of spiritualising the Old Testament, without, however, attempting a systematic reconstruction of tradition. But all those who in the first century undertook to furnish Christian practice with the foundation of a complete systematic knowledge [a "gnosis"—WVR], she declared false Christians, Christians only in name. Historical enquiry cannot accept this judgment. On the contrary, it sees in Gnosticism a series of undertakings, which in a certain way is analogous to the Catholic embodiment of Christianity, in doctrine, morals, and worship. The great distinction here consists essentially in the fact that the Gnostic systems represent the acute secularising or hellenising of Christianity, with the rejection of the Old Testament; while the Catholic system, on the other hand, represents a gradual process of the same kind with the conservation of the Old Testament. . . It is therefore no paradox to say that Gnosticism, which is just Hellenism, has in Catholicism obtained half a victory.[28]

It is obvious from these remarks that any struggle against Gnosticism would be a struggle against Hellenism by an already Hellenized church. As Harnack explains it this struggle provided Christianity with the opportunity to oppose externally the very process of Hellenization that was taking place within it, and on which many of its victories in Hellenic culture were to be based.

The struggle against Gnosticism was not a "positive" endeavor of apologetic evangelization, but a "negative" defense of the church's identity and even of its existence. But as we can see from the remarks cited above, Harnack is not concerned with the simple fact that "anti-Gnosis" was "negative" because in it the church defended itself against the counter force of Hellenization. What interests him—and what is subtle about his treatment of Gnosticism—is the fact that precisely through this defense and negation of a counter force, the counter force gained entry into, and victory over, the church. In other words, the very struggle against acute Hellenization further Hellenized the church.

We must remember that the positive process of Hellenization had already brought "dogma" into being. We must also remember that dogma, in Harnack's view, was not an expression, but rather an intellectualistic kind of Christianity, a "mischievous" form of Christianity.[29] The irony of the struggle against Gnosticism—against acute Hellenization—is that it strengthened rather than weakened the intellectualism of the "Dogmatic Church." This is because the church waged this struggle by making logically tighter and more rigidly creedal the already systematic network of its "doctrines."[30]

To that extent the struggle against Gnosticism not only furthered the process of Hellenization in the church but placed a kind of seal upon it. That is because from now on Hellenization was useful not merely in the church's positive evangelical efforts; it was something indispensable in its defense against the enemy.[31] As Harnack writes elsewhere,

> The struggle with Gnosticism compelled the church to put its teaching, it worship, and its discipline into fixed forms and ordinances, and to exclude everyone who would not yield them obedience.... If by "Catholic" we mean the church of doctrine and of law, then the Catholic church had its origin in the struggle with Gnosticism. It had to pay a heavy price for the victory which kept that tendency at bay; we may almost say that the vanquished imposed their terms upon the Victor: *Victi victoribus legem dederunt.* It kept Dualism and the acute phase of Hellenism at bay; but by becoming a community with a fully worked out scheme of doctrine, and a definite form of public worship, it was of necessity compelled to take on forms analogous to those which it combated in the Gnostics. To

encounter our enemies' theses by setting up others one by one, is to change over to his ground.[32]

The "high price"—in Harnack's opinion—that was paid for waging battle against Gnosticism, and for winning a victory over it, is actually seen in four crucial changes wrought in the church: (1) the sacrifice of evangelical freedom to a church bound by dogma and law; (2) the intellectualism of a Dogmatic Christianity, or the penetration of the church by Greek philosophy; (3) the church's becoming an "institution"; and (4) the decline of evangelization.[33]

The Problem of "Harnack and Hellenization"
At the outset of the paper I raised the question whether elements traceable to the ancient Greeks, or at least to Hellenistic civilization, are still being assimilated into our culture and into Christianity in the twentieth century. If we imagine these elements in the broadest way, we may ask how Harnack's own work as a whole is related to Hellenization in this sense.

The answer to this question is: Harnack is very much involved with the on-going problem of Hellenization. In fact, his *concept* of Hellenization is rooted in this involvement. The form of Hellenization that continues to concern him is "Dogmatic Christianity," the identification of Christian faith with assent to authoritative dogmas.

We may find this judgment applicable or inapplicable, depending on where we are located in twentieth century Christianity. In his own time Harnack found it applicable to the churches of the Reformation. Harnack's concern, or even alarm, over Hellenization in the churches of the Reformation is rooted in his perception of the Reformation tradition as an anti-Hellenizing force in the church, one that draws upon Augustine's struggles at the end of the Patristic period.

It is Harnack's view that, because of their inheritance of this tradition, the churches of the Protestant Reformation contain the only real promise (humanly speaking, he would allow) of reversing the process of Hellenization and of keeping New Testament faith alive in the church. In the following passage he points out that

Dogmatic Christianity continues into the present day because it draws its life from a Hellenized world, but that this Hellenized world itself is limited and cannot endure forever. He then cites the "reforming impulse" of Protestantism as an avenue leading out of Dogmatic Christianity. Taking "dogma" in the pregnant sense of the word, as in the "History of Dogma," which he regarded as his life's work, Harnack concludes with the claim that a "History of Dogma" will "hasten this process."

> Dogma [is] that type of Christianity which was formed in ecclesiastical antiquity. . . . But the Christian religion, as it was not born of the culture of the ancient world, is not for ever chained to it. The form and the new contents which the Gospel received when it entered into that world have only the same guarantee of endurance as that world itself. And that endurance is limited. . . . In consequence of the reforming impulse in Protestantism, the way was opened up for a conception which does not identify Gospel and Dogma, which does not disfigure the latter by changing or paring down its meaning while failing to come up to the former. . . . The Gospel since the Reformation, in spite of retrograde movements which have not been wanting, is working itself out of the forms which it was once compelled to assume, and a true comprehension of its history will also contribute to hasten this process.[34]

If this sounds self-congratulatory coming from a Protestant, we should consider that Harnack's whole sense of danger, not merely his hope, was directed at the Protestantism of his day. Harnack sensed precisely in the churches of the Reformation the danger of Hellenization, namely the temptation to a doctrinal Christianity:

> The counter-church which . . . rapidly arose in opposition to the Roman church . . . perceived . . . that its truth and its title lay in the re-establishment of the Gospel. But the thought also stole in surreptitiously: We, that is to say, the particular churches which had now sprung up, are the true church. Luther, of

course, was never able to forget that the true church was the
sacred community of the faithful; but still he had no clear ideas
as to the relation between it and the visible new church which
had now arisen, and subsequent generations settled down more
and more into the sad misunderstanding: We are the true
church because we have the right "doctrine". . . . Not, perhaps,
in theory, but certainly in practice, a double form of Christianity
arose, just as in Catholicism; and in spite of the efforts of the
Pietistic movement, it still remains with us today. The
theologian and the clergyman must defend the whole doctrine,
and be orthodox; for the layman it suffices if he adheres to
certain leading points and refrains from attacking the orthodox
creed.[35]

But even if the churches of the Reformation "catholicize" themselves with dogma, says Harnack, this will never destroy the
Gospel.[36] Here we can see in what sense the academic study of the
history of dogma can "hasten" or at least encourage the reforming
process of anti-Hellenization, for Harnack bolsters his hope in the
indestructibility of the Gospel from his study of Hellenization in the
early church.

Even in the outwardly decorated but inwardly decayed temples
of the Greek and Roman church [the Gospel] has not been
effaced. "Venture onwards! Deep down in a vault you will still
find the altar and its sacred, ever-burning lamp!" This Gospel,
associated as it was with the speculative ideas and the mystery-
worship of the Greeks, yet did not perish in them; united with
the Roman Empire, it held its own even in this fusion, nay, out
of it gave birth to the Reformation.[37]

Hence, with Harnack that self-satisfied and whiggish nineteenth
century feeling of living in the culminating period of all Western
history, the feeling that pervades those Hegelian histories of dogma
written in the generation before Harnack,[38] has come to an end. It
has been replaced by the twentieth century feeling, or "anxiety," that

an age-old configuration might finally be broken—we might even say de-constructed—and something new, something "authentically" Christian, put in its place. It is in connection with this feeling, that is, from his "prophetic" stance toward the on-going process of Hellenization, that Harnack formed his "concept" of Hellenization in the early church.

Some Concluding Critical Remarks

I would like to conclude with some critical remarks regarding Harnack's claim that dogma represents the "spirit of Greek philosophy" in the Christian church. We may consider Harnack's assertion that "dogma" represented an identification of something philosophical with something ecclesiastical from both sides of the equation. We will begin with the philosophical side first.

The first question we must ask about Harnack's idea of the spirit of Greek philosophy is: Which philosophy of the Greeks does Harnack have in mind? In my opinion it is not satisfactory to lump all of Greek philosophy together under a heading such as "the spirit of Greek philosophy." Certainly there are common traits and connecting threads that we can trace in the Hellenic philosophical tradition as a whole. But it is doubtful that a single "spirit" was at work in all expressions of this tradition.

When a phrase such as "the spirit of Greek philosophy" is used and heard, what really happens is that the writer as well as the audience are drawn toward the convenient opinion that the ethos of Greek philosophy in general is embodied in one particular Hellenic thinker or school. This seems in fact to have been Harnack's understanding. The "spirit of Greek philosophy" is, for Harnack, "the spirit of Platonism." "We are here concerned," he writes, "with that influx of the Greek spirit which was marked by the absorption of Greek philosophy and, particularly, of Platonism."[39]

If, for the sake of argument, one included under the rubric of "Platonism" the philosopher who was arguably—or at least from a certain point of view—the greatest Platonist of ancient times, Aristotle, and then considered the impact which Plato and Aristotle between them exercised upon the entire Christian tradition, then it would be understandable—although, in my opinion, still incorrect—to say that the notion of "dogma" reflects the "spirit of Platonic philosophy." But it will not do to allow the spirit of Platonism by itself to represent "the spirit of Greek philosophy" as a whole.

We must ask a second question about Harnack's idea of the spirit of Greek philosophy, or rather of Platonic philosophy. Is "dogma" really indicative of, or even essential to, the spirit of this philosophy? It seems that Harnack saw in the Platonic emphasis on *logos* the same (intellectual) spirit that appeared as "dogma" in the Christian church. We have seen how important the Logos speculation of the Apologists was for Harnack's account of Hellenization. Nevertheless, certain considerations seem to rule out an identification of "dogma" with the spirit of Platonism, its emphasis on *logos* notwithstanding.

One consideration is that "dogma" in Platonism would have to be understood as the soul's adherence to certain views, especially to such views (even if they are not mere "opinions:" *doxai*!) as can be passed on through teaching. According to Plato, both in the *Phaedo* and in the *Republic*, such views, such *logoi*, remain hypothetical until they are grounded in an insight into those "things themselves" of which they speak.[40] Moreover, according to the seventh of the epistles traditionally ascribed to Plato, such direct insight into the Ideas is said to surpass all *logoi*. Therefore it cannot be fully conveyed in speech, let alone through writing.[41]

Another consideration is that Aristotle would have understood "dogma" as related to the rational *hexis*, the acquired mental trait or "habit" of the intellectual part of the soul, that he calls *doxa*. Of course, following Plato, Aristotle excludes *doxa* from the list of intellectual "excellences" (*aretai*) or virtues on the ground that its affirmations concerning truth may in fact be false.[42]

But, quite apart from the error to which *doxa* (opinion) is naturally liable, Aristotle also excludes it from the highest levels of the soul's activity simply because it is a *hexis*, a habit. As important as habit in general (and intellectual habit in particular) may be for Aristotle, habit still represents a kind of holding pattern for the soul (*hexis* referring to a "having" or "holding," from *echein* meaning "to have" or "hold"). Habit therefore falls under the category of "potentiality," as differentiated from "actuality." In rational souls, habit is necessarily something other, and less, than a fully en-acted focus (the *energeia*) upon, for example, truth, such as we find in the intellectual virtue of "nous," its intelligence or insight.[43] Intelligence is the soul's true virtue (*arete*) and happiness (*eudaimonia*), but only when actually enacted and not when present in mere potentiality as a habit or *hexis*.[44]

I would argue that it is here, in the notion of "intelligence" as *nous* or *theorein*, that we come closer to the so-called "spirit of Platonic philosophy," especially as broadly defined to include Aristotle. *Theorein* or *theoria* is not only more actual than any *hexis*, but also more profound—at least for Aristotle—than any technical or practical "logistic," or any scientific and dialectical *dianoia* ("thought"). As *nous* (intellection), *theorein* implies having a vision rather than holding a view.

It would seem, then, if we consider everything really fundamental in Platonism, that the notion of "logos" does not truly reflect its Spirit. This holds even for the Christian-ecclesiastical notion of "dogma." In fact, the *gnōsis* of the Hellenistic Gnostics would seem to reflect "the spirit of Greek philosophy" in a much deeper way than does the notion of "dogma" in the early church.

After all, would not philosophers in the Hellenistic period have considered a "dogmatic" philosophy to be one in which the Greek spirit is already dead? Isn't this the point of skepticism, especially in the Academy after Plato? Even the church father, Augustine, for whom the philosophical and theological question of the *Logos* was paramount, could still see in Academic skepticism an attempt to conceal and shelter the genuine meaning—one might even say the "spirit"—of Platonism in a profoundly unphilosophical age.[45] How could Augustine have come to such conclusions regarding skepticism if, as Harnack sees it, an adherence to dogmas were essential to the spirit of Greek philosophy?

Turning to the ecclesiastical side of Harnack's equation—"dogma is the spirit of Greek philosophy in the church"—we may ask whether church "dogma" was really all that intellectual. If we consider the symbolic nature of the creeds—that is, their function in determining membership in the Body of Christ[46]—it is clear that "dogma" took shape over and against "heresy." This is a point Harnack himself makes in a brilliant way, especially in his treatment of what we called "the negative form" of Hellenization that took shape during the church's struggle against Gnosticism.

But if we may reverse this insight, we will not only see that dogmas were aimed "symbolically" against heresy, but that heresies themselves were symbolic. That is, heresies were assertions of "counter-creeds" for the Christian church, and therefore were attempts to divide the Body of Christ. Originally "heresy" was understood not so much as a "view," but as a posture, that is, as a "standing apart" (*apostasis*) from the Body of Christ *because* of, or on the pretext of some view, usually a new view. "Heresy" therefore originally meant "sect."

In keeping with what is really essential about a sect, the word "heresy" actually points not to something intellectual but rather voluntaristic, namely, one's *choice* to stand apart. "Heresy" in Greek is *hairesis*; "choice" is *prohairesis*.[47] The common root of the two words suggests that for the church "dogma" was an attack upon the apostate *decisions* underlying certain views, and not upon these *views*, considered abstractly or intellectually in and by themselves. Perhaps the element of "views," or the *doxic* element is really secondary to the "voluntaristic" element, since dogmas are aimed against something "sectarian" in the sense described above. If this is the case, it is impossible to identify "dogma" with the intellectual spirit of Greek philosophy, no matter how widely or narrowly this philosophical spirit is defined.

One last critical point: Although Harnack does not regard the Gospel to be merely historical in nature, he does regard adaptation of the Gospel to the Hellenistic world, namely the process that resulted in the "Catholic Church," as a wholly historical process.

Harnack's work is founded upon an "historicizing" tendency, a tendency to view the process of Hellenization as essentially "historical." For this reason he assigns the historian of dogma a crucial role in reforming this process.

But there is something ominous about Harnack's "historicism," especially in combination with his view of Hellenization as unfortunate for the church and hence to be rooted out and avoided. An "historicistic" treatment of Hellenization is combined in Harnack with a negative relationship to everything Hellenistic.

Viewed in this light, Harnack's historicistic and negative position on Hellenization is not far removed from the now widespread view that the Gospel itself is essentially historical, meaning a product of history. Many historians of religion would argue that as long as we hold out (as Harnack still did) for something like an "essence" of Christianity, our thinking remains trapped by the gravitational pull of Hellenism, specifically of the *ousia*, the supra-temporal "substance" of Greek philosophy.

In other words, the historicistic criticism of Hellenization in the early church, which was brought to such heights in Harnack's own work, has been carried so far that the very idea of an "essence" of the Gospel, or of Christianity as such, is defeated in advance by the two-edged sword Harnack taught us to wield. Any conviction regarding the supra-temporal "essence" of Christianity now seems both (1) naive from the historical point of view, and (2) too Hellenistic from the philosophical point of view. If Harnack's work can be placed in the context of this dual "historicistic/anti-Hellenistic" tendency, then it has ironically contributed to an outlook that has finally taken a self-destructive turn. For Harnack's "concept" of Hellenization, as we saw, depends upon his relationship to Hellenization, a negative relationship that was rooted in his conviction regarding the "essence" of the Gospel. Contemporary historians working with Harnack's own legacy have now perhaps brought these researches to a point of crisis by calling into question what Harnack still regarded as the "Christian" basis on which they rested.

Notes

1. See E. P. Meijering, *Die Hellenisierung des Christentums im Urteil Adolf von Harnacks* (Amsterdam: North-Holland Publishing Company, 1985), esp. 122-42. See also William V. Rowe, "A Critical Study of E. P. Meijering's *Die Hellenisierung des Christentum im Urteil Adolf von Harnacks*," *Philosophia Reformata* 57 (1992): 78-85.

2. See Werner Jaeger, *Early Christianity and Greek Paideia* (London: Oxford University Press, 1961), 6 and 107, note 6. See also M. Hengel, *Jews, Greeks and Barbarians* (Philadelphia: Fortress Press, 1980), 52f.

3. A. von Harnack, *History of Dogma*, Neil Buchanan, trans. (New York: Dover Publications, 1961), vol. I, 47; *Lehrbuch des Dogmengeschichte*, (subsequently *LD*), Dritte Auflage (Freiburg in Breisgau and Leipzig: J. C. B. Mohr, 1894), vol. 4, 46.

4. Ibid., 56, n.1; *LD*, I, 55, n.1.

5. *History of Dogma*, vol. I, 48, n.1; *LD*, I, 47, n.1.

6. This is an interpretation we may rightly dispute in view of the nature of God's covenant with Abraham.

7. *History of Dogma*, vol. I, 47; *LD*, I, 46-47.

8. Ibid., 43-44; *LD*, I, 43.

9. Ibid., 46-47; *LD*, I, 45-46.

10. Ibid., 47f; *LD*, I, 46f.

11. Von Harnack, *What Is Christianity?*, Thomas Bailey Saunders, trans. (New York: Harper & Row, 1957), 199-200.

12. "It is very gratifying to find an investigator so conservative as Sohm, now fully admitting that 'Christian theology grew up in the second and third centuries, when its foundations were laid for all time (?), the last great production of the Hellenic Spirit' " (Kirchengeschichte im Grundriss, 1888, 37): *History of Dogma*, vol. I, 39, n.1; *LD*, I, 38, n.1 (38-9). Harnack places a question mark in this quote after the words "were laid for all time" because of the conservatism evident in them.

13. For example, Harnack is the first to make extensive use of the treatise of Celsus against Christianity.

14. A summary statement of these stages can be found in Adolf von Harnack, *What is Christianity?* (n.11) 201:

> The first stage of any real influx of definitely Greek thought and Greek life is to be fixed at about the year 130. It was then that the religious philosophy of Greece began to effect an entrance, and it went straight to the centre of the new religion. It sought to get into inner touch with Christianity, and, conversely, Christianity itself held out a hand to this ally. We are speaking of Greek *philosophy*; as yet, there is no trace of mythology, Greek worship, and so on; all [i. e., the only thing, WVR] that was taken up into the church, cautiously and under proper guarantees, was the great capital which philosophy had amassed since the days of Socrates. A century or so later, about the year 220 or 230, the second stage begins: Greek mysteries, and Greek civilisation in the whole range of its development, exercise their influence on the church, but not mythology and polytheism; these were still to come. Another century, however, had in its turn to elapse before Hellenism as a whole and in every phase of its development was established in the church.

15. *What Is Christianity?* 202.

16. "Ancient teachers before them had also called Christ 'the Logos' among the many predicates which they ascribed to him; one of them, John, had already formulated the proposition: 'The Logos is Jesus Christ.' But with John this proposition had not become the basis of every speculative idea about Christ; with him, too, 'the Logos' was only a predicate. But now teachers came forward who previous to their conversion had been adherents of the platonico-stoical philosophy, and with whom the conception 'Logos' formed an inalienable part of a general philosophy of the world. They proclaimed that Jesus Christ was the Logos incarnate. . . . In the place of the entirely unintelligible conception 'Messiah,' an intelligible one was acquired at a stroke; Christology, tottering under the exuberance of its own affirmations, received a stable basis; Christ's significance for the world was established; his mysterious relation to

God was explained; the cosmos, reason, and ethics, were comprehended as one. . . . [Hence] the identification of the Logos with Christ was the determining factor in the fusion of Greek philosophy with the apostolic inheritance." *What Is Christianity?*, 203-204.

17. ". . . The parallel between the ecclesiastical dogmas and those of ancient schools of philosophy appears to be in point of form complete. The only difference is that revelation is here put as authority in the place of human knowledge, although the later philosophic schools appealed to revelation also. The theoretical as well as the practical doctrines which embraced the peculiar conception of the world and the ethics of the school, together with their rationales, were described in these schools as dogmas. Now, in so far as the adherents of the Christian religion possess dogmas in this sense, and form a community which has gained an understanding of its religious faith by analysis and by scientific definition and grounding, *they appear as a great philosophic school in the ancient sense of the word*" (emphasis mine, WVR). *History of Dogma*, vol. I, 15; *LD*, I, 15.

18. "The foolishness of identifying dogma and Greek philosophy never entered my mind," *History of Dogma*, vol. I, 21; *LD*, I, 22.

19. "To a much larger extent than the earlier speculative ideas about Christ, [the Logos idea of the Apologetes] absorbed men's interest; it withdrew their minds from the simplicity of the Gospel, and increasingly transformed it into a philosophy of religion," *What Is Christianity?*, 204.

20. *History of Dogma*, vol. I, 17; *LD*, I, 17-18.

21. *History of Dogma*, vol. I, 14-15 and 15-16; *LD*, I, 16-17.

22. *History of Dogma*, vol. I, 20; *LD*, I, 20.

23. Although this would certainly be to miswrite it, in Harnack's opinion. "It can in no way be conducive to historical knowledge to regard as indifferent the peculiar character of the expression of Christian faith as dogma, and allow the history of dogma to be absorbed in a general history of the various conceptions of Christianity. Such a 'liberal' view would not agree either with the teaching of history or with the actual situation of the Protestant churches of the present day: for it is, above all, of crucial importance to perceive that it is a peculiar stage in the development of the human spirit which is described by dogma. On this stage, parallel with dogma and inwardly united with it, stands a definite psychology, metaphysic and natural philosophy, as well as a view of history of a definite type. This is the conception of the world obtained by antiquity after almost a thousand years' labour, and it is the same connection of theoretic perceptions and practical ideas which it accomplished." *History of Dogma*, 20; *LD*, I, 21.

24. "I have given . . . little ground for the accusation that I look upon the whole development of the history of dogma as a pathological development within the history of the Gospel. I do not even look upon the history of the origin of the Papacy as such a process, not to speak of the history of dogma. But the perception that 'everything must happen as it has happened' does not absolve the historian from the task of ascertaining the powers which have formed the history, and distinguishing between the original and later, permanent and transitory, nor from the duty of stating his own opinion." *History of Dogma*, vol. I, 22; *LD*, I, 22.

25. *History of Dogma*, vol. I, 17; *LD*, I, 18.

26. "Parallel with the slow influx of the element of Greek philosophy, experiments were being made all along the line in the direction of what may be briefly called 'acute Hellenisation.' While they offer us a most magnificent historical spectacle, in the period itself they were a terrible danger." *What Is Christianity?*, 205.

27. *History of Dogma*, vol. I, 224-25.

28. *History of Dogma*, vol. I, 227-28.

29. "The Christian religion is assuredly informed with the desire to come to terms with all knowledge and with intellectual life as a whole; but when achievements in this field—even presuming that they always accord with truth and reality—are held to be equally binding with the evangelical message, or even to be a necessary preliminary to it, mischief is done to the cause of religion. This mischief is already unmistakably present at the beginning of the third century." *What Is Christianity?*, 211-12.

30. "How much of its original freedom the church sacrificed! It was now forced to say: You are no Christian, you cannot come into any relation with god at all, unless you have first of all acknowledged these doctrines, yielded obedience to these ordinances, and followed out definite forms of mediation. Nor was anyone to think a religious experience legitimate that had not been sanctioned by sound doctrine and approved by the priests. The church found no other way and no other means of maintaining itself against Gnosticism, and what was set up as a protection against enemies from without became the Palladium, nay, the very foundation within." *What Is Christianity?*, 207.

31. "It is in the second century, and with the apologists, that Intellectualism commences; and, supported by the struggle with the Gnostics and by the Alexandrian school of religious philosophers in the church, it manages to prevail." *What Is Christianity?*, 216.

32. *What Is Christianity?*, 207.

33. *What Is Christianity?*, 211-12.

34. *History of Dogma*, vol. I, 20-21; *LD*, I, 20, 21-22.

35. *What is Christianity?*, 293.

36. "Who can guarantee that those [Reformation] churches, too, will not become 'Catholic' which had their origin in 'the liberty of a Christian man?' That, however, would not involve the destruction of the Gospel: so much, at least, history proves. It would be still traceable like a red thread in the centre of the web, and somewhere or other it would emerge afresh, and free itself from its entangling connexions." *What Is Christianity?*, 298.

37. *What Is Christianity?*, 293-95.

38. See *History of Dogma*, vol. I, 23-40; *LD*, I, 23-40.

39. *What Is Christianity?*, 201.

40. *Phaedo* 100B, *Republic*, 510B-511D.

41. *Epistle* VII, 341C.

42. *Nicomachean Ethics*, VI, 3, 1039b 15-17.

43. *Nicomachean Ethics*, VI, 6, 1140b 30-1141a 8 and 1143a 35-1143 b 6.

44. *Nicomachean Ethics*, I, 8, 1098b 32-4; and X, 6, 1176a 34-1176 b 5.

45. *Contra Academicos*, III, xvii-xviii.

46. See J. N. D. Kelly, *Early Christian Creeds* (London: Longmans, 1972), 52-61.

47. See M. Desjardins, "Bauer and Beyond: On Recent Scholarly Discussions of *Hairesis* in the Early Christian Era," *The Second Century* 8 (1991): 65-82, especially 73-75.

Alexandria or Athens as the Essence of Hellenization

A Historian Responds to a Philosopher

Barry W. Henaut

The Problem of Definition

Beware the respondent who announces "I have not come to bury this paper, but to praise it." Imagine my chagrin when a third of the way through Rowe's paper I realized he had entirely undercut my best criticism. For Harnack and Rowe both demonstrate how intimately connected every topic is to our own past history and present expectations. We usually apply to a topic only our own previous strengths; and readers will undoubtedly notice "sins of omission" arising from long-standing weaknesses.

The central problem is one of definition. What is "Hellenization?" For the historian of early Christianity "Hellenization" usually refers to Greek culture from the time of Alexander the Great (356-323 BCE) as it makes its impact throughout the Greco-Roman empire. It is largely an urban phenomenon, and manifested itself in popular philosophies such as Platonic Dualism, Stoicism, and Cynicism. Symbolically, it is best represented by the city of Alexandria, the center of learning and culture founded by its namesake in 331 BCE. Its ethos is manifestly distinct from that of the Pre-Socratics, Plato and even Aristotle, despite the short chronological distance from the latter, for the classical Greek philosophers were more closely associated with the Greek city-states, the most famous being Athens. The general acceptance of the given definition of "Hellenization" for the historian may be recognized in New Testament textbooks and courses which usually begin with Alexander the Great rather than with Athens and Plato.[1]

It is of no small importance that, for Harnack, the essence of Hellenization in the church is to be found with that form of Greek culture best represented by Athens, rather than Alexandria, and best characterized as "philosophical." This definitional starting point allows Harnack to assert that the first stage of Hellenization in the church begins circa 130 CE, when "the religious philosophy of Greece began to effect an entrance."[2] The definition likewise allows Harnack to equate Hellenization with "dogma" and philosophical theology of the second century.[3]

The distinction is more than semantics. One can always identify a historical process and consistently apply a particular term without any harm being done. In the present instance, however, Harnack's term is both inappropriate and inconsistently applied, and it leads to a number of insupportable conclusions. Rowe identifies one of the primary reasons, namely the relationship of historical inquiry and the process of Hellenization itself to the present.

Historical Inquiry and Hellenization
As Rowe notes, the very topic of "Harnack and the Concept of Hellenization" conceals and implies another topic: the relationship of Hellenization and the work of Harnack. The process of Hellenization cannot be assumed to have ended after the third century CE. Thus we may well ask to what extent the process continues in Harnack and even the twentieth century. The question also applies to ourselves; the topic is not simply a curiosity of the past but reflects upon the present.

When we ask how Harnack, and we ourselves, are affected by Hellenization and investigate the motives for exploring this question, the first problem emerges. Rowe acknowledges a number of diverse and contradictory reasons for exploring this topic, namely "repristination" of one's own tradition, or establishing a model for relating with secular culture. He notes Harnack's own theological concerns; for Harnack, Hellenization, as the rise of "dogmatic" theology, represents a contemporary problem. It threatens the evangelical freedom of the gospel known in the "primitive church" of the first century and regained with the Reformation. Harnack regarded the study of Hellenization as an academic antidote for this plague. Arising from a twentieth century anxiety, Harnack's historical inquiry is thus clearly distinct from the Whig histories of the nineteenth century.[4]

Harnack's desire to provide an antidote to modern problems has, I believe, led him to an inappropriate definition of Hellenization. The term is fortuitously chosen, perhaps unconsciously, because it allows for a number of distinctions necessary for apologetical purposes. Harnack first describes Hellenism as a movement that "having its origin among a small people, became a universal spiritual power, which, severed from its original nationality, had for that very reason penetrated foreign nations."[5] The importance of this definition is that for Harnack, the spread of Hellenistic culture is a paradigm for the universal mission of the church; he almost identifies Hellenization with that process of history inaugurated by Alexander, that is, the spread of Greek culture throughout most of the Mediterranean world. But notice that the paradigm also calls for the church to be "severed from its original nationality," i. e., Judaism; and this separation accounts for its success at "foreign penetration."

The contrast with Judaism is unfortunate, and insupportable historically. As Rowe points out, Harnack assumes that Judaism is "limited to the horizon of the Hebrew nation," an assumption which he disputes "in view of the nature of God's covenant with Abraham."[6] It is well to remind ourselves that biblical Judaism and Judaism of the second Temple era made provision for inclusion of Gentiles into the covenant people of Yahweh, while the letters of Paul reflect great tensions within the early church over the Gentile mission and the requirements of admission for the "new community." Hence, note the assumptions within the telic force of Harnack's assertion:

> The Gospel was a message for humanity even when there was no break with Judaism; but it seemed impossible to bring this message home to men who were not Jews in any other way than by leaving the Jewish Church [sic]. But to leave that Church was to declare it to be worthless.[7]

It is not too strong to see here a type of apologetic work which Willard Oxtoby in another context characterizes as "more forgiving toward the symbolic statements of the authors own tradition than toward those of another."[8]

A different view of Hellenization within the early church, and its relationship to Judaism, emerges when Hellenization is taken to refer to the influence of Greek culture as it was introduced by Alexander. From this perspective it would make no sense to regard Hellenization of the church as movement away from a non-Hellenistic condition. For the church was truly "Hellenistic" from the start! As Harnack admits there "is no single writing of the New Testament which does not betray the influence of the mode of thought and general conditions of the culture of the time which resulted from the Hellenising of the east."[9] Within the church over the centuries different aspects of Hellenism have come and gone, but the church did not become increasingly Hellenized. Even more damaging for Harnack's program, the implied contrast between a non-Hellenistic Judaism and an increasingly Hellenistic (and universal) church withers away. As Martin Hengel has shown:

> From about the middle of the third century BCE *all Judaism* must really be designated *"Hellenistic Judaism"* in the strict sense, and a better differentiation could be made between the Greek-speaking Judaism of the Western Diaspora and the Aramaic/Hebrew-speaking Judaism of Palestine and Babylonia.[10]

The starting point of what constitutes "Hellenization," therefore, is no small matter. But beyond the problem of comparison, Harnack's definition leads to a related issue, that of the relationship of history and culture.

History and Culture

Harnack's definition of Hellenization as the rise of dogmatic, philosophical theology raises another key issue regarding our interpretation of the historical process. It is, I believe, no accident that for Harnack "true Hellenization" involves the rise of philosophical analysis identified with Platonism and "Athens." This implies a value judgment regarding the "popular," less "philosophical" culture of the Hellenistic era as somehow less deserving.

According to such a view, history "proper" is the history of thought. This is perhaps best expressed by R. G. Collingwood, who views the study of history as the re-enactment of thought; since nature has no experience of thought, there can be no history of nature:

> Of everything other than thought, there can be no history. Thus a biography, for example, however much history it contains, is constructed on principles that are not only non-historical but anti-historical. Its limits are biological events, the birth and death of a human organism: its framework is thus a framework not of thought but of natural process.[11]

This exaltation of "thought" above all else lies behind Harnack's identification of Hellenization with philosophical theology. It is also the motivating force behind his sequential ordering of the process of Hellenization within the early church. During the first stage, after 130 CE, for Harnack "as yet, there is no trace of mythology, Greek worship, and so on" while even a century later in the second stage, "Greek mysteries, and Greek civilisation in the whole range of its development, exercise their influence on the Church, but not mythology and polytheism."[12]

Entire generations of scholars have spent a lifetime lost in the blind alley of the "Myth versus History" debate. It is unfortunate that when Bultmann framed his analysis of early Christianity he gave the impression that myth was nothing more than the decayed wineskins that are quickly to be discarded when we bring out the real vintage of the *Kerygma*, the gospel proclamation. But if we place myth within a broad range of figurative language including parable, metaphor, and symbol, I believe we can place Harnack's assumption in a different light. Metaphor, parable, and myth may have a different role and function within our human culture, but they are no less, or more valuable than philosophy.

And in terms of the philosophy of history, more recent theorists have challenged Harnack and Collingwood's essentially reductionist views. We can see this, for example, in Thomas McIntire's insight that our reality consists of three dimensions which he calls historical, structural and ultimate. Under the historical he places "all phenomena, whether human or nonhuman," since they all exist in time and undergo "the temporal process of coming into being, carrying on, modifying, perhaps developing, and then passing away."[13]

Harnack's definition also raises another issue of method—one which I will only briefly consider. How do we relate religion and culture? Harnack implies that the essence of the gospel is "neither Jew nor Greek." It is born of its (non-Hellenistic) parent Judaism, quickly separates to embrace a universal mission, and then undergoes Hellenization, which is both a strength and danger. For Rowe points out that, positively, Hellenization allowed the church to vanquish its adversaries. Negatively, it infiltrated the church like a parasite, robbing it of evangelical freedom and demanding the exclusion of those who refuse to assent to its demands. Throughout it all, the "essence" of the "gospel" can, as it were, be distilled and separated from its cultural context. For Harnack it exists like Plato's true forms, independent of any one particular manifestation. But as an aspect of human culture and part of the historical process, can we really abstract religion from its context in this way? As McIntire observes, "Human phenomena come into being by culture-making and pass away by what we might call culture-unmaking. Human phenomena do not just come into being; we *bring* them into being by our creative acts."[14]

Notes

1. See, e. g., Norman Perrin and D. C. Duling, *The New Testament: An Introduction*, 2nd ed. (New York: Harcourt Brace Jovanovich, 1982).
2. Adolf von Harnack, *What is Christianity?*, 201; see Rowe, "Adolf von Harnack and the Concept of Hellenization," n.14 above, 94.
3. See Harnack, *History of Dogma*, 20; Rowe, "Harnack and Hellenization," in this volume, 80-81.
4. Rowe's apt reference—and usurpation of my best critique!—is to Herbert Butterfield, *The Whig Interpretation of History* (London: Penguin, 1931, 1971). However, in distinction from Rowe (85-88), I believe that the elements of value and moral judgments implicit in Harnack suggest that he, although anticipating well the ethos of early twentieth century anxiety, still retains key elements of twentieth century Whig historians.
5. Harnack, *History of Dogma*, 47; Rowe, 71.
6. Rowe, "Harnack and Hellenization," 72, and n.6.
7. Harnack, *History of Dogma*, vol. I, 43-44; see Rowe, 73.
8. Willard G. Oxtoby, *The Meaning of Other Faiths* (Philadelphia: Westminster, 1983), 73-74. Also 83, "It is a cardinal sin in the comparison of religious traditions and communities to compare the ideals of one's own with the achievements of another."
9. Harnack, *History of Dogma*, vol. I, 48, n.1; see Rowe, 72.
10. Martin Hengel, *Judaism and Hellenism: Studies in their Encounter in Palestine during the Early Hellenistic Period*, John Bowden, trans. (London: SCM, 1974), I, 104.
11. R. G. Collingwood, *The Idea of History* (London and New York: Oxford University, 1946), 304.
12. Harnack, *What is Christianity?*, 201; see Rowe, n.14 (on p. 94).

13. C. T. McIntire, "Historical Study and the Historical Dimension of Our World," in *History and Historical Understanding*, C. T. McIntire and Ronald A. Wells, eds. (Grand Rapids: Eerdmans, 1984), 20.

14. McIntire, "Historical Study," 31.

Creatio ex nihilo in Philo

Albert M. Wolters

In this paper I propose to discuss the question: "Did Philo Judaeus hold to a doctrine of creation which can be legitimately described in the terms of classical Jewish and Christian orthodoxy, namely as *creatio ex nihilo*?" I shall divide my discussion into four stages, dealing first with the question itself, specifically the meaning of *creatio ex nihilo*, and the significance of its presence or absence in Philo, then with the state of Philonic scholarship on this issue, thirdly with the main arguments which are adduced in support of the important different positions taken on the problem, and finally with some considerations which are important in evaluating the issue as a question of scholarship. My goal will not be to offer a new solution to the problem, but rather to clarify the issue, and to offer some perspective on the scholarly debate.

The Question
It is necessary first of all to clarify our terms. To begin with, the word *creatio* and its modern derivatives or equivalents (*creazione*, *Schöpfung*, etc.) are notoriously ambiguous. Not only do they denote an action as well as the result of that action (in Greek: respectively *ktisis* and *ktisma*); they are also commonly used to designate an absolute "causing-to-exist" and a "transformation" of raw materials into a new product, in the manner of a sculptor or a carpenter. In

the modern age, moreover, we must contend with connotations of the word "creation," particularly its derivatives "creative" and "creativity," coming from Romantic ideas concerning artistic production.

When we speak of *creatio ex nihilo*, however, we must be clear that the first term of this phrase is a *nomen actionis*; it refers to the *act* of creating and has nothing to do (at least in its classical formulation) with the aesthetics of Romanticism. Matters are less clear for the second ambiguity which we mentioned: "absolute causing-to-exist" versus "transformation." Indeed, the formulation "creatio *ex nihilo*" first arose from reflection on this ambiguity. The phrase *ex nihilo* is designed to remove the ambiguity in question, to exclude the understanding of creation as the transformation of raw materials, for it denies the presence of preexistent material for the product of creation.

It should also be clear that *creatio ex nihilo* refers to an action which is divine in origin and cosmic in scope. God is the subject and the world is the object. Creating in this sense is something which only God can do, and it is no doubt for that reason that the Bible reserves the Hebrew verb *bārā'* and the Greek verb *ktizein* for this exclusively divine activity.[1] Moreover, the formula *creatio ex nihilo* is traditionally applied only to that universal coming-to-be of all things "in the beginning."

To summarize our discussion of the classic formula, we can say that *creatio ex nihilo* refers to God's causing the world to exist without the benefit of an already existing material.

Given this definition, why is it significant or interesting to determine whether Philo subscribed to such a view? The answer to this question seems to be twofold. It is of interest, first, for the history of ideas. If Philo does hold to a systematically articulated doctrine of *creatio ex nihilo*, then it can be argued that he was the first to do so, and he may be regarded as the author of an enormously influential doctrine in subsequent philosophy and theology. In the second place, the doctrine of creation is a key aspect of the broader issue regarding the relationship of Judaism and Hellenism in Philo's thought. Again, if Philo does hold to a legitimate version of *creatio ex nihilo*, this lends strong support to the view that Philo is primarily Jewish and modifies Greek philosophy to conform to orthodox Judaism, since *creatio ex nihilo* is consistent with elements found in pre-Philonic Judaism. If he does not, he would appear to have subordinated his Jewish faith to Greek philosophy. Let me elaborate briefly on each of these two points.

It is commonly held that the doctrine of *creatio ex nihilo* is a relatively late development in Jewish and Christian thinking. Although 2 Maccabees 7:28 (dated second century BCE) is often cited as the first explicit formulation of the doctrine, this is widely challenged today. David Winston, for example, argued in 1971 that the verse will not bear this interpretation, and concludes that "the first explicit formulation of *creatio ex nihilo* appeared in second-century Christian literature."[2] Winston's view is elaborated and defended by Gerhard May in his detailed monograph *Schöpfung aus dem Nichts* in 1978.[3] Over against this view we find the position of H. A. Wolfson, who argues that although *creatio ex nihilo* may not be taught in 2 Maccabees 7:28, it definitely *is* found in Philo.[4] In this way Wolfson strengthens his overall view that Philo stands at the beginning of a great new phase in the history of philosophy, which lasted until Spinoza. The question of *creatio ex nihilo* in Philo thus plays an important role in Wolfson's grand panoramic vision of the history of Western philosophy.

Closely related to this question is the issue of Philo's "Jewishness." The contrast between the biblical and the Hellenic traditions with respect to the origin of the cosmos can be stated in very stark terms. In his commentary on the apocryphal Book of Wisdom, J. Reider writes:

> The Jews believed in creation out of nothing; the Greeks believed in creation out of formless matter which was eternal. On the one hand religious monism (God alone is eternal); on the other philosophic dualism (God and matter are eternal).[5]

We can find equally definite and sweeping statements in the writings of Étienne Gilson, who frequently formulates the difference between the biblical and Greek conceptions on this point in terms of the *contingency* of the world.[6] This is a concept which is quite foreign to the tradition of Hellenic philosophy, while it is foundational to biblical religion.

Viewed in the light of this contrast, the question of *creatio ex nihilo* in Philo becomes a litmus test of his Jewish orthodoxy or faithfulness to the biblical worldview. At stake here is the sovereignty of God: is there an ontological principle which exists alongside and independently of God, on which he is in fact dependent in creating the world? Or is *everything* outside of God utterly dependent for its existence on the sovereign will of the Creator?

Rephrased with reference to Philo: did Philo compromise the biblical teaching concerning the sovereignty of God by accommodating it to the Greek idea of an eternal preexistent matter? Or did he safeguard his Jewish faith and biblical teaching by insisting on a preexistent matter which was itself created by God? Depending on one's interpretation of Philo on this score he will appear more as one who has sold out his Jewish religious heritage to Greek thought, or as the genius who transformed philosophy on the basis of his Jewish faith. So here too the topic we are treating plays a significant role in overall perspectives of Philo interpretation. What is at stake is more than detailed questions of exegesis, but fundamentally different conceptions of the history of ideas.

The State of the Question

Partly because of these broader issues of interpretation, and partly because of the ambiguous and apparently contradictory evidence in Philo's writings, there is little consensus in the scholarly literature on the issue of *creatio ex nihilo* in Philo. Leading scholars disagree strongly on the question—not only whether the doctrine is found at all, but also in what sense it does or does not appear. What we propose to do in what follows is to sketch briefly the principal variant interpretations, reserving critical analysis for the following section.

Perhaps the simplest view is that Philo was a loyal Jew, and that therefore he must be interpreted as teaching *creatio ex nihilo*. This is the argument of F. V. Courneen in an article entitled "Philo Iudaeus Had the Concept of Creation," published in 1941.[7] However, as Louis Feldman has observed, "This is begging the question, since, despite Philo's protestations, there is much room for doubting his Orthodoxy."[8] To this we might add that Courneen also takes for granted another debated point, namely that the doctrine of "creation out of nothing" was part of orthodox Judaism in Philo's day.

We find the same view reflected in Samuel Sandmel's work *Philo of Alexandria*, published in 1979.[9] In outlining the content of Philo's treatise *On the Creation*, he writes:

> Two themes, which one might call Jewish, recur in the treatise. One is that God created the world out of nothing. That is to say, there did not preexist some matter, some material, which God, at creation, utilized, shaping it into the form of the world.[10]

In a note on this passage he adds: "See Wisdom of Solomon 11:17 which seems to assert that God made the world out of matter without form. Philo seems to be rejecting this view."[11]

The opposite extreme on the interpretive spectrum is represented by Emil Schürer, author of the monumental *Geschichte des jüdischen Volkes im Zeitalter Jesu Christi*, (Leipzig, 1909). In an article written for the ninth edition of the *Encyclopaedia Britannica*, Schürer described Philo's position as follows:

> The world can be ascribed to God only insofar as it is a cosmos or orderly world; its material substratum is not even indirectly referable to God. Matter . . . is a second principle, but in itself an empty one, its essence being a mere negation of all true being. It is a lifeless, unmoved, shapeless mass out of which God formed the actual world by means of the Logos and divine forces. Strictly, the world is only formed, not created, since matter did not originate with God.[12]

In this interpretation, God creates the world out of a matter which functions as a second uncreated principle independent of him. Carl Siegfried, in an article for *The Jewish Encyclopedia*, draws out the religious implications of this view:

> Philo's conception of the matter out of which the world was created is entirely un-Biblical and un-Jewish; he is here wholly at one with Plato and the Stoics. According to him, God does not create the world-stuff, but finds it ready to hand. God can not create it, as in its nature it resists all contact with the divine.[13]

This conception of creation in Philo was the prevailing one in the late nineteenth and early twentieth century. It was represented by such influential expositors as E. Zeller[14] and E. Bréhier,[15] and is still found in the article on Philo in the current edition of *Die Religion in Geschichte und Gegenwart* (1961) by C. Colpe.[16] In fact, as recently as 1987 it appeared in the English revision by Jenny Morris of the section on Philo in Schürer's *magnum opus*.[17]

However, since the 1948 publication of Wolfson's two-volume study of Philo a mediating position between the two extreme interpretations has become dominant. By and large, the simple alternatives: "creation out of nothing" versus "creation out of uncreated matter" have been avoided in recent decades. Instead, we can say that Wolfson's interpretation has dominated the field, to be challenged in recent years by Winston.

Wolfson develops his view in the first volume of his major study *Philo: Foundations of Religious Philosophy in Judaism, Christianity and Islam*.[18] For our present purposes it will suffice to quote a summarizing statement by Wolfson from his article on Philo in *The Encyclopedia of Philosophy*. The relevant passage reads as follows:

> . . . Philo also could not accept the view commonly held by contemporary students of Plato that the pre-existent matter out

of which, in the *Timaeus*, the world was created was eternal. But as a philosopher he did not like to reject altogether the reputable Platonic conception of a pre-existent matter. And so here, too, he solved the difficulty by the method of harmonization. There was indeed a pre-existent matter, but that pre- existent matter was created. There were thus to him two creations, the creation of the pre-existent matter out of nothing and the creation of the world out of that pre-existent matter.[19]

In effect, Wolfson is conceding the point that the actual account of the creation of the physical world which Philo gives in connection with Genesis 1 does not describe a *creatio ex nihilo* but an ordering of a formless matter as Plato describes it. But he saves Philo's orthodoxy on this point by arguing that Philo does hold to a *creatio ex nihilo* with respect to formless matter. In this way Philo can have it both ways; creation out of nothing can be simultaneously affirmed and denied. In Hegelian fashion the affirmation of Courneen and his followers, and the denial of Schürer and his followers, are resolved into the higher synthesis of Wolfson's interpretation.

Wolfson's view of the matter was attractive and persuasive, and proved to be very influential. Until recently it was the prevailing interpretation.[20] Representative of this broad consensus is the un- qualified statement found in the article on Philo in the current *Encyclopaedia Britannica* (the one which replaces the older one by Schürer, quoted above): "Philo did not reject the Platonic view of a preexistent matter but insisted that this matter too was created."[21] Although the word "insisted" here goes beyond what Wolfson would have claimed, it is clearly his view that is being summarized. We find the same interpretation echoed in the recent Italian history of ancient philosophy by G. Reale.[22]

Although widely accepted since 1947, Wolfson's reading of Philo's doctrine of creation has not gone unchallenged. Apart from an unpublished German dissertation completed in 1955,[23] it has been subjected to a searching critique by David Winston in 1975;[24] he restated both his critique and his alternative interpretation in

1981.[25] Leaving aside for the moment the details of his argumentation, we quote two passages from his 1981 discussion:

> Logically, of course, God is, for Philo, indirectly the source of preexistent matter, but Philo would have recoiled from ascribing it to the *creative* activity of God, just as he recoiled from ascribing even the *shaping* of matter directly to God.[26]

> . . . Even the virtually non-existent void [i. e., the matter from which the world is created—AW] is but a shadow reflection of an idea in God. Hence what in Philo's view was the crucial defect in the Platonists' doctrine of eternal matter (i. e., the elevation of matter into an autonomous albeit passive principle) has carefully been eliminated from his own version of that theory.[27]

In Winston's view, therefore, we cannot speak of *creatio ex nihilo* in Philo, not even with respect to preexistent matter (*pace* Wolfson). Instead, matter is a "shadow reflection" of an idea in God, and therefore still finds in him, albeit "indirectly," its ontological "source." Consequently, matter is robbed of its Platonic autonomy as independent principle.

Despite the differences between them, Wolfson and Winston, who today probably represent the two most authoritative interpretations of creation in Philo, are not as far apart as Winston's critique might indicate. Both agree that for Philo creation takes place from a preexistent matter, that this matter is not an independent principle, and that Plato's account must be modified to safeguard God's sovereignty. Their differences focus on the relatively narrow issue of the sense in which preexistent matter owes its existence to God. On that issue Wolfson argues for, and Wilson against, the applicability of the formula *creatio ex nihilo* to Philo's cosmogony.

The Arguments

This section will not discuss in detail all the arguments adduced for and against *creatio ex nihilo* by the authors mentioned. We will focus on the argumentation of Wolfson and Winston, since these can be said to dominate the present state of the scholarly discussion on this issue.

Wolfson, after a survey of previous scholarship on the question, and of the relevant Philonic passages on various sides of the issue, announces that a new approach is called for.

> If, therefore, an answer is to be found to the question of Philo's position on the subject, it will have to be found in some passage in which he definitely and unmistakably states that the preexistent matter out of which the world was created was itself created by God.[28]

"Such a passage," he continues, "is to be found in his revision of the creation story of the *Timaeus*."

In that story, Plato distinguishes between an unlimited void (the abode of the ideas) and a limited void called, among other things, "Receptacle" and "Space." Within that limited void there are copies (*mimēmata*) of the ideal four elements. Now it is from these copies that the world is created by the demiurge, first by transforming them into the four elements and then by creating the world from the latter. In Philo's interpretation of Plato the limited void and the *mimēmata* which it contains together constitute preexistent matter.[29]

According to Wolfson, this Platonic account fails to make clear not only whether the unlimited void with its ideas was created, but also whether the limited void and its *mimēmata* were created. All he says about the latter is that they come to be "in a fashion marvellous and hard to describe." Philo, however, in his revision of the Platonic account, removes these ambiguities. The unlimited void is abolished altogether and its ideas declared to be created. As for the Receptacle and its element-copies, Wolfson argues, they too are declared by Philo to be created.[30]

Since these two together constitute preexistent matter, we are here at the crux of the issue. In Wolfson's view, the createdness of this preexistent matter can be shown to be held by Philo from the section of the *On the Creation* in which he deals with the first day of creation.

In that section, Philo asserts that the first day deals with the creation of the *intelligible* world. When the biblical text (quoted according to the Septuagint) speaks of God's making the *heaven* and the *earth*, this really refers to the incorporeal heaven (the idea of fire) and to the invisible earth (the idea of earth). Similarly, *darkness* really refers to the idea of air, and *water* to the idea of water. Thus we have the creation of Plato's ideal four elements. Moreover, *Spirit of God* represents the ideas of mind and soul, and *light* represents the celestial bodies.

Wolfson points out that this interpretation of Genesis 1:1-3, although it follows the *Timaeus* account on many essentials, nevertheless also diverges from it on some significant points. One of these is that the ideal four elements are said to be created: "Philo . . . definitely says that the ideas of the four elements are created *and consequently the copies of the ideal four elements in the limited void are also created.*"[31]

The italicized words (emphasis mine) give the conclusion which Wolfson draws from Philo's view, that the ideal elements are created. If *they* are created, Wolfson is saying, then it follows that their copies (*mimēmata*) are also created. Consequently, at least one of the two components of preexistent matter can be said to be created.

That leaves the other component, the limited void. It is here that Philo's interpretation of another term in the Genesis account becomes significant, the term that in the Septuagint is rendered *abyssos*. Wolfson writes: ". . . In his comment on the term 'abyss' he clears up the ambiguity in Plato with regard to the origin of the limited void."[32] "Abyss" is explained by Philo as referring to "the idea of the void." This is described as *achanes*, which is reminiscent of Hesiod's *chaos*, which in turn is connected with Plato's "Receptacle" or "Space."

> Consequently when Philo speaks of the creation of the idea of void, he means that the idea of Plato's "Receptacle" or "Space"

was created *and hence Plato's Receptacle or Space itself was also created* [my emphasis].[33]

In other words, the other component of preexistent matter can also be said to be created.

It should be noted that Wolfson's argument involves two separate chains of inference. The first links "abyss" with Plato's Receptacle. The second (indicated by the words emphasized in the last quotation) infers the createdness of a copy from the createdness of its idea.

Wolfson thus claims to have shown that for Philo both components of preexistent matter (the *mimēmata* of the ideal elements and the Receptacle/Space) are created by God. He finds confirmation of this view in a direct statement which Philo makes in another treatise, *On the Confusion of Tongues*. God, it is there stated, "created space (*chōra*) and place (*topos*) simultaneously with bodies (*sōmata*)."[34] According to Wolfson, *chōra* here refers to the "Space" of limited void, *topos* refers to three-dimensional extension, and *sōmata* has a double reference: both to the copies of the ideal elements (which correlates with *chōra*) and to extended bodies (which correlates with *topos*).[35]

Thus Wolfson completes his widely influential case for the createdness of preexistent matter, and therefore *creatio ex nihilo*, in Philo. His argumentation is lucid, learned, and very ingenious, but it may be doubted whether he has produced a passage in Philo "in which he definitely and unmistakably states" that preexistent matter was created.

We turn now to Winston's critique of Wolfson and the details of his alternative, basing our account on his 1981 "Introduction." Winston agrees with Wolfson that Philo's preexistent matter may fairly be said to be composed of the *mimēmata* and the Receptacle/Space.[36] What he disputes is the inference that, if the ideal Forms/Ideas of these realities were created, then the copy-realities must also be created. The fact is that Plato himself is "vague on the manner in which the copies of the eternal Forms came into being." Certainly he does not attribute their creation to the demiurge.

Instead, they seem to arise as "some sort of automatic reflection of the Forms in the Receptacle." There is no reason to believe that the copy-Form relation in Philo is any different from that in Plato, so that Wolfson's inference of a divine *creation* of the copies is hardly necessary.[37]

Furthermore, if Philo *had* taught the creation of preexistent matter, he would have been inconsistent with himself. Elsewhere, Philo insists that what God creates is orderly and good, yet on Wolfson's interpretation, he created something which was disorderly and evil, since the *mimēmata* are the source of matter's chaotic character, and matter itself is inherently "faulted." If God cannot be said directly to *shape* matter, we must certainly deny that he directly *created* it. As for Wolfson's claim that Philo held to a creation *ex nihilo*, this conflicts directly with Philo's expressed opinion elsewhere that "nothing comes into being from the non-existent."[38]

Finally, Philo's statement that "God created *chōra* and *topos* simultaneously with *sōmata*," which Wolfson used as the clincher of his argument, is much more plausibly interpreted as referring to the creation of three-dimensional space (designated by the synonyms *chōra* and *topos*) concurrently with three-dimensional bodies. There is no necessity to introduce a subtle distinction between *chōra* and *topos*, or to postulate a double sense for *sōmata*.[39]

In elaborating his own view of the ontological status of preexistent matter, Winston enters into the question of the eternity of the world. He defends the thesis that Philo "taught a doctrine of eternal creation:"[40]

> In the mystical monotheism of Philo nothing really exists or acts except God; all else is but a shadow reality ultimately deriving from the truly Existent. Unlike Plato, who was a pluralist, Philo was thus unwilling to allow even for a self-existing void, and therefore made its pattern an eternal idea within the Divine Mind.[41]

In Winston's view, therefore, even though preexistent matter was not created in the strict sense, it has no subsistence in itself, and cannot be conceived as a principle of creation alongside God. "Even the virtually non-existent void is but the shadow reflection of an idea of God." Nor does this dependency-relation have a beginning in time, since God is always actively thinking his thoughts or ideas: "God's thinking is eternally bringing matter into being and simultaneously ordering it."[42] Passages in Philo which seem to speak of a temporal beginning of the world must not be taken literally. In short, we might say that, for Winston, Philo can be said to hold a view of cosmogony which closely resembles the later Neoplatonic interpretation of the *Timaeus*.

As we have stated above, Wolfson and Winston espouse interpretations which are remarkably similar despite their differences. They are so similar that one wonders whether some of Winston's criticisms of Wolfson don't apply to himself. For example, if the creation of primordial matter is inconsistent with Philo's view that God only creates what is orderly and good, we may well ask whether a disorderly and evil matter can plausibly be taken as an "automatic reflection" of God's eternal ideas. As David Runia has argued, Winston's view

> . . . is in the final analysis a metaphysically refined variant of the *creatio ex nihilo* thesis. Although matter would be only indirectly created by God, it is still the result of divine activity. There must be postulated a higher prototype of matter, an indefinite dyad or *noētē hylē*, for the existence of which God is directly responsible. Can the Philonic conviction that God is in no way responsible for the imperfect nature of material reality then still be seriously maintained?[43]

Runia answers his own question by stating that "matter possesses for Philo the status of an eternal constituent of reality with an existence (if that word can be used) in some way independent of God."

And so the pendulum swings. There seems to be an inherent ambiguity in the status of matter for Philo, a vacillation between independence and dependence with respect to the creator. It seems that no coherent interpretation can do full justice to both tendencies in Philo.

Concluding Observations
By way of conclusion, I offer a number of reflections on the interpretive problem we have been discussing. They are presented as points of view which may illumine the seemingly unsatisfactory conclusion of our survey.

(1) The central fact about Philo is that he seeks to achieve a synthesis of Greek philosophy and the Hebrew Bible, more specifically of Plato and Moses. These two traditions of thought each have their own individuality, and cannot be synthesized without conflict. However we describe the basic contrast between them, it is clear that on the point of cosmogony there are mutually exclusive conceptions. For Plato and his heirs the world is constituted by the conjunction of irrational matter and rational form. At bottom form and matter are independent realities which are at odds with each other, evil being associated with matter, and good with form. For Moses (the Pentateuch) the world is constituted by the sovereign will of the creator. All things are dependent for their existence and their identity upon the almighty fiat of YHWH. Goodness inheres in creation; evil results from human sin. In synthesizing these two fundamentally dissimilar conceptions, Philo attempted to correlate form with the creator and matter with creation, and was forced to postulate various intermediate stages between the extremes.

As a result, creation was conceived as the imposition of divine form upon non-divine matter. But since matter in the original scheme is an independent principle associated with evil, it does not comport well with a cosmogony in which God is sovereign and creation is very good. As long as creation is conceived in Platonic terms, therefore, matter will have an ambiguous and contradictory status. To the degree that it is independent, it clashes with God's sovereignty; to the degree that it is created or dependent it clashes with its own role as disorderly foil to form.

(2) Since Philo incorporates in his thinking both the Platonic motif of form and matter and the Mosaic motif of sovereign creation,

all the interpretations we have surveyed have some legitimacy. To the extent, however, that they attempt to find a single harmonious overall conception in which Platonic and biblical themes all fit equally neatly, they are also illegitimate, because they fail to appreciate the inherent incompatibility of some of the basic themes involved. A satisfactory interpretation of Philo's cosmogony must recognize the necessity of inconsistencies for someone engaged in Philo's project. Such inconsistencies must not be ignored or smoothed over, but shown to be the result of a fundamental tension between Plato and Moses.

(3) If *creatio ex nihilo* is defined, as we have done, as "God's causing the world to exist *without* the benefit of an already existing material," then it is clear that Philo does not hold to such a conception. That a case can nevertheless be made for the created or dependent status of the already existing material in Philo again shows the fundamental tension in his thought. What he had given away with his left hand he seeks to retrieve with his right.

(4) The doctrine of *creatio ex nihilo* is a later formulation, forged in the polemical context of the confrontation of the Hellenic and biblical traditions. In one sense it is anachronistic to ask whether Philo subscribed to such a doctrine, because the theological *doctrine* had not yet been formulated. But in another sense it is not, because the doctrine is implicit in the biblical account of creation. What is at stake is the absolute sovereignty of the biblical creator, who simply commands things to be, and they are, even if there is no raw material to work with.

(5) Though Philo cannot be said to be the first to formulate or espouse the doctrine of *creatio ex nihilo*, Wolfson was nevertheless right in recognizing the significance of cosmogonic speculation within the philosophical construct worked out by Philo. It is not the doctrine which is crucial, but the attempt itself to fuse the Greek form-matter motif and the biblical creation motif. Philo set the terms of a problem which was to remain foundational throughout patristic, medieval and early modern philosophy.

Notes

1. See W. Foerster's article on *ktizō* and cognates in *TWNT* 3.999-1034, esp. 1007, line 34, and 1027, line 21.
2. D. Winston, "The Book of Wisdom's Theory of Cosmogony," *History of Religions* 2 (1971): 191.
3. Berlin and New York: W. de Gruyter, 1978.
4. H. A. Wolfson, *Philo: Foundations of Religious Philosophy in Judaism, Christianity and Islam*, 2 vols. (Cambridge MA: Harvard University Press, 1947), 1.303f.
5. J. Reider, *The Book of Wisdom* (New York: Harper and Bros., 1957).
6. É. Gilson, *La philosophie au Moyen Age*, 2d ed. (Paris: Payot, 1962), 9f.
7. *New Scholasticism* 15 (1941): 46-58.
8. Louis Feldman, *Scholarship on Philo and Josephus (1937-1962)* (New York: Yeshiva University, n.d. [1963]) 16. @NOTES = 9. Samuel Sandmel, *Philo of Alexandria: An Introduction* (New York: Oxford University Press, 1979).
10. Sandmel, *Philo*, 53.
11. Sandmel, *Philo*, 178, note 40.
12. "Philo," *Encyclopaedia Britannica*, Ninth Edition (1899), 17.762. Schürer's article was retained, though occasionally revised, in subsequent editions of the *Britannica*. The passage cited is still found in the Fourteenth Edition (1971), 17.861.
13. "Philo Judaeus," *The Jewish Encyclopedia* (New York: Funk and Wagnalls, 1905), 10.13.
14. E. Zeller, *Die Philosophie der Griechen in ihrer geschichtlichen Entwicklung*, III, 2.2 (Leipzig: Reisland, 1903), 436f.
15. E. Bréhier, *Les idées philosophiques et religieuses de Philon d'-Alexandrie*, 2d ed. (Paris, 1925), 80-82.
16. "Philo von Alexandria," *RGG*, col. 343: "Geschaffen aber ist die Welt . . . von Gott, jedoch aus einer ungeschaffenen Hyle."
17. See E. Schürer, *The History of the Jewish People in the Age of Jesus Christ (175 B.C.-A.D. 135)*. Rev. and Ed. by G. Vermes and F. Millar, 3 vols. in 4 (Edinburgh: Clark, 1973-1987), III.2.885.

18. Wolfson, *Philo* (n.4), 1.300-310.

19. "Philo Judaeus," *The Encyclopedia of Philosophy* (New York: Macmillan, 1967), 6.152.

20. According to D. Winston, Wolfson's interpretation is adopted by G. Lindeskog, R. M. Grant, C. de Vogel and R. Arnaldez. See the "Introduction" to his *Philo of Alexandria: The Contemplative Life, The Giants, and Selections* (New York: Paulist Press, 1981), 304, note 25.

21. "Philo," *The New Encyclopaedia Britannica*. Fifteenth Edition (1985), *Micropaedia*, 9.386.

22. G. Reale, *Storia della filosofia antica. IV. Le scuole dell' età imperiale* (Milan: Vita e Pensiero, 1978), 282: "la creazione stessa della materia."

23. K. Bormann, *Die Ideen- und Logoslehre Philons von Alexandrien: Eine Auseinandersetzung mit H. A. Wolfson* (Unpub. dissertation, Cologne, 1955), 42-44. See Feldman, *Scholarship* (n.8), 15.

24. D. Winston, "Philo's Theory of Cosmogony," chapter 8 in *Religious Syncretism in Antiquity*, B. A. Pearson, ed. (Missoula: Scholars Press, 1975).

25. Winston, "Introduction," (n.19), 7-13.

26. Winston, "Introduction," 12.

27. Winston, "Introduction," 16.

28. Wolfson, *Philo*, (n.4), 1.303.

29. Wolfson, *Philo*, 1.308.

30. Wolfson, *Philo*, 1.305.

31. Wolfson, *Philo*, 1.308.

32. Wolfson, *Philo*, 1.308.

33. Wolfson, *Philo*, 1.308.

34. Philo, *De Confusione Linguarum*, 27.136.

35. Wolfson, *Philo*, 1.309.

36. Winston, "Introduction," 9-10.

37. Winston, "Introduction," 11.

38. Philo, *De Aeternitate Mundi*. 5; cf. *De Specialibus Legibus*, 1.266.

39. Winston, "Introduction," 13.

40. Winston, "Introduction," 14.

41. Winston, "Introduction," 16.
42. Winston, "Introduction," 16.
43. D. T. Runia, *Philo of Alexandria and the Timaeus of Plato* (Leiden: Brill, 1986), 454.

Mastery of the Passions: Philo, 4 Maccabees and Earliest Christianity

David C. Aune

Throughout this work we are focusing our discussion of Hellenistic Judaism almost entirely upon Philo of Alexandria, and there is some justification for this.[1] However, when considering the theme of self-mastery (understood here as the conquering or controlling of human passions), the document known as 4 Maccabees (4 Macc) should also be considered.[2] There are many similarities between Philo and the author of 4 Macc: both take it for granted that human passions should be controlled, and both argue repeatedly that the Jewish religion offers a superior method of self-mastery. However, there are also some important differences, especially in terms of the role of ascetic practice.[3] The purpose of this inquiry is to explore the treatment of the passions by Philo and the author of 4 Macc and then to suggest some implications for understanding mastery of the passions in the first two centuries of early Christianity.

We begin by offering a working definition of the terms *pathē* and *apatheia*. It is generally accepted that, with a few important modifications, Stoicism is the most important philosophical background for the ethical theory of both Philo and the author of 4 Macc.[4] Stoics viewed the *pathē* as diseased, irrational impulses of the soul, often categorized under the four most troublesome ones (referred to as the "Stoic tetrachord"): pleasure (*hēdonē*), desire (*epithumia*), grief (*lupē*) and fear *(phobos)*. The highest ethical ideal for the Stoics was the attainment of *apatheia*, which did not signify the elimination of all emotions but only of the diseased ones, the *pathē*. Those who attain *apatheia* are guided by right reason, experience the "good emotions" *(eupatheiai)* and are therefore free from anything that is contrary to Nature (which for the Stoics was equivalent to the will of God).[5]

Mastery of the Passions in Philo's Writings[6]

Philo's treatment of the passions can best be described as a blending of Platonic psychology with Stoic moral theory which is then used for interpreting the Bible and defending the Jewish faith. On the one hand, Philo accepts the Platonic tripartite division of the soul into parts which are rational (*logikos*), high-spirited (*thumikos*), and lustful (*epithumētikos*), which he links, respectively, with the head, chest and stomach.[7] On the other hand, Philo offers the standard Stoic definition of passion as both an "immoderate and excessive impulse" (*ametros kai pleonazousa hormē*) and an "irrational and unnatural movement of the soul" (*tēs psychēs hē alogos kai para phusin kinēsis*).[8] He accepts the Stoic "tetrachord"[9] and from his extensive use of medical terminology it is clear that Philo also accepts the Stoic notion of passions as diseases of the soul.[10]

The result of Philo's Platonic-Stoic synthesis is that the "high-spirited" and "lustful" portions of the soul (as well as the corresponding parts of the body—the chest, stomach and what lies below the stomach) are by nature irrational and diseased. Those who attain moral perfection will radically excise these irrational portions of the soul. Others must remain content with allowing the rational portion of the soul to rule over the irrational elements. Like a charioteer, reason has been placed over these "high-spirited" and "lustful" elements to bridle them (*epistomizein*) and hold them in check.[11] Or like the stake which the Israelites used for digging latrines outside the camp, reason is used to dig out the passions from the soul and to prevent them from spreading out beyond their proper bounds.[12] Philo's Jewish piety can be seen clearly in his views about self-mastery: the Torah contains the actual utterances of God which are the "royal road" of true and genuine philosophy (*On the Posterity and Exile of Cain* 101-12). Therefore, to obey the Torah means to be guided by "divine reason"[13] and to live "according to nature."[14]

Philo considers some passions to be more troublesome than others. Here, as elsewhere in his exegetical writings, his discussion of ethical matters develops out of an allegorical interpretation of specific texts. In his treatment of Genesis 3:1f., Philo associates pleasure (*hēdonē*) with the serpent in the garden of Eden and declares it to be the source of the other three:

[Pleasure] is at the bottom of all [the passions], as something of a starting-point and foundation. Desire comes about as the love of pleasure; grief enters in when pleasure is taken away. Fear, again, is born because of the dread of being without pleasure. It is clear, then, that all of the passions depend upon pleasure (*Allegorical Interpretation* III 113).

Building upon the idea that the serpent was cursed to go on his breast (*stēthos*) and on his belly (*koilia*), Philo argues that passion comes to reside in the lower regions of the body, which correspond to the lustful (*epithumetikōs*) part of the soul. (On this these see also the essay of P. Booth, "The Voice of the Serpent: Philo's Epicureanism" in this volume, 159-72.)

Later, in his exposition of the tenth commandment at *On the Decalogue* 142-53, Philo claims that desire is the most problematic because it originates "with ourselves and is voluntary (*hekousios*)." This interpretation is influenced by the Greek translation of the tenth commandment as *ouk epithumēseis*: control of desire is required by God. Elsewhere, Philo argues that desire was the source of evil: "Of the passions, none is so troublesome as desire. . . . Desire, then, is such an exceedingly great evil or, rather, it may be said, the fountainhead of all evils (*On the Special Laws* IV 80, 84)."[15]

This leads us to ask the question: can all persons expect to achieve complete mastery over pleasure, desire and the other passions by obeying the Torah? And, if not, how does therapy for the passions differ for persons of various "soul-types"? Philo's prescription for the passions is often described as a two-stage ethical program in which a very few persons attain *apatheia* but the vast majority attain only *metriopatheia*, a moderation of, or limited control over, the passions.[16] I would like to modify this view slightly by suggesting that Philo's program for self-mastery is far more adaptable than is often recognized. For Philo, the highest goal for humankind is to become like God.[17] To the extent that God is without passions,[18] Philo can speak of *apatheia* as an ideal ethical state.[19] But the failure to attain this ideal state is not always a negative judgment upon those who continue to strive against the passions. Instead, Philo both accepts the fact that persons are at different stages in their moral development and acknowledges that development toward the ideal can be a good in itself.[20]

To illustrate Philo's adaptable ascetic program, we will focus first upon representative biblical figures in his exegetical writings. Then, secondly, we will evaluate his description of the ascetic communities known as the Essenes and the Therapeutae. Finally, we will look briefly at some autobiographical statements in which Philo describes his own attempts at self-mastery. While Philo uses a wide range of metaphors to describe the mastery of the passions, we will be paying special attention to his use of medical imagery.[21]

It is important for Philo that Moses, the giver of the law, did in fact achieve a state of *apatheia*. In *On the Sacrifice of Abel and Cain* 9, Moses is described as being sent by God "as a loan to the earthly sphere," gifted with "no ordinary excellence" and "fully strengthened (*ana kratos*) to rule the passions of the soul." Combining the qualities of king, philosopher, law-giver, priest and prophet in his person, Moses exemplifies the virtuous life (*Moses* II 3-7). As such, Moses is the master surgeon, considering it necessary to "excise and cut out all of the *thumos* from the soul, not being content with *metriopatheia* but only complete *apatheia*."[22] The result of this surgery is that the "rational portion of the soul which remains [after the emotions have been cut out] may exercise its truly free and noble

hould also take into consideration a person's willingness
ed: "laws and teachings . . . urge those willing to obey in
ms, but those most disobedient in the firmest possible way,
bodily and external goods and consider as one's goal the
ue. . ." (*On the Virtues* 15).[34]
presents many examples of successful self-mastery
his writings, but two ascetic communities deserve special
he Essenes and the Therapeutae.[35] Although he admits
who attain great goodness are rare" (*Every Good Man*
Philo emphasizes that they can be found: "Of the wise
st and the virtuous, the number is small . . . but not
t" (*Every Good Man is Free* 72). The Essenes are
s examples of virtuous behavior who, through close study
ic law and commitment to strict communal principles,
h degree of piety and self-mastery. These "athletes of
eve their exemplary state of near moral perfection by
rking at [*diaponousin*] the ethical part [of philosophy],
ws of their fathers as their trainers" (*Every Good Man*

the Therapeutae and Therapeutrides (female ascetics)
ate and practice a simple lifestyle of contemplation,
ayer. Although Philo does not use the term *apatheia* to
r ascetic achievements, members of this community
successful "cure" for the passions through their life of
e women in this community deserve special mention
willingness to devote themselves freely to virginity
eriority of their ascetic program: "Most of [the women
ins, who have kept their chastity not under compulsion,
he Greek priestesses, but of their own free will in their
ng for wisdom" (*On the Contemplative Life* 68).[36] In his
d treatment of these two communities, Philo agai
wo of his major concerns: the Jewish way of life lead
form of self-mastery, and training in virtue must b
e's abilities and aptitudes.

impulses towards all things beautiful, with nothing pulling against it any longer or dragging it in another direction" (*On the Migration of Abraham* 67). Again (*On the Unchangeableness of God* 68) Moses is described as "the best of physicians for the passions and diseases of the soul, [who] set before himself one work and one purpose, to make a radical excision of the diseases of the mind."

In his attainment of *apatheia*, Moses experiences no pain or toil (*ponos*): "without pain is the one on whom God bestows with great abundance the good things of perfection. The one who acquires virtue by means of pain is found to fall short of perfection, as compared with Moses, who received [virtue] easily and without pain from God" (*Allegorical Interpretations* III 135).[23] Because God created and sustains the world without toil (*aneu ponōn—On the Sacrifices of Abel and Cain* 40), "lack of weariness" (*akamatos*) is a condition most befitting divinity. To the extent that Moses represents God in a state of near divinity, he too achieves this perfection without *ponos*.[24]

In contrast to Moses, the one "making moral progress" (*prokoptōn*). Unable to cut out the passions entirely, Aaron controls them and bridles them through reason and virtuous conduct. Philo's use of medical imagery here is again quite graphic: Aaron does not perform surgery on the passions but cures them with the saving medicines (*sōtēriois pharmakois*) of reason and virtue (*Allegorical Interpretations* III. 128-29). Rather than *apatheia*, Aaron practices *metriopatheia*: "The one making moral progress, holding a secondary position, practices moderation of passions, as I have said, for he is not able to cut out the breast and the high-spirited element but he brings to it reason and the other virtues, as charioteer and guide" (*Allegorical Interpretations* III. 132).[25] The control of passions is a process for the *prokoptōn*, who needs to be reminded continually of the "thought of God" in order to experience the healing of all sicknesses of the soul (*Allegorical Interpretations* III. 215-16).[26]

An important triad for Philo is that of Abraham, Isaac and Jacob, three soul types which represent the movement toward perfection. Of these, Isaac, the self-taught sage, represents moral perfection in the form of joy (*chara*), one of the *eupatheiai* "good passions."[27] It is important to note that Isaac's perfection is a divine gift: endowed with a simple and pure nature, he has no need of training (*askēsis*) or education (*On the Preliminary Studies* 36). As such, Isaac is described *In the Worse Attacks the Better* 46 as being "the only example of *apatheia* among its kind (*en genesei*)."[28]

Abraham offers an interesting case study of a biblical character whose self-mastery is described as conquest of certain passions but moderation of others. In the tractate devoted to his moral progress, Abraham symbolizes the soul's journey from pagan practices to the knowledge of God (*On Abraham* 66-71). Philo praises Abraham as a "sage"[29] who "passes most of his life joyfully, rejoicing in contemplation of the world" (*On Abraham* 207). In describing his willingness to sacrifice Isaac, Philo uses language which suggests complete mastery over his passions: "[Abraham] showed no change of color nor yielding of the soul but remained steadfast. . . . Mastered by his love for God he was fully strengthened (*ana kratos*) to conquer all the names and love-charms of family ties" (*On Abraham* 170). Later, Abraham proves himself to be victorious over the four passions and the five senses again "fully strengthened" (*ana kratos*) for the task (*On Abraham* 244).

Abraham's seemingly successful conquest of the passions throughout his life makes Philo's description of him after Sarah's death all the more surprising (*On Abraham* 256-7). After acknowledging the importance of reason (*logismos*) as the antagonist of passion, Philo explains that

[Abraham] should not struggle beyond measure as at a new and unknown misfortune, nor be without passion [*apatheia*] as though nothing painful had happened, but choose the middle way rather than the extremes and aim at moderation of passion [*metriopathein*], not being discontented that nature should receive the debt which it is due, but making it easier to bear through quietness and gentleness.

We must be careful not press th advocated in other philosophical bereavement.[30] But there is, it seer Philo's part that cures for the passi circumstances.

The other "holy man" of Abrah by training (*askēsis*).[31] As such, Jacc discipline and ascetic practice, rece God."[32] Trained by his grandfatl healthy state through his studies ((44) and passes on this moral str times, those being "trained in wisd practical and contemplative aspec indifferent as indeed indifferent, lusts, always eager to take thei passions. . ." (*On the Special Lu askētai* fall away before finishing their training in virtue, turn aside *tions* I 89). In either case, trainir divine help: "Upon the one knowledge, he gives both adva and also that of never withdr *Interpretations* I 89).

An important passage in th clear example of Philo's progra humanity into three categorie *prokoptousi* (those making m reached perfection (*teteleiōm* moral perfection is of course t that persons are at different s tains that, like physicians wh those making moral progres: ruined by evil, "and if some se little, it should be cherished (*On the Sacrifices of Abel and*

passions s to be hea gentler ter to disdain life of virtu

Philo throughou mention: t that "those is Free 63), and the ju non-existen presented a of the Mos attain a hig virtue" achi "intently wo taking the la is Free 80).

Likewise remain celit study and pr describe the have found a devotion. Th because thei shows the su are] aged virg like some of t ardent yearni highly idealiz underscores t to a superior adapted to on

We conclude our discussion of Philo by presenting two autobiographical statements which give us a glimpse into his own attempts at self-mastery. First, Philo expresses an idea, common among later Christian monastic writers, that contemplation of divine things is closely related to the control of one's passions and does not come about automatically by withdrawal from the world:

Many a time have I myself forsaken friends and family members and country and come into a wilderness, to give my attention to some subject worthy of contemplation, and derived no advantage from doing so, but my mind scattered or bitten by passion has wandered off to matters of the contrary kind. Sometimes, on the other hand, while in the midst of a great throng I have a clear mind. God has dispersed the crowd around my soul and taught me that a favorable and unfavorable condition are not brought about by differences of place, but by God who moves and leads the carriage of the soul in whatever way He pleases. (*Allegorical Interpretations* II 85)

Elsewhere, Philo describes how the control of passions was achieved in his own experience:

Often I have gone to difficult social gatherings or extravagant dinners. If I did not arrive with reason, I would become a slave to the things provided, being led by untamable masters of sight and sound and all that brings pleasure to the nostrils and tastebuds. But if I arrive with persuasive reason [*hairountos logou*], I become master rather than slave and, fully strengthened [*ana kratos*], I achieve the good victory of endurance and rational self-restraint, standing against and striving against everything that incites the unruly desires to burst forth. (*Allegorical Interpretations* III 156)

Philo can emerge victorious from his battle against the passions when he has reason (*logos*) as a dinner companion; he applies to himself the term *ana kratos* which had previously been used to describe both Moses and Abraham.

We see, then, that while very few individuals attain *apatheia*, both the biblical figures of "high worth" and the members of ascetic communities in Philo's day serve as examples of self-mastery. Philo's ascetic program takes into account a variety of factors such as one's natural ability and one's place along the path of moral development. Admittedly, most persons remain as *prokoptōn* throughout their life, but study of and obedience to divine truths can bring them quite close to a passionless state.

Mastery of the Passions in 4 Maccabees

Turning now to consider 4 Macc, we find another author who combines Stoic ideas with his own particular understanding of Judaism.[37] In a discourse which can be dated to the mid-first century CE,[38] this unknown but rhetorically sophisticated author writes to other Jews, exhorting them to remain faithful to the laws of their ancestors. His thesis, that "pious reasoning" can master the passions, and his method for developing the thesis, a series of logical arguments and encomiums on heroic figures in the past, could easily have been presented in the Greek philosophical schools of his time. Furthermore, a comparison of this document with its most important primary source, 2 Macc, shows that the elaborations and additions are often directly informed by moral philosophy.[39] In effect, the author uses a *Greek* literary form to argue that the standard virtues celebrated by *Greek culture* can best be attained by meeting the obligations of the *Jewish* Law.[40]

At 1.20-27, the author classifies the passions under two main headings: pleasure (*hēdonē*) and pain (*ponos*). The image given is that of two branches, pleasure and pain, growing respectively out of the body and the soul, each with multiple offshoots. Associated with pleasure are desire (*epithumia*), joy (*chara*) and other passions related to a malicious disposition (*kakoēthēs*). Associated with pain are fear (*phobos*) and grief (*lupē*). Anger (*thumos*) is, according to human experience, common to both pleasure and pain.

While this categorization of the passions is curious for a number of reasons,[41] its uniqueness can be explained by the author's intentions in this document. Pleasure and pain are highlighted as passions in order to emphasize that the Maccabean martyrs are not led astray by the pleasures of this world, and are able to endure horrible amounts of pain without succumbing to their torturer's demands. Other variations can be explained by the notion that obedience to the Law takes precedence over every other aspect of life. Even the seemingly positive emotions of joy and parental love can be regarded as destructive passions if they get in the way of following the Law.[42] From gruesome descriptions of torture in the second half of the document, it also becomes clear that the author construes *pathos* to include both excessive impulses and human suffering.[43]

Before proceeding further, we would do well to examine closely the phrase, *ho eusebēs logismos*, translated here as "pious reasoning." As far as I have been able to determine, 4 Macc is the first (and only) occurrence of this phrase in the standard Greek literature previous to the second century CE.[44] It is, however, similar to certain of Philo's formulations, especially "holy reasonings" (*hosious . . . logismōn*) which are separated from unholy reasonings by those who love God (*Who is the Heir* 201). The author of 4 Macc uses his phrase to mean "reasoning in accordance with the ways of God," which is to say reasoning in accordance with a strict interpretation and application of Torah.[45] A specific method for mastering the passions by "pious reasoning" is suggested throughout this discourse, a method which is almost identical to that which Philo prescribed for the *prokoptōn*: allow the mind to be guided by the Law and the virtues which come from obedience to it.

In a few places throughout this document, the author maintains that while the passions can be mastered, they cannot be completely rooted out. An important text in this regard is 3.2-5:

No one is able to cut out [*ekkopsai*] desire, but reasoning can provide a way for us not to be enslaved to desire. No one can cut out anger from your soul, for reasoning can aid [in dealing with] anger. No one can cut out malicious disposition, but reasoning can fight at our side so that we are not overcome by malicious disposition. For reasoning is not the uprooter of the passions, but their antagonist.[46]

This text in particular has led many commentators to suggest that author of 4 Macc rejects early Stoicism in favor of Platonism or a more eclectic philosophical position. However, the views expressed here have much in common with the Middle Stoicism of Posidonius, who likewise argued for mastery and control but not extirpation of the passions.[47] Another passage suggests that the author of 4 Macc specifically rejects the Platonic tripartite division of the soul: "When God created human beings, he planted in them passions [*pathē*] and inclinations [*ēthē*], but at the same time he enthroned the mind among the senses [*noun . . . dia tōn aisthēstēriōn*] as a sacred ruler over all" (2.21-3). Therefore, since passions are not part of a lower, "lustful" portion of the human soul, he cannot conceive of them as being completely removed from the soul.

However, while the author of 4 Macc consistently emphasizes mastery rather than extirpation, the examples of Eleazar, the seven brothers and the mother clearly suggest the *apatheia* which was attained by the Cynic and Stoic sages. If we take as our definition for *apatheia* the previously discussed notion of the elimination of *pathē*, the freedom from external forces contrary to nature, and the accompanying experience of *aponia* ("toil-lessness" or lack of pain), we see that the author of 4 Macc believes the attainment of *apatheia* to be possible by strict adherence to the Law. For the author of 4 Macc, complete mastery of the passions is essentially equivalent to the attainment of *apatheia*.

When Eleazar is tortured, he is "in no way moved" (*oudena tropon metetrepeto*),[48] and although his body collapses, his reasoning remains "straight and unbent" (6.7). Eleazar is extolled as one who "shattered the frenzied surge of the emotions,"[49] a model priest, philosopher and king. Although he is compared with the biblical figures of Isaac and Aaron, there are also close parallels between the description of Eleazar and those of the Cynic wise men (especially Antisthenes and Diogenes) idealized by Stoic writers of the Roman period.[50]

The seven brothers and the mother are also described as being completely free from the passions which trouble them the most. One by one, the brothers step forward and willingly endure the horrible tortures, fearlessly proclaiming their faith until finally they are silenced by death. Note, for example, the bold witness of the first brother: "Cut my limbs, burn my flesh and twist my joints. Through all these tortures I will convince you that sons of the Hebrews alone are invincible where virtue is concerned."[51] Likewise, the mother is presented as enduring mental anguish and exhibiting heroic amounts of courage and perseverance (15.29-31). She is both a "champion of the Law" who carried away the prize "in the contest of the inner parts" (15.29) and a "soldier of God" who "vanquished even the tyrant" (16.14). In her steadfastness and endurance she is portrayed as having super-human strength and courage. Even in her death she models extraordinary virtue: rather than allow herself to be defiled by the hands of her assailants, she flings herself into the fire (17.1).[52] By repeatedly emphasizing that these courageous martyrs experience no human suffering, the author demonstrates his thesis that "pious reason" overcomes the passions.

This leads us to the final question of whether or not moral perfection is attainable by those who live rightly. The author addresses this question directly at 7.17-23, which is quoted here at length:

Some may say that not all are able to master their emotions, because not all possess sound judgement in their reasoning [*phronimon ton logismon*]. But, as many as attend to piety with their whole heart will be able to master the passions of their human nature, believing that they, like the patriarchs Abraham, Isaac and Jacob, do not die to God but live to God. Therefore, no contradiction arises when certain ones are not able to master their passions because of weak reason [*asthenē logismon*]. Who, then, living as a philosopher by the whole rule of philosophy, trusting in God and knowing that it is blessed to endure all pain for the sake of virtue would not be able to master their passions because of their devotion to God? For only the wise and courageous person is master of the passions.

To paraphrase the author's argument: mastery of the passions (which is, as we said, essentially equivalent to the attainment of *apatheia*) is possible for those who are fully devoted to God. Unlike Philo, the author of 4 Macc does not advocate any adaptable program of ascetic practice: all persons, whatever their natural abilities and whatever their stage of moral development, should expect to master their passions completely if they obey the Torah.

This interpretation finds support in the presentation of the martyrs as individuals who are not hindered by the obstacles of old age, youth and gender. The argument builds from Eleazar, "an aged man" (7.16) through the seven "young men" (8.1) to the mother, who represents the climax of the story because "the mind of a woman [sic] despised even more diverse kinds of sufferings (14.11)." Therefore, when he reaches the exhortation to "obey this Law" in 18.1, the author has in effect stated that it is possible for all persons to do so, whatever their inherent disabilities. Failure to attain mastery of the passions is due to the weakness (or, sickness)[53] of one's reason (7.20), which is strengthened (or healed) by obedience to the Law.

Related to this is the message that even an *aponos apatheia* is attainable by those who live rightly. Remember that for Philo, one test of true *apatheia* is whether or not it can be accomplished without *ponos*. In 4 Macc, even those most susceptible to pain are described as being able to overcome it and, indeed, be free from it. Note, for example, the statement of the second brother: "I relieve the burden of pain by the pleasures which come from virtue" (9.31) and the sixth: "Your fire is cold to us, and the catapults painless (*aponos*), and your violence powerless . . . ; therefore, unconquered, we hold fast to reason" (11.26-27, RSV trans.). To use Philo's language of moral development, the author of 4 Macc suggests that even the *prokoptōn* can attain *apatheia* through strict obedience to the Law.

We will now summarize our findings thus far. Despite their similarities, Philo and 4 Macc represent different perspectives on self-mastery. Philo, who has a Platonic tripartite understanding of the human soul, suggests that moral perfection consists in a complete extirpation of the diseased *pathē*. But since *apatheia* is rare, the vast majority of humanity will spend their lives struggling to control their passions by right reason. Adducing moral exemplars from Hellenistic philosophy, the Jewish scriptures and the ascetic communities of his day, Philo offers an adaptable ascetic program which acknowledges that some persons go further in moral advancement than others. On the other hand, the author of 4 Macc, while not using the term *apatheia* or describing the passions as being entirely rooted out, suggests that complete mastery over the passions is possible for anyone who is willing to obey the Law. As a rhetorical discourse with many ecomiastic features, we find no program of asceticism outlined in 4 Macc. Instead, we have a highly idealized account of Jewish heroes who remain uncompromisingly faithful to the commandments of God and experience complete freedom from their passions, especially pleasure and pain.

Implications for Understanding Self-Mastery in Early Christianity
It is undoubtedly true that both Philo and 4 Macc paved the way for early Christian adaptation of Greek philosophical ideas regarding mastery of the passions. By the fourth century, Christian authors could suggest that Philo met with the apostle Peter on a journey to Rome during the reign of Claudius, and that Philo's Therapeutae were in fact early Christian monastics.[54] Jerome includes Philo in his list of Church fathers and quotes a saying that "either Philo platonizes or Plato philonizes."[55] While most modern scholars stress the unlikelihood of a direct relationship between Philo's description of the Therapeutae and later Christian monasticism, all would agree that, like Philo, Christian ascetics drew on themes (like renunciation and withdrawal from the world) which were common among philosophical writers of the first few centuries of our era.[56]

Early Christians were even more willing to claim the Maccabean martyrs as their own. In the second and third century CE, the book of 4 Macc was used as a source for early Christian martyrologies.[57] We find in many of these Christian writings an emphasis on moral perfection which is quite similar to 4 Macc: unwavering obedience to God results in complete freedom from troublesome bodily sensations.[58] By the early fourth century the Maccabean martyrs were themselves venerated as Christian saints[59] and many homilies were written to celebrate both the martyrs' courage and the central theme of 4 Macc, that pious reason masters the passions.[60]

With these Jewish writers, then, Christians found examples of how a belief system based upon the Bible could successfully provide individuals with Greek virtues such as *enkrateia*. While we cannot presume to undertake a thoroughgoing treatment of this topic here, in what follows I will sketch out a few ways in which some of the earliest Christian writers developed the topic of self-mastery. My comments will be limited primarily to select writings from the first two centuries CE.[61]

First, we note the differences. For the most part, the first generation of Christian writers are not influenced by Platonic or Stoic conceptions of the passions. In the New Testament, the word *pathos* occurs only at Romans 1:26, Colossians 3:5 and 1 Thessalonians 4:5, and is used in a more limited fashion than in Philo or 4 Macc.[62] More frequent is the related word *pathēma*, which sometimes does carry the meaning of "passion" in the sense of evil or sinful desires (as at Romans 7:5: *ta pathēmata tōn hamartiōn* and Galatians 5:24: *tois pathēmasin kai tais epithumiais*) but most often refers to various kinds of "suffering," including the suffering (passion) of Christ.[63] This notion is, as we saw, also present in 4 Macc and it is this sense of the word which carried the day in the Christian writings of the late first and early second century, developed most fully by Ignatius,[64] but also evident in Barnabas[65] and Justin Martyr.[66]

When individual "passions" such as *hēdonē* and *epithumia* are discussed in the New Testament, the emphasis is upon disobedience to divine commands rather than irrational movements of the soul.[67] Some writings do suggest, with Philo, the view that evil desires are the root of evil[68] and many link the passions with heretical teachings.[69] A far more common paradigm in the New Testament is that of purity and pollution, as is evident in the words of Jesus in Mark 7:20-21: "What comes out of a person is what defiles the person. For from within, out of the heart of human beings come evil thoughts [*dialogismoi kakoi*], fornication, . . ."

Consequently, the method for controlling the passions in the New Testament also differs from that of Philo and the author of 4 Macc. The cravings associated with pleasure and desire are not viewed as diseased portions of the soul which need to be treated by surgery, ascetic practice or the therapy of right reason. Instead, one's entire soul needs to be made new through belief in and identification with Jesus Christ (Romans 6:5-11; 1 Peter 1:22-23). And whereas both Philo and the author of 4 Macc argued strenuously that life in accordance with the Torah provides the means for self-mastery, this notion is rejected outright by the earliest Christian writers, especially the apostle Paul. In a number of places, Paul develops the idea that the Law has no power over the passions.[70] One contrast between 4 Macc and the book of Romans is particularly striking: in 4 Macc 2.6 the author writes, "Since it is the Law which has forbidden us to desire, I shall much more easily persuade you that reason is able to master the desires" but Paul, in Romans 7:8 writes, "Sin, finding opportunity in the commandment ['do not desire'], produced all kinds of desires in me." For Paul, sinful passions are to be dealt with not by control but by being crucified with Christ: "Those who belong to Christ Jesus have crucified the flesh with its passions and desires" (Galatians 5:24). It is not unlikely that the opponents of Paul in both Romans and Galatians were pious Jews who sought to impose upon newly converted Gentiles the idea that the Law can help them achieve mastery of the passions.[71]

However, despite these differences between the New Testament and the Stoicized Jewish writings of Philo and 4 Macc, the point should not be missed that self-mastery was, from the beginning of the Christian movement, an important aspect of membership in the body of Christ.[72] Paul devotes a large portion of his letter to the Romans to the problem of "sinful passions" (1:18-32; 6:1-23; 7:7-25), compares himself to an athlete who exercises self-mastery in all things (1 Corinthians 9:24-27) and presents self-mastery as a "fruit of the Spirit" available to all believers (Galatians 5:23). In the view of many New Testament scholars, Paul's self-identity was shaped to some extent by the Cynic-Stoic depiction of the sage who struggled against adversities of many kinds, including the passions.[73] Indeed, the preaching of Paul in Acts is described as including the Greek virtues of justice and self-mastery (Acts 24:25).

In a number of documents which are usually dated near the beginning of the second century, Christian writers began more intentionally to blend ethical teachings drawn from the philosophical schools with their understanding of Christianity. Thus we find in the Pastoral epistles long lists of ethical requirements for church leaders (1 Timothy 3:1-13; Titus 1:7-8) and exhortations for the young "to flee youthful lusts" (2 Timothy 2:22) and "to exercise self-restraint" (*sōphronein*—Titus 2:6).[74] In 2 Peter 1:5, the readers are exhorted to "make every effort by means of your faith to supply virtue, and with virtue knowledge, and with knowledge self-mastery . . ." and in 1 Clement the readers are likewise enjoined to live virtuous lives and, interestingly, to "root out (*ekkopsēte*) lawless, wrathful jealousy" (*1 Clement* 63:2).[75] Mastery of the passions is especially important for the *Shepherd of Hermas*: his first vision begins with the accusation of an "evil desire of wickedness" rising up in his heart and throughout his writings the importance of *enkrateia* is stressed.[76]

With Clement of Alexandria we have perhaps the best example of an early Christian writer whose understanding of self-mastery draws directly upon Hellenistic philosophy. Clement's understanding of the relationship between Christianity and Greek philosophy is one of the clearest examples of the *praeparatio evangelica* motif in early Christian literature. For Clement, philosophy was, before the Lord's coming, "necessary to the Greeks for righteousness and now becomes useful for piety, being a kind of preparatory training [*propaideia*] to those who are reaping the benefits of faith through demonstration."[77] This attitude is quite evident in his discussion of the passions, where the passions are equated with sinfulness:

> Everything contrary to right reason is a sin. The philosophers, for example, maintained that the more generic passions are defined in some such way as this: desire is a longing which is disobedient to reason; fear is an aversion which is disobedient to reason; pleasure is an elation of the soul disobedient to reason and grief is a contraction of the soul disobedient to reason. If, then, it is in its relationship to reason [*logos*] that disobedience is the origin of sin, is it not necessarily true that obedience to the Word [*logos*], which we call faith, is the very substance of a person's moral duty?[78]

We note first that Clement accepts the standard Stoic definition of the passions: four generic impulses which are disobedient to right reason. But Clement uses his familiarity with Stoic terminology to argue that faith in the true *Logos* (i. e., Christ) fulfils the moral duty set forth by philosophy. Later in this passage his theological framework becomes even more evident as he links the origin of the passions to the first act of disobedience against God. Human beings have become like irrational, pleasure-seeking beasts as a punishment for their sin.[79]

Clement, anticipating Origen and others in the Alexandrian tradition, borrows a great deal from Philo's writings.[80] Like Philo, Clement argues that the Mosaic Law provided the basis for the Greek virtue of moral self-restraint (*Miscellanies* 2.18). Even more, Clement suggests that Jewish dietary laws were indeed effective in curbing the passions of pleasure and desire:

> The divine Law, while keeping in mind all virtue, trains human beings especially to self-control [*enkrateia*] . . . and disciplines us beforehand to the attainment of self-control by forbidding us to partake of such things as are by nature fat, as the breed of pigs, which is full-fleshed. . . . If, then we are able to exercise control over the stomach, and what is below the stomach, it is clear that

we have heard of old from the Lord that we are able to destroy the desires through the Law.[81]

Of course Clement's program moves beyond the Old Testament into the New and, in the final analysis, the Jewish Law functions for Clement like the Greek philosophical writings, as a preparation for the gospel.

In his description of moral progress Clement shows many affinities with Philo's understanding of the passions. Thus in the *The Educator* he uses medical imagery to describe the healing of the passions: "The Educator strengthens souls with persuasion . . . then gives the nourishing mild medicine of His loving counsel to the sick person that he may come to a full knowledge of the truth;" and again, "The Word [*logos*] is our Educator who heals the unnatural passions of our soul with His counsel."[82] From instructions about proper behavior at banquets and the public baths to guidelines about simple clothing and food, Clement specifies how the passions of pleasure and desire can be curbed, concluding that just as "a horse is led by a bit, an ox by a yoke and a wild beast is snared by a trap, man is reformed by the Word [*logos*] by whom he is tamed . . . caught . . . and restrained."[83]

However, there are some important differences between Clement and Philo. For Clement the *Logos*, as a personification of God himself, assumes the qualities of passionlessness and sinlessness which Philo had attributed to God alone.[84] Furthermore, Clement is less inclined than Philo to accept persons at varying stages in their moral development. There is, in Clement, both a tendency to view all persons as equally lost and in need of salvation[85] and an emphasis on perfectionism represented by his "true Gnostic."[86] Clement seems much more positive than Philo about the attainability of moral perfection: those who are properly instructed by Christ are healed of their passions and will become like God.[87] Therefore, while he apparently does not know of 4 Macc,[88] Clement is closer to 4 Macc than to Philo on the question of who can attain *apatheia*.

Clement's understanding of self-mastery is representative of an approach which was to become quite prominent among Christian writers of the third and fourth centuries. Important figures like Origen, the Cappadocian fathers, Ambrose and Jerome are all influenced by Stoic and Middle Platonic views about the passions. While differences did develop on the question of how to cure the passions, there was little dispute that passions were problematic and needed in some way to be controlled. We have, then, in the concern for self-mastery, an example of how certain influential forms of Judaism and Christianity blended their ideas with Greek philosophy in late antiquity.[89]

Notes

1. As other contributors to this volume indicate, Philo's writings shed light on a number of concerns which are important for scholars of religion in late antiquity. Thus H. Chadwick, "Philo," *The Cambridge History of Later Greek and Early Medieval Philosophy*, A. H. Armstrong, ed. (Cambridge: Cambridge University Press, 1967), 137, could declare that "the history of Christian philosophy begins not with a Christian but with a Jew, Philo of Alexandria."

2. Two other important Jewish writings in Greek from this period dealing with self-mastery include the *Wisdom of Solomon* and *Pseudo-Phocylides*. In *Wis*, 2.1f, impious and ungodly individuals are described as having reasonings (*logisamenoi*) which are not right (*orthōs*). Specific passions include "desire" *(epithumia)* which perverts the innocent mind (4.12) and fear *(phobos)*, which is described as a betrayal of *logismos* (17.12). God provides victory over these passions through his gift of wisdom (6.12f). *Ps-Phoc.* 59-69 advocates a moderate position, which may be due to Aristotelian influences: "Let your passions be those which are commonly accepted; neither great nor overwhelming. . . . Moderation is best in all things, excesses are troublesome."

3. Ascetic practice is defined here as the voluntary exercise of any activity which promotes inner moral strength and self-control. Usually this takes the form of renunciation and self-denial. For both Philo and the author of 4 Macc, as for later Christian writers, the

goal of asceticism is the achievement of greater access to and closer union with God.

4. For the importance of Stoicism in Philo see David Winston, "Philo's Ethical Theory," *Aufstieg und Niedergang der römischen Welt (ANRW)* II.21.1 (Berlin: Walter de Gruyter, 1984), 400-14. However, even here Philo's eclecticism is evident, as is stressed by M. Pohlenz, "Philon von Alexandreia," *Kleine Schriften*, H. Dörrie, ed. (Hildesheim: G. Olms, 1965) 1.305-83, and D. Hay, "Psychology of Faith," *ANRW* II. 20.2 (Berlin: Walter de Gruyter, 1987) 898-902. For 4 Macc see Robert Renehan, "The Greek Philosophical Background of Fourth Maccabees," *Rheinisches Museum für Philologie* 115 (1972): 223-38, who convincingly shows connections between 4 Macc and the "Middle Stoicism" of Posidonius.

5. Nicholas P. White, "Two Notes on Stoic Terminology," *American Journal of Philology* 99 (1978): 115-19; Michael Frede, "The Stoic Doctrine of the Affections of the Soul," *The Norms of Nature: Studies in Hellenistic Ethics*, Malcolm Schofield and Gisela Striker, eds. (Cambridge: Cambridge University Press, 1986), 93-110, and Martha Nussbaum, "The Stoics on the Extirpation of the Passions," *Apeiron* 20 (1987): 129-77. One interesting modification made by Philo in *Ques. Gen.* 2.57 is discussed by J. Dillon and A. Terian, "Philo and the Stoic doctrine of *Eupatheiai*," *Studia Philonica* 4 (1976-77): 17-24.

6. Citations of Philo's works are drawn from the ten volume edition (with two supplements) in the *Loeb Classical Library (LCL)*: *Philo, with an English translation*, F. H. Colson, G. H. Whitaker, trans. (Cambridge, Mass.: Harvard University Press, 1958-62). Abbreviations and titles follow the format of the *LCL Philo*. Other abbreviations follow the *Oxford Classical Dictionary*. Unless otherwise indicated, translations presented here are my own modifications of the Loeb translation.

7. Described in detail at *Allegorical Interpretations* I. 69-70. For this background in Plato, see especially *Phaedrus* 246f.; *Timaeus* 69C; and *Republic* 439D. Sometimes the division of the soul is presented as bipartite, with a simple distinction made between rational and

irrational elements; on this see the helpful discussion in Brad In-
wood, *Ethics and Human Action in Early Stoicism* (Oxford: Clarendon Press, 1985), 139-43.

8. *On the Special Laws* IV. 79. Cf. also *Allegorical Interpretations* III
185 where passion is likewise described as an "irrational impulse"
(*alogos hormē*). For the Stoic background, see *Stoicorum Veterum
Fragmenta (SVF)* vol. 3, especially fragments 391, 459, 462, 463, 480.
English translations of these and other related texts are available in
A. A. Long and D. N. Sedley, *The Hellenistic Philosophers*, vol. 1
(Cambridge: Cambridge University Press, 1987), 410-23.

9. *Op.* 79; *Allegorical Interpretations* II 8; *Allegorical Interpretations* III
113; *Vita Cont.* 2. According to *Allegorical Interpretations* III. 140,
Philo devoted special attention to the subject of the four passions
in another treatise which is not extant.

10. So *Quod Deus* 67: *tas tēs dianoias nosous; Every Good Man is Free*
12: *noson psuchēs*, and the description of the Therapeutae in *Vit.
Cont.* 2: "Their [therapy] treats souls oppressed with grievous and
well-night incurable diseases, inflicted by pleasures and desires and
griefs and fears, by acts of covetousness, folly and injustice and the
countless host of the other passions and vices" (Colson, trans., in
LCL).

11. This image of the charioteer is a favorite of Philo's: see, especially, *Allegorical Interpretations* III 118, 127-28, 138; 13. As noted
above, Plato's dialogues are an important background here; the
image of the charioteer derives from the *Phaedrus* 246a.

12. *Leg. All.* III. 153, on Deut. 23:13 (LXX). The analogy betweeen
passions and excrement would certainly not have been lost upon
readers of the Jewish scriptures. Philo here also adds to his discussion the text from Exod. 12:11, "Your loins should be girded up,"
and states: "For God would have us gird up our passions and not
wear them flowing and loose" (Colson, trans., LCL).

13. This concept is variously described at *Allegorical Interpretations*
III. 118 as "sacred reason" (*hieros logos*), at *Cher.* 36 as "divine
reason" (*logos theios*) and at *On the Sacrifices of Abel and Cain* 51
as "right reason" (*orthos logos*).

14. H. Koester, "*Nomos Phuseōs*: The Concept of Natural Law in Greek Thought," *Religions in Antiquity: Essays in Memory of E. R. Goodenough*, J. Neusner, ed. (Leiden: Brill, 1968), 521-41.
15. On this point, Philo is in agreement with many other Jewish writers of the Roman period. See, e.g., *Apoc. Mos.* (Greek recension of the Life of Adam and Eve) 19.3: "desire (*epithumia*) is the origin (*kephalē*) of every sin," and *Apoc. On Abraham*. 24.9: "I saw there desire and in her hand (was) the head of every kind of lawlessness" (Rubinkiewicz, trans., in *The Old Testament Pseudepigrapha [OTP]* 1, 701).
16. So Winston, "Ethical Theory " (n.4), 405-14. Perhaps the clearest elaboration of this view is to be found in S. Lilla, "Middle Platonism, Neoplatonism and Jewish-Alexandrine Philosophy in the Terminology of Clement of Alexandria's Ethics," *Archivio Italiano per la Storia Della Pieta* 3 (1962): 30-36. My position is closer to that of E. Bréhier, *Les idées philosophiques et religieuses de Philon d'Alexandrie* (Paris: J. Vrin, 1925), 250-310.
17. So, e.g., *On the Virtues* 168: "A person should seek to imitate God as much as possible and neglect nothing which would make this assimilation possible." See also *On the Special Laws* IV.188; *Fug.* 63; *Ques. Gen.* IV.188. The concept is drawn from Plato's *Theaetetus* 176A-B. Philo's emphasis on likeness to God is rightly stressed by T. Rüther, *Die sittliche Forderung der Apatheia in den beiden ersten christlichen Jahrhunderten und bei Klemens von Alexandrien* (Freiburg: Herder, 1949), 17-18. Cf. W. Helleman, "Philo of Alexandria on Deification and Assimilation to God," *Studia Philonica Annual* 2 (1990): 51-71.
18. So *On Abraham* 202: "The nature of God is without any grief or fear and does not partake in any passion. . . ." See also *Op.* 8 and *Quod Deus* 51.
19. Stated most clearly in *Allegorical Interpretations* III 132: "The perfect person makes freedom from passion his continuous concern." So also *Allegorical Interpretations* II. 99-102, where *apatheia* is described as *sōtēria* (salvation) and *On the Virtues* 31, where the ideal soldier is described as one for whom passion has found no entry.

20. I am indebted to S. K. Stowers for this understanding of adaptability as a pedagogical strategy in antiquity. For a defense of adaptability in the moral teachings of Paul, see Clarence Glad, *Early Christian and Epicurean Psychagogy: Paul and Philodemus*, unpubl. Ph.D. thesis, Brown University, 1992. Whereas Glad focuses on the adaptability of the psychagogue (the "soul-guide"), this discussion of Philo focuses on the different moral states of those being guided.
21. Other metaphors which have been explored by scholars include military imagery: A. Pelletier, "Les passions à l'assaut de l'âme Philon," *Revue des études grecques* 78 (1965): 52-60, and athletic imagery: V. Pfitzner, *Paul and the Agon Motif* (Leiden: E.J. Brill, 1967), 38-48. Medical imagery is frequently employed by Philo but has received little attention by scholars.
22. *Allegorical Interpretations* III, 129: *holon ton thumon ektemnein kai apokoptein oietai dein tēs psuchēs, ou metriopatheian alla sunolōs apatheian agapōn*. Philo here combines the *apatheia* of the Stoic sage with the text in Lev. 8:29 about removing the breast from the ram of consecration before offering it to the Lord.
23. But see Philo's extended discussion at *On the Sacrifices of Abel and Cain* 35-42 about the benefits of *ponos* for those still making moral progress.
24. Winston, "Ethical Theory" (n.4), 401, rightly states that since Philo's sages achieve the state of *apatheia* without toil, they differ from the Cynic sages for whom toil was an important part of the process of perfection. Philo's sages are heavenly and therefore do not experience the virtues corresponding to a natural, earthly existence.
25. Given that *metriopatheia* was the position advocated by many Platonists, Peripatetics and Epicureans, it seems likely that Philo is here engaged in a polemic against those philosophical positions which were unwilling to accept the Stoic notion of moral perfection.
26. Another moral state is described at *On Husbandry* 161: the wise person who is unaware of their wisdom (*dialelēthotes sophoi*). See

SVF 3.539-40 and the discussion in Winston, "Ethical Theory" (n.4), 410.

27. See especially *On the Sacrifices of Abel and Cain* 7: "[Isaac has] left behind human instruction and has become an apt student of God. . . ." Cf. also *Fug.* 78 and *On Abraham* 168.

28. Colson and Whitaker in the Loeb edition translate as follows: "the only example of freedom from passion beneath the sun." But the context clearly suggests a comparison between Isaac and his other family members (Abraham and Jacob).

29. One of the most common appellations for Abraham is *sophos*: *On Abraham* 77, 80, 83, 132, 142, 199, 202, 207, 213, 255, etc.

30. As Colson points out in the Loeb edition, both Plutarch, *Cons. ad Apoll.* 102D and Cicero, *Tusc. Disput..* 3.12, quote Crantor's *Peri Penthous*, which advocates *metriopathein* for dealing with grief.

31. Jacob is quoted often as "supplanter" of the passions (*Allegorical Interpretations* II 89) and "the wrestler" or the one in training (*Allegorical Interpretations* III 18, 190-91).

32. Described in detail at *Mut.* 81f., taking the name of "Israel" to mean "one who sees God." Cf. also *Som.* 171.

33. E. Bréhier, *Les idées philosophiques* (n.16), 267-71, offers a particularly good treatment of this passage.

34. Likewise, for Philo, persons in varying stages of spiritual development hold different conceptions of God: see *Mut.* 19f. and *On Abraham* 119f.

35. Descriptions of the Essenes can be found in *Every Good Man is Free* 75-91 and *Hyp.* 11.1-18. The Therapeutae and Therapeutrides (hereafter simply referred to as "Therapeutae") are the subject of *Vit. Cont.* Philo's idealized presentation of these communities has been much discussed; see, especially, G. Vermes, "Essenes and Therapeutae," *Revue de Qumran* 3 (1961): 495-504; D. Mendels, "Hellenistic Utopia and the Essenes," *HTR* 72 (1979): 207-22, and V. Nikiprowetzky, "Le 'De Vita Contemplativa' revisité," in *Sagesse et Religion: Colloque de Strasbourg Octobre 1976*, E. Jacob, ed. (Paris: Presses Universitaires de France, 1979), 105-25.

36. On the benefits of virginity see also *Post.* 135; *Fug.* 50 and *Mos.* 2.68.

37. My understanding of 4 Macc has been shaped by J. Collins, *Between Athens and Jerusalem* (New York: Crossroad, 1983), 187-94; H. Anderson, "4 *Maccabees*: A New Translation and Introduction," *OTP* 2.531-64 and especially S. K. Stowers, "4 Maccabees," *Harper's Biblical Commentary* (San Francisco: Harper and Row, 1988), 923-34. See also A. Dupont-Sommer, *Le Quatrième Livre des Machabées* (Paris: Champion, 1939) and M. Hadas, *The Third and Fourth Book of Maccabees* (Dropsie College Edition; New York: Harper and Bros., 1953). Unless otherwise indicated, translations are my own.

38. See the arguments advanced by E. Bickerman, "The Date of Fourth Maccabees," *Louis Ginzberg Jubilee Volume*, S. Lieberman, et al., eds. (New York: The American Academy for Jewish Research, 1945) English Section: 105-12.

39. E. g., the discussion of Greek virtues, the description of the martyrs as "philosophers," and even the notion that reason masters the passions are all absent from 2 Macc. On the relationship between the two books, see especially Dupont-Sommer, *Quatrième Machabées*, 30f.

40. On the question of what is meant by "Law" in this document, I am in essential agreement with the conclusions of Paul Redditt, "The Concept of *Nomos* in Fourth Maccabees," *Catholic Biblical Quarterly*: 45 (1983), 249-50: "The term *nomos* refers to the Pentateuch in the Hebrew Bible, which the author of 4 Maccabees considers divinely promulgated. Further, *nomos* functions to inspire not simply pious behavior, but rational living." When I use the term "Law," it is the Pentateuch (Torah) of the Hebrew Bible which is meant.

41. Lists of the passions were very common among the Hellenistic philosophers, but those who categorized the passions under the rubric of "pleasure and pain" typically used the word *lupē* (for which I prefer the translation "grief"), not *ponos* (so, e.g., Plato, *Phlb.* 31c, Aristotle, *Eth. Nic.* 1105 b 21 and Albinus, *Epit.* 32.3). Furthermore, the author of 4 Macc lists joy (*chara*), an emotion generally considered to be a *eupatheia*, as a *pathos* associated with pleasure. For the ways in which 4 Macc compares with other "passion lists," see especially Urs Breitenstein, *Beobachtungen zu Sprache, Stil und Gedankengut des Vierten Makkabäerbuchs* (Basel/Stuttgart: Schwabe & Co., 1978), 134-43.

42. See, e.g., 2.10-14 and especially 15.2-3 and 11: "Two courses were open to this mother, that of piety and that of preserving her seven sons . . . ; she loved piety more, piety which preserves to eternal life according to God. . . . Though so many factors concerning love for her children influenced the mother to suffer with them (*sumpatheian*), yet in the case of none of them were the various tortures strong enough to sway her reasoning. . . ."

43. The connection between "passions" and human suffering is discussed briefly by D. Seeley, *The Noble Death: Graeco-Roman Martyrology and Paul's Concept of Salvation* (Sheffield: JSOT Press, 1990), 96-97.

44. This statement is based upon a recent search which I conducted on the *Thesaurus Linguae Graecae*. The *TLG* is an ongoing project based at the University of California at Irvine; an exhaustive listing of the texts in this databank can be found in Luci Berkowitz, et al., *Thesaurus Linguae Graecae: Canon of Greek Authors and Works*, second ed. (New York: Oxford University Press, 1986). My findings are in essential agreeeement with S. Lauer, "*Eusebēs Logismos* in 4 Macc," *Journal of Jewish Studies* 6 (1955): 170-71.

45. That the author did not have in mind some abstract quality of piety here is clear from texts like 5.20, where *eusebeia* refers to a strict adherence to the Torah, "in matters both small and great." For more on this, see Collins, *Between Athens and Jerusalem* (n.37), 187f., who argues that one of the most distinctive features of 4 Macc is the defense of "the Jewish law in all its particularity."

46. Likewise, the use of agricultural imagery suggests control rather than extirpation: reason is the "universal gardener [who] purges, prunes, binds up, waters and thoroughly irrigates and thus tames the wild growth of inclinations and passions" (1.29).

47. So Renehan, "Philosophical Background" (n.4), 223-38.

48. The verb *metatrepein* and its cognates are used throughout this document to describe a turning or swerving from pious reason: see especially 7.12 ("Eleazar did not swerve in his reason") and 15.11 ("the manifold tortures [of the mother] could not influence a swerving of her reason").

49. 7.5, Hadas, trans. (n.37).

50. Cf., e.g, *Diog. Laert.* 6. 3,5,13; Sen. *Constant.* 3.4-5 and, especially, Arr. *Epict. Diss.* 3.22.48f. On the relationship between Eleazar and the Stoic sage see Stowers, "4 Maccabees" (n.37), 929-30.

51. 9.17-18, RSV trans. Virtue is displayed in the dispassionate endurance of torture.

52. On the mother, see R. D. Young, "The 'Woman with the Soul of Abraham': Traditions about the Mother of the Maccabean Martyrs," in *"Women like This": New Perspectives on Jewish Women in the Greco-Roman World*, A.-J. Levine, ed. (Atlanta: Scholars Press, 1991), 67-81.

53. The word *asthenēs* is often used by philosophical writers to describe moral weakness in the sense of sickness, e. g., *SVF* 3.421 and 473. In this usage it is nearly synonymous with *nosos*.

54. Eusebius *Ecclesiastical History* 2.17. For Eusebius, it is unthinkable that any group but Christian monastics could renounce their property, embrace virginity and contemplate the Scriptures in the way that Philo describes. On this see J. Bruns, "Philo Christianus, The Debris of a Legend," *HTR* 66 (1973): 141-45 who argues that Eusebius uses Hegesippus as a source for his accounts about Philo.

55. Both the list of fathers and this quote, which Jerome claims is "current among the Greeks," are in *Vir. Illus.* 11.

56. Good discussions include F. Daumas "La 'solitude' des Thérapeutes et les antécédents égyptiens du monachisme chrétien," and A. Guillaumont, "Philon et les origines du monachisme," *Philon D'Alexandrie. Lyon 11-15 Septembre 1966: colloques nationaux du Centre national de la recherche scientifique* (Paris: Éditions du Centre national de la recherche scientifique, 1967) 347-58; 361-73. Even more doubtful about a correspondence between Jewish and Christian asceticism is M. Simon, "L'ascétisme dans les sectes juives," *La* *tradizione dell' enkrateia: Motivationi ontologische e protologische. atti del Colloquio internazionale Milano, 20-23 aprile 1982*, U. Bianchi, ed. (Rome: Edizioni dell' Ateneo, 1985), 393-426.

57. See especially O. Perler, "Das Vierte Makkabaeerbuch, Ignatius von Antiochien und die aeltesten Martyrerberichte," *Rivista Di archeologia cristiana* 25 (1949): 47-72.

58. So, e. g., Polycarp's prediction that "The One who enables me to endure the fire will enable me to remain in the fire, unharmed (*askulton*). . . ." (*Mart. Pol.* 13.3) is fulfilled as he is shielded from the blaze (15.2) and Perpetua is depicted as a noble and steadfast sage who marches to her death with "a shining countenance and calm step. . ." (Musurillo trans.). But also present in Christian martyrdoms is the *imitatio Christi* motif so that the martyrs are often described as joining in the sufferings of Jesus.

59. An important, though dated, discussion is M. Maas, "Die Maccabäer als christlicher Heilige," *Monatsschrift für Geschichte und Wissenschaft des Judentums* 44 (1900): 145-56. For a more recent assessment of the evidence see M. Schatkin, "The Maccabean Martyrs," *Vigiliae Christianae* 28 (1974) 97-113.

60. These include John Chrysostom, *De Maccabaeos homilae* (*PG* 50.617-28) and *De Eleazaro et de septum pueris* (*PG* 63.523-30); Gregory Nazianzus *In Maccabaeorem Laudem* (*PG* 35.911-34) and Ambrose of Milan, *De Iacob et vita beata* (*CSEL* 32.2); *Saint Ambrose: Seven Exegetical Works*, M. McHugh, trans. (*Fathers of the Church* 65; Washington: Catholic University Press, 1972), 119-84.

61. My approach here follows the definitions and guidelines set forth by A. Wolters, "Christianity and the Classics: A Typology of Attitudes," *Christianity and the Classics: The Acceptance of a Heritage*, Wendy E. Helleman, ed. (Lanham: University Press of America, 1990), 189-203.

62. In Romans 1:26, the *pathē atimias* refer to same-sex activities between females and between males; the *pathos* of Col. 3:5 and the *pathei epithumiais* of 1 Thess. 4:5 are both associated with unspecified sexual immorality (*porneia*). Wilhelm Michaelis in "*Pathos,*" *Theological Dictionary of the New Testament* 5.928 rightly argues that Paul's usage of these terms is close to the (non-philosophical) uses of Josephus and the *Testament of Joseph* 7.8.

63. So 2 Cor. 1:5, Phil. 3:10, Heb. 2:9-10, 1 Pet. 1:11, 4:13 and 5:1 (*pathēmata Christou* stated or implied). For references to sufferings of a more general nature, see Rom. 8:18, 2 Cor. 1:6-7, Col. 1:24, 2 Tim. 3:11, Heb. 10:32, 1 Pet. 5:9.

64. Used 15 times in his seven letters to refer to the suffering and death of Christ; see especially W. Schoedel, *Ignatius of Antioch* (Philadelphia: Fortress Press, 1985).

65. E. g., Barnabas 6.7: *to pathos*.

66. E. g., *Apol.* 1.22.4, 32.7; *Dial.* 31.1 and 40.3. Two notable exceptions in which *pathos* refers to a diseased or evil state of the soul are *Herm. Mand.* 4.1.6 and *Sim.* 6.5.5.

67. For *hēdonē* see James 4:1,3 and 2 Pet. 2:13; for *epithumia*, see Rom. 6:12, Gal. 5:16, Eph. 2:3, 1 John. 2:16, *Herm. Vis.* 3.7.2, etc. These two terms are used together in Titus 3:3.

68. So Rom. 7:7 and especially Jas. 4:1-2.

69. Especially 2 Peter 2:2 and Jude 16.

70. See, especially, Rom. 7:4-25 and the contrast between Spirit and law in Gal. 5:16-24.

71. This thesis is developed by S. K. Stowers, *Justice, the Jews and Others: A Re-reading of Paul's Letter to the Romans* (forthcoming from Yale University Press).

72. H. Crouzel, "Les sources bibliques de l' *enkrateia* chrétienne," *La tradizione dell' enkrateia* (n.56), 505-26, rightly maintains that the Stoic and Platonic influences on early Christian asceticism ought not to be stressed to the exclusion of the biblical (chiefly Pauline) background. See also the second chapter of Stowers, *Justice, the Jews and Others* (forthcoming).

73. See especially J. T. Fitzgerald, *Cracks in an Earthen Vessel: An Examination of the Catalogues of Hardships in the Corinthian Correspondence* (Chico: Scholars Press, 1984) and A. Malherbe, "The Beasts at Ephesus," *Journal of Biblical Literature* 87 (1968): 71-80.

74. The philosophical background of the Pastoral epistles has recently been explored in works such as B. Fiore, *The Function of*

Personal Example in the Socratic and Pastoral Epistles (Rome: Biblical Institute Press, 1986) and L. Donelson, *Pseudepigraphy and Ethical Argument in the Pastoral Epistles* (Tübingen: J. C. B. Mohr, 1986). See also the excellent commentary by M. Dibelius and H. Conzelmann, *The Pastoral Epistles* (Hermeneia; Philadelphia: Fortress, 1972).

75. The verb *ekkoptō* and its synonym *apokoptō* were often used in a philosophical sense to describe the extirpation of the passions; cf. Philo *Allegorical Interpretations* III. 129 and discussion above. 1 Clement, like other Christian literature of this period, also stresses the importance of *enkrateia* (35.2; 64.1).

76. *Herm. Vis.* 3.8.1; *Herm. Man.* 6.1.1; *Herm. Sim.* 9.15.2. A fuller treatment of the earliest Christian adaptations of Stoic notions about the passions can be found in Rüther, *Apatheia* (n.17), 29-49.

77. *Strom.* 1.5 (28.1), but Clement's argument about the preparatory value of philosophy continues through chapter 7; on this theme see D. N. Jastram, "The *Praeparatio Evangelica* and *Spoliatio* Motifs as Patterns of Hellenistic Judaism in Philo of Alexandria, in this volume, 189-203. While I have consulted a variety of English editions of the *Stromateis*, translations presented here are my own and citations in parenthesis refer to the edition of O. Stählin in *Die griechischen christlichen Schriftsteller der ersten drei Jahrhunderte*, vol. 2 (Leipzig: J. C. Hinrichs, 1905-36).

78. *Paed.* 1.13 (101). The edition consulted for the *Paidagōgos* is H-I. Marrou and M. Harl, Le pédagogue, 3 vols., *Sources Chrétiennes* 70, 108, 158; (Paris: Les Editions du Cerf, 1960-70) but the English translation is from *Clement of Alexandria: Christ the Educator of Little Ones*, S. Wood, trans. (New York: Fathers of the Church, 1954), 23. Cf. *Strom* 2.13 .(59.6), where Clement defines passion as "an excessive appetite exceeding the measures of reason, or appetite unbridled and disobedient to the reason. Passions, then, are a movement of the soul contrary to nature."

79. *Paed.* 1.13 (101-2) and descriptions of immoral behavior throughout *Paed.* book 2. The background of Romans 1:18-32 is certainly as important as the Stoic notion of persons with unbridled desires acting against Nature.

80. On the nature and extent of Clement's borrowing from Philo see especially A. van den Hoek, *Clement of Alexandria and His Use of Philo in the Stromateis* (Leiden: E. J. Brill, 1988).

81. *Strom.* 2.20 (105.1; 106.2). Clement's positive evaluation of the Jewish laws should be read against the background of Marcionite tendencies to reject the Jewish Scriptures. See van den Hoek, *Clement's Use of Philo*, 228; also in this volume, D. H. Williams, "Harnack, Marcion and the Argument of Antiquity," 223-40, and J. Martens, "*Nomos Empsychos* in Philo and Clement of Alexandria," 323-38.

82. *Paed.* 1.1 (3) and 1.2 (6).

83. *Paed.* 3.12 (99). The analogy between human beings and animals captures well Clement's understanding that passions are part of the baser, more bestial elements of human behavior. On his instructions regarding behavior see also M. E. Irwin, "Clement of Alexandria: Instructions on How Women Should Live," in this volume, 395-407.

84. *Paed.* 1.2 (4): the *logos* is *apathēs*. This point is rightly stressed by van den Hoek, *Clement's Use of Philo* (n.80), 227.

85. So, e. g., in *Paed.* 1.9 (75f.), Clement describes the different means by which Christ, the educator, will bring salvation to his people (warning, blaming, rebuking, etc.), but there is no suggestion that some persons are less in need of help than others. Instead, all persons are morally deficient and in need of God's care: "we need the Savior because we are sick from the reprehensible lusts of our lives, and from blameworthy vices and from diseases caused by our other passions. . . . In a word, throughout the whole of our human lives, we need Jesus that we many not go astray and at length merit condemnation as sinners. . ." (83).

86. *Strom.* 2.20 (103.1f.). See also his discussion of baptism in *Paed.* 1.6 (26): "When we are baptized . . . we are made perfect. . . . Perfection lies ahead, in the resurrection of the faithful, but it consists in obtaining the promise which has already been given to us." The fullest treatment of this topic remains W. Völker, *Der wahre Gnostiker nach Clemens Alexandrinus* (Berlin: Akademie, 1952).

87. Seen, e. g., in *Paed.* 1.12 (100): "He [Christ] corrects evil, diagnoses the cause for passion, extracts the roots of unreasonable lusts, advises what we should avoid and applies all the remedies of salvation to those who are sick." Rüther, *Apatheia* (n.17), 66-79 shows that, for Clement, likeness to Christ leads the believer to a state of passionlessness. In essential agreement is S. Lilla, *Clement of Alexandria: A Study in Christian Platonism and Gnosticism* (Oxford: Oxford University Press, 1971), 60-117, who concludes, "Moral perfection is for Clement the necessary condition which man must satisfy if he wants to possess *gnōsis*: only he who, with the help of Christ, has become *apathēs and homoios* to God is admitted to the higher knowledge of the divinity or *gnōsis* " (117).

88. In *Strom.* 1.21 (123.3) Clement mentions the *biblion to tōn Maccabaikōn* ("book of the Maccabees") but from *Strom.* 5.14 (97.7.2) it seems clear that 2 Macc is in mind. Furthermore, the fact that Clement does not mention Eleazar, the mother and seven brothers in his discussion of martyrdom (*Strom.* 4) suggests he doesn't have access to the highly philosophical retelling of the story in 4 Macc.

89. I would like to express my gratitude to Michael Stone, Stanley Stowers and Susan Harvey, members of the seminar on asceticism in early Christianity at Brown University (Fall, 1991), and especially to Wendy Helleman for their helpful comments on earlier drafts of this paper.

The Voice of the Serpent: Philo's Epicureanism

A. Peter Booth

In his attitude towards Greek philosophy, which was for the most part a positive one,[1] Philo of Alexandria anticipated patristic positions in some, but certainly not in all respects. Philo regarded his own Hebraic tradition as more ancient.[2] He did not regard it primarily as a perfection or fulfilment of the Greek tradition in the sense of a *praeparation evangelica*; yet a foreshadowing of the *spoliatio* motif appears clearly in his attempt to include Greek philosophy in his great project of refining Judaism.[3] In a sense Philo is superimposing one world on the other, fitting the Greek to the Hebrew. In his interpretation of the Mosaic text, Philo often asks why it is that Moses makes a particular statement; often the answer comes from Greek philosophy.

Yet it is readily apparent that for two extremely important issues, (1) that of divine creativity[4] and (2) that of the existence of evil as an external and somehow independent force, the combination of worlds is an uneasy one. There is no proper equivalent for either of these basic Mosaic teachings in the mainstream of Greek philosophy. Undoubtedly Plato's *Timaeus* proved useful on the question of creation.[5]

In this paper I will argue that Epicureanism served Philo well in the discussion of evil. But Philo was much influenced by Middle Platonism,[6] and for the most part he accepted that school's assessment of Epicurus's teaching. My position is that it was not Epicureanism proper which served his purpose, but rather the caricature of Epicureanism as it was portrayed by its opponents. Of course, if Philo is to be faulted for what he attributed to Epicurus without recourse to the actual Epicurean documents, we will also have to recognize that in this practice he had many pagan predecessors.

Opposites in Scripture
Since Philo's work was primarily of an exegetical nature, commenting on the Mosaic text, it is hazardous to speak of doctrines and unshifting, clearly defined positions. Recurrent themes, and the impressions created by these, provide a more reliable indication of his positions. For example, he often speaks of pairs of opposites: virtue contrasted with pleasure, the spirit with the flesh, male with female, Platonism with the teachings of Epicurus, unity with multiplicity, allegory with a literal reading of the text. It is important to note the pervasiveness of this bilateral symmetry and the significance he attaches to it:

> That is the nature of opposites; it is through the existence of the one that we chiefly recognize the existence of the other (*On the Giants* 3).[7]

> . . . Everybody knows that practically nothing at all which exists is intelligible by itself and in itself, but everything is appreciated only by comparison with its opposite. . . . We only know the profitable through the hurtful, the noble by contrast with the base, the just and good in general by comparison with the unjust and evil (*On Drunkenness* 186-87).

> . . . In couples of opposites it is impossible that one member should exist and the other not (*On the Eternity of the World* 104).

In each of the given pairs the first is positive, while the second is negative. And positives and negatives reinforce one another respectively. Thus in his allegorical interpretation of the Law, Philo is willing to use Epicurean rejection of anthropomorphic terms to illustrate the folly of those who take Scripture literally:

> ... If the Existent Being has a face, and he that wishes to quit its sight can with perfect ease remove elsewhere, what ground have we for rejecting the impious doctrines of Epicurus (*On the Posterity and Exile of Cain* 2)?

In this interesting passage Philo shows that he is capable of using Epicureanism both to defend his allegorical reading of the text against Jewish literalists, and to defend the given words of Scripture against Greeks who belittle such expressions.

Plato and Epicurus
The rather surprising contention of *On Drunkenness* 186-87 (quoted above) that good is known particularly by contrast with evil, taken at face value, may help to shed light on the antipathy between Epicureanism and the teachings of Plato in Philo's thought. Given what Epicurus taught concerning "pleasure," it was not difficult to approve of Platonism and Stoic ethics. The Platonic portrayal of the tripartite soul clearly appealed to Philo,[8] and was often used because it reinforced his own view on the need to deny the body: "God," he contends, "has conceived a hatred for pleasure and the body (*Allegorical Interpretation* III, 139). The Epicurean definition of 'the good' in terms of pleasure, *especially as its enemies defined Epicurean pleasure*, could not be more at odds with the Platonic good, and Philo's negative appraisal of Epicureanism in turn helped to reinforce his favorable attitude to Platonism.

The Role of the Serpent: On the Creation 157-58
In a text of great importance for later Christian writers who continued to regard the serpent, from Genesis through Revelation, as a type of the Evil One, Philo refers to Epicurean teaching to explain

the otherwise embarrassing reference to the serpent's voice. The method of approach is similar to that of *On the Posterity and Exile of Cain* 2. He asks, "Why does the serpent speak with a human voice in the Mosaic account of the temptation of Eve?"

> . . . Because pleasure employs ten thousand champions and defenders who have undertaken to look after her and stand up for her, and who dare to spread the doctrine that she has assumed universal sovereignty over small and great, and that no one whatever is exempt therefrom. . . . And they tell us that every living creature hastens after pleasure as its most necessary and essential end, and man above all (*On the Creation* 157-62).

Although pleasure's claim to primacy is elsewhere linked with atomism,[9] allusions to *pleasure's* claim to "sovereignty" and *pleasure* as nature's "necessary and essential end" clearly indicate a reference to Epicureanism, even though the school is not named.[10]

However, in the discussion of Genesis 3, there is much more at stake than the elucidation of an embarrassing anthropomorphism, the serpent's speaking with a human voice. Epicureanism as the philosophical advocate of pleasure becomes the voice of the Evil One, for "what a serpent does to a man, that pleasure does to the soul" (*Allegorical Interpretation* III 236).

In a passage reminiscent of the language of Epicureanism, pleasure is typified by the worst of the wild beasts:

> [The serpent, pleasure] is cursed also beyond all the wild beasts. By this I mean the passions of the soul, for by these the mind is wounded and destroyed, a kind of starting point and foundation. Lust comes into play through love of pleasure; pain arises as pleasure is withdrawn; fear again is engendered owing to a dread of being without pleasure (*Allegorical Interpretation* III 113).[11]

The serpent/pleasure identification is an obvious and forceful method of associating Epicureanism with evil: pleasure is a "subtle and snake-like passion" (*Allegorical Interpretation* II 84). If the

Platonic depiction of the tripartite soul did not sufficiently regard evil as external to human nature, a necessity from the viewpoint of the Mosaic text, Epicurus's definition of the good in terms of pleasure has served Philo's purpose well.

Disobedience and the Fall
Philo read the Mosaic account of the fall as an act of idolatrous disobedience by

> . . . those who have of their own free choice turned away and departed from the Existent Being, transcending the utmost limit of wickedness itself—for no evil could be found equivalent to it (*On the Posterity and Exile of Cain* 9).

But the fall from grace, according to Philo, occurs in stages beginning with Adam's reception of the woman God created for him.[12] The aetiology of marriage ("Therefore a man leaves his father and mother and cleaves to his wife;" Genesis 2:24) becomes an allegory of the beginnings of apostasy:

> For the sake of sense-perception the Mind, when it has become her slave, abandons both God the Father of the universe, and God's excellence and wisdom, the Mother of all things, and cleaves to and becomes one with sense-perception and is resolved into sense-perception so that the two become one flesh and the one experience . . . [and] the man, then, of whom the prophet speaks . . . prefers the love of his passions to the love of God (*Allegorical Interpretation* II 49-50).

The full act of apostasy follows, for the Mind then "shows itself to be without God and full of self-love, when it deems itself as on a par with God" (*Allegorical Interpretation* I 49). Eve is an allegory of the senses, standing as such between Adam and the serpent, who speaks to her, not to Adam. Adam and Eve together, Mind and the Senses, are allegories of humanity; and as we have seen, the serpent presents an allegory of pleasure, an external force acting upon the human mind through the senses.

Thus mind is incited to wickedness by those "champions and defenders [of pleasure]," namely, Epicureans "who dare to spread the doctrine that she has assumed universal sovereignty over small and great" (*On the Creation* 160). Mind, having once succumbed to the senses, lives "under the rule and dominion of pleasure to which the prophet gave the figurative name of a serpent" (*Allegorical Interpretation* II 72). Pleasure itself remains an external, independent force. Philo's "rationalizing"[13] reading of the passage as an allegory of the serpent is not that of the Mosaic text; nor is his reading that found in the New Testament. But as he emphasizes the allure of pleasure in human disobedient turning away from God, and associates this with Epicureanism, Philo paves the way for an even more damaging association between the appealing voice of the Evil One and the philosophy of pleasure.

Mosaic and Epicurean Views of the Good

According to Philo, Moses discredits the Epicurean teaching that feelings of pleasure and pain reveal the nature of good and evil: "Pleasure does not report the object to the mind as it is, but artfully falsifies it" (*Allegorical Interpretation* III 61). His account of the patriarchs, who are said not to have "known" their wives (*On the Cherubim* 40-41), also denies the reliability of the senses. Furthermore, Moses is said to contest Epicurus's definition of pleasure in its highest and most reliable form, as tranquillity.[14]

Yet while Philo denied the validity of what Epicurus said about pleasure, he still continued to treat as Epicurean views which the philosopher himself specifically rejected: for Philo's "pleasure" is not Epicurean. Even so, Philo seems to have been familiar with Epicurus's writings, particularly through what appear to be verbal reminiscences, as in references to the smooth movements of pleasure, to pleasure's "titillations," or to the sufficiency of the plainest of food and drink.[15] The latter recalls Epicurus's letter to Menoeceus in which the master not only denies that true pleasure has anything to do with the pleasures of the licentious, but refers to others who do misconstrue his teaching thus.[16]

Indeed Philo's frequent reference to pleasure, in terms of "the belly and the parts below," is a commonplace of *anti-Epicurean* literature in antiquity. Nor did Philo reject only the more extreme forms of such pleasure; even moderate pleasures of legitimate foods or of one's own wife are repudiated and said to be comparable with that

> . . . mighty force felt throughout the whole inhabited world, no part of which has escaped domination . . . even natural pleasure in often greatly to blame (*On the Special Laws* III 8-9),

for "it is for the sake of pleasure that we do wrong" (*Allegorical Interpretation* II 108). Sense perception is neither good nor bad in itself, whereas

> . . . the serpent, pleasure, is bad of itself; and therefore it is not found at all in a good man. . . . [Pleasure] has in her no seed from which virtue might spring, but is always and everywhere guilty and foul (*Allegorical Interpretation* III 68).

Adam's natural desire is comparable to that of those who marry sterile women and "copulate like pigs or goats" for the sheer pleasure of it; and they, like pederasts, bestialists and harlots, are "impious adversaries of God" (*On the Special Laws* III 36). Again and again pleasure is characterized as evil, and a continuity between its most innocuous and most vicious forms is stressed: it is for the sake of pleasure that we do wrong.

Pleasure in the Old Testament
The kind of associative process with which Philo slides from one end of the scale of pleasure to the other, from pleasures natural and permitted to those of a degenerate nature, characterizes also the parade of "Epicurean" or pleasure-loving figures. Cain, for example, when banished for his brother's murder, defends himself like

an Epicurean, that is, one for whom virtue is sought only as a means of obtaining pleasure.[17] Onan, who refused to beget children in his brother's name (Genesis 38:8-10), is presented as an allegory of those who "pursue only their own profit and think not of others" (*On the Unchangeableness of God* 18-19).

Philo likewise, consistently draws an equation between the mind as masculine and the senses as feminine. In so doing he treats that which is said of the woman or femininity as an allegory of the senses.[18] On a literal reading culpability is assigned to the woman for the transgression she instigated in response to pleasure's appeal. But on the deeper level of allegory, culpability is assigned to an element of human nature which is always prone to pleasure's appeal. And the effeminate philosophy of the senses, Epicureanism, incites this element to wickedness. The outcry of the Sodomites, prefigurations of Epicureans,

> . . . denotes something which is usually found among licentious and intemperate men, and is even greater than impiety. For they do not believe that there is an overseer or inspector of human affairs, nor do they believe that there is a providence over such things as seem good [to Him]. And they do nothing else but what is contrary to what He says, and they send forth voices that are hostile to the Father and His truth (*Questions and Answers on Genesis* IV 42).

So in the attack on various philosophical positions with which Philo ends his first book on the special laws, he identifies those who are forbidden entrance to the sanctuary because of mutilation with those who have

> . . . lost by castration the conception of the Generator of all things. They are impotent to beget wisdom and practice the worst of wickedness, atheism (*On the Special Laws* I 330).

In this way polytheism, as it corresponds with the multitude of devotees of pleasure, is associated with effeminacy or loss of generative powers:

[Polytheists] have infected the world with the idea of a multiplicity of sovereigns in order to geld from the mind of man the conception of the one and truly existent being (*On the Special Laws* I 331).

Pleasures are many, and wickedness is manifold; their devotees and practitioners are also without number. So too there is a "multitude of so-called philosophers," among whom are those who "assert that the universe is infinite," and who "refuse to connect it with any ruler or governor, but make it dependent on the automatic action of an unreasoning force" (*On Drunkenness* 198-99).

And so, through the voice of the serpent and the outcry of the Sodomites, the Epicurean denial of providence in the name of pleasure is transformed from a comparatively passive and innocuous deism, to become the equivalent of an active missionary endeavour on the part of the devil.

Conclusions

The light of revelation cast upon pagan philosophy must have seemed, from Philo's point of view, a redemptive light. The law of Moses constituted the criterion by which to judge what was good and what was evil in the Greek tradition. Conversely, Greek philosophy also served to illustrate the allegorical prefigurations of the Mosaic law. For Philo "pleasure" was most useful in illustrating the presence and power of evil, represented by Moses in the form of the serpent in the garden. The alleged philosophy of pleasure, which in its atomic doctrine denied providence, served to illustrate the voice of the serpent.

Philo's dualism of mind and body, or spirit and matter, favored Platonism and the ethical emphases of the Stoics. Epicureanism was radically at odds with both of these. Of all the pagan schools, Philo is consistently hostile only to Epicureanism. The essence of that hostility expressed itself in his antagonism to "pleasure," and his redefinition of what Epicurus meant by that term. Thus Philo's general sympathy with Greek philosophy shaped his attitude towards Epicureanism. In this he anticipated and probably influenced Justin Martyr.[19] In his identification of the voice of the serpent with that of the philosophy of pleasure he foreshadowed Irenaeus's ascription of the Valentinian heresy to Epicurean roots, at least partially.[20] He also anticipated Clement of Alexandria's reference to the sowing of the tares (in the parable of Matthew 13:24-30) as the work of Epicurus,[21] and Tertullian's attribution of some positions of Marcion to that same source.[22]

But the "voice of the serpent" contains a warning: Philo's Epicureanism was in fact only a perversion of Epicurus's own teaching as it was disseminated by its enemies. Yet as such it was accepted by many, including Philo and the Christian Fathers,[23] who found it suitable for their own ends. The lesson for us is that Christianity's own appropriation of the classical tradition, for its ends, may well be equally prone to a dangerous misappropriation of the same sort.

Notes

1. See, for example, H. A. Wolfson, *Philo: Foundations of Religious Philosophy in Judaism, Christianity and Islam* (Cambridge, Mass.: Harvard University Press, 1962), and S. Sandmel, "Philo Judaeus: An Introduction to the Man, his Writings, and his Significance," in *Aufstieg und Niedergang der römischen Welt* (1984) II 21.1, 3-46.
2. S. R. C. Lilla, *Clement of Alexandria: A Study in Christian Platonism and Gnosticism* (Oxford: Oxford University Press, 1971), refers to lost works of Philo on the basis of Clement's evidence, 31, n.1.
3. See Wolters' comment on Augustine's use of Exodus 12:35-36 in *Christianity and the Classics*, W. E. Helleman, ed. (Lanham, MD: University Press of America, 1990), 198-99. Philo treated the passage as history rather than as allegory (*Mos.* I, 140-42). Wolters' reference to Augustine, "All the riches of classical antiquity . . . are drawn into a great project of Christianization" could well be applied,

as here, also to Philo. Wolfson's description of the work of the Alexandrian Jews and Philo, "who consciously and deliberately and systematically set about remaking Greek philosophy according to the pattern of a belief and tradition of an entirely different origin" (op. cit., 4), recalls the Augustinian *convertenda*. See also the treatment of D. M. Jastram in this volume, "The *Praeparatio Evangelica* and *Spoliatio* Motifs," 189-203.

4. A. H. Armstrong, *An Introduction to Ancient Philosophy* (London: Methuen, 1947; Boston: Beacon Press, 1968 reprint), 168. On this theme see the analysis of A. Wolters in his *"Creatio ex nihilo* in Philo,"* in this volume, 107-24.

5. Ibid., 157-67. See also D. T. Runia, *Philo of Alexandria and the Timaeus* of Plato, (Leiden: E. J. Brill, 1986).

6. Ibid., 161f. On middle-Platonism as the context of Philo's work, see J. Dillon, *The Middle Platonists* (London: Duckworth, 1977), 139-83.

7. The text and translations of Philo's work used will be those of the Loeb edition, and the abbreviations of titles those used in the indices, vol. X of that edition.

8. E. g., *Allegorical Interpretation* I, 70: "our soul is threefold;" *Agr.*, 73: "Desire and high spirit are horses . . .", an allusion to Plato's *Phaedrus* 246a.

9. Moses' killing of the Egyptian (Exodus 2) is taken to be an allegory of the victory of virtue over godless pleasure: the Egyptian had been assailing the Hebrew, the soul, "from the vantage-ground of pleasure" and Moses, after striking him down, covered him with sand, "a drifting, disconnected substance," for he, Moses, evidently "regarded both doctrines as having the same author, the doctrine that pleasure is the prime and greatest good, and the doctrine that atoms are the elementary principles of the universe" (*Fug.* 148).

Compare Philo's wording: ἡδονὴν ὡς πρῶτον καὶ μέγιστον ἀγαθὸν, and καὶ ἀτόμους ὡς τῶν ὅλων ἀρχάς, with that of Epicurus: καὶ διὰ τοῦτο τὴν ἡδονὴν ἀρχὴν καὶ τέλος λέγομεν εἶναι τοῦ μακαρίως ζῆν· ταύτην γὰρ ἀγαθὸν πρῶτον καὶ συγγενικὸν ἔγνωμεν... καὶ ἐπεὶ πρῶτον ἀγαθὸν τοῦτο καὶ σύμφυτον, *Letter to Menoeceus* 128-29, and ὥστε τὰς ἀρχὰς

ἀτόμους ἀναγνκαῖον εἶναι σωμάτων φύσεις, *Letter to Herodotus*
41. Text and Translation of Epicurus is by C.Bailey, *Epicurus: The Extant Remains*, (Oxford: Clarendon, 1926).

10. In the extant works, Philo refers to Epicurus and his teachings only twice by name; on neither occasion does he mention the doctrine of pleasure: *Aet.* 8, where Epicurus is listed with Democritus and the Stoics as maintaining a theory of the creation and destruction of the world, and *On the Posterity and Exile of Cain*, 2; yet that is no indication of the extent of the implicit, recurring association of Epicureanism with pleasure.

11. Cf. Epicurus: "For it is then that we have need of pleasure, when we feel pain owing to the absence of pleasure; but when we do not feel pain, we no longer need pleasure. And for this cause we call pleasure the beginning (ἀρχὴν) and end of the blessed life" (*Letter to Menoeceus*, 128). On this passage in Philo see also D. Aune, "Mastery of the Passions, 125-58 in this volume.

12. A. H. Armstrong, *Ancient Philosophy* (n.4), 160: "The book of Genesis in particular is not considered by him as a record of historical fact, but as a kind of Platonic myth describing the creation of Intelligence, higher and lower, and Soul by God together with the intelligible and sensible worlds, a Platonic 'fall' of the intelligence seduced by the senses, and the ways by which it can return to its original state."

13. S. Sandmel, "Philo Judaeus" (n.1), 38: "Paul lived in a world inhabited by a devil, and governed by principalities, the 'elements' of this world; Philo, a rationalist, reflects none of this."

14. "Epicurus in the work on *Choice* speaks as follows: 'Freedom from trouble in the mind and from pain in the body are static pleasures:' " καταστηματικαί εἰσιν ἡδοναί, Diogenes Laertius X 136). Philo: καταστηματικὴν εἶναι τὴν ἡδονήν, *Leg. All.* III, 160.

15. For the reference to "smooth movement" see *ad loc., Post*, 79f. (*LCL, Philo*, II, 370, 499) and on pleasure's "titillations" *ad loc. Leg. All.* III, 160 (*LCL, Philo* I. 406-409). The *Letter to Menoeceus*, 131: "plain savours (λιτοὶ χυλοί) bring us a pleasure equal to a luxurious diet, when all the pain due to want is removed; and bread and water

(μᾶζα καὶ ὕδωρ) produce the highest pleasure, when one who needs them puts them to his lips." Cf. Philo: "Food and drink nourishes us, though it be the plainest barley-cake and water from the spring": κἂν ᾖ εὐτελεστάτη μᾶζα καὶ ὕδωρ ναματιαῖον, *Som.* II 48); the word χυλοί also occurs a little later in the same work (51).
16. "When, therefore, we maintain that pleasure is the end, we do not mean the pleasures of profligates and those that consist in sensuality, as is supposed by some who are either ignorant or disagree with us or do not understand, but freedom from pain in the body and from trouble in the mind" (*Letter to Menoeceus*, 131). It is noteworthy that Clement of Alexandria will also quote from the opening lines of the *Letter to Menoeceus* and acknowledge the work as though he had it in front of him (*Stromata* IV, viii, 71), and then either deliberately misrepresent Epicurus on pleasure as set out in that letter or rely on handbooks from which he is actually quoting and which assembled things like "views of philosophers on philosophy." Philo makes reference to such handbooks at *Agr*, 10, and they may well have been his source of information on Epicureanism in both cases.
17. *Det.*, 156-57; see the Loeb commentators *ad loc* (*LCL, Philo* II, 306-307, 496-97).
18. See D. Sly, "The Plight of Woman: Philo's Blind Spot?" in this volume, 173-87.
19. Lilla, *Clement of Alexandria* (n.2), ch. 1, "Clement's Views on the Origin and Value of Greek Philosophy," 9-59.
20. Irenaeus: "And not only are they convicted of bringing forward, as if their own [original ideas], those things which are to be found among the comic poets, but they also bring together the things which have been said by all those who were ignorant of God, and who are termed philosophers; and sewing together, as it were, a motley garment out of a heap of miserable rags, they have, by their subtle manner of expression, furnished themselves with a cloak which is really not their own . . . adopting the [ideas of] shade and vacuity from Democritus and Epicurus, they have fitted these to their own views, following upon those [teachers] who had already talked a

great deal about a vacuum and atoms. . . . In like manner, these men call those things which are within the *Pleroma* real existences, just as those philosophers did the atoms; while they maintain that those which are without the *Pleroma* have no true existence, even as those did respecting the vacuum" (*Adv. Haer.* II, xiv, 2-3; *Ante-Nicene Christian Library (ANCL)*, A. Roberts and J. Donaldson, eds. (Edinburgh: T. T. Clark, 1885; repr. Grand Rapids, Mich.: Eerdmans, 1956), vol. I.

21. Clement of Alexandria: "And as in the Barbarian philosophy, so also in the Hellenic, 'tares were sown' by the proper husbandman of the tares; whence also heresies grew up among us along with the productive wheat; and those who in the Hellenic philosophy preach the impiety and voluptuousness of Epicurus, and whatever other tenets are disseminated contrary to right reason, exist among the Greeks as spurious fruits of the divinely bestowed husbandry" (*Strom.* VI, viii; *ANCL*, vol. 2).

22. Tertullian: "If (Marcion) chose to take any one of the school of Epicurus, and entitle him God in the name of Christ, on the ground that what is happy and incorruptible can bring no trouble either on itself or anything else (for Marcion, while poring over this opinion of the divine indifference, has removed from him all the severity and energy of the judicial character), it was his duty to have developed his conceptions into some imperturbable and listless god. . . ." *Adv. Marc.* I, xxv; *ANCL* vol. 3.

23. With Philo's influence on the eastern Fathers as concerns Epicureanism we might compare that of Cicero in the west: both redefine Epicurean pleasure and argue that Epicureanism is the easiest and most popular of the philosophical schools, with many pleasure-loving adherents. Cicero and Philo can therefore be regarded as providing independent attestations of an older anti-Epicurean distortion.

The Plight of Woman:
Philo's Blind Spot?

Dorothy Sly

In the Introduction to the publication based on the 1984 "Christianity and the Classics" conference, W. Helleman observed:

> From its very beginning Christianity was concerned [among
> other things] . . . with the position of women in the family or in
> society. These issues are still of interest and may provide an
> indicator for the type of questions with which we can approach
> the classical texts today.

She continued, "Not only do we find there [in classical literature]
the roots of our own culture; the very distance by which we are
removed from it allows us to see more clearly the consequences of
positions taken."[1]

Helleman has provided a succinct rationale for what follows
here: a brief study of the attitudes toward women revealed in the
extant writings of Philo of Alexandria. Once we understand Philo's
view of women, we may also be able to detect the further influence
of his view. It is my aspiration to trace Philo's concept of woman
through some of the early Christian church fathers, as David Aune
has traced Philo's understanding of the passions.[2] But in the present

essay I shall only begin this project by considering the picture of
women that Philo himself presents.

For the most part, when we question the Philonic text on the
position of women, we are addressing questions with which Philo
did not deal directly. And we are sailing in largely uncharted waters.[3]
Yet the subject deserves attention. As Isaak Heinemann observed,

> Es verdient nur Beachtung, dass sein Rationalismus, sein Glaube
> an die Unentbehrlichkeit der Philosophie für die wahre
> Lebensführung, ihn nicht einmal das Problem der Frauenbil-
> dung hat sehen lassen.[4]

For this task one must be prepared to dig beneath the surface
of the text, and to accept the challenge issued years ago by the great
Philo scholar, Harry Wolfson, ". . . to reconstruct the latent processes of his reasoning, of which his uttered words, we may assume, are
only the conclusions."[5]

Gender Distinctions
Even the casual reader of Philo will notice the gender distinctions
which are so liberally sprinkled throughout his work. That which is
strong, intellectual, virtuous, or active is designated "masculine;"
what is weak, soft, passion-driven, or passive is "feminine." How
much weight should we put on such verbal idiosyncrasies? Does
Philo's choice of words have anything to do with human gender, or
is he simply playing with figurative language? We know that Philo
leans heavily on analogy and allegory; is this only a matter of style?
Can we agree with the assertion of one scholar that "there is no
pejorative judgment on women made by the author, who is only
making use of a language"?[6] I have long suspected that Philo's
gender distinctions should not be dismissed so easily.

My suspicions have been supported by discoveries in the social
scientific discussion of language, to the effect that there is a circular
or spiral relationship between one's language and one's view of
reality: each affects the other. Further, one's language reflects the

socialization process that begins in earliest childhood.[7] That process frequently employs analogy.[8]

The anthropologist Mary Douglas has developed a theory that institutions legitimate their way of doing things by citing self-evident analogies, for example "female/male, left/right, people/king." She notes that the formulation of these patterns is not fortuitous; rather, it is a powerful device for legitimizing social relations, division of labor and political hierarchy.[9]

Philo does assume that "nothing at all which exists is intelligible by itself and in itself, but everything is appreciated only by comparison with its opposite" (*On Drunkenness* 186). But the decision regarding what constitutes opposites and how pairs of opposites are analogous to one another is not questioned. Philo also assumes that the readers will accept his choices as self-evident: male is to female as active to passive, strong to weak, spiritual to carnal, intellectual to sensual.

Convinced that Philo's gender distinctions permeate his thought, I have insisted that we must move beyond Baer's position which attempts to keep them within the bounds of the non-personal and the allegorical. Baer concludes that for Philo sexuality represents the lower nature, designated "feminine" or "womanish," whereas asexuality represents the higher nature, termed either "masculine" or "virgin." The goal of a man's life is to eliminate the feminine within himself. But according to Baer, this cannot be translated into the sphere of real male-female relations, for God ordained human sexual reproduction, and woman must therefore be of some good. Thus Baer concludes that Philo advocates that the female be cut out when he speaks non-personally or allegorically; when he speaks personally, he takes a different position, allowing that she be tolerated.[10]

I do not believe that this distinction holds for Philo. I base my conviction on the following passage:

The words "Depart out of these" [weak, feminine things] are not equivalent to "Sever thyself from them absolutely," since to issue such a command as that would be to prescribe death. No, the words import "Make thyself a stranger to them in judgement and purpose; let none of them cling to thee; rise superior to them all; they are thy subjects, never treat them as sovereign lords; thou art a king, school thyself once and for all to rule, not to be ruled (*On the Migration of Abraham* 7f).[11]

Thus I maintain that on all levels Philo advocates the control, not the elimination or the toleration, of the feminine. According to the law of nature, the superior should rule and the inferior be ruled. Since masculine is superior and feminine inferior, the masculine must always rule or control the feminine. The feminine is a necessary aspect of life; indeed, if properly controlled, it can contribute to the general good. This happens on the interpersonal level as well as in other contexts.

Women's Roles

Sexuality
From this discussion of the all-pervasiveness of Philo's gender distinctions, I wish to proceed by examining Philo's understanding of women's role in life, the area which Baer did not discuss. The female role is always considered in relationship to the good for a man. Women's first function is to reproduce. And, as I have mentioned earlier, human reproduction is good, for it is ordained by God. The sex drive is necessary for reproduction. But the sex drive is also a passion, an aspect of the lower nature. It pulls a man away from the life of the mind, namely life in search of God. Alone in paradise Adam had no sex drive and therefore could contemplate God unhindered. But when he laid eyes on Eve he experienced passion. Universalizing Adam's experience, Philo concludes that woman is the direct cause of evil to man, distracting him from his quest for God. In Philo's words, she "becomes for him the beginning of blameworthy life," a life "of mortality and wretchedness in lieu of ... immortality and bliss" (*On the Creation* 151f.). The only solution is that he control her.

Philo associates sexuality primarily with woman. Man certainly has sexual impulses—in fact Philo speaks of man's desire for woman as the most imperious of the passions. But he also holds that man can turn his sexuality off and on at will; for Philo this is the deeper meaning of circumcision. For a man it symbolizes "the excision of pleasures which bewitch the mind" (*On the Special Laws* I. 9). Woman, on the other hand, is passion personified. According to Philo, the Mosaic law provides the societal controls which are absolutely necessary for the woman. For the good of the family and of the community, she must submit to these controls, and they are to be imposed by the men in her life.

What options are open to women, as Philo sees them? First, they should be virgins till they reach puberty, marry and bear children. Philo does not say much about the early stage of life, except that the girl's father is obliged to guard her virginity, and that a husband can expect a virgin bride (*On the Special Laws* III 81, based on Deut. 22:21). The bride of a priest remains a perpetual virgin, although here Philo does venture into the realm of allegory (*On Dreams* II 185). The wives of the patriarchs were likewise allegorically virgin (*On the Cherubim* 50).[12] But in real life, the time from puberty to menopause is the period of full womanhood, associated with menstruation, passion, sexual relations or "defilement" and childbearing. In Philo's scheme every woman marries.

This, of course, raises the question of the women Therapeutae, whom he calls "aged virgins." Did not these women come from a society in which marriage was the norm? The answer may lie in the fact that in Greco-Roman antiquity a post-menopausal woman was once more regarded as a virgin. She would no longer be dangerous to men. In fact, she appears to have the spiritual potential of the average man.

Virginity
One cannot help but note the importance which men like Philo placed upon virginity, for they used it widely as a metaphor for the unsullied life.[13] Earlier in this paper I alluded to Baer's observation of the equivalence of "virginity" and "masculinity" in Philo's

thought. Accordingly, virginity represents the absence of the danger typically posed by the female.

Here again social scientific observations corroborate literary study. Anthropologists have characterized Mediterranean societies by the fact that the honor of the social group, particularly its men, is determined by the comportment of their women. Men are obsessed with the fear of losing that most precious possession, the virginity of their women; if that should happen, their honor would turn to shame. This phenomenon, still observed today, is rooted in the ancient world, according to Jane Schneider.[14] Indeed biblical scholar Bruce Malina has profitably applied the honor/shame code to New Testament studies.[15] Endeavours such as these help to elucidate why male writers of antiquity, like Philo, were so engrossed with female virginity.

The Good Woman

As Philo views the two sexes, woman is passion-driven but man can choose whether or not to be ruled by his sexuality. The good man practically ignores it. True, he marries and procreates, but he chooses a wife after the model of Jacob's Leah—the good woman, Wisdom personified (Proverbs). Sometimes Philo likens her to the hated wife of Deuteronomy 21, severe and august; indeed he goes so far as to characterize her as "rough, ungentle, crabbed and our bitter enemy" (*On Sobriety* 23; *On the Sacrifices of Abel and Cain* 20). The good man, according to Philo, should run no risk of being ensnared by any type of sexual allure. He is always in charge of his sexuality. Besides this, he is in control of the women assigned to him by law, his daughters and his wife. Thus, as well as allegorically controlling the female within himself, he literally controls the female persons of his household. The less vigilant man succumbs to sexuality, both within himself and in the person of his wife, and the fact that she is his wife does not absolve him of guilt (*On the Special Laws* III 9), He is, as it were, paralyzed and seduced, and all unawares allows his marriage and household to be corrupted (*On the Embassy to Gaius* 39f.). To sum up, Philo says that males in general are charged with the responsibility of keeping femaleness

(i. e., sexuality) under control. Women, on the other hand, have no choice and no direct responsibility.

Three Types of Women
One can divide the women Philo talks about into two main groups: the women of the Bible, and women of his own society, i. e., the Jewish community in first century Alexandria. In both of these groups there are three types, and they parallel each another. The best state for a woman is that which is closest to maleness, virginity. The second best is to be under male domination. The worst is to run uncontrolled.

Virgins
Of the biblical women the most admirable are those who through allegory become virgins. These are the wives of Moses and the Patriarchs. They are not persons so much as adjuncts or complements to their husbands. In the expository or more literal works, these same women fall into the second class; i.e., they are subservient to their husbands. Philo retells the old biblical stories so as to take all the steel out of resourceful women like Sarah and Rebecca. In his account they are docile and obedient. Some lesser women of the Bible also fall into this second properly controlled class. They invariably cooperate with, assist and enhance men. Thirdly there are the women who seduce, disturb, question or challenge men. Philo's list of these "bad" biblical women includes Eve, Potiphar's wife, the Moabite women, Hagar and Lot's wife.

And what of the women of his own day? Corresponding to the biblical virgins are the female Therapeutae who, as we have noticed, are not women at all, but virgins. They live in community with men in a manner that seems egalitarian, until one examines the text more closely to discover that there are subtle distinctions which keep the female Therapeutae subordinate. The real women fall into two classes, as did the biblical women. And here Philo is just as dualistic. There are good women and bad women, ladies and harlots, *astai* and *pornai*. There is no middle ground.

Harlots

Much of Philo's material about women of his own day occurs in the four books of *Special Laws*. Near the beginning of the first book, and before the discussion of specific laws, Philo tells the story of Phineas (55f.), linking it with the story of the Levites and the golden calf (79). In both stories pious men—Phineas and the Levites, respectively—took up the sword against their own people in order to avert a worse evil. Ordinary custom would deplore such action. But according to Philo these men were justified. They were obeying a higher law. For custom is female, and the law of nature is male (*On Drunkenness* 68). One must destroy the female in order to preserve the male. Impulsively, bypassing judges and councils, the heroes put God's enemies to the sword.

One of the most noticeable features of the *Special Laws* is the frequency with which Philo cries out for an immediate death penalty (2.232; 3.11, 31, 38, 51, 102, 106, 108). But when one considers the tone set by the introductory stories one realizes that Philo sees his own community in a position analogous to that of Israel surrounded by the Canaanites. Their further survival would depend upon a united observance of the law.

The story of Phineas has an added twist, namely, that women are portrayed as instigating apostasy. According to Philo's reading of Numbers 25 the crime of the Israelite men was triggered by lust for women. Balaam had advised Balak that the one way he could defeat the Israelites was by preying on their greatest weakness, their sex drive. So Balak encouraged his young Moabite women to seduce the Israelite men, and in so doing to require the men first to worship the Moabite gods. Of course the men succumbed. Looking back on the story we might comment that the main guilt lies with the men for apostasy. But according to Philo the *women* are culpable. They have conspired to reverse the order set up by nature, i. e., by God. They have stepped out of their natural role, becoming active and seductive. The apostasy of the men thus becomes an inevitable consequence. In this way the Phineas story encapsulates Philo's fear of women's sexuality as the greatest potential danger to man and society. It also prepares us to expect two things: first, that he would intensify the scope and the harshness of the biblical laws regarding women, and second, that his disapproval of woman would be expressed in terms of her misuse of sexuality. This brings us to his laws regarding harlots.

Who, specifically, are the harlots in Philo's world? He uses the term "harlot" without precision. We have seen earlier that Philo thinks dichotomously, classifying women as either *astai* or *pornai*, ladies or harlots. A woman who does not fit into his pattern of submissive passivity earns Philo's disapproval; and an effective way to insult a woman of whom one disapproves is to call her a harlot. She may in fact be a woman who deals in love charms, or who has joined another religion, earning thus also the epithets "abominable and licentious" (*On the Special Laws* I 323). "Harlot" may indeed denote a woman of irregular sexual conduct, but we should note that in his biblical commentary he uses the term to mark the victim of rape: Philo denies the rape of Dinah, apparently because it would have contravened the law that there be no *porne* among the daughters of Israel (*On the Migration of Abraham* 224; Deut. 23:17).

What does the law say of the harlot? Philo demands punishment that goes beyond anything in Scripture.[16] "With us a courtesan is not even permitted to live, and death is the penalty appointed for women who ply this trade" (*On Joseph* 43). "A pest, a scourge, a plague-spot to the public, let her be stoned to death—she who has corrupted the graces bestowed by nature, instead of making them, as she should, the ornament of noble conduct" (*On the Special Laws* III 51). In the world of the Old Testament the penalty of stoning was levied for the most heinous crimes, when the fabric of society, indeed of cosmic order, was seen to be threatened.[17] And this is the penalty Philo demands for the harlot. For him harlotry is the one sin which cannot be erased by repentance. This in spite of the fact that in a different context (in the same treatise) he can say that "God . . . has given to repentance the same honor as to innocence from sin." But not, apparently, in the case of the harlot, for Philo says of her that "In the souls of the repentant there remain, in spite of all, the scars and prints of their old misdeeds" (*On the Special Laws* I 103), thus making convenient use of Plato's teaching that at death scars remain on both body and soul (*Gorgias* 524E).

Ladies

Philo's other term for classifying woman is *astē*, "lady," by which he means the wife or daughter of a free member of the Jewish community in good standing. Since we know that Philo belonged to the upper stratum, we may assume that he is thinking of his own social group. In fact, this appears to be the only type of woman he knows first-hand. This is evident from his remark that women are weak and their life "is naturally peaceful and domestic" (*On the Special Laws* IV   223, 225). On another occasion he generalizes about wives as "the dainty product of the luxury that has grown up with them from their earliest years" (*On Rewards and Punishments* 146). To meet Philo's description a woman would have to be mistress of a wealthy household.

In his longest continuous passage on good women, Philo prescribes the following:

> A woman should not be a busybody, meddling with matters outside her household concerns, but should seek a life of seclusion. She should not shew herself off like a vagrant in the streets before the eyes of other men, except when she has to go to the temple [*hieron*], and even then she should take pains to go, not when the market is full, but when most people have gone home, and so like a free-born lady worthy of the name, with everything quiet around her, make her oblations and offer her prayers to avert the evil and to gain the good (*On the Special Laws* III   171-74).

Obviously this prescription could be followed only in families wealthy enough to afford the household help that would free the wife from running ordinary errands. The depiction of a society where all respectable women can afford to stay home in seclusion hardly fits S. W. Baron's picture of first century Alexandria where "the masses lived in dark, congested and unhealthy quarters," and Jews, as in the rest of the Diaspora, were known for poverty rather than wealth.[18] Philo's work reveals no empathy with the mass of ordinary women.

This is virtually the only passage where Philo speaks of the religious obligations or attainments of women. The good woman makes offerings and prayers "to avert the evil and to obtain the good." With this he implies that her interests are not those of the most purely spiritual, namely those who love God for his own sake. She fits into Philo's second or third class of religious people, those who worship out of self-interest, whether to obtain the blessing of religious reward or to avoid punishment, as he explains in the treatise *On Abraham* 125-30. It is not surprising that such is the highest spiritual attainment Philo holds out for women of his day, since he states in the *Hypothetica* (or *Defence of the Jews*) that women's religion is derivative: "Wives must be in servitude to their husbands." They do not attend the synagogue, for "the husband seems competent to transmit knowledge of the laws to his wife" (7.3, 14).

Conclusions
In conclusion, it is clear that Philo does not have his finger on the pulse of the society of his day, particularly that of the Jewish Alexandrian community, nor is he aware of any but a small segment of the women. His writing is nonetheless immensely valuable in setting out for us a *perception* of women—one that for the most part conforms to the presuppositions with which he was raised, as well as those of his Greek and biblical Judaic education.[19] Suffice it to say that in his writing one can find no single passage in which he treats the woman as a person, capable of engaging in the spiritual Odyssey—the great religious breakthrough which Philo so eloquently designed for men.

Notes

1. *Christianity and the Classics: The Acceptance of a Heritage*, W. E. Helleman, ed. (Lanham, MD: University Press of America, 1990), 27.

2. D. Aune, "Mastery of the Passions: Philo, 4 Maccabees and Earliest Christianity," in this volume, 125-58.

3. Credit for initial work goes to Richard Baer, Jr., for *Philo's Use of the Categories Male and Female* (Leiden: Brill, 1970). See also my published doctoral dissertation, *Philo's Perception of Women*, Brown Judaic Series 209 (Atlanta: Scholars Press, 1990).

4. In his *Philons griechische und jüdische Bildung* (Hildesheim, New York: George Olms, 1973), 236.

5. *Philo* (Cambridge, Mass.: Harvard University Press, 1947), vol. 1, 106. No doubt, I am carrying Wolfson's challenge into areas he would not have dreamed of entering. Methodologically, I have been guided by Sheila Briggs, "Can an Enslaved God Liberate? Hermeneutical Reflections on Philippians 2:6-11," *Semeia* 47 (1989): 137-53, and Fokkelein van Dijk-Hemmes, "The Imagination of Power and the Power of Imagination," *Journal for the Study of the Old Testament* 44 (1989): 75-88.

6. Jean LaPorte, *The Role of Women in Early Christianity* (New York and Toronto: Edwin Mellen Press, 1982), 4.

7. See Peter L. Berger and Thomas Lückmann, *The Social Construction of Reality* (Garden City, NY: Doubleday, 1967), 94-96; Bruce Malina, "The Social Science and Biblical Interpretation," in *The Bible and Liberation*, Norman K. Gottwald, ed. (Maryknoll, New York: 1983), 12: "Language inevitably imparts meanings which are rooted in a social system."

8. *The Oxford English Dictionary, Compact Edition*, gives the following definition of analogy: "A name for the fact that the relation borne to any object by some attribute or circumstance, corresponds to the relation existing between another object and some attribute or circumstance pertaining to it." To take an example that might come from our own life experience: think of the child who from the time she is first strapped into the baby seat of the car repeatedly hears her father utter the expression "Woman driver!" She grows up absorbing both the thought and the emotion behind the expression and, unless she makes a conscious effort to analyze and reject it, she may even adopt it as part of her own speech and thought: in a proper world one draws parallels between the pairs woman/man and passenger/driver; therefore one sees the conjunction of "woman" and "driver" as anomalous. I believe that allegory is extended analogy, i. e., it assumes a similarity of relationship between two extended sets, rather than between two pairs. On Philo's use of pairs of opposites see the article in this volume by P. Booth, "The Voice of the Serpent," 159-72.

9. In her book *How Institutions Think* (Syracuse, NY: Syracuse University Press, 1986), 48f., Mary Douglas explains that for an incipient institution to become stabilized "There needs to be an analogy by which the formal structure of a crucial set of social relations is found in the physical world, or in the supernatural world, or in eternity, anywhere, so long as it is not seen as a socially contrived arrangement. When the analogy is applied back and forth from one set of social relations to another and from these back to nature, its recurring formal structure becomes easily recognized and endowed with self-validating truth." Douglas calls this the "naturalization of social classifications." See further, ibid., 63f.:

> Socially based analogies assign disparate items to classes and load them with moral and political content. . . . And the submerged classification justifies a particular lot assigned to women in the division of labor, whether as agricultural workers and load carriers or as pretty little things incapable of thought. It also justifies feminine behavior of spontaneity, easy tears, inconsistent wants, and nurturing care.

10. Baer, *Categories* (n.3), 75.

11. *Migr.* 7f. All quotations are from the *Loeb Classical Library (LCL)*, *Philo*, F. H. Colson and G. H. Whitaker, trans. (Cambridge, Mass.: Harvard University Press, 1958-62).

12. Cf. the discussion of D. Aune in this volume, "Mastery of the Passions," regarding Moses and Isaac, who were untouched by the passions (128-38). See the same contribution for a discussion of the question of control or excision of troublesome passions of the soul in Philo's writings (126-29; cf. 135-36).

13. This practice was carried into the early Christian world. Elizabeth Castelli observes that in the early fourth century the ideal of virginity functioned as a continuation of the earlier ideal of martyrdom. See her article "Women's Sexuality in Early Christianity," *Journal of Feminist Studies in Religion* 2 (Spring, 1986): 61-88. See also Shaye J. D. Cohen, "Menstruants and the Sacred in Judaism and Christianity," in S. Pomeroy, ed., *Women's History and Ancient History* (Chapel Hill, NC: University of North Carolina Press, 1991), 273-99; and G. P. Corrington, " 'The Divine Woman?' Propaganda and the Power of Chastity in the New Testament Apocrypha," in M. Skinner, ed., *Rescuing Creusa: Women in Antiquity* (Lubbock, Texas: Texas Tech University Press, 1987), 151-62.

14. J. Schneider, "Of Vigilance and Virgins: Honor, Shame and Access to Resources in Mediterranean Societies," *Ethnology* 10 (1971): 1-24.

15. B. Malina, *The New Testament World: Insights from Cultural Anthropology* (Louisville: John Knox, 1981), passim.

16. See the *Encyclopedia Judaica* (New York: MacMillan, 1991-92), s. v. "Sexual offences."

17. J. J. Finkelstein, *The Ox that Gored* (Philadelphia, 1981), 26f.

18. S. W. Baron, *A Social and Religious History of the Jews* (New York and London: Columbia University Press, 1952), vol. 1, 265f. Valuable insight into urban life can also be gained from T. F. Carney, *The Shape of the Past: Models and Antiquity* (Lawrence, Kansas: Coronado Press, 1975), and from Ramsay MacMullen, *Roman Social Relations* (New Haven and London: Yale University Press, 1974).

19. In *Philo's Perception of Women* I argue that Philo views woman through two lenses: the biblical one which sees her as man's helpmate, and the Platonic-Aristotelian one which accepts her as either a defective member of the same species, or as a being more akin to the body than the mind. For further study in the latter, I recommend the bibliography in Genevieve Lloyd, *The Man of Reason: "Male" and "Female" in Western Philosophy* (Minneapolis: University of Minneapolis Press, 1984). See also the essay of Judith Romney Wegner, "Philo's Portrayal of Women—Hebraic or Hellenic?" in A.-J. Levine, ed., *"Women Like This," New Perspectives on Jewish Women in the Greco-Roman World* (Atlanta: Scholars Press, 1991), 41-44; she concludes that Philo's disparaging depiction of women owes far more to Greek than to authentic Jewish traditions (65).

The Praeparatio Evangelica and Spoliatio Motifs as Patterns of Hellenistic Judaism in Philo of Alexandria

Daniel N. Jastram

Introduction

The question under consideration in this study of Philo of Alexandria is: what are the patterns of interaction between his faith and his culture, between his Judaism and his Hellenism? This study finds that Philo operated with a three-part, rather than a two-part framework: the issue was not Judaism versus Hellenism, but a new cosmopolitan ideal versus an inadequate Judaism as well as an inadequate Hellenism.

The perceived inadequacy of both traditional Judaism and Hellenism finds implicit validation from two well-known motifs used to show patterns of interaction between faith and culture: the *praeparatio evangelica* and *spoliatio* motifs. Both make assumptions of inadequacy. If Greek learning is only a preparation for the truth it is clearly unable on its own to attain full truth. If, on the other hand, in line with the *spoliatio* motif, Greek learning is a field from which one chooses things of value in order to incorporate them into one's own system of truth, the assumption is that one's state would be the poorer without these goods.[1]

Whichever pattern is adopted, it will fit somewhere on a continuum of attitudes and responses in the interaction between faith and culture: total rejection on one extreme, total assimilation on the other; right in the middle one finds the response of an appropriation in which one's faith is not destroyed by the addition of culture. This middle region of appropriation is usually considered as one which includes the greatest diversity: it may be an appropriation based on a thorough critique of culture, or a cautious appropriation resulting in transformation, as that culture becomes associated with the faith; it may even be an extremely flexible appropriation which invites syncretism.[2]

It should be noted that this faith-culture continuum, as a whole, assumes a mono-cultural perspective, i. e., a view from one side of the fence; for we find ourselves asking the question: how much of what is on the other side of the fence will be tolerated on this side, and in what manner? The one extreme, "total rejection," keeps everything out. The other extreme, "total assimilation," tears down the fence. The middle position, "appropriation," maintains the fence, but allows passage from one side to the other.[3]

Historical Context

As a Jew, Philo of Alexandria (d. ca. 45 CE) faced the same predicament that Christians did: dissonance between faith and culture. Because he was a writer of substantial influence, both in his own time and for later Christian authors, the patterns of response which Philo adopted merit close attention.

As an Alexandrian Jew, Philo shared with many Diaspora Jews a significant degree of Jewish Hellenism. Hellenism is evident in part by the use of the Greek language. The Septuagint, inscriptions, and papyri show that Jews used Greek in their religious, literary, and personal lives. Use of Greek names and Greek symbols also indicates a high degree of appropriation of Greek culture.[4]

Philo's family, the noblest and wealthiest of the Alexandrian Jews, had connections with the Herodian dynasty through Philo's brother, Alexander Lysimachus, and also with the Roman court through Philo's nephew, Tiberius Julius Alexander.[5] Philo was certainly in a social and financial position to benefit from Greek education and culture as it was available for a Jew of his stature. That he did so is evident from his many quotations from Greek philosophers and dramatists, from his Platonizing perspective, and from his intimate acquaintance with all aspects of Greek culture, even the social life of dining, drinking, music, theater, painting and sculpture, and a wide variety of athletic pursuits, especially those of the gymnasium: the celebrated institution through which one obtained Greek citizenship.[6] All of these factors suggest that one could apply to Philo that famous encomium reportedly spoken by Aristotle of a Jewish traveller: not only did the man talk like a Greek, but he also had the soul of a Greek.[7]

And yet it is evident from his treatise *On the Unchangeableness of God* (17-18) that Philo was firmly Jewish, advocating the sacrifice of life itself rather than abandoning Jewish laws. It was because of his unquestioned Judaism that the Alexandrian Jews chose him to lead their delegation to the Roman Emperor, Caligula, to plead their cause against Flaccus, the prefect of Alexandria and Egypt.

Thus Philo's background neither inclined him to reject Greek learning totally (Jewish use of the Greek language itself made that impractical), nor to become assimilated totally into Greek culture (as did his nephew, Tiberius Julius Alexander, who lost his faith completely).[8] Philo took on a mediating position, one of appropriation; and even here, he placed himself in the middle of the middle position. For his appropriation was not based on an extreme critique of culture, nor would he allow appropriation to degenerate into syncretism. Philo judiciously accepted from culture that which could be harmonized with his faith. As a result, he was thoroughly both Jew and Greek, not just a Jew with Greek education.

Spoliatio Motifs

As part of this pattern of appropriation, Philo included *spoliatio* motifs in his writings.[9] In *Who is the Heir* (247), he complains about those he calls sophists, who constantly differ in their answers to questions of philosophy. Stating that the history of philosophy is full of discordance, he compares conflicting philosophical opinions to the birds of prey which swarm down upon the half-pieces of animals divided in sacrifice by Abraham (Genesis 15:11). They swarm about,

> Until the man-midwife who is also the judge takes his seat in their midst and observes the brood of each disputant's soul, throws away all that is not worth rearing, but saves what is worth saving and approves it for such careful treatment as is required (*Who Is the Heir*, 247).

This is Philo's picture of a wise, faithful eclectic like himself: one who chooses appropriately from the opinions of the philosophers, whether they be Plato, Aristotle, Zeno, Pythagoras, or the Skeptics. And many Christian writers emulated Philo in this eclectic approach (following the *spoliatio* motif), selectively choosing the flowers from which they, like bees, would draw pollen for their honey.[10]

More dominant for Philo, however, is a "double *spoliatio*" motif, which portrays Jews taking back wisdom which others have previously taken from them.[11] In *Every Good Man is Free* (57) Philo, while making a point about the differences between the wise and the foolish, cites Zeno and adds the comment: "We may well suppose that the fountain from which Zeno drew this thought was the law-book of the Jews. . . ."

In *Who Is the Heir* (213-14), while discussing the passage "He placed the sections facing opposite each other" (Genesis 15:10, concerning Abraham's covenantal sacrifice), Philo writes:

> For the two opposites together form a single whole, by the division of which the opposites are known. Is not this the truth which according to the Greek Heracleitus, whose greatness they celebrate so loudly, put in the forefront of his philosophy and vaunted it as a new discovery? Actually, as has been clearly shown, it was Moses who long ago discovered the truth that opposites are formed from the same whole, to which they stand in the relation of sections or divisions.

In *On the Special Laws* (IV. 61), while explaining the Mosaic law about not accepting "idle hearing" as legal evidence, Philo comments:

> Some Grecian legislators did well when they copied from the most sacred tables of Moses the enactment that hearing is not accepted as evidence. . . .

When Philo discusses the flood of Noah and the destruction of Sodom and Gomorrah in *On the Eternity of the World* (146 f.) and related passages, and speaks of these as examples of destructions also described by Plato, he again indicates that whatever truth there may be in Plato's story must ultimately have come from Moses.[12] Among the passages (e. g., in *Allegorical Interpretation* II 15 and *Moses* II 12) that extol Moses in his various aspects as philosopher, king, lawgiver, high-priest, and prophet, as Philo compares Moses with his non-Jewish counterparts, he repeatedly claims the primacy of Moses, whether among philosophers or lawgivers.

Praeparatio Evangelica Motifs
In addition to *spoliatio* motifs, Philo also includes *praeparatio evangelica* motifs in his treatises; here again we will see that he does so with a surprising twist. Early Church Fathers with a positive perspective on Greek learning thought that Greek philosophy could prepare pagans for conversion just as the Torah prepared Jews for the Gospel. In his *Miscellanies* Clement used the image of rain on a field: although rain (i. e., pagan learning) helps to grow weeds, it also brings forth fruitful crops.[13] Philo also regarded Greek learning positively: a vital, necessary element for attaining the goal of faith, i. e., as preparation for spiritual conversion.

True to his mediating position between Judaism and Hellenism, Philo constantly advocated Greek learning (*paideia*), especially in its general curricular form (the *encyclios paideia*).[14] As a middle education (*mesē paideia*) it is a preparation (*encyclia propaideumata*) through which one attains to the study of philosophy. Philo saw this Greek education as a stepping-stone to higher things, a mental training for the soul; for like a house, the soul was prepared by means of the *encyclios paideia* to receive the Divine Lodger. Greek learning was like the milk which must precede the meat, as the preliminary source of spiritual strength. Again he compared it to the handmaiden with whom the young soul mates (as Abraham did with Hagar) before it can mate with true wisdom. Thus Philo endowed the *encyclia* with inherent spiritual value, for through it ordinary human beings could reflect on the wonders of the universe and so gain a knowledge of God at their own level.[15]

Philo advocated the *encyclia* so enthusiastically because he saw it as the "preparation" by which Greeks could reach philosophy and become converted to the ultimate truth, of which they had but partial knowledge. It was also the "preparation" by which Jews could arrive at the same truth, of which they too had partial, though more complete, knowledge. Through allegory and Platonism (the latter provided the ontological parallel to the former, literary means) the spiritual meaning of the Torah was available together with its literal meaning. This means that Philo regarded the *encyclia* as a preparation for attaining ultimate truth, both for Greeks and Jews. Traditional Greek and Jewish learning were both inadequate: Greek learning, because it often produced sophists with misguided opinions, pederasts, or others who were only in love with things of this world, materialists who never passed on to true philosophy; and Jewish learning, because it produced either dull-witted simple-tons who could only see the surface (i. e., literal) meaning of the Torah, or over-enthusiastic allegorists who wanted to sweep away the literal sense of the Torah completely. True philosophy should be the goal for all, as Philo showed by citing the Magi of Persia, the Gymnosophists of India, the Essenes of Palestine, and the Therapeutae of Egypt.

Aristotle's Golden Mean

A Third Position for Culture
As a consequence, Philo adopted a third cultural position which transcended both the common Greek and common Jewish one. He did not view Greek learning from the Jewish side of the fence, asking

how much of it (if any) should be allowed on his side. He expressed disapproval even for his own Jewish side of the fence. Rather, he took a position in the middle of the road: the Aristotelian golden mean, the *aurea mediocritas*. Philo called it the king's highway, the royal road. This framework assumed three positions rather than two. A simple contrast between Greek and barbarian, Jew and Gentile was inadequate. And both elements of the contrast were inadequate. Philo's bi-cultural Alexandrian and Judaic background led him to a third, trans-cultural, middle position of the golden mean rather than one either Greek or Jewish. Thus, the "us" versus "them," or the "Jew versus Greek" paradigm was transformed into an ideal, cosmopolitan "us" (including cosmopolitan Jews and Greeks) versus an inadequate "us" (i. e., traditional Jews) and an inadequate "them" (i. e., traditional Greeks). Philo characterized this third cultural position cosmopolitan "us" primarily by philosophical and ethical ideology focusing on the distinction between virtue and vice, good and bad, wise and foolish, all of which hinge on the presence or absence of *paideia*. This ethical focus, in turn, also incorporated a third position.[16]

A Third Position for Ethics

Philo's focus, therefore, was not on Greek or Jewish culture itself characterized as good or bad, but on philosophy as the road to ethics. Just as he recast the simple cultural dichotomy between Jew and Greek into a three-part framework, he also recast the simple ethical dichotomy between good and bad into a three-part framework. In this framework there are two extremes, both of which are bad; and one mean, which is good. In each of the ethical dichotomies mentioned above (virtue-vice, good-bad, wise-foolish), Philo's third position (the golden mean) uses the first term of each pair: virtue, good, and wise, to signify the result of *paideia* in the cosmopolitan Jew or Greek. The second term of each pair (vice, bad, and foolish) signifies ethical extremes characterized by the absence of *paideia*. The opposite extremes on either side of the golden mean are characterized by insufficiency or excess of the ethical quality in question.[17]

The three-part nature of this ethical framework is clearly defined by Philo in his treatise *On the Unchangeableness of God* (164):

> Therefore, that we may not be forced to turn aside and have dealings with the vices that war against us, let us wish and pray that we may walk straightly along the middle path or mean. Courage is the mean between rashness and cowardice, economy between careless extravagance and illiberal parsimony, prudence between knavery and folly, and finally piety between superstition and impiety.

A Third Position for Faith

As the last phrase of the above quotation shows, Philo applied the three-part framework to matters of faith as well as culture and ethics. He recasts the simple contrast of piety and impiety into two extremes and a golden mean. Thus piety is the virtuous mean, while impiety and superstition, both corruptions of piety, are the vicious extremes: one has too little religion, while the other has too much.[18] In *On the Special Laws*, (IV 147) Philo clarifies this in his comment about piety: "Addition will beget superstition and subtraction will beget impiety."

This is also why, in *On the Sacrifices of Abel and Cain* (15), he calls superstition the sister of piety: altering piety, by adding or subtracting, produces a mutation. In *The Worse Attacks the Better* (18), he refers to those who do not practice religion at all as impious; those who practice it in mutilated form are called superstitious. Again in *On Noah's Work as a Planter* (107-108), when Philo likens piety to a plant troubled by addition of parasitic outgrowth (i. e., superstition) which is to be removed, he writes:

> Sacred ministrations and the holy service of sacrifices is a plant most fair, but it has a parasitic growth that is evil, namely superstition, and it is well to apply the knife to this before its green leaves appear. For some have imagined that it is piety to slaughter oxen, and allot to the altars portions of what they have got by stealing, or by repudiating debts, or by defrauding creditors, or by seizing property and cattle-lifting, thinking, in

their gross defilement, that impunity for their offenses is a thing that can be bought. . . . He [i. e., God] takes no delight in blazing altar fires fed by the unhallowed sacrifices of men to whose hearts sacrifice is unknown.

So, those who disingenuously try to manipulate God by carrying out deeds of religion without their deeper meaning practice superstition. Speaking about insincerity in *On the Unchangeableness of God* (102-103), Philo writes:

What of those who render an insincere worship to the only wise God, those who as on a stage assume a highly sanctified creed and profession of life, which does no more than make an exhibition to the assembled spectators?

Their true nature, as Philo describes them, is disguised with the symbols, or wrappings of religion, but when these are shed the hypocrisy of their insincerity will be revealed.

Unlike such hypocritical practitioners of religion, the simple-minded commoners who are not able to accept the higher spiritual and allegorical truths of the Torah are also described as superstitious in *On the Unchangeableness of God* (138). In *On the Cherubim* (42), for example, Philo writes:

When I purpose to speak of them [i. e., the higher and allegorical truths of the Torah], let them who corrupt religion into superstition close their ears or depart. For this is a divine mystery, and its lesson is for the initiated who are worthy to receive the holiest secret, even those who in simplicity of heart practice the piety which is true and genuine, free from all tawdry ornament. The sacred revelation is not for those others who, under the spell of the deadly curse of vanity, have no other standards for measuring what is pure and holy but their barren words and phrases and their silly usages and ritual.

In such passages decrying superstition, Philo sounds surprisingly like Gentile detractors who characterize the Jews as misanthropic and superstitious because they appear anti-social and unreasonably scrupulous in their religious observances. Yet, Philo clearly upheld the literal understanding of the Torah as well as the spiritual meaning behind its laws. In *On the Embassy to Gaius* (361) Philo records that when he led the Jewish delegation to the Emperor Caligula and finally gained an audience to complain about the oppression of Flaccus, Caligula shot back with the question, "Why do you refuse to eat pork?" Philo did not deny the validity of the question. He also accepted the validity of the practice under attack. This means that where he denounces Jewish usages and ritual his focus is on practices resulting not from the written code but from oral tradition: practices like the *erub*, the means by which Pharisees allowed greater freedom of movement on the Sabbath, or the strict observances concerning what is clean or unclean in Jewish associations with the Gentiles.

Philo upheld piety, including a literal observance of the laws of the Torah. He denounced both their rejection and their mutations, calling the former impiety and the latter superstition. According to Philo, true piety is cosmopolitan because Moses, the pre-eminent philosopher, king, lawgiver, high-priest, and prophet has revealed true piety, and other philosophers only echo Moses in their approximation of that piety.

Conclusions

This study has considered the question: what patterns of interaction are evident in Philo between his faith and his culture, between his Judaism and his Hellenism? Our conclusion is that Philo's perspective included a three-part framework for each of the areas of religion, ethics, and culture. He developed a new cosmopolitan ideal, working from the highly Hellenized milieu of his Jewish-Alexandrian context. His was not a simple mono-cultural antagonism, looking from one side of the fence and asking what interaction with the other side, if any, is appropriate. His was a fundamentally and thoroughly trans-cultural perspective which advocated a new cosmopolitan ideal, through which the best of Greek learning produced a philosophic piety, which would lead both Jews and Greeks to universal Truth.

Notes

1. For a recent discussion of these two motifs in the context of Greco-Roman antiquity see W. E. Helleman, ed., *Christianity and the Classics: The Acceptance of a Heritage* (Lanham, MD.: University Press of America, 1990). There Helleman, in her study on "Basil's *Ad Adolescentes*: Guidelines for Reading the Classics," 31-51, shows how Basil defended the use of pagan authors as a *praeparatio evangelica* in which one must take what is useful, but pass over what is not. In the same volume A. M. Wolters, in his study, "Christianity and the Classics: A Typology of Attitudes," 189-203, explains the *praeparatio evangelica* motif as a pattern of interaction between faith and culture in which "grace perfects nature," and the *spoliatio* motif as one in which "grace restores nature." Both assume the inadequacy of Greek learning: according to the former it must be perfected; according to the latter it must be restored, converted, or transformed for use by others.

2. See Cornelia J. de Vogel, "Platonism and Christianity: A Mere Antagonism or a Profound Common Ground?" *Vigiliae Christianae* 39 (1985): 19f., and H. Richard Niebuhr, *Christ and Culture* (New York: Harper and Row, 1951), for various positions within this faith-culture continuum.

3. Alan Mendelson's *Philo's Jewish Identity* (Atlanta, Georgia: Scholars Press, 1988), provides a detailed study of this issue as it relates to Philo. His chapter 5 (115-38), "Drawing the Line," is especially relevant to the issue of a mono-cultural perspective as seen from one side of the fence.

4. On Jewish use of the Greek language, see Martin Hengel, *Judaism and Hellenism: Studies in Their Encounter in Palestine during the Early Hellenistic Period*, 2 vols., John Bowden, trans. (Philadelphia: Fortress Press, 1974), esp. vol. 1, 58-64; and Louis W. D. Davies and Louis Finkelstein, eds., *The Cambridge History of Judaism*, 2 vols.

(Cambridge, England: Cambridge University Press, 1984-89), esp. vol. 2, chapter 3, 79-114: "Hebrew, Aramaic and Greek in the Hellenistic Age." Philo makes a revealing identification of Greek as "our language" in distinction from Hebrew, in his *On the Confusion of Tongues* (129), noted by Victor Tcherikover, *Hellenistic Civilization and the Jews*, S. Applebaum, trans. (New York: Atheneum, 1970), 347. On the use of Greek personal names among the Jews, see the *Corpus Papyrorum Judaicarum*, 3 vols., V. Tcherikover, A. Fuks, and M. Stern, eds. (Cambridge, Mass.: Harvard University Press, 1957-64), 27-29; and Tcherikover (1970) (see above), esp. 346f.; also Davies and Finkelstein (see above), 102f. On the use of Greek symbols, see Erwin R. Goodenough, *Jewish Symbols in the Greco-Roman Period*, 13 vols. (New York: Pantheon Books, 1953-68), esp. vol. 1, 30-32, 178.

5. Davies and Finkelstein (n.4), vol. 2, 164, note that Philo's elder brother, Gaius Julius Alexander, was a very rich man who managed the estates of emperor Claudius's mother, Antonia.

6. Aside from Philo's constant quotations of, and allusions to, Greek writers and philosophers, he provides numerous other instances of intimate acquaintance with the characteristic aspects of everyday cultured Greek life, all of which strongly suggests personal involvement. A cursory check reveals over 200 passages (excluding quotations and allusions mentioned above) which hint of personal participation in the social life of cultured Greeks in Alexandria. See Tcherikover (1970) (n.4 above), 350, for evidence of Jewish names in lists of the *epheboi* of the gymnasium. See also Davies and Finkelstein (n.4 above), vol. 2, 162, on Jewish youths attending the gymnasium and participating in athletic contests. See A. T. Kraabel, "Paganism and Judaism: The Sardis Evidence," in *Paganisme, judaisme, christianisme: Influences et affrontements dans le monde antique*, Mélanges offerts à Marcel Simon (Paris: E. de Boccard, 1978), 13-33, on archaeological remains of a synagogue in Sardis devastated in 17 CE, and evidently a segment of a mammoth gymnasium complex.

7. Citations of this account can be found in Menachem Stern, *Greek and Latin Authors on Jews and Judaism: From Herodotus to Plutarch* (Jerusalem: Israel Academy of Sciences and Humanities, 1974-84), 47-52, cited prominently by Alan Mendelson in his *Secular Education in Philo of Alexandria* (Cincinnati: Hebrew Union College Press, 1982), xvii.

8. See Josephus, *The Antiquities of the Jews*, 20. 100, on this last point, noted by Davies and Finkelstein (n.4), vol. 2, 164.

9. But Philo never uses the motif explicitly or with any reference to the Exodus story (Exod. 12:35-36; 3:21-22; 11:2). His only direct reference to the Jewish *spoliatio* of the Egyptians occurs in *Moses* I, 141-42, where he gives alternate justifications for the event but no recognition of the event as symbolic of a *spoliatio* motif. As we see below, his *spoliatio* motifs assume the form of eclecticism, which was appropriate to him as an Alexandrian who was both Jew and Greek; see further n.11. All quotations in this essay are taken from the Loeb *Philo*, F. H. Colson and G. H. Whitaker, trans. (Cambridge, Mass.: Harvard University Press, 1958-62). Titles and abbreviations also follow the format of the Loeb edition of *Philo*.

10. This imagery is used by Basil of Caesarea, *Ad Adulescentes* (iv. 8, Loeb ed.), as Pauline Allen notes in "Some Aspects of Hellenism in Early Greek Church Historians," *Traditio* 43 (1987): 373; it is also discussed by Helleman (n.1), 42.

11. This motif reflects Abraham's recovery of Lot and his possessions from four neighboring kings in Genesis 14:16, more than the Jewish *spoliatio* of the Egyptians. See also Norman Roth, "The 'Theft of Philosophy' by the Greeks from the Jews," *Classical Folia* 32 (1978): 53-67, tracing this theme through Philo to the early Christian apologists. Elsewhere in this volume, in " 'Spoils from Egypt' between Jews and Gnostics" (383-93), Lawrence E. Frizzell notes that Jewish *spoliatio* of the Egyptians, as recorded in Exodus, is often justified by claims that the wealth appropriated was commensurable (1) with the value of the previous years of labor rendered by the Jews, or (2) with the value of punitive damages for the loss of freedom through enslavement by the Egyptians, or (3) with the value associated with Joseph's leadership on behalf of the Egyptians in the past (see the *Book of Jubilees* 48:18-19; Philo, *Moses* I. 140-42; Irenaeus, *Adv. Haer.* iv. 30; Clement of Alexandria, *Strom.* i. 23; Tertullian, *Adv. Mar.* ii. 20, ii. 28, iv. 24). In each case the Egyptians are seen as having acquired something from the Jews which the Jews are now reappropriating.

12. See especially Colson's note "d" *ad. loc.*, also his note on sections 147f. in the Appendix of the Loeb volume VII. 530, of Philo's work.

13. C. A. Contreras discusses the position of Clement, together with other Church Fathers, in his "Christian Views of Paganism," *Aufstieg und Niedergang der römischen Welt*, II, 23. 2 (1980): 980-82.

14. On *encyclios paideia* see: Mendelson (1982) (n.7 above), especially his bibliography, 113-17; Monique Alexandre, *De Congressu eruditionis gratia: Introduction, traduction et notes*, vol. 16 of *Les Oeuvres de Philon d'Alexandrie*, R. Arnaldez, C. Mondésert, and J. Pouilloux, eds. (Paris: Ed. du Cerf, 1967), esp. 27f.; and A. P. Bos, *Cosmic and Meta-Cosmic Theology in Aristotle's Lost Dialogues* (Leiden: E. J. Brill, 1989), esp. ch. 11: "*Exoterikoi logoi* and *enkyklioi logoi* in the *Corpus Aristotelicum* and the origin of the idea of the *enkyklios paideia*," 113-52.

15. See Mendelson (1982) (n.7), xxiv, and 76-79; also David Runia's review of this book in *Mnemosyne* 39 (1986): 494.

16. Hengel (n.4), 65, refers to Strabo I, 4, 9 (66f.), a passage which records Eratosthenes' proposal that people should no longer be classed as Greeks or barbarians, but according to the virtue and vice resulting from *paideia*. On Philo's use of pairs of opposites see also in this volume P. Booth, "The Voice of the Serpent," 160-61, and D. Sly, "The Plight of Women," 175.

17. In other words, the nature of the two-part framework, or simple contrast, can be pictured easily as a sheet of paper with one end labelled "good" and the other "bad;" that of the three-part framework (with a good mean and two bad extremes) can be pictured as the same sheet of paper with both ends as bad extremes pushed toward each other, and the raised middle of the sheet as the golden mean: i. e., the hump of the sheet is the middle way, or the king's highway, and the two extremes of the sheet are the ditches, one on each side of the highway.

18. All ten cases of Philo's use of "superstition" (*deisidaimonia*) listed in Gunter Mayer's *Index Philoneus* (Berlin: De Gruyter, 1974), 69, have a negative meaning, although elsewhere the word has the more positive meaning associated with a religious feeling of fear and respect, or with piety towards the gods.

Muddying the Water: Metaphors for Exegesis

John H. Corbett

In Greco-Roman, Jewish and Christian texts one can find a number of striking images which feature human interaction with water as a metaphor for exegesis. The extent and complexity of this apparently straightforward metaphoric system is impressive and also revealing.

Fresh water is necessary for life and often serves as a symbol for life, especially in areas of scanty rainfall. In ancient Mediterranean cultures the experience of water is expressed in a common typology most familiar to us from the Bible. The sea is the realm of death, while fresh water is associated with life, and with the divine gift as the source of all life. Running water, however, is ambivalent: abundant streams are welcome in the long dry Mediterranean summer, but winter torrents may bring destruction and death. Control of running water is difficult but rewarding; thus irrigation receives special attention.

In terms of topography, weather patterns, rainfall and water resources the Mediterranean environment is uniform. Metaphors reflecting that environment also appear strikingly uniform. Yet variations against a common theme impart a distinctive character to different traditions, revealing cultural contrasts. Particularly metaphors which draw on human experience with water as a model for

human experience of divine interaction, and for exegesis of a divine-
ly-given text, help us define the varying relationships among Greco-
Roman, Jewish and Christian traditions. I would suggest that this
metaphoric system which reflects the experience of water shows a
distinctive development in Jewish and Christian traditions. Study of
this metaphoric system reveals the scriptural world view as a "restoration" of the value system of the Greco-Roman world—that is,
as a "return" to a more fundamentally correct system of values.

Poetic Popularization as a Muddy Cup
St. Martin, Bishop of Tours (371-397), became the dominant model
of sanctity for western Europe in his own lifetime, thanks to the *Life
of St. Martin* of his younger contemporary and disciple Sulpicius
Severus.[1] Martin's cult received little official promotion until Per-
petuus (Bishop at Tours from 458 to 488) transformed the small
shrine into a large basilica and commissioned Paulinus of Périgueux
to recast first the *Life*, then the *Dialogues* of Sulpicius, into a
powerful poem. This is the poem in which Paulinus makes striking
use of water imagery to describe his own work as an interpreter of
the life of St. Martin.[2] Of particular interest is the dedication at the
beginning of the fourth book as, upon completion of the *Life*, he
begins the task of translating Sulpicius's *Dialogues*:

> Not so that there might shine forth more brightly from (my)
> wretched mouth,
> What the page of so perceptive a heart had marked out,
> For the force of (his) words, sparkling with living power,
> Loses its inborn vigour when softened by verse;
> Rather because not all seek out the recesses of the pure fount,
> (For these must be searched out more closely); a great many
> often drink
> The waters which lie open near to hand, neglecting the hill;
> So too I, who can publish nothing worthy of the learned,
> Shall offer muddy cups at no great distance to the slow.

(Paulinus,*Life* IV 5-13)

Note the contrast he offers between the work of Sulpicius and his own. He states that whereas (1) people *do* participate in liturgical reading of Sulpicius's *Life of St. Martin* (the pure fount); (2) many prefer to listen to an account (muddy cups) which is more accessible; and thus (3) Paulinus offers his *"translatio"* as a poem which is close at hand for a mass audience. Paulinus states clearly that his work is not intended as an improvement on Sulpicius's *Life*; close study demonstrates that he faithfully paraphrases Sulpicius, omitting almost nothing, with only the addition of an occasional digressive hymn of praise and free expansion when it serves to clarify the story. Paulinus clearly saw his work as one of "popularization." To bring the holy story closer to a wider audience, "earth" had to be mixed with the "pure water." A recent study by G. Malsbary has clearly shown that the expansions give details which help embody the narrative in a more "realistic" context.[3] The divine element does not appear directly; it had been "embodied" already twice before—in Martin himself and in Sulpicius's *Life*. So Paulinus is only continuing this process, adding more earth to the pure water of tradition, and making mud—or "muddy cups" (*turbida pocula*). Thus the mixing of mud and water provides a central image for the exegetical activity through which he attempts to portray the divine in human clay.[4]

Paulinus also refers to his poetic task as a *"translatio,"* literally "carrying across" material from one form to another. In Christian Greco-Roman antiquity, *translatio* was used for the process by which (re-discovered) remains of the Holy Dead were taken out of obscurity and brought into a prominent place, like a church, to be accessible to all believers.[5] And sometimes, indeed, the celebration of such "translations" was marked by the blessing of rain after long drought, giving a Christian echo of the experience of Elijah.[6] Thus, in the "translation" of the Holy Dead, participating believers often experienced redemptive *charisma*.[7]

There are some obvious homologies between such *translatio* and that of Paulinus: the intention of *translatio* (in both senses) was one of bringing the divine closer to a wider audience or congregation. Such a process involved human intervention; and this might appear to "contaminate" the Holy while bringing it close to hand. Paulinus's poem is offered as a "muddy cup," that is, as an exegetical paraphrase in verse. Before their translation, the remains of the Holy Dead were dust. The recognition, translation, liturgical celebration and particularly the preparation of narrative accounts of their lives and holy deeds effected a re-animating of the Holy Dead: re-embodying them in the experience of believers. Thus both kinds of "translation" represented the mingling of dust with water; in both cases water represents the divine, and dust the material of inanimate creation, but mud and water mixed together yield animate life always embodying the divine.

Numbers 21:16-18, Living Water from the Well
Symbolic identification of (fresh) water and Torah has long characterized the Jewish tradition.[8] Pre-eminent was the theme of water as a gift in the wilderness: at Marah, Elim, and Rephidim (Exodus 15:25,27 and 17:1-17) and especially from Moses' striking the rock (Numbers 20:11). Moses' rod merits special attention; an early *midrash* on Wisdom (11:1-14) expands on water as a means of divine correction or reward. Already in this explanation we see a close association between the leadership and teaching of Moses and the presence of water, made available through the staff.

The early interpretive tradition (*targum* and *midrash*) emphasized the role of leaders, especially Moses. What is missing here is a suggestion regarding how their example might be implemented by their followers. In contrast, the song of Israel at Beer suggests a striking model:

> Spring up, O well—sing ye unto it—
> The well which the princes digged
> Which the nobles of the people delved
> With a stave and with their staffs
> And from the wilderness, a gift.   Numbers 21:16-18[9]

Here, as elsewhere, the *targumim* were concerned to emphasize those for whom (or through whom) the well was given; they were identified in the first place as the patriarchs, but included also the seventy sages, the Sanhedrin and others.[10] The expression "with a stave" (*BIMChOQEQ*) has attracted the attention of exegetes, both ancient and modern.[11] The *targumim* have compressed the "stave" and "staff" into the neutral "walking stick," but they typically distinguish between the patriarchs who have dug the well and Moses and Aaron who measure or draw it out with their sticks. The Septuagint usually interprets "stave" to indicate royal authority, but here it refers to *gentile* kings!

The *targumim*, the Tannaitic *midrashim* (and some later ones) here take "stave" (*MeChOQEQ*) in its regular sense, as referring to scribes or teachers (of Torah).[12] The ambiguity in the exegetical tradition: "ruler," or "teacher/scribe," is fundamental; the primary meaning of the verbal root *ChQQ* refers to scratching. The meaning "engraving" could be derived from this and, by extension, also the "giving of laws." The idea of "rule" was probably implicit already from the beginning in the image of holding or wielding a stave. The same basic idea of "scratching" could later be applied to writing and, by extension, to scribal activity and teaching in general. If the word translated "stave" in Numbers 21:18 is indeed a noun, the meaning "scratcher" (that is, "stave") seems especially appropriate,[13] and preferable to the abstract "sceptre" (that is, "rod of command"). Many modern commentators have missed the presence of a root idea of "scratching" or "digging" here in Numbers 21:18, since it does not appear in other biblical contexts where this word is used.[14] In my opinion, the passage is *primarily* focused on the stave used as a digging stick to find and bring out water. It was this primary image of digging for water (in Numbers 21:16-18) which was explicitly (re)captured by noted exegetes and irrigationists in the community at Qumran.

The Damascus Rule: Torah and the Well of Life

A foundational document from the Qumran community exhorts those "who enter the New Covenant in the land of Damascus" (*CD* VIII 21), and provides a detailed outline of the community "Rule."[15] Recounting how some few "men of the covenant" (*CD* VI 2) turned back from the way of error and rebellion, this text presents a striking exegesis of Numbers 21:16-18. It quotes the biblical text and continues:

> The well is the Law and those who dug it were the converts (penitents) of Israel who went out of the land of Judah to sojourn in the land of Damascus. God called them all princes because they sought Him, and their renown was disputed by no man. The stave is the interpreter of the Law of whom Isaiah said, "He makes a tool for His work" (Isaiah 54:16); and the nobles of the people are those who come to dig the well with the staves with which the stave ordained ("staved") that they should walk in all the age of wickedness—and without them they shall find nothing—until he comes who shall teach righteousness at the end of days. (CD VI 4-11, following Vermes)

Texts from Qumran often recognize the significance of water. Contrasting the faithful "remnant" with non-believers, the author of the "Rule" asserts:

> And they dug a well rich in water;[16]
> but he who despises it shall not live.   (*CD* III 16-17)

Again this text claims that one "who turns away, commits treachery, and departs from the well of living water will not be reckoned in the council of the people" (*CD* XIX 33-35).[17]

Elsewhere the "teachers of lies" are said to "withhold from the thirsty the drink of knowledge" (I *QH* IV 11); while in the *Community Rule* the phrase "the drink of the many" (Vermes: "drink of the congregation") is the special drink which symbolizes full membership in the community (I *QS* VI 20, Vermes 82).[18]

The association of this symbolic complex with the well in Numbers 21:16-18 is patent. Consistent use of the word "well" (*BeER*), to represent the source of knowledge and life, and especially the reference to the "digging" of the faithful believers, suggests that

Numbers 21:16-18 provides the source of this symbolic complex, so central to the self-understanding of the Qumran community. The well represents the Torah; the diggers are the penitents of Israel who have left the land of Judah to sojourn in the land of Damascus.[19] These penitents are called "princes" because "they *sought* him." Noteworthy here is the specific use of the word for "seeking," *DARASH*, which supplies the normative term for exegesis, *MIDRASH*. The key word "stave" is first identified with the exegete himself, the one who "seeks out or interprets Torah." Isaiah 54:16 is cited in support of this view: "(God) makes a tool for his work."[20] Finally, the nobles of the people are those who come to dig and open the well "with the staves with which the stave staved (that is, ordained) that they should walk;" in other words, all the members of the community who follow the practice of their leader participate in digging the well and thus interpreting Torah. The "stave" here represents both the authoritative teacher and the authoritative tradition of exegesis as it helps the faithful in their own "walking." Again it is noteworthy that *Halakah*, literally "walking," gives the normative word for a life lived in obedience to Torah. In this community of scholarly exegetes and skilled irrigation workers, emphasis falls on the mode of life, behavior and learning which constitutes seeking out God and his Torah, understood metaphorically as "digging the well." Other texts from Qumran depict the Torah as a well of living water *freely given* to those who dig; this reveals the same tradition in its *aggadic* dimension, namely, as it reflects an *immediate experience* of divine presence, distinct from that achieved through study and ethical conduct.

The Thanksgiving Hymn: The Poet as Irrigation Worker
Human beings living in marginal environments soon learn that effort in finding and bringing out water vastly improves the quality of life. It is scarcely surprising that the Qumran community was obsessed with water and water imagery. As it is used in one of the Thanksgiving hymns, the imagery suggests a sophistication of irrigation technology, which is not usually appreciated. The texts are quite clear, none more so than the neglected and powerful *Thanksgiving Hymn*

(or *Hodayot*: I *QH* VIII 4-40). It is a long complex poem, rich in biblical allusions and natural imagery; the text is partially defective but the main movement of thought is clear.

In the opening (lines 1-5) the poet thanks God for placing him beside "a fountain of streams in a dry land."[21] Next (5-11) he develops the related image of a "fountain of mystery" giving "living waters" for "trees of life." In the following stanza (12-14) the echoes of Genesis become more explicit: the "wellspring of life" is hedged in by angelic forces and "whirling flames of fire." As yet there is no evidence of *human* activity. In the third stanza (16-20) the tone changes; the poet presents himself as the conduit of God's rain ("You, O my God, have put into my mouth as it were an early fall of rain for all, and a fount of living waters. . . ." However, the word for rain (*GESHEM*) is uncommon in the Qumran texts. And the expression "an early fall of rain" (*YOREH GESHEM*) suggests the word play so favoured by the community: *YOREH/MOREH*, as "early fall (of rain)" or "teaching." The central image appears clearly in stanza four (21-26), the heart of the poem: here the poet specifies his own active role as God's irrigation worker, with rich allusion to the technical vocabulary of irrigation agriculture: "By my hand you have opened their fountain, together with their ditches" (21).[22] The seemingly innocuous phrase "when I lift my hand to dig its ditches" (22-23) again suggests the presumption of the poet's claim.[23]

This poem, thus, makes some astonishing claims: the Holy Spirit, or by implication, God's hand in history, is present in (the swinging of) the poet's hand, as God is present in his mouth. And this is taken to represent an early fall of rain, which, through word-play, also suggests teaching. If rainfall represents the presence of God on earth, then the swinging hand is that of the *darshan*, the authoritative exegete and teacher; and irrigation work explicitly appears as the symbolic equivalent of exegesis.

Conclusion

The passages examined from Paulinus, Numbers 21:16-18 (together with the exegetical tradition, especially *CD* VI 1-11), and the *Thanksgiving Hymn* share an important theme in their common use of water imagery. Numbers 21:16-18 presents us with a picture of the well, the diggers and their instruments; the diggers are here identified with the elite of Israel. The exegesis of the Qumran text *CD* VI 4-11 also concerns itself particularly with the diggers and the stave; while it shares the Jewish exegetical concern with authoritative teaching, it also suggests clearly that the whole sectarian community, a group between the elite few and the indolent many, could participate in digging the well and seeking out the Torah. The metaphorical dimension implicit in the biblical narrative of Numbers is developed extensively in the Qumran exegesis. Although the Qumran community would not have denied the "historicity" of the Numbers narrative, the Qumranic exegesis is here clearly more typological than allegorical. The *Thanksgiving Hymn* (I *QH* VII 4-40) focuses its attention on the role of the poet in bringing out the water, first using the image of an early fall of rain, as a fountain of living waters placed by God in the mouth of the speaker.

The second image is borrowed from the experience of irrigation. The ditches here closely resemble in function the muddy cups of Paulinus. For Paulinus contrasts the few who seek the pure fount with the many who prefer warmer water close at hand; to the latter he offers his muddy cups. If the text of the Thanksgiving Hymn is correctly restored at line 16, and the water of God's law is intended for "*all* who thirst," this provides a striking contrast to our usual understanding of the Qumran sect as in-turned and exclusive.[24] Finally, the image of water and earth mixed to produce mud is also strongly present at Qumran—not least in the *Thanksgiving Hymns*— as an image for the way human beings have been fashioned by God, through mixture of water (from the divine) with inanimate dust.[25]

The Qumran texts and Paulinus thus are both much concerned with bringing water to the thirsty; both recognize that this water must be provided in muddy cups, or through ditches, where mud represents what has been added in the process of exegesis (that is, digging or ditching) necessary to bring the divine water to the world. But the mixture of mud and water suggests not only the exegetical process, but beyond that the creation of humanity, and the incarnation of the divine. By contrast the emphasis in Numbers 21:16-18 is on the act of digging and the identity or character of the digger, though the presence and use of the "stave" opens the way to a metaphorical interpretation which is much more concerned with the character of the tool and the manner of its use.

Despite the differences of emphasis in the texts which we have examined thus far, most of the symbolic elements are closely affiliated. This may be explained through the influence of the biblical text at Qumran and for Paulinus.[26] We would do well also to recognize here the formative influence of the *experience* of water in the Mediterranean world. My purpose here, in the first place, has not been to trace textually-based historical traditions or environmental determinants; rather, taking these as given in the literature, it is my concern to examine the metaphorical structure of these groups of symbols. A brief examination of a contrasting use of water imagery in Philo will help us recognize the distinctive features of biblical metaphors so far examined.

Philo is familiar with biblical water imagery and its traditional interpretation; but his own views are strikingly at odds with what we have seen so far. For Philo the digging of the well in Numbers symbolizes the discovery of wisdom or knowledge; but his concern is typically private and intellectual, rather than communal and ethical (*On Dreams* II 270/1: *LCL* V 562-5). He has little to say about the role of Moses here.[27] The river in Pharaoh's dream is identified as speech which may be either good or bad.[28] The experience of Jacob and Isaac at the "well of the oath" suggests that no human can attain full knowledge.[29] Philo's elitism stands out even more distinctly in his interpretation of the metaphor of the spring: the great man's ideas are tantamount to revelation (the spring), his words to exegesis (its outflow).[30] Finally, Philo uses the image of drinking from a muddy spring in a way which directly opposed that of Paulinus and the Qumran exegetes: an unsatisfied desire to drink from the fountain of peace, according to Philo, is better than drinking from a muddy spring (*On Dreams* II 149-54 especially 150: *LCL* V 510/1). When we are driven to drink from the muddy waters, irrationality attacks and overpowers reason within the soul, as it were like a herd run wild. Although we must remember that Philo uses his images as symbols of forces *within* the soul, the muddy fountain and wild herd both compare unfavourably to the reasonable and restrained elite. The elements of the metaphor are familiar; but their symbolic value for Philo is starkly opposed to that of the other texts examined.

All our texts work with an underlying image: water from a spring (or a well) flows down through a river and loses its original cold purity as it becomes warm and is mixed with mud; however the "muddy cups" or ditches bring it closer to more would-be drinkers— as long as we know how to "mix the cups" (through *translatio*), to dig the wells or ditches, and wield the stave of exegesis (in the process of "seeking out"). For Paulinus, for the children of Israel at the well, and for the sectaries at Qumran the context is communal and social; the one who "digs" offers an example (of behavior) to be imitated. For Philo, on the contrary, muddy springs are to be avoided as manifestations of mass unreason; here the root metaphor is recast to exalt an experience that is private rather than communal, and intellectual rather than behavior-oriented. Shared natural experience of water in the Mediterranean world has offered the basic metaphor; but the particular experiences and values of different communities have also led to profound variations in emphasis, and these are mediated by historical traditions. The "muddy cups" of Paulinus thus appear as a Christian "restoration" of values based in biblical texts and broadly affirmed in Jewish exegetical traditions. Philo's opposition to this version of the root metaphor (with which he is clearly familiar) could not be more patent: the role of Moses' staff, and waters for the unreasoning masses are both clearly rejected; no mud is wanted here!

Notes

1. For Sulpicius and the *Life of St. Martin* see C. Stancliffe, *Saint Martin and his Hagiographer: History and Miracle in Sulpicius Severus* (Oxford University Press, 1983).

2. Paulinus of Périgueux, *Libri VI De Vita S. Martini*, M. Petschenig, ed., *CSEL* 16 (1898), 16-159.

3. G. Malsbary, *The Epic Hagiography of Paulinus of Périgueux*, unpub. Ph. D. Thesis, University of Toronto, 1987.

4. See J. H. Corbett, "Hagiography and the Experience of the Holy in the Work of Gregory of Tours," *Florilegium* 7 (1985): 40-54.

5. For the larger social context see P. Brown, *The Cult of the Saints* (Chicago: University of Chicago Press, 1981); for *translatio* see M. Heinzelmann, *Translationsberichte und andere Quellen des Reliquienkultes* (Turnhout: Brepols, 1979).

6. See R. Sharpe, "Goscelin's St. Augustine and St. Mildreth: Hagiography and History in Context," *Journal of Theological Studies* ns. 41 (1990): 502-16 esp. 513f: rain ending a long drought at the translation of Mildreth from Thanet to Canterbury (May 18, 1030 CE) and the subsequent repetition of this blessing, with explicit reference to Elijah (1 Kings 18:41-45). I am indebted to the work of Sharpe for bringing to my attention this instance and the rich dossier concerning St. Mildreth; beyond this Sharpe deserves credit for the scope of this seminal study and the acuity of his insight into the complex relationship of hagiographic texts, liturgy and social experience.

7. For the manifestation of redemptive *charisma* associated with the commemoration of St. Martin, his "passing" and his translation, see the ample evidence recorded by Gregory of Tours in his *Libri IV de Virtutibus S. Martini*, B. Krusch, ed., *Monumenta Germaniae Historica, Scriptores Rerum Merovingicarum II ii* (new edition, Hannover, 1969); cf. J. H. Corbett, "*Praesentium Signorum Munera*: The Cult of the Saints in the World of Gregory of Tours," *Florilegium* 5 (1983): 44-61 for discussion and tabular presentation of the evidence.

8. Especially so in the traditions associated with the "gift of water" in the story of the exodus; for this and what follows see G. Bienaimé, *Moise et le don de l'eau dans la tradition juive ancienne: targum et midrash* (Rome: Biblical Institute Press, 1984). This excellent book offers a comprehensive and insightful overview of a vast topic. An

early Targum makes the identification of fresh water and Torah explicit: the children of Israel found no water in the wilderness because they had strayed from the Law (*PsJ* on Exodus 15:22). Other early sources also attest to the identification: see Sirach 24:23-31, esp. 24, 30/1 with strong imagery of irrigation; *Hodayot* I QH II 17-18; VIII 21. Particularly striking are the images in *Avot* 2,8 (the sage is a "plastered cistern" or an "everflowing spring"); cf. Bienaimé 9f. Wrong teaching is evil (or poisonous) water: the disciples who drink from it die (*Avot* 1,11—reported in the name of Abtalion, hence before ca. 10 CE).

9. *JPS* version with the last line interpreted following Bienaimé: in the second last line I have altered "sceptre," "stave" and "staves" to "staffs" in the JPS version for the sake of clarity in the following discussion.

10. Thus the well at Beer was given "by the merit of Miriam" according to the *targum Pseudo-Jonathan (PsJ)*; it was dug by Abraham, Isaac and Jacob the chiefs of the people and measured/brought out by Moses and Aaron, the masters/scribes of Israel (so *PsJ* and commonly in the *targum* tradition); see Bienaimé (n.8) 157-64 for *targumim* on Numbers 21:16-18.

11. For what follows see G. Vermes, *Scripture and Tradition in Judaism*, ed. 2 (Leiden: Brill, 1973), 49-55, esp. 50/51 where the very complex exegetical questions are well reported, in a somewhat oversimplified discussion (focusing on the meaning of *MeCHOQEQ*);cf. Bienaimé (n.8), 161-63 for a more comprehensive discussion of the whole tradition.

12. Cf. Vermes, *Scripture and Tradition*, 52: "With the exception of Judges V 14, Palestinian exegetical tradition relates *MChQQ* to the teaching of the Torah. The teacher is either God, who gave the Law, or Moses, who is the *SIFRA* par excellence, or the scribes in general."

13. Otherwise the unvocalized letters could denote (1) "the one who scratches = commands, writes" (*nomen agentis*), hence Moses pre-eminently in early *midrash*, or (2) the action of "scratching/marking" (verbal noun) under the influence of the Aramaic *peal* which forms its infinitive with *mem* preformative (so Bienaimé (n.8), 186).

14. As Bienaimé suggests (186), the *targumim* and other early midrashic evidence support a paraphrase along the following lines: "the princes (i. e., the patriarchs) dug it with their staffs, Moses and Aaron brought it out by scratching." This latter picture suits very well the natural conditions in which "wells" are produced in the Sinai and Negev!

15. The Hebrew text of the document (commonly known as the *Damascus Document* or *Damascus Rule*) is conveniently consulted in E. Lohse, *Die Texte aus Qumran* (Darmstadt, 1971) 63f.; (*CD* I-XX in the conventional numbering system). The history and original structure of this text is even more complex than usual for the "Dead Sea Scrolls." A plausible reordering is offered by Vermes in *The Dead Sea Scrolls in English* (Penguin ed. 2, 1975), 95f. See B. Wacholder, *The Dawn of Qumran* (Cincinnati: HUC Press, 1983), 101f. for a detailed study of this major text.

16. So Vermes; more literally "to many waters;" the Hebrew phrase has a special resonance, suggesting the cosmic waters of the "depths."

17. Lohse, *Die Texte*, 102; cf. Vermes *Scrolls in English*, 106: from this point on only the "B text" is preserved.

18. Apart from the congregational drink which was the privilege of membership, water played a major role in ritual bathing: e. g., *CD* X 10-13 ("concerning purification by water"), *CD* XI 21-23 (washing required before entering the House of Worship).

19. Of course, we must be alert to the special resonance of these terms for members of the Qumran community. Here the comprehensive study of B. Wacholder provides useful guidance: *The Dawn of Qumran* (Cincinnati: HUC Press, 1983), esp. 128-29 and n.122. Just as the diggers are identified as "penitents of Israel," so the "stave" (*MeChQQ*; Wacholder translates this as "staff") is to be interpreted as referring to the community "lawgiver," identified with Zadok the founder of the sect who will return as the "Teacher of Righteousness" at the end of days. Then, in Wacholder's view, the

Torah identified with the well in this passage is to be understood as the "sectarian Torah," an idea which gains added piquancy if we believe with Wacholder that the ark in which Zadok claims to have found sealed the *Sefer Torah* hidden in the time of Joshua (see *CD* V 2-3) was itself buried in a "pit" or "well": "The Damascus Document seems to be saying that Zadok claims to have found the sealed Torah in a box, a . . . (well or pit) in the nomenclature of the Numbers passage. This may explain the Qumranic tradition of wrapping parchments and placing them in containers in caves, thus contributing to the preservation of the sect's library" (Wacholder, *The Dawn*, 128-29, n.122). Of special interest to the present study is the impulse to see symbolic systems "realized" in life (the Torah is "living water," so it should come from a well). Perhaps this impulse is simply to be understood as reflecting the immediacy of the primary experience of water in an arid environment: water is the type and Torah its fulfillment. This symbolic system is better described as typological than allegorical: as with ritual bathing or baptism the water and its fulfillment are simultaneously present in the experience of believers. It is to be noted also that the Hebrew phrase "teacher of righteousness" commonly, at Qumran and in rabbinic exegesis, gives rise to the primary interpretation "teacher" = "early fall (of rain)" for which see, e. g., *Megillat Ta'anit* and the discussion below. In any case we should resist the tendency (evident in the work of Wacholder) to distinguish the sectarian understanding of these ideas/images (such as well, Torah, stave, teacher, etc.) too sharply from the larger experience of "Jewish" life and faith in the 2nd Temple/early rabbinic period. I would prefer to emphasize the common experience of water in the Mediterranean environment, for instance, and the wide play of symbolic systems within their own parameters (which it is our task to discover).

20. As is the usual practice in rabbinic exegesis, a practice already established as a foundation stone of Pharisaic methodology and also, surprisingly—or perhaps not so—found at Qumran, the whole passage of Isaiah is to be brought before us (in the manner of a *haftarah* or prophetic portion on the Torah reading); and the vision of Isaiah

is appropriate here: God promises restoration, comfort, peace and protection to all the children of Israel; he has "created a tool for his work," conventionally interpreted in Bible versions as "weapon" but here more appropriately translated with the more inclusive "tool."

21. With a cumulation of analogous imagery strongly reminiscent of Isaiah and the Psalms; cf. Isaiah 33:7; 44:3; 49:10; Psalms 63:2; 78:16, *inter alia*.

22. The poet continues with allusions to planting "by the plumb line of the sun" (22) and the plants which are thus able to flourish in time of heat though their roots are in rocks of flint. All this is drawn from the technical vocabulary and experience of irrigation agriculture. Conversely biblical allusions are not notable here. The cord and the plumbline, however, are found elsewhere (cf. Isaiah 28:17; 34:17; 2 Kings 21:15), not least in the surveying image in Ezekiel's great vision (47:1-12, esp. 3).

23. The common verb used here for "lift" seems not to be thus used in the Bible. By contrast it is used a number of times in the *Thanksgiving Hymns* of the poet's experiencing the presence of the Holy Spirit (I *QH* VII 7, XVII 26; cf. frag. 2,9; 2,13); in the *War Scroll* the same word refers to God's decisive hand in history (I *QM* XVII 9). The expression recurs in this hymn (33) when the inability to "swing the hand" symbolizes the poet's own incapacity.

24. In another passage the "teachers of lies and seers of falsehood" are said to "withhold from the thirsty the drink of knowledge and assuage their thirst with vinegar" (I *QH* IV 9-11; so Vermes, *Scrolls in English*, 161).

25. I *QH* I 21: "And yet I ?????? a shape of clay, kneaded in water, a ground of shame and a source of pollution . . ."; cf. III 24. Sometimes the image is quite neutral (I *QH* XII 24/5;XIII 14/15).

26. Ecclesiasticus/Sirach 24:23-31 may well provide the obvious model for Paulinus and the Qumran texts (as was suggested by a commentator on an earlier version of this paper): Wisdom is an overflowing river, and the "author" compares himself to "a canal leading from a river, a watercourse into a pleasure garden." It would be ill-advised to deny the formative role of any number of biblical texts; but I am not concerned here, in the first place, with an historical critical analysis of a textual tradition whether Jewish, Christian or Greco-Roman.

27. Or when he strikes the rock; of course, the *Life of Moses* as a whole contains very straightforward interpretation of incidents in the life of Moses.

28. *On Dreams* II 236-67: *LCL* V 550-63. Striking here is the symbolic ambivalence of "rivers" (Philo is very sure that rivers can be good or bad)—something characteristic of biblical water typology reflecting, at the level of immediate experience, the utility of river water to human life on the one hand, and the potential for drowning, on the other.

29. *On Dreams* I 4-40: *LCL* V 297-317 on Genesis 28:10f; cf. Genesis 26:32. Such is Philo's interpretation of the biblical text, as he read it (Isaac did *not* find water in this well!). The biblical text of Genesis 26:32, as we commonly know it, asserts that Isaac's servants *did* find water at the "well of the oath."

30. *The Migration of Abraham*, 71: *LCL* IV 173 on Genesis 12:1-4 (the blessing of Abraham): *Logos* is both thought and speech, "one resembling a spring, the other its outflow." This image recurs in Philo's interpretation of the symbolic meaning of the vestments of the priests (*Life of Moses* II 127 cf. 129: *LCL* VI 511). Why is the reason seat doubled? "The *logos* is twofold, as well in the universe as in human nature. . . . With man in one form it resides within, in the other it passes out from him in utterance. The former is like a spring and is the source from which the latter, the spoken, flows" (127).

Harnack, Marcion and the Argument of Antiquity

Daniel H. Williams

Surely no study on the problem of Hellenism in early Christianity can be undertaken without considering the contributions of Adolf von Harnack. Nor can the study of Harnack's legacies be sufficiently appreciated without considering the figure of Marcion. For Harnack, Marcion played a central role at a critical juncture of Christian history; he regarded Marcion's work of "radical reconstruction of tradition,"[1] as an attempt to correct influences alien to the original Christian *kerygma*. Such a purist inclination held a special fascination for the German historian; he shared many of the perspectives of Marcion's quest, as he himself admitted, "It is a joy to occupy oneself with a deeply religious man of intellectual purity, one who rejects all syncretism, allegory and sophistry."[2]

Looking at Marcion was like looking into a mirror for Harnack, for he characterized syncretism as the inevitable but unfortunate product of Hellenism, or dogmatic development in the early church, in contrast with its original conditions of religious power and freedom.

In this paper I wish to examine (1) Harnack's view of Marcion as a counterforce to the spirit of Hellenism in early Christianity, and (2) the assumptions on which Harnack built his portrait of this controversial and elusive figure. Our knowledge of Marcion has for so long been dependent on Harnack's conclusions that any reassessment of Marcion must begin with a reconsideration of Harnack. And it is clear that Harnack's theological prejudices not only shaped his interpretation of Marcion's teaching but also determined how he reconstructed the evidence.[3]

It is generally recognized that Marcionite teaching as presented by Harnack provided a prototype of that articulated in the sixteenth century Reformation as Old Testament law versus New Testament grace: "It was Luther who once again gave a central position to the Pauline-Marcionite recognition of the distinction between law and Gospel."[4] Indeed, Harnack shared fully Neander's view of Marcion as the first Protestant.[5] It should not surprise us, therefore, that Harnack mitigated the contrast between Marcion's absolute rejection of the Old Testament and the Christian tradition (with exception of Gnosticism). Accordingly, I wish to examine particularly how Harnack's theological agenda and view of Law and Gospel in Marcionite thought affected his analysis of the early church's acceptance of the Old Testament. For his perspective did not account for the unique and necessary role of the Old Testament in the second and third centuries, namely the apologetical argument of antiquity. S. G. Wilson has commented on the attitude of Marcionites (and Harnack) toward Judaism, and discussed Marcion's response to the Jewish-Christian problem of the second century.[6] It remains for us to examine the factors ignored by Harnack, yet crucial for the response of the early church to Marcion's rejection of the Old Testament.[7]

Marcion as a Counterforce to Hellenism

According to Harnack, "Original Christianity" was in appearance "Christian Judaism, the creation of a universal religion on Old Testament soil."[8] From the beginning tensions existed within the nascent faith as recipients of the Gospel struggled to realize their identity, possessing a Jewish heritage actuated within the cultural atmosphere of Hellenism.[9] The effect of Hellenization was inevitable as Christianity disengaged itself from its Jewish roots. But this also was the beginning of its woes, for Hellenism became an agent in the transmutation of the Gospel into forms quite foreign to the intentions of its founder.

The worst of these transmutations for Harnack was Gnosticism. Even though Gnosticism was a manifestation that Christian communities were seeking the permanence of apostolic standards to govern their faith,[10] it was nevertheless the "first to transform Christianity into a system of doctrines." Gnostics are described as those who "in a swift advance, attempted to capture Christianity for Hellenic culture," converting the Gospel into an "absolute philosophy of religion;" this Harnack has epitomized as the "acute secularizing or Hellenizing of the Christian faith."[11]

A dualistic conception was fundamental to Gnosticism, for it made a radical separation between the God of the Israelites and the supreme or unknown God; this, as Harnack well knew, entailed the rejection of the Old Testament in many Gnostic systems. Many Gnostics believed that the Hebrew scriptures either contained no revelations from the Supreme God or did so only in certain parts.[12] Given the complex Gnostic cosmology, which viewed the material creation itself as product of the Fall, the Old Testament was considered irrelevant to the drama of salvation being played out since Jesus' appearance.

Traditional Christianity, or what Harnack calls "Catholicism" (*fides catholica*),[13] fared no better than Gnosticism on the Hellenization problem. The development of "Catholicism" into a body characterized by dogmatics and politics was alien to the spirit of primitive Christianity. We know, Harnack declares, that to Jesus "all traditions, doctrines and forms were essentially the same, if only God was acknowledged, his will followed, and his kingdom given room."[14] But the rise of dogma came about as Christian-Jewish communities, affected by the "Greek spirit," attempted to "fix" the apostolic tradition, and so began to systematize the Gospel message as an absolute. Part of this systematization arose from tensions between covenantal Judaism and the Gospel which Catholic Christianity still maintained. In order to preserve the relevance of the Old Testament, Christians had to develop a hermeneutic which consciously appropriated the Old Testament through allegory. In doing so, it fatefully passed into a philosophic interpretation of religion.

> The view of the Old Testament as a document of deepest wisdom [being interpreted spiritually], transmitted to those who knew how to read it as such, unfettered the intellectual interest which would not rest until it had entirely transferred the new religion [of Christianity] from the world of feelings, actions and hopes into the world of Hellenic conceptions, and transformed it into a metaphysic.[15]

If Gnosticism exhibited a Hellenized world view through its rejection of the God of the Old Testament, Catholics were affected by the same problem for the opposite reason, through its justification and allegorizing of the Old Testament as a distinctly Christian book. The Hellenization of Christianity was inevitable as long as Christianity maintained the Old Testament as its own possession.

Thus Harnack speaks of a "crisis" in the beginning of the second century; a crisis in determining how one constitutes an essential Christian faith. On one side, he says, "stood the formless, uncrystallized Christian proclamation, bound to the Old Testament" as authoritative, yet determined to draw its message into the apostolic sphere and preserve both the spirit and the letter; on the other side stood those who presented a clear *gnōsis* of God and a message of redemption which had no relevance to its Jewish heritage. Christianity was in danger, either of being resolved into a mass of philosophical speculations, or of being completely detached from its original conditions.[16]

In the midst of this crisis Marcion entered with a solution. According to Harnack, Marcion saw himself called to liberate Christianity, not by a syncretistic system, but through "simplification, unification and clarity of what bore the Christian label . . . [a] plain religious message was to be set in opposition to the immense and ambiguous complex of what was handed down in tradition" [namely

Catholicism].[17] In his book, *Marcion: The Gospel of the Alien God*,[18] Harnack contended that Marcion offered a viable alternative to the problem of Hellenization, a solution which was neither Gnostic nor Catholic, and in which neither cosmological dialectic nor Semitic religious wisdom corrupted the pristine purity of the Gospel. In short, he regarded Marcionism as a reform movement:[19] Marcion, the most devoted pupil of the apostle Paul, exercised radical Paulinism to detach Christianity from the soil of the Old Testament, and thus return the Christian faith to the unsullied message of the Gospel.[20] Harnack admits that Paul would doubtless have been horrified at Marcion's denial of the birth of Christ and the genuineness of his flesh; nevertheless, there is no question in Harnack's mind that Paul would have been a Marcionite had he lived in the second century!

> No doubt Paul would have taken note of the development of Christian syncretism with pain and dismay, would have joined in the Marcionite criticism of Christianity on the most important points, would also have condemned this Christianity as a flock that had been led astray, but would have seen in the man who here appeared as a reformer his own authentic pupil.[21]

For Marcion, the Pauline "spirit" meant the abolition of Old Testament law as unrelated to the saving work of Christ's death and resurrection. True, Christianity had rejected circumcision, ordinances regarding feast days, and sacrifices, but the Catholicism which prevailed over Pauline teaching[22] proclaimed the two covenants as correlatives, and denied the essence of the Christian message through such distortions.[23]

Numerous scholars have already commented on the debatable nature of Harnack's historical and theological interpretations of the patristic sources.[24] Most questionable is Harnack's assumption that Marcion himself was only superficially affected by elements common to many Gnostic theologies. Hans Jonas (among others) has accused Harnack of underestimating the influence which Gnosticism had on

Marcion.[25] We may agree with Harnack that the impact of the Syrian
Gnostic Cerdo on Marcion as reported by Irenaeus is exaggerated,
and that Marcion never shared the cosmological intricacies which
are typically attributed to many Gnostic systems. Nonetheless,
Marcion's presuppositions about the "alien" Supreme God, his
negative view of the created order, and his distantiation of the
Supreme God from the creation is far more Gnostic than Harnack
allows. Nor can it be correct, as Harnack claims, to exclude Marcion
from the Gnostics because he was guided by soteriological interests,
not by cosmological speculations.[26] Surely Gnosticism was at its
heart a religious movement in search of salvation and escape from
the material (i. e., evil) world of the Creator.

Also problematic is Harnack's characterization of the conflict
between Marcion and Catholicism over the role of the Old Testament in the Christian faith: "Marcion wanted to free Christianity
from the Old Testament, but the church preserved it." Harnack's
overzealous identification of Marcionism with Pauline theology lay
at the root of this rejection. At the same time, Harnack gives a strong
indication that he shares Marcion's sense of the incompatibility of
law and Gospel. The question is raised in *Marcion*, Chapter X: "Was
he [Marcion] right or was the church, which did not detach itself
from the book?"

> If one carefully thinks through with Paul and Marcion the
> contrast between "righteousness that is by faith" and the
> "righteousness that is by works" and is persuaded also of the
> inadequacy of the means by which Paul thought he could
> maintain the canonical recognition of the Old Testament, con-
> sistent thinking will not be able to tolerate the validity of the
> Old Testament as canonical documents in the Christian
> church.[27]

Still, Harnack does not deny that the second century made the
right decision against the Marcionite challenge in accepting the Old
Testament. After all, the teaching of Jesus was clearly "on the soil"

of the Old Testament and could not be dispensed with. But the church had won a Pyrrhic victory in defeating Marcion. The uneasy relationship between grace and law would continue to smoulder within Christianity, only to burst forth again under Luther's critical judgment upon the church's tradition, including the canonical status of the Old Testament. Even so, Luther, like Paul, never judged the inspiration of the Old Testament to be inferior to that of the New Testament. And yet, says Harnack, "What an unburdening of Christianity and its doctrine it would have been if Luther had taken this step!"[28]

Given Harnack's historical agenda, the Old Testament becomes the "ball and chain" which the church of the Gospel must bear because of the weight of tradition:

> It may also be stated as an assured fact that the church maintained the Old Testament not so much for reasons of content and substance as for reasons of history.[29]

And the consequence of this preservation was the religious and ecclesiastical crippling of early Christianity. The continued acceptance of the Old Testament presented the church with major interpretive hurdles to cross:

> The Old Testament brought Christianity into a tragic conflict [of Law and Gospel]. . . . From the close of the second century onward the church managed to cope with the problem and eliminated at least some of the oppressive difficulties and . . . place[d] the Old Testament on a lower level.[30]

Yet this distinction continued to be threatened by the church's view of a single inspiration.

Thus, Harnack's interpretation of Law and Gospel suffers from an encrustation of theological prejudices that seriously taint the outcome. His view of the Old Testament as an exegetical burden for the early church in its determination to regard ancient Judaism as an integral part of the Christian inheritance, hardly does justice to the evidence. The preservation of the Old Testament may well have dragged the church into a conflict between Law and Gospel. But we must not overlook the socio-political role of the Old Testament in validating the claim of early Christianity to be a reputable religion through its strong link to Judaism, a recognized religion of antiquity. Harnack underestimates what was at stake in the church's acceptance of the Old Testament. One may argue, instead, that the Marcionite theology and canon threatened early Christianity with being uprooted from its vital link with religious tradition. For Christian apologists of the second century were at great pains to affirm their legitimacy through a connection with older Judaism.

The Apologetic Value of the Old Testament
One of the standard charges against the Christians in the second and third centuries was the novelty of their beliefs and writings. New religions were automatically suspect because they lacked the time-honored respect of tradition. In the *Octavius*, Minucius Felix puts the golden rule for an acceptable religion in the Greco-Roman world into the mouth of the pagan, Caelius: "As a general principle, the greater the age that ceremonies and shrines accumulate, the more hallowed these institutions become."[31] This sentiment expressed by Minucius unmistakably echoes Cicero's influential dialogue, *De natura deorum*,[32] in which traditional authority persuades even the most skeptical to believe in the gods.

It should be noted that Christians never attempted to reject this premise; instead, in apologetic treatises they demonstrate at length that Christianity adequately meets the criterion by claiming a direct connection with a religion of recognized antiquity: Judaism.[33] Justin's use of this already common argument may be traced back to Philo who also claimed that Moses was of greater antiquity than the Greek philosophers.[34] According to Justin, Plato learned about the creation of the material world and the divine nature of the universe from Moses.[35] Similarly, Theophilus of Antioch claims that the "sacred books" preceded all other writers of antiquity, Egyptian or Greek, and that well before the Trojan war.[36] Thus, says

Theophilus, "One can see the antiquity of the prophetical writings and the divinity of our doctrine, that the doctrine is not recent, nor our tenets mythical and false, as some think, but very ancient and true."[37] We find almost exactly the same claim in other writers, such as Irenaeus, Pseudo-Justin and Tertullian, the latter admitting that "our religion" dates to a recent period, but is supported "by the writings of the Jews, the oldest which exist."[38]

Of course the main link between the Christian faith and Judaism was forged by recognizing the prophetic role of the Old Testament. Origen's claim that the person and work of Christ, including his resurrection, were foretold by the prophets,[39] represents a view which had already been indelibly stamped on Christian consciousness from its beginning. Tertullian, among others, defended the integral role of Judaism and its scriptures, even though the law was said to be abolished in the new dispensation. According to Tertullian, Judaism retains its prophetic significance of leading us to the Gospel, and thus "our building (i. e., the church) is to stand in Christ upon the foundation of the ancient prophets."[40] A linkage to the history of the Jews via the Old Testament provided Christians with an argument against pagan criticisms of their recent appearance.[41] It also lent credibility to the Christian insistence that the new order under Christ was a fulfillment of prophecies uttered ages before. The success of making this contention was especially important since religious pagans also placed much emphasis on the authority of prophetic sayings and oracles.[42]

Marcion's View of the Old Testament

Turning to Marcion, we find a very different approach to the relationship of old and new covenants. It is universally acknowledged by anti-Marcionite writers that for Marcion the Old Testament provided no preparation for the Gospel brought by Christ. The redeemer God, the Father of Jesus, is wholly distinct from and even unknown to the creator god of the Old Testament. Thus, Marcion would never have agreed with Irenaeus, that "the writings of Moses are the words of Christ." Revelation of the unknown God, for Marcion, came only through the manifestation of Christ, whose appearance in this world was unexpected and unheralded. As son of the alien God, Jesus had no association with the creator god and his world, nor with the written testimonies of the law and the prophets. For Marcion, the Old Testament contained no element of *praeparatio evangelica* because the creator God was not even aware of the Supreme and Good God, and thus could not inspire prophecy about his forthcoming deeds.[43] In sum, the revelation brought by Christ was not intended to supplant or fulfil Judaism, but to displace it entirely; the one had no connection with the other.

It was this radical discontinuity between Gospel and the Hebrew scriptures which scandalized Catholic Christians, not merely for theological reasons, but because such a discontinuity was problematic for those who wished to remain contiguous with, yet also act as transformers of contemporary culture. Marcionism had no interest in transformation. It insisted on a clean break between the past and the present, cutting apostolic Christianity off from any mooring in tradition or antiquity. A small but insightful illustration of this separation may be found in Marcion's (expurgated) *Gospel of Luke*, where Jesus' words in 5:39, "The old is good," are completely deleted. Religious novelty was not to be shunned, but highlighted as proof that the redeemer God had once and for all made himself known through Christ.

Christian apologists agreed with Marcion that Christ's advent represented a new age of redemption, for Tertullian writes in *De oratione* 1:

> [W]hatever had been in bygone days, has either been quite changed, as circumcision, or else supplemented, as the rest of the law; or else fulfilled, as prophecy; or else perfected, as faith itself. For the new grace of God has renewed all things from carnal to the spiritual, by superinducing the Gospel, the obliterator of the whole ancient bygone system.

But one finds here also the language of tension that did exist in the mind of the early church regarding the exact relation between the Old Testament and the apostolic writings. Marcion (and with him, Harnack) were eager to claim that the Gospel introduced a spiritual reign, and altogether obliterated the former works of the law. Yet this new dispensation of grace had been announced long before in the Old Testament by the Lord himself; how can Marcion claim the prophets are from another god than the God of the Gospel, asks Irenaeus, if the whole life and all the doctrine and sufferings of the Lord were predicted through the prophets?[44] The novelty of redemption through Christ, therefore, was carefully linked to the prophetic past.

Confusion of Marcionites with Catholics
An even greater reason for concern among the Catholics, beyond the heretical teachings of Marcion, was the failure of non-Christian critics to distinguish Marcionites from Catholics. For example, Celsus, a pagan intellectual of the second century, epitomized the Christian position as claiming that Jesus was the only supra-human being to visit the human race. Celsus is said to have drawn this view from the followers of Marcion, though it really comes from Apelles, Marcion's more radical disciple. If, as Origen tells us in his refutation, Celsus was drawing on Marcionite sources, it would not be surprising that the pagan polemicist found reasons to claim that Christianity was a *new* phenomenon with the appearance of Jesus. Origen's reply, that according to the Old Testament many other supra-human creatures (i. e., angels) had visited the earth,[45] was an attempt to indicate continuity between angelic visits in the Old Testament and the appearance of Christ.

Origen realized that objections of Celsus against Christians were founded on Marcionite theology, which was not distinguished, he says, "from ours." He complains of Marcionite alterations of the gospel texts which are attributed to Christian "believers."[46] Marcion's cosmogony was used to describe the Christian interpretation of Genesis;[47] and he took issue with Celsus's critique of Marcion's theology as if it applied to the Catholic position.[48]

Origen's observations about Celsus are by no means unique. It appears that non-Christians regularly conflated Marcionite beliefs and practices with those of Catholics. After all, Marcion was the founder of a church which so resembled the liturgy and organization of Catholics that we hear Cyril of Jerusalem warning members of his flock not to wander into a Marcionite place of worship by mistake.[49] Yet, we would expect someone like Celsus, who was generally well informed about Christian and Gnostic doctrines,[50] to discriminate between the two; but he does so only in name,[51] whether out of ignorance or intentionally. This problem serves to confirm Justin's observation that in Rome Marcionites were called "Christians" by their pagan neighbors.[52] The fact that Marcionites were persecuted equally along with the Catholics would underline the point that the Roman authorities did not make any distinctions. Eusebius of Caesarea records several Marcionite martyrs during the Decian and Diocletian persecutions.[53] The "Anonymous" heresiologist in Eusebius's *Historia Ecclesiastica* V.16 tells us how those "who are called Marcionites, say that they had vast numbers who were martyrs for Christ."[54] It is significant that this writer, obviously a contemporary, does not attempt to dispute the claim but says only "They do not confess Christ in truth."

To what degree did the pagan confusion of "Catholicism" with Marcionism actually contribute to the charges of religious novelty laid against Christians? Given the evidence we have reviewed, there are sufficient grounds for believing that Marcionism presented a real danger to the standard Catholic position. A Marcionite faith would not have allowed Christians to claim that they were adherents of a tradition that went back to Moses. It would also have derailed a certain socio-cultural acceptability that Catholics were seeking in the eyes of those from whom they attempted to gain toleration.

Marcionism, on the other hand, was concerned with no such apologetics. Since redemption in Christ liberates believers from nothing less than the world itself,[55] it stands to reason that Marcionite theology demanded an explicit rejection of all concerns of cultural and social life; all of these represented the works of the creator. Marcionite baptism for instance, was not a washing away of sin, but a sacramental disavowal of the creator's world.[56] Marcionism was, in effect, a refusal to participate in the same cultural and philosophical presuppositions as the Catholics. Contemporary society had no value whatsoever, and this was undoubtedly the rationale for the extreme ascetic practices of Marcionite communities, whose ethic has been described as one of a life of protest.[57]

Conclusions

We have seen that Harnack's evaluation of the Old Testament in the development of early Christianity was much encumbered with his theological presuppositions about the role of Marcion as a reformer. Whatever role the Old Testament could have played as a *praeparatio evangelica* is vitiated because it encouraged Christian interpretation towards allegory and syncretism. Yet we have seen that the price of Marcion's solution to the problem of Hellenism was too high for the early church, since the surrender of the Old Testament would have, *inter alia*, undercut Christianity's apologetic claim to be a religion of tradition. Ironically, Harnack may well have been correct in accusing Catholicism of succumbing to Hellenist influences for at least one reason he does not mention: Catholic arguments for the preservation of the Jewish heritage were motivated, not only for its value as prophecy, but for the benefit of religio-cultural acceptance which Christians were eager to win in a hostile world. Surely this attitude too was a result of the "spirit" of Hellenism.

Notes

1. A. von Harnack, *History of Dogma*, trans. from the 3rd edition by N. Buchanan, vol. II (New York: Dover, 1961), 23.
2. *Marcion: The Gospel of the Alien God*, trans. from the 2nd German edition by John E. Steely and Lyle D. Bierma (Durham, NC: The Labyrinth Press, 1990), 14. All citations from Harnack's *Marcion* in the present article are from this translation. On the publication see below n.18.
3. D. L. Balas, "Marcion Revisited: A 'Post-Harnack' Perspective," in W. E. March, ed., *Texts and Testaments: Critical Essays on the Bible*

and the Early Church Fathers (San Antonio: Trinity University Press, 1980), 96.

4. *Marcion*, 134.

5. Ibid., 124.

6. S. G. Wilson, "Marcion and the Jews," in S. G. Wilson, ed., *Anti-Judaism in Early Christianity*; vol. 2: *Separation and Polemic* (Waterloo, Ont.: Wilfrid Laurier Press, 1986), 45-58.

7. For a general introduction to Marcion and Marcionism, consult J. Quasten, *Patrology* I. 268-72, *et passim*; E. C. Blackman, *Marcion and His Influence* (London: SPCK, 1948); R. M. Grant, *Gnosticism and Early Christianity* (New York: Columbia University Press, 1948), 122f. There is very little interest in Marcion among patristic scholars at present; this is reflected in the paucity of new studies. A recent full-scale examination of Marcionism by R. J. Hoffman, *Marcion: On the Restitution of Christianity* (Chico, CA: Scholars Press, 1984) appears to have subscribed to many of Harnack's theses about Marcion as a Paulinist.

8. *History of Dogma*, III, 287.

9. For an exploration of the definition of Hellenism and Hellenization, see William Rowe's article in this volume, pages 70f.

10. "The *gnōsis* which subjected religion to a critical examination awoke in proportion as religious life from generation to generation lost its warmth and spontaneity." "The Gnostics were not solely to blame for that. They rather show us merely the excess of a continuous transformation which no community could escape." *History of Dogma* II, 24-25.

11. *History of Dogma* III, 227.

12. Ibid., 258.

13. For Harnack's definition of "catholic," see *History of Dogma* II, 18, n.1. I shall use the term to refer to that part of the church often characterized as "orthodox," or traditional, mainline.

14. *Marcion*, 5. Cf. *History of Dogma* II, 25.

15. *History of Dogma* III, 225.

16. Ibid., II, 23.

17. *Marcion*, 12.

18. The first German edition was published by J. C. Hinrich in 1921, *Marcion, Das Evangelium von fremden Gott*. After this publication of *Marcion*, Harnack responded to criticisms raised by Walter Bauer, H. F. von Soden and others, in *Neue Studien zu Marcion* (= TU 44) (1923), and then issued a revised version of *Marcion* in 1924 (= TU 45) also published by J. C. Hinrich. This second edition was reprinted by Wissenschaftliche Buchgesellschaft (Darmstadt) in 1960.

19. Harnack believed Marcion truly did understand Pauline thought even if it was pushed to practical extremes in Marcion's application. In fact, Marcion (had he been generally accepted) considered himself able to purify the church of pharisaism, accomplishing a work which Paul was never able to realize. *History of Dogma* III, 283.

20. "Marcion, like Paul, felt that the religious value of a statutory law with commandments and ceremonies was very different from that of a uniform law of love." *History of Dogma* III, 69. Cf. *Marcion* ch. 3, for Harnack's stylization of Marcion as a Pauline reformer.

21. *Marcion*, 124.

22. As a reformer, Marcion believed that Paul preached a Gospel totally different from that of the original apostles, who had corrupted Jesus' original teachings. *Marcion*, 128.

23. Harnack has been much criticized for his view that the atemporal message of the Gospel can be distinguished from its social or intellectual environment so that one can discuss the "essence" (*Wesen*) of the Christian faith quite apart from its Jewish or Greco-Roman antecedents. See L. Michael White, "Adolf Harnack and the 'Expansion' of Early Christianity: A Reappraisal of Social History," *The Second Century* 5 (1985/86): 97-127.

24. Balas, "Marcion Revisited," 97f., briefly lists a number of areas in Harnack that require a thorough re-evaluation. See also B. Aland, "Marcion: Versuch einer neuen Interpretation", *Zeitschrift für Theologie und Kirche* 70 (1973): 420-47.

25. *The Gnostic Religion*, 2nd ed. (Boston: Beacon Press, 1963), 138. Cf. J. Quasten, *Patrology* I. 269; R. M. Grant, *Gnosticism and Early Christianity* (n.7), 25f.

26. *History of Dogma*, III, 267. For an analysis of the tenets of
Marcion compared to Gnosticism, see *Marcion*, 173, n.1. In the
History of Dogma (which seems to be more moderate in its account
of Marcion), Harnack admits some Gnostic influence on Marcion,
especially in shared characteristics such as the antithesis between
spirit and matter. However, such an antithesis was also shared by
Paul, and Marcion's position revealed his teaching to be religious in
nature, not a set of principles, which for Harnack meant the systematic cosmogony of Gnosticism (270-73).
27. *Marcion*, 133. "The question must be posed, for we are confronted not by some theologian without a following or influence but
by the man who established the New Testament and created a great
church that flourished for centuries. He may rightly lay claim to the
honor of deserving to be taken seriously today" (134).
28. *Marcion*, 135. Harnack believed that the question of the status
of the Old Testament still confronts modern Protestantism. We
cannot, he says, accept Marcion's reasons for rejecting the Old
Testament as a "false" book, indeed we cannot reject the Old
Testament at all. "Rather, this book will be everywhere esteemed
and treasured in its distinctiveness and its significance (the
prophets) only when the canonical authority to which it is not
entitled is withdrawn from it" (138).
29. Ibid., 133.
30. Ibid., 134.
31. *Octavius*, 6.
32. Even the format of the *Octavius* is probably modeled on Cicero's
work; see the discussion of J. M. Ross, "Introduction," *The Nature
of the Gods* (London: Penguin Books, 1972), 53.
33. Tacitus, *Annales* V. 5: "Jewish worship is vindicated by its
antiquity."
34. C. J. De Vogel, "Platonism and Christianity: A Mere Antagonism
or a Profound Common Ground," *Vigiliae Christianae* 39 (1985):
9-10.
35. 1 *Apol., 59-60.*
36. *Ad Autolycum* II., 23.

37. Ibid., II, 29.

38. *Apology*, 6. Cf. Pseudo-Justin, *Cohortatio ad Graecos*, is thought to have been written no earlier than the third century. Chapters 8-12 are devoted to the task of showing the antiquity of Christian teachers and writers since Moses "was our first religious teacher" and the Greek writers were dependent on him.

39. *Contra Celsum* I. 34.

40. *Adversus Marcionem* V. 2, 17.

41. *Apology*, 6. The pagan Celsus argued that Christians have no authority for their doctrines because Christianity lacks the approval of antiquity. *Contra Celsum* III. 14; V. 33; V. 65.

42. Cf. Balbus's speech in *De natura deorum* showing the significance of prophecies (c. 10-12); on Celsus' high regard for oracles, cf. *Contra Celsum* VII. 2; VIII. 45.

43. *Marcion*, 79.

44. *Adv. Haer.* IV. 34.1.

45. *Contra Celsum* V. 54.

46. Ibid., II. 27.

47. Ibid., VI. 52. Cf. "After this, as if he [Celsus] were addressing us who believe that this world is the creation of some alien and strange God. . ." (VI. 53).

48. Ibid., VI. 74.

49. *Cat.* 18. 26. Marcionites also practised signing on the foreheads, used the sacraments (with water instead of wine), and had a hierarchical structure similar to that of Catholics. Tertullian, *Adv. Marc.* 3, 22; *De praescr.* 41.

50. H. Chadwick, trans., *Origen: Contra Celsum* (Cambridge: University Press, 1953), pp. xxviii-xixx.

51. *Contra Celsum* V. 62. From his perspective, Celsus was not incorrect in portraying Marcionism as another faction within Christianity.

52. 1 *Apol.*, 26.

53. R. S. Wilson, *Marcion: A Study of a Second-Century Heretic* (London: SPCK, 1933), 73-74.

54. It is of interest also that Marcionite martyrs from Apamea on the Menander viewed martyrs from Montanist communities as heretics and had no communion with them.
55. *Marcion*, 23.
56. Tertullian, *Adv. Marc.* I. 38.
57. A. Vööbus, "The History of Asceticism in the Syrian Orient," *CSCO* subsidia 14 (1958): 49.

The Acts of John: The Gnostic Transformation of a Christian Community

Paul G. Schneider

Adolf von Harnack described Gnosticism as "the acute secularising or Hellenising of Christianity," which included the rejection of Hebrew scripture and the adoption of a Platonic idealism.[1] Harnack's definition has been challenged by scholars who have pointed to the non-Hellenic (Babylonian and Iranian) elements and especially the Jewish roots of the various gnostic systems, and have argued against perceiving Gnosticism only as a Christian phenomenon or heresy.[2]

But Harnack might not have been entirely wrong, for the *Acts of John* (*AJn*) a second century account of the apostle's exploits in Asia Minor, might be a witness to a similar process. Through the diverse stories that its author had collected and redacted about John, the *Acts* introduces us to the beliefs and practices of a highly Hellenized Christian community from Egypt.[3] At an early stage in its transmission, the Johannine *Acts* and its community were transformed by the addition of a large and clearly gnostic interpolation (chaps. 94-102).[4] Thus, the *AJn* offers us a unique opportunity. By examining how the original author and community of the Johannine *Acts* understood their faith, and how it was changed by a later interpolator-redactor, we can see how this community developed into a form of Gnosticism, or left itself open to gnostic proselytizing.

The Christianity of the Acts of John

Conversion-Resurrection-Transformation

Like Apollos of Alexandria, the Egyptian author of the *AJn* did not know Christian baptism.[5] One of the most extraordinary features of the Johannine *Acts* is that none of John's converts were baptized, while all of them had been raised from the dead, whether they were physically dead or not.[6] For instance, the apostle resurrected a man who had been murdered by his son (chaps. 48-54). Despite being brought back to life, the father was not happy, because while he was dead he did not have to endure his son's abuse. John agreed with the man, that it would be better to remain dead than to be restored to his former life, but John reassured the father that he has raised him to a better life—the life of a Christian (52). That is the purpose of John's resurrections: not to return people to their former lives but to convert them and those who witnessed these miracles.[7]

That people would become Christians because an apostle performed a miracle is not entirely distinctive to the *AJn*. According to the *Acts of Andrew*, a proconsul and his household were baptized after Andrew created an earthquake (2), and "all believed and were baptized" when Andrew raised an Egyptian boy (3).[8] There is, however, an essential difference in the *AJn*. While in the other apocryphal *Acts* the focus is upon those who were led to believe and to convert because an apostle raised someone from the dead, in the Johannine *Acts* the focus is upon those who had been revivified, and little if any distinction is made between their "resurrection" and "conversion." Those who have been resurrected by John are already "converted," in that they have been given new lives as Christians. For some, their conversion appears automatic, while others need only accept their new lives.[9] This point is emphasized when our author informs his readers about one person who chose otherwise: Fortunatus, the steward of a Christian couple, Drusiana and Andronicus (chaps. 63-86).

Under Satan's influence, a certain Callimachus had fallen in love with Drusiana. Callimachus's friends told him that his love for Drusiana was folly, for not only was she married but, since she was a Christian, she was also celibate. But Callimachus did not heed his friends' advice and constantly pursued Drusiana, which so distressed her that she willed herself to death. The story does not end with Drusiana's death, however, because Callimachus was so dominated by his lust that he bribed Fortunatus to open Drusiana's tomb so he might have his way with her body. But before they could commit this crime, a snake bit Fortunatus—killing him—and terrified Callimachus into a "dead" faint.

Upon discovering the bodies on the following day, the apostle raised Callimachus, who told him that an angel, appearing as a beautiful young man, had said to him, "Callimachus, you must die in order to live."[10] Callimachus readily affirmed the angel's words, for the man he once was, was now dead. Like the murdered father, Callimachus had not returned to his previous life, but to the true life of a Christian. The apostle then revivified Drusiana, who in turn raised Fortunatus. But, to everyone's surprise, Fortunatus vehemently rejected his resurrection, and eventually died again from the serpent's bite. So it was not enough to be raised physically from the dead. One must be spiritually raised as a Christian, and accept this new life. For our author and his community, that is the true resurrection.[11] And, one wonders if the Ephesians 5:14 citation from an earlier Christian hymn may indicate the background of the *Acts'* resurrection-conversion motif.

Christian Life
John's converts are not only remarkable because of the manner in which they became Christians, but also for the stability of their souls. According to the *Acts'* author, the true Christian lives vigorously, soberly and unhindered by all the things that cause emotional distress (chaps. 68-69). And, our author demonstrates this Christian ideal with a set of positive and negative examples: Cleopatra and Lycomedes (chaps. 19-24). When John first met Cleopatra she was in a coma. Lycomedes, her husband, was so distraught over his

wife's condition that he lost control of himself and became "lifeless" (ἄπνους). When John raised Cleopatra, she immediately asked about her husband. But, before showing her Lycomedes' body, John ordered Cleopatra not to become upset about her husband's condition, but to keep her soul "immovable" (ἀκίνητον) and "unwavering" (ἀμετάτρεπτον) (23). And despite her anguish, Cleopatra obeyed the apostle; following his instructions, she raised Lycomedes from the "dead," and thus exemplified what it meant to be a Christian for the *Acts* community.

From this episode and others,[12] it appears that for the author and the community of the *AJn*, a (true) Christian was one whose soul had become immovable to one's passions.[13] Thus, our author's concept of a Christian is very similar to Philo's description of immovable persons[14] such as Abraham and Moses, who remained unmoved by their emotions, even in the presence of God (Gen. 18:22; Deut. 5:31). According to Philo, emotional stability is the hallmark of a wise person, for,

> ... the mind of the Sage, released from storms and wars, with calm still weather and profound peace around it, is superior to men, but less than God. For the human mind of the common sort shakes and swirls under the force of chance events, while the other, in virtue of its blessedness and felicity, is exempt from evil. The good man indeed is on the border-line, so that we may say, quite properly, that he is neither God nor man, but bounded at either end by the two, by mortality because of his manhood, by incorruption because of his virtue (*On Dreams* 2.229-230).[15]

Philo's blurring of the sage's humanity is intriguing because the apostle's humanity is also somewhat obscured in the *AJn*. The *Acts* portrays John as God's intermediary, through whom the Lord reveals his power and mercy. Yet there are times when the *Acts'* description of the apostle hints at his being divine, himself.[16] Like Philo's wise man, John is human, yet something more.

At the other end of the spectrum are those persons who are controlled by their emotions (*On Preliminary Studies* 59). According to Philo, it is characteristic of such a person to be:

> . . . ever moving contrary to right reason, and to be averse to rest and quietness, and never to plant himself firmly and fixedly on any principle. He has one set of views at one time, another set at another, and sometimes holds conflicting views about the same matters, though no fresh element has been introduced into them. He becomes great and small, foe and friend, and nearly every other pair of opposites in a moment of time (*On the Posterity and Exile of Cain* 24-25).[17]

For Philo, Cain was the prototype of the unstable person because he deliberately blinded the eyes of his soul (*On the Posterity and Exile of Cain* 21, cf. 22-23). The emotional Lycomedes is the prototype in the *AJn*.[18] By contrast, Cleopatra, like Philo's wise person, has stilled the swelling and tossing of her soul (cf. *Allegorical Interpretation* II.90). Thus, although Cleopatra and Lycomedes faced the same predicament—a "lifeless" spouse—they reacted differently. While the frenetic Lycomedes could only faint (die), the immovable Cleopatra was able to raise her husband from the dead. So, Cleopatra, too, is now something more than human for she can raise someone from the dead.[19]

The Christology of the Acts of John

The Johannine *Acts* identifies Christ as the "God of all Ages," who is "exceedingly great," "incomprehensible" (79), "invincible" (104), immutable (104), but also polymorphic! Throughout the *Acts*, the Lord (κύριοs is the preferred title) appears in various human guises but never with a human body.[20] The Lord never closes his eyes (89) or eats (93); nor does he leave any footprints (93). An important feature of the *Acts'* polymorphic Christology is introduced in its account of the calling of James and John:

For when he had chosen Peter and Andrew, who were brothers, he came to me and to my brother James, saying "I need you; come with me!" And my brother said this to me, "John, what does he want, this child on the shore who called us?" And I said, "Which child?" And he answered me, "The one who is beckoning to us." And I said "This is because of the long watch we have kept at sea. You are not seeing straight, brother James. Do you not see the man standing there who is handsome, fair and cheerful looking?" But he said to me, "I do not see that man, my brother. But let us go, and we will see what this means."

And when we had brought the boat to land we saw how he also helped us to beach the boat. And as we left the place, wishing to follow him, he appeared to me again as rather bald(-headed) but with a thick flowing beard, but to James as a young man whose beard was just beginning (chaps. 88-89).[21]

Eric Junod and Jean-Daniel Kaestli have claimed an Egyptian origin for the Lord's polymorphism.[22] As Horus manifested himself as an infant, a young man, a man and an old man to express his eternity and absolute permanence, so does the *Acts'* Lord. But, while the *Acts'* Christology might have its roots in ancient Egyptian religion, the importance of this story is that the Lord appeared in two pairs of *contrasting* forms. And, with James always seeing younger forms of the Lord, as compared to those witnessed by John, it is easy to see the two brothers representing two groups of Christians, with John representing those who have a more mature Christology or spirituality.[23] This division between Christians does not entail hostility, because James's visions of the Lord are not incorrect, just younger than those seen by John. That John and James are brothers should not be overlooked, for both brothers (i. e., both communities) were called by the Lord. Plus, with James and John seeing progressively older manifestations of the Lord, the spirituality of both groups of Christians should be seen as maturing.[24]

Salvation
The surviving chapters of the original *AJn* only once refer to the Lord as Savior (108). And, when the apostle and others celebrated the Eucharist (chaps. 85; 108-109), no mention was made of the Lord's passion and death. This is not very surprising, since the *Acts'* community believed that the Lord never had a body. Whatever significance these Christians saw in Christ's death, it is unlikely that salvation was a part of it. So, we are left with a mystery: how did these Christians understand salvation and Christ's role in it?[25]

The Gnosticism of the Acts of John
The author of the *AJn* has left us with several questions. (1) How did the community of the Johannine *Acts* continue the apostle's method of conversion?[26] (2) How did the *Acts'* author and his community view salvation?[27] (3) Who was the Lord's heavenly twin? (4) Finally, in the *AJn* we find a Christian community that is more at home with Philo and Platonic thought. Despite the parallels with Philo, the Christians of the Johannine *Acts* have long ago severed their ties (if any) with Judaism.[28] There is not the slightest trace of Jewish scripture in the *Acts*, and allusions to "New Testament" writings are restricted to the *Acts'* versions of the calling of James and John and the transfiguration.[29] So, in what direction is this form of Christianity heading?

An unknown Christian gnostic answered these questions by injecting into the *AJn* the material that became chapters 94-102. According to these chapters, Jesus had initiated his disciples into a secret sacrament before his arrest,[30] and appeared to John in a cave at the Mount of Olives *during* the crucifixion.[31] In this cave, the Lord introduced John to a luminous, supernatural cross, which he (now a disembodied voice) identified as "Logos," "Jesus," "Christ," "Son," "Spirit," "Father" and "Grace" (98). The apostle saw people surrounding this Cross of Light and another group within it. Those outside the cross were identified by the Lord as belonging to the cosmic-demonic forces (98). Those within the cross are described as having a similar likeness, for according to the Lord, " . . . when human nature is taken up, and the race that comes to me [i. e., the Lord] and obeys my voice, then he who now hears me shall be united with this (race) and shall no longer be what he now is, but (shall be) above them as I am now. For so long as you do not call yourself mine, I am not what I am; but if you hear me, you also as hearer shall be as I am. . ." (100).[32] Salvation, therefore, according to our interpolator, is the ascension and transformation of the *Acts'* immovable Christians into members of a spiritual race who resemble the Lord.

Our interpolator's concept of salvation might not have been totally alien to the original author of the *Acts* or his community. They knew of a time (92) when Jesus had been visited by someone who had descended from heaven. This supernatural being, who resembled the Lord, said, "Jesus, those whom you have chosen still disbelieve you." Jesus agreed, "You are right; for they are human." Does this mean that the disciples will never believe; or will they become something other than human? If this is true then both the *AJn* and Origen associate the Lord's or the Logos's polymorphism with a change in Christians.[33] We don't know how the *Acts'* community first answered these questions, but our gnostic interpolator's answer was a definite "yes," for according to him, this transformation was accomplished by the sacrament—a mystery rite—that Jesus had instituted in the Upper Room (chaps. 94-96). Those who participated in the Lord's mystery received his *gnōsis* and became members of the Lord's kindred (συγγενής), a spiritual race that bears his image and likeness (chaps. 100-101).[34]

Expectations and Results
From what we have observed in the original chapters of the *AJn*, it might not have been all that hard for the *Acts* community to accept the interpolator's revision (and progression?) of their faith.[35] The *Acts* had described the apostle's converts as those who had been spiritually resurrected. The interpolator saw, and the *Acts'* readers would now see in these resurrections their spiritual rebirth and transformation into the Lord's kindred. Cleopatra, the *Acts'* ideal

Christian, whose transformed soul remained immovable in the face of adversity and grief, became the Gnostic who had been transformed as a member of the Lord's ·spiritual race. The apostle's account of the Lord being visited by a heavenly twin would stand out, for not only would the *Acts* community identify him as a member of the Lord's kindred, whose members are identical to the Lord, but it would also identify him as that which they were to become by participating in the Lord's mystery rite. The existence of this esoteric sacrament also might not have been a great surprise, for when the apostle cursed Satan because of Fortunatus, he mentioned a "resurrection to God"(ἀνάστασις πρὸς θεόν) along with fastings, prayers, holy washing, Eucharist, *agape* meals, and funerals.[36] The *Acts'* interpolator could have understood or wanted the *Acts'* readers to see this phrase as an allusion to the Lord's secret sacrament; a conclusion that the members of the *Acts* community could have easily reached on their own (if they had not already done so).

The result of our Gnostic inserting his material into the *Acts* was even more profound, for he transformed its community's faith into something very similar to both Valentinian[37] and Sethian Gnosticism. The combination of the *Acts'* Christology, with its division between mature and immature Christians with the interpolation's transformation motif, creates something quite similar to the *Gospel of Philip* (*Gos. Phil.*). Like the Lord of the *AJn*, this gospel's Jesus "did not reveal himself in the manner [in which] he was, but it was in the manner in which [they would] be able to see him. . ." (II,3, p. 57, 28f.). Again like the Johannine *Acts*, the *Gos. Phil.* also divides Christians into two groups, for "[He revealed himself] to the great as great. He [revealed himself] to the small as small."[38] In the Johannine *Acts* this scheme is illustrated in its account of the calling of James and John (chaps. 88-89), but also in its version of the transfiguration (90). According to the *AJn*, Jesus transformed himself into a supernatural giant, whose head reached the heavens. When John saw this manifestation of the Lord, he became afraid and doubted. The Lord responded to John's change of heart by becoming a small man. Thus, the Lord revealed himself to John as great, when John was great in faith. When John was small in faith, the Lord also became small.

Both the *Gos. Phil.* and the interpolated *AJn* contain a transformation motif. Like the participants of the Lord's secret sacrament, the Christians of the *Gos. Phil.* become Christ (II,3, p. 61, 21f.). For the community of the *AJn*, they could see in John's actions the result of such a transformation. In chapter 88, John tells those with him, "I must adapt myself to your hearing and according to each man's capacity"[39] about the Lord's polymorphism. John's statement is reminiscent of the *Gos. Phil.*'s Jesus appearing in forms appropriate for his audience's ability to understand and the *Acts'* Lord appearing in forms that, at least, reflect one's spiritual maturity. Why would the apostle mimic the Lord? Our gnostic interpolator provides the answer: John has already become one of the Lord's kindred (100). Now that he is like the Lord, John also must conform himself to his audience's level of comprehension. It is only by doing so that John's audience will understand his stories about the Lord's polymorphism, which are (now) the first step toward their becoming the "transformed hearers" of the revelatory discourse (101).[40]

The parallels between the *AJn* and Valentinianism are striking,[41] but so are the similarities to Sethian Gnosticism. The combination of the *Acts'* immovable soul and the interpolation's spiritual race is very similar to what we find in Sethian Gnosticism, and as particularly expressed in the *Apocryphon of John* (*Ap. John*). The *Apocryphon*'s savior informs our apostle about an immovable race[42] that is made up of those who have accepted the salvific *gnōsis* and have perfected themselves by transcending their passions. By keeping their focus on the "incorruption," they can endure the instability of the created world. These people will be saved immediately, and join the seed of the heavenly Seth on the third eternal realm (Daueithei; II,1, p. 25, 24-26, 6).

The *Apocryphon*'s description of the immovable race closely corresponds to the *Acts'* characterization of the "true" Christian as being a member of a class of immovable humans who have transcended their passions by their being spiritually resurrected from the dead.[43] Whereas the members of the *Apocryphon*'s immovable race live "without anger or envy or jealousy or desire and greed of everything" (25, 30-32), the author of the Johannine *Acts* describes the Christian soul as one that has "had the constancy not to be set on fire by filthy pleasure, not to yield to indolence, not to be ensnared by love of money, not to be betrayed by the vigor of the body and by anger" (69).[44] And, while the *Apocryphon*'s readers know that they will dwell on the third eternal realm and be joined with the immovable race of the heavenly Seth, the readers of the interpolated *AJn* are to believe they will ascend and join the Lord's spiritual race in the Cross of Light, if they participate in the Lord's mystery.[45]

For both the interpolated *AJn* and Sethian Gnosticism, membership in such a supernatural race is not predetermined.[46] According to the *Gospel of the Egyptians (Gos. Eg.)*, membership in the immovable race is open to those who are pure and worthy, and who have carried out the proper rites ("the begetting of Seth's seed"; III,2, p. 59, 9-61, 2; 63, 4-64, 3).[47] For the Sethians, baptism(s) was (were) the predominant form of the ritual by which one became a member of Seth's immovable race.[48] For the community of the interpolated Johannine *Acts*, membership in the Lord's supernatural race was made possible by participating in his mystery.[49] Thus, everyone has the potential to be saved—to become one of Seth's children or a member of the Lord's kindred.[50]

Conclusions
Whether or not our interpolator had been a Valentinian or a Sethian, or a member of the *Acts* community,[51] we can see why the Johannine *Acts* would have been so inviting to him, but also how receptive the *Acts* community would have been to his efforts. Through stories that had once circulated independently, the author of the *AJn* has revealed a Christian community that, true to Harnack's view of early Christianity, had discarded Hebrew scripture and visualized their faith as almost a Platonic ideal. Their resurrection- conversions,[52] their immovable souls, their Christology and even their opinion of other Christians, all have suggested

the presence of gnostic thought or a development toward some form of Gnosticism. But, it was the addition of chapters 94-102 that ultimately resulted in, or completed, the evolution of their beliefs. Our Gnostic's interpolation cast a new light on the very same episodes that these Christians knew so well and revealed the truth (the *gnōsis*) that lay behind them. In fact, the combination of the *Acts'* original stories with the interpolator's sacrament and revelatory discourse present such a cohesive presentation that one could almost imagine the *Acts'* author to have compiled and reworked the various stories about John to be a solid foundation from which the interpolator could work. And, with his "help" (or as demonstrated by his interpolation) these Christians saw the fulfilment of their faith in the Lord's salvific *gnōsis* and membership in his spiritual race. By participating in the Lord's mystery, not only will these Christians transcend all passions, but as members of the Lord's kindred, their unwavering and tranquil souls will also be indestructible to the cosmic forces that would prevent them from ascending to the luminous cross. Thus, for those who accepted the interpolator's addition and participated in the Lord's mystery rite, both they and their faith were changed forever.

Notes

1. A. von Harnack, *History of Dogma*, 4 vols., 3rd ed., N. Buchanan, trans. (Gloucester, MA: Peter Smith, 1961), 1:227-29.
2. R. Reitzenstein, *Hellenistic Mystery-Religions: Their Basic Ideas and Significance*, J. E. Steely, trans. (Pittsburgh: The Pickwick Press, 1978); *Poimandres: Studien zur griechisch-ägyptischen und frühchristlichen Literatur* (Leipzig: B. G. Teubner, 1904); W. Bousset, *Hauptprobleme der Gnosis* (Göttingen: Vandenhoeck & Ruprecht, 1907); R. M. Grant, *Gnosticism and Early Christianity*, 2nd ed. (New York: Harper & Row, 1966). Also C. Schneider, *Geistesgeschichte des antiken Christentums* (Munich: Beck, 1954), 1: 268 places Gnosticism within the history of late Platonism.
3. Asia Minor has usually been identified as the *Acts'* place of origin because it focuses upon John's activities in that area (E. g., K.

Schäferdiek, "Acts of John," in *New Testament Apocrypha*, E. Hennecke and W. Schneemelcher, eds.; R. McL. Wilson, trans. and ed. (Philadelphia: Westminster, 1965), 2: 214. However, the *Acts'* author betrays no knowledge of Asia Minor. An Egyptian origin is more likely because of the parallels between the *Acts* and the Alexandrian Origen (see nn.24 and 32 below) and Philo (see n.27 below). Also, "Clement of Alexandria, *Adumbrationes*," O. Stählin, ed., *Clemens Alexandrinus, Die griechischen christlichen Schriftsteller der ersten drei Jahrhunderte*, 2nd ed., Ludwig Früchtel (Berlin: Akademie, 1970), 3:210 is the only witness to the Johannine *Acts'* tradition about the Lord's polymorphism. E. Junod and J.-D. Kaestli, *Acta Iohannis*, Corpus Christianorum, Series Apocryphorum (Turnhout: Brepols, 1983), 2:692-94 present other arguments for an Egyptian origin. As for its date of composition, the *Acts'* theological and literary character suggests a dating between 150-200.

Before going further, it might be wise for me to clarify what I mean by the phrase, "highly Hellenized." I have used this phrase, for the lack of a better expression, to describe a Christian community whose members have abandoned the Jewish heritage of their religion for that of Platonism. It is not that they interpret their faith by means of Platonism, but that being a Christian meant to them being a participant in the stability of the Transcendent. See n.13 below.

4. The identification of chapters 94-102 as a later addition to the *AJn* was first made by Junod and Kaestli (*Acta Iohannis*, 2:425-26; 466; 581-642). I have serious reservations about some of their arguments for identifying these chapters as an interpolation; cf. P. G. Schneider, *The Mystery of the Acts of John* (Lewiston: Mellen Research University Press, 1991), 209-19; however, I also believe that chaps. 94-102 are a later addition to the text. Where I truly part company with Junod and Kaestli is over the previous history of this material, the question of why this material was placed in the *AJn*, and whether our interpolator could have been a member of the *Acts'* own community. It is beyond the limitations of this paper to discuss fully all the reasons and methods of our interpolator. See my paper

"Perfect Fit: The Major Interpolation in the *Acts of John*," in *1991 SBL Seminar Papers* (Atlanta: Scholars Press, 1991), 518-20.

5. It would be remiss of me not to mention a 1974 article by Junod and Kaestli, "Un fragment inédit des *Actes de Jean*: La guérison des fils d'Antipatros à Smyrne," *Museum Helveticum* 31 (1974): 96-104, in which they argue for replacing the episode of "John and the Partridge" (chaps. 56-57) with an account of the healing of Antipatros's two sons by the apostle; cf. Junod and Kaestli, *Acta Iohannis*, 1:75, 92-96. This story concludes with the apostle instructing the father and his sons concerning the Father, the Son and the Holy Spirit and then baptizing them. This in itself is problematic, for according to the Johannine *Acts*, Christ and God are one and the same, with no distinction between the Father and the Son. And, since Junod and Kaestli believe this episode had been altered to include the addition of the baptisms, the absence of baptism in the Johannine *Acts* is all the more conspicuous. Moreover, while our author never mentions baptism (neither βαπτίζω, βάπτισμα, nor βαπτισμός are mentioned in the *AJn*), he definitely knew about some sort of ritual washing (chap. 84).

6. In fact, the majority of those raised-converted from the "dead" were actually still alive, although they are described as "lifeless." There are also instances of what could be described as "mass resurrections." For example, those who witnessed the destruction of Artemis's temple in Ephesus (chaps. 37-44) confessed faith in John's god and prostrated themselves before the apostle. John then *raised them up* through prayer and speeches (cf. 46-47).

7. This is clearly the case with Lycomedes and Cleopatra (cc. 19-24), who were not resurrected for their own sake, but that God could convert those present: καταμαθόντες γὰρ τὴν δυναστείαν σου διὰ τοῦ ἐγηγέρθαι τοὺς ἀποψύξαντας σωθήσονταί τινες αὐτῶν, c.22. The resurrection of this couple is the "vehicle" by which others can be converted. This was also the reason for the miraculous healing of the elderly women of Ephesus (33). The Greek text of the *AJn* is that of M. Bonnet's *Acta Apostolorum Apocrypha*, vol. 2 (Hildesheim: Georg Olms Verlagsbuchhandlung, reprint 1959). The

English translation (with some modifications), is that of K. Schäferdiek's "Acts of John," in *New Testament Apocrypha* (n.3).

8. M. R. James, "Acts of Andrew," in *The Apocryphal New Testament* (Oxford: Clarendon Press, 1924), 338. And, in the *Acts of Peter*, the apostle is told by some converts that they had become Christians because Paul had raised people from the dead and had healed the sick (2:4; *Actus Vercellenses Aa*, I, 48; W. Schneemelcher, "The *Acts of Peter*," in *New Testament Apocrypha* (n.3), 2:283.

9. Thus it appears that the author and the community of the Johannine *Acts* did not know or, most likely, did not recognize Christian baptism as the way to become a member of their community. Our author, however, definitely knew about some sort of ritual washing (λουτρόν), which he has John mention along with other liturgical or sacramental practices (84). See nn.4 and 33.

10. "Καλλίμαχε, ἀπόθανε ἵνα ζήσῃς." (76).

11. The *Acts'* spiritual resurrection-conversions call into question the direction that its Christian community is taking. Tertullian, in his *Liber de Resurrectione Carnis* 19 (*Patrologia cursus completus: Series Latina*, Tomus Posterior, col. 865-66) clearly identified such a motif as gnostic. And C. L. Sturhan, in *Die Christologie der ältesten apokryphen Apostelakten* (unpublished Doctoral Dissertation, Göttingen, 1952, 46f.), argued that Gnosticism lies behind the *Acts'* motif, with these physical and spiritual resurrections illustrating the awakening of the one redeemed by *gnōsis*. Sturhan saw in Callimachus's fainting an external symbol of his bondage to the world of sensuality, that is, the world of death. His resuscitation therefore points to his redemption, as he sees through that former bondage and simultaneously recognizes his true purpose in life (ibid., 45). Sturhan also saw this motif behind the apostle ordering Lycomedes to awaken his soul, and to cast off the heavy sleep (21). Lycomedes had revealed his "unredeemed" status by accusing and challenging God, and by the sensuality that tied him to the pleasures of the transient world (ibid., 48). The theme of the Gnostic being asleep or drunk is well attested (*Concept of the Great Power*, NHC VI, 4, p. 39,33-40,4; *Apocryphon of John*, NHC II, 1, p. 21,15), and a Gnostic could understand the

Acts' resurrection-conversions in that light. Whether the members of the *Acts'* community originally understood their conversions in a similar fashion is an open question, although it might have been a small leap for them to adopt such an interpretation. Still, this motif is also found in the New Testament, especially Eph. 5:14, ". . . for it is light that makes everything visible. This is why it is said: 'Wake up, O sleeper, rise from the dead, and Christ will shine on you.' "

12. The *Acts'* ideal of the unwavering, tranquil and obedient soul is clearly present in the episodes about the resurrection of Artemis's priest (46-47); the fratricide (54), as well as in John's words to Lycomedes concerning the true Christian soul (29) and his speech at Drusiana's funeral (chaps. 67-69). Our author was also willing to emphasize this Christian ideal with a humorous story about bedbugs (chaps. 60-61) that would have been familiar to his readers; (cf. Diodorus of Siculus, *The Library of History*, C. H. Oldfather, trans. (Cambridge, MA: Harvard University Press, 1961) 4.22, in vol. 2, 414; and Claudius Aelianus, *On the Characteristics of Animals*, A. F. Scholfield, trans., 3 vols. (Cambridge, MA: Harvard University Press, 1958), 3.37, in vol. 1, 198).

13. That the members of the *Acts* community seem to have envisioned themselves as having transcended movement and change suggests that they saw themselves as belonging to the Platonic realm of the immutable. According to our author, entrance into this realm is by one's spiritual (and at times also physical) resurrection from the dead. On this point, we have a curious parallel with the first century BCE *Axiochus*, in which the soul is described as having a sort of calm (after)life, untroubled by evils and at ease in immovable tranquillity in the world beyond death (370D). For the author and the community of the *AJn*, that "world beyond death" is Christianity.

14. According to Philo (*Mosis*, 1.158-59), Moses entered this Platonic realm when he climbed Mt. Sinai to receive the Torah. All references to Philo's writings are from the Loeb Classical Library, F. H. Colson and G. H. Whitaker, trans., 10 vols. (Cambridge, Mass.: Harvard University Press; 1929-1962). I am especially indebted to Michael Williams' study of this motif in his book, *The Immovable*

Race, A Gnostic Designation and the Theme of Stability in Late
Antiquity, Nag Hammadi Studies 29 (Leiden: E.J. Brill, 1985).
15. " ὅτι ἡ τοῦ σοφοῦ διάνοια χειμώνων μὲν καὶ πολέμων
ἀπαλλαγεῖσα, νηνέμῳ δὲ γαλήνῃ καὶ βαθείᾳ εἰρήνης χρωμένη
κρείττων μέν ἐστιν ἀνθρώπου, θεοῦ δὲ ἐλάττων. ὁ μὲν γὰρ
ἀγελαῖος ἀνθρώπειος νοῦς σείεται καὶ κυκᾶται πρὸς τῶν
ἐπιτυχόντων, ὁ δ   ἅτε μακάριος καὶ εὐδαίμων ἀμέτοχος κακῶν·
μεθόριος δὲ ὁ ἀστεῖος, ὡς κυρίως εἰπεῖν μήτε θεὸν αὐτὸν εἶναι
μήτε ἄνθρωπον, ἀλλὰ τῶν ἄκρων ἐφαπτόμενον, ἀνθρωπότητι
μὲν θνητοῦ γένους, ἀρετῇ δὲ ἀφθάρτου. " (De Somnii 2.229-30).
16. For instance, Lycomedes had a portrait secretly made of John
(chaps. 26-29). When the portrait was finished, Lycomedes placed
an altar before it, so that he and others could pray before it (worship
the apostle?). When John discovered the painting, he believed it was
the portrait of a god and chided Lycomedes for committing idolatry
(27). When Lycomedes told John that the portrait was of him, the
apostle did not then rebuke Lycomedes for worshipping him as a
god. For John, the problem with the portrait was that the painting
only records the apostle's physical resemblance. Yet, the lack of a
rebuke against worshipping an apostle as a god suggests a distinctive
understanding of the role of apostle. One could argue that the Acts'
readers were to assume that Lycomedes was rebuked for worshipping the apostle as a god. Yet, the absence of such a criticism is
startling in comparison to incidents in other apocryphal Acts. For
example, according to the Acts of Peter (8:29; Actus Vercellenses, Aa
I, 78), Peter, too, had been venerated as a god after he raised a child
from the dead. But, while the Petrine Acts does not mention Peter
criticizing such veneration, it did emphasize his humanity, with the
apostle, himself, stating, "You men of Rome, seeing that I too am
one of you, wearing human flesh, and a sinner, but have obtained
mercy, do not look at me, as though by my own power I were doing
what I do; (the power is) my Lord Jesus Christ's. . ." (8:28; Actus
Vercellenses, Aa I, 74-75). No such statement is found in the Johannine Acts. Furthermore, the apostle's initial reaction to learning that
the portrait was of himself was to exclaim, "Παίζεις με τέκνον

τοιοῦτός εἰμι τῇ μορφῇ τὸν κύριόν σου " (28). The apostle's comment has not been well preserved, but from what has survived, it is possible to see the apostle admitting a resemblance to the Lord. If he did, then the apostle's humanity has been further obscured by his physical resemblance to the Lord.

17. "...αἰεὶ παρὰ τὸν ὀρθὸν λόγον κινούμενος ἠρεμίᾳ καὶ ἀναπαύσει δυσμενὴς εἶναι καὶ ἐπὶ μηδενὸς ἑστάναι παγίως καὶ ἐρηρεῖσθαι δόγματος. ἄλλοτε δοῦν ἀλλοῖα δοξάζει καὶ περὶ τῶν αὐτῶν ἔστιν ὅτε μηδενὸς περὶ αὐτὰ συμβεβηκότος καινοτέρου τἀναντία, μέγας καὶ μικρὸς καὶ ἐχθρὸς καὶ φίλος καὶ πάνθ᾽, ὡς ἔπος εἰπεῖν, τὰ μαχόμενα ἐν ἀκαρεῖ χρόνου γινόμενος" (*De Posteritate Caini* 24-25).

18. The *Acts'* parricide (chaps. 48-54) would be another example, for Lycomedes' emotional instability resulted in murder and self-castration. It was only when he became *quiet* that he was truly able to repent and become a Christian.

19. Perhaps John's prayer in c. 114 has a similar division in mind: " δεξιοὶ τόποι στηκέτωσαν, ἀριστεροὶ μὴ μενέτωσαν. "

20. Not only does the Lord change his appearance, he can also alter the consistency of his "body" from hard to soft (89), material to immaterial (93). The Lord never closes his eyes (89) or eats (93); nor does he leave any footprints (93).

21. " ὅτε γάρ ἐξελέξατο Πέτρον καὶ Ἀνδρέαν ἀδελφοὺς ὄντας, ἔρχεται πρός με καὶ τὸν ἀδελφόν μου Ἰάκωβον εἰπών· Χρήζω ὑμῶν, ἔλθατε πρός με. Καὶ ὁ ἀδελφός μου τοῦτο εἶπεν· Ἰωάννη, τὸ παιδίον τοῦτο ἐπὶ τοῦ αἰγιαλοῦ καλέσαν ἡμᾶς τί βούλεται; Κἀγὼ εἶπον· Ποῖον παιδίον; Ὁ δέ μοι πάλιν· Τὸ νεῦον ἡμῖν. Κἀγὼ ἀπεκρινάμην· Διὰ τὴν πολλὴν ἡμῶν ἀγρυπνίαν τὴν κατὰ θάλασσαν γεγονυῖαν οὐ σὺ ὁρᾷς ἀδελφέ μοῦ Ἰάκωβε; οὐχ ὁρᾷς δὲ τὸν ἑστῶτα ἄνδρα εὔμορφον καλὸν ἱλαροπρόσωπον; Ὁ δέ μοι εἶπεν· Τούτου οὐχ ὁρῶ ἀδελφέ· ἀλλ᾽ ἐξέλθωμε καὶ ὀψόμεθα τὸ τί βούλεται.

Καὶ οὕτως σιγῇ τὸ πλοῖον ἀγαγόντες εἴδομεν καὶ αὐτὸν ἅμα ἡμῖν βοηθοῦντα ὅπως τὸ πλοῖον ἑδράσωμεν. ὡς δὲ ἀπέστημεν τοῦ τόπου αὐτῷ βουληθέντες ἕπεσθαι, πάλιν ὤφθη ἐμοὶ ὑπόψιλον ἔχων, τὸ δὲ γένειον δασὶν καταγόμενον, τῷ δὲ

'Ιακώβῳ ἀρχιγένειος νεανίσκος. ὑποροῦν μὲν οὖν ἀμφότεροι ὅ τι βούλεται τὸ ὁραθὲν ἡμῖν " (cc. 88-89).

22. Junod and Kaestli, *Acta Iohannis*, 2:470f.; E. Junod, "Polymorphie du Dieu sauveur," in J. Ries, ed., *Gnosticisme et le monde hellénistique*, Publications de l'Institut Orientaliste de Louvain 27 (Louvain-la-Neuve: Institut Orientaliste, 1982), 41f.

23. This division between "mature" and "immature" Christians also appears in the *Acts'* portrayal of Peter, James and John after the transfiguration (91). Peter and James are somewhat vexed with John because he is talking with the Lord. They are also confused about what had happened, for they want to know who was speaking with the Lord. This question is puzzling, because we know from the *Acts'* account that only John and the Lord were on the mountaintop. Yet, Peter and James ask John who was talking with the Lord. Wouldn't they have recognized John's voice? Why didn't John admit that the only other voice was his? It is possible that the divine voice was originally present in this version of the transfiguration, but our author deleted it because, according to his Christology, the Lord would be talking to himself. Why, then, didn't our author also omit their question? It is because he wanted to contrast Peter's and James' perplexity to John's growing awareness of the Lord's identity.

24. Origen (*Contra Celsum* 2.64) similarly claimed that the Logos did not appear in like fashion to all who saw him, but according to each disciple's power of perception, and is therefore capable of an apparently unlimited number of transformations. These levels of capacity are not static, because as a Christian matures, the Logos's form also progresses (4.15-16). Thus, for Origen, the Logos's polymorphism is a tool by which everyone, no matter what their capability, can receive and understand him at their own level. This scheme of spiritual progress can be seen behind the *Acts'* account of the transfiguration (90). When the Lord appeared as a supernatural giant (representing the highest level of understanding so far reached by John), the apostle became afraid and doubtful. The Lord responded to John's lack of spiritual maturity by transforming him-

self into a small man. So John's shift in faith was visibly displayed by the Lord's transmutation from a *giant* to *small* man. References to Origen's *Contra Celsum* are from the *Patrologia cursus completus: Series Graeca*, vol. 11, J. P. Migne, ed. (Paris: Migne, 1857).

25. But if it is not by his death that salvation came to the world, aren't we left with one other alternative? Would it not have been by what he taught—his *gnōsis*? If this is what the community of the original *Acts* believed, then it would appear that these Christians were already taking the first step toward Gnosticism.

26. The *Acts* does contain stories of other Christians performing resurrections (e. g., Cleopatra, Drusiana), but did these resurrection-conversions continue after John had moved on to another town (or had died)? See n.33 below.

27. And what was their view of humanity in relation to their concept of salvation? With Callimachus and Fortunatus, one can see a division between those who accept their new lives as Christians (Callimachus) and those who do not (Fortunatus). But, John called Fortunatus the Devil's son (84), because of his "unbending soul" (ἀμετάθετον ψυχήν) and "unchanged nature" (φύσις ἀφύσικος, (c.84), and once mentioned "souls who are able to hope and be saved" (ψυχὰς δυναμένας ἐλπίσαι καὶ σωθῆναι, 23). All of this suggests an ontological division of humanity between those who can be saved (Callimachus) and those who cannot (Fortunatus). But if this is true, why did John rebuke Callimachus's opposition to resuscitating Fortunatus, and allow Drusiana to raise Fortunatus? What about John's brother James and the Christians he represents? Does their spiritual immaturity (as contrasted to John's) prevent them from being saved? The surviving chapters of the Johannine *Acts* do not offer a coherent understanding of humanity that answers all of these questions, but our interpolator might have done so (see n.51 below).

28. It might well be that our author did not even know Philo. The similarities that we have seen between these two Egyptian authors could lead one to conclude that our author knew at least some of Philo's writings. The author of the *AJn* evidently did not feel any restraint when it came to sources. He was perfectly willing, for example, to use stories that would have been familiar to those who had read Diodorus Siculus or Claudius Aelianus. So, it might have been quite simple for him to have added Philo as another source. But, his including a description of the Jews as "lawless" and their "lawgiver" (Moses) as a "lawless serpent" (94) makes it questionable as to whether he would have used a Jewish source. And, as Williams (*The Immovable Race*, [n.14], 8-34.) has clearly established, the theme of stability was one known by a large segment of the ancient world, and so it could well be that both our Egyptian authors reflect well-known concepts.

29. Despite the fact that the motif of God's immovable people can be found in Hebrew scripture (e. g., LXX Ps. 14:5; 15:8; 45:5f.; 61:3; 1 Chron. 16:30), and subtly appears in Heb. 12:25-28.

30. According to Mark 14:26 (cf. Matt. 26:30), Jesus and his twelve disciples sang a hymn after the Last Supper. This hymn was presumably the Hallel (Ps. 113-118) sung with the last cup of wine at the end of the Passover meal. But, according to our Gnostic's tradition (chaps. 94-96), Jesus had ordered those with him to hold hands and form a circle, and with himself in the middle they began to sing. As they were singing, the Lord performed a dance and commanded the disciples to join him in the dance. When they had finished dancing and singing, the Lord explained to the disciples what they had just experienced, ordered them to remain silent, and after a brief, final doxology, he left. Previous scholarship, although recognizing the fact that Jesus and the disciples had danced, had been chiefly interested in the hymnic material of these chapters and attempted to reconstruct a single hymn from it. The most notable reconstructions of the hymn or sacrament are: M. Brioso, "Sobre el 'Tanzhymnus' de Acta Iohannis 94-6," *Emérita* 40 (1972): 31-45; D. I. Pallas, "Ὁ ὕμνος τῶν πράξεων τοῦ Ἰωάννου κεφ. 94-97," in *Mélanges Octave et Melpo Merlier*, (Athènes: Institut Français, 1956) II.221-44. J. Schattenmann, *Studien zum neutestamentlichen Prosahymnus* (München: C. H. Beck, 1965), 97-100; Schneider, *Mystery of the Acts of John* (n.4), 147-60, 223-26.

31. The interpolator made use of the *Acts'* mature/immature motif in his account of the crucifixion, for the Lord appeared to John in a cave at the Mount of Olives during the crucifixion, while for those "below" he appeared on the cross (97). According to our interpolator, the crucifixion was only another one of the Lord's various manifestations, but also one that divides Christians between those whose understanding of the Lord stops with the crucifixion (the immature), and for those whose spirituality goes beyond (the mature). Thus, the interpolator's Lord can claim that he suffered and that he did not (chaps. 99, 101-102). Such a paradox is characteristic of some Valentinian works. The author of the *Gospel of Truth* can state that Jesus "was nailed to a tree," and affirm his "imperishability" (I,3, p. 20, 20-30; cf. p. 23, 33-24, 9). The *Tripartite Tractate* also declares the Savior, who "for their sake . . . became manifest in an involuntary suffering . . . ," but who is also the "eternally, and unbegotten, impassable Logos. . ." (I,5 113, 35-38). Yet, we are also reminded of Zostrianos referring to the one "who suffers although he is unable to suffer" (*Zost*, VIII,1, p. 48, 27). References to the *Gospel of Truth* and the *Tripartite Tractate* are from the translations by G. W. MacRae, H. W. Attridge and Dieter Mueller in *The Nag Hammadi Library In English*, J. M. Robinson, ed. (San Francisco: Harper & Row; Leiden: E. J. Brill, 1977). See Schneider, "Perfect Fit: The Major Interpolation in the *Acts* of John," 528-32, and *Mystery of the Acts of John*, 127-31, 220-22.

32. "ὅταν .... ἀναληφθῇ ἄνθρωποι φύσις καὶ γένος προσχωροῦν ἐπ᾽ ἐμὲ φωνῇ τῇ ἐμῇ πειθόμενον, ὃν νῦν ἀκούω με σὺ τοῦτο γενήσεται, καὶ οὐκέτι ἔσται ὃ νῦν ἔστιν. ἀλλ᾽ ὑπὲρ αὐτῶν ὡς κἀγὼ νῦν· μέχρι γὰρ μήπω ἴδιόν μου λέγεις ἑαυτὸν τοῦτο οὐκ εἰμὶ ὅ εἰμι· ἐὰν δέ με ἀκούσῃς, ἀκούων καὶ σὺ μένε ὡς κἀγώ..." (c.100).

33. According to Origen (*Contra Celsum* 6.68; see n.24), Christ also transforms his disciples so they may see his glorious form. However, for Origen, the transformed Christians remain human—just as Origen also affirms Christ's humanity(?)—whereas Jesus' reply in the Johannine *Acts* suggests that the disciples will become something other than human.

34. Schneider, *Mystery of the Acts of John* (n.4), 161-200.

35. Provided that he was not a member of the *Acts'* community at a later time. See nn. 48 and 50.

36. "καταργήθητι ... ἀπὸ ἀναστάσεως τῆς πρὸς θεόν· ἀπὸ εὐωδίας ἧς κοινωνεῖν μέλλεις· ἀπὸ νηστειῶν· ἀπὸ δεήσεων· ἀπὸ λουτροῦ ἁγίου· ἀπὸ εὐχαριστίας ... ἀπὸ ἀγάπης· ἀπὸ ἀκηδίας· ἀπὸ ἐγκρατείας..." (c.84). We should take note again that the author of the *AJn* never uses terms such as βάπτισμα or βαπτισμός, but instead refers to λουτρὸν ἅγιον. Curiously, the same holds true for the Lord's secret sacrament, in which the initiates claim that they want to be cleansed: λούσασθαι θέλω καὶ λούειν θέλω. R. H. Miller, "Liturgical Materials in the *Acts* of John," *Studia Patristica*, XIII, Papers presented to the Sixth International Conference on Patristic Studies held in Oxford, E. A. Livingstone, ed. (Berlin: Akademie, 1975), 378 has seen in John's statement a reference to Christian initiation, "resurrection to God" (ἀναστάσις πρὸς θεόν), with εὐωδία referring to prebaptism anointing; "fastings" (νηστεία) and "prayer"(δέησις) alluding to the preparation before the sacrament, and then the "holy washing" (λουτρόν ἁγίου): baptism itself. The "eucharist" (εὐχαριστία) completes the act of initiation. The main problem with Miller's interpretation is that the phrase, "resurrection to God" cannot be a reference to baptism, because John (and his community) does not baptize, but literally resurrects people to God. Thus, the phrase could simply mean "conversion," but the presence of this phrase in a list of sacraments and pious practices could be taken as evidence of these spiritual resurrections having taken some liturgical form. After all, if we see in the apostle's spiritual resurrection-conversions a reflection of the *Acts* community, then, how did one become a member after John's death and that of his converts?

37. Many scholars have seen Valentinianism or something akin to it behind these chapters (see Schäferdiek, "Acts of John" 2:212-14 and especially Junod and Kaestli, *Acta Iohannis* 581-632). Most scholars point to the mention of the Ogdoad and the "twelfth number" in the sacrament (See n.39 below), but especially to the Lord's description of the Cross of Light as the division of all things and the elevation of what is firmly fixed out of what is *unstable* (98). This function is identical with that of the Valentinian Stauros-Horos, which can be described as also separating "the All from what is created and inferior; what is firm and what is without foundation" (cf. Irenaeus *Adv. Haer.* 1.3.5). The Cross of Light was also responsible for the "harmonizing of wisdom," which naturally suggests that our interpolator's cosmogony is comparable to the Valentinians', with the Cross of Light, i. e., Christ, healing the errant aeon of her passions and re-establishing the order that her actions had disturbed. With the discourse's single reference to the harmonization of wisdom, one could deduce also a simple cosmogonic myth behind it, with a single Sophia being detached from the Pleroma and a single redemptive intervention by the Cross of Light. Such a myth would be close to Valentinus's teaching and the Oriental Valentinianism (Theodotus), which also present a single Sophia and a single redemptive intervention. However, in their systems the emission of the demiurge and of the powers of the left and the right occurred before Sophia had been healed of her passions, while our revelatory discourse has the order reversed (98). Thus, the revelatory discourse is closer to Ptolemy's system (Irenaeus, *Adv. Haer.* 1.5.1) in which the advent of these powers is a consequence of Sophia's restoration.

38. E. Pagels, "The Gospel of Philip" in *Documents for the Study of the Gospels*, D. R. Cartlidge and D. L. Dungan, eds. (Philadelphia: Fortress Press, 1980), 59-62.

39. " δεῖ με πρὸς τὰς ἀκοὰς ὑμῶν ἁρμόσασθαι, καὶ καθ᾽ ἃ χωρεῖ ἕκαστος ἐκείνῳ ὑμῖν κοινωνήσω ὧν ἀκροαταὶ δύνασθε γενέσθαι" (c.88).

40. There is also a possible parallel to the *Acts'* mystery rite: the Valentinian sacrament of redemption as described in the *Gos. Phil.* (II,3, p. 67,9-27). Both sacraments express the desire for resurrection, rebirth and restoration. Like the initiates of the *Acts'* mystery sacrament, the participants of this Valentinian sacrament are not only reborn and resurrected, they have also been empowered to return safely to the Pleroma (II,3, p. 74, 20f.; 86, 4-15). And, the Lord's secret sacrament does include the participation of the Ogdoad and the "twelfth number" (Dodecad?). Irenaeus (*Adv. Haer.* 1.21.1,3-5), who claims that the Valentinians had numerous versions of their sacrament of redemption, could have easily added the Johannine sacrament to his list. In fact, Junod and Kaestli (*Acta Iohannis*, 2:631) have done just that. Cf. *Excerpta ex Theodoto*, 80.1-3.

41. This is particularly true because the parallels are not always dependent on the interpolator. For instance, the *Acts'* Christology and division of mature and immature Christians is similar to the *Gos. Phil.*'s. Such parallels could be taken as evidence of the *Acts'* community moving toward Valentinianism or something like it.

42. The theme of the immovable race is also found in the *Three Steles of Seth* (*Steles Seth*), *Zostrianos* (*Zost.*), and the *Sophia of Jesus Christ* (*Soph. Jes. Chr.*). See Williams, *The Immovable Race* for a complete examination of this theme.

43. The revelatory discourse of *Ap. John* ends with a poem which includes the lines, "And *I raised him up* and sealed him in the light of the water with five seals, in order that death might not have power over him from this time on" (II,1 p. 31, 22-25). Thus, the members of this gnostic community, like the *Acts'*, have been *raised up* by the savior, who then baptizes them in opposition to death.

44. "..τὴν ὑπομείνασαν ὑπὸ ἡδονῆς ῥυπαρᾶς μὴ ἐκλυθῆναι, ὑπὸ ῥαθυμίας μὴ ἡττηθῆναι, ὑπὸ φιλαργυρίας μηδὲ δελεασθῆναι, ὑπὸ ἀκμῆς σώματος καὶ ὀργῆς μὴ προδοθῆναι" (c.69). Cleopatra and Drusiana would have been perfect examples for the apocryphon also. Despite the "lifeless" condition of her husband, Cleopatra's soul remained "unmoved and unwavering," and was therefore able to raise her husband from the "dead." Drusiana, like the apocryphon's immovable race (II,1, p. 25, 30), kept herself free from the contamination of sexual intercourse. Twice, she chose to die (chaps. 63-86), rather than have sex with her unconverted husband and Callimachus.

45. Furthermore, while the members of the apocryphon's immovable race can endure the instability of the created world, the *Acts'* transformed Gnostics must also endure whatever befalls them, particularly persecution: Schneider, "Perfect Fit: The Major Interpolation in the *Acts of John* (n.4)," 528-32, and *Mystery of the Acts of John*, 127-31, 220-22.

46. The apocryphon's savior does speak of the spiritual awakening of the Gnostic (II, 1 p. 22, 3-23, 35), which would seem to suggest that one cannot attain *gnōsis* or membership in the immovable race. But, the apocryphon also makes it clear that salvation or membership in the immovable race is not a birthright, but the result of personal initiative. According to the apocryphon, everyone possesses Seth's seed and the Spirit of life. But, while every human being possesses this seed, not everyone is receptive to the awakening *gnōsis* (see n.49 below. Those who became members of the immovable race did so because they *decided* to *become* perfect by overcoming their passions.

The interpolated *AJn* appears to take a similar stance. On the one hand, the *Acts'* Lord informs John that the crowd within the Cross of Light is not yet complete because, "not every one who has come down has been gathered again" (...οὐδέπω τὸ πᾶν τοῦ κατελθόντος συνελήφθη μέλος, c.100). This statement naturally suggests a predetermined number, but the Lord immediately states that those who are to be gathered up are to be transformed, which implies just the opposite. Furthermore, the Lord had instituted a sacrament so that people could become members of his spiritual kindred, something that would be unnecessary for members of a "predetermined" group.

47. Unlike the *Ap. John*, the *Gos. Eg.* maintains that everyone does not possess Seth's seed. According to Williams (*Immovable Race* (n.14), 164), the preexistence of the Seth's seed "means only that this mechanism for salvation, for spiritual begetting, already exists to be received by those who turn out to be worthy of it." The inclusiveness of the *Ap. John*, the *AJn* and the *Gos. Eg.* is also found in the *Steles Seth* and *Zost.* In the *Steles Seth* there is no suggestion of the immovable race being made up of predetermined individuals. For example, at the end of the first stele Seth says, "And those whom thou hast willed, thou hast saved. But thou dost will to be saved all who are worthy" (VII,5, p. 121, 12-14). And when Zostrianos descended into the perceptible world, he went out to preach the truth to all (VIII,1, p. 130, 9), not solely to a select group, and those who accept the truth are those who chose salvation, listened when invited and sought to understand (cf. VIII,1, p. 44, 1-4).

48. Hans-Martin Schenke, "The Phenomenon and Significance of Gnostic Sethianism," in *Sethian Gnosticism*, vol. 2, *The Rediscovery of Gnosticism*, B. Layton, ed. (Leiden: E. J. Brill, 1981), 606-607; John D. Turner, "Sethian Gnosticism: A Literary History" in *Nag Hammadi, Gnosticism, and Early Christianity*, C. W. Hedrick and R. Hodgson, Jr., eds. (Peabody, MA: Hendrickson Publishers, 1986), 68-69.

49. In light of this, what the Lord of the Johannine *Acts* had referred to as having descended might be the preexistent spiritual seed, not the Gnostics themselves. And, just as according to the *Gos. Eg.*, this seed is not sown into people until they have been ritually begotten-transformed, so the sacrament of the *AJn* could be that community's sacramental "begetting" of the spiritual race (or of what has descended?). Curiously, Schenke, "The Phenomenon and Significance of Gnostic Sethianism" (n.48), 601-602) believes the Sethians also possessed a sacrament that might have been of a higher order: "a mystery of ascension," whose etiology is found in the liturgical *Steles Seth*. One could describe the *Acts'* sacrament also as "a mystery of ascension" since the initiates do transcend to the Pleroma. But, this does not mean that the *AJn* contains a Sethian sacrament. Nor do the parallels between the interpolated *AJn* and Sethian Gnosticism indicate that our interpolator was a Sethian. What these parallels do show is that for both the Sethians and our interpolator, *gnōsis* and salvation were not things to be attained "intellectually" for a predetermined group, but "liturgically" and for all.

50. But not everyone does become a member, or as quickly. In addition to those souls who immediately respond to the truth and become members of the immovable race, the apocryphon's savior also informed our apostle about souls that do not immediately respond to the power of the Spirit of life. They might not know who they are and they could do evil deeds under the influence of the Opposing Spirit, but they can still attain salvation. It might take the souls several reincarnations before these souls receive the *gnōsis* and are saved (II,1, p. 27, 10f.). According to the apocryphon, the only souls that are denied salvation are those who attained *gnōsis*, but rejected it. They no longer have the options of reincarnation and repentance. These souls are taken to the power where the angels of poverty exist, to be tortured for eternity. Thus, according to the *Ap. John* there are three groups (not types of souls; cf. *Zost.*, VIII,1, p. 27, 13-28, 14), with the first group made up of those to whom the attainment of this *gnōsis* comes easily. These Christians will endure anything that befalls them. They have transcended all passions, such as anger, envy, jealousy, desire, greed. In the *AJn*, they are represented by John, who has a mature understanding/vision of the Lord, and by Cleopatra who has transcended her own emotions. The second group in the *Ap. John* includes souls who gradually respond to the *gnōsis*, through the power of the Spirit of life. James and the Christians he represents can be identified as such, for although their perception of the Lord is not as mature as John's, it is progressing. And in the end they, too, will be saved, though it will take them longer. Finally, the apocryphon speaks of souls that have attained *gnōsis* but rejected it. It takes little effort to identify Fortunatus as one who had encountered the Lord's *gnōsis* (or the *Acts'* "spiritual resurrection"), but rejected it. In the eyes of the apocryphon's author, Fortunatus and those like him have been overcome by the Opposing Spirit (Satan in the *Acts*). Thus, it is possible to see in the *AJn* a tripartite view of humanity that corresponds more closely to the *Ap. John* than to western Valentinianism.

51. As we have observed, much of what our interpolator introduced to the *Acts'* community might not have been so unexpected. That the interpolation and the rest of the Johannine *Acts* complement and enlighten each other so well about the Lord's polymorphism,

salvation and the apostle's spiritual resurrection-transformations could be taken as evidence for recognizing chaps. 94-102 as a product of and witness to the *Acts'* community at a later stage of its development, rather than the intrusion of an "outsider." One could almost imagine that the *Acts'* author had compiled and reworked the various stories about John so that they could be a solid foundation from which the interpolator could work.

52. See n.11 above.

Trimorphic Protennoia and the Wisdom Tradition

Rosemary Halford

Thematic analysis of Nag Hammadi Codex XIII, 1, *Trimorphic Protennoia* (*Trim. Prot.*), presents difficulties because the text underwent several stages of redaction. Two major commentators on *Trim. Prot.*, John Turner and Gesine Schenke Robinson, have recognized the complex compositional history of this document.[1]

In his discussion of *Trim. Prot.* and the Prologue of the Fourth Gospel, Craig Evans has concluded that these share a wisdom background, but while in the Gospel the wisdom motif of descent is expressed as incarnational theology, this is represented as gnostic cosmology in *Trim. Prot.*[2] Such a conclusion rests on inadequate appreciation of stratigraphy. While *Trim. Prot.* certainly does contain Sethian cosmology, an incarnational theology may also be recognized in *Trim. Prot.* at the original compositional level. This incarnational theology reveals Protennoia as a gnostic re-interpretation of Sophia.

P.-H. Poirier has also insisted on the need for redactional analysis of this treatise. While his discussion of descent and restraint cites only Sethian material, his conclusions refer to the work as a whole.[3] In contrast, the references of Kurt Rudolph to *Trim. Prot.* in his classic work, *Gnosis*, cite only aretalogical material.[4] The reader may justifiably complain that these authors are comparing apples and oranges.

Redactional Layers of Trim. Prot.

Redaction criticism is often described through the image of an onion; one peels away redactional material in layers indicated by changes of theme and of vocabulary. In *Trim. Prot.* it is possible to remove redactional layers to isolate an aretalogical kernel which has clear parallels with the Jewish wisdom tradition. The latest and most obvious redactional layer is a superficial Christianization, a very thin veneer indeed. For the text has been Christianized in the simplest way: the word "Christ" has been added wherever lists of characteristics or titles of a divinity occur, as at 37,34 and 38,23; both are embedded in Sethian material. Even Yvonne Janssens, who established the critical edition and originally referred to *Trim. Prot.* as a Christian gnostic work, has more recently accepted a secondary Christianization for this work.[5]

Carston Colpe has classified it as a Sethian work, indeed "a classic within the Sethian corpus."[6] Although commentators do not agree on what constitutes "Sethianism" (if indeed such exists!) *Trim. Prot.* fails to meet some very basic criteria for Sethianism, such as the occurrence of the name "Seth," who is never mentioned. Nevertheless, there are sections in *Trim. Prot.*, such as the one devoted to cosmogony, 38,30-40,7, which parallels Sethian material in *The Gospel of the Egyptians*. This section lacks literary integrity, and is incomprehensible without information from other gnostic writings. The passage refers to four luminaries or light-bearers (38,30-39,5), but their role is not explained. An interesting passage on baptismal practice (47,35-49,11) similarly represents an interpolation, not an intrinsic part of *Trim. Prot.*

My position is that the writing has been Sethianized;[7] a writer familiar with the Sethian system has reworked and clarified the original *Trim. Prot.*. This is a defensible position for there are clear grammatical indications of change in writing style and thought. One may note, for example, the change from use of the first person singular to the third person singular or plural. B. Layton's translation of the document in his *The Gnostic Scriptures* (1987) signals these changes by switching from poetry to prose.[8]

Analysis of the stratigraphy of *Trim. Prot.* which isolates the aretalogical kernel embedded within Christian and Sethian interpolations reveals an original writing which probably included an introduction, followed by descriptions of Protennoia's three descents as Father or Thought, as Mother or Voice and Sound, and finally as Son or Word. Most of this material is presented in the *ego eimi* format: "It is I who am first thought" (35,1), "It is I who am perception and acquaintance" (36,12), "It is I who am the Mother of the sound" (42,9), "I am the verbal expression" (46,5) (Layton trans.).

This aretalogical material is in strong contrast with Sethian interpolations. For example, with regard to creation, the great demon (presumably Sakla) is described as ordering the eternal realms or aeons (40,4-6); use of the third person singular here indicates Sethian material. But in contrast to this Sethian material, *Protennoia* in the kernel layer asserts: "I radiated on the darkness. It is I who brought forth the water. . . . It is I who, within my thinking, radiated the entirety part by part" (36,5-8). Such *ego eimi* (first person) proclamations contrast with third person singular statements in Sethian passages discussing the same theme of creation. Protennoia's language is much closer to that of Proverbs 8, which describes Sophia at the Lord's side at the time of creation, although the biblical passage does not use the *ego eimi* construction.

This kernel of aretalogical material has its own literary integrity; it can be understood on its own without reference to other gnostic works. The material of this layer has interesting parallels with Isis aretalogies, with some of the speeches of Sophia in the Hebrew wisdom tradition,[9] and with other gnostic writings such as *The Thunder* or *Perfect Mind* (*NHC* VI,2).[10]

Protennoia and Sophia

Kurt Rudolph has pointed out the similarity between the figures Protennoia and Sophia.[11] In his analysis of that similarity in "The Jewish Background of the Gnostic Sophia Myth,"[12] George Mac-

Rae provides a list of wisdom characteristics which includes twelve motifs also appearing in *Trim. Prot.* For example, she is an hypostatized being, in intimate union with the divine. She proclaims, "It is I who am First Thought, the thinking that exists . . ." (35,1); "I am the life of my afterthought" (35,12); "It is I who am the entirety" (35,31). Protennoia is pre-existent, and (as we have already seen) instrumental in creation. She is identified with a holy spirit. As Sophia is a breath of the power of God (Wisdom of Solomon 7:24-25), Protennoia declares that she puts breath into her own and injects the holy spirit into them (45,28-29).

There is a strong resemblance between Sophia and Protennoia not only in the way that they are described but also in their actions. Protennoia is a classic gnostic redeemer figure—she descends and reascends, taking her posterity with her into the holy light (50,18). The theme of reascent is of interest because it demonstrates the fluidity of the wisdom tradition, and shows how a gnostic author could exploit tension within the tradition. In Sirach 24,8-12 Sophia is identified with Torah; she does not return to heaven but is domesticated in the Torah. Non-canonical writings describe how Sophia is rebuffed and returns to heaven; rejected among the "sons of man," she takes a seat in the midst of the angels (1 Enoch 42:1-2). Partisan groups, such as Essenes and Gnostics, have claimed Sophia as their own, since she legitimizes their claim to have the truth.

Trim. Prot. and the Jewish Wisdom Tradition

The move from universal Sophia of canonical writings to partisan Sophia of the Gnostics indicates the flexibility of the wisdom tradition. The author of *Trim. Prot.* has a rich heritage from which to develop images to express the importance of the gnostic redeemer Protennoia.

Of fifteen characteristics or motifs found in the wisdom tradition given by MacRae, Protennoia has a positive correlation with fourteen of them: (1) a personal being, (2) intimate union with God, (3) pre-existence, (4) spatial imagery, such as dwelling in the clouds, (5) imagery concerning status and authority, such as enthronement, (6) identification with the Holy Spirit, (7) instrument of creation, (8) soteriological role, (9) descent to the material world, (10) reascent, (11) familial imagery, (12) identification with life. I add to MacRae's list of wisdom characteristics: (14) use of imagery concerning light, and (15) rewards bestowed by the wisdom figure; Protennoia does exhibit parallels with all of these wisdom motifs.

The only characteristic described by MacRae which does not have any comparable use in *Trim. Prot.* is (13) identification of Sophia with a tree of life. This latter is a motif used with such vehemence by some gnostic authors—see for example the diatribe against the trees of paradise in the *Apocryphon of John* (21,26 -22,9)—that the theme may have been consciously avoided by the author of *Trim. Prot.*

Conclusions

This comparison between *Trim. Prot.* and the wisdom tradition leads to several conclusions. First, respect for the literary stratigraphy is a prerequisite for commentary on the treatise. Only then can the thoroughly sapiential kernel of the writing be recognized for what it is: Protennoia of the aretalogical layer and Sophia are very closely related indeed.

Second, *Trim. Prot.* should suggest the futility of any wisdom-gnostic dichotomy. On the basis of *Trim. Prot.* it is possible to argue that the Jewish wisdom tradition was becoming more gnosticized; the existence of a sectarian and pre-gnostic wisdom school merits further investigation. The wisdom tradition provides the matrix which a gnostic author could use to portray Protennia as a classic gnostic redeemer figure, or a Christian author to describe the Jesus of the Fourth Gospel.

Third, *Trim. Prot.* presents a sapiential redeemer figure in a document contemporary with early Christian writings. I would therefore suggest that *Trim. Prot.* supports James Robinson's position regarding a wisdom Christology of early Christianity; Robinson laments the loss of this "stillborn Christology."[13] Since Sophia Christology did not come to fruition in western Christianity, it is "less a recording of a traceable strand of Christian history than a nostalgic reminiscence of what might have been."[14]

In his response to Robinson's article, Charles Hedrick is less pessimistic concerning a sapiential Jesus. He holds that a Christian wisdom writing of the Nag Hammadi library, *The Teaching of Silvanus*, (*NHC* VII,4) presents the same type of wisdom Christology that Robinson finds in Q.[15] Since *Silvanus* dates from the late second or early third century, Sophia Christology cannot have been stillborn; there was an ongoing trajectory.

I suggest that *Trim. Prot.* witnesses this ongoing trajectory of a lost wisdom Christology, precisely because it is so thoroughly sapiential in its understanding of a gnostic redeemer figure. The estimated early date of *Trim. Prot.*'s composition and redaction[16] lends support for Robinson's position regarding early Christian thinkers and writers who used similar wisdom motifs to try to express the reality of Jesus Christ.

Hedrick uses the water image of a trajectory, namely a series of unconnected yet similar ebbs, flows and eddies.[17] I would suggest that in the wisdom trajectory, *Trim. Prot.* is a fascinating, swirling eddy, one that we are aware of only because of the fortunate rediscovery of the Nag Hammadi library. It may be an eddy with no direct outcome nor clearly logical outflow. Nevertheless, it does suggest that other sapiential understandings, such as the sapiential Jesus, whose loss is lamented by Robinson, were available at least to some early Christian communities.

Notes

1. John Turner, "Sethian Gnosticism: A Literary History," *Nag Hammadi, Gnosticism and Early Christianity*, H. W. Hedrick and R. Hodgson, eds. (Peabody, MA: Hendrickson, 1986), 55-86; Gesine Robinson, "Trimorphic Protennoia (*NHC* XIII, 1)," *Anchor Bible Dictionary* (Garden City, NY: Doubleday, 1992), VI:663. See also Robinson's article, "The Trimorphic Protennoia and the Prologue of the Fourth Gospel," *Gnosticism and the Early Christian World*, J. E. Goehring, C. W. Hendrick, J. T. Sanders and H. D. Betz, eds. (Sonoma, CA: Polebridge Press, 1990), 37-50.

2. Craig Evans, "On the Prologue of John and the Trimorphic Protennoia," *New Testament Studies* 27 (1980-81): 399.

3. P.-H. Poirier, "La Prôtennoia Trimorphe (*NH* XIII,1) et le vocabulaire du *Descensus ad inferos*," *Le Muséon* 96 (1983): 193-204.

4. Kurt Rudolph, *Gnosis: The Nature and History of Gnosticism*, P. W. Coxon and K. H. Kuhn, trans., R. McL. Wilson, ed. (San Francisco: Harper and Row, 1984), 141-44.

5. Yvonne Janssens, "The Trimorphic Protennoia and the Fourth Gospel," *The New Testament and Gnosis: Essays in Honour of Robert McLachan Wilson*, A. H. B. Logan and A. J. Wedderburn, eds. (Edinburgh: T. & T. Clark, 1983), 242.

6. Carsten Colpe, "Heidnische, jüdische und christliche Uber-lieferung in den Schriften aus Nag Hammadi III," *Jahrbuch für Antike und Christentum*, 17 (1974): 122-23. Cited from an un-published translation, "Pagan, Jewish and Christian Traditions in the Texts from Nag Hammadi III," by John S. Kloppenborg.

7. *Trim. Prot.* is certainly not the only writing in the Nag Hammadi corpus to have been subjected to Sethianization. See the article by Louis Painchaud, "The Redactions of The Writing Without Title (*CG* II,5)," *The Second Century* 8 (1991): 217-34.

8. Bentley Layton, *The Gnostic Scriptures* (Garden City, NY: Doubleday, 1987), 86-100; Layton's translations are used throughout this paper.

9. John Kloppenborg, "Isis and Sophia in the Book of Wisdom," *Harvard Theological Review*, 75 (1982): 57-84, especially 67-68.

10. George MacRae, "The Ego-Proclamation in Gnostic Sources," *The Trial of Jesus*, Cambridge Studies in honor of C. D. F. Moule, E. Bammel, ed. (London: SCM, 1970), 122-34.

11. Rudolph, *Gnosis* (n.4), 141.

12. George MacRae, "The Jewish Background of the Gnostic Sophia," *Novum Testamentum* 12 (1970): 86-101. I reject two of MacRae's characteristics (Sophia's identification with a sevenfold cosmic structure and her identification with Adam), since they are too weakly attested to be really indicative of the wisdom tradition.

13. James Robinson, "Very Goddess and Very Man: Jesus' Better Self," *Images of the Feminine in Gnosticism: Studies in Antiquity and Christianity*, Karen King, ed. (Philadelphia: Fortress Press, 1988), 113-27.

14. Robinson, "Very Goddess" (n.13), 126.

15. Charles Hedrick, "A Response to 'Very Goddess and Very Man: Jesus' Better Self' by James M. Robinson," *in Images of the Feminine in Gnosticism* (n.13), 133.

16. Turner suggests that the first compositional layer of *Trim. Prot.*, the aretalogical material, probably existed before 100 CE. See "Sethian Gnosticism" (n.1), 71. G. Robinson holds ("Trimorphic Protennoia" [n.1], 663) that the final form of *Trim. Prot.* may have been reached by the beginning of the second century.

17. Hedrick, "Response" (n.15), 130.

Gnosis, Theology and Historical Method

Schuyler Brown

Paul and Gnosis

Criticism of *gnōsis* at various times in the church's history provides us with a litmus test for the current state of Christian theology. The earliest and briefest critique of *gnōsis* comes from the apostle Paul: "*Gnōsis* puffs up" (1 Cor. 8:1).[1]

Since *religious* knowledge seems to be at issue here, Paul cannot be referring to the arrogance which is sometimes associated with superior intellectual gifts. Rather, Paul's astute observation has to do with a phenomenon for which modern depth psychology provides us with fresh insight.

Unlike the religious knowledge which comes from without, through the preached word (cf. Rom. 10:17), *gnōsis* comes from within, through transformative experience. *Gnōsis*, in this paper, refers to such *introverted religious knowledge*. This *psychological* understanding clearly differs from attempts to provide a *doctrinal* definition of *gnōsis*;[2] it would fall under what E. M. Yamauchi refers to as "Gnosticism" in the "broad sense."[3]

The paradigm for this type of transformative experience is Paul's own confrontation by Christ on the Damascus road, about which C. G. Jung observes:

True though it may be that this Christ of St. Paul's would hardly have been possible without the historical Jesus, the apparition of Christ came to St. Paul not from the historical Jesus but from the depths of his own unconscious.[4]

When the Gnostics fail to distinguish themselves from the numinous source of this inner knowledge, the result is psychological inflation: "*Gnōsis* puffs up." Commenting on a passage from the *Acts of John*, Jung observes:

This overweening attitude arises from an inflation caused by the fact that the enlightened John has identified with his own light and confused his ego with the self.[5]

Paul declares that the whole purpose of his life is the knowledge of Christ and of the power of Christ's resurrection (Phil. 3:10). The experiential character of this knowledge is brought out in the NEB translation: "All I care for is to *know* Christ, to *experience* the power of his resurrection."[6]

However, Paul was also aware of the need for something to compensate for the inflationary effect of *gnōsis*. Speaking of his revelatory experiences, he says: "To keep me from being too elated by the abundance of revelations, a thorn was given me in the flesh" (2 Cor. 12:7).[7] The balance in Paul's personal life between revelatory experience and the "thorn in the flesh"—whatever that may refer to specifically—is expressed theologically in a dialectical relationship between existence in this world and the resurrection. For Paul the resurrection is present in human experience only under the paradoxical sign of the cross.

The Gnostics who denied the need for any future resurrection (1 Cor. 15:12) seem not to have acknowledged any such compensation for their numinous experiences. Their rejection of any eschatological reservation expressed the unqualified ultimacy of their present experience. Like the two persons mentioned in 2 Tim. 2:18, they seem to have believed that "the resurrection is past already." This position represents, according to K. H. Rengstorf, "a trivialization of the reality of death."[8]

Two Views of Nature and Grace
Ironically, in the period following Paul's death, it is the Gnostics, rather than the orthodox, who uphold the dialectical relationship between cross and resurrection.[9] In the famous passage from 1 Clement about the phoenix, the resurrection is represented as the logical extension of God's way of working in nature. The author asks rhetorically:

> Do we, then, consider it a great and marvelous thing that the Creator of all things should raise those who have given him holy service through the confidence of a noble faith, when even through a bird he shows us the greatness of his promise? (XXVI)[10]

No such inference from nature could be made by the Gnostics, for whom the creator or demiurge is an ignorant abortion, who enslaves the inhabitants of the lower world through their ignorance of "the unknown Father." Such language, so offensive to Catholic orthodoxy, continues the language of Paul himself, who speaks of "the god of this world," who "has blinded the minds of unbelievers" (2 Cor. 4:4).

Scholastic theology maintains that "grace builds on nature," but theology in the Pauline trajectory upholds the absolute discontinuity between nature and grace.[11] The latter position corresponds to the psychological recognition of the unconscious as radically "other," in relation to rational consciousness.

Gnosis and the Heresiologists
The root of the conflict between *gnōsis* and the emerging Catholic church was not so much "heretical" teaching as it was the challenge to ecclesiastical power.[12] For the pneumatic, knowledge of the truth is knowledge of one's own true self. Such knowledge is quite inde-

pendent of those ecclesiastical institutions which the *Apocalypse of Peter* refers to as "dry canals" (79:30). Although the Gnostics did not reject church structures outright and actually developed their own forms of community life, they did not *need* these structures, and such elitism posed an insupportable challenge to local church authorities.

In his attack on "what is falsely called *gnōsis*" (1 Tim. 6:20), the author of 1 Timothy declares that the Gnostic is "puffed up with conceit" (v.4)[13]—again a reference to psychological inflation. He "knows nothing" (v.4), for here truth is identical with the "sound doctrine" proclaimed by the church (v. 3; cf. 1:10; 2 Tim. 1:13; 4:3; Tit. 1:9, 13; 2:1, 2).

The dating of the Pastoral Epistles ranges all the way from 60 to 160. A late dating would make the author a possible contemporary of Irenaeus (130-200), who explicitly affirms the ecclesial nature of the "sound doctrine" which is opposed in the Pastorals to the "myths" and "genealogies" of the Gnostics (1 Tim. 1:4; 4:7; 2 Tim. 4:4; Tit. 1:14; 3:9):

> True knowledge is that which consists in the doctrine of the apostles, and the ancient constitution of the church throughout all the world, and the distinctive manifestation of the body of Christ according to the successions of the bishops, by which they have handed down that church which exists in every place (*Against the Heresies* IV.33.8)

For Irenaeus, the church "is the entrance to life; all others are thieves and robbers" (III.4.1). The crime of the Gnostics was therefore "treason" against the church.

Gnosis in the New Testament

Adolf von Harnack's diagnosis of *gnōsis* as "the acute Hellenization of Christianity" will be considered in our final section. It is to Rudolf Bultmann that we owe the recognition of *gnōsis* within the New Testament, particularly in Paul and the Fourth Gospel.[14] This position has been continued by Bultmann's students, especially James Robinson and Helmut Koester.

It is challenged by E. M. Yamauchi, who adopts the position defended by Simone Pétrement at the Messina Conference, namely, that "Gnosticism" is "a post-Christian heresy."[15] Critical for this debate are the two matters discussed earlier:[16] the neologism "Gnosticism" and the definition of *gnōsis*. Since Yamauchi is talking about "a fully developed Gnosticism,"[17] our "broad" understanding of the phenomenon in question is really not affected.

Although introverted religious knowledge is naturally expressed through myth, the presence of the gnostic redemption myth is not essential for a text or an author to be considered gnostic. Both in Paul and in the Johannine corpus we find a positive evaluation of spiritual knowledge, though in the context of a community situation. This is in striking contrast to the Pastorals, where the emphasis falls one-sidedly on the "sound doctrine" of the church.

Gnosis, Feminism, and Sexual Imagery
Today feminism is a principal theological interest. It therefore comes as no surprise that the centrality of female figures in gnostic literature has attracted attention.

An impressive witness to this interest is the collection of essays from the 1985 conference in Claremont.[18] Despite the erudition of the contributors, I was struck by the meager results of the historical method, when applied to the Nag Hammadi writings. For as the editor candidly observes, "Gnosticism is simply not interested in history."[19]

Although the interests of ancient authors need not always tie the hands of modern scholars,[20] the Nag Hammadi writings seem to be so entirely the creation of the religious imagination that no convincing answers can be given to the historical questions which they raise: What was the place of women in gnostic communities? Were some of the Nag Hammadi texts actually written by women?

The presence of female figures like Sophia, Norea, Edem, and Epinoia in gnostic writings is part of a broader characteristic of these texts: an interest in sexual imagery, which includes both male and female.[21] The importance of androgyny in gnostic mythology suggests that a psychological interpretation of these texts might be more illuminating than attempts at historical reconstruction.[22]

Writing before the Nag Hammadi library became accessible, C. G. Jung made this connection between mythology and psychology:

> Most of [the Gnostics] were in reality theologians who, unlike the more orthodox ones, allowed themselves to be influenced in large measure by inner experience. They are therefore, like the alchemists, a veritable mine of information concerning all those natural symbols arising out of the repercussions of the Christian message.[23]

A great deal is lost if the gnostic myth is regarded simply as the imaginative garb for gnostic teaching. Whatever is unknown to consciousness can only be known through projection. Therefore, in a pre-psychological age, psychological contents find expression in what is perceived to be external, e. g., the cosmic drama of redemption. If the modern interpreter places undue emphasis on the conscious process of doctrinal formulation, the text's proximity to the unconscious is overlooked.

Harnack, Rowe, and Hellenization

According to Ps.-Dionysius, theology includes "not only learning divine things but also experiencing them."[24] Institutional Christianity tends to regard religious experience with suspicion. The doctrinal emphasis of the church has favored the "upper" realm of spiritual light over that transformative process, familiar to the mystics, which always involves "the dark night of the soul." Although the Apostle's Creed contains the *descensus ad inferos*,[25] Christ's descent to the underworld has usually been thought to exempt Christians from undergoing a similar experience.

In this Dionysian experience, where human reasoning is of no avail, the imaginative function of mythology takes on crucial significance. Jung has written:

To the intellect, all my mythologizing is futile speculation. To the emotions, however, it is a healing and valid activity.[26]

In Harnack's view, the Hellenistic legacy includes both philosophy and mythology.[27] Yet, while he views the *logos* specula-tion of the Christian apologists as "the positive form of Helleniza-tion,"[28] he thinks that *gnōsis*, where mythology has a crucial role, represents "the negative form of Hellenization."[29] Ironically, "the very struggle against acute Hellenization further Hellenized the Church."[30]

Problematical in Harnack's analysis is his representation of philosophy and mythology as antithetical elements in the Hellenistic legacy to the church. In this, ironically, he exemplifies the doctrinal bias of mainline Christianity. In fact, the "Apollonian" and "Dionysian" aspects of Hellenism are closely related. Rowe astutely observes that "the *gnōsis* of the Hellenistic Gnostics would seem to reflect the 'spirit of Greek philosophy' in a much deeper way than does the notion of 'dogma' in the early church."[31]

The tragic irony in the conflict over *gnōsis* was that each side really needed the other. However, the church chould see *gnōsis* only as a challenge to its authority, not as an enrichment of its life. Consequently, the "victory" of the church resulted, on the one hand, in the dogmatic Christianity which Harnack deplored, and on the other, in a sectarian movement which would quickly vanish from the historical scene.

As in other schisms in the history of the Christian church, both sides were left impoverished: "For the layman it suffices if he adheres to certain leading points and refrains from attacking the orthodox creed."[32] But religion, as the quotation from Ps.-Dionysius suggests, is both conceptual and experiential.

When the mystic journey is undertaken in total isolation from the believing community, if often bears strange fruit. Jung ap-preciated better than Harnack the need for ecclesiastical doctrine:

Recognizing the danger of Gnostic irrealism, the Church, more practical in these matters, has always insisted on the concretism of the historical events. . . .[33]

One example of a mystical vision which was "elaborated" with the help of dogma is the so-called "Trinity Vision" of Brother Nicholas of Flüe. Ecclesiastical teaching provided Nicholas with a container for "a sight so terrible that his own countenance was changed by it."[34]

However, Jung also recognized that the rationalism of western Christianity, intensified by the Reformation and the Enlightenment, was driving spiritually minded people to the religions of the East; but for these, according to Jung, our western psychology is not well adapted.

When the church denigrates and suppresses religious experience, it turns itself into a rigid and authoritarian system, more concerned with its own power than with its true mission: "that they may have life, and have it abundantly" (John 10:10).[35]

The perennial attraction of "repristination,"[36] i. e., the return to "the simplicity of the Gospel,"[37] is illusory, for it is never possible to annul a lengthy process of historical development. As Harnack realized, the churches of the Reformation, which sought to separate Gospel from dogma, also succumbed to "the temptation to a doctrinal Christianity."[38]

The present challenge arises out of the fact that European culture, the descendant of both Hellenism and Christianity, is no longer universal. If, as Harnack affirms, "the Christian religion, as it was not born of the culture of the ancient world, is not forever chained to it,"[39] then the Christian religion must be enculturated in lands of whose very existence the second century was unaware.

In this process *gnōsis* has a crucial role, because, unlike either Hellenism or European culture, such knowledge is truly universal: it "enlightens everyone coming into the world" (John 1:9, RSV alternate translation).

Historical methodology is useful in suggesting how one religious tradition may depend on another,[40] but it cannot account for those remarkable similarities between religious traditions which have had no historical contacts. For these phenomena the "subterranean" influence of *gnōsis* is a plausible hypothesis.[41]

Conclusions

Yamauchi concludes his article with the observation: "Whether [the demise of the Gnostics] is a matter of gratification or lament is a highly personal issue. . . ."[42]

Some share the heresiologists' negative assessment of *gnōsis* and use the label "Gnostic" to discredit any movement in the church of which they disapprove.[43] Others share the view of the ancient Gnostics themselves that *gnōsis* renders the church superfluous.

Clearly, the fall-out from this ancient schism still weighs heavily upon us; yet church and *gnōsis* need each other. The fatal split between doctrine and experience can only be healed through a genuine *conjunctio oppositorum*.

As Jung prophetically observed,

> Disparagement and vilification of Gnosticism are an anachronism. Its obviously psychological symbolism could serve many people today as a bridge to a more living appreciation of Christian tradition.[44]

Notes

1. Ἡ γνῶσις φυσιοῖ (1 Cor 8:1).
2. Attempts at doctrinal definition have led scholars to distinguish *"gnōsis"* from "Gnosticism," and "Gnostic" from "proto-Gnostic," "enthusiast," and "mystic." The definition of an ancient religious movement and the identification of its literature are tasks of modern scholarship which pursue, consciously or unconsciously, contemporary academic or theological interests. The "Gnostics," however they are defined, did not usually *call* themselves "Gnostics," just as the authors of the New Testament writings did not usually *call*

themselves "Christians." Yamauchi's survey article ("Gnosticism and Early Christianity," in this volume, 29-61, illustrates how competent scholars, evaluating the same evidence, come to strikingly different conclusions. Nor is this surprising. There is an inevitable circularity in the doctrinal definition of *gnōsis* and the identification of gnostic texts: a teaching is considered "gnostic" if it is found in a "gnostic" text, but for a text to be judged "gnostic," it must contain "gnostic" teaching. A similar problem occurs in the definition of "apocalyptic" and the identification of "apocalyptic" texts. William Rowe ("Adolf von Harnack and the Concept of Hellenization," in this volume, 69-98, implicitly criticizes the doctrinal definition of *gnōsis* when he writes: "Originally 'heresy' was understood not so much as a 'view,' but as a posture, that is, as a 'standing apart' (*apostasis*) from the Body of Christ. . . ." (91).

3. Yamauchi (above, 29). A broad definition of *gnōsis* is not useful for purposes of tracing specific historical dependencies, but that is not my object in this paper. I have avoided the English neologism "Gnosticism," which has no equivalent in German scholarship. In the English translation of K. Rudolph's book, *Gnosis* (see note 14), the sub-title reads: *The Nature and History of Gnosticism*. In the German original the sub-title reads: *Wesen und Geschichte einer spätantiken Religion*. Furthermore, the distinction between *gnōsis* and Gnosticism involves some questionable assumptions. Cf. J. M. Robinson, "On Bridging the Gulf from Q to the Gospel of Thomas (or Vice Versa)," *Nag Hammadi, Gnosticism, and Early Christianity*, C. W. Hedrick and R. Hodgson, Jr., eds. (Peabody, MA: Hendrickson Publishers, 1986), especially the section, "The Messina Definition of Gnosticism," 128-35.

4. *The Archetypes and the Collective Unconscious* = *The Collected Works of C. G. Jung* (*CW*), R. F. C. Hull, trans. (Princeton, NJ: Princeton University Press, 1980), vol. 9, pt. I, 121.

5. "Transformation Symbolism in the Mass," *Psychology and Religion: West and East* = *CW*, vol. 11 (1977): 287.

6. The Greek text has a single infinitive: τοῦ γνῶναι αὐτὸν καὶ τὴν δύναμιν τῆς ἀναστάσεως αὐτοῦ (Phil.3:10).

7. The verb ὑπεραίρομαι occurs only here (2 Cor. 12:7) in the New Testament.

8. "Eine Verkürzung der Realität des Todes." I. Korintherbrief, Wintersemester 1966/67, Westfälische Wilhelms-Universität, Münster. C. G. Jung made a similar comment upon returning from India: "Man must come to terms with the problem of suffering. Eastern man wants to free himself from suffering by brushing suffering away. Western man tries to suppress suffering with drugs. But suffering must be overcome, and it is overcome only by being borne. That we can only learn from Him," i. e., Christ on the cross. Quoted by W. Uhsadel, *Evangelische Seelsorge* (Heidelberg, 1966), 121; quoted in *C. G. Jung, Word and Image*, A. Jaffé, ed. (Princeton: Princeton University Press, 1979), 177-78.

9. A similar shift of positions is observable in the relationship between Christian faith and the Old Testament. In the opinion of J. Louis Martyn, Paul's position on this matter was: "You can't get here from there." However, in the post-Pauline period, it was the "heretic" Marcion who declared the strict discontinuity between the Old Testament and the New, while the "orthodox" position maintained that Christianity was the fulfillment of Judaism. "How my mind has changed or stayed the same," General Meeting of the Society of Biblical Literature in New Orleans, Nov. 18, 1990.

10. Μέγα καὶ θαυμαστὸν οὖν νομίζομεν εἶναι, εἰ ὁ δημιουργὸς τῶν ἁπάντων ἀνάστασιν ποιήσεται τῶν ὁσίως αὐτῷ δουλευσάντων ἐν πεποιθήσει πίστεως ἀγαθῆς, ὅπου καὶ δι' ὀρνέου δείκνυσιν ἡμῖν τὸ μεγαλεῖον τῆς ἐπαγγελίας αὐτοῦ; (XXVI)

11. Carl J. Peter, "A Roman Catholic Contribution to the Quest of a Credible Eschatology," *CTSA Proceedings*, 29 (1974): 255-71, and my response, *ibid.*, 279-82.

12. S. Brown, *The Origins of Christianity: A Historical Introduction to the New Testament* (New York: Oxford University Press, 1993), 161-63. This view of the gnostic "threat" differs from that given by W. Helleman in the proposal for a manuscript based on the June 1991 Conference at the Institute for Christian Studies: "Threatened

by gnostic reinterpretations of central beliefs concerning Jesus Christ, Christians found they had to clarify their own positions."
13. (I Tim. 6:4).
14. K. Rudolph, *Gnosis: The Nature and History of Gnosticism*, R. McL. Wilson, trans. (San Francisco: Harper & Row, 1987), 300.
15. Yamauchi (n.2), 45, this volume.
16. See above, notes 2 and 3.
17. Yamauchi (n.2), 45, this volume.
18. *Images of the Feminine in Gnosticism*, K. King, ed. (Philadelphia: Fortress Press, 1988). See my review in the *Toronto Journal of Theology* 7/2 (Fall 1991): 293-95.
19. Ibid., 159.
20. *Origins* (n.12), 2-3.
21. M. A. Williams, "Variety in Gnostic Perspectives on Gender," *Images* (n.17), 5: "Such gnostic texts are frequently manifesting a greater proclivity toward gender imagery at large, both male *and* female imagery."
22. J. Singer, *Androgyny: Toward a New Theory of Sexuality* (Garden City, N.Y.: Anchor Press/Doubleday, 1977).
23. *Aion: Researches into the Phenomenology of the Self* = *CW*, vol. 9, pt. II (1979), 269.
24. οὐ μόνον μαθὼν ἀλλὰ καὶ παθὼν τὰ θεῖα. Ps.-Dionysius,*De Divinis Nominibus*, 2.9. Cf. Hebr 5:8, ἔμαθεν ἀφ' ὧν ἔπαθεν, which, in turn, alludes to the Greek aphorism, πάθει μάθος (Aeschylus, *Agamemnon* v.177).
25. In her 1984 M.A. Research Paper at the Centre for Religious Studies (University of Toronto), Leslie Kobayashi traced the complex history of the *"Descensus ad Inferos,"* showing how scripture was accommodated in order to make room for a conception with wide-spread parallels in Greco-Roman mythology.
26. *Memories, Dreams, Reflections*, R. & C. Winston, trans. (New York: Vintage Books, 1963), 300.
27. Harnack, quoted by Rowe (n.2), in his note 14, p. 94 above.
28. Ibid., 78.
29. Ibid., 81f.

30. Ibid., 84.

31. Ibid., 90.

32. Harnack, quoted by Rowe, 87.

33. *Transformation* (n.5), 287. Compare Yamauchi's statement: "The Gnostics . . . lost their moorings in history" (above, 46).

34. *Archetypes* (n.4), 9.

35. C. Brown, "Religious Imagination—Then and Now," *The Bible Today*, vol. 29, 4 (July 1991): 237-41.

36. Rowe (n.2), 70.

37. Harnack, quoted by Rowe (n.2), in his note 19, p. 95.

38. Rowe (n.2), 86.

39. Harnack, quoted by Rowe (n.2), 86.

40. A good example is Yamauchi's derivation of Qur'an 4:157 from Manichaeanism; see his "The Crucifixion and Docetic Christology," *Concordia Theological Quarterly* 46 (1982): 1-20, esp. 13-14.

41. S. Brown, "The True Light," *Toronto Journal of Theology* 1/2 (Fall 1985): 222-26.

42. Yamauchi (n.2), 47.

43. Philip J. Lee, *Against the Protestant Gnostics* (New York: Oxford University Press, 1987).

44. *Transformation*, (n.5), 292.

Gnosticism and the Classical Tradition

Scott T. Carroll

Gnosticism played an important role in the formative stages of Christian doctrine. In its confrontations with Gnosticism, early Christianity was moved to refine its own theological positions. Nineteenth century scholars, relying on the patristic record, made broad-sweeping generalizations about the role of Gnosticism and its relation to Hellenistic thought. However, the more recent discovery of gnostic sources has prompted significant re-evaluation of such theories; both the patristic record and the gnostic sources are seen to pose their own interpretive difficulties. In this paper I wish to examine the relationship between Gnosticism and Hellenism from the vantage point of a Greek philosopher of late antiquity, Plotinus (d. 270), particularly through his tract against the Gnostics (II.9), which gives a lucid critique of gnostic adaptation of Greek thought.

Gnosticism and Hellenism

Prior to the 1945 discovery of the Nag Hammadi codices, and their publication starting in 1959, most of what was known about Gnosticism came from patristic anti-gnostic writings.[1] With their sources scattered, burned or buried, the Gnostics were condemned to speak primarily through the writings of their enemies. Aside from some passages in Irenaeus there is substantial lack of agreement between patristic accounts and recently-found gnostic writings.[2] Thus modern critical study of the anti-gnostic heresiological works[3] has moved in the direction of source criticism. Scholars have attempted to discover evidence of philosophical influence particularly because the heresiologists frequently claimed that Gnostics were misled by Greek philosophical positions.

Armed with new critical presuppositions, post-Enlightenment scholars have taken a different approach to the history of early Christianity. F. C. Baur (d. 1860), the founder of the influential Tübingen school, had opened the modern era of gnostic research by reinterpreting the heresiologists:[4] he rejected the patristic complaint that Greek philosophical speculation led to heresy. Instead, Baur regarded the Gnostics as the first Christian philosophers in a succession that culminated with Hegel and the theology of German Idealism. According to Baur, the Gnostics heralded a new age of religious philosophy, unshackled from oppressive (ecclesiastical) authority. It was his suggestion that Gnosticism emerged from Jewish circles conversant with pagan religion and philosophy. Others have extended his thesis by suggesting that *gnōsis* was rooted in Hellenistic metaphysical speculation applied to scripture by Hellenized Jews.[5]

Adolf von Harnack (d. 1930), the eminent German Lutheran historian, regarded Gnosticism as the "acute Hellenization of Christianity."[6] Although Harnack's concept of "Hellenization" was not well-defined, it was integral to his view of the development of Christian doctrine. Harnack was deeply suspicious of tradition and of a triumphalistic interpretation of the development of doctrine, which he regarded as a process similar to, but slower than the "Hellenization" which characterized Gnosticism. His negative view of the "Hellenization" of Christian dogma was also influenced by his deep suspicion of "modernist" theology in which, according to him, use of Greek rationalism undermined the gospel.

Both Baur and Harnack were products of their time, using their analysis of the Gnostics and Hellenization for their own agenda: Baur positively, and Harnack negatively. In the early twentieth century few scholars still defended the formative influence of a Greek speculative tradition on the development of Gnosticism, whether positively or negatively. Through their interest in comparative religion, members of the History of Religions school turned, instead, to the influence of Eastern myth and religion on Gnosticism.

With the recent publication of the Nag Hammadi codices, scholars for the first time were faced with the complex variegations of gnostic thought.[7] The question of the relationship of Gnosticism and Platonism has been reopened with an enthusiastic search for parallels between these.[8] Morton Smith has been one of the most outspoken advocates for a strong genetic link between Gnosticism and Platonism,[9] but S. Pétrement has recommended the need for a more cautious, empirical study of apparent similarities between gnostic and Platonic thought.[10] Pétrement's sentiments are echoed by the eminent historian of ancient philosophy A. H. Armstrong.[11] Recent scholarship has heeded their advice.

How must we evaluate the use of Hellenistic ideas in Gnosticism? To explore this question I would like to focus on the founder of Neoplatonism, Plotinus, who informs us regarding a group of Gnostics flourishing in Rome in the third century; among them were his own (disaffected) disciples. Plotinus's critique of the Platonism of his gnostic opponents is particularly directed at their view of the world-soul, and provides an insightful analysis of the Gnostics' use of Platonic speculation.

Plotinus on Gnosticism

Plotinus was concerned with similarities between Gnosticism and Platonism[12] and wrote *Ennead* II 9 as a treatise against unnamed opponents who based their teachings on a misunderstanding of Plato.[13] Recent scholars have argued convincingly that this shorter tract was originally part of a more extensive tract comprising *Enneads* III 8; V 8; V 5; and II 9,[14] and have identified the opponents, who attended Plotinus's lectures as Gnostics.[15] Some of the "deluded students" were actually his friends. If this "Longer Work" was originally a single treatise against the Gnostics, Plotinus was clearly concerned about the inroads that Gnostics had made into his school. This, in turn, leads us to reconsider the current understanding of the relationship between Plotinus, or later Platonism, and the gnostic opponents. Indeed, a thorough and insightful study of M. J. Edwards has recently argued that information culled from Plotinus's presentation of his gnostic opponents is compatible with both patristic testimony and certain gnostic texts.[16]

Plotinus's chief informant on Christianity was, doubtless, Porphyry, his disciple, editor, biographer and infamous author of a treatise *Against the Christians*.[17] In his biography of Plotinus he provides an intriguing description of his master's gnostic opponents; a problematic, but critical passage (16.2) which reads, αἱρετικοὶ δὲ παλαιᾶς φιλοσοφίας ἀνηγμένοι, is usually understood as affirming that the gnostic opponents of Plotinus were "sectarians from the ancient philosophy [i. e., Platonism]."[18] This would imply that the Gnostics were at one time closely associated with Platonism, and they eventually abandoned Platonic speculation. But, in fact, the passage is more correctly translated as affirming that these Gnostics "used the ancient philosophy [i. e., Platonism] *as a first principle.*"[19] Much to the consternation of the Neoplatonists, the Gnostics claimed that their ideas originated from Plato himself. Out of concern for the perceived credibility of their system, they thought that such an appeal to Plato would give them instant credibility.

Pagan and Christian anti-gnostic polemics are undeniably different. While heresiologists insisted on a genetic connection between Gnosticism and Greek philosophy, Neoplatonists rejected the Gnostics' Platonic claims; in fact, they stripped the Gnostics of their claim to Platonic authority in the same way that the church fathers countered heretical claims to apostolic authority.

In the biographical treatise Porphyry lists several gnostic teachers, but none of these can easily be identified. He also mentions certain gnostic works: "revelations of Zoroaster, of Zostrianos, of Nikotheos, of the *Foreigner*, of Messos, and of other such figures."[20] Two of the works, *Zostrianos* and *The Foreigner*, (or *Allogenes*), have been found among the codices of Nag Hammadi and have been ascribed to Sethian Gnosticism.[21] These and other Sethian works have been culled for evidence of Platonism, and this in turn may provide more information about Plotinus's gnostic opponents.[22] Plotinus's disciples did continue to oppose the Gnostics. Amelius Gentilianus wrote a work against the *Book of Zostrianos* and Porphyry wrote against a certain *Book of Zoroaster*. However, these refutations have not survived.[23]

It is not necessary, and is beyond the scope of the present essay, to compile a long list of allusions to Platonic thought in gnostic texts. Such an approach is methodologically flawed and ultimately counter-productive. To avoid the temptations of "parallelomania" these concluding observations will be limited to Plotinus's diatribe against the Gnostics: Plotinus had much to say about Gnostic use and abuse of the classical tradition, and Plato in particular.

In *Ennead* II 9 Plotinus systematically corrects gnostic teaching and allegation regarding a relationship to the Platonic tradition. He argues that gnostic mythology is an alien import, and complains that Gnostics camouflage their true opposition to the Platonic philosophical tradition by hiding behind familiar Platonic ideas taken out of context. Gnostic belief in a deficient demiurge, their multiplication of hypostases, their concept of matter, exclusivity and moral ineptitude betray a fundamental antipathy for traditional Greek philosophy.

In a detailed analysis of the relationship between the Gnostics and Plato, Plotinus asserts,

> Generally speaking, some of these peoples' doctrines have been taken from Plato, but others, all the new ideas they have brought in to establish a philosophy of their own, are things they have found outside of the truth. (*Ennead* II 9, 6. 10-12)

He lists mythological ideas which he regarded as coming directly from Plato. But none of these allegedly borrowed ideas are essential to Gnosticism. And so the traces of Platonic thought in the gnostic system are not significant. Where parallels appear to be more dramatic, Plotinus accuses the Gnostics of plagiarism, a common rhetorical device.[24]

What upset Plotinus more was the way in which Gnostics abused Platonism by intertwining strange teachings with Platonic language. For instance, Gnostics used imagery of the individual human soul shedding its wings and falling, from Plato's *Phaedrus*, to describe the fall of the world-soul. Ignoring the original intention, Gnostics brazenly adopted a well-known term while radically transforming its meaning.

Plotinus also disagreed with the gnostic portrayal of hypostases intervening between the Transcendent One and the material realm. While Plotinus claimed the authority of Plato in maintaining a maximum of three hypostases: the One, the Nous, and the Soul, the Gnostics multiplied intellects with their numerous aeons, thereby destroying the economy of the three hypostases:

> And the making a plurality in the intelligible world, Being and Intellect and the Maker different from Intellect, and Soul, is taken from the words in the *Timaeus*: for Plato says, "The maker of this universe thought that it should contain all the forms that intelligence discerns contained in the Living Being that truly is." But they did not understand, and took it to mean that there is one mind which contains in it in repose all realities, and another mind different from it which contemplates them, and another which plans ... and they think that this is the maker according to Plato, being a long way from knowing who the maker is. (*Ennead* II 9, 6. 14-24)

Thus Plotinus accuses the Gnostics of using Plato's *Timaeus* 39C 6-7 to proof-text their notion of the hypostases while missing the plain meaning of the passage. Of course Plotinus's own position on the hypostases was not entirely unlike that of his gnostic opponents. Although a normal reading of the *Timaeus* would not have suggested the gnostic teaching of the three intellects, Plotinus also looked to the *Timaeus* for his view of the triad: Being, Life and Mind *within* Nous. Either these ideas were mediated by contemporary Middle-Platonic sources, or they were the independent product of gnostic reflection in this period.[25]

Plotinus made the strong polemical charge that the Gnostics were either masters of deceit, or ignorant. Using the evidence of Plotinus, one might argue that the heresiologists over-emphasized the potential dangers of Greek philosophy because they too confronted the brazen use of classical Greek philosophy that Plotinus describes. The Gnostics were cunning, not ignorant. They obviously were deeply concerned about the philosophical credibility of their mythology. They attended Plotinus's lectures, kept up with contemporary philosophical discussion, and were attentive to critique. If gnostic proof-texting was intentional, it is revealing, for it shows that the Gnostics attempted to buttress their mythology with sources that were both normative and authoritative, regardless of whether these quotations were entirely consistent with their system. Ironically, they may have been following a precedent set by Plotinus himself.

Plotinus's accusation of arrogance also used by Christian heresiologists, is exemplified in the following. He wrote,

> And in general they falsify Plato's account of the manner of the making, and a great deal else, and degrade the great man's teachings as if they had understood the intelligible nature, but he and the other blessed philosophers had not. (*Ennead* II 9,6.24-28)

Plotinus admitted that there was nothing wrong in disagreeing with the ancient sages, as long as there was open discussion; but Gnostics sought fame "censuring men who have been judged good from ancient times by men of worth and by saying that they themselves are better than the Greeks." (*Ennead* II 9,6.50-53)

Plotinus commended the ancient philosophers over the Gnostics. He was concerned that the uneducated and gullible would be duped by gnostic claims to antiquity; the learned would readily recognize gnostic interjection of alien concepts into earlier teachings. In his irritation over the departure of some of his students to Gnosticism, Plotinus suggested that a harsher response would be more appropriate

> ... to repel those who have the insolence to pull to pieces what godlike men of antiquity have said nobly and in accordance with the truth. So let us leave that detailed examination; for those who have grasped precisely what we have been saying up till now will be able to know what the real state of the case is as regards all their other doctrines. (*Ennead* II 9,10.12-17)

Some Concluding Observations

Gnosticism addressed itself to significant issues in the history of thought: questions about God, creation, evil and eternity. Similarities between Platonic and gnostic thought have not gone unnoticed from the earliest times. From Plotinus's account we learn that Gnostics freely cited Plato to substantiate their doctrines. Although some minor concepts were borrowed directly, others, according to Plotinus, were taken out of context and transformed to suit the Gnostic systems. And again, the Gnostics quoted an ancient authority simply to win approval from those who recognized the philosophical tradition.

Some tentative conclusions may be drawn concerning the relationship between Gnosticism and classical Greek philosophy. First, the Gnostics were certainly influenced, consciously and unconsciously, by the world in which they lived and were educated; it is impossible to disentangle ourselves from our own experiences. Second, many of the gnostic cardinal ideas can be seen to derive from a variety of sources: biblical, Hellenistic, Jewish, or even pedestrian, contemporary Platonism. Not that we would wish to strip the Gnostics of innovation or creativity, for certainly they possessed both. Third, in their use of Platonic sources, the Gnostics were no more plagiarisers than their contemporaries, Middle- or Neo-Platonists. They footnoted their mythology with the master, not always careful of his original intention, but in the hope of impressing a Hellenized audience. One might suggest that the Gnostics constructed an elaborate mythological system from the spoils of Judaism, Christianity, and also Greek philosophy.

Notes

1. A complete modern language translation was not available before 1977. For general works on Gnosticism consult H. Jonas, *The Gnostic Religion: The Message of the Alien God and the Beginnings of Christianity*, 2nd ed. (Boston: Beacon Press, 1963); K. Rudolph, *Gnosis: The Nature and History of Gnosticism*, R. McL. Wilson, et al., trans. (New York: Harper and Row, 1987); and G. Filoramo, *A History of Gnosticism*, A. Alcock, trans. (Oxford: Basil Blackwell, 1990). For standard editions of gnostic and patristic sources see J. M. Robinson, ed., *The Nag Hammadi Library*, 2nd rev. ed. (San Francisco: Harper and Row, 1988); B. Layton, *The Gnostic Scriptures* (Garden City, N. Y.: Doubleday, 1987); and W. Förster, ed., *Gnosis I: Patristic Evidence*, R. McL. Wilson, trans. (Oxford: Oxford University Press, 1972).
2. For critical studies that appeared after the publication of the Nag Hammadi codices consult F. Wisse, "The Nag Hammadi Library and the Heresiologists," *Vigiliae Christianae* 25 (1971): 205-23; K. Koschorke, *Hippolyt's Ketzerbekämpfung und Polemik gegen die Gnostiker* (Wiesbaden: Harrassowitz, 1975); B. Aland, "Gnosis und Kirchenväter," in *Gnosis, Festschrift für Hans Jonas*, B. Aland, ed. (Göttingen: Vandenhoeck und Ruprecht, 1978), 158-215; Gérard Vallée, *A Study in Anti-Gnostic Polemics: Irenaeus, Hippolytus, and Epiphanius*, Studies in Christianity and Judaism 1 (Waterloo: Wilfrid Laurier University Press, 1981); Pheme Perkins, "Irenaeus and the Gnostics," *Vigiliae Christianae* 30 (1976): 193-200; Idem., "Ordering the Cosmos," in *Nag Hammadi, Gnosticism, and Early Christianity*, C. W. Hedrick and R. Hodgson, Jr., eds. (Peabody, MA: Hendrickson, 1986), 221-38; and M. J. Edwards, "Gnostics and Valentinians

in the Church Fathers," *Journal of Theological Studies* 40 (1989): 27-47.

3. R. A. Lipsius, *Die Quellen der ältesten Ketzergeschichte* (Leipzig: Barth, 1875); A. von Harnack, "Zur Quellenkritik Geschichte des Gnostizismus," *Zeitschrift für die historische Theologie* (1874): 143-226; and A. Hilgenfeld, *Die Ketzergeschichte des Urchristentums* (Leipzig: Fues, 1884).

4. F. C. Baur, *Die christliche Gnosis oder die christliche Religionsphilosophie in ihrer geschichtlichen Entwicklung* (Tübingen: Osiander, 1835); P. C. Hodgson, *The Formation of Historical Theology: A Study of F. C. Baur* (New York: Harper and Row, 1966); Idem., *Ferdinand Christian Baur on the Writing of Church History* (New York: Oxford University Press, 1968); and H. Harris, *The Tübingen School* (Oxford: Oxford University Press, 1975).

5. H. Graetz, *Gnosticismus und Judenthum* (Krotoschin: B. L. Monasch und Sohn, 1846); M. Joël, *Blicke in die Religionsgeschichte zu Anfang des zweiten christlichen Jahrhunderts*, vol. I (Breslau: Schottlander, 1880); M. Friedländer, *Der vorchristliche jüdische Gnosticismus* (Göttingen: Vandenhoeck und Ruprecht, 1898; repr. Farnborough: Gregg International, 1972); and B. Pearson, *Gnosticism, Judaism, and Early Christianity* (Minneapolis: Fortress Press, 1990).

6. A. von Harnack, *Lehrbuch der Dogmengeschichte*, 3rd ed., vol. I (Freiburg-Leipzig: Mohr, 1894). Harnack later admitted to Jewish influences on the development of Gnosticism and to the existence of a vulgar, non-Christian Syrian Gnosticism, which he disregarded.

7. A portion of Plato's *Republic*, (588a-589b), included among the gnostic tractates in the Nag Hammadi Library (*NHC* VI,5), confirmed for some a connection between Gnosticism and Platonism. This fragment precedes the Hermetic tractates (*NHC* VI,6,7,8), which may indicate that *NHC* VI,5-8 came to the Coptic translator as a unit. This particular section of the *Republic* was immensely popular in late antiquity and may have come from a philosophical anthology. However, the fact that the fragment was included in the Nag Hammadi Library probably indicates less about the nature of impulses towards all things beautiful, with nothing pulling against it any longer or dragging it in another direction" (*On the Migration of Abraham* 67). Again (*On the Unchangeableness of God* 68) Moses is described as "the best of physicians for the passions and diseases of the soul, [who] set before himself one work and one purpose, to make a radical excision of the diseases of the mind."

In his attainment of *apatheia*, Moses experiences no pain or toil (*ponos*): "without pain is the one on whom God bestows with great abundance the good things of perfection. The one who acquires virtue by means of pain is found to fall short of perfection, as compared with Moses, who received [virtue] easily and without pain from God" (*Allegorical Interpretations* III 135).[23] Because God created and sustains the world without toil (*aneu ponōn—On the Sacrifices of Abel and Cain* 40), "lack of weariness" (*akamatos*) is a condition most befitting divinity. To the extent that Moses represents God in a state of near divinity, he too achieves this perfection without *ponos*.[24]

In contrast to Moses, the one "making moral progress" (*prokoptōn*). Unable to cut out the passions entirely, Aaron controls them and bridles them through reason and virtuous conduct. Philo's use of medical imagery here is again quite graphic: Aaron does not perform surgery on the passions but cures them with the saving medicines (*sōtēriois pharmakois*) of reason and virtue (*Allegorical Interpretations* III. 128-29). Rather than *apatheia*, Aaron practices *metriopatheia*: "The one making moral progress, holding a secondary position, practices moderation of passions, as I have said, for he is not able to cut out the breast and the high-spirited element but he brings to it reason and the other virtues, as charioteer and guide" (*Allegorical Interpretations* III. 132).[25] The control of passions is a process for the *prokoptōn*, who needs to be reminded continually of the "thought of God" in order to experience the healing of all sicknesses of the soul (*Allegorical Interpretations* III. 215-16).[26]

An important triad for Philo is that of Abraham, Isaac and Jacob, three soul types which represent the movement toward perfection. Of these, Isaac, the self-taught sage, represents moral perfection in the form of joy (*chara*), one of the *eupatheiai* "good passions."[27] It is important to note that Isaac's perfection is a divine gift: endowed with a simple and pure nature, he has no need of training (*askēsis*) or education (*On the Preliminary Studies* 36). As such, Isaac is described *In the Worse Attacks the Better* 46 as being "the only example of *apatheia* among its kind (*en genesei*)."[28]

Abraham offers an interesting case study of a biblical character whose self-mastery is described as conquest of certain passions but moderation of others. In the tractate devoted to his moral progress, Abraham symbolizes the soul's journey from pagan practices to the knowledge of God (*On Abraham* 66-71). Philo praises Abraham as a "sage"[29] who "passes most of his life joyfully, rejoicing in contemplation of the world" (*On Abraham* 207). In describing his willingness to sacrifice Isaac, Philo uses language which suggests complete mastery over his passions: "[Abraham] showed no change of color nor yielding of the soul but remained steadfast. . . . Mastered by his love for God he was fully strengthened (*ana kratos*) to conquer all the names and love-charms of family ties" (*On Abraham* 170). Later, Abraham proves himself to be victorious over the four passions and the five senses again "fully strengthened" (*ana kratos*) for the task (*On Abraham* 244).

Abraham's seemingly successful conquest of the passions throughout his life makes Philo's description of him after Sarah's death all the more surprising (*On Abraham* 256-7). After acknowledging the importance of reason (*logismos*) as the antagonist of passion, Philo explains that

> [Abraham] should not struggle beyond measure as at a new and unknown misfortune, nor be without passion [*apatheia*] as though nothing painful had happened, but choose the middle way rather than the extremes and aim at moderation of passion [*metriopathein*], not being discontented that nature should receive the debt which it is due, but making it easier to bear through quietness and gentleness.

We must be careful not press this text too far: *metriopathein* is advocated in other philosophical writings as a treatment for bereavement.[30] But there is, it seems to me, an understanding on Philo's part that cures for the passions must be adapted to certain circumstances.

The other "holy man" of Abraham's clan, Jacob, acquires virtue by training (*askēsis*).[31] As such, Jacob represents those who, through discipline and ascetic practice, receive the victorious prize of "seeing God."[32] Trained by his grandfather Abraham, Jacob achieves a healthy state through his studies (*On the Sacrifices of Abel and Cain* 44) and passes on this moral strength to his descendants, 49. At times, those being "trained in wisdom" emerge victorious in both the practical and contemplative aspects of life, "schooled to hold things indifferent as indeed indifferent, armed against the pleasures and lusts, always eager to take their stand in a position above the passions. . ." (*On the Special Laws* II 44-46). At other times, the *askētai* fall away before finishing the course: "many, after beginning their training in virtue, turn aside at the end" (*Allegorical Interpretations* I 89). In either case, training in virtue cannot be done without divine help: "Upon the one to whom God bestows secure knowledge, he gives both advantages, that of working the virtues and also that of never withdrawing from them. . ." (*Allegorical Interpretations* I 89).

An important passage in the treatise *On Husbandry* provides a clear example of Philo's program for moral development. He divides humanity into three categories: the *archomenois* (beginners), the *prokoptousi* (those making moral progress) and those who have reached perfection (*teteleiōmenois*—*On Husbandry* 159).[33] While moral perfection is of course the ideal for all, Philo accepts the fact that persons are at different stages of growth. Elsewhere he maintains that, like physicians who are willing to treat hopeless cases, those making moral progress should try to rescue persons being ruined by evil, "and if some seed of recovery should appear, however little, it should be cherished as we fan an ember with every care" (*On the Sacrifices of Abel and Cain* 123, *LCL* trans.). Therapy for the passions should also take into consideration a person's willingness to be healed: "laws and teachings . . . urge those willing to obey in gentler terms, but those most disobedient in the firmest possible way, to disdain bodily and external goods and consider as one's goal the life of virtue. . ." (*On the Virtues* 15).[34]

Philo presents many examples of successful self-mastery throughout his writings, but two ascetic communities deserve special mention: the Essenes and the Therapeutae.[35] Although he admits that "those who attain great goodness are rare" (*Every Good Man is Free* 63), Philo emphasizes that they can be found: "Of the wise and the just and the virtuous, the number is small . . . but not non-existent" (*Every Good Man is Free* 72). The Essenes are presented as examples of virtuous behavior who, through close study of the Mosaic law and commitment to strict communal principles, attain a high degree of piety and self-mastery. These "athletes of virtue" achieve their exemplary state of near moral perfection by "intently working at [*diaponousin*] the ethical part [of philosophy], taking the laws of their fathers as their trainers" (*Every Good Man is Free* 80).

Likewise, the Therapeutae and Therapeutrides (female ascetics) remain celibate and practice a simple lifestyle of contemplation, study and prayer. Although Philo does not use the term *apatheia* to describe their ascetic achievements, members of this community have found a successful "cure" for the passions through their life of devotion. The women in this community deserve special mention because their willingness to devote themselves freely to virginity shows the superiority of their ascetic program: "Most of [the women are] aged virgins, who have kept their chastity not under compulsion, like some of the Greek priestesses, but of their own free will in their ardent yearning for wisdom" (*On the Contemplative Life* 68).[36] In his highly idealized treatment of these two communities, Philo again underscores two of his major concerns: the Jewish way of life leads to a superior form of self-mastery, and training in virtue must be adapted to one's abilities and aptitudes.

Gnosticism than it does about the predilection of the compilers of the library, particularly if the collection was an orthodox anti-heretical library. For an overview of the complex relationship between the *Hermetica* and Gnosticism see E. M. Yamauchi, *Pre-Christian Gnosticism: A Survey of the Proposed Evidences*, 2nd ed. (Grand Rapids, MI: Baker, 1983), 69-72; and 204-206.

8. See for example W. Theiler, "Gott und Seele im kaiserzeitlichen Denken," in *Forschungen zum Neuplatonismus* (Berlin: Walter de Gruyter, 1966), 113; A. D. Nock, "Gnosticism," in *Essays on Religion and the Ancient World*, Z. Stewart, ed. (Cambridge, MA: Harvard University Press, 1972), 2. 949; H. J. Krämer, *Der Ursprung der Geistmetaphysik* (Amsterdam: Schippers, 1964), 223-64; and J. M. Dillon, *The Middle Platonists* (London: Duckworth, 1977), 384-96.

9. M. Smith, "History of the Term *Gnostikos*," in *The Rediscovery of Gnosticism* (see n.21 below), 2. 796-807. See S. Pétrement's critique of Smith's paper in *A Separate God: The Christian Origins of Gnosticism*, C. Harrison, trans. (San Francisco: Harper Collins, 1990), 359-62; originally published as *Le Dieu séparé: Les origines du gnosticisme* (Paris: Les Editions du Cerf, 1984).

10. S. Pétrement has evolved in her own thinking about Gnosticism and Platonism; see S. Pétrement, "Un platonisme romantique," in *Le dualisme chez Platon, les Gnostiques et les Manichéens* (Paris: Presses Universitaires de France, 1947), 129; "La notion de gnosticisme," *Revue de Métaphysique et de Morale* 65 (1960): 418; "Le Colloque de Messine et le problème du gnosticisme," *Revue de Métaphysique et de Morale* 72 (1967): 370; and *A Separate God*, 486; see also 211.

11. A. H. Armstrong, "*Gnosis* and Greek Philosophy," in *Gnosis: Festschrift für Hans Jonas*, B. Aland, ed. (Göttingen: Vandenhoeck und Ruprecht, 1978), 87-124; and idem., "Dualism, Platonic, Gnostic and Christian," in *Plotinus amid Gnostics and Christians*, D. T. Runia, ed. (Amsterdam: Free University Press, 1984), 37-41.

12. For discussion of recent Plotinian scholarship see H. J. Blumenthal, "Plotinus in the Light of Twenty Years' Scholarship, 1951-1971," *Aufstieg und Niedergang der römischen Welt* II. 36. 1 (1987):

528-70; and K. Corrigan and P. O'Cleirigh, "The Course of Plotinian Scholarship from 1971 to 1986," in *ANRW* II. 36. 1 (1987): 571-623.
13. For the critical text of the *Enneads* consult *Editio minor*, Oxford Classical Text, 3 vols., P. Henry and H. Schwyzer, eds. (Oxford: Oxford University Press, 1964-); translations of Plotinus in this paper are from A. H. Armstrong, *Plotinus: Works*, Text and English translation, *Loeb Classical Library*, 6 vols. (Cambridge, MA: Harvard University Press, 1966-1980). For a complete bibliography on Plotinus consult the 2 vols. of *ANRW* (n.12 above).
14. First suggested by H. Jonas, *Gnōsis und spätantiker Geist*, Teil i (Göttingen: Vandenhoeck und Ruprecht, 1934); later argued by R. Harder, "Ein Neue Schrift Plotins," *Hermes* 7 (1936): 1-10. For commentaries on the "Long Text," which were, regrettably, completed prior to the complete publication of the Nag Hammadi Codices, consult V. Cilento, *Paideia Antignostica: Ricostruzione d'un unico scritto da Enneadi III,8 V,8, V,5 II,9* (Firenze: le Monnier, 1971); and D. Roloff, *Plotin: Die Grossschrift III,8-V,8-V,5-II,9*, Untersuch. zur antiken Lit. und Gesch. 8 (Berlin-New York: de Gruyter, 1971). The author is presently completing an English translation and commentary of the reconstructed text.
15. Explicit reference to the "Gnostics" as such is somewhat misleading, since the name is not used in the text of the treatise. It was Porphyry who attached the title "Against the Gnostics" to *Ennead* II 9. Porphyry's second choice for a title, according to the *Vita Plotini* 16, was "Against those who say the Maker of the Universe is Malign." *Ennead* II 9, 15: "those who already know," may be a derogatory reference to his opponents' self-designation as the Gnostics. C. Schmidt's identification of Plotinus's opponents was based on descriptions from Epiphanius *Adv. Haer.* 39 and 40; Irenaeus *Adv. Haer.* 1. 29; those represented in the *Apocryphon of John* (BG); as well as the untitled text in the *Bruce Codex*; and without the further assistance of the recently discovered Nag Hammadi codices (an obvious deficiency). He nonetheless came to remarkable conclusions about the nature of Plotinus's gnostic adversaries. See his *Plotins*

Stellung zum Gnosticismus und kirchlichen Christentum, TU 20 (Leipzig: Hinrichs, 1901).

16. M. J. Edwards, "Neglected Texts-in the Study of Gnosticism," *Journal of Theological Studies* 41,1 (1990): 26-50.

17. For fragments of the work consult *Greek and Latin Authors on Jews and Judaism*, M. Stern, ed. (Jerusalem: KTAV, 1980). See also A. Merideth, "Porphyry and Julian against the Christians," in *ANRW* 28,2 (1979), 1130-36. Porphyry was apparently an attentive critic of Christianity. Acquainted with both the Old and New Testaments, he refuted those who derived Christian doctrine from Greek thought. His polemic illustrates a learned sensitivity, lacking the vociferous rhetoric of previous critics. The significance of his work against the Christians, when compared with his brief description of the Gnostics, is that he clearly recognized the Gnostics to be Christians and yet also outside of emerging Christian orthodoxy.

18. Porphyry, *Vita Plotini*, 16.2, αἱρετικοί. A. H. Armstrong translates this as follows: "There were in this time many Christians and others, and sectarians who had abandoned the old philosophy. . . ."

19. Porphyry *Vita Plotini* 16.2. See J. Igal, "The Gnostics and 'The Ancient Philosophy' in Plotinus," in *Neoplatonism and Early Christian Thought. Essays in Honour of A. H. Armstrong*, H. J. Blumenthal and R. A. Markus, eds. (London: Variorum, 1981), 138-49; and Edwards, "The Study of Gnosticism (n.16)," 33-37. The entire translation rests on the meaning of αἱρετικοί (either 'sectarian,' or more normally 'able to choose') and (the perfect middle participle of ἀνάγω, meaning "deriving from, or using as a first principle;" see also Plutarch, *Moralia* 592f.).

20. *Vita Plotini* 16.5-8. Nikotheos is associated with Marsanes in the Bruce Codex, Chapter 7; see C. Schmidt, ed., and V. MacDermot, trans., *The Books of Jeu and the Untitled Text in the Bruce Codex*, Nag Hammadi Studies 13 (Leiden: Brill, 1978), 235. For other sources see B. A. Pearson, *Commentary on the Nag Hammadi Codices IX and X* (Leiden: Brill, 1981), 226f. The most substantive information about Nikotheos is contained in the *Treatise on the Omega* by

Zosimus of Panopolis; see W. Scott, *Hermetica* (Oxford: Clarendon, 1924-36), 4, 104-53.

21. The following tractates have been categorized as Sethian: *The Apocryphon of John* (*NHC* II,1; III,1; IV,1; BG 2); *The Hypostasis of the Archons* (*NHC* II,4); *The Gospel of the Egyptians* (*NHC* III,2; IV,2); *The Apocalypse of Adam* (*NHC* V,5); *The Three Steles of Seth* (*NHC* VII,5); *Zostrianos* (*NHC* VII,1); *Melchizedek* (*NHC* IX,1); *The Thought of Norea* (*NHC* IX,2); *Marsanes* (*NHC* X,1); *Allogenes* (*NHC* XI,3); *Trimorphic Protennoia* (*NHC* XIII,1); and the *Untitled Bruce Codex*, according to H.-M. Schenke, "The Phenomenon and Significance of Gnostic Sethianism," in *The Rediscovery of Gnosticism: Proceedings of the International Conference on Gnosticism at Yale, New Haven, Connecticut, March 28-31, 1978,* 2 vols.; B. Layton, ed., *Studies in the History of Religion* 41 (Leiden: Brill, 1980-81), 588; see also J. D. Turner, "Sethian Gnosticism: A Literary History," in *Nag Hammadi, Gnosticism, and Early Christianity,* 55-86. C. Colpe, "Heidnische, jüdische, und christliche Überlieferung in den Schriften aus Nag Hammadi II," *Jahrbuch für Antike und Christentum* 16 (1973): 113 includes *The Paraphrase of Shem*; and L. Painchaud, *Deuxième Traité du Grand Seth* Bibliothèque copte de Nag Hammadi, Textes 6 (Québec: L'Université Laval, 1982) has also argued that *The Second Treatise of the Great Seth* (*NHC* VII,2) reflects Sethian mythology.

22. For a study of Platonic elements in various Sethian tracts see B. A. Pearson, "Gnosticism as Platonism," *Harvard Theological Review* 77 (1984): 55-72; reprinted and updated in *Gnosticism, Judaism, and Egyptian Christianity* (Philadelphia: Fortress Press, 1990), 148-64, see esp. 150 n.9. Edwards sees the Christian and Platonic elements to be later additions; see "The Study of Gnosticism" (n.16), 48. H.-C. Puech, "Plotin et les gnostiques," in *Les sources de Plotin,* Entretiens Hardt 5 (Geneva: Fond. Hardt, 1960), 160-90; his appendix in *En Quête de la Gnose* (Paris: Gallimard, 1980), 1. 110-16; and F. García Bazán, *Plotino y la gnosis* (Buenos Aires: Fundacion para Educacion, la Ciencia y la Cultura, 1981) argue unconvincingly that Plotinus opposed Valentinians. In the most detailed study of

Plotinus and the Gnostics, Cristoph Elsas, in *Neuplatonische und gnostische Weltablehnung in der Schule Plotins* (Berlin: Walter de Gruyter, 1975), identifies the Elchasaites as Plotinus's opponents and downplays any connection with the Sethians. His work was unfortunately published prior to the publication of several significant Platonized Sethian tracts: *The Three Steles of Seth, Allogenes, Zostrianos*, and *Marsanes*.

23. Porphyry, *Vita Plotini* 16.13-19; and M. J. Edwards, "How Many Zoroasters?" *Vigiliae Christianae* 42,3 (1988): 282-89, argues for the existence of a gnostic version of what they purported to be the Zoroastrian original of Plato's myth.

24. See for example Hippolytus, *Ref.* 5. 2; and 7. 5; and Plotinus, *Ennead* II 9, 6. Other stock features in his polemic include charges of immorality and insulting adversaries with their own phrases; on these see Edwards, "The Study of Gnosticism," 33 and 37-38.

25. There is a striking similarity between Numenius's triad (Being, Mind and Life) and the triad found in the Sethian *Zostrianos* and *Allogenes* (Vitality, Mentality and Existence). According to Numenius, Life generated the material world as a result of an indiscretion, providing another fascinating parallel to gnostic myth. See also Porphyry, *Vita Plotini*, 17-18.

Judaism and Gnosticism

Michel Desjardins

One of the earliest surviving descriptions of Gnosticism, prepared by Irenaeus of Lyons ca. 180 CE in order to expose and refute what he perceived as the gnostic threat to Christianity, attributes the source of this Christian "heresy" to a heterodox Jew, Simon of Samaria, from whom all the heresies derived.[1] The Jewish connection continues to tantalize students of Gnosticism.

Two areas of research have proven to be particularly fruitful in this regard. The first concerns the specific nature of the overlap. Gnosticism has long been seen to contain elements found in several contemporary religious and philosophical systems: this has prompted many to call it "syncretistic," in an attempt to describe the remarkable number of parallels it shares with those traditions more commonly classified as Christian, Iranian, Hellenistic, Egyptian and Jewish. In this context the Jewish presence in Gnosticism has most certainly not gone unnoticed.

The second area of research is more etiological than phenomenological: Did Gnosticism emerge primarily out of Judaism? This question now dominates the search for gnostic origins, although the answers given, whether positive or negative, are far from uniform, and the solution is not yet in sight.

The following discussion presents an overview of the recent direction of research in these two related areas. In keeping with much of modern scholarship I assume, first, that "Judaism" and

"Gnosticism" represent a remarkably wide range of religious possibilities in the ancient world, yet contain enough common elements to warrant being grouped as "-isms;" and second, that regardless of the degree of overlap which exists between them, they represent two distinct and often competing ways of addressing religious concerns.

Schuyler Brown's remarks in this volume, in "*Gnōsis*, Theology and Historical Method" (279-91), provide a healthy reminder that even scholarly consensus is no guarantee of truth. "Gnosticism" in particular may owe more to modern scholarly imagination than to anything else.

The Jewish Components to Gnosticism
Fundamental to first and second century Judaism was the supremacy of Yahweh and the intrinsic goodness of his creation, the salvific value of Torah and its study, and belief in the election of Israel. Less widespread, but still important among certain Jewish groups was a pessimistic, dualistic world view, combined with the struggle to understand the presence of evil and anticipate the end of the present age. The gnostic texts repeatedly reflect these factors. At times, especially when dealing with biblical interpretation and a dualistic understanding of reality, the concerns appear quite Jewish; frequently, however, the texts seem to incorporate and invert the Jewish factors. Yahweh, for instance, becomes a second-rate god and his creation is anything but good. Indeed, one is left, typically, with simultaneous Judaic and anti-Judaic flavors.

The use and interpretation of the Jewish Bible and post-biblical traditions is now an amply-documented feature of the extant gnostic works. Well over a century ago H. Grätz's *Gnosticismus und Juden-thum* explored the links between Judaism and Gnosticism,[2] and modern interpreters have not hesitated to follow his lead. For example, I. Gruenwald has highlighted the links between Jewish apocalyptic thought and Gnosticism;[3] G. Stroumsa has done so more systematically in his *Another Seed: Studies in Gnostic Mythology*.[4] For connections between Jewish mystical traditions and Gnosticism the classic work remains G. Scholem's *Jewish Gnosticism, Merkabah Mysticism, and Talmudic Traditions*.[5] B. Pearson's studies, though, have most consistently and forcefully reinforced the biblical components to Gnosticism (especially his *Gnosticism, Judaism, and Egyptian Christianity*).[6]

Genesis 1-3 in particular was mined for meaning by Gnostics in antiquity, and several figures from those chapters (e.g., Adam, Eve, Seth) recur frequently in the extant texts.[7] Similarly, later biblical and extra-biblical Jewish traditions, especially concerning Adam and Eve, Melchizedek, Wisdom, Norea/Na'amath, find their way onto the pages of gnostic treatises, as do targumic, midrashic and talmudic ways of interpreting those texts and traditions. It comes as no surprise, then, that some of the Nag Hammadi tractates (e. g., *The Apocryphon of John, The Hypostasis of the Archons, On the Origin of the World*) may well have been directed toward potential Jewish converts.[8]

Alongside this gnostic concern for Jewish Scripture, traditions and modes of interpretation are an attack on Judaism. This anti-Judaism rarely denigrates Jews as individuals.[9] What it does, however, in its critique of the cosmos, is to deconstruct and undermine the core elements of Judaism. The heart of the issue revolves around theology. The Jewish notion of a spiritual, transcendent deity and realm finds its parallel in gnostic systems; so too, however, does a lower creator figure who is often clearly equated with Yahweh.[10] This demiurge is thought to have created, in ignorance, a flawed cosmos; often with malice, he keeps its inhabitants enslaved. The Jewish God, then, is considerably reduced in status, his Torah serves to keep humans subservient, and his chosen people dwell in ignorance. This understanding of theology and cosmology can be termed "cosmic anti-semitism" insofar as it denigrates fundamental Jewish theological concepts rather than individuals.

Complicating the picture is the gnostic belief that sparks from the spiritual realm have entered the cosmos, including humanity itself, thereby undermining the enslaving cosmic system and allowing humans to gain knowledge of a superior realm. Accordingly, the supreme deity considers people worthy of "salvation," and those who gain this *gnōsis* become the new elect. In that process parts of the Torah are seen as helpful when read with the proper insight. Indeed, the building blocks of Judaism (election, the value of Torah, the essential goodness of the supreme deity) recur even within this polemical anti-Judaic framework.

Several factors have recently led scholars to make this Jewish connection a major feature in gnostic studies. The papyrus find near Nag Hammadi in 1945 is the most important. It eventually resulted in the publication of several primary gnostic sources which, the more closely they are examined, reveal multiple Jewish connections. This initially came as a surprise, as did the discovery of the Jewish scrolls near the Dead Sea in 1947, which raised to prominence the presence of ascetic and apocalyptically-oriented Jewish works readily comparable to Gnosticism. Renewed interest among New Testament scholars, after the horrors of this century's Holocaust, in approaching early Judaism positively has also contributed to the inclusion of Judaism in discussions about Gnosticism. Aiding this process, and encouraged by the Dead Sea Scrolls, was the heightened appreciation for the diversity of first and second century Judaism. Another factor has been G. Scholem's early dating of some of the Jewish mystical (Merkabah) traditions, hitherto placed in the Middle Ages; his dates would allow for the possibility of examining points of contact between esoteric Jewish and gnostic teachings. Scholem has not actually convinced many that Jewish mystical texts are essentially "gnostic," or that they emerged in the first two centuries. But he has helped to bring to the surface possible Jewish connections, thereby fulfilling his closing wish to "provide us with enough material to set us thinking" in this regard.[11] Together, these factors have led to a situation in which one rarely speaks of Gnosticism without also mentioning Judaism.

A Jewish Origin for Gnosticism?

It is one thing to note the parallels between Judaism and Gnosticism; it is another to claim that Gnosticism emerged primarily and directly out of Judaism. In fact, scholars have continued to hold quite different opinions about the origins of Gnosticism. Some argue for a *genetrix* other than Judaism, the leading representatives being

Hellenism,[12] Christianity,[13] and Iranian[14] or Egyptian[15] thought. Others (e. g., E. M. Yamauchi, R. M. Grant), refusing to limit the origin to a single source, find roots in several.[16] There are also those (e. g., G. P. Luttikhuizen, K. W. Tröger, W. C. van Unnik, and H. Jonas) who, rather than holding a particular position themselves, prefer to underline the weaknesses behind the "Jewish origins" stance.[17] And a few, now most notably I. P. Couliano, insist on the *sui generis* nature of Gnosticism and decry attempts to ground it in anything else.[18] Still, in recent years the Jewish origin to Gnosticism has become the dominant hypothesis, particularly in North American circles. This section explores the factors supporting this position.

The leading modern proponent for a Jewish origin to Gnosticism is Birger Pearson, whose views on this matter over the last twenty years are now collected in his *Gnosticism, Judaism, and Egyptian Christianity* (1990).[19] Throughout these essays, Pearson argues for the use by Gnostics of Jewish Scripture and traditions of biblical exegesis. In his opinion, Gnosticism is a pre- (less likely para-) Christian phenomenon which emerged out of sectarian Jewish circles, rejected the traditional forms of Judaism, and in the process became a new religion. He deems the relationship between Judaism and emerging Gnosticism "parasitical . . . in that the essential building blocks of the basic Gnostic myth constitute a (revolutionary) borrowing and reinterpretation of Jewish scripture and traditions. But the resulting religious system is anything but Jewish."[20]

Pearson, like others,[21] begins to build his case on the extent of the Jewish parallels, and the degree to which those parallels seem integrated into the gnostic systems. This suggests a close proximity to Judaism. He adds to this base the realization that the Jewish motifs also appear in non-Christian (or mildly Christianized) gnostic writings.[22] This suggests that those Jewish motifs need not have come *via* Christianity. Most importantly, through comparative and detailed exegetical analyses, he argues for an appreciation of the wide range of parallels—not only to parts of the Bible, but to later apocalyptic and mystical traditions, and to sophisticated midrashic techniques. This suggests knowledge by insiders rather than outsiders. Together, these pieces contribute the main arguments in favor of a Jewish origin to Gnosticism.

In this discussion of origins, the anti-Judaism of the gnostic texts is invariably addressed in order to explain how a movement which emerged out of Judaism in places could be so anti-Jewish. Proponents of a Jewish setting exhibit an imaginatively creative range of ideas to resolve this problem. One type of solution is to place the originators of Gnosticism on the fringes of Judaism, thereby making them in a sense Jews . . . but not quite Jews.[23] This linkage is made, geographically, to the Alexandrian hinterland,[24] Samaria,[25] and the Qumran community;[26] or, more generally, to mystically and apocalyptically-minded segments of the Jewish population.[27]

A. Segal's perspective, expressed in several notable publications since the mid-1970s, provides the most important recent statement on this issue. Careful to posit a theory which explains only some types of Gnosticism, and sensitive to the difficulties of speaking about "Judaism" and "Gnosticism" as though they were single entities, Segal argues that Christianity, rabbinic Judaism and Gnosticism developed together during the first two centuries—and all emerged from a common Jewish matrix. He likens rabbinic Judaism and Christianity to "Rebecca's children," locked in a competitive embrace from the time of conception.[28] More importantly, for our purposes, he grounds Gnosticism in a Jewish side-stream pre-dating Philo, distinguished by an enduring fascination with the possible existence of a second divine power, whether complementary or opposing:

> From the rabbinic perspective, both Christianity and gnosticism were virulent and vituperative varieties of "two powers" heresy, but the heresy with a complementary divine economy arose earlier than the heresy with an opposing one. This evidence gives limited and disinterested support to the church fathers'

contention that gnosticism arose later than Christianity. But it further implies that both Christianity and gnosticism arose out of Hellenistic and apocalyptic Judaism by sharing heretical traditions of scriptural interpretations which speculated on a principal angelic mediator of God.[29]

Another type of explanation for the anti-Judaism is to set the emergence of Gnosticism within a specific socio-historical context which would explain its distinctive mix of Jewish and anti-Jewish features. Two examples stand out. H. Green, basing himself on economic and social factors, argues for a first century Alexandrian setting among marginalized, alienated Jews. In his view, the transformation of the Egyptian economy by the Romans at that time from state to private ownership, while providing new economic opportunities for some, created a crisis for urban Jewish intellectuals whose religious adherence thwarted their economic and social aspirations.[30] S. G. Wilson, for his part, is more comfortable with the theory that the shock, anger and disillusionment felt by a segment of the Jewish population at the outcome of their wars against Rome (whether 70 or 117, but more likely 135 CE) would suffice to explain the emergence of a new religious movement that was both Jewish and anti-Yahweh.[31] These theories, each in their own way, support the position that gnostic anti-Judaism need not undercut the claim for a Jewish origin—indeed, that it further supports the Jewishness of the extant gnostic material.

A contemporary feature of gnostic studies, then, is that it takes seriously not only the overlap between Judaism and Gnosticism, but also the possibility that Gnosticism developed directly out of Judaism. What helps to give this approach a modern ring is that the Jewish connection is not raised, as it was by Irenaeus, to denigrate the Gnostics, but in order to understand them—and at times, using A. Segal's perspective, to see Judaism, Christianity and at least some forms of Gnosticism as siblings, struggling to comprehend God and humanity while competing with one another for legitimacy.

Notes

1. Irenaeus, *Adversus Haereses* I.23.2 (*Sources chrétiennes* 293, A. Rousseau and L. Doutreleau, eds.). We cannot be certain that Simon considered himself a Jew.

2. Krotoschin: B. L. Monasch & Sohn, 1846.

3. Many of his essays can now be found in his *From Apocalypticism to Gnosticism: Apocalypticism, Merkavah Mysticism and Gnosticism* (Frankfurt a. M: Peter Lang, 1988). On the link between apocalyptic and gnostic thought: "Apocalypticism . . . in all likelihood provided Gnosticism with its particular concept of knowledge and the soteriological function of this knowledge, and it could have also provided Gnosticism with its version of extreme dualism" (97).

4. Leiden: Brill, 1989.

5. New York: Jewish Theological Seminary, 1965.

6. Minneapolis: Fortress, 1990. Still relevant is G. W. MacRae, "The Jewish Background of the Gnostic Sophia Myth," *Novum Testamentum* 12 (1970): 86-101; reprinted in his collected *Studies in the New Testament and Gnosticism* (Wilmington, Del.: Michael Glazier, 1987).

7. Note E. Pagels' perceptive comment: "Gnostic Christians . . . understood [Genesis 1-3] . . . not so much [as] *history with a moral* but as *myth with meaning* . . . rather like a fugal melody upon which they continually improvised new variations," from *Adam, Eve, and the Serpent* (New York: Random House, 1988), 63-64.

8. This Jewish matrix to some Nag Hammadi documents is highlighted, e. g., in L. Painchaud's edition of *On the Origin of the World*, forthcoming in the Laval series, "Bibliothèque copte de Nag Hammadi."

9. For a more detailed discussion of this phenomenon, see J. Gager, *The Origins of Anti-Semitism* (Oxford: Oxford University Press, 1983), 167-83.

10. See, e. g., Pearson's *Gnosticism* (n.7), 124-29.

11. Scholem, *Jewish Gnosticism* (n.6), notably 83. See in particular M. S. Cohen's *The Shi'ur Qomah: Liturgy and Theurgy in Pre-Kabbalistic Jewish Mysticism* (Lanham, MD: University Press of

America, 1983), which dates the *Shi'ur Qomah* and the rest of the *merkabah* mysticism corpus to 500-800 CE (51-76).

12. E. g., U. Bianchi, "Le problème des origines du gnosticisme," in U. Bianchi, ed. *The Origins of Gnosticism: Colloquium of Messina 13-18 April 1966* (Leiden: E. J. Brill, 1967), 1-27; also his "Le gnosticisme: Concept, terminologie, origines, delimitations," in B. Aland, ed., *Gnosis: Festschrift für Hans Jonas* (Göttingen: Vandenhoeck & Ruprecht, 1978), 33-64; and R. Grant, *Gods and One God* (Philadelphia: Westminster Press, 1986), esp. 86-87, 106-13. Grant previously argued for a Jewish *Sitz*, emerging out of the disillusionment of post-70 CE Judaism; see his *Gnosticism and Early Christianity* (New York: Columbia University Press, 1959).

13. Most importantly now see S. Pétrement, *Le Dieu séparé: Les origines du gnosticisme* (Paris: Les Éditions du Cerf, 1984; English translation 1990).

14. The Iranian position originates with the German "history of religions" school, whose two most important books are: W. Anz, *Zur Frage nach dem Ursprung des Gnostizismus: Ein religionsgeschichtlicher Versuch* (Leipzig: Hinrichs, 1897), and W. Bousset, *Hauptprobleme der Gnosis* (Göttingen: Vandenhoeck und Ruprecht, 1907). A strong critique of this school, including its view on gnostic origins, was prepared by C. Colpe, *Die religionsgeschichtliche Schule: Darstellung und Kritik ihres Bildes vom gnostischen Erlösermythus* (Göttingen: Vandenhoeck & Ruprecht, 1961). Few scholars today argue for Iran as the primary source for the emergence of Gnosticism; see, however, G. Widengren, "Der iranische Hintergrund der Gnosis," *Zeitschrift für Religions- und Geistesgeschichte* 4 (1952): 97-114.

15. For Egyptian roots, see C. J. Bleeker, "The Egyptian Background of Gnosticism," and L. Kákosy, "Gnosis und ägyptische Religion," both in *The Origins of Gnosticism* (n.12), 229-47. The most important contribution in this regard promises to be Daniel McBride's forthcoming University of Toronto doctoral dissertation, "The Egyptian Origins of *Gnosis*: Dualist Expression in the Graeco-Roman Era." McBride argues that the fundamental components of

Gnosticism can all be found in pre-Christian Egyptian thought, and that *gnōsis* taps into a non-Christian perspective of reality.
16. See in particular E. M. Yamauchi, *Pre-Christian Gnosticism: A Survey of the Proposed Evidences* (London: Tyndale Press, 1973, rev. 1983); also his "Jewish Gnosticism? The Prologue of John, Mandaean Parallels, and the *Trimorphic Protennoia*," in R. van den Broek and M. J. Vermaseren, eds., *Studies in Gnosticism and Hellenistic Religions: Presented to Gilles Quispel on the Occasion of his 65th Birthday* (Leiden: E. J. Brill, 1981), 467-97. Note, for example: "No single source can satisfactorily explain all the facets of a syncretistic religion like Gnosticism which has no historic founder. We must therefore adopt a polyphyletic rather than a monophyletic model of origins" (494). Yamauchi, though, has come to accord Judaism an important role in the emergence of Gnosticism, considering the post Bar Cochba period (135-) as the likeliest setting; see his paper in this volume, "Gnosticism and Early Christianity" 34-35. R. McL. Wilson shares this desire to highlight the Jewish contribution while not denying other possible contributory factors; see his *The Gnostic Problem: A Study of the Relations between Hellenistic Judaism and the Gnostic Heresy* (London: A. R. Mowbray and Co., 1958): "Clear evidence for Jewish influence upon Gnosticism in any particular case is seldom available, but there is more to show that Judaism was a contributory factor" (263).
17. E. g., G. P. Luttikhuizen, "The Jewish Factor in the Development of the Gnostic Myth of Origins: Some Observations," in T. Baarda, et al., eds., *Text and Testimony: Essays on New Testament and Apocryphal Literature in Honour of A. F. J. Klijn* (Kampen: J. H. Kok, 1988), 152-61; K. W. Tröger, "The Attitude of the Gnostic Religion towards Judaism," in B. Barc, ed., *Colloque international sur les textes de Nag Hammadi* (Quebéc: Les Presses de l'Université Laval, 1981), 86-98; W. C. van Unnik, "Gnosis und Judentum," in *Festschrift für Hans Jonas* (n.13), 65-86 (e. g., "Im Judentum kann man nach meinem Dafürhalten den Ursprung der Gnosis nicht finden," 86). H. Jonas, while insisting that "Gnosticism originated in close vicinity and in partial reaction to Judaism," has continued to argue against

those who would posit a narrow Jewish *Sitz*. He considers Gnosticism to be not a revolt within Judaism but against Judaism. See his "Delimitation of the Gnostic Phenomenon: Typological and Historical," in *The Origins of Gnosticism*, 98-112 (the quotation above is from 102), reprinted in his *Philosophical Essays: From Ancient Creed to Technological Man* (Chicago: University of Chicago Press, 1974), 263-76, under the title "The Gnostic Syndrome: Typology of its Thought, Imagination, and Mood;" see also his "Response to G. Quispel's 'Gnosticism and the New Testament': 1. The Hymn of the Pearl. 2. Jewish Origins of Gnosticism?' " in J. P. Hyatt, ed., *The Bible in Modern Scholarship* (Nashville: Abingdon Press, 1965), 279-93.

18. I. P. Couliano, *The Tree of Gnosis: Gnostic Mythology from Early Christianity to Modern Nihilism*, H. S. Wiesner and I. P. Couliano, trans. (San Francisco: Harper, 1992), e. g., xiii. See my review in *Method and Theory in the Study of Religion* 5/1 (1993), 75-82.

19. Chapters 2-9 are particularly relevant. See also Pearson's "The Problem of 'Jewish Gnostic' Literature," in C. W. Hedrick and R. Hodgson, Jr., eds., *Nag Hammadi, Gnosticism, and Early Christianity* (Peabody, Mass.: Hendrickson, 1986), 15-35.

20. *Gnosticism*, 9. Pearson ("The Problem," 35) has compared this perspective to a quotation from Irenaeus concerning the Basilidian Gnostics: "They say they are no longer Jews, but not yet Christians" (*Adv. haer.* I.24.6).

21. For surveys, see most notably S. G. Wilson's forthcoming *Jewish-Christian Relations: 70-170 CE*, to which I am much indebted. Also important is H. A. Green, *The Economic and Social Origins of Gnosticism* (Atlanta: Scholars Press, 1985), 176-95.

22. Commonly-cited examples of non-Christian writings include *Eugnostos, The Paraphrase of Shem, The Thunder, Perfect Mind*, and *The Apocalypse of Adam*. Lightly-Christianized writings include *The Sophia Jesu Christi, The Gospel of the Egyptians, The Hypostasis of the Archons*, and *On the Origin of the World*.

23. See, e. g., K. Rudolph, *Gnosis: The Nature and History of Gnosticism*, R. McL. Wilson, trans. (San Francisco: Harper and Row,

1983, German edition 1977), 275-94, and his "Randerscheinungen des Judentums und das Problem der Enstehung des Gnostizismus," *Kairos* 9 (1967): 105-22. G. Quispel has long held this theory; see his "Christliche Gnosis und jüdische Heterodoxie," *Evangelische Theologie* 14 (1954): 474-84, and "Gnosis," in M. J. Vermaseren, ed., *Die orientalischen Religionen im Römerreich* (Leiden: E. J. Brill, 1981), 413-35.

24. A. Hönig, *Die Ophiten: Ein Beitrag zur Geschichte des jüdischen Gnosticismus* (Berlin: Manner-Müller, 1889), and M. Friedländer, *Der vorchristliche jüdische Gnosticismus* (Göttingen: Vandenhoeck & Ruprecht, 1898) both argued that the earliest Gnostics were Egyptian Jews. Friedländer in particular opted for an Alexandrian setting, and considered Philo to have directed some of his attacks against them. Subsequently, Philo has been seen to contain more proto-gnostic than anti-gnostic elements. See, e. g., M. Simon, "Éléments gnostiques chez Philon," in *The Origins of Gnosticism*, 359-76; and Green, *The Economic and Social Origins* (n.21), 174-210.

25. See W. Betz, "Samaritanertum und Gnosis," in K.-W. Tröger, ed., *Gnosis und Neues Testament: Studien aus Religionswissenschaft und Theologie* (Berlin: Evangelische Verlanganstalt), 1973, 89-95; and in particular J. Fossum, *The Name of God and the Angel of the Lord: Samaritan and Jewish Concepts of Intermediation and the Origin of Gnosticism* (Tübingen: J. C. B. Mohr, 1985). In an attempt to explain how Jews themselves could have produced the idea of the gnostic demiurge, Fossum notes that gnostic sources do not all present equally negative and demonic images of the demiurge, and then proceeds to point to the Samaritan "angel of the Lord," God's second in command, as the likeliest source.

26. See the articles by H. Ringgren, "Qumran and Gnosticism," and M. Mansoor, "The Nature of Gnosticism in Qumran," in *The Origins of Gnosticism* (n.12), 379-400.

27. See Scholem, *Jewish Gnosticism* and Gruenwald, *From Apocalypticism to Gnosticism* (nn.4 and 6). The most important study now is Stroumsa's *Another Seed* (n.4). Stroumsa argues that at the root of Gnosticism lies a concern to explain the presence of evil. He grounds this concern in Jewish apocalyptic thought, and finds that the root cause emerges from reflections on the Genesis myth concerning the "sons of God" and their sexual acts with humans. Gnostics, in his view, saw themselves as children of Seth (=another seed), untainted by the evil archons.

28. A. Segal, *Rebecca's Children: Judaism and Christianity in the Roman World* (Cambridge: Harvard University Press, 1986). The following (p. 1) is representative: "The time of Jesus marks the beginning not of one but two great religions of the West, Judaism and Christianity.... So great is the contrast between previous Jewish religious systems and rabbinism that Judaism and Christianity can essentially claim a twin birth.... Like Jacob and Esau, the twin sons of Isaac and Rebecca, the two religions fought in the womb. Throughout their youth they followed very different paths, quarreling frequently about their father's blessings. As was the case with Rebecca's children, the conflict between Judaism and Christianity molded their character and determined their destinies."

29. Segal, *Two Powers in Heaven: Early Rabbinic Reports about Christianity and Gnosticism* (Leiden: E. J. Brill, 1977), xi. See also "Dualism in Judaism, Christianity, and Gnosticism: A Definitive Issue," in his *The Other Judaisms of Late Antiquity* (Atlanta: Scholars Press, 1987), 38.

30. Green, *The Economic and Social Origins* (n.21). This work is often cited and praised, but its central thesis has not proved convincing.

31. Wilson, "Gnostics and Marcionites," in his forthcoming *Jewish-Christian Relations*. He expresses his indebtedness to R. Grant's earlier (and now discarded) theory that the roots of Gnosticism are to be traced to Jews disenchanted with their God and their faith after the fall of Jerusalem in 70 CE (see note 12 above); but Wilson prefers a post-135 date following the failed Bar Cochba rebellion. This view is shared—albeit with less conviction—by Yamauchi in his "Jewish Gnosticism?" (n.16), and most recently in his "Gnosticism and Early Christianity," in this volume, 34-35.

Nomos Empsychos in Philo and Clement of Alexandria

John Martens

Scholarship on Clement and the concept of the "living law" (*nomos empsychos*), such as it is, has generally concentrated on the link between Clement and Philo.[1] There is obvious justification for this connection, but there is another aspect to Clement's use of the *nomos empsychos* ideal which has been neglected in the scholarship on Clement, namely, his use of this ideal based on Hellenistic Pythagorean fragments. In this essay I hope to show that the "living law" ideal as outlined in these Hellenistic sources actually suits Clement's needs as a Christian apologist far better than the ideal as it is portrayed in Philo's work.

The concept of the *nomos empsychos* as it is used by Clement serves three purposes: (1) to indicate a close link between the Mosaic law and the Logos (Christ); (2) to portray Christ as the true sage in Greco-Roman philosophical terms; and (3) to show that Christ, the "living law," is both superior to the Mosaic law and the fulfilment of Greco-Roman philosophical ideals. In adopting the concept of *nomos empsychos* and in "Christianizing" it, Clement draws not only upon Philo, but perhaps more importantly upon other Hellenistic sources now available to us only as fragments. It is of interest that, as scholars of the Hellenistic fragments have noted,

Clement preserves a fragment of one of these texts, although he attributes it to a different author. This appears not to have been noted by scholars of Clement in the context of *nomos empsychos* discussions, possibly because the term *nomos empsychos* itself does not appear in the text.

The Idea of the Nomos Empsychos Before Philo

The *nomos empsychos* ideal is located in a group of fragments found in Stobaeus and attributed to followers of Pythagoras, namely, Ecphantus, Sthenidas of Lokri, Diotogenes, and Archytas of Tarentum.[2] All these texts, with the possible exception of Archytas's material, are considered pseudonymous. They are usually dated to the Hellenistic period, generally the late third to early second century BCE, when much was being published on the theme of "Kingship."[3] These fragments deal with the perfect king, and *nomos empsychos*, the "living law," is the most evocative title these authors use to describe the king.

As with most ideal Greek views of kingship, the king embodying *nomos empsychos* was to be perfect and just.[4] He was to be a benefactor (*euergetēs*) to his subjects. He was to be a saviour (*sōtēr*) for them. These attributes are common to Greek kingship, especially the "kingship" speculation of the Hellenistic era.[5] What sets the *nomos empsychos* ideal of these (Pythagorean) fragments apart from other Greek views of kingship is found in the king's relationship with God, his relationship with his subjects, and his ability to become the law for his subjects.

The king is the unique creation of God; he resembles the rest of humanity in outer form, but he is not only human, for he exists in a realm between humanity and God (*Ecphantus*: 4.7.64; *Diotogenes*: 4.7.61). He is a friend of God and shares a special *koinōnia* with him (*Ecphantus*: 4.7.64; *Diotogenes*: 4.7.62). He is also, preeminently, an imitator of God, and his imitation (*mimēsis*) brings *harmonia* to the *kosmos*, to the state, and to individual persons subject to him (*Ecphantus*: 4.7.64,65; *Sthenidas*: 4.7.63).

He becomes a "god among men" (*Diotogenes*: 4.7.61).[6] His subjects are to enter into *koinōnia* with him and to become imitators of him; to do so is to bring harmony to their microcosm, the state, and to themselves (*Diotogenes*: 4.7.62). If they imitate the king and accept his *logos*, they are able to follow the right path and have sin and corruption driven from them (*Ecphantus*: 4.7.64; *Diotogenes*: 4.7.62).

The king becomes their *nomos empsychos* (*Archytas*: 4.1.135; *Ecphantus*: 4.7.64; *Diotogenes*: 4.7.61). The Hellenistic Pythagorean texts contrast the written law, which is *apsychos*, with the king, who is *nomos empsychos* (*Archytas*: 4.1.136). The king who follows God is truly lawful; because of his lawfulness, he is able to replace the written law and become a fuller representation of the divine law. The written law, thus, becomes unnecessary for the subjects of the king, for the king himself perfectly embodies the law.

Also in other sources, such as the pseudo-Aristotelian *Rhetorica ad Alexandrum* (1420a, 21-25), Cicero (*De leg.* 3.2-3; *De rep.* 1.52; *De off.* 2.41-42), Musonius Rufus (*Stob.* 4.7, 67),[7] and Plutarch (*Ad Ineruditum Principem* 780c), the term *nomos empsychos* (or *logos empsychos*) is used to contrast the written law and the king as law. All of these texts, like the Hellenistic Pythagorean texts, maintain the basic distinction of the *nomos empsychos* ideal: the law is either written or it is embodied in the king, the living law.

The Nomos Empsychos in Philo
The term *nomos empsychos* appears in Philo's work as many times as in the Pythagorean fragments (*Moses* 1.162; 2.4; *Abraham* 5). However, Philo breaks down the distinction between the law being *either* written *or* embodied as living law. This innovation is due to his need to protect the law of Moses. The Patriarchs, who according to Philo follow the law of nature and become *agraphoi nomoi*, become *nomoi empsychoi* as well (*Abraham* 5-6). They do not, however, replace the law of Moses, for Philo is intent on both explaining how the Patriarchs follow the Mosaic law *before* it is written, and showing that the law of Moses is in agreement with Greco-Roman forms of law. Thus the either/or character of the contrast is broken down. A *nomos empsychos*, properly understood,

would not replace the written law; he would follow the written law—if this written law were the Mosaic law.

Philo refers to Moses as the "living law" twice: in *Moses* 1.162 and 2.4. He elaborates on Moses as the "living law" particularly in *Moses* 1.148-162, where he uses the language of *nomos empsychos* tractates to describe Moses as king. In fact, Philo's description of Moses in this context resembles that of the king of the Hellenistic fragments in almost all respects. Philo, furthermore, uses language appropriate for royalty and close friendship with God only for the description of Moses. In the language of the exclusive kingship model, only Moses is the true "king."

When Philo also refers to the Patriarchs as living laws (*Abraham* 5), he diminishes the exclusivity of the designation characteristic of the Hellenistic fragments. Yet the "living law" designation for Patriarchs does not attribute royal exclusivity to them in the same way it does for Moses. Rather, it gives them the status of the "Sage."[8] Thus, unlike the Hellenistic fragments, Philo creates two levels of *nomoi empsychoi*, those of king and of sage.

The Nomos Empsychos in Clement
Elements of both the Hellenistic and the Philonic ideal are found in the thought of Clement. In fact, Clement seems intent on maintaining the relationship which Philo sees between the *nomos empsychos* and the (written) law of Moses, while he also retains the Hellenistic idea that the written law is replaced by the "living law."

The Influence of Philo
Clement's use of the *nomos empsychos* in *Miscellanies* 1.26, 167: "now Moses was, so to say, a living law, governed by (*kybernomenos*) the right word,"[9] clearly reveals the influence of Philo, for no other author made the connection between Moses and the "living law." But although Clement does not elaborate here on his designation of Moses as "living law," he is evidently familiar with Philo's discussion of Moses as lawgiver and king or "living law" in *Moses* 1.148-62. Yet when he calls Moses a *nomos empsychos*, he uses the term also applied elsewhere to Jesus. For this reason Clement avoids use of

royal language to describe Moses as the "living law." Rather he claims that Moses too was "governed" by the *orthos logos*, that is, by Christ. Clement cannot say that Moses is the equivalent of Christ, although in using the language of the *nomos empsychos* he comes close to intimating this.

Clement's intention in adopting the title *nomos empsychos* for Moses must be to show close relationship between the law of Moses and its true lawgiver: the Logos, Christ. They exist on a continuum. Yet by describing Moses as the living law, Clement does approximate Philo's equation: the law of Moses equals the *nomos empsychos*. This is why Clement must create another stratum upon which Jesus exists as the "living law."

The Influence of the Hellenistic Pythagorean Texts
By designating Moses as the "living law," Clement not only indicates the close relationship between Moses and the Logos, but between Moses' law and the Logos. However, when Clement also calls Jesus the "living law," (specifically in *Miscellanies* 2.18,3-19,4), interest is focused on Jesus' royalty and on the contrast between Jesus and written law. In this passage Clement says,

> ... Sages are sages by virtue of wisdom and those who are under the law are lawful by virtue of the law, and so the Christians, followers of Christ, are royal by virtue of Christ the King (18,3). This will be made clear presently: "That which is Right is truly lawful, and law, by nature, is right reason, and not that which resides in letters or in other objects." The Eleatic Stranger demonstrates that the royal and political man is a living law (18,4).[10] And such is he who, on the one hand, fulfils the law, and, on the other hand, "does the will of the Father,"[11] written openly upon a raised cross, set forth as an example of divine virtue for those who are capable to see clearly (19,1). The Greeks know that the dispatches of the Ephors in Lacedaemonia have been, by law, written on pieces of wood; but my law, as I said earlier, is royal, living, and right reason: "the law, king of all, living and dead," as the Boeotian Pindar

says (19,2).[12] For Speusippus, in his first book to Cleophon, seems to write the same things as those in Plato: "For if kingship is a worthy choice, and only the sage is king and ruler, the law, being right reason, is equally worthy." And this it is (19,3). But the Stoic philosophers expound their doctrine, attributing only to the sage kingship, priesthood, prophecy, legislative power, wealth, true beauty, nobility, and freedom; but the sage, and it is granted by them, is difficult to find (19,4).[13]

There is much to unpack in this passage, apart from Clement twice calling Jesus the "living law." Clement is operating with a triangle of concerns in this passage, particularly because Moses already earlier has been designated as a living law. Clement is concerned with (1) the Sage, that is, the Greco-Roman wise man; (2) those under the Mosaic law which governs the Jews; and (3) the convergence and fulfilment of Jewish and Christian concerns in the person of Christ.

Concentration on Jesus' royalty is not, of course, foreign to Christianity; but in light of the double use of the term *nomos empsychos*, stress on Jesus' royalty is probably related here to Clement's use of the "living law" ideal. Clement has not emphasized the royal quality of the "living law" as it applies to Moses, although it was stressed by Philo. But Clement does note that Christians are royal, and lawful, by the grace of Christ.[14] The idea that Christ's salvific act should serve to make royal those who participate in it is, again, not foreign to Christianity, but the language of royalty and the participatory nature of righteousness here again recall the ideal in the Hellenistic *nomos empsychos* tractates: by following the king, his subjects become lawful and just.

Clement also contrasts law as "right reason" with law "which resides in letters or in other objects," and then says that the Eleatic Stranger calls such a royal and political man a "living law." The term does not, in fact, appear in any of Plato's works. Important for our purposes, however, is the contrast Clement presents between the "written law" and the "living law," for it is the contrast which is found in the Hellenistic fragments, although ignored by Philo. We know that for Clement this living law is Jesus.

Clement returns again to contrast the royal and living law, Jesus, the *orthos logos*, with Spartan law written on wood. Then, using a statement of Speusippus he stresses the identity between true law, the *orthos logos*, and the true sage and king, Jesus. Clement also plays on the Stoics' difficulty in finding the Sage, both to explain why Jesus was not generally considered a Sage, and why such a Sage was not recognized before the coming of Christ.[15]

We find, therefore, that Clement describes Jesus as the living law, the equivalent of *orthos logos*, and does so in kingly and royal terms. Jesus is twice compared to written law, once generally and once to Spartan law. As with the Hellenistic Pythagorean fragments, the *nomos empsychos* replaces and is superior to the written law. Jesus is not contrasted with the Mosaic law; but there is, implicit in Clement's account, a devaluation of the law of Moses with respect to Jesus, the true law, the living law, and *orthos logos*.[16]

While Moses, a living law, is governed by the *orthos logos* (as is his law), Jesus, the living law, *is* the *orthos logos*. Clement is walking a fine line. With Philo he maintains an intimate connection between the *orthos logos*, the *nomos empsychos*, and the law of Moses (cf. *The Educator* 1.88, 2f; 2.75, 1f). And this serves Clement's purpose, especially in his debate with Gnostics, in demonstrating the continuity of revelation: for the law had a divine purpose and was not to be ignored altogether.[17]

There is one major difference. For Clement, as for Philo, Moses is governed by right reason; but for Clement, Jesus *is* right reason: this is more than Philo would, or could, claim for any person. Clement has raised the stakes of Philo's game: he can protect the law of Moses, and call Moses a "living law," without regarding either Moses or the Mosaic law as the equal of Jesus. This is because the true law, Jesus Christ, though intimately connected to the law of Moses, *is* the *orthos logos* and is not simply governed by the *orthos logos*, as is Moses, according to Philo.

But Clement's purposes not only coincide with Philo's, they go beyond them. Clement wants to argue that the true *nomos empsychos*, the *orthos logos*, the King, has come; and he replaces and transcends the written law, even the law of Moses.[18] Thus it is Clement's Christian purpose to portray Jesus as the true law. But this is also in line with the Hellenistic Pythagorean fragments: the written law is superseded when the living law, the king, comes. And there is good reason to believe that Clement knew these Hellenistic texts, or others related to them.

The Fragment of Eurysos: Miscellanies 5.5, 29[19]

The fragment of Eurysos is a puzzling passage for scholars of the Hellenistic fragments. It reproduces, almost exactly, a passage attributed by Stobaeus to Ecphantus in *Stob.* 4.7.64 (Hense 272,11-14). But Clement attributes his passage to Eurysos the Pythagorean.[20] And Clement also alters the sense of the passage. In Clement the passage reads, "The earthly form is like the others, in that it is made from the same material, but it is fashioned by the Supreme Artificer, who in making it used himself as the Archetype."

The passage in Ecphantus reads, "On the one hand the King claims the most of the better elements in our common nature, on the other hand his earthly form is like the others, in that it is made from the same material, but he is fashioned by the Supreme Artificer, who in making him used himself as an Archetype."

Unlike Ecphantus, Clement is not concerned with the king in this passage; he is concerned with showing the agreement between Genesis 1:26-27 and Greek philosophy: human beings are different from and superior to the rest of God's creation.[21] Ecphantus's point is that the king is a unique creation of God.[22] But this appears to have been Eurysos's point as well, as is revealed in a companion piece to this passage, located in *Stob.* 1.6.19 (1,89), and pointed out by E. R. Goodenough.[23] Whether Ecphantus copied Eurysos, or whether Eurysos copied Ecphantus is a difficult question; but with Walter Burkert I believe that Eurysos copied Ecphantus.[24] It cannot seriously be maintained that they are the same person, or that Eurysos is a citation mistake for Eurytos.[25] Important for us, however, is that Eurysos was also speaking of the king.[26] We may be certain, therefore, that Eurysos knew even more of the kingship ideal, and we may also be certain that Clement knew more of the ideal.[27] How Clement alters his source to provide a parallel with Genesis 1:26-27 is in itself interesting and instructive; but the fact that Clement has direct knowledge of texts dealing with the *nomos empsychos* ideal, and is not dependent only on Philo's presentation, is of paramount concern.

This allows us to confirm the suspicion that Clement knew the *nomos empsychos* ideal both from Philo and from its initial elaboration in the Pythagorean texts. In making use of these varied sources, however, Clement creates something new. Jewish law and Greek wisdom converge in the person of Christ.

Conclusions
For Clement the law of Moses is in agreement with the Logos: thus its promulgator, Moses, is a "living law" governed by the Logos. But the true, kingly living law, the Greco-Roman sage *par excellence* who replaces the written law, whether Mosaic or Spartan, is itself the *orthos logos*, Jesus Christ.

Clement has used Philo's claim that the "living law" is in agreement with the law of Moses, and the claim of the fragments that the living law replaces the written law. Clement also maintains Philo's distinction between two strata of *nomoi empsychoi*: one is the person governed by right reason (for Philo, identified with the Patriarchs, and for Clement, with Moses); the other is the only king, the friend of God (for Philo this was Moses, but for Clement it was Jesus).

For Clement, however, the true "living law" is the *orthos logos*. This is certainly more than Philo claimed, and very different from any claim made in the Hellenistic Pythagorean writings. There is an obvious Stoic influence on Clement in the claim that Christ is the *orthos logos*: for the Stoic sage embodied the *orthos logos*,[28] while the Hellenistic Pythagorean texts never describe the king as the *orthos logos*. Thus Clement brings together Stoic and Pythagorean claims about the sage.

We should not, however, overlook Clement's own concerns; his Christian concerns did motivate and drive him. Clement's reasons for utilizing the concept of the *nomos empsychos* are his own as a Christian apologist. His battle with Gnosticism over the place of the Mosaic law demanded that Clement make sense of the place of the law in salvation history, and locate it on a continuum which maintained its importance. But his desire to show Jesus as the true law, the true king, and the true wise man necessitated that the place of the law be secondary. Using the ideal of the *nomos empsychos* not only from Philo's writings, but particularly from the Hellenistic Pythagorean writings, allowed him to maintain both of these claims. In his use of the *nomos empsychos* ideal, Clement incorporates both Jewish and Greek elements as he recreates it in light of Christian belief.

This intellectual creation both marks Clement's originality and places him in the mainstream of Christian apology, especially with respect to the *praeparatio evangelica* motif. Clement sees not only Jewish but also Greek history and thought as a preparation for the incarnation of Christ and the Gospel.[29] In this he builds on Philo's initial forays into the relationship between reason and revelation.

Yet Clement sees Judaism as only one step on the road to truth; and so he relegates Philo's apex to the base of the pyramid. In the synthesis of Clement, Judaism and Hellenism provide cornerstones in salvation history, but their function, it is clear, was only a support along the ascent to the top: the person and message of Jesus Christ. They provided preparatory steps for a journey which ends with faith in Christ.

Clement's use of the *nomos empsychos* ideal represents its grandest synthesis, and not only among Christians. His insights, however, were not maintained. When next we meet the *nomos empsychos* ideal in a Christian context it is in Justinian's *Corpus Iuris Civile: Novellae*. In *Novella* 105, chap. 4, lines 7-15, we find Justinian referring to the king as the "living law" in the context of a discussion of the *hypateia*, or "consular governor." The king is given to his subjects as a special honor, says Justinian, and God counsels him regarding the laws. He becomes, therefore, a "living law." This is a return to the language of the kingship tractates and of Clement, but both their mysticism and Clement's religious insights are missing. The ideal of the *nomos empsychos* has become but another description of the function of the earthly Emperor.

Notes

1. W. Richardson, "Christ as *ho nomos empsychos* in Clement of Alexandria and Some Trends in Current Theology," in *Studia Patristica*, 15/1, Elizabeth A. Livingstone, ed. (Berlin: Akademie, 1984), 361-67; id., "The Basis of Ethics: Chrysippus and Clement of Alexandria," in *Studia Patristica*, 9/3, F. L. Cross, ed. (Berlin: Akademie, 1966), 88; id., "*Nomos empsychos*: Marcion, Clement of Alexandria and St. Luke's Gospel," in *Studia Patristica*, vol. 6, F. L. Cross, ed. (Berlin: Akademie, 1964), 191; Salvatore Lilla, *Clement of Alexandria: A Study in Christian Platonism and Gnosticism* (London: Oxford University Press, 1971), 76; Annewies van den Hoek, *Clement of Alexandria and His Use of Philo in the Stromateis* (Leiden: E. J. Brill, 1990), 59-64; Cl. Mondésert, *Clément d'Alexandrie. Les Stromates II*, Sources Chrétiennes 38 (Paris: Editions du Cerf, 1966), 46 n.7 ; Otto Stählin, *Clemens Alexandrinus. Stromata Buch I-VI*, Band 2 (Berlin: Akademie, 1960); André Méhat, *Étude sur les 'Stromates' de Clément d'Alexandrie,*Patristica Sorbonnensia 7 (Paris: Éditions du Seuil, 1966), 380, 390.

2. Ecphantus: *Stob.* 4.7.22,64; Diotogenes: *Stob.* 4.7.61,62; Sthenidas: *Stob.* 4.7.63; Archytas: *Stob.* 4.1.135-138. All further references to these texts will refer to the book, chapter, and section numbers in *Stobaeus*.

3. I would be remiss not to mention the problem of dating. Some scholars, particularly Louis Delatte (*Les traités de la royauté d'-Ecphante, Diotogène et Sthénidas*, Bibliothèque de la Faculté de Philosophie et Lettres de l'Université de Liège 97, 1942) and Walter Burkert ("Zur geistesgeschichtlichen Einordnung einiger Pseudopythagorica" in *Fondation Hardt: Pour L'Étude de L'Antiquité Classique Entretiens: Tome XVIII, Pseudepigrapha I* [Genève: Fondation

Hardt, 1972]) do not believe these texts are Hellenistic; they date
them to the 2nd or 3rd century CE. I have not found this late dating
convincing. My own position is in agreement with that of E. R.
Goodenough, "The Political Philosophy of Hellenistic Kingship,"
Yale Classical Studies 1 (1928): 55-128; Holger Thesleff, *An Intro-
duction to the Pythagorean Writings of the Hellenistic Period* (Åbo:
Åbo Akademie, 1961); id., "On the Problem of the Doric Pseudo-
Pythagorica: An Alternative Theory of Date and Purpose," *Fonda-
tion Hardt: Pour L'Étude de L'Antiquité Classique Entretiens: Tome
XVIII Pseudepigrapha I* (Genève: Fondation Hardt, 1972); *The
Pythagorean Texts of the Hellenistic Period*, Acta Academiae Aboen-
sis, Ser. A: Humaniora, v. 30, no. 1 (Abo: Abo Akademie, 1965);
Francis Dvornik, *Early Christian and Byzantine Political Philosophy:
Origins and Background*, vol. I, Dumbarton Oaks Center for Byzan-
tine Studies (Locust Valley, N.Y.: J. J. Augustin, 1966), and Glenn
Chesnut, "The Ruler and the Logos in Neopythagorean, Middle
Platonic, and Late Stoic Political Philosophy," in *ANRW* II. 16.2,
1310-32.

Armand Delatte in his *Essai sur la politique pythagoricienne*
(Bibliothèque de la Faculté de Philosophie et Lettres de l'Université
de Liège, 1922), argued that the work of Archytas was genuine. I am
not certain that anyone else holds this position, but there is a noted
difference in the treatment of Archytas and that of Ecphantus,
Sthenidas, and Diotogenes. L. Delatte does not, for instance, deal
with Archytas in his book; he considers him earlier. Thesleff also
considers Archytas's work earlier than that of the other three. So,
too, does Burkert, who believes that the Pythagorean writings of the
Hellenistic period in general may be based upon genuine writings of
Archytas.
4. Plato, *Pol.* 300c; *Rep.* 425a-c; Aristotle, *Pol.* 3.11,13. Cf. also
Jerome Hall, "Plato's Legal Philosophy" in *Indiana Law Journal* 31
(1956): 183, 192. See L. Delatte's discussion in *Les traités*, 123-63,
for the development of the kingship ideal with special attention to
the *nomos empsychos* ideal in Greek thought.

5. W. W. Tarn, *Hellenistic Civilization* (Cleveland and New York: Meridian Books, 1964), 48-57; W. S. Ferguson in *The Cambridge Ancient History VIII: The Hellenistic Monarchs and the Rise of Rome*, F. E. Adcock, S. A. Cook, and M. P. Charlesworth, eds. (Cambridge: University Press, 1954), 17-18; Lily Ross Taylor, *The Divinity of the Roman Emperor* (Chico, CA.: Scholars Press; a reprint of the 1931 edn., Middletown, Conn.: American Philological Association), 17-31; Cuthbert Lattey, "The Diadochi and the Rise of King Worship," *The English Historical Review* 32 (1917): 321f; Julius Kaerst, *Geschichte des Hellenismus*, Band II (Leipzig and Berlin: B.G. Teubner, 1926), 380f, esp.385; Francis Dvornik, *Early Christian and Byzantine Political Philosophy: Origins and Background*, vol. I, 210-33; Wilhelm Schubart, "Das Hellenistische Konigsideal nach Inschriften und Papyri," in *Archiv für Papyrusforschung und verwandte Gebiete*, Band 12 (Leipzig and Berlin: B.G. Teubner, 1937), 1-26.

6. Cf. Aristotle, *Pol.* 1264a

7. Cf. Cora Lutz, "Musonius Rufus: The Roman Socrates," *Yale Classical Studies* 10 (1947): 64-65.

8. Van den Hoek, *Clement* (n.1), 59.

9. The verb used by Clement, *kybernaō*, to describe the relationship of Moses, the "living law," to the *orthos logos* is not used by Philo to describe Moses as the "living law." It is interesting to note, however, that in a discussion of Melchizedek as the king (based on Gen. 14:18), and in the allegorical interpretation which follows, Philo says the king is governed (*kybernomenon*) by the *orthos logos* (*Leg. All.* 3.79-80).

10. The term does not appear in Plato. Mondésert, *Clément d'Alexandrie. Les Stromates II*; and Stählin, *Clemens Alexandrinus. Stromata Buch I-VI*, Band 2, point to *Pol.* 295e and 311bc.

11. Cf. Matt. 7:21; 21:31; 1 John 2:17.

12. Pindar, frag. 169.

13. The translation is my own.

14. Méhat, *Étude*, 380, n.224.

15. Nevertheless, in Clement's *Protrepticus* 10.86, he states that when Christ came he was neither "disbelieved" nor "unrecognized."

16. Van den Hoek, *Clement* (n.1), 46: "Clement determines the rank of his concepts to a significant degree on the basis of time: that is, whether they are before or after the advent of Christ. Law and philosophy are ranked together since they belong to the earlier phase. They are necessary before the advent and useful but not indispensable after it."

17. W. Richardson, *"Nomos Empsychos*: Clement, Marcion" (n.1), 192. Clement walked a fine line in his debate with the Gnostics, for he himself had gnostic sensibilities and his orthodoxy was somewhat in question in the ancient church; H. B. Timothy, *The Early Christian Apologists and Greek Philosophy* (Assen: Van Gorcum, 1973), 77-79, 91-98; Elizabeth A. Clark, *Clement's Use of Aristotle* (New York and Toronto: Edwin Mellen Press, 1977), 7, 23-26, 33-36; Lilla, *Clement of Alexandria* (n.1), 226-34. For this paper, "Gnosticism" is defined on Clement's terms: "false" Gnostics are those whose life is too austere, and so mock the goodness of creation; or those who accept rules and laws of moral conduct as matters of indifference (*Strom.* 3.5.40, 2-3).

Clement finds in the *nomos empsychos* ideal a welcome response to Gnostic contentions that the Mosaic law simply caused fear (*Strom.* 2.8.39, 4-5) and that Christianity represented a clean break from the errors of Old Testament teaching. Clement affirms the importance of law while simultaneously affirming the pre-eminence of Jesus Christ and the true, spiritual nature of law. The Mosaic law, it is true, was only a measure of grace until the fulness of Jesus Christ—as, in a sense, was Greek philosophy—but Clement felt it necessary to defend the place of the law in order to defend basic rules of moral conduct among Christians, and to proclaim the active role of God throughout history.

18. Van den Hoek, *Clement* (n.1), 46: "The law of Moses, the keystone of Philo's structure, is devalued in a certain sense by Clement when he puts the law on the level of worldly culture as a preparatory phase and makes the two, so to speak, a pair of symmetrical buttresses for the essential edifice." Cf. Clement, *The Rich Man's Salvation*, 8.939-940; 9.940.

19. Also found in *Fragmenta Philosophorum Graecorum* (*FPG*), vol. 2., Friedrich Wilhelm August Mullach, ed. (Paris: Firmin-Didot & Sociis, 1928-1935), as Eurysos, frag. 1, 112.

20. The passage is found in Ecphantus word for word. The only differences that I can see are two case endings. The only other fragment attributed to Eurysos is located in *Stob.* 1.6.19 (Hense 210, 25-212, 17; also found in Mullach, *FPG*, vol. II, as Eurysos, frag. 2, 112). No information regarding his birthplace or date is provided. The ideas, however, are in line with those in his other fragment— they are concerned with the true and false nature of things—and he even mentions the nature of the king. Perhaps as significantly, the text is written in Doric. One of his rare words, *autautothen*, is located also in Archytas, Diotogenes, and Ecphantus (cf. also n.27). Because of Clement's use of his work and because he is not gathered with the other Pythagorean fragments, I choose to regard him as a follower of these Hellenistic authors. This remains hypothetical.

21. The point which Clement is intent on making in this passage may be related to his polemic against idolatry. He glosses Gen. 1:26 in the context of a polemic against idolatry elsewhere and makes much of the fact that only humans are made in the image and likeness of God (*Protrepticus* 10.79-84; cf. 12.93). Clement also shows anger at Alexander's supposed deification (*Protrepticus* 10.77) and claims that the human being *sui generis* was made by the Supreme Artist (*ho aristotechnas pater*) as a living statue (*agalma empsychon*, 10.78).

22. Philo preserves a statement similar to Ecphantus's in terms of the superiority of the king's creation, but he does not share similar language. Philo, fragment *apud Antonius Melissa, Sententiae sive loci communes, Pars II, sermo 2* (Jacques Paul Migne, *Patrologiae cursus completus. Series Graeca*. 136, col. 1012bc). Cf. Glenn Chesnut, "The Ruler and the Logos in Neopythagorean, Middle Platonic, and Late Stoic Political Philosophy," in *ANRW* II.16.2, 1328, for the text and English translation.

23. E. R. Goodenough, "The Political Philosophy of Hellenistic Kingship," *Yale Classical Studies* 1 (1928): 76.

24. Walter Burkert, "Zur geistesgeschichtlichen Einordnung einiger Pseudopythagorica" (n.3), 52, insists correctly that Eurysos cannot be a citation mistake for Ecphantus. But could it be a citation mistake for someone else? Could it be the Pythagorean Eurytos (Diogenes Laertius 8.45; Iamblichus, *vit. Pyth.* 146, 148, 267-69), about whom we know much more? This is a tempting proposal, but see the following note on the impossibility of this suggestion.

25. Thesleff, *An Introduction* (n.4), 69; *Texts*, 87-88, maintains that Eurysos is a citation mistake for Ecphantus, but this would mean that Clement not only cited Eurytos for Ecphantus, but that his misspelling was the same as that of *Stobaeus* in 1.6,19! Eurysos would then be the creation of a citation mistake and two misspellings.

26. Delatte, *Les traités*, 177-80 suggests that Ecphantus copied Philo in adopting the "living law" ideal. This leads to an incredible hypothesis. Ecphantus, he suggests, borrowed Philo's view of humankind created in the image of God, and altered it to apply only to the king in the *nomos empsychos* ideal, for which he was also dependent upon Philo. Eurysos then borrowed this view of the unique king and modified it in line with general Jewish claims regarding the creation of all humanity. Clement then borrowed this passage to support a Judeo-Christian view of human creation. It is far more likely that Clement adapted the ideal of the unique king, the living law, as found in Eurysos to suit his Christian claims about the creation of humankind.

27. The passage which Goodenough located in *Stob.* 1.6,19 would appear to be dependent upon a passage which Stobaeus attributed to Diotogenes (*Peri Hosiotētos*: 4.1,133). The case cannot be argued here.

28. Cf. also Plutarch, *Ad Ineruditum Principem*, 780c; and the pseudo-Aristotelian *Rhetorica ad Alexandrum*, 1420a, 21-25. The phrase *logos empsychos* appears in both of these cases.

29. H. B. Timothy, *The Early Christian Apologists and Greek Philosophy* (n.17), 59-71.

Gnosticism as Heresy: The Response of Irenaeus

Terrance Tiessen

Introduction

At the first (1984) conference on "Christianity and the Classics," Albert Wolters distinguished two main phases in the relationship of Christianity to classical, that is "pagan Greco-Roman" culture.[1] In the first phase, that culture was the very atmosphere within which the church lived and thought, while in the second phase, the church drew on written remains of that earlier culture. Irenaeus falls within the first phase. For him, the gnostic teachings and writings were not historical artifacts but living and dangerous realities. This chapter will not describe in detail what Irenaeus understood to be the gnostic teaching but will focus on the reasons for his view of that teaching as dangerous heresy, and on the manner in which he responded to it. We will observe the manner in which Irenaeus evaluated views which purported to be Christian, but which he considered to be even worse than pagan.

Until the relatively recent discovery of the gnostic texts at Nag Hammadi, scholars were largely dependent on early Christian apologetic writings for their knowledge of Gnosticism. Irenaeus provided us with the earliest clear exposition of gnostic teaching; much of the subsequent discussion of Gnosticism is clearly dependent on him.[2] Irenaeus claimed to give an accurate exposition of the gnostic teachings in order to provide the church with an adequate critical response. He himself indicates that he wrote his apology after conversations with Gnostics and reading the *Commentaries* of the disciples of Valentinus and of Ptolemaeus (*Against the Heresies [AH]* I, Pref. 2). Although the reliability of Irenaeus's representation of Gnosticism has been questioned by some,[3] it has been defended by many others. The Nag Hammadi discoveries have, for the most part, confirmed the reliability of Irenaeus and demonstrated his knowledge of the various gnostic traditions which appear in those texts.[4] Among these texts, two have been of particular interest in regard to the work of Irenaeus: *The Apocryphon of John* and the *Gospel of Truth;*[5] others, such as the *Apocalypse of Peter*, were clearly known to Irenaeus (*AH* III,12,1-7; III,13,2).[6] Irenaeus himself testified to the great diversity of gnostic teaching, but indicated that he endeavoured to represent the gnostic position accurately so that he would not undermine his own polemic (*AH* I,11,1-4).

Gnosticism as a Threat to Christian Truth

The complaint has been made that Irenaeus used the term "gnostic" indiscriminately, applying it to all his enemies, or presenting them as descendants and secret followers of the creed.[7] M. J. Edwards demonstrates that this is not an accurate assessment.[8] Irenaeus did recognize the conventional nature of the name "gnostic;" he was also aware that as a heresy Gnosticism appeared earlier than Valentinianism, which he regarded as an adaptation of the gnostic system (*AH* I,11,1).[9]

False Interpretations of Jesus

Irenaeus complained that the Gnostics "falsify the words of the Lord and become evil interpreters of what has been well said" (*AH* I, Pref. 1), thus destroying the faith of many people, turning them away under the pretext of a special knowledge which others do not have. What made the apologetic task of Irenaeus particularly difficult was that Gnosticism was not a clearly organized sect; it was not even strictly a Christian sect.[10] The gnostic movements which existed were

fragmented and disunited.[11] To complicate matters further, the lines
between orthodoxy and heresy were also not clearly drawn within
the Christian church.[12] Irenaeus was dealing with something like a
guerilla movement; its origins appeared to be non-Christian, but it
had certainly appropriated Christian theological terminology and
developed gnostic Christian groups.[13]

Though one could describe Gnosticism as a "world religion"
distinct from Christianity,[14] it is clear that the particular Gnostics
with whom Irenaeus contended considered themselves members of
the larger Christian community.[15] From the perspective of Irenaeus,
however, these Gnostics were even worse than the pagans, for
pagans at least ascribed first place to the deity who made the
universe, even if they actually worshipped the creature rather than
the Creator (*AH* II,9,2).

Syncretism and Dualism
Irenaeus accused the Gnostics of syncretism in their use of pagan
thought, charging that names given to the Aeons were recognizable
for pagans by association with their own gods; according to Irenaeus,
Gnosticism claimed that the pagan gods were in fact images of the
gnostic Aeons (*AH* II,14,9).[16]

By way of counter-charge, the Gnostics in turn asserted that
the apostolic witness to the oneness of God was an accommodation
to the beliefs of Jewish and early Christian hearers, and not an
essential truth. Some Gnostics recognized that the apostolic teaching concerning Jesus and his heavenly Father was identical with that
of Irenaeus, and differed substantially from their own dualistic and
emanationist position. However, they attributed this to the fact that
the apostles could not declare to the Jews a God different from the
one in whom they believed (*AH* III,12,6). Such an approach to
Scripture left the way open for a pluralistic approach to truth and
revelation, but the Gnostics did not themselves take this route.

Pheme Perkins has suggested that at its core, gnostic teaching
was universalistic, that their distinction between those who would
or would not be saved was operative only when conflict with non-

Gnostics showed them that not all would accept their teaching. In her view a dualistic soteriology

> . . . does not represent gnostic anthropology generally. The elevation of humanity above the Creator and the cosmos assures its transcosmic destiny. Metaphors of the true human soul as part of the light lost by the Mother would seem to require that all are eventually to reach that destiny.[17]

If this is an accurate construction of gnostic anthropology and soteriology, it certainly does not appear among the Christianized gnostic views discussed and refuted by Irenaeus. He encountered a Gnosticism which recognized a threefold classification of humanity and clearly set itself apart as the saved, i. e., the pneumatic. It offered some hope to those like Irenaeus, who were "psychical," but none to those who were "material" by nature (*AH* I,6,1; I,7,5). As Gérard Vallée has noted, Irenaeus was concerned with two aspects of the gnostic system: the "emanationist scheme expressed in the doctrine of the aeons and, . . . its dualistic outlook." It was particularly the latter to which Irenaeus addressed much of his attack.[18]

Secret Knowledge of God
For Gnostics the great distance between the Father and humanity was bridged by many Aeons; nonetheless, it left the Father, as distinguished from the Creator, or demiurge, completely unknowable for most human beings (*AH* IV,9,3). The Gnostics contended, however, that as a spiritual or pneumatic class of people they had a superior knowledge of God which they had received from Jesus, the creature produced by the whole Pleroma of the Aeons (*AH* I,2,6). For during a period of eighteen months on earth after the resurrection, Jesus had secretly taught the clear truth to a few disciples who had the capacity to understand such mysteries (*AH* I,30,14). These men, in turn, had handed on that knowledge (*AH* II,2,2). By making a sharp distinction between the God revealed by the prophets and the one revealed by Jesus, the Gnostics established their distinctiveness in relation to the Jewish religion. Moreover, by claiming supe-

rior knowledge of the teaching of Jesus through oral traditions handed down from the apostles they set themselves above the teaching of the church as represented by Irenaeus.

The Response of Irenaeus

The Use of Classical Rhetorical Form
In rejecting what he regarded as confusing and contradictory heretical teachings, Irenaeus put much emphasis on the reasonability and coherence of Christian truth. Significant work has been done on the rhetorical form of Irenaeus's response to Gnosticism.[19] It is now recognized that Irenaeus was acquainted with and mastered the rhetorical arguments and techniques of the Hellenistic schools, showing a "predilection for the dilemma and the question," and excelling "in the use of irony and the *ad hominem* retort."[20] In the first two books of *Against the Heresies* Irenaeus made extensive use of the technique of demonstrating the opponent's self-contradictions, contending that the gnostic system harmonizes neither with what exists, nor with right reason (*AH* II,25,1), neither with human experience (*AH* II,27,1), nor with common sense (*AH* II,26,3; I,16,3).[21]

The order of the arguments in Books II-V also indicates acquaintance with classical rhetorical form: "It was a common rhetorical technique to hold back the decisive arguments for the later parts of the development and to present the weaker ones first."[22] Thus Irenaeus begins with his philosophical arguments, and moves on to the more critical arguments from Scripture. Yet, appeals to Scripture were difficult because of the lack of an established canon and standards for interpretation. This is why Irenaeus appealed to the reasonable character of Christian teaching; indeed, Frederick Wisse proposes that "it is only in terms of an appeal to 'reason' that we can speak of orthodoxy in the true sense of the word. The rational coherence of ideas provided an internal standard of truth. Only what coheres with traditional dogma is acceptable; what does not cohere with it is heresy."[23]

The Philosophical Response

Irenaeus was not a philosopher[24] and his accusation that gnostic teachings were borrowed from philosophy, and were themselves philosophy (*AH* II,14,2-7; IV,33,3) was intended to discredit these teachers, for he regarded philosophy as "the source of wrong doctrines."[25] The only occasion that Irenaeus commended a philosopher, it was small praise: granting that Plato was more religious than Marcion (*AH* III,25,5). Thus Vallée is right in claiming that "if one persists in calling Irenaeus's arguments at this point philosophical, they should be qualified as popular philosophy or popular wisdom. They do not, in themselves, constitute the over-throw of Gnosis that has been promised;" this is conceded by Irenaeus himself in presenting these arguments first.[26]

According to P. Perkins, the response of Irenaeus to this system "reveals a pattern of anti-Platonist polemic that derives from an earlier attempt to compare the superior Christian account of crea-tion, God, and providence with accounts that were common in philosophical circles."[27] Historians of Middle Platonism refer to the system of Valentinus as "underworld Platonism;"[28] Irenaeus's argu-ments against the Valentinians parallel those of Philo against the Platonists, and were possibly learned in Smyrna, the home of two famous second century Platonists, Albinus and Theon.[29]

Philosophical treatises of Epicureans or Stoics often appealed to the argument from "universal agreement."[30] Irenaeus's own standard was the universally accepted "rule of truth" or faith (*AH* I,10,2; III,2,1), but, according to Perkins, "he carefully includes the broader appeal in his use of the argument from consensus against his opponent's view of the creator."[31] According to Irenaeus, what the pagans learn from nature, all believers have learned from Scrip-ture, namely, that it is the one God and Father who created and ordered the cosmos. The pattern of Irenaeus's argument concerning the cosmos is so much like an argument used by Plutarch against the Stoics, that Perkins concludes that Irenaeus has borrowed it and reapplied it in his debate with the Gnostics.[32] This is not to suggest, however, that Irenaeus came upon it through extensive knowledge of the philosophers. As Perkins notes, "He has most likely learned this argument from Christian polemic against philosophers, that is, from a tradition of Christian polemic less favorably disposed toward Platonism, than, for example, the Alexandrian tradition."[33]

The Socio-Political Concern
Irenaeus's concern for peace and unity has been well demonstrated by G. Vallée.[34] This concern made Irenaeus more severe in his treatment of the Gnostics than he was of the Jews or the pagans. He saw gnostic preaching as divisive and dangerous to the mission of the church (*AH* I,27,4; I,25,3) not only because it was theologically erroneous; it was socially subversive. According to Vallée, this explains two factors in the work of Irenaeus: (1) his focus on dualism in the arguments against Gnosticism, and (2) the apparent lack of concern about the Montanists, with whom Irenaeus must have been familiar, and whose doctrines could also be considered dangerous.[35]

Henry Green has concluded that Gnosticism died out ultimately not because of the effective attacks on its teachings, but because of its failure to develop an integrated (social) structure like that of the orthodox church.[36] If Green is right, the effectiveness of opposition against the Gnostics was more sociological than ideological.

The Ethical Concern
A common concern among the critics of heresies like Gnosticism was that their teaching provided legitimacy for immoral behavior. Irenaeus did attack the behaviour of the Simonians and the Carpocratians (*AH* II,32,1-2). However, the kind of libertinism to which he alludes has not been supported from the Nag Hammadi texts; these documents indicate a tendency, rather, to asceticism.

The Theological Response
Where Gnostics accused ordinary Christians of being ignorant, Irenaeus countered with the charge that the Gnostics were ignorant of truth. In particular, they were ignorant of the "rule of truth or of faith," the "ultimate authority which guides Irenaeus's criticism and

to which all other authorities are subordinated."[37] Too much was at stake for Irenaeus to be content with philosophical arguments against Gnosticism. His key contribution is an exposition of the truth which had faithfully been held by the church, and taught by the Scriptures, the Lord, the apostles, and those who had remained true to the tradition handed down by the apostles.

Irenaeus had no desire to be a theological innovator. He wanted to be faithful in passing on the apostolic tradition. Yet, as William Loewe demonstrates, his response to Gnosticism led him to bring together "diverse elements of the Christian tradition into a myth the comprehensiveness of which matched that of the Gnostics." It was the structure of this myth, "governed by the notions of dispensation, recapitulation, and the Pauline Christ-Adam typology" that expressed Irenaeus's own "creative originality." Loewe suggests that the Christian counter-myth with which Irenaeus met the gnostic myth matched the comprehensive sweep of the gnostic teaching as no other before Irenaeus.[38] In this paper we shall not expound Irenaeus's creative restatement of Christian truth. In consideration of the relationship between Christianity and pagan culture, however, three themes assume importance: (1) the role of the church in transmission of the truth, (2) the state of "pagans," and (3) the value of natural revelation.

The Role of the Church in Transmission of the Truth

At the close of Book II of *Against the Heresies* and in the Preface of Book III, Irenaeus declares his intention to prove from the Scriptures of the Lord the arguments that he has brought against the errors of his opponents (*AH* II,35,4; III, Pref.); much of Book II is devoted to rational argument from Scripture. His attention is quickly drawn, however, to the problem of the oral tradition, since the Gnostics rejected the authority of Scripture in deference to secretly transmitted apostolic traditions. The Gnostics contended that without knowledge of these, it was impossible to find truth in the Scriptures (*AH* III,2,1). Irenaeus responded by pressing the claim to the succession of bishops whose lineage could be traced back to the apostles, and who faithfully preserved their teaching. Irenaeus also came to the realization that Marcion was right at least in one thing, the necessity of a canon of authoritative New Testament writings.[39]

With respect to the secrecy and great diversity of gnostic teachings, Irenaeus affirmed the public world-wide proclamation of the church, and the unity and consistency characteristic of its preaching and teaching. The debate with Gnostics led Irenaeus "to apply the word 'tradition' in a novel and restricted sense, specifically to the church's oral teaching as distinct from that contained in Scripture."[40] It was clearly the assumption of Irenaeus that all who accepted the truth of the apostolic teaching, as proclaimed by the church, were part of the church, and all who rejected that teaching were cut off from the church. From this Henry Green has drawn the challenging conclusion that "the Church Fathers reacted to Gnosticism in the way that Rabbinic Judaism reacted to Christianity; they made their religion exclusive and defined their membership by ideology."[41]

The State of "Pagans"

While insisting that knowledge of God, and hence salvation, is not possible outside of the church, where the Holy Spirit is at work, Irenaeus nevertheless allowed for gradations in the evil of human error. Plato, for instance, was "more religious" than the Marcionites because he attributed both goodness and justice to God, and acknowledged God's providence (*AH* III,25,5). André Méhat has pointed out that the major objection of both Tertullian and Irenaeus against the philosophers was that they were the source of heresies. About the year 225, the *Refutation*, generally attributed to Hippolytus of Rome, took up that thesis and showed that each heresy corresponded to a school of philosophy.[42]

From the perspective of Irenaeus the Gnostics were more evil than the pagans because they described the Creator as the product of a defect among the Aeons, and attributed evil to him (*AH* II,9,2). In a discussion of Psalm 1:1 Irenaeus recognizes various gradations of evil; from the "ungodly" who have no knowledge of God,[43] he recognizes next the "sinners," "who have knowledge of God, and do not keep his commandments,"[44] and finally, the "pestilential," who corrupt not only themselves but others with "wicked and perverse doctrine," namely, the heretical teachers.[45]

Irenaeus drew a strong contrast between the gods worshipped by pagans and the true God, citing both Old Testament prophets (*AH* III,6,3) and the apostle Paul (*AH* III,6,5). There is no suggestion that one might be worshipping the true God through sincere, though ignorant, worship of idols, for Irenaeus regarded these in fact as "idols of demons" (*AH* III,6,3). Evangelization of pagans was viewed as more difficult than that of the Jews because one could not appeal to the Old Testament Scripture as witness to Christ. Unlike Clement of Alexandria, or Justin, Irenaeus makes no suggestion that other scriptures—religious or philosophical—might serve a parallel, preparatory function for those who did not have the Old Testament.

For Irenaeus, the "seed of Christ" in Scripture was the announcement of Christ in the Old Testament, not the presence of the Word in creation or the creature, as in the Stoic idea of *logos spermatikos* (*AH* IV,10,1).[46] Irenaeus rejected the charge by the Gnostics that the apostles were guilty of syncretism and accommodationism in their missionary preaching. They did not accommodate their message to the ideas of the pagans (Gentiles), but boldly told them that their gods were not gods at all (*AH* III,12,6). Had Irenaeus conceded this point to the Gnostics, he could not have avoided a relativism and pluralism, which in turn would certainly have undermined his polemic against the Gnostics. His whole argument depended on the assumption that what the apostles declared to the Jews and to the Gentiles was divine truth, uncompromised by accommodation to the errors of their hearers, and that he had access to the truth via a chain of Christian leaders.

The Value of Natural Revelation
Assessment of the truth value of classical (pagan) thought and writing, from a Christian perspective, necessarily raises the question of the value of general, natural, or creational revelation. In response

to the gnostic way of salvation through special knowledge of their secret traditions, Irenaeus stresses the uniqueness of Jesus Christ as the only one through whom saving knowledge of the Father can be achieved, citing passages such as John 1:18 (*AH* III,11,6), Matthew 11:27 and Luke 10:22 (*AH* I,20,3; II,6,1; II,14,7; IV,6,1,3,7; IV,7,4). Both Jews and Gnostics made the mistake of believing that they could come to know God without the mediation of the Son. The Ptolemaeans cited Matthew 11:27 to demonstrate that Jesus announced a God who was unknown until that time (*AH* IV,6,1). Irenaeus cites the text nine times, arguing that it is the statement of an eternal truth: no one has ever known the Father (though he was previously known) except by means of the Son's manifestation. According to Irenaeus, this text does not announce the unknowability of the Father, but the exclusive role of the Son as revealer of the Father. Whatever knowledge people might have of God could not have come through alternative means. Thus Peter did not declare a new God to Cornelius and his household, nor did Philip preach a new God to the Ethiopian eunuch, as Marcionites and Ptolemaean Gnostics claimed (*AH* III,12,7-8).

On the other hand, Irenaeus did have a very clearly enunciated doctrine of revelation by the Word through creation and providence (*AH* IV,6,6-7). He proposed that before the Law of Moses was given, people who observed the precepts of the natural law "were justified and . . . pleased God" (*AH* IV,13,1). In this context, Irenaeus is demonstrating the unity of the testaments against the Marcionites, and points to the continuity from the natural law (God's law of which people had innate knowledge before Sinai), through the Mosaic code, to the Lord's commandments which did not abrogate the Old Testament law, but extended and fulfilled it. As John Hochban points out, "the context seems clearly to indicate that the verb *justificare* is here used in a rather loose sense, . . . since in the phrase that immediately follows justification is ascribed to 'faith'." Hochban draws a parallel to Tertullian's "*naturalia legis justitia*" (*Against the Jews* 2) and cites other passages in Irenaeus which clearly refer Abraham's justification to faith, and ground his righteousness on the redemption accomplished by Christ.[47] Nevertheless, Irenaeus does acknowledge a period during which God left people with natural precepts, given from the beginning and implanted within human beings. These precepts were the same as those eventually written in the decalogue (*AH* IV,15,1).[48] It is important to remember, however, that the patriarchs were not left with natural law alone, for they had encounters with the pre-incarnate Word in theophanic appearances, and had various typical revelations which created a Christological anticipation (*AH* IV,5,3-5; V,17,1-2; *Proof* 12,24,25,44,45).

Irenaeus understood the creation of the world by the Word to be a revelation of God the Creator which necessitates a response of faith, just as does the (New Testament) revelation of the Father by the Son.

> For by creation itself, the Word reveals God the Creator; and by the world he reveals the Lord the Maker of the world; and by the thing formed the craftsman who formed it, and by the Son the Father who generated the Son: and these things do indeed address all people in the same manner, but not all believe them in the same way (*AH* IV,6,6).

If all are addressed in the same manner in general and special revelation, but not all believe, it is apparent that at least some do. Irenaeus affirms that divine self-revelation in creation and providence was "for all humans without exception, who, from the beginning, according to their capacity, in their generation both feared and loved God, and practised justice and piety toward their neighbour, and desired to see Christ and to hear his voice" (*AH* IV,22,2). To understand Irenaeus's position it should be remembered that Irenaeus had no concept of people who, in his own day, were restricted to natural revelation, since he considered the whole world to have had contact with the church.[49] Because of the expectation that those who "feared and loved God" were people who "desired to see Christ and to hear his voice," it would seem risky to press too far the extent to which natural revelation alone would be sufficient to lead one to saving knowledge of God.

The issue of revelation through creation and providence was important to Irenaeus because he realized that Gnostic denial of this providence of God posed the barrier for their knowledge of the true God. In the gnostic system of the Aeons, the demiurge or Creator of the world was ignorant of the Almighty Father, although purportedly a creature of the Father. Irenaeus was prepared to grant that God would be unknown because of his great eminence, yet his creatures could not be totally ignorant of him because of his providence (*AH* II,6). At this point Irenaeus appealed to universal consensus regarding God as the Creator of the world. Even the pagans assented to this truth, having learned it from creation itself (*AH* II,9,1). Some pagans (*ethnicorum*), on the other hand, had been moved by providence to declare that the Maker of this universe is a Father who takes care of all things and administers our world (*AH* III,25,1). Even Plato confessed God to be just and good, with power over all, exercising judgment. Thus one could say that he, in witnessing to the providence of God, showed himself more religious than the Gnostics (III,25,5). At this point in the presentation Irenaeus is particularly indebted to the Stoics as he enumerates the natural phenomena which point to God's existence (*AH* II,27,2).

One final point for attention is the controversial passage in *AH* II,6,1. Alexander Roberts translates the passage as follows:

> For since His invisible essence is mighty, it confers on all a profound mental intuition and perception of his most powerful, yea, omnipotent greatness. Wherefore, although "no one knows the Father, except the Son, nor the Son except the Father, and those to whom the Son will reveal Him," yet all [beings] do know this one fact at least, because reason, implanted in their minds, moves them, and reveals to them [the truth] that there is one God, the Lord of all.[50]

Roberts' translation of the phrase *quando ratio mentibus infixa*, "because reason, implanted in their minds," appears to support natural knowledge of God. A similar interpretation is given in the work of M. A. DuFourq, M. Vernet,[51] and Jules Lebreton.[52] More recently, some scholars have argued that *ratio* ought to be read as *Logos*, representing religious knowledge, based on the illumination of the Word rather than on purely natural knowledge.[53] This reading can appeal to antecedents in the work of Justin and Clement of Alexandria, as well as in Stoic philosophy. A more satisfying approach is taken by Antonio Orbe, who does not begin his analysis with Irenaeus's dependence on other Christian or Greek authors before him, but with the context of Irenaeus's controversy with the Gnostics.[54] Irenaeus differed significantly from Gnostics on the issue of a "natural knowledge of God." If they accepted Stoic arguments regarding the visibility of God in his providence, Gnostics like Ptolemy assigned such providence to the demiurge, granting that Gentiles (i. e., hylics or materialists) were equally able with psychics to contemplate the sensible creation. Thus people of this lowest category were capable of true worship of God, of reasoning from creation to the Creator, and of rising from the sensible world to the demiurge.[55] But, according to the Gnostics, people of the hylic or psychic level are altogether unable to acquire knowledge of the Father through nature. They could only come to knowledge of the Father through revelation of two kinds: the Gospels (i. e., literary traditions of the Gnostics), and individual illumination.[56]

Orbe thus proposes that Irenaeus uses the argument that all beings, including angels and demons, have knowledge of the existence of the one God—as is evident from their invocation of the Almighty (*AH* II,6,2)—to reveal the absurdity of the Valentinian claim that even the Demiurge and his angels, creatures of the Father who live in his house, do not know the existence of the Father, let alone his essence.

The pagan argument for the knowledge of God from providence serves him well here. Granted, no one really knows the Father except the Son and those to whom the Son reveals him. Yet, beside this special knowledge, simple rational knowledge of the existence of God, the Lord of the universe, is available even to the terrestrial spirits. The pagans who acknowledged the good disposition of the sensible world and acquired this kind of knowledge included people such as Plato (*AH* III,25,1,5), the Stoics, and perhaps even middle-Platonists.[57]

Thus Irenaeus, in his discussion with the Gnostics, insists on two ways of knowing God: from tradition "by the Son," and from creation "by reason." Yet the Son is involved in both ways, for he is involved in creation and providence; more importantly, it is he who mediates all saving knowledge of God. Revelation in nature is not inadequate, but has saving value only when accompanied by supernatural revelation of the Word.[58]

Conclusions
In this brief look at a few items of Irenaeus's controversy with the Gnostics, we have seen that Christianized Gnostics were viewed by Irenaeus as a threat to Christianity. They argued for an apostolic tradition different from that which came down through the bishops of the Christian church. More important, they rejected the role of the Word as exclusive revealer of the Father at every stage of human history. For Irenaeus, knowledge of God is possible because God, the one God who is both Father and Creator, has revealed himself through creation and providence, and through a law written on the hearts of his human creatures. The Word was instrumental in every form of revelation. Those who know of God's existence, and acknowledge him as Creator and Lord through their knowledge of God's creation and providence, have a knowledge of God that is enabled by the Word's role in that creation. Irenaeus insisted that reason alone, unaided by an illumination of the Word, could know God the Creator. For knowledge of God to be salvific, however, it must be accompanied by illumination through the Word, which enables the response of faith. If on the one hand Irenaeus regarded Gnostics as worse than pagan Greek philosophers who acknowledged the goodness of God and recognized him as creator of the cosmos, he also emphasized that only the Christ of the Scriptures provided saving knowledge of the Father. This is central in his response to the gnostic claim of special knowledge conveyed through the secret traditions safeguarded by "pneumatic Christians."

Notes

1. Albert M. Wolters, "Christianity and the Classics: A Typology of Attitudes," in *Christianity and the Classics: The Acceptance of a Heritage*, Wendy E. Helleman, ed. (Lanham, MD: University Press of America, 1990), 190.

2. George W. MacRae, "Why the Church Rejected Gnosticism," in *Jewish and Christian Self-Definition*, vol. 1, *The Shaping of Christianity in the Second and Third Centuries*, E. P. Sanders, ed. (Philadelphia: Fortress Press, 1980), 127.

3. E. g., Elaine H. Pagels, "Conflicting Versions of Valentinian Eschatology: Irenaeus's Treatise Versus the Excerpts from Theodotus," *Harvard Theological Review* 67 (1974): 35-53.

4. For arguments in support of Irenaeus's reliability, see Simon Tugwell, "Irenaeus and the Gnostic Challenge," *Clergy Review* 66 (April 1981): 127-30, and 135-37; Pheme Perkins, "Irenaeus and the Gnostics: Rhetoric and Composition in *Adversus Haereses* Book One," *Vigiliae Christianae* 30 (1976): 193-200; id., *The Gnostic Dialogue: the Early Church and the Crisis of Gnosticism* (New York: Paulist Press, 1980); Jean Daniélou, *Gospel Message and Hellenistic Culture: A History of Early Christian Doctrine Before the Council of Nicaea*, vol. 2, John Austin Baker, trans. and ed. (Philadelphia: Westminster Press, 1973), 339; J. F. McCue, "Conflicting Versions of Valentinianism? Irenaeus and the *Excerpta ex Theodote*" in *The Rediscovery of Gnosticism*, Proceedings of the International Conference on Gnosticism at Yale, March 28-31, 1978, vol. 1; *The School of Valentinus*, Studies in the History of Religions, Supplements to *Numen*, 41, Bentley Layton, ed. (Leiden: E. J. Brill, 1980), 404-16; cited by Einar Thomassen in *Journal of the American Academy of Religion* 50 (June 1982): 298. M. J. Edwards concludes from comparison of the *Apocryphon of John* and the work of Irenaeus (especially *AH* I,29) that Irenaeus was "an honest reader and capable critic;" see his "Gnostics and Valentinians in the Church Fathers," *Journal of Theological Studies*, ns. 40 (April 1989): 37. For a methodological discussion see M. Desjardins, "The Sources for Valentinian

Gnosticism: A Question of Methodology," *Vigiliae Christianae* 40 (1986): 342-47.

5. See particularly the reference to the *Veritatis Evangelium* in *AH* III,11,9 and discussion by W. C. van Unnik, "The 'Gospel of Truth' and the New Testament," in *The Jung Codex, a Newly Recovered Gnostic Papyrus; Three Studies* (London: Mowbray, 1955), 96; Martin Krause, "Introduction to the 'Gospel of Truth'," in *Gnosis: A Selection of Gnostic Texts*, vol. 2: *Coptic and Mandean Sources*, Werner Foerster, R. L. McL. Wilson, trans. and ed. (Oxford: Clarendon Press, 1974), 54; George W. MacRae, "Introduction to the 'Gospel of Truth,' " in *The Nag Hammadi Library in English* (San Francisco: Harper & Row, 1977), 37.

6. Cf. Perkins, *The Gnostic Dialogue* (n.4), 115-18.

7. Morton Smith, "The History of the Term *gnostikos*," in *The Rediscovery of Gnosticism*, vol. 2 (Leiden, 1981), 796-807.

8. M. J. Edwards, "Gnostics and Valentinians" (n.4), 27-30.

9. Ibid., 30.

10. R. McL. Wilson, "Slippery Words II: *Gnosis*, Gnostic, Gnosticism," *Expository Times* 89 (July 1978): 300.

11. Henry Alan Green, "Suggested Sociological Themes in the Study of Gnosticism," *Vigiliae Christianae* 31 (1977): 175.

12. R. McL. Wilson, "Slippery Words" (n.10), 299; Gérard Vallée, *A Study in Anti-Gnostic Polemics: Irenaeus, Hippolytus, and Epiphanius*. Studies in Christianity and Judaism, vol. 1 (Waterloo, Ont: Wilfrid Laurier University Press, 1981), 11.

13. A case has been made for Gnosticism as a Christian heresy by Edwin M. Yamauchi, *Pre-Christian Gnosticism: A Survey of the Proposed Evidences*, 2nd ed. (Grand Rapids: Baker, 1983), and a more recent summation of the case has been provided by Simone Pétrement, *Le Dieu séparé: Les origines du gnosticisme* (Paris: Cerf, 1984); Edited and trans. in 1990 as *A Separate God: The Christian Origins of Gnosticism*. Others argue for a pre-Christian form of Gnosticism, e. g., Birger A. Pearson, "Jewish Elements in Gnosticism and the Development of Gnostic Self-Definition," in *Jewish and Christian Self-Definition*, E. P. Sanders, ed., vol. 1, 159; and id. "Early

Christianity and Gnosticism: A Review Essay," *Religious Studies Review* 13 (Jan. 1987): 3.

14. W. C. van Unnik, "Newly Discovered Gnostic Writings: A Preliminary Survey of the Nag Hammadi Find," *Studies in Biblical Theology* (Naperville, Illinois: Allenson, 1960), 23; Birger A. Pearson, "A Review Essay," *Religious Studies Review*: 3.

15. Perkins, *The Gnostic Dialogue* (n.4), 12.

16. "Valentinus became the greatest enemy of the Fathers because he used Plato, not to repudiate the Gnostics (as both Plotinus and Clement do) but to entice their intractable doctrines into the service of a teaching which claimed the support of St. John and St. Paul. He was thus the one man who could draw his creed simultaneously from Plato and the 'so-called gnostic heresy,' yet aspire to the see of Rome." Edwards, "Gnostics and Valentinians" (n.4), 46.

17. Perkins, *The Gnostic Dialogue* (n.4), 183.

18. Gérard Vallée, "Theological and Non-Theological Motives in Irenaeus's Refutation of the Gnostics," in *Jewish and Christian Self-Definition* (n.2), E. P. Sanders, ed., 180.

19. See for example, W. R. Schoedel, "Philosophy and Rhetoric in the *Adversus Haereses* of Irenaeus," *Vigiliae Christianae* 13 (1959): 22-32; R. M. Grant, "Irenaeus and Hellenistic Culture," *Harvard Theological Review*, 42 (1949): 41-51; Pheme Perkins, "Irenaeus and the Gnostics" (n.4); D. B. Reynders, "La polémique de saint Irénée. Méthode et principes," *Recherches de théologie ancienne et mediévale* 7 (1935): 5-27.

20. Vallée, *Anti-Gnostic Polemics* (n.12), 13.

21. Pheme Perkins points out that "the Epicurean school opens (*Nat. Deor.* I.8-15) with a condensed catalogue of paradoxes of other schools much like summaries that Irenaeus uses in *Haer* II," in "Ordering the Cosmos: Irenaeus and the Gnostics," in *Nag Hammadi, Gnosticism, and Early Christianity*, Charles W. Hedrick and Robert Hodgson Jr., eds. (Peabody, Mass: Hendrickson, 1986), n.15, 225. See also Vallée, *Anti-Gnostic Polemics* (n.12), 12.

22. Vallée, *Anti-Gnostic Polemics* (n.12), 13.

23. Frederick Wisse, "The Use of Early Christian Literature as Evidence of Inner Diversity and Conflict," in *Nag Hammadi, Gnosticism, and Early Christianity* (n.21), 186.

24. Robert M. Grant, "Carpocratians and Curriculum: Irenaeus's Reply," *Harvard Theological Review* 79, no. 1-3 (June-July 1986): 127; W. R. Schoedel, "Philosophy and Rhetoric" (n.19) 22, 31.

25. Vallée, *Anti-Gnostic Polemics* (n.12), 14.

26. Ibid., 16.

27. Perkins, "Ordering the Cosmos" (n.21), 221.

28. J. Dillon, *The Middle Platonists. A Study of Platonism 80 B.C. to A.D. 220* (London: Duckworth, 1977), 384-89; cited by Perkins, "Ordering the Cosmos" (n.21), 222.

29. Ibid., 223-24.

30. Ibid., 226.

31. Ibid.

32. Ibid., 227.

33. Ibid.

34. Vallée, *Anti-Gnostic Polemics* (n.12), 24.

35. Ibid., 30: "The emanation principle is not seen as socially subversive; it is only said to be arbitrary and absurd. But the dualist outlook represents a social threat. It spares no mundane authority, criticizes what is universally received, and challenges the status quo. Its potential for disturbing peace and order knows no limit; consequently, Gnostics are seen as dangerous radicals."

36. Henry Alan Green, "Suggested Sociological Themes" (n.11) 175-80.

37. Vallée, *Anti-Gnostic Polemics* (n.12), 17.

38. William P. Loewe, "Myth and Counter-Myth: Irenaeus's Story of Salvation," in *Interpreting Tradition: The Art of Theological Reflection*, Jane Kopas, ed., *The Annual Publication of the College Theology Society*, 1983, vol. 29 (Chico, CA: Scholar's Press, 1984), 40.

39. Henry Chadwick, *The Early Church* (Baltimore, Maryland: Penguin Books, 1967), 81.

40. J. N. D. Kelly, *Early Christian Doctrines*, 2nd ed. (New York: Harper and Row, 1960), 37.

41. Henry Allen Green, "Suggested Sociological Themes" (n.11), 175.

42. It should be noted, however, that Clement of Alexandria was aware of Christian hostility to the Greek philosophers, but did not share it. Cf. André Méhat, "La philosophie du troisième testament? La pensée grecque et la foi selon Clément d'Alexandrie," *Lumière et vie* 32 (1983): 17.

43. From *Proof of the Apostolic Preaching*, trans. and annotated by Joseph P. Smith, S. J., *Ancient Christian Writers*, no. 16 (New York: Newman Press, 1952).

44. J. P. Smith here suggests that Irenaeus is referring also to the arrogance of Gnostics who regarded good works as necessary for the initiate; *Proof*, 134, n.15.

45. Elsewhere, Irenaeus likens three groups of people to different categories of the unclean animals in the Old Testament. The Gentiles, or pagans, who do not have faith in God, are like the animals that neither chew the cud nor have a cloven hoof. The Jews have the words of God (i. e., chew the cud), but are not fixed firmly in the Father and the Son (i. e., do not have the surefootedness of the divided hoof). The heretics claim to believe in the Father and the Son (i. e., have a divided hoof), but they do not meditate on God's words with a view to growing in obedience and righteousness (*AH* V,8,3).

46. Cf. Albert Houssiau, *La christologie de saint Irénée* (Louvain: Publications Universitaires de Louvain, 1955), 85.

47. John Hochban, "St. Irenaeus on the Atonement," *Theological Studies* 7 (December 1946): 546. Cf. *AH* IV,5,5; IV,8,1-2; IV,22,2.

48. The importance of a "clear conscience" in the worship of God and in the offering of an acceptable sacrifice is borne out in the case of Cain, whose heart was full of envy and ill-will to his brother. It is the pure conscience that sanctifies the sacrifice (IV,18,3).

49. Terrance Tiessen, "The Missiological Context of Irenaeus's View of the Non-Christian," *Divine Revelation and the Non-Christian in the Theology of Irenaeus* (Unpublished dissertation, Ateneo de Manila University, 1984), 64-81.

50. *Ante-Nicene Christian Library*, 1:365.

51. Cited by Louis Escoula, "Saint Irénée et la connaissance naturelle de Dieu," *Revue des Sciences Religieuses* 20 (May-October 1940): 252.

52. Jules Lebreton, *Histoire du dogme de la Trinité des origines au Concile de Nicée*, vol. 2 (Paris: Gabriel Beauchesne, 1928), 528f.

53. E.g., Louis Escoula (n.51), 255-70; Juan Ochagavia, *Visibile Patris Filius: A Study of Irenaeus' Teaching on Revelation and Tradition*. Orientalia Christiana Analecta, no. 171 (Rome: Pont. Institutum Orientalium Studiorum, 1964), 77-80; Albert Houssiau, "L'exégèse de Matthieu 11, 27b selon saint Irenée," *Ephemerides Theologicae Lovanienses* 29 (1953): 334-36.

54. Antonio Orbe, "San Ireneo y el conocimiento natural de Dios," *Gregorianum* 47 (1966): 441-77, 710-47.

55. Ibid., 448-50.

56. Ibid., 461.

57. Ibid., 719, n.91.

58. Ibid., 731.

Tertullian on Athens and Jerusalem

Wendy E. Helleman

Quid ergo Athenis et Hierosolymis?
Quid Academiae et Ecclesiae?
Quid haereticis et christianis?   *De Praes.*7.9

"What does Athens have in common with Jerusalem? the academy with the church? heretics with Christians?"

This quotation has echoed down the centuries. It is found in innumerable discussions of early Christianity. Often its use is only tangentially connected with Tertullian himself. And although numerous recent studies have demonstrated that only a naive reading would take this quotation to be representative of Tertullian's own approach, such investigations have not put an end to its use.[1] Where Justin Martyr or Clement of Alexandria have been regarded as taking a more conciliatory approach to the wisdom of the Greeks, Tertullian is still for many the prototype of intransigence, staunchly opposed to compromise, accommodation, or synthesis. The quotation has become a symbol for an isolationist or oppositionist approach, a tag for those who would argue for a decisive separation between Christians and "the world," Christ and culture.[2]

In the present discussion of the quotation and the motif which it represents, I would like to investigate why the statement of Tertullian has so persistently been identified with the isolationist position. To do so I wish to turn first to Tertullian's own use of the Athens/Jerusalem theme in its original context, the treatise *De Praescriptionibus* (*On Prescriptive Rules*).[3] Secondly, I wish to examine a recent study of the Athens/Jerusalem theme in Jean-Claude Fredouille's *Tertullien et la conversion de la culture antique*, a work which by its very title would appear to challenge the older interpretation.[4] And finally I would like to examine a short study of Rudolf Boon, *Antiquitas Graeco-Romana et Dignitas Israelitica*, with the subtitle: "The Athens/Rome/Jerusalem controversy as a fundamental factor in the Western European process of secularization;" this discussion highlights a number of factors which are helpful in exploring the continued popularity of the Athens/Jerusalem motif.[5] Clarification of Tertullian's view of the relationship between Athens and Jerusalem is significant for our discussion of Hellenistic Judaism and Gnosticism within the context of early Christianity, not only because the motif reflects an early Christian attitude to pagan (classical) culture, but because the quotation in its original context occurs as part of a discussion of heresy, with special reference to Gnosticism.

Tertullian's De Praescriptionibus: An Analysis

The full title of Tertullian's treatise is *De Praescriptionibus adversus haereses omnes* or "On *a priori* arguments (or principles) to be used against all heresies."[6] *Praescriptio* has an exact legal meaning: "interdiction, or formal objection,"[7] and in the treatise Tertullian does appear to have a semi-legal situation in mind when he speaks of heretics as *trespassers* who use scriptural evidence while they have no clear title to these writings (*Praes*.37). Nonetheless, the basic purpose of the treatise is pastoral, especially as Tertullian warns Christians against discussing scripture with heretics who do not share a basic agreement on the rule of faith (*Praes*.15-19).[8] Accordingly, the semi-legal aspects of the discussion are to be understood in a metaphorical sense. In this treatise Tertullian provides basic principles; implications of such principles will receive attention in other treatises with more specific arguments directed at particular heretical positions.[9]

Tertullian begins the treatise by reminding Christians that they ought not to be surprised at the number and vigor of heresies; the apostle Paul had already warned that these would come as a testing of faith (*Praes*.1-4).[10] Heresies are like fevers consuming the body, drawing strength in proportion to the body's weakness (2); like wolves in sheep's clothing (Matt. 7:15), false prophets are all the more dangerous because they pretend to profess Christ (4) but destroy the unity of faith (5). Heretics have made their choice, their *hairesis*: they have refused to submit to the authority of the church which possesses the truth of the gospel as it was handed on from Christ himself to the apostles and the churches they founded (6).[11]

With this remark Tertullian comes to the climax of the introductory *exordium*: heretics propagate foolishness by choosing human wisdom, looking to the school of Plato, the Stoics, or even Epicurus when discussing issues such as the origin of evil, of human beings, or even of God.[12] Calling on Paul's advice in Colossians 2:8, "See that no one take you captive through hollow and deceptive philosophy which depends on human tradition", and the apostle's discussion with the philosophers of Athens in Acts 17:16f., Tertullian exclaims, "What has Athens in common with Jerusalem, the Academy with the church, or heretics with Christians? Our instruction comes from the Portico of Solomon, where we are taught to seek the Lord with simplicity of heart. Away then with Stoic, Platonic, or dialectic Christianity. After possessing Christ there is no room for further curiosity."[13]

Responding to heretical use of the text "Seek and you will find" (Matt. 7:7) to warrant inquiry into deeper questions, Tertullian asserts that for Christians the purpose of searching is to find Christ and to believe in him (*Praes*.8-14). Further search for knowledge about God, if it is not to be endless (12), must respect the rule of faith which, as he summarizes in chapter 13, follows closely on the "apostolic" creed of the ante-Nicene church.

With chapter 15 we come to Tertullian's central statement concerning the dangers which heretical use of the scriptures pose for Christians. According to Tertullian, heretics have no right to use the scriptures. The scriptures belong not to them, but only to those who by the rule of apostolic succession can be shown to have clear title. For Tertullian it is axiomatic that truth precedes falsehood, that true doctrine has preceded its distortion and mutilation in heretical teaching (*Praes*.31 and 39). In discussing the proper use and understanding of scripture Tertullian stresses the role of the *regula fidei*, the rule of faith (19-21). To protect Christians against useless arguments over the interpretation of scripture Tertullian advises preliminary agreement on the rule of faith as summarized in the creed, since it is attested as faithfully representing the message which Christ himself entrusted to the apostles, and they in turn to the churches they founded (20-22).[14]

It is precisely because the proponents of heretical teachings cannot produce lists of bishops going back in unbroken succession to the apostles that Tertullian, in a dramatically-worded chapter (37), insists that they are trespassers, enemies, and strangers in a territory for which only those who submit to the rule of faith have clear title (cf.15).

For a proper appreciation of the Athens/Jerusalem motif in this treatise it is important first to recognize that the exclamation occurs at a climactic point in the introductory discussion. In his study of Tertullian and rhetoric, Robert Sider has demonstrated that precisely at this point one might expect a clearly stated contrast or opposition, as well as rhetorical exaggeration.[15] The triple nature of the exclamation, together with the given context in the treatise, also indicates that Tertullian used the Athens/Jerusalem opposition with the intent of undermining the teaching of heretics, especially where these were closely linked with philosophical schools, as in Valentinus's use of Platonism. Even Plotinus in his treatise against the Gnostics (II 9) complained of their abuse of the authority of Plato.[16]

Tertullian certainly had reservations about philosophy; it may have represented the highest achievement of the Greeks but as such it was a purely human wisdom. When for teachers like Valentinus its role obviously took precedence to that of the faith, and *deter-*

mined the nature of the quest for knowledge about God and human nature, Tertullian regarded it as a dangerous occupation. Through the Athens/Jerusalem motif in the *De Praescriptionibus* he thus presents the reader with a sharp contrast between those who have the confidence of faith because they submit to the rule of faith, and those whose expression of the faith is determined by philosophical positions.

Tertullien et la conversion de la culture antique

Jean-Claude Fredouille's study of Tertullian puts him in the context of Roman North Africa of the second and third century, presenting him as a Christian engaged with the culture of his time and actively transforming that which he has inherited.[17] The present analysis will focus on the chapters where Fredouille discusses the Athens/ Jerusalem motif, to examine how he understands Tertullian's *conversion* or *transformation* of ancient culture. We will begin by looking at what Fredouille means by "ancient culture;" next, how he understands "conversion;" and, finally, how he has interpreted the Athens/Jerusalem motif.

Ancient culture

From his statement of purpose it is clear that Fredouille hoped to correct a negative image of Tertullian by focusing on "la vie profonde de l'auteur, le rythme propre de son oeuvre" (*Tertullien*, 1972: 17-8). And these phrases are certainly indicative of what he means by "la culture de Tertullien." Discussion of cultural forms such as drama and public festivals takes second place to a focus on inner culture, or cultivation based on education. Tertullian emerges as a man of literary taste and refined sensibility, particularly as *rhetor*: a speaker and writer.

In his account of Tertullian's education Fredouille emphasizes the inspiration of Cicero who advocated the study of history, jurisprudence, and philosophy for the *orator*.[18] Three aspects of Tertullian's writings which reflect his education are given special attention: rhetoric, breadth of interest (or *curiositas*), and "true culture."

Although Tertullian repudiated the orators together with philosophers when these seek their own glory, his frequent use of rhetorical figures like caricature, paradox, and antithesis give evidence of mastery of oratorical style (481-82). Fredouille concludes that for Tertullian rhetoric had a legitimate role in the defense of the faith and the effective education of fellow Christians.

The second aspect, his *curiositas*, or wide-ranging interest in philosophical and theological issues, is similarly regarded positively, in the tradition of a philosopher like Aristotle. He denounced only the *curiositas* of heretical groups who asked impossible questions regarding the origin of God, or of evil (432).[19]

The third characteristic, "true culture," although crucial for Fredouille's main thesis, is not as convincingly presented. Fredouille emphasizes that were Tertullian's culture not truly *une formation d'esprit* (484), one could not imagine the spiritual depth of the inner life transformed by faith. Clearly, Fredouille regards "ancient culture" as a highly personalized if not privatized factor. In reading Tertullian he has focused primarily on the categories of thought evident in the treatises, and has recognized these to be characteristic of a highly cultivated and well-educated person (18-19). In fact, he regards the coherence and success of Tertullian's writings as the result of a harmony between his own categories of thought and those imposed on him by his education (18).

But Fredouille's analysis of Tertullian's personal journey from paganism through Christianity to Montanism has its pitfalls. The writings we have of Tertullian all date from the period after his conversion. It is no easy task to distinguish clearly between the categories of Tertullian's own thought and those derived from his education using sources which reflect primarily Tertullian the Christian. Although not oblivious to the problem, Fredouille has not altogether avoided the dangers of circular reasoning on this question.[20] Discerning the transition from non-Christian to Christian thought demands attentive reading and a degree of identification, which inevitably introduces an element of subjectivity into the analysis. As we shall see below, it is particularly on this question of delineating the transition from paganism to Christianity that Fredouille's study is less convincing.

Conversion

The theme of "conversion" takes us to the heart of Fredouille's argument. He is particularly interested in the impact of conversion on Tertullian as a writer, and begins by stating that for Tertullian conversion to Christianity was not a matter of simply rejecting the rhetoric, dialectic, and philosophy of his education; nor was it a matter of adding faith and dogma (19-20, 481). Even to say that ancient culture gave him the tools to analyze, expound, and defend Christian teaching, or to use his training in the service of truth, is inadequate (484). What Fredouille calls *la rencontre en lui de l'Antiquité et du Christianisme* was a more complex matter (481). In his endeavor to get behind the polemics to find the actual person Fredouille focuses on the transition to a new world of thought, an adaptation of older cultural forms to new ways of thinking. In this process Tertullian continued to use older patterns of thought and expression, although he rejected more blatant forms of paganism, like idolatry, the polytheism of poets, and immoralities of myths (19-20, 481).[21]

Tertullian's conversion is described as a *process* (19-20, 485). To explain this process he refers to (Stoic) imagery of plant growth and grafting.[22] Fredouille refers to Tertullian's new faith as one that does not uproot ancient culture but is grafted onto it, and thus "converts" it, i. e., by turning it in a different direction. In fact, for conversion Fredouille prefers the Stoic term *prokopē*: a process of growth and change, rather than the more traditional term *metanoia* (25, 481, 485). And he concludes that Stoic categories of thought are crucial for Tertullian's description of the role of faith and of moral progress (484-85). Tertullian could not deny his past, the training of his youth (481).

Fredouille thus regards the metaphor of plant growth helpful to explain the process of conversion, and to provide unity and coherence to his portrayal of Tertullian as a writer and person. This approach does allow for a reconciliation of some inner contradictions in the traditional picture; its weakness lies in its inability to account for the oppositionist language which Tertullian does use (18, 24-25, 484-85).

The Jerusalem/Athens motif

In his discussion of the Jerusalem/Athens theme in Tertullian's work, especially *De Praes.* 7.9, Fredouille is in agreement with Sider and others in recognizing the polemical context. Analysis of the many references to philosophers in the treatises has convinced him that Tertullian could not have intended a simple rejection of philosophy or of ancient culture represented by Athens.[23] He compares this passage with that of *Apology* 46, where Tertullian also climaxes a long debate with a statement which rejects the identification of Christianity with philosophy: "What do the philosopher and the Christian have in common, the one a disciple of Hellas, the other of Heaven . . . the one corrupting the truth, the other restoring it." This repetition of a stylistic device should, according to Fredouille, alert us to its true source, the Pauline exclamation of 2 Corinthians 6:14-16: "Do not be yoked together with unbelievers. For what do righteousness and wickedness have in common? Or what fellowship can light have with darkness? What harmony is there between Christ and Belial? . . ."[24]

Fredouille concludes that if Tertullian opposed the identification of Christianity with a philosophy it was not because he wished to reject philosophy as such, but to indicate the superiority of Christianity. The philosophers have only the pretence of truth and a reputation of wisdom, but even that they have corrupted in their desire for fame and glory. The scriptures present the truth which is more ancient than any system of philosophy.[25]

To summarize Fredouille's analysis, the Athens/Jerusalem motif in the *De Praescriptionibus* is to be regarded as a rejection not of philosophy as such but of the particular use of philosophy (i. e., by Gnostics) to create a Stoicizing or Platonizing Christianity in which the philosophical element dominates. If Tertullian's adaptation of ancient culture aimed at a synthesis, as Fredouille claims, it was a synthesis in which Christianity was to be accorded supremacy in its use of those aspects of ancient culture which were seen to be compatible with the faith.

The portrayal of Tertullian which emerges from the work of Fredouille is undoubtedly an attractive one. His Tertullian is not the rigorous oppositionist of the traditional picture; according to Fredouille, his views more closely approximate those of Justin Martyr or Clement of Alexandria.[26] Where he differs from them, according to Fredouille, it is primarily a matter of emphasis, reflecting a typically Roman sceptical attitude to philosophy. Indeed, with his presentation of Tertullian's argument for the superiority of Christianity over pagan philosophy and culture, Fredouille may have vindicated the assessment of Harnack, who considered Tertullian a precursor of scholastics for whom Christianity represented the completion and perfection of pagan culture.[27]

Fredouille's image of conversion as a process of grafting the new faith onto the older plant of ancient culture is central to this portrayal of Tertullian. Fredouille is certainly justified in acknowledging the continued influence of categories of thought from pagan culture through an education which could not easily be dismissed. But he also claims that in matters as fundamental as the role of faith, older patterns of thought continued to have a decisive role. We must then ask, if pagan Greco-Roman cultural forms have so thoroughly determined the expression of the faith, can faith still truly be said to have transformed or converted that culture?

We must return to the question of the line of demarcation between the old and the new, between pagan and Christian elements in Tertullian's work. In his concern to find unity and coherence Fredouille appears to have sacrificed some of the sharp edges of Tertullian's thought. The fact that we must rely on what are primarily Christian treatises for a study which aims to discover the process of adaptation of the old to the new may have helped to blur the distinction between them. And surely one could expect a search for unity under such circumstances to be inclined toward emphasizing the integration of the new with the old, at the expense of the distinctions between them.

Undeniably, ancient culture continued to play an important role in Tertullian's life and thought. Deeply engrained patterns of behavior, training, and education are not quickly eradicated. The perspective of history allows us to see even more clearly how much Tertullian was a part of the Roman world of the late second century. Yet I would argue that his contribution as an author does not lie only, or even primarily in the way he reflected that world; it is rather to be found in his critical examination of that culture in terms of his new-found faith. And Tertullian does give us a clear indication of the line of separation between Christianity and the pagan world of classical antiquity. The clue is to be found in the significance of the "rule of faith" in his thought. In the passages examined, *De Praes.* 7.9, and its parallel in *Apology* 46, especially as one studies them in context, one finds that the *regula fidei* had a decisive role in casting the Christian faith and life in undeniable opposition to ancient culture especially as that culture was represented by philosophy. Where philosophy would teach anything incompatible or contrary to the rule of faith it too is to be rejected. Where it attempts to usurp the fundamental role of the rule of faith it cannot be tolerated.

Antiquitas Graeco-Romana et Dignitas Israelitica

Rudolf Boon approaches the question of Athens and Jerusalem quite differently from those who regard Tertullian as the prototype of an oppositionist approach, or those who wish to correct such a portrayal of Tertullian. In his *Antiquitas Graeco-Romana*,[28] Boon makes no direct reference to Tertullian but assumes acquaintance with the Athens/Jerusalem motif throughout. For him Jerusalem represents the heritage of Israel; he regards repudiation of the Judaic heritage within modern European culture as the critical factor in the process of secularization within this culture during the past two centuries (20f.).

Boon argues that such a repudiation is primarily to be traced to a number of Enlightenment *Lumières* and to Romantic Neo-Classicism. Among Enlightenment figures Boon points especially to Voltaire and d'Holbach, whose thought reveals both racism and anti-semitism. They regarded Judaism as superstitious; it represented everything opposed to the ideals of the Enlightenment: truth, wisdom, and reason. But such a rejection of Judaism also concealed a repudiation of Christianity as the corruption of true European culture, the pure spirit inherited from Greece and Rome (47-48).[29]

By thus undermining the *"dignitas israelitica,"* these Enlightenment figures gave a significant impetus to the process of secularization. Their approach found a strong echo in Romantic Neo-Classicism, the movement inspired by the classical ideal of beauty, a movement which glorified Hellas and idealized Spartan simplicity, Athenian democracy, and the civic virtues of Republican Rome. Such idealization of the spirit of classical antiquity had little patience with the role of Jerusalem as an active participant in Greco-Roman antiquity. Herder's appreciation for Israel and Hebrew language proved to be an exception; Goethe pointedly contrasted the beauty of Homer with the barbarism of the Jewish scriptures (40-46). Repudiating centuries of Christian appreciation and adaptation of the classical heritage in European culture, Romantic Neo-Hellenism found its inspiration in the pagan spirit of ancient Hellas (24-39). As a result, where Tertullian asked: "What has Athens in common with Jerusalem?" Neo-Classicists turned the question around: "What has Jerusalem in common with Athens?"

According to Boon, Christians have not been sufficiently alert to the implications of this repudiation of Jerusalem and the Judaic heritage, to the enormous repercussions for cultural values and for an education which has routinely relegated the Hebrew literature to the orientalists, denying its rightful place within the European and Western tradition (40f.).

The older tradition which incorporated Greek wisdom within Judeo-Christian society and culture has been disintegrating apace during the past two centuries. This process has had a profound impact on our culture and on the study of classical languages and literature. According to Boon the study of the classics has lost the sense of identity it had when integrated with a culture where the Jerusalem heritage prevailed (51). Nor has it retained the independence which the Romantic Neo-Hellenists sought for it as they opposed the centuries-long tradition in which elements of the classical heritage were integrated with a Christian culture.[30] Rather, it has suffered renewed dispersal, supporting a variety of areas of study, and providing "building blocks" for a variety of contemporary philosophies or ideologies, whether (atheistic) materialism, historicism, or positivism. At their core such ideologies share a common rejection of Christianity. If the time has come to re-evaluate the Enlightenment and Romantic Neo-Hellenism, the time has come also to evaluate anew the impact of these movements on the study of classical Greco-Roman culture. In our Western world the horrors of the holocaust have served as a compelling reason for a thorough re-examination of the role of "Jerusalem" in the history of Europe as well as the ancient Near East.

Boon concludes that if we are to look for a future beyond secularization, a position advocating irreconcilable opposition between Athens and Jerusalem is not in the best interest for Christianity, any more than for a proper understanding of classical antiquity as the context within which Christianity had its beginning (52). Recognition of the distinctive significance of Jerusalem for human history can provide the key to opening a new chapter in the encounter of Christianity and the many peoples and cultures of our globe, and in the study of early Christianity in the context of classical Greco-Roman culture.

Conclusions

In this brief study of the Athens/Jerusalem theme we have seen that the motif, though initiated by Tertullian, has certainly taken on a life of its own during the last few centuries. It is therefore all the more urgent that we take a careful look at its original appearance in the context of his *De Praescriptionibus* if we are to properly assess its meaning, and recognize that Tertullian ought not to be regarded as the quintessential representative of the isolationist position.

With his substantive work on Tertullian, Fredouille has done much to challenge the traditional portrayal, presenting the church father as creatively engaging himself with the Greco-Roman culture of his time. The success of his effort has been widely acclaimed. We would, however, question his presentation of Tertullian's "conversion" as a transformation of culture, in part because of the rather specialized and personalized interpretation of culture in terms of categories of thought; also because Fredouille is more successful in demonstrating Tertullian's understanding of Christianity as *superior* to ancient culture, than in showing how it actually *transformed* that culture. His description of Tertullian's adaptation of classical categories for Christian thought-patterns opens the door for a blurring of the distinction between the old and the new, and is at least in part the result of a failure to recognize the crucial role of the "rule of faith."

And finally, if Tertullian's motif has been widely retained regardless of recent revision in our understanding of his work, an important clue to its continued popularity may be found in the essay of Rudolf Boon. The "Athens/Jerusalem" motif has served as a symbol for an attitude in the study of Christianity and the classics which has enjoyed widespread support since the Enlightenment and romantic neo-Hellenism. From a purist position, classicists have regarded the study of Judaism and the church fathers as a contamination of orientalizing thought, and promoted a separation between study of the "classics" and investigation of literature based on Jerusalem or the new Israel: Christianity. It has been the aim of the present study to demonstrate that one cannot justifiably appeal to Tertullian as an advocate of such a position.

If indeed Tertullian is to be regarded as representing a "transformational" rather than an "oppositionist" approach on the issue of the relationship between "Christ and culture," we must now return to the question with which this study began: "What has Athens in common with Jerusalem?" It is often thought that Tertullian would have given the answer: "Nothing at all!" On the basis of the present inquiry I would suggest that the answer implied by Tertullian was rather: "Far too much!"

Notes

1. Aside from the work of Jean-Claude Fredouille, *Tertullien et la conversion de la culture antique* (Paris: Études Augustiniennes, 1972), (whose view of Tertullian will be examined below, 4f.), two other important studies of Tertullian were published almost simultaneously: Timothy David Barnes, *Tertullian, a Historical and Literary Study* (Oxford: Clarendon, 1971), who refers to the Athens/Jerusalem theme on p. 210; and Robert D. Sider, *Ancient Rhetoric and the Art of Tertullian* (Oxford: Clarendon, 1971), who discusses *De Praes.* on pp. 25-26.

R. D. Sider also dealt with the issue briefly in "*Credo quia absurdum?*", *Classical World* 73 (1980): 417-19. Understanding the disjunction of Athens and Jerusalem as one of Greek philosophy over against biblical truth or revelation, he argues that Tertullian did not reject philosophy from an anti-rationalist or fideist position, but was willing to use both reason and philosophy in persuading others of the truth. He did so because he recognized God as a God of reason and order; one could therefore expect such rational order also to be reflected in the world created by him. Pagan philosophers, according to Tertullian, have recognized such order only in a distorted way, yet not without some valid glimpses of truth; cf. *Apol.* 46.5, or *De An.*20.1, "Seneca saepe noster." Disorderly behavior and thinking typified, rather, the heretics (*Praes.*41). Sider claims that Tertullian's position does not differ substantially from that of Clement or Origen (419).

Although there is at present no unanimity on Tertullian's appreciation of philosophy, there is substantial scholarly agreement on Tertullian's attitude to reason. In an important bibliographical article, "Approaches to Tertullian: A Study of Recent Scholarship," *The Second Century* 2 (1982): 228-60, especially 247-50, Sider indicates that many scholars now acknowledge that Tertullian was not radically hostile to reason; cf. Joseph Moignt, *Théologie trinitaire de Tertullien*, vol. 1 (Paris: Aubier, 1966), 153f., and Justo L. González, "Athens and Jerusalem Revisited: Reason and Authority in Tertullian," *Church History* 43 (1974): 17-27. Tertullian's attitude to philosophy is discussed below, 364-65, 368.

2. H. R. Niebuhr's classic, *Christ and Culture* (New York: Harper and Row, 1951), presented the following five historic positions taken by Christians on the relationship between Christ and culture: parallel status, identity, superiority, isolation, and transformation. For Niebuhr Tertullian represented the epitome of the "Christ against culture" position (55). Tertullian's role in typifying the isolationist approach is also discussed briefly by A. Wolters in his typology of attitudes to classical culture in Wendy E. Helleman, ed., *Christianity and the Classics: The Acceptance of a Heritage* (Lanham MD: University Press of America, 1990), 196.

3. Of the different forms of the title which have accompanied this treatise, *De Praescriptione Haereticorum* has the authority of the oldest manuscripts and is frequently used. This does not necessarily mean that it would have been the title assigned by Tertullian himself; introductory or final words in a treatise are important indicators of the title intended. Alternative titles given in the manuscripts are *De Praescriptionibus Haereticorum* and *De Praescriptionibus Adversus Haereticos*; cf. T. H. Bindley, ed., *Tertulliani De Praescriptione Haereticorum* (Oxford: Clarendon, 1893), 27. J.-P. Migne's *Patrologia Latina*, vol. 2, (which like vol. 1 is devoted to Tertullian) gives the title *De Praescriptionibus adversus Haereticos*. He defends this title by referring to the words with which Tertullian concludes the treatise, ". . . generaliter actum est nobis adversus haereses omnes certis et justis et necessariis praescriptionibus . . . ", *Praes.* 44.13; cf. *Praes.* 35.1, and *De Carn. Christi* 2.5-6. For use of the plural *"praescriptionibus"* see also the extensive discussion of *"praescriptio,"* its meaning and use in Tertullian's work, by J.-C.Fredouille, *Tertullien et la conversion de la culture antique* (Paris: Etudes Augustiniennes, 1972), 195-234, especially 228-30. See further p. 362 and nn.6 and 7.

4. The central argument of this full-length study, (cf. n.3), may also be found in the shorter article "Tertullien et la culture antique" published in *Mélanges Etienne Gareau* (Ed. University of Ottawa, 1982), 197-206.

5. Rudolf Boon, *Antiquitas Graeco-Romana et Dignitas Israelitica, De controverse 'Athene,' 'Rome,'-'Jerusalem' als fundamentele factor in het westeuropese secularisatie-proces* (Amsterdam: Vrije Universiteit, 1989). I have used Boon's essay because he presents clearly the contemporary re-evaluation of the place of Jerusalem in our culture and draws out some implications for the study of classical Greco-Roman civilization. His analysis is paralleled in other studies; an extensive discussion of interconnections between attitudes to classical antiquity and anti-semitism can be found in Martin Bernal's *Black Athena, The Afroasiatic Roots of Classical Civilization* (London: Free Association Books, 1987).

6. This is the reconstruction of the title for which J.-C.Fredouille argues, *Tertullien* (n.3), 228-30. The treatise was probably written early in the third century. Fredouille (487) proposes a date between 198 and 206; Barnes, *Tertullian* (n.1), 55, assigns the treatise to the year 203.

7. A useful introductory discussion of this term as a clue to the interpretation of the treatise may be found in the introduction of R.-F.Refoulé for his edition of Tertullian's *De Praescriptionibus: Tertullien, Traité de la Prescription contre les hérétiques*, Sources Chrétiennes, vol. 46 (Paris: Ed. du Cerf, 1957), 20-45. Two other studies are noteworthy: J. Stirnimann, *Die Praescriptio Tertullians im Lichte des römischen Rechts und der Theologie* (Fribourg en Suisse: Paulus-Verlag, 1949), and D. Michaélidès, *Foi, écritures, et tradition: Les "praescriptiones" chez Tertullien* (Paris: Anbier, 1969). In his lengthy discussion of various possible meanings of *praescriptivo* as it is used in different passages, Fredouille, *Tertullien*, (1972), analyzes different positions taken, and wisely cautions the reader to study the context to determine the precise meaning intended in any particular passage. See n.3 above.

8. Fredouille rejects the position of numerous studies of the past century which have sought to identify Tertullian, the church father, with the jurist of the same name; cf. T. D. Barnes, *Tertullian* (n.1):

22-29, and R. D. Sider, "Approaches" (n.1), 238. Accordingly, Tertullian's use of legal terminology is not to be regarded as evidence of the work of a lawyer as much as the trademark of the *rhetor*. Fredouille prefers to compare Tertullian with Cicero, *Tertullien* (n.3), 1972: 483-84. See also n.18 below.

9. *Praes*. 44.14. Aside from the treatise "against all heresies," there are the specific treatises against Hermogenes, against the Valentinians, against Marcion, and against Praxeas.

10. As in 1 Tim. 4 or 1 Cor. 11:19.

11. Although in his treatise *Against all Heresies*, ch. 1, Tertullian refers to heretical groups among the Jews (Sadducees, Pharisees, or Herodians), it is important to remember that Tertullian's primary concern is for those heresies which take the Christian gospel as their point of departure. Such perversion of the truth, according to Tertullian, brings on a persecution which is particularly cruel for it produces the shame of apostasy instead of the glory of martyrdom.

12. The Valentinians were associated with Plato, and Marcion with the Stoics. Epicurus is not so readily to be identified with one of the heretical groups. In this passage, as in *De Res. Car.* 1, Tertullian is particularly interested in Epicurus's denial of the survival of the soul after death, and may be alluding to controversies of the first decades of the church with those Jews who also denied the resurrection (cf. 1 Cor. 15:12f.).

13. The final lines of *Praes*. 7 are as follows:

Quid ergo Athenis et Hierosolymis? quid academiae et ecclesiae? quid haereticis et christianis? Nostra institutio de porticu Solomonis est qui et ipse tradiderat Dominum in simplicitate cordis esse quaerendum. Viderint qui Stoicum et Platonicum et dialecticum christianismum protulerunt. Nobis curiositate opus non est post Christum Iesum nec inquisitione post evangelium. Cum credimus nihil desideramus ultra credere. Hoc enim prius credimus non esse quod ultra credere debeamus (Ed. Refoulé, n.7).

14. In his discussion of the *regula fidei*, L. Wm. Countryman, "Tertullian and the *Regula Fidei*," *The Second Century* 2 (1982): 208-27, notes the connection of the *regula* with baptismal confession and the catechumenate (219-21), and the antiheretical context of its use (223-25). Anthony J. Guerra, "Polemical Christianity: Tertullian's Search for Certitude," *The Second Century* 8 (1991): 109-23, notes the traditional character of the *regula* (118).

15. R. Sider, *Ancient Rhetoric* (n.1), 25-26.

16. Plotinus's treatise II 9 has the subtitle "Against those who consider the maker of the universe to be evil." Plotinus is particularly vehement in his arguments against these Gnostics precisely because they appeal to the authority of Plato to defend what he regards as a perversion of Plato's views on human nature and the cosmos.

17. The full-scale study of 1972 (n.3), giving a thorough examination of many of Tertullian's treatises, represents Fredouille's doctoral thesis at the Sorbonne in Paris; the more abbreviated restatement, "Tertullien et la culture antique" (n.4), was presented at the University of Ottawa and elsewhere in Canada in 1981, and published in 1982.

18. In the treatises Tertullian amply demonstrates his familiarity with *exempla* from the historians, a general if not always precise use of juridical terms, and broad acquaintance with the doxographical "manual style" statements and general themes of the philosophers (Fredouille, *Tertullien* [n.3], 483-84). At present the identification of our Tertullian with the jurist mentioned in the Justinian code is no longer widely accepted (cf. n.8 above). Fredouille appeals to Cicero, Seneca and Quintilian as examples of other Romans who studied jurisprudence and/or philosophy in support of an education in rhetoric; cf. T. D. Barnes, *Tertullian*, 24, 213, 228-31. Although Fredouille recognizes affinities between Tertullian and the Second Sophistic movement of the second century (*Tertullien*, 182-84), he would not go so far as Barnes who regards Tertullian as a Christian sophist. Barnes's study was published in 1971; it does not appear in Fredouille's (1972) bibliography. Rather, Fredouille (17) acknowledges other writers who have approached the work of Tertullian with differing interests: those of the theologian or historian of religion/Gnosticism (J. Steinman, A. d'Alès), the literary stylist (P. Monceaux, P. de Labriolle), or historian (J. Fontaine).

19. On the intertwinement of rhetoric with the teaching of philosophy in the early Academy after Plato, as well as in the school of Aristotle, see M. L. Clarke, *Higher Education in the Ancient World* (London: Routledge and Keegan Paul, 1971), 67f., and 88f. Also T. D. Barnes, *Tertullian*, 228-31.

20. This danger is increased by the fact that in comparison with other periods, like the late Republic, early Empire, or later centuries such as the fourth, we do not possess an abundance of literature with which to compare Tertullian's work.

The question of Tertullian's conversion as a conversion of culture is dealt with on p. 367-70; we may note here that in recent years a number of studies have been devoted to the nature and motivation of Tertullian's conversion. The influence of Judaism on Tertullian, and the nature of his adherence to the Montanists have received attention (cf. Sider, "Approaches" [n.1], 233-38). Barnes, *Tertullian*, (n.1), 247, recognized the difficulty of reconstructing the true nature of his conversion. Indeed, studies such as those of J. Klein, *Tertullian: Christliches Bewusstsein und sittliche Forderungen* (Hildesheim: H. A. Gerstenberg, 1975; 1st ed., Dusseldorf, 1940), or A. Quacquarelli, "La cultura indigena di Tertulliano e i Tertullianisti di Cartagine," *Vetera Christianorum* 15 (1978): 207-21, which have nonetheless attempted to explain Tertullian's conversion, often reveal as much about the authors' own understanding of conversion and the Christian life as they inform us about Tertullian himself. For Fredouille's work as well it is important to recognize the structuralist presuppositions which are assumed throughout, and are particularly important in his analysis of Tertullian's "culture" and his "conversion" as an ongoing process.

21. Cf. Fredouille, "Tertullien et la culture antique" (1982, n.4), 205.

22. Fredouille does not make an explicit reference to the New Testament use of this image. In Romans 11 Paul describes the relationship between Jews and Gentiles in terms of a wild olive shoot grafted to an older tree; the Gentiles are compared to the shoot grafted on the tree of Judaic faith. For Paul the image portrays the transition from a faith exclusively for Jews, to one which includes all other nations on the earth. Fredouille, however, applies this image to the process of conversion as a transition from the absence to the presence of faith. Use of this image is crucial in his effort to link Tertullian more closely with Justin Martyr and Clement of Alexandria; see 365.

23. Fredouille's conclusions are based on studies of the past decades analyzing Tertullian's attitude to philosophy, e.g., F. Refoulé, "Tertullien et la philosophie," *Revue des Sciences religieuses* 30 (1956): 42-45, and R. Braun, "Tertullien et la philosophie païenne: Essai de mise au point," *Bulletin de l'association Guillaume Budé* (1971): 231-51. In his bibliographical article, "Approaches to Tertullian" (n.1), R. Sider draws attention to the important role of J.-C. Fredouille in recent discussions of this issue (247f.).

24. Fredouille, "Tertullien" (n.4), 199.

25. *Apol.* 46.1 and 7. In the *Ad Nationes* 2, 2.4 Tertullian refers to Christianity as *plena atque perfecta sapientia.* And he concludes the *De Pallio* by calling Christianity a *melior philosophia* (6.2). Cf. Fredouille, "Tertullien" (n.4), 199-200, 203-206.

25. *Apol.* 46.1; cf. Fredouille, "Tertullien" (n.4), 199-200.

26. Tertullian's discussion of Jesus the *logos* as word and reason in the *Adv. Praxean* 5 is perhaps the clearest indication of a link with the views of Justin Martyr. Also noteworthy is the tribute given Justin: "philosophus et martyr," as well as Miltiades, "philosophus," in the treatise against the Valentinians (5.1).

27. A. Harnack, *Lehrbuch der Dogmengeschichte. Band III, Die Entwicklung des kirchlichen Dogmas.*, 4 Aufl. (Tübingen: Mohr, 1910), 16. Cf. F. Refoulé, "Tertullien" (n.23), 43.

28. Cf. n.5 above.

29. M. Bernal has documented the racist and anti-semitic views which arose from the Enlightenment, in *Black Athena* (n.5), especially 239-40, 338-44, 387-88. In the field of Christian Origins, anti-semitic views of European scholarship have now been exposed in depth. For a discussion of this matter, including bibliographic details, see E. P. Sanders, *Paul and Palestinian Judaism* (Philadelphia: Fortress Press, 1977), particularly the introductory remarks.

30. Decline in the study of classical literature in Europe and North America in the last decades is at least partly due to a more general decline in support for the humanities. It is ironic, however, that a strong factor in a minor revival in the study of classical languages at the undergraduate and secondary levels in the USA is the supportive role such study provides for enhancing the students' facility in the English language.

"Spoils from Egypt," between Jews and Gnostics

Lawrence E. Frizzell

In the first "Christianity and the Classics" conference, A. Wolters offered a useful typology of attitudes for the relationship between the biblically grounded Christian tradition and the Greco-Roman culture.[1] He examined five attitudes of Christians to the classics: (1) overt rejection, (2) *praeparatio evangelica*, (3) classics as a parallel authority, (4) the *spoliatio* motif, and (5) the classics equated with Christian truth.[2] For present purposes the classics may be defined as the texts and traditions which embody the best in the ancient Greek and Roman cultures. Yet basic questions, already posed by early Christians who tried to live their faith in the context of the ancient Mediterranean culture, still face Christians of subsequent centuries. Thus, both the issues and the response of early Christian leaders maintain their relevance.

For some Christians the Gospel is so new that it seems impossible to link it with the world in which they live; for them the call to become a fool for Christ implies world-flight. Other Christians recognize that wisdom and goodness can be perceived in each culture. Christian teachers can draw upon such elements in their heritage as a "preparation" for the Gospel. Again, practical wisdom teaching a morally upright life may provide parallels with the biblical message. As a fourth model, Christians may be moved to appropriate the best elements of a pagan culture, and to place it at the service of the faith. Here we may turn to the example of Israelites who borrowed gold, silver and garments from their Egyptian neighbors at the time of the Exodus. A fifth approach attributes equal value to the truth contained in the classics and Christian truth. Wolters gives the work of Marsilio Ficino (1433-1499) as an example of the identification of Plotinus's thought and the Gospel.[3] But could one imagine a teacher of the early centuries presenting such an approach? Why, then, would anyone convert to Christianity?

Wolters has defined *praeparatio evangelica* as "grace perfecting nature," and *spoliatio* as "grace restoring nature." Yet one may discern a close link between the two approaches, for both place intellectual and artistic aspects of pagan culture at the service of the Christian message. In this paper only the *spoliatio* theme will be examined.

Beginning with the interpretation of Exodus passages which speak of "despoiling the Egyptians" (Exodus 3:21,22; 11:2,3; 12:35-37), we find that various perspectives were developed in the history of Jewish and Christian exegesis. Our main interest, however, will focus on the use of these passages as a paradigm for Christian appropriation of wisdom from the pagan world.

The Biblical Texts
The passages concerning "spoils from Egypt" do not appear to be among the most significant of the great dramatic encounters of the "Sinai-Exodus" experience of the Hebrew people. Yet as both Jews and Christians of later centuries pondered carefully the words of the sacred text, this theme did achieve a certain prominence. Our survey will be limited to the period that ends with Origen.

Already in Genesis Abram was promised great possessions upon the departure of his descendants from Egypt. Genesis 15:13,14 gives the promise of God's covenant with Abram, as the patriarch is told in a dream:

Know with certitude that your descendants will be sojourners in a land that is not theirs, and will be slaves there, and they will be oppressed for 400 years; and I will bring judgment on the nation which they serve, and afterward they shall come out *with great possessions.*

The first account of Israel's reception of precious items and clothing from the Egyptians follows on the promise of God's mighty deeds to liberate the Israelites from Pharaoh's dominion:

I will give this people favour in the sight of the Egyptians; and when you go, you shall not go empty, but each woman shall ask of her neighbour, and of her who sojourns in her house, jewelry of silver and gold and clothing, and you shall put them on your sons and on your daughters; thus you shall despoil the Egyptians (Exod. 3:21-22).

This passage may be regarded as the logical antecedent of two later events, (1) the making of the golden calf (Exod. 32:1-6) and (2) the construction of the tabernacle with its beautiful ornaments (Exod. 25-40). No one would need to ask where former slaves obtained such precious metals and cloth.

In a thorough study of the biblical texts, Yehuda T. Radday has recently suggested that the gifts from the Egyptians were not intended as compensation for years of slavery, but rather as tokens of good will to be used by the Israelites as an offering to God for their pilgrimage into the desert.[4] But Radday has ignored the earlier work of David Daube, one of the great scholars of comparative Jewish and Roman law.[5] In his explanation of the statement "You shall not go empty" (Exod. 3:21), Daube has accented the law of freeing a Hebrew slave: "And when you let him go free from you, you shall not let him go empty-handed . . ." (Deut. 15:13).[6] This provides a parallel for the early Jewish explanation that silver and gold constituted compensation for the slave labor that Israelites had endured.[7] This point was already made in the Book of Jubilees, a retelling of Genesis and Exodus chapters 1-12 (dated approximately in the second century BCE):

> On the 14th day we (angels) bound him (Prince Mastema) so that he might not accuse the children of Israel on the day when they were requesting vessels and clothing from the men of Egypt—vessels of silver, gold and bronze—so that they might plunder the Egyptians in exchange for the servitude to which they subjected them by force. And we did not bring the children of Israel from Egypt in their nakedness (*Jubilees* 48:18-19).[8]

In his elaboration on this explanation, Philo of Alexandria reveals sensitivity of the Jews to possible anti-semitic use of this passage:

> The Hebrews ... were not oblivious of the injustices which malice had inflicted on them; for they took out with them much spoil . . . not in avarice or, as their accusers might say, in covetousness of what belonged to others. . . . In the first place they were but receiving a bare wage for all their time of service; secondly, they were retaliating, not on an equal but on a lesser scale, for their enslavement. . . . (*Moses* 1, 140-41).[9]

The Exodus Texts among Greek Christians

Christians of Gentile as well as Jewish background revered the Old Testament because the link with a very ancient heritage was crucial for binding disparate groups into a unified community of faith. In early centuries, however, quotations or allusions to passages such as "the spoils from Egypt" only occur infrequently in apologies or treatises.

Irenaeus

Irenaeus (ca. 130-200, and from ca. 178 Bishop of Lyons) deals with the theme of "spoils" in *Against the Heresies/Adversus Haereses (AH)*, his defense of the Christian faith against Gnosticism. For the Gnostics had used the divine command to despoil the Egyptians of Exodus 3:21-22 to argue that the God of the Jewish Scriptures is inferior to the God revealed by Jesus. In response Irenaeus explains that the tent of meeting, or tabernacle in the desert was made from the precious vessels and garments which had been brought from Egypt (*AH* 4.30,1), and he also maintains that the Egyptians were debtors for their very lives, through the kindness shown by the patriarch Joseph. Undoubtedly this refers to his successful administration of Egypt's resources during time of famine (Genesis 41): "Joseph gathered all the silver that was found in the land of Egypt and in the land of Canaan, for the grain that they bought . . ." (Gen. 47:14).

Moreover, Irenaeus notes, the Israelites were reduced to the worst form of servitude (Exod. 1:13-14); the gifts of the Egyptians were but a minimal wage for their labor.

> This is the type of our Exodus, which refers to the faith in which we are constituted, whereby we are taken from the number of the nations. Like those who departed from the Egyptians who did not know God, we build within ourselves the tabernacle of God, for God dwells with those who do good (*AH* 4.30,3).[10]

Clearly Irenaeus, in refuting the Gnostics, has studied the Exodus passage carefully to anchor the Christian faith in the much older tradition through his development of a typology for the church.

Clement of Alexandria

Clement of Alexandria (ca. 150-215) acknowledged that *gnōsis*, as spiritual illumination, was central to the Christian search for perfection, but he agreed with Irenaeus that it presupposed the faith of the Christian church. In his defense of the Hebrews for "spoiling the Egyptians" he follows the argument of Philo:

> The Egyptians refused to believe Moses' teaching concerning God's power. . . . In their departure, the Hebrews carried with them considerable booty taken from the Egyptians, not by

cupidity as people accuse them . . . but first, as an indispensable remuneration for services rendered to the Egyptians during their entire sojourn; secondly, by way of reprisal: they vexed the Egyptians, so attached to their silver . . . just as the Egyptians had vexed those who served them. Thus, if one considers this to be a state of war, they believed themselves authorized to carry off the goods of their enemies, conquered like the stronger do to the weaker. . . . They despoiled the Egyptians to recuperate the salary which the latter for a long time refused to give them (*Miscellanies* 1:157,2).[11]

Thus Clement argued that the contest between the God of Israel and the Egyptian Pharaoh, and between Moses and the magicians constituted nothing less than war, hereby anticipating the exegetical work of Huesman and Clifford.[12] However, Clement has put greater emphasis on the idea of compensation for slave labor.

Origen

As might be expected, Clement's disciple Origen (ca.185-254) brought new dimensions to the theme. Imbued with a profound respect for divine revelation in the Scriptures, he recognized that the teachings of Gentile sages could be dangerous, like the plagues inflicted on the Egyptians (*Homily on Exodus* 4.6) or the pagan wives of King Solomon (*Homily on Numbers* 20.3).[13] Yet from the advice that Moses received from his pagan father-in-law Jethro (Exod. 18:17-23), Origen argued:

If we sometimes find a statement expressed with wisdom by the Gentiles, we must not spurn, along with the name of the author, what he says . . . but as the Apostle said, "Test everything; hold fast to what is good" (1 Thess. 5:21; *Homily on Exodus* 11.6).

Excerpts of Origen's writings compiled by Basil and his friend Gregory of Nazianzen include a "Letter to Gregory the Wonder-worker" (*Philocalia* XIII), with the interesting subtitle (probably provided by the Cappadocian editors): "Under what circumstances

and to whom are the philosophical disciplines useful for the interpretation of the Holy Scriptures?" To answer this question, Origen
turns to the passage from Exodus:

> God in person told the children of Israel to ask of their neigh-
> bours and household companions vessels of gold and silver, as
> well as garments. Thus, they would despoil the Egyptians to find
> in what they would receive the materials that would serve for
> divine worship. From the spoils taken from the Egyptians by the
> children of Israel would be made the tent of the Holy of Holies,
> the ark with its cover, the cherubim, the propitiatory, the golden
> vessel to hold the manna, the bread of angels. These objects were
> made from the most beautiful gold of the Egyptians . . .
> (*Philocalia* XIII.2).[14]

Origen notes that Egyptians had not used the precious objects
as they ought; however, through divine wisdom the Hebrews dedi-
cated them to the honor of God. Nonetheless, Origen realized that
it could be dangerous to dwell among the Egyptians (that is, the
disciplines of the world) after being nourished by God's law and true
worship, for when Jeroboam fled to Egypt (1 Kings 11:26-40), he
learned idolatry. "Thus, when he returned to the land of Israel, it
was to rend the people of God in two and to teach them to say to
the golden calves: 'These are your gods, O Israel, who brought you
out of Egypt' " (1 Kings 12:28).

> Myself, I have learned by experience and I can say to you that
> rare are the men who have taken in Egypt what is useful and
> who, then departing from that country, have made objects des-
> tined for divine worship. But many are the brothers of the
> Edomite Ader (Hadad). They are the ones who have profited
> by their Hellenic learning to conceive heretical thoughts and to
> construct, as it were, golden calves at Bethel . . . (*Philocalia*
> XIII.3).[15]

Origen concludes by exhorting Gregory to apply himself to reading the Sacred Scriptures in a spirit of prayer, in order to understand divine realities (8.4).

Thus the great Alexandrian biblical scholar and theologian shows great caution regarding the appropriation of Greek philosophy and literary interpretive tools for biblical study. This may seem ironic, because it was precisely the school of Alexandria associated with Clement and Origen which developed the allegorical interpretation of Scripture practised by Jews like Philo. These in turn had accepted this method for understanding ancient texts from Greek scholars who spiritualized or allegorized the older literature to overcome embarrassing episodes, particularly in Homeric epic.[16] Since the Alexandrian Jewish community had shown the way, the school of Pantaenus and Clement felt at home with allegory as a method of biblical exegesis.

One might think that Origen could have used an analogy to make his point: just as the ancient Hebrews had a right to take silver, gold and garments from Egypt, so Christians could appropriate the intellectual fruit of pagan labor. Instead, after acknowledging that divine wisdom alone gives the capacity to use natural gifts for divine service, Origen identifies "the Egyptians" as "the disciplines of the world." Although he begins with the historical reading of the text, and recognizes that the "spoils" provided materials from which Israel made objects for the service of God, he moves on to the allegorical level and uses Egypt as the symbol of secular disciplines having a propensity to lead people into idolatry. The only way to avoid compromise and heresy is to study the Scriptures in a spirit of prayer, ever mindful of the relation between Scripture and divine worship. In extant Christian literature, Origen seems to be the first to draw this allegorical lesson from the texts about Israel taking spoils from Egypt.[17]

Origen has developed the same theme in his discussion of the comely captive of Deuteronomy 21:10-14. In a homily he comments on the passage which requires thirty days for rituals like shaving the head and cutting the nails, by which the woman mourns her parents before she can be taken in marriage:[18]

> Frequently, I too have gone to war against my enemies and have found among my spoils a beautiful woman. Indeed, we find good and reasonable things even among our enemies; so, if we read wise and learned words from one of them, we must purify them, taking the insight and cutting away all that is dead or useless, such are the hair of the heads and nails of this woman taken among the spoils from the enemy. Then we can make her a wife when she does not have anything that could be called dead through infidelity. . . . For us, whose spiritual warfare involves not human weapons but the power of God to destroy (false) counsels, if it is discovered that the adversary has a beautiful woman, that is some rational discipline, then we purify it as just indicated (*Homily on Leviticus* 7:6).[19]

Conclusions

The genius of Origen made a profound impression on his contemporaries, and also on succeeding generations of Christians. The image of "despoiling the Egyptians" is found in Gregory of Nyssa's reflections on the *Life of Moses*. Augustine of Hippo also discussed the gold and silver from the Egyptians in his *83 Diverse Questions* (Q. 53), and used the allegory in his important treatise *On Christian Instruction* (2.11,60) as well as the *Confessions* (7.9). Augustine's writings did much to popularize Origen's allegorical image for the Latin Church; because of his great influence it became a common theme among medieval theologians.

As new generations of Christians grapple with age-old questions of relating to their own world and cultural context, it is useful to review early Christian insights and paradigms for the use of the treasures provided by a non-Christian heritage. Although many early Christian leaders expressed appreciation for the value of the pagan classics, they also expressed their reserve by advising the subordination of these treasures to the divine wisdom found in the Scriptures.

Notes

1. Albert M. Wolters, "Christianity and the Classics: A Typology of Attitudes," in *Christianity and the Classics: The Acceptance of a Heritage*, Wendy E. Helleman, ed. (Lanham, MD: University Press of America, 1990), 195-201.

2. Ibid., 195-201.

3. Ibid., 199-200.

4. Yehuda T. Radday, "The spoils of Egypt," *Annual of the Swedish Theological Institute* 12 (1983): 127-47.

5. David Daube, *The Exodus Pattern in the Bible* (London: Faber & Faber, 1963), 55-61. See also Julian Morgenstern, "The despoiling of the Egyptians," *Journal of Biblical Literature* 68 (1949): 1-27; he interprets *kalah* to mean "bride" rather than "completely" (following Joseph Coppens). The mention of gold and silver objects and garments describes how a bride adorns herself (Isaiah 49:18; 61:10; Jeremiah 2:32). When Israelite *women* (noted in the text) were sent forth from Egypt, they were garbed as brides.

6. Explanations drawn from other biblical records are found in the commentaries on Exodus in the *Jerome Biblical Commentary* (John Huesman cites 1 Samuel 6:3f.) and the *New Jerome Biblical Commentary* (Richard Clifford refers to victors despoiling their enemies after battle, as in Joshua 7:21; Judges 5:30).

7. On this point see also the Babylonian Talmud, Sanhedrin 91a.

8. This is the translation of O. S. Wintermute in *The Old Testament Pseudepigrapha*, James H. Charlesworth, ed. (Garden City, NY: Doubleday, 1985), vol. 2, 140.

9. This translation is from F. H. Colson, *Philo* (Cambridge: Harvard University Press, 1935) volume VI, 349. J. G. Gager in *Moses in Greco-Roman Paganism* (Nashville: Abingdon, 1972), 51, describes the relations between Jews and the general population in Egypt during the Second Temple period. Aspersions were cast on the generation that left Egypt under Moses, so Philo argued that the Hebrews were entitled to "occult compensation." See Eusebius, *Commentaria in Psalmos, Patrologia Graeca*, vol. 23, column 1309.

10. Adelin Rousseau et al., eds., *Adv. Haer.*, Sources Chrétiennes 100 (Paris: Éditions du Cerf, 1965), 782. The argument is similar to that of the Babylonian Talmud; see above n.7.

11. Marcel Caster, *Les Stromates*, Sources Chrétiennes (Paris: Cerf, 1951).

12. On their work, see above n.6.

13. See Marcel Borret, *Origène, homélies sur L'Exode*, Sources Chrétiennes 321 (Paris: Cerf, 1985), 346, n.3 (see 14-16, 407-408). Recent general surveys of this issue include John H. Corbett, "Paganism and Christianity" in the *Encyclopedia of Early Christianity*, Everett Ferguson, ed. (New York: Garland, 1990), 674-78; P. R. C. Hanson, "The Christian Attitude to Pagan Religions up to the Time of Constantine the Great" in *Aufstieg und Niedergang der römischen Welt* 23.2 (1980), 910-73, followed by "Christian Views of Paganism" by Carlos Contreras, 974-1001. See also H. Dörrie, "Die andere Theologie. Wie stellten die frühchristlichen Theologen des 2-4 Jahrhunderts ihren Lesern die 'Griechische Weisheit' (den Platonismus) dar?" *Theologie und Philosophie* 56 (1981): 1-46 and A. M. Ritter, "Platonismus und Christentum in der Spätantike," *Theologische Rundschau* 49 (1984): 31-56; Christian Gnilka, "La conversione della cultura antica vista dai Padri della Chiesa," *Cristianesimo nella Storia* 11 (1991): 593-615.

14. Origen develops the description in detail, describing four types of gold brought from Egypt. In *Origène: Philocalie, 1-20 sur les Écritures*, Sources Chrétiennes 302 (Paris: Cerf, 1983), 402 n.2, M. Harl comments that Origen seems to depend on Jewish traditions which are not found in the Bible.

15. Origen here "fuses" the account of Hadad the Edomite of 1 Kings 11:14-25 with the subsequent account of Jeroboam.

16. See David Dawson, *Allegorical Readers and Cultural Revision in Ancient Alexandria* (Berkeley: University of California Press, 1992) for a discussion of the pagan writers in Philo, Valentinus and Clement. He does not consider our precise theme.

17. See Henri Crouzel, *Grégoire le thaumaturge: Remerciement à Origène suivi par la Lettre d'Origène à Grégoire*, Sources Chrétiennes

148 (Paris: Cerf, 1969), 90, n.2. In "The Medieval *accessus ad auctores*," *Traditio* 3 (1945): 223, Edwin A. Quain states that it was probably introduced by St. Augustine. "This theme . . . was the most important influence in giving a *rationale* to the study of pagan literature by Christians."

18. The passage shows respect for the woman's personal dignity and demands her freedom if the man later rejects her. Clement of Alexandria points to the thirty-day waiting period as a time for the man to evaluate his intention regarding the purpose of marriage, which is the begetting of children (*Stromateis* III: 11,71). See John Oulton and Henry Chadwick, *Alexandrian Christianity* (Philadelphia: Westminister, 1954), 73.

19. See Marcel Borret, *Origène: Homélies sur le Lévitique* 6 (390-91) (Paris: Cerf, 1981) I, 346-48. See also Henri de Lubac, *Exégèse mediévale: Les quatre sens de l'écriture* (Paris: Aubier, 1959), I, 290-92.

Clement of Alexandria: Instructions on How Women Should Live

M. Eleanor Irwin

In his *Paidagōgos*, or *The Educator*, Clement instructs men and women who have accepted the Christian faith on appropriate behavior and attire. The community he addresses—educated, cultured and wealthy—lived in Alexandria, one of the largest cities of the Mediterranean world. New Testament writers had exhorted their readers, most of whom were not noble, powerful or wise,[1] to hospitality, kindness, obedience and love for one another. They paid but scant attention to outward appearances. In books 2 and 3 of *The Educator*, Clement provides what is missing. He establishes detailed guidelines for Christian living, for eating and drinking, entertainment and bathing, clothing and adornment and a variety of similar niceties on which the New Testament kept silent.[2]

Clement drew upon his Greek background and particularly the philosophical education which had made a deep impression on him.[3] He regarded philosophy as instruction for the Greeks in the same way that the law instructed the Jews; he called it a *praeparatio evangelica* or a *paidagōgos* to lead them to Christ, the true *Paidagōgos*, or *Educator*. Where philosophy agreed with Christian principles it gave him a framework and models for living.[4]

For Clement all Christians, whether or not they have enjoyed a literary education, are philosophers. This is clear from a passage toward the end of *Paidagōgos* (3.78), where he exploits the root meaning of the verb *philosophein*, "to love wisdom," when he asks, "How do you love God and your neighbour if you do not love wisdom, i. e., philosophize?"[5]

Clement accepts the equality of men and women, based on Paul's remark that in Jesus there is "neither male nor female" (Gal. 3:28). Yet he is not willing to obliterate all the differences between them. Accordingly, near the beginning of *Paidagogos* (1.10.1-11.1) he asserts[6] that men and women have a common name: *anthrōpos*[6]; they are the same with respect to their relationship to God; both are taught by the same Instructor, Christ the Word; and the important virtues of self-control (*sōphrosyne*) and modesty (*aidōs*), are the same for both.[7]

Although the guidelines Clement gives in *Paidagōgos* are designed to develop self-control and modesty in both sexes, he varies what is demanded of men and women, for he allows women a number of small luxuries and comforts which are denied to men. He also allows more freedom in social activities for married in comparison with unmarried women. Clement was motivated by a concern for what he regarded as the physical weakness and vulnerability of women, and by a desire to control encounters between women and men. He disapproved strongly of men who were like women: the *androgynoi*. And while he did not specifically censure women who were like men, many of the distinctions he made between attire appropriate for women and for men reflect his desire to discourage women from living like men.

In classical Greek thought, "male" and "female" represented polar opposites, like day and night, light and dark, right and left, up and down; they were not typically regarded as two forms of one entity.[8] In a list attributed to the Pythagoreans, men were associated with light, day, right and up, while women belonged with dark, night, left and down. "Good" appears on the right with male, and "bad" on the left with female. Clement did struggle against such an opposi-

tion of men to women, for he insisted on the essential unity of the
sexes, emphasizing that both men and women were *anthrōpoi*, and
that both should strive for the same virtues. Yet his ideas of masculinity and femininity and of the roles typically associated with each
were heavily influenced by Greek cultural traditions. He dismissed
outright the non-traditional lifestyles portrayed by women in other
Christian communities.

In the present essay I have selected examples of Clement's
instructions to women in *Paidagōgos* to show how he expected
women to dress and adorn themselves, and how to behave in church,
at the baths and at dinner parties.[9] On the basis of these instructions
I have described differences between standards for women and
those for men, and discussed the varying degrees of freedom given
to married and unmarried women.

Clothing and Adornment
Women's clothing was to be simple in style, covering the entire body
and reaching the ground. It was not to be decorated with gold
embroidery. Clothing should be white in color, but might be dyed,
as long as the dye was not purple. Gold jewellery, pearls and precious
stones were not to be worn. It may appear surprising that Clement
allowed women to wear colored clothing when men could wear
white only; he also permitted women, but not men, to wear scented
oils. This is best understood as part of Clement's program to ensure
that women were attractive to their husbands or suitors.

Clement quotes both Scripture and Greek literature to illustrate
the connection between clothing and the virtue of the wearer. "Dyed
garments," he says "do not satisfy the demands either of necessity
or of truth" (2.108.1), i. e., white clothing is as good as colored, and
dye by which color is achieved is not the true color. The particularly
offensive dye, purple, represented the ultimate in extravagance in
the ancient world.[10] White clothing, on the other hand, had connotations of cleanliness as well as the goodness that comes from
being sincere—without pretence—because no dye has been used to
change the natural appearance.

Sin had long been clothed in purple and scarlet, from the time of the prophet Isaiah who (1:18) contrasted the scarlet of sin with the white of sinlessness. Perhaps the strongest association between sin and scarlet in Scripture occurs in the description of the two cities personified at the end of the Revelation. The whore of Babylon is clothed in scarlet and purple, and adorned with gold, pearls and precious stones while the new Jerusalem, the bride of Christ, is robed in the pure white of the righteous deeds of the saints.[11]

Greek attitudes and traditions certainly influenced Clement as well. He praises the Spartans for "allowing only prostitutes to wear brightly colored clothing and gold ornaments. In this way . . . they bred into their good women a reluctance to adorn themselves" (2.105.2). He cites Prodicus of Ceos (2.10.110) whose story of the "Choice of Heracles" was related many years before by Xenophon. In it, Heracles as a young man on the threshold of maturity was confronted with the choice between Virtue and Vice.[12] Virtue (*Aretē*) was not only dressed in pure white; her eyes were modest and her stance virtuous, while the bold eyes of Vice (*Kakia*), her voluptuous body, makeup and clinging clothing told what kind of woman she was.

Only the wealthy could afford purple dyed clothing. Clement wanted members of his community to use their wealth to help the poor, not merely to spend it on their own pleasures.[13] He reminds his readers of the rich man in Jesus' parable who was "clothed in purple and fine linen" but ignored the needy beggar Lazarus who "lay at his gate, covered with sores" (2.105.1). Later (2.120) Clement accuses wearers of gold and jewellery (men as well as women) of shirking their responsibility to the poor and ignoring them as the rich man had ignored Lazarus. He concludes, "It is wicked for one to live in luxury while many are in want" (2.120.6).

In prescribing that women wear clothing which reached to the ground, Clement was almost certainly thinking with disapproval of women mentioned in the apocryphal Acts who adopted male clothing and moved about with the freedom of men.[14] Clothing which reached the ground kept legs modestly hidden but also impeded movement. Men, conversely, were not to let their clothes trail on the ground because it was important for them to move freely.[15]

Women in men's clothing had predecessors in several of the philosophical schools, including Plato's Academy.[16] Among these female philosophers the Pythagorean women modelled the modesty and decorum of which Clement approved. One of these, Theano, was at a banquet when a male guest admired her exposed arm.[17] She took the compliment as a proposition and replied that her arm was "not public property."[18] In thus preserving her dignity, Theano provides Clement with a role model for Christian women who want to fend off amorous advances. He improves upon the original story and recommends (2.114.2) that when a woman's arm is admired, she answer "it is not public property;" when her legs are admired, she reply "they belong to my husband;" and when her face is admired, she say "only for him to whom I am married."

Pythagorean women were paradigms of womanly behavior for Clement not only for the stories of their virtue, but because treatises attributed to them gave advice on clothing and luxuries very much like his own, and for much the same reasons. A treatise attributed to Perictione, for example, advised women to avoid purple-dyed clothing, jewellery, cosmetics and a lot of bathing. A woman was to love "her husband, her children and her entire household" even if her husband did not treat her well. She was "to preserve the law and not emulate men."[19] Like Perictione, Clement too advises women to avoid useless luxuries; both reinforce the role of women as wives and mothers, rather than as rivals to men.

Clement also addresses the matter of appropriate footgear for women. He reminds his readers that women's shoes have two purposes: covering and protection. Thus shoes for women should cover the feet modestly, and protect them from the hazards of the road. Women might wear a simple white sandal for everyday and a heavier, oiled sandal when travelling. Women going barefoot outside the house[20] are suspected of loose conduct, like the women worshippers of Dionysus who kicked off their sandals, untied their hair and arched their necks in orgiastic delight. These Maenads were suspected of drunkenness, immodesty and sexual immorality; Christian women must not risk being taken for such by going about in bare feet.

In contrast, bare feet were thought to be appropriate for men. Athletes went barefoot; so did Socrates, and his imperviousness to cold and physical discomfort was well known.[21] Because footwear offered protection, going barefoot (except when necessary on military campaigns) was a sign of manliness and toughness; this was not a message a woman should be communicating. Because footwear was tied on to the foot, men might reject shoes as symbols of bondage, whereas a barefoot woman was unbound, i. e., out of control.

Clement's comments on jewellery are directed chiefly to women. Although he quotes Paul, Clement took Peter[22] as his authority for forbidding women to wear gold ornaments (2.127.2):

> Women should dress themselves modestly and decently in suitable clothing, not with their hair braided, or with gold, pearls, or expensive clothes, but with good works, as is proper for women who profess reverence for God (1 Tim. 2:9-10).

While protesting weariness and disgust, Clement allowed a riot of references to personal adornment in classical authors roll off his pen to express his concern for excessive and inappropriate ornamentation. These references demonstrate the frequency with which Greek authors, particularly the comic poets, inveighed against the women who adorned themselves with jewellery, and the cost to men who would try to buy and retain their affection in this way.

Clement was particularly critical of "silly rich women" who had gold chamber pots (2.39.2),[23] tried to look younger by coloring their grey hair (2.69.4) and justified their gold ornaments, precious stones and pearls by claiming that since God made these beautiful things they had the right to enjoy them (2.118.3, 119.2). Clement disapproved of the useless expenditures of these wealthy women on luxuries. It is also likely that he targeted them because through their wealth the women were influential in the community.

Different Standards
Clement in several places distinguishes what is appropriate for married women and for unmarried women, with the intent of protecting unmarried women from unwanted, inappropriate attention, while encouraging married women to appear attractive to their husbands. He acknowledges that married women might use fragrances which are "not overpowering to a husband;" thus he recognizes the legitimate physical attraction between husband and wife. But he advises unmarried women to refrain from using perfume on the grounds that perfume entices men, as prostitutes know only too well. Clement disapproves of unmarried women attending banquets, though he does permit married women to accompany their husbands. When women attend church services, they are cautioned by Clement to wrap themselves in a cloak, and thus cover their arms and legs from the gaze of men (3.79.3-5).

Clement accepts and reaffirms the traditional Greek separation of roles for men and women; women were typically expected to work within the house and men outside. In his discussion of exercise for good health (3.49.1-52.2), Clement recommends that men use the gymnasium, wrestle and play ball, or engage in less strenuous exercises like walking, and useful exercises like hoeing. However, for women his recommendation is that they spin, weave, cook, grind flour and serve their husband's meals. Clement is probably recalling the advice which Ischomachus gives to his young wife (Xenophon, *Oeconomicus* 7-10), assuring her that weaving, kneading bread and making beds would keep her slim, make her cheeks glow with natural color, guarantee her continued attractiveness to her husband and keep his eye from roving to a servant girl.

Clement acknowledges the need for men and women to bathe, but not too often or too long. Too much time spent there would be enervating, "undermining strength . . . inducing lassitude and even fainting spells" (3.46-7). There are other dangers as well. He is indignant that some women are attended by male servants who

accompany them even when they are undressed, and give massages
(3.31). The baths threaten self-control and modesty. If women use
the occasion to display themselves to men, they leave both themselves and the men open to temptation. It is of interest to note that the
Pythagorean treatises warned in similar terms against the dangers
of too much bathing. Rather than assuming that "cleanliness is next
to godliness," the Greeks had their unwashed holy prophets and
wise men.[24]

Thus we see that although the rhetorical pronouncements of
Clement claim that both men and women are members of the
Christian community and both are to be instructed regarding the
attainment of the same virtues, in practice he reinforces traditional
Greek roles for men and women. Women belong within the house
and are vulnerable when outside of it, while the prior allegiance of
men is to the city, outside the house, and their movement is not
restricted. Women need protection from men, a protection which
they achieve ultimately through marriage. It was for this reason that
women should not neglect their appearance; a husband must be
found for them and kept by them.

Before we condemn Clement for reinforcing the traditional
roles of the Greco-Roman world of his time, we must ask what other
options were available for the lives of Christian women. I would
suggest that within the Christian communities there were three
models, namely those portrayed by ascetics, misogynists and martyrs.
The first and third were adopted and developed by women, while
the second is associated with literature written by men.

Ascetic women typically rejected marriage, revelled in their
independence, wore men's clothes and travelled unchaperoned.
The combination was no accident. Stories of their adventures, often
involving the refusal of a proposal of marriage, would almost certainly have been current in Clement's time,[25] but he rejected any
model which proposed independence from men for women.

The misogynist tradition of the ancient world, most clearly
represented by Semonides and his infamous satire "On Women,"
treated women as irrational creatures susceptible to deceit and in

need of control. Both Philo of Alexandria and Tertullian are typically regarded as belonging within this category.[26] But Clement also rejected a model which did not regard women as capable of achieving Christian virtue and maturity.

A third model for women in the Christian community was portrayed by the female martyrs who suffered along with men for their faith in Christ. The stories of their deeds were recorded and were widely known. These women showed a characteristic usually attributed to men: courage and endurance in the face of physical suffering; yet they also retained their dignity and modesty as women.[27] In the early accounts of the Martyrdom at Vienne and Lyons (177 CE) and the Martyrdom of Perpetua and Felicity (203 CE), women martyrs were the central figures.[28] As they assumed a role of spiritual leadership among their companions in prison and in the arena, such heroic women showed the strength of which they were capable. When called to account for their faith, they were beyond the protection of husbands and fathers, and thus took on responsibility for themselves.[29] Whether they were slaves or nobles, rich or poor, all faced martyrdom on the same terms. Yet if Clement reflected on the prospect of persecution, he would have hoped that the day would never come when women would be called upon to suffer like men.

If Clement rejected these alternative lifestyles for women, he had good reasons. If he was beguiled by his society's view of women as wives and mothers, he nonetheless granted them a dignity which was not always found in Christian circles. He did not treat them as the "devil's gateway," to remind them of the role of Eve in sin's first entry among humankind. He wanted women to live in the way which he believed most conducive to virtue, the life of a respectable woman, cared for by a man and caring for him in turn. He wanted women to be philosophers in their hearts but not in outward appearance. The philosopher's cloak was for men.

Notes

1. Cf. 1 Cor. 1:26.

2. 1 Peter 3:3-4 and 1 Timothy 2:9-10 do, however, mention women's adornment.

3. Clement treated virtue as a mean in *Paidagogos*, cf. Salvatore R. C. Lilla, *Clement of Alexandria: A Study in Christian Platonism and Gnosticism* (Oxford: Oxford University Press, 1971), 99, n.3.

4. He did not accept all philosophers. Clement took material from Platonic, Pythagorean and Stoic teaching and rejected that of Cynics, Skeptics and Epicureans, whom he regarded as hostile to Christian values. For a discussion of the influence of Greek philosophy on Clement, cf. H. I. Marrou, "Clément D'Alexandrie" in *Recherches sur la tradition platonicienne* (Vandoeuvres-Genève. 12-20 Août 1955), 183-200; Eric F. Osborn, *The Philosophy of Clement of Alexandria* (Cambridge: The University Press, 1957); H. Chadwick, *Early Christian Thought and the Classical Tradition* (Oxford: Clarendon, 1966), 40-65.

5. References to Clement are to the edition of Otto Stählin (1905) in the series *Die griechischen christlichen Schriftsteller der ersten Jahrhunderte*, revised in three volumes: vol. 1 *Protrepticus und Paidagogos*, Ursula Treu, ed. (Berlin: Akademe, 1972), vol. 2 *Stromata Buch 1-VI*, Ludwig Früchtel, ed. (Berlin: Akademie, 1960), vol. 3 *Stromata VII u. VIII* (with other minor works), L Früchtel and U. Treu, eds. (Berlin: Akademie, 1970).

6. *Anthrōpos*, "human being," though commonly masculine, can be feminine in gender and may refer to a woman or a man, LSJ s.v. The distinction in *Strom.* 4.118.1-134.4 between the "perfect man" or Gnostic and his female counterpart as the "good wife" is comparable.

7. "A common life, a common grace and a common salvation," a Stoic theme; cf. *Clément d'Alexandrie: Le Pédagogue*, Livre 1, introduction and notes, H.-I. Marrou, M. Harl, trans. (Paris: Cerf, 1960), 128, n.1.

8. Cf. W. K. C. Guthrie, *A History of Greek Philosophy*, vol. 1 (Cambridge: Cambridge University Press, 1962), 245, for the table of Pythagorean opposites; on the ancient Greek habit of treating male and female as opposites, cf. G. E. R. Lloyd, *Polarity and*

Analogy: Two types of argumentation in early Greek thought (Cambridge: Cambridge University Press, 1966), esp. 42, 48-49, 149. In this volume see also the paper of D. Sly, "The Plight of Woman," 174-76.

9. The closing chapters of the second book of the *Paidagogos* deal with personal adornment, clothing (2.102-115), shoes (2.116-7) and jewellery (2.118-127). In 3.11, Clement reviews Christian behavior.

10. Cf. M. Reinhold, *History of Purple as a Status Symbol in Antiquity* (Bruxelles: Latomus, 1970).

11. References from Revelation: Babylon, 17:4, (17:18), 18:16; Jerusalem, 19:18, (21:2). For a further discussion of the connotations of purple, white and dye, cf. M. E. Irwin, "Colourful Sheep in the Golden Age: Vergil, *Eclogues* 4:42-45," *Echos du Monde Classique/Classical Views* 23 n.s. 8 (1989): 23-37.

12. Xenophon, *Memorabilia*, 1. 2.21-34.

13. Wealth was not an evil in itself; cf. his sermon "Who is the rich man who is being saved?" a homily on Mark 10:17-31, and Charles Avila, *Ownership: Early Christian Teaching* (London: Sheed and Ward, 1983), 33-46 on Clement's teaching about property and wealth.

14. Cf. Stevan L. Davies, *Revolt of the Widows: The Social World of the Apocryphal Acts* (Carbondale: Southern Illinois University, 1980), 58-61, for Thecla cutting her hair like a man, wearing a man's cloak, and for Paul's initial disapproval and ultimate acceptance of her way of life.

15. This test (impediment to movement) explains many fashions to which women have submitted over the years, like high-heeled shoes and pencil-slim skirts.

16. Female philosophers were commonly regarded as no better than prostitutes. They were often foreigners and represented "female intrusion into male territory;" cf. Jane M. Snyder, *The Woman and the Lyre: Women Writers in Classical Greece and Rome* (Carbondale: Southern Illinois University, 1989), 121. Cf. her general discussion of women philosophers (99-121), which includes treatment of Epicureans (101-105), Cynics (105-108), Pythagoreans (108-13).

Hipparchia, an Athenian of the third century BCE, chose to be the partner of Crates, a Cynic philosopher, wearing the same clothing he wore and accompanying him everywhere. She gave up the loom, the most womanly of occupations, (*Diogenes Laertius* 6.96-8).

17. Perhaps she was wearing a Doric chiton with sleeves open to the shoulder; cf. L. Whibley, *A Companion to Greek Studies* (New York and London: Hafner Pub., 1931/1963), 624, fig. 146, 147.

18. *Strom.* 4.121.2 *all' ou demosios*. The adversative *alla* alerts us to the attempted seduction, cf. J. D. Denniston, *Greek Particles* (Oxford: Oxford University Press, 1959) s.v. *alla*, l.(ii) 1-2. Cf. also *LSJ* s.v. *demosios* I.1.b "used by the public;" II c. subst. "prostitute." Besides telling this story about her, Clement quotes Theano with approval, *Strom.* 4. 44. 2.

19. Holger Thesleff, *The Pythagorean Texts of the Hellenistic Period* (Abo: Abo Akademie, 1965) 142-45 = Stob. 4.28.10. For a translation and discussion, cf. S. B. Pomeroy, *Goddesses, Whores, Wives and Slaves: Women in Classical Antiquity* (New York: Scribners, 1975), 134-36. Another Pythagorean treatise (*Thesleff*, 151-54) discusses chastity, "woman's greatest virtue," and describes the appropriate adornment of a woman: no cosmetics, no jewellery, no clinging, silk or dyed clothing.

20. It was the normal practice in ancient Greece for women to go barefoot inside the house and to wear shoes when going out in public cf. Whibley, *A Companion* (n.17), 632.

21. Cf. Plato, *Symposium* 174 A 3-5; Socrates rarely bathed and rarely wore shoes.

22. What Peter said (1 Pet. 3:3-4) was: "Do not adorn yourselves outwardly by braiding your hair, and by wearing gold ornaments or fine clothing; rather let your adornment be the inner self with the lasting beauty of a gentle and quiet spirit, which is very precious in God's sight." Clement has conflated the two references, making one suspect that they were often quoted.

23. Clement was also critical of men who had useless luxuries like silver feet on the legs of their beds, silver urinals and crystal chamber pots.

24. E. g., *Selloi,* prophets of Zeus at Dodona, with unwashed feet: Homer, *Iliad* 16. 234-35; Socrates in Aristoph., *Birds* 1554-55 and n.22.

25. Cf. Davies, *Revolt* (n.14), 3, for dating of apocryphal Acts to the end of the second and beginning of the third centuries, contemporary with Clement. Cf. also Virginia Burrus, *Chastity as Autonomy: Women in the stories of Apocryphal Acts* (Lewiston/Queenston: Mellen, 1987), 125-27, for summaries of stories.

26. Tertullian, a contemporary of Clement, displayed misogynist tendencies in some of his writings; in *De cultu feminarum* he calls women "the devil's gateway," and blames women as "daughters of Eve" for the Fall. Philo's attitude to women is discussed in this volume in the essay of D. Sly, "The Plight of Woman: Philo's Blind Spot," 173-87.

27. Women suffered martyrdom from New Testament times; Acts 9:2, also 1 Clement 5:6, and the discussion of the mother of seven sones in 4 Maccabees, in this volume, D. Aune, "Mastery of the Passions," 137-38.

28. Texts and translations are conveniently found in H. Musurillo, *Acts of the Christian Martyrs* (Oxford: Clarendon, 1972); Vienne and Lyons, 62-85; Perpetua and Felicity, 106-31.

29. Women martyrs, unlike the virgins of the apocryphal Acts, might be married (Perpetua) and have given birth (Perpetua and Felicity).

Symbol and Science in Early Christian Gnosis

Padraig O'Cleirigh

Comparison of the proponents of Christian *gnōsis* in the second and third centuries CE supports the thesis that the more orthodox such a *gnōsis* is, the more rational it is. The converse is equally true. The grounds for this thesis are examined in the present paper, which aims to show that Clement and Origen allow greater scope for reasoning than do the Valentinian masters. The significance of such an alliance of orthodoxy with rationality will be assessed, particularly in terms of the implications for Harnack's theory of the early development of Christianity.

Valentinian and Ptolemaean Gnosis

Study of Hellenistic religion and philosophy shows that the knowledge represented by *gnōsis* is not necessarily, and certainly not chiefly, a rational knowledge. [1] Although in the period under consideration, the second and third centuries CE, the content of *gnōsis* is always "reality," in some cases this "reality" is exclusive, that is, restricted to what is "most real": the world of spirits and their transcendent source. In other instances *gnōsis* also embraces this phenomenal world at a lower level of reality.

But knowledge of spiritual reality comes only by illumination; it can be grasped by human thought, and expressed in human language only indirectly and inadequately by symbols.[2] Knowledge of this embodied world may be obtained and transmitted in the same way—by illumination and symbol, respectively. But this world in its dispersion can also be known through the discursive procedures of analysis, conceptualization, rational inference and demonstration.

In this context Valentinians differ from orthodox Christian Gnostics only in the degree of emphasis. All these thinkers use symbols, all use conceptual arguments. It is simply a question of how much of the latter is combined with the former mode of apprehension and communication and how well the two approaches to knowledge are integrated.

The great Valentinian myth reveals both divine and earthly mysteries.[3] Its discourse is symbolical rather than rational. Yet it has considerable rational elements in its account of this world. In particular it is concerned with giving a rational account of the transformations of matter.

We see in the account of Irenaeus, their adversary, that the Ptolemaeans did have an interest in physical philosophy:

> They declare that this (the consequence of the fall of the lower Sophia) was the origin and substance of the matter from which this world was formed; from her conversion came forth the whole soul of the world and the Demiurge: all other things owed their beginning to her terror and sorrow. For from her tears all that is of a liquid nature was formed; from her smile all that is lucent; and from her grief and perplexity all the corporeal elements of the world. . . . Now what follows from all this? No light tragedy comes out of it as the fancy of every man among them pompously explains, one in one way and another in another, from what kind of passion and from what element matter derived its origin.[4]

The sarcasm of Irenaeus does not destroy the power of the Valentinian suggestion on the genesis of matter. Moreover he tells us that *all* their teachers emphasized this part of their system. And we can see from his subsequent remarks (as in *Against the Heresies (AH)* 1.4,5) that the construction of the world was then explained in philosophical as well as those poetic terms. The Savior

> . . . separated and set apart her passions from Achamoth and commingled and condensed them, changing them from incorporeal passions into incorporeal matter. He then by this process conferred on them a fitness to become concretions and corporeal structures[5].

The demiurge "formed the earthy human being from the invisible substance, from fluid and unorganised matter."[6]

Although this account has rational elements the myth as a whole is critical of reasoning, particularly if, with eminent Valentinian scholars G. Quispel and W. Foerster, we understand Sophia to represent this reasoning.[7]

Moreover it is doubtful that the saving *gnōsis* of the Valentinians involves a complete understanding of this visible world. At any rate, although he records the Ptolemaean claim to have acquired the knowledge of all things, Irenaeus feels confident in challenging them to supply an answer for selected earthly mysteries as a pledge of their knowledge of more important subjects:

> If any . . . imagine that he has acquired not a partial but a universal knowledge of all that exists—being such a one as Valentinus or Ptolemaeus . . .—let him tell us the reasons (which we know not) of those things which are in this world . . . so that we may credit him also with respect to more important points.[8]

Some texts from Nag Hammadi show a more positive attitude to the knowledge of this world, especially *Marsanes* 5, as noted and

translated by Birger Pearson. "I have deliberated and have attained
to the boundary of the sense-perceptible world; I have come to
know, when I was deliberating whether in every respect the sense-
perceptible world is worthy of being saved entirely." Pearson attributes this remarkable attenuation of gnostic acosmism to the
profound effect of Platonism on the writer.[9] But this treatise is
neither Valentinian nor Christian in content.[10]

The Gospel of Truth, which does have Valentinian connections,
shows no concern with this world except as a negative pole to the
plenitude of the divine spiritual world. *The Tripartite Tractate* (109:
Nag Hammadi Library [NHL], 89f.) mentions different accounts of
this world, but this world does not occur in the description of
knowledge in the fullest sense (127: *NHL*, 98f.).

Note however the distinction made between elementary les-
sons and complete instruction in *The Gospel of Philip* (*NHL*, 157)
and the following characterization of the Revealer in *The Gospel of
Truth*: "in schools he appeared and he spoke the word like a teacher"
(*NHL*, 41). Note also the double valuation of word as opposed to
thought: on the one hand the word is beggarly compared to the
vision (*NHL*, 101), yet despite the deceptive nature of worldly names
it is not possible to learn the Truth without these names (*NHL*,
142f.). The scholastic note which is prominent in these passages
shows the authors' readiness to engage in discursive exposition of
their knowledge. Such exposition is most marked in Ptolemaeus's
Letter to Flora, a work characterized by clear analysis of concepts.

The Valentinians certainly do not avoid using discursive
reasoning. It must now be seen whether they use such reasoning as
extensively as their orthodox counterparts.

Clement of Alexandria
Turning to Clement of Alexandria, we notice at once his more
explicit interest in rational knowledge:

> The expression . . . "know thyself" . . . may be an injunction to
> the pursuit of knowledge. For it is not possible to know the parts

without the essence of the whole, and one must study the genesis of the universe, that thereby we may be able to learn the nature of man.[11]

The true dialectic is the science which analyses the objects of thought and shows abstractly and by itself the individual substratum of existences, or the power of dividing things into genera, which descends to their most special properties and presents each individual object to be contemplated simply such as it is.[12]

Clement defines *gnōsis* as "that light which is lit in the soul as a result of obedience to the commandments, a light which makes clear everything on earth, which enables man to know himself and teaches him to participate in God."[13]

It is clear enough from these quotations that Clement includes a precise knowledge of earthly matters in his idea of *gnōsis*. In fact when he excludes God from the grasp of demonstrative science we infer that for Clement most realities fall within the scope of such science.[14]

Indeed we may agree with the view of Mondésert that Clement attempts to "raisonner le symbolisme."[15] In this view Clement considers symbolism to be essentially adapted to the psychology of human beings, an instrument of evocation by means of interior analogies, prior to writing and even to language, especially in regard to divine matters.

All those who have so to speak discoursed on divine matters, whether barbarian or Greek, have covered with a veil the final reasons of things and they have passed on the truth only by enigmas and symbols, allegories, metaphors and analogous figures.[16]

One would be inclined to credit Clement with the distinction between an abstractive way of thinking, which always keeps the mind within the limits of the human λόγος (ratio) . . . and a different way of knowing and thinking, marked by an impetus (ἐπιβολή) of the intellect and a momentum which carries the νοῦς beyond itself. . . . On the one hand a philosophy which is conceptualizing, abstractive, Aristotelian; on the other a philosophy which is based on intuition and symbol and is wholly Platonist.[17]

Still Clement attempts to apply reason methodically to the interpretation of symbols and he does this with more clarity than his Valentinian counterparts.[18]

Origen

Clement's great interest in rational knowledge is surpassed by that of Origen. Origen repeatedly speaks of a complete knowledge of lower realities as an indispensable preliminary to the higher. In his *On First Principles* 2,11 Origen sketches the rewards for goodness: after death there will be instruction in every detail of this world (sect. 6-7). It will complete inquiry begun while one was embodied. It will even supply the neglect of inquiry while one was embodied, but in this case the instruction will take longer. No one will be exempted from this course.[19]

> I think that the saints as they depart from this life will remain in some place situated on the earth, which the divine scripture calls "paradise." This will be a place of instruction and, so to speak, a lecture room or school for souls, in which they may be taught about all that they had seen on earth. . . . This leads us to suppose that no small interval of time may pass before the reason merely of things on earth can be shown.

The same process of rational learning recurs to the saints at each level as they ascend from earth through the air and the spheres.

They will remain there for some time, until they learn the reason of the ordering of all that goes on in the air, in its twofold form. By twofold form I mean, for example, when we were on earth we saw animals or trees and we perceived the differences among them and also the very great diversity among men. But when we saw these things we did not understand the reasons for them . . . when we have comprehended it in its fullness we shall comprehend in twofold form the things we saw on earth . . . . In each sphere the saint will first observe all that happens there and then learn the reason why it happens.[20]

In the heavenly places God will show them the causes of things, of stars that exist or even might exist, and so, on to invisible realities.

It is true that Origen does not always write so positively about knowledge of the embodied world. For instance in the Prologue to the *Commentary on the Song of Songs* he suggests that the use of the study of nature is to convince us of nature's uselessness. He learns from Ecclesiastes and the study of physics that:

> . . . all visible and corporeal things are fleeting and brittle, and surely once the seeker after wisdom has grasped that these things are so, he is bound to spurn and despise them; renouncing the world bag and baggage, if I may put it that way, he will surely reach out for the things unseen and eternal.[21]

Still, Origen does not exempt the reader from the study of nature. Rather he urges perpetual progress from inferior to the superior studies, recognizing, even so, that the inferior will not be exhausted in this life.

His practice in teaching at Caesarea in the 240's was to include the study of nature as a regular stage in the curriculum. Gregory's evidence in his *Address of Thanksgiving*, 8, is that Origen explained each being by dividing it into its primary elements; he spoke on the nature of the All and the nature of each part as well as on the variety and change of things in this world. He filled his students with rational admiration for the sacred arrangement of the universe, using his own as well as traditional arguments. Physics was taught in so rational a manner that admirers of Origen's devotion to the mystery have felt compelled to doubt the evidence of Gregory— either Gregory misunderstood Origen (Völker) or came away with a one-sided view of his meaning (Crouzel).[22]

Aside from the use of reason in investigating physical questions, Origen examines ethical questions in an increasingly analytic manner:

> (the soul) should know whether its disposition is good or not and whether its intention is right or not; if its intention is right, does the soul have the same relationship to all the virtues, both in understanding them and practicing them . . . is it in such a state that it will progress and increase in the understanding of realities?

Knowledge of one's moral state should be grounded in a philosophical grasp of the nature of the soul.

> It ought to know what its essence is—is it corporeal or incorporeal . . . is it simple or composed of two, three or more elements. . . . To know itself, the soul will ask if there are some spirits similar to it in nature and yet different in condition, and why this is so.[23]

While Origen places such unprecedented emphasis on the necessity of discursive reasoning in Christian *gnōsis*, he nonetheless wholly integrates this rational procedure with symbolic language. One may note the concurrent use of conceptual terms and metaphors from scripture on most pages of Origen's works; but there is a single passage in the *Reply to Celsus* (6, 9) where he converts philosophical science into Christian symbolism. Celsus had quoted Plato's *Seventh Letter* (342 ab) on the five elements constituting knowledge: the name, the description, the image, the scientific grasp and the real and knowable object. Origen rewrites these elements in the language of Christian understanding: the voice in the wilderness (John the Precursor or the Old Testament), the incarnate Logos (the Jesus of history), the mark of the wounds made by the Logos in the individual soul, Christ as wisdom in the perfect, and finally—though Origen is not explicit here—Christ as the Intelligible World. The importance of this passage has been well elucidated by Crouzel.[24] Origen is discussing the same philosophical certainty as Celsus but he has integrated the discussion with the symbols of his religious belief.

Origen acknowledged the rationality of the Valentinians. They were more rational than the simple believers.[25] They found problems in the world and in scripture, and Origen agrees that these problems are real. Poetic presentation does not obscure the conceptual theses they advance on salvation and providence. Still Origen attacks their solutions. He finds it easy to criticize their logic and lack of cautious expression.

The most likely reason for the Valentinian lack of interest in applying reason more thoroughly to the realities of this world is their view of the transitoriness of this material world of ignorance and illusion. This would link their low interest in rational thinking with their alienation from this world, and so with a major criterion for what is gnostic.[26] By contrast orthodox writers like Origen affirm the worth both of the world and the knowledge of the world despite the lower value of both, despite their transitoriness.

Is it a simple coincidence that the Christian *gnōsis* which became more orthodox is also more rational? Probably not. The connection between orthodoxy and rationality was made in the second half of the second century by the Apologists and indeed probably with an anti-gnostic purpose.[27] This connection was maintained by Irenaeus in his anti-gnostic polemics but it was more positively developed by those promoters of Christian *gnōsis*, Clement and Origen.[28]

The fact, however, that rational argument serves a polemical purpose does not necessarily entail the absence of a more fundamental purpose in its use: that is, the exercise of the soul's powers in comprehending all that exists. It may be moot whether one should credit this pure intellectual interest to Irenaeus or some of the Apologists, but we have seen both Clement and Origen insist on the need to know all earthly things. For them, as later for Augustine, the knowledge of higher and lower reality is more than the knowledge of the higher alone.

Conclusions: Harnack, Gnosis and Hellenization
Whatever the fundamental relationship between symbol and science, it is clear from the passages examined—and I think these passages fairly representative—that while all Christian Gnostics express themselves by symbols as well as by concepts, Clement writes more analytically than the Valentinian authors and Origen is even more insistent than Clement on the need to appropriate rationally the realities of this embodied cosmos. I conclude with a suggestion of the relevance of this fact for the thesis of Harnack that Gnosticism constituted the "acute" Hellenization of Christianity while Catholicism achieved its "chronic" Hellenization.[29]

In writing of "Hellenization," which is his more specific term for "secularization," Harnack is referring to the stage of Hellenic culture contemporary with the emergence of Christian *gnōsis*. This culture certainly includes rational thinking as part of the inherited conglomerate[30] but the rational appropriation of reality is not its chief interest. Salvation, both in this life and thereafter, is the last end of knowledge and the salvation of knowledge comes more radically from revelation than from rational discourse:

> The union of the traditions and rites of the Oriental religions, viewed as mysteries, with the spirit of Greek philosophy is the characteristic of the epoch. . . . It may, however, be asserted that Gnosticism anticipated the general development, and that not only with regard to Catholicism, but also with regard to Neoplatonism, which represents the last stage in the inner

history of Hellenism. The Valentinians have already got as far as Jamblichus.[31]

Gnōsis starts from the great problem of this world, but occupies itself with a higher world, and does not wish to be an exact philosophy, but a philosophy of religion.[32] The *gnōsis* is free from the rationalistic interest of the Stoa. . . . The only guide to this world is a μάθησις (not exact philosophy) resting upon a revelation and allied with μυσταγωγία .[33]

Precisely here we must ask how the orthodox Alexandrian *gnōsis* with its comprehensive interest in the philosophy of nature fits with Harnack's scheme of the development of Christian doctrine through two different phases of Hellenization. The rational interests of the orthodox are anomalous to the main line of development which Harnack is sketching. Of course, the rational interests of Plotinus and Proclus are equally anomalous. Harnack expressly limits his thesis to the history of Christian doctrine and so does not recognize the need to deal in detail with the history of thought in general. Still, the less he acknowledges general developments in Hellenistic philosophy the more paradoxical his formula of Hellenization appears.[34] For Harnack the spirit of Greek philosophy characteristic of the epoch seems to have lost all rationality.

Yet Harnack was certainly aware of the increased rational ambitions of the orthodox Christian Gnostics: "The Gospel was being transformed into a system of complete knowledge in order to subdue the world."[35] Moreover, Christianity in particular

seemed to put no limits to the character and extent of the knowledge, least of all to such knowledge as was able to allow all that was transmitted to remain, and at the same time to abolish it by transforming it into mysterious symbols.[36]

These passages give a good account of the activity of the orthodox Gnostics. They depict a more liberal, rather than a more gradual, Hellenization of the Gospel. And this process of accommodation is indeed given expression by Harnack, though not in so lapidary a formula.[37] The liberal Hellenization was in fact a fuller "Verweltlichung" in taking account not only of the spirit of the times but of the world itself as well. But this was a process which characterized also heterodox Gnostics of the second and third generations[38]. Its importance is inadequately assessed in the Hellenistic schema of Harnack's great history of Christian dogma.

Notes

1. While *gnōsis* always means knowledge, the complexity of this concept increased with the development of epistemology. The definition of *gnōsis* in the context of ancient Gnosticism is notoriously difficult and one would gratefully assent to the formula proposed in the Final Document of the Messina Colloquium on the origins of Gnosticism—if only the document did not beg so many questions and beget so many dissenters in its turn. That document's definition of *gnōsis* is the "knowledge of divine mysteries reserved for an elite": U. Bianchi, ed., *Le origini dello Gnosticismo* (Leiden: Brill, 1967), xxvi. Obviously this definition excludes from the start any knowledge of earthly mysteries. While it focuses on the most important content of *gnōsis* in Late Antiquity, it is excessively acosmic. *Gnōsis* should include a knowledge of the mysteries of this world, at least as a secondary part of its content. It does so in all the thinkers I am discussing here. Moreover the definition should include mention of the revelation of the reserved mysteries.

2. I am using "symbols" in the broadest sense, to represent any expression which means more than it says literally, and in this way hints at the nature of the mysterious source and the mystery in its products. While symbols are essentially non-scientific, scientific concepts may well be used as symbols. The precision of scientific thought precludes such versatility.

The contrast of symbolic and conceptual reasoning is prevalent in all the writers I am studying here. While at times they distinguish "symbol" from "allegory" or "enigma," "symbol" is most often a very general term which includes these distinctions. One can philosophize with symbols even better than with concepts.

3. Irenaeus, *Adversus Haereses* 1,1-8.

4. The English translations from Irenaeus are by A. Roberts in *The Ante Nicene Fathers*, A. Roberts and J. Donaldson, eds. (Grand Rapids: Eerdmans, 1975), vol. 1. The original Greek and the Latin translation of this work come from the edition by A. Rousseau and L. Doutreleau: *Irénée de Lyon, Contre les Hérésies, livre 1* (Paris: Cerf, 1979). Ταύτην σύστασιν καὶ οὐσίαν τῆς ὕλης γεγενῆσθαι λέγουσιν, ἐξ ἧς ὅδε ὁ κόσμος συνέστηκεν. Ἐκ μὲν γὰρ τῆς ἐπιστροφῆς τὴν τοῦ κόσμου καὶ τοῦ Δημιουργοῦ πᾶσαν ψυχὴν τὴν γένεσιν εἰληφέναι, ἐκ δὲ τοῦ φόβου καὶ τῆς λύπης τὰ λοιπὰ τὴν ἀρχὴν ἐσχηκέναι· ἀπὸ γὰρ τῶν δακρύων αὐτῆς γεγονέναι πᾶσαν ἔνυγρον οὐσίαν, ἀπὸ δὲ τοῦ γέλωτος τὴν φωτεινήν, ἀπὸ δὲ τῆς λύπης καὶ ἐκπλήξεως τὰ σωματικὰ τοῦ κόσμου στοιχεῖα... Καὶ τί γάρ; Τραγῳδία πολλὴ λοιπὸν ἐνθάδε καὶ φαντασία ἑνὸς ἑκάστου αὐτῶν ἄλλως καὶ ἄλλως σοβαρῶς ἐκδιηγουμένου ἐκ ποταμοῦ πάθους ⟨καὶ ⟩ ἐκ ποίου στοιχείου ἡ οὐσία τὴν γένεσιν εἴληφεν· (*Adv. haer.* 1.4,2-3).

5. ἀλλ ἀποκρίναντα χωρὶς συγχέαι καὶ πῆξαι καὶ ἐξ ἀσωμάτου πάθους εἰς ἀσώματον ⟨τὴν⟩ ὕλην μεταβαλεῖν αὐτά· εἶθ οὕτως ἐπιτηδειότητα καὶ φύσιν ἐμπεποιηκέναι αὐτοῖς ὥστε εἰς συγκρίματα καὶ σώματα ἐλθεῖν. *Adv. haer.* 1.4,5. This emphasis on invisible matter helps make the transition from incorporeal passions to corporeal (elemental) matter by positing an entity which is still incorporeal but is already matter. Of course it shows the narrator's acquaintance with philosophical speculation on prime matter. Note the identical doctrine in Clem. Alex,. *Excerpta ex Theodoto*, 46-48, and Hippolytus, *Refutatio Omnium Haeresium*, 6.32,6. We find mention of invisible matter also in *The Tripartite Tractate*, 104, 5-6. The Laval commentary on this treatise by E. Thomassen and L. Painchaud suggests that the Coptic word means blindness as well as invisibility, an inability to see as well as an inability to be seen: *Le Traité Tripartite (NH 1,5)* (Québec: L'Université Laval, 1989), 401.

This is an excellent instance of a scientific concept being harnessed for symbolical expression.

6. " ...τεποιηκέναι καὶ τὸν ἄνθρωπον τὸν χοϊκόν, οὐκ ἀπὸ ταύτης δὲ τῆς ξηρᾶς γῆς, ἀλλ ἀπὸ τῆς ἀοράτου οὐσίας, ἀπὸ τοῦ κεχυμένου καὶ ῥευστοῦ τῆς ὕλης λαβόντα..." 1,5,5. The fluidity of matter is also mentioned in *The Tripartite Tractate* passage referred to in the previous note.

7. Quispel does so in *Gnosis als Weltreligion* (Zurich: Origo, 1951), 37 and Foerster in "Die Grundzüge der ptolemaeischen *Gnosis*," *New Testament Studies* 6 (1960): 22.

8. si . . . quis . . . putet se non ex parte sed universaliter universam cepisse eorum quae sunt additionem . . . causas eorum quae in hoc sunt mundo adnuntiet nobis ut ei de maioribus quoque credamus *Adv. haer.* 2, 28, 9. And see, for instance, *Adversus Haereses* 1.21,4: " . . . they affirm that the inner and spiritual man is redeemed by means of knowledge, and that they, having acquired the knowledge of all things, stand thenceforward in need of nothing else": ὥστ εἶναι τὴν ἀπολύτρωσιν τοῦ ἔνδον ἀνθρώπου.....Λυτροῦσθαι γὰρ διὰ γνώσεως τὸν ἔνδον ἄνθρωπον τὸν πνευματικὸν καὶ ἀρκεῖσθαι αὐτοὺς τῇ τῶν ὅλων ἐπιγνώσει....

9. Cf. his comment in *The Nag Hammadi Library in English*, J. Robinson, ed., 3rd revised edition (San Francisco: Harper, 1988) (hereafter indicated as *NHL*), 463. References to the treatises recovered at Nag Hammadi are taken, for the most part, from this volume.

10. Nevertheless one should notice the plan of "demonstration from first principles" mentioned in the *Origin of the World* (*NHL*, 172), later followed by "a description of the structure of our world" (187). "The author works with direct or indirect quotations, references, summaries, explanations and etymologies, which stand in sharp contrast to the otherwise dominant narrative style. This way of working, of defending one's own view by appeal or reference to other works, is intended as a demonstration of a substantive and convincing argumentation." But again this treatise is only slightly if at all connected with Valentinian teaching.

11. Τὸ μὲν οὖν "γνῶθι σαυτὸν" ... δύναται δὲ γνῶσιν ἐγκελεύεσθαι μεταδιώκειν. οὐκ ἔστι γὰρ ἄνευ τῆς τῶν ὅλων οὐσίας εἰδέναι τὰ μέρη· δεῖ δὴ τὴν γένεσιν τοῦ κόσμου πολυπραγμονῆσαι, δι ἧς καὶ τὴν τοῦ ἀνθρώπου φύσιν καταμαθεῖν ἐξέσται.
ι *Strom.* 14,60.3.

12. " ...αὕτη γὰρ τῷ ὄντι ἡ διαλεκτικὴ φρόνησίς ἐστι περὶ τὰ νοητὰ διαιρετική, ἑκάστου τῶν ὄντων ἀμίκτως τε καὶ εἰλικρινῶς τοῦ ὑποκειμένου δεικτική, ἢ δύναμις περὶ τὰ τῶν πραγμάτων γένη διαιρετική, μέχρι τῶν ἰδιωτάτων καταβαίνουσα, παρεχομένη ἕκαστον τῶν ὄντων καθαρὸν οἷον ἔστι φαίνεσθαι."
1 *Strom.* 28.17,2)

13. " ... τὴν γνῶσίν φαμεν... τινα ἐπιστήμην θείαν καὶ φῶς ἐκεῖνο τὸ ἐν τῇ ψυχῇ ἐγγενόμενον ἐκ τῆς κατὰ τὰς ἐντολὰς ὑπακοῆς τὸ πάντα κατάδηλα ποιοῦν τὰ ⟨τε⟩ ἐν γενέσει αὐτόν τε τὸν ἄνθρωπον ἑαυτόν τε γινώσκειν παρασκευάζον καὶ τοῦ θεοῦ ἐπήβολον καθίστασθαι διδάσκον." 3 *Strom..* 5.44,3.

14. "Nor any more is He apprehended by the science of demonstration. For it depends on primary and better known principles. But there is nothing antecedent to the Unbegotten." ἀλλ οὐδὲ ἐπιστήμη λαμβάνεται τῇ ἀποδεικτικῇ· αὕτη γὰρ ἐκ προτέρων καὶ γνωριμωτέρων συνίσταται, τοῦ δὲ ἀγεννήτου οὐδὲν προϋπάρχει. 5 *Strom.* 12.81,6.

15. See Claude Mondésert, "Le symbolisme chez Clément D'-Alexandrie" in *Recherches du science religieuse* 26 (1936): 158-80.

16. Πάντες οὖν, ὡς ἔπος εἰπεῖν, οἱ θεολογήσαντες βάρβαροί τε καὶ Ἕλληνες τὰς μὲν ἀρχὰς τῶν πραγμάτων ἀπεκρύψαντο, τὴν δὲ ἀλήθειαν αἰνίγμασι καὶ συμβόλοις ἀλληγορίαις τε αὖ καὶ μεταφοραῖς καὶ τοιούτοις τισι τρόποις παραδεδώκασιν.... 5 *Strom.* 4.21,4.

17. C. Mondésert, "Le Symbolisme" (n.15), 169.

18. The clarity of Clement's expression may owe much to the influence on him of the Aristotelian writings. See E. A. Clark,

Clement's Use of Aristotle: The Aristotelian Contribution to Clement of Alexandria's Refutation of Gnosticism (New York/Toronto: Mellen, 1977). But this clarity should not serve to mark Aristotle as a confident rationalist. Note Professor Bos's argument in his paper in this volume, "Cosmic and Metacosmic Theology," 7, that the relatively low ranking of discursive reasoning by Aristotle contributed substantially to the gnostic attitude to reason.

19. On this section see my "Knowledge of this World in Origen" in *Origeniana Quarta*, Lothar Lies, ed. (Innsbruck: Tyrolia, 1987), 249f.

20. Puto enim quod sancti quique discedentes ex hac vita permanebunt in loco aliquo in terra posito, quem "paradisum" dicit scriptura divina, velut in quodam eruditionis loco et, ut ita dixerim, auditorio vel schola animarum, in quo de omnibus his, quae in terra viderant, doceantur. . . . Ex quibus omnibus putandum est quod interim non parum temporis transeat, usquequo eorum tantummodo, quae super terram sunt, ratio post vitae abscessum dignis et bene meritis ostendatur . . . putandum est igitur quod tamdiu sancti ibi permaneant, usquequo utriusque modi rationem dispensationis eorum, quae in aere geruntur, agnoscant. Quod autem dixi "utriusque modi," hoc est: verbi gratia, cum in terre essemus, vidimus vel animalia vel arbores, et differentias eorum perspeximus sed et diversitatem quam plurimam inter homines; verum videntes haec, rationes eorum non intelleximus . . . cum ergo comprehenderimus integre eius rationem, tunc "utroque modo" comprehendemus ea, quae vidimus super terram . . . in quibus (globis vel caelis)singulis perspiciet primo quidem ea quae inibi geruntur, secundo vero etiam rationem quare gerantur agnoscet . . .: *De Principiis* 2,11,5-6. I cite Rufinus's translation from H. Görgemanns and H. Karpp, *Origenis De Principiis Libri IV* (Darmstadt: Wissenschaftliche Buchgesellschaft, 1976). The translation is from G. W. Butterworth, *Origen on First Principles* (London: SPCK, 1936).

21. R. P. Lawson, trans., *Origen The Song of Songs: Commentary and Homilies* (Westminster/London: Newman Press, 1957).

22. See W. Völker, *Das Vollkommenheitsideal des Origenes* (Tübingen: Mohr, 1931), 229f., and H. Crouzel, *Remerciement à Origène* (Paris: Cerf, 1969), 89f.

23. *Com. Cant.* II 11 (trans. Lawson; see note 21).

24. H. Crouzel, *Origène* (Paris: Lethielleaux, 1984), 155f., and *Origène et la connaissance mystique* (Bruges: Desclée de Brouwer, 1961), 324-70.

25. Origen, *Com. John* 5.8. The parallel of Augustine finding the Manichees persuasive until he entered on physical speculations was adduced during discussion by Professor Yamauchi.

26. When dealing with *gnōsis*, a comprehensive form of knowledge, is not the epistemological aversion from this world the most important feature of gnostic anticosmism?

27. See Robert Joly, *Christianisme et philosophie: Études sur Justin et les apologistes grecs du deuxième siècle* (Bruxelles: Editions de l'Université de Bruxelles, 1973), 154f.: "Il est fort possible que la lutte contre la gnose, qui ne pouvait pas ne pas mobiliser nos Apologistes, même ceux dont nous ignorons s'ils ont écrit contre les gnostiques, a favorisé, elle aussi, l'expression de ce christianisme rationnel. La connaissance (*gnose*) des gnostiques n'avait rien de logique, d'intellectuel, de dialectique, comme on voudra. Il faut qu'elle soit absolument surnaturelle, à la mesure de Dieu, son objet absolument transcendant. Le déferlement mythologique de la plupart des apocalypses gnostiques avait de quoi irriter une mentalité grecque plus intellectuelle et plus classique. Et par réaction contre cette gnose abominée, il était assez normal de trouver des appuis dans un hellenisme traditionel."

28. See E. F. Osborn, "Reason and the Rule of Faith in the 2nd Century A.D." in *The Making of Orthodoxy*, Rowan Williams, ed. (Cambridge: Cambridge University Press, 1989): 40-61. "Irenaeus is seen to present the rationality of the divine economy . . . in contrast to the irrationality of the Gnostic accounts" (46); "To the end Clement insists that the failure of the heretic is logical and intellectual. The rule of the church which guides the interpretation of scripture makes no sense apart from argument" (53).

29. Die geschichtliche Betrachtung . . . erkennt . . . in dem Gnosticismus—sofern er ein dogmengeschichtlicher Faktor geworden ist— eine Reihe von Unternehmungen, derer in gewisser Weise die katholische Ausprägung des Christenthums in Lehre, Sitte und Cultus analog ist. Der grosse Unterschied hier besteht aber wesentlich darin, dass sich in den gnostischen Bildungen die akute Verweltlichung, resp. Hellenisirung des Christenthums darstellt (mit Verwerfung des A. T.), in dem katholischen System dagegen ein allmählich gewordene (mit Conservirung des A. T.): *Lehrbuch der Dogmengeschichte* 1 (Tübingen: Mohr, 1990; repr. of 1909 edition), 249f.

My concluding suggestion will be best considered in the context of the paper of W. Rowe and the response to it by B. W. Henaut, included in this volume.

30. Harnack himself claimed that the Gnostics produced the first "scientific theological" literature in Christianity. These works "form in every respect the counterpart to the scientific works which proceeded from the contemporary philosophic schools." Ibid., 242.

31. A. Harnack, *History of Dogma*, N. Buchanan, trans. (New York: Dover, 1961), vol. 1, 230-31. The latter statement is true only of the union of philosophy and religion, not of the independent elaboration of philosophy, as for instance in the case of Plotinus.

32. Ibid., 233.

33. Ibid.

34. R. Mortley has recently maintained, with plausibility, that cosmology is integral to religious doctrine in this period: ". . . at the end of the Hellenistic period powerful religious forces were appropriating the language of rationalism for the purposes of advancing a cosmology which combined a deistic view with an emphasis on the importance of reason in the making of reality, and in man's experience of reality." *From Word to Silence* 1 (Bonn: Hanstein, 1986), 39.

35. A. Harnack, *Outlines of the History of Dogma*, E. K. Mitchell, trans. (Boston: Starr King Press, 1957 repr.).

36. *History of Dogma* (n.31), vol. 1, 226.

37. ". . . der langsamen und, man darf sagen, schonender Umbildung, der man sie (die überlieferte Religion) unterwarf, leistete sie nur geringen Widerstand, ja hat sie in der Regel gar nicht empfunden." *Lehrbuch* (n.19), 250.

38. This phenomenon may be accounted for as an expansion of a simpler original pattern. Such is Jonas's account of the main gnostic movement. According to him the structure of *gnōsis* tends to plenitude: that which is grasped first intuitively is later explored discursively. He claims that such expansion derives from the autonomous spiritual substance of pure *gnōsis*; this is how he accounts for the emergence of the great systems of the 3rd century. See H. Jonas, *The Gnostic Religion*, 2nd rev. ed. (Boston: Beacon, 1970), 36. This complex question of the nature of gnostic thought is dealt with quite differently by A. Böhlig in "Zur Struktur gnostischen Denkens," *New Testament Studies* 24 (1978): 496-509. He claims there is a special faculty for gnostic thinking parallel to, and so underived from, other mental capabilities. For a less radical explanation of this expansion of interest in rational cosmology, one could point to the recovery of confidence in rational speculation in the philosophical schools of the period, the building on this renewed confidence by Christian thinkers of the main church, and the subsequent attempt of the heterodox Gnostics to follow suit.

Epilogue

Wendy E. Helleman

At a time when Christianity is expanding rapidly in non-Western countries, yet virtually under siege in much of Europe and North America, it is surely appropriate to return to the issue of "Hellenization," to re-examine the usefulness of cultural, philosophical and theological forms inherited from early Christianity.

Current principles of apologetics and missiology still accent the need for contextualization and indigenization of the gospel; the message must be communicated in language which speaks clearly to those for whom it is intended.[1] From this perspective it is often maintained that theological formulations and creeds based on disputes of early Christianity within the Greco-Roman world do not adequately answer the questions of Christians in very different times and cultural environments. "Hellenization," it is argued, has added unwarranted complexity to the original simple message of the gospel by intellectualizing Christianity. In the interest of a relevant and vital faith it is necessary to "de-Hellenize" Christianity, namely, to strip Christian teachings of the "Hellenic" expressions and forms which have shaped them from earliest times, and thus reclaim a simpler, less encumbered and purer expression of the faith.[2]

What then is the status of the "Hellenic" contribution for the history of Christianity? Is it truly a liability, not to be communicated to young Christian communities of the "two-thirds world?" And do we, in maintaining the significance of those early theological discussions, whether in creeds or doctrinal decisions, impose on emerging churches an impossible burden, one even we ourselves no longer tolerate?

Harnack and Hellenization

The theme of the "Hellenization" of Christianity has a long history, particularly within Protestant Christianity. Since the Reformation many have appealed to this theme to characterize heretical movements, and to categorize undesirable aspects of Christianity seen to result from dangerous accommodation of the faith or paganizing syncretism. Unitarians have long directed such accusations at the trinitarian formulations resulting from the Nicene settlement; terminology for the sacraments as mysteries of faith, supposedly derived from Greco-Roman mystery-religions, has also been identified as evidence of the negative influence of "Greek" ideas on primitive Christianity.[3] Use of the "Hellenization" theme in this way was foreshadowed in the Reformers' call for a return *ad fontes*. Their primary concern was the rejection of accumulated traditions in favour of a return to scripture as the ultimate source of truth. Nonetheless, the theme of return served to reinforce purist claims for early Christianity. Inasmuch as "return to the source" assumes an original "purity" which can be corrupted, an appeal to "Hellenization" could well be strengthened as the explanation why Catholic Christianity went astray.[4] The blame for introducing concepts which contaminated and complicated the message of the gospel has most frequently been directed at philosophical schools, especially the Platonists.

Within our own century the work of Adolf von Harnack (1851-1930) on the history of Christianity has certainly provided significant impetus for reconsideration of the Hellenic heritage as a legitimate component and ongoing factor within Christianity.[5] Aspects of the argumentation are clearly dated, and the historical critical method with which he was so closely identified is now itself the subject of critique.[6] But Harnack's stature has not diminished significantly, nor has his influence been undermined. The scope of his work is such that even after the better part of a century of critical reflection students of early Christianity can return to it with profit, though they may not expect to agree with all of his views. Particularly because Harnack's work has been popularized and perpetuated through widely used texts such as those of K. Latourette his influence has continued long after his death in 1930.[7]

For the present collection of essays interest has focused particularly on Harnack's characterization of Gnosticism as an "acute Hellenization" of the gospel.[8] Harnack took a special interest in Gnosticism from his earliest scholarly work. His first dissertation, written at Leipzig in 1872, has as its title *Source Criticism and the History of Gnosticism*.[9] It was at the time acclaimed for rigorous application of textual-historical criticism in its use of sources. Harnack's first course of lectures in 1875 also focused on the Gnostics.

Toward the end of his life Harnack returned to an early interest with his substantive and highly influential study of Marcion (1921). Harnack did not, however, present him as a Gnostic, since Marcion's views were not characterized by the cosmological speculation with which he identified other Gnostics. In his essay on Marcion in this volume, D. H. Williams shows that Harnack portrayed Marcion as an early reformer, anticipating Luther in purifying early Christianity, calling it back to an earlier simplicity.[10] Marcion's radical interpretation of the Pauline epistles, and his rejection of the Judaic heritage from the Old Testament may be explained from this perspective; he was detaching the gospel from its Old Testament association with "law." For Harnack Marcion's work was also significant for interrupting the process of Hellenization which was then changing the gospel into a form unrecognizable and unacceptable to its true founders. This is similar to the interpretation of Marcion in the *History of Dogma*; Harnack identified "Hellenization" as the key factor in transforming the Christian religion from a living faith to an intellectual affirmation of theological statements, or dogma.[11]

The essays of this collection focus on the "Hellenization" of early Christianity, and the respective roles of Gnosticism and

Judaism in this process; the question has been approached from a variety of directions. An important and central issue is the clarification of what "Hellenization" meant for Harnack himself. How did the concept function in his understanding of the history of Christianity; which aspects of the Greek heritage were significant? A second issue is the role of Gnosticism as a form of "Hellenization," or the question of the respective roles of Greek and non-Greek philosophical and theological/religious themes in the Gnostic documents. And a third is the more general issue of "Hellenization" in antiquity as a historical and political process associated with the conquests of Alexander the Great and his successors, particularly the Ptolemies and Seleucids. The nature of the Hellenization of Palestine has been the focus of significant scholarly attention in recent years. In a second section of this epilogue the more general question of religion and culture will be explored, as we return to the question of motifs of interaction and of "synthesis" as an interpretation of patristic use of Greek philosophical positions.

Harnack's Concept of "Hellenization"

In order to understand Harnack's characterization of Gnosticism as the "acute Hellenization" of the gospel it is important to recognize the multi-faceted nature of "Hellenization;" various aspects may be implied in discussions of this issue at any given point. It is, therefore, important to discern whether the question of Hellenization is primarily one of *language*: Greek vs. Hebrew or Aramaic; or are we dealing with a question of *ethnicity*, Hellenes vs. the children of Abraham in the line of Isaac and Jacob? Is it a *political* question of rulers and subjects, of Ptolemies, Seleucids and Maccabeans, and the right to collect taxes, or to possess the *land*? Is it a question of *culture*, the customs typical to a people: ideologies and philosophies, literature, or sculpture and architecture? Or is it primarily a question of *religion*, not just in terms of cult and ritual, forms of worship, sacrifices, and festivals, whether these be monotheistic or polytheistic, but also as a question of conscience and ultimate allegiance?[12]

For Harnack, aspects of religion and philosophy (or culture) are the focus of attention, as one might expect, for the analysis of

Gnosticism as "acute Hellenization" occurred within a discussion of early Christian dogma. The role which Harnack assigned to Gnosticism is somewhat analogous to that which Protestant theologians have often assigned to Greek philosophers, particularly the Platonists: one of undermining the power of the gospel, and threatening the vitality of Christianity.[13] Although Harnack may well have been attracted to some Gnostic positions, he does appear to have accepted the verdict of patristic writers in characterizing Gnosticism as the epitome of heresy. Initial appreciation for Harnack's argument was certainly related to his identification with this long tradition.[14]

Nonetheless, as W. Rowe has indicated in his discussion in this volume, Harnack's use of the concept of "Hellenization" is not lacking in subtlety. Questions of language, ethnicity, and political power are not excluded. Indeed, the attractiveness of this concept for Harnack is particularly evident from its primary function of explaining the geographical and religious *universality* of the Christian faith, in contrast with the more ethnically confined and exclusivist Judaism of Old Testament religion.[15] It is, further, clear from this use of the term "Hellenization" that the phase of Greek culture and history referred to is that of the Hellenistic kingdoms, even as these in turn were incorporated in the Roman empire; only at this point was Greek culture characterized by a certain universality, in contrast with the more parochial character of the classical Greek culture of an earlier period such as the fifth century BCE.[16]

Harnack applied the term "Hellenization" positively also for the incorporation of the concept of *logos* by apologists like Justin Martyr. In their identification of Jesus with the *logos* Harnack recognized a useful apologetic strategy of presenting the Redeemer in terms familiar to the Greco-Roman world of the time. Through fusion of a basic theme from Greek philosophy, that of an active rational principle uniting all phenomena within the cosmos, with a depiction of Christ as the Word or *logos* of God in the gospel of John, the apologists were preparing Christianity for its ultimate triumph, its acceptance as a philosophical religion within the Roman

Empire.[17] Christians were fully involved in the Greco-Roman world of their time and took seriously the challenge of giving an account of their faith; they were ready to engage the best minds of the day, whether in the market place, the schools, or at the imperial court. At the same time, however, they discovered that the impact of such ventures was never only a one-way matter.

For Harnack Hellenization as a strategy of using philosophical forms and concepts to represent religious themes took a negative turn with Gnostic speculation. At this point Harnack identifies the process of Hellenization as one of secularization, or accommodation to the spirit of the times, *Verweltlichung*.[18] Use of Greek philosophy has become ominous. Harnack's identification of Gnostics like Valentinus or Basilides as theologians is not altogether a compliment. They are not in the first place philosophers, although evidently influenced by philosophy. Theirs is a philosophy of religion. The religious tracts, exegetical works, hymns, acts and gospels which they composed provided a counterpart to the "scientific" or scholarly and intellectual (*wissenschaftlich*) work of the philosophical schools of the time.[19]

Gnosticism as such posed a real threat of "acute Hellenization;" but, according to Harnack, a slower and eventually more dangerous process of Hellenization occurred when the Christian church reacted to Gnosticism in a struggle for its own identity. Again, in the tension and dialectical interaction with Gnosticism both parties were deeply affected. T. Tiessen in his essay on Irenaeus in this volume reflects on one aspect of such a dialectical interaction when he claims that the scope and creativity of Irenaeus's comprehensive theological construction may well have been motivated by a desire to match the originality of Gnostic cosmological mythologizing.[20] P. O'Cleirigh, on the other hand, in his essay has focused on the inconsistencies of Harnack's use of one term: "Hellenization," whether acute or chronic, to explain the work of both orthodox Gnostics like Clement or Origen and heterodox Gnostics like Valentinus. Harnack insisted that heterodox Gnostics were far more inclined to use mythical and symbolic language; the orthodox

Gnostics, on the other hand, with their positive evaluation of embodied reality as good creation, had the greater appreciation of rational argument as source of truth. If Harnack was primarily interested in discovering how the Christian faith was converted into an intellectual affirmation of theological statements, O'Cleirigh argues, he may have been right in using "Hellenization" to describe the work of Clement or Origen, but should not also have applied the term to the Gnostics.[21]

In dealing with Gnosticism early Christianity clearly responded by developing the creeds as theological and dogmatic formulations of the faith. It also tightened its hierarchical institutional structure, granting more authority to the bishops. Intellectualization and institutionalization were, according to Harnack, the twin evils resulting from the impact of Gnosticism. Harnack's work recognized the element of Gnosticism which infected the church in its response to Gnosticism; and likewise the element of Hellenization which infected the church in its response to Hellenization. He regarded the Gnostic repudiation of the Old Testament as the only major factor distinguishing Gnostic and later Catholic theologians.[22]

But even for Catholic acceptance of the Old Testament as a Christian document negative "Hellenization" had its influence, this time through Judaism. For the Old Testament was maintained only by "spiritualizing" it through allegorical interpretation; for this, Harnack explains, the way had been paved within philosophical Judaism particularly by those who, like Philo, had regarded the Old Testament message as one in which reason emancipates the soul from the control of the passions.[23] Williams, in his discussion of Marcion, has examined the impact of Harnack's "Lutheran" view of the incompatibility of law and gospel on his arguments for early Catholic acceptance of the Old Testament; Williams suggests that exegetical challenges were far outweighed by the positive role of the Old Testament to portray Christianity with a respectable antiquity. While Marcion denied the *praeparatio evangelica* argument, Catholic Christians accepted the Old Testament as an indispensable witness to link the creator God of Genesis with the Supreme God and Father of Jesus.[24]

Although for Harnack the negative aspects such as institutionalization and intellectualism seem to predominate, it is nonetheless clear that the concept of Hellenization also had a positive side, for it was important in explaining the universality of the faith. Depicting the interaction of Gnosticism and Catholic Christianity as a matter of dialectical tension may also, indirectly, be recognized for a positive element in the Hellenization process. For, as B. Henaut has recognized in his evaluation of Harnack as historian, Harnack was himself far too much the intellectual to denigrate altogether the role of intellectual discussion in the history of Christianity.[25] According to Harnack, however, the negative factors combined to dissipate evangelical fervour, the enthusiasm of the faith.

Dogmatic formulation as an illegitimate expression of the faith was the focus of Harnack's interest in dealing with "Hellenization." Recognition of this is crucial for understanding why Harnack characterized Gnosticism as well as much of Catholic Christianity as "Hellenization" of that faith. Authentic Christianity, according to Harnack, is not to be found in a religion of creeds and doctrines to which one may give intellectual assent; rather, it is a matter of experience, a living relationship and simple trust. Dogmatic Christianity with its philosophical theology posed a threat to a pure evangelical religion, that of Jesus and Paul, a religion he characterized by feeling, hopes, action and enthusiasm.[26] This view of original Christianity, which is highly idealized and certainly reflects Romantic influence, provided the background for Harnack's critical study of the history of dogma. It was his hope that the Christian church could be recalled to such an original state when purified of its contamination, whether the more acute Hellenization identified as Gnosticism, or the more chronic, gradual Hellenization characterizing Catholicism with its heritage of dogmatic theology and metaphysical speculation. This was his goal in writing a history of dogma; this was also his hope for reforming the church.[27]

Harnack's lectures on the "essence" of Christianity were enormously popular in his time.[28] The acceptance of such an a-temporal "essence" of Christianity allowed Harnack to avoid the danger of relativism which looms when Christianity is altogether reduced to its historical dimension, a danger which has not been avoided by his successors. But Harnack's contemporaries also recognized and challenged the idealization which characterized such a view of "original" Christianity.[29] In his concluding assessment Rowe questions Harnack's characterization of *dogma* as a true reflection of the spirit of Greek philosophy, suggesting that *gnōsis* might be a better candidate.[30] He also asks whether Harnack's critical historical approach to the early centuries of Christianity would not inevitably also affect historical understanding of the gospel itself, resulting in a historicism which would regard it too as no more than a product of history.[31] During the past decades the historical critical approach, epitomized in Harnack's work, has increasingly been questioned. As a methodology for uncovering the "truth" closely associated with positivism in the sciences, its limitations are now more fully recognized.[32]

Gnosticism and Greek Philosophy
Although Harnack was certainly influenced by the Tübingen school in his understanding of the New Testament, he did not altogether agree with F. C. Baur's position on the Gnostics as having their origin with Judaism and as the first Christian philosophers in a succession ending with Hegel and German idealism.[33] In his view of Judaism as a significant influence on the Gnostics, Baur anticipated later, more well-known scholars like Grätz and Friedlander, who looked to sectarian Judaism, influenced by non-Jewish contemporary philosophical or theological reflection, for the origin or at least the context of Gnosticism. It is not surprising that Harnack, with his tendency to regard Hellenism and Judaism as polar opposites, was almost totally indifferent to the role of Judaism for his analysis of Gnosticism.[34] By interpreting *gnōsis* as "absolute knowledge" Harnack managed to avoid the dilemma of the relative importance of religious or philosophical elements in Gnosticism. For Harnack the

Gnostics were primarily theologians whose attention focused on intellectual questions.[35] It would appear that Harnack's primary interest in (history of) dogma and his aversion to rationalistic dogmatic formulations of patristic theology was decisive in motivating his focus on the philosophical or scholarly nature of Gnosticism as it affected early Christian theological discussions.

Harnack's understanding of Gnosticism as an expression of Greek philosophical speculation has not received broad acceptance in this century. Even in his own time the *religionsgeschichtliche Schule* followed the lead of Reitzenstein in turning to Oriental religion, to Babylonian and Iranian myths, in search of key elements in Gnostic thought, particularly the dualistic view of human nature and the cosmos evident in the strong contrast between light and dark, matter and spirit. Adherents of the "history-of-religions" school regarded Gnosticism as essentially religious and non-Hellenic in origin.[36] This approach, as E. Yamauchi has noted, does not have strong representation in current discussion of Gnostic origins; indeed, few scholars at present consistently defend the position of the "history-of-religions" school.[37] Instead, numerous scholars now regard Gnosticism as a religious movement of the Hellenistic world which is essentially independent in origin, or at least pre-Christian; and they consider it worthy of being studied in its own right, not just as a heretical form of Christianity.[38]

This approach is well represented by scholars who have followed in the footsteps of R. Bultmann: K. Rudolph, H.-M. Schenke, H. Koester and J. M. Robinson. Such scholars are usually willing to accept a formative if not decisive role for Judaism among the sources for Gnosticism.[39] In the present collection R. Halford most closely represents such an approach in her analysis of the Gnostic document *Trimorphic Protennoia*.[40]

Yamauchi, on the other hand, in this collection presents an update on the position he has argued particularly in his major publication, *Pre-Christian Gnosticism*. He has vigorously denied the validity of accepting Gnosticism, certainly in a meaningful sense of the term, as a phenomenon of pre-Christian times.[41] As M. Desjardins has noted in his response, Yamauchi's argument aims at undermining an understanding of the New Testament which currently enjoys extensive popularity, and is best represented in North America by H. Koester.[42]

Yamauchi also maintains his view in opposition to Walter Bauer's thesis on the variety of early "Christianities" and the priority of so-called unorthodox or heterodox Christianity. The German edition of this book was published in 1934; only recently has it been translated into English as *Orthodoxy and Heresy in Earliest Christianity* (1971).[43] Bauer's position not only supports those who regard Gnosticism as "pre-Christian," but would be particularly damaging for the purist view of the early church operative in Protestant views of early Christianity, and also accepted by Harnack. However, Bauer's reinterpretation of first and second century documents to support his thesis regarding early prevalence of heretical positions has now been widely questioned on text-critical grounds.[44] Yamauchi is evidently sympathetic to Harnack's purist view of early Christianity, although he comments on the issue only indirectly in his conclusions.[45]

To return to the question of origins, in the present century the focus has clearly shifted to Judaism as a significant background for Gnosticism. Many have followed Grätz and others in looking to sectarian and syncretizing Judaism for the key, if not the source of Gnosticism. The discovery of the Nag Hammadi documents has also encouraged such a trend, for the texts are frequently characterized by revelatory pronouncement and mythologizing exposition, as well as numerous references to Old Testament themes, particularly from early chapters of the book of Genesis.[46] This position on the origin of Gnosticism has been popularized by G.Quispel; at present it is best represented by Birger Pearson, who links Gnosticism with the Judaism of a sectarian group which broke with traditional Judaism and gave it a radical reinterpretation.[47]

One may ask, then, whether Harnack's view of Gnosticism as a "Hellenization" of the gospel can still be defended; is it even useful to reconsider his position as a viable option? An approach to

Gnosticism which regards it as a corruption of Christianity, or as a heresy within the context of early Christianity can still be found; however, it is certainly not widely appreciated in contemporary study of Gnosticism. At the 1966 Messina conference on Gnostic origins Simone Pétrement was alone in her defense of Gnosticism as a heresy parasitic on Christianity. As Yamauchi explains, however, there are at present certainly more scholars willing to agree on the assumption of a Christian context for fully developed Gnosticism.[48]

But neither E. Yamauchi nor S. Carroll, whose essay in this collection deals specifically with the relationship of Platonism and Gnosticism, is impressed by arguments for regarding Greek philosophy, particularly the Platonists, as the origin of Gnosticism. According to Yamauchi, the discovery of portions of Plato's *Republic* among Nag Hammadi documents is not without significance, but Harnack's characterization of Gnosticism as a "Hellenization" is too simplistic.[49] Carroll, recognizing the accusations of heresiologists like Irenaeus and Tertullian regarding philosophical influence on Gnostic positions, dismisses the significance of these claims through comparison with Plotinus's discussion of the Gnostic appeal to Plato. In his treatise II,9, against the Gnostics, Plotinus accuses them of arrogance, plagiarism, gross misunderstanding and misrepresentation of the master; Carroll concludes that the Gnostic claim to an association with Platonism was primarily a clever strategy to impress potential adherents, and to gain credibility in the contemporary intellectual climate.[50]

It is significant, also, that scholars of ancient Greek philosophy like A. H. Armstrong continue to urge strong caution against accepting anything more than superficial influence of Greek philosophical ideas on the Gnostics. In his contribution to the *Festschrift* for Hans Jonas, Armstrong warned against linking the pessimistic views of the cosmos, the demiurge, and cosmic powers, or themes of alienation and estrangement which characterize Gnostic documents with the positions of the Greek philosophers.[51] Even Simone Pétrement, as Carroll has noted, is cautious in her assessment of similarities in views of Platonists and Gnostics.[52]

Nonetheless in his lead paper Bos provides a strong argument for reconsideration of a Greek philosophical position, namely that of Aristotle, as the background, if not the immediate source for important themes in Gnosticism. In his discussion of the role of Aristotle in ancient Greek philosophy Bos examines the scholarly reinterpretation of Aristotle which has followed on the rejection of Jaeger's views, particularly the renewed attention to the important role of theological discussion in the work of Aristotle. From his own reconstruction of fragments from the lost works of Aristotle and *testimonia* from later writers, Bos concludes that Aristotle was not averse to the use of myth in his work, any more than his great teacher Plato. Important themes in Gnosticism, such as (1) the double theology of an unknown remote God and a subordinate creator/demiurge, (2) the depreciation of rational thought at the expense of intuition, and (3) the ambivalent portrayal of the demiurge as "sleeping world-soul" (based on an Aristotelian myth of "dreaming Kronos") can be traced back to Aristotle by way of Middle Platonism.[53]

Although cognizant of various key definitions which have been offered for Gnosticism, particularly that of R. McL. Wilson (1968) who focused on the distinction between the unknown God and the demiurge, the divine spark defining true humanity, a pre-mundane fall, and *gnōsis* as a means of deliverance and return, Bos himself emphasizes the supernatural character of the knowledge represented by *gnōsis*. It refers to knowledge concerning one's origin; and that origin is in turn identical with the transcendent origin of all reality. Bos focuses on Gnostic acceptance of an important philosophical distinction, namely the distinction between material and immaterial reality, between the natural and the spiritual or transcendent worlds. Greek thinkers posited this very basic distinction through the use of theoretical abstraction, a philosophical tool characteristic of neither Jewish nor Christian thought until introduced later through Greek influence.[54]

Where Bos focuses on the definition of the term *gnōsis* and Gnosticism as a religious and philosophical movement, P. Schneider's discussion of the community of believers reflected in the *Acts of John* goes even further than Bos in partially vindicating the views of Harnack. Schneider argues for progressive Hellenization in the *Acts* from its first forms to its later interpolations. This community already had a docetic view of Christ, understood conversion to Christian faith as resurrection, and emphasized the concept of impassability in its understanding of the Christian life.[55] Such an emphasis argues strongly for influence from Hellenistic philosophy, as is evident from numerous other papers, particularly those of P. Booth and D. Sly who have focused on Philo, and even more from that of D. Aune, who specifically focuses on this theme as it is used by both Philo and the author of 4 Maccabees. The interpolated passage, particularly chapters 94-102 of the *Acts*, while it reinforces the role of resurrection as conversion, also introduces a clearly Gnosticizing description of Christ, the sacraments and salvation.[56]

Judaism and Hellenization as Historical Phenomena

It is clear from the above discussion that examination of the process of Hellenization in early Christianity cannot ignore the role of Judaism, any more than it can neglect the obvious significance of Gnosticism. Although much attention has been directed at Judaism as a source of Gnosticism, important questions remain concerning absence, in Gnostic texts, of crucial Judaic themes: the unity of God, the authority of Torah, role of the Messiah, or the covenant.[57] With H. Jonas, J. Daniélou has argued that Gnosticism, in some respects at least, is better regarded as anti-Judaic. Indeed, when Judaism is regarded as background or origin of Gnostic positions most scholars are careful to refer to sectarian or heterodox Judaism: the Essenes, mystics, groups comfortable with mythical speculation from Babylonians or Persians, or writers like Philo whose views were closely associated with contemporary philosophical positions from which later Judaism dissociated itself.[58] Accordingly, they typically assume a plurality of "Judaisms" in this period, avoiding the issue of a normative definition.

Jewish Exclusivism Modified

If we are to take seriously Harnack's approach to Gnosticism and Hellenization, one of the most important issues for discussion is the unfortunate character of Harnack's polarization of Judaism and Hellenism as these affect early Christianity; this was recognized in Rowe's analysis, and re-emphasized in Henaut's response.[59] The disjunction of Judaism and Hellenism was not only a mistaken notion; because it was crucial to his argument for Hellenization as a universalizing factor, it had a significant impact on Harnack's understanding of early Christianity.

As a people, the Jews were ethnically defined as the descendants of Abraham, Isaac and Jacob, yet as a people of the covenant with Yahweh their identity was certainly more flexible. Especially the book of Isaiah testifies that the promises to Israel extended beyond their narrow territorial and ethnic confines, thus echoing the promise of Genesis 12:3 that all the nations would be blessed through Abraham.[60] It is also important to recognize that of the Jews exiled in Babylon only a small percentage returned to Palestine to rebuild the temple and occupy their ancestral lands; most Jews continued to live elsewhere throughout the known ancient world in *diaspora*, the extent of which is clearly documented in Acts.[61] Through payment of the temple-tax the link with Palestine was maintained; many regularly made the pilgrimage to Jerusalem for the high festivals.

Even as a scattered people the Jews maintained their identity; extensive literary evidence testifies to this. They valued highly such distinctive traits as Sabbath observance, dietary restrictions like abstinence from pork, circumcision, aniconic worship, and weekly assembly in a synagogue or place of prayer.[62] Such traits fostered a sense of belonging and unity, all the more needed because of their scattered existence. The degree of unity thus achieved, however, does not add up to the exclusivism of Harnack's interpretation.

Greek Universalism Refined

If the exclusivism of Jews needs to be redefined, the universalism of the Greeks in the Hellenistic empires has also been the subject of re-examination. Well before the extensive conquests of Alexander Isocrates had claimed that being "Hellene" was not in the first place a matter of race or blood, but rather a question of language and culture.[63] Since the studies of Tarn and Griffith earlier this century it is often assumed that acquaintance with the Greek language and culture was wide-spread and provided the culturally dominant note in the Hellenistic empires of the ancient Near East.[64]

Hellenistic culture was focused particularly on the Greek cities founded by Alexander as the hub of Greek civilization in the farflung kingdoms. To maintain Greek ways, social life was organized around the gymnasium, stadium, and theatre.[65] Such institutions had historic associations with Greek gods and heroes like Heracles; and these in turn were often identified with local deities in syncretistic fusion, as symbols of the new era. The Greek language followed Greek traders and soldiers as a *lingua franca*; those of the local populace who wished to take advantage of trade, or climb the political and military ladder would find it in their interest to learn the language. They would also wish to make provision for their children to learn the language and perhaps even take on citizenship through the traditional rite by which Greek youths made the transition to adulthood, the ephebate.[66]

Yet it is important not to overestimate the use of Greek as a common language, for it has been demonstrated that in the Seleucid empire Aramaic was more likely to be a second language of choice for trade or administration, and in Egypt demotic continued to be used in administrative documents.[67] Various studies of the past years have also demonstrated the relative superficiality of Hellenization as a cultural influence; the continuation and even thriving of local cultural traditions and literary efforts, whether in Egypt or Syria and Phoenicia reveal the inability to penetrate local cultures with any depth.[68]

Hellenization in Palestine

It has long been assumed that even if Judaism in the *diaspora* was thoroughly affected by Hellenization, at least in Palestine its impact was not so strong, for there the Maccabean uprising against the Hellenizers provided evidence of a strong movement of resistance. However, the portrayal of Hellenization in Palestine has been modified in the last decades particularly as a result of the work of Martin Hengel, who has demonstrated that the strong differentiation between Hellenism in Palestine and that in the rest of the Hellenistic empire is no longer acceptable. Hengel's work builds on the historical investigations of V. Tcherikover who argued that the Hasmonean rulers were not primarily interested in guarding religious autonomy for the Jews, but in supplanting the power of the traditional aristocracy, particularly its control of the important position of the high priest.[69] Under Ptolemaic and Seleucid rulers the Palestinian Jews did not resist Hellenization. Numerous cities had been founded and were governed by a council according to a Greek constitution. Hellenistic administration was felt particularly in the form of taxes imposed, and traders took advantage of the crossroads position of Palestine. Both administration and trade was carried on with use of Greek language, although Greek certainly did not supplant the use of Aramaic.

The Maccabean uprising had as its ostensible goal the removal of Hellenizing influences; 1 Maccabees 1:11-15 speaks of propaganda in favor of Greek customs like use of the gymnasium, nudity in sports, and removal of the sign of circumcision, the sign of the covenant with Yahweh. It has traditionally been assumed that the issue of religious freedom was significant for the resistance to Hellenization; current scholarly treatment, however, questions the role of the Maccabeans and Hasidim in opposing "Greek ways." Even after the Maccabean crisis evidence for continued use of the Greek language, literary forms, philosophical concepts and educational structures, particularly the gymnasium, is extensive; clearly, Palestine did not cease to exist as a part of the Hellenistic world.[70] The resistance to elements of Hellenistic culture, like sports and use of the gymnasium, is now thought to have focused on these institutions primarily as symbols of arrogant and oppressive "colonial" power, retaliating with anti-Greek propaganda in return. Accordingly, current scholarship assumes that the term "Hellenization" in these conflicts was used primarily as a political slogan, a catch-word to express hostility against a ruling power, to rally opposition; religious (and other cultural) aspects were a secondary consideration.[71]

Although they have been challenged, Hengel's conclusions regarding Hellenization of Palestine have not been overturned; indeed, recent discussions of the Hellenization of the Jews confirm the results of Hengel's work.[72] Current scholarly work no longer assumes a strong contrast between the Judaism of Palestine and that of the *diaspora* in the Hellenistic kingdoms; neither does it accept the strong disjunction which typified Harnack's polarization of Judaism and Hellenism as such. Hellenization is recognized as a complex phenomenon touching on many different aspect of life: political structures, language and literature, and philosophical ideas. As a historical process affecting Palestine "Hellenization" is regarded primarily as a matter of political and cultural power, whereas Judaism is typically categorized as "religion;" accordingly, it is unacceptable to assume, even theoretically, a mutual exclusion of the two, or to assume that becoming "Hellenized" meant inevitable betrayal of Judaism.[73] It is not difficult to demonstrate that many who professed loyalty to Judaism did not oppose Hellenistic culture; nor did "Hellenizers" necessarily believe that their policies would involve them in compromise or betrayal of their Judaism. Philo of Alexandria is often cited as an example of a Jew who was comfortable in both. When it came to clearly unacceptable demands on their beliefs, like requests to honor Greco-Roman deities and worship at the imperial shrines, the Jews invariably resisted. Their views on worship were well-known and for the most part respected in antiquity, particularly in the Roman Empire.

New Understanding of Hellenistic Judaism and Early Christianity
Thus it appears that much more emphasis has recently been placed
on the congruence of Palestinian Judaism(s) with Judaism elsewhere in the Hellenistic kingdoms and Roman empire; the discussion has focused on the role of the Greek language and literature,
philosophical reflection and educational institutions (gymnasium,
ephebate), as well as political and administrative structures. Particularly the openness of Palestinian Jews to Hellenistic cultural
forms which is assumed in these discussions is far removed from
Harnack's treatment of Judaism in his work on early Christianity
and Hellenization. A more significant role for Judaism, whether in
the transmission of philosophical and theological positions from the
Hellenistic world, or in the formative stages of the development of
Gnosticism, is at present a much more tenable position.

Our understanding of the historical situation of Christianity of
the first two centuries has also undergone a significant shift during
the past century. One example illustrates this well: if New Testament
Greek was once thought to be a language peculiar to these documents, the publication of numerous inscriptions and papyri from the
Hellenistic Near East, associated with names like W. Ramsay, B. P.
Grenfell, and A. S. Hunt, caused dramatic re-evaluation of that
position. It has become clear that the Greek language of the New
Testament was no more esoteric than the language commonly used
in the Eastern parts of the Roman Empire, *koine* Greek.[74] To
explain the peculiarity of some New Testament words, the scholar
is still well advised to turn to the Greek of the Old Testament, the
Septuagint. Continuity of early Christianity with Judaism has never
been seriously questioned. But the papyri have provided good
evidence that the everyday, common language of its environment in
the Greco-Roman world has been a significant factor influencing
terminology of New Testament documents.

We may therefore safely conclude that from its very beginning
early Christianity was "Hellenized" not only because the Jews of
Palestine lived in a Hellenized context. When Paul and other mis-
sionaries sought out Jews in the *diaspora*, and through, or despite,

them sought out Gentiles, "Hellenization" in terms of language and cultural forms was even more a reality.

Hellenization and Gnosticism as Contamination
From our discussion it is clear that the question of Hellenization, particularly as it has arisen from Harnack's work on early Christianity, is a question of the Hellenic contribution to early Christian theological discussions, resulting in dogmatic formulation whether on the deity of Christ, as with *logos* theology, or on the Trinity with the Nicene settlement. For Harnack, and many others who preceded him, "Hellenization" was primarily a question of philosophical influence on religious and theological forms. "Hellenization" represented an intellectualization of the Christian faith, and as such introduced a complication, if not a corruption of the primitive simplicity of the gospel message.

It is obvious that clarification of the meaning and extent of "Hellenization" must be settled before proceeding to the second question of Gnosticism as an instance of such a process of "Hellenization." Here it is important to discern whether philosophical or religious aspects are more important. Is it primarily a question of the influence of themes from Greek philosophy on Gnostic positions, i. e., a question of the history of thought; or is it primarily a question of Gnostic influence on early Christianity, introducing an intellectualistic element which is at odds with the "primitive simplicity" of Christianity? Clearly, the latter is uppermost for Harnack. It is certainly difficult to comprehend why Harnack would have accented the philosophical character of Gnosticism unless one realizes the context of Harnack's discussion of early Christianity. As an instance of Hellenization, Gnosticism presents Harnack with a severe case of contamination.

Still one must not forget that it was in his capacity as a historian of Christianity that Harnack's contribution has been valued; neglecting a critical examination of the question from the historical point of view would not do him justice. Indeed, with respect to study of Gnostic documents this century has witnessed a lively discussion of both the nature and origin of Gnosticism. Historical study of the

Hellenistic kingdoms has also examined the influence of Hellenization as a political, cultural or religious question. As a historical process Hellenization was an issue for Judaism long before it became an concern to Christianity. The transfer of Hellenic cultural forms within the Hellenistic kingdoms, Judaic as well as others, was an undeniable reality. Of particular interest for our study, however, is the conclusion of contemporary historians that at a critical point in Judaic history, at the time of the Maccabean revolt, the theme of "Hellenization" represented a political slogan, a catch-word to rally support against those thought to be selling out to foreign rulers. Even so, the term represents a betrayal, a process all the more critical as it was perceived to result in loss of identity for Judaism.

Methodology and Religious Identity
It would appear that before the question of the relative significance of various factors in Hellenization, whether political and historical/cultural, or philosophical and theological/religious, can be resolved a prior question needs to be asked, a question of methodology. This is the question of the identity, or defining character of the faith, and of the ways it might be threatened by aspects of (Greek) culture, whether that be defined by political or administrative structures, educational matters, or themes in Greek philosophy or theology. It is important to discern in a more general way how cultural factors threaten the identity (or even independent existence) of a group characterized by a distinctive religion, like Christianity or Judaism. If a clear division between spheres of politics and religion is a realistic assessment, how is it that such groups have often felt threatened within a supposedly neutral environment, fearing secularization, compromise or paganizing syncretism? Are processes of accommodation and possible contamination truly avoidable?

Historical investigation alone can not answer such a question, as even Harnack realized at least implicitly; for a historical examination of Hellenization as a corrupting influence on early Christianity assumes a prior uncontaminated status, an identifiable original condition of the faith which may be regarded as having a normative status. Adjectives like "pure," "original" or "simple" are indeed often used to express what is genuine in dealing with the issue of identity. And from a methodological perspective, the question of identity is presupposed in issues of contamination, corruption or betrayal. Contamination, on the other hand, is often characterized in terms of secularization, syncretism, or paganizing idolatry; "heresy" is used for a more extreme threat or betrayal of the faith. For philosophical and cultural issues the corresponding terms are: compromise, accommodation, or synthesis.

Harnack himself had some difficulty in providing a satisfactory description of an original condition of the Christian situation, mainly because the elements of religion which he favored were matters of experience and action, trust, hope and enthusiasm.[75] Aversion to rational discourse as a Hellenic inheritance led him to focus on those elements which, however indispensable for a living religion, are not easily expressed and discussed, for language necessarily communicates by means of words and sentences. His view of primitive Christianity also reflects a degree of nostalgia for a time when issues were apparently less complicated, and religion characterized by pristine purity. Such a romanticized idealization of early Christianity was challenged, and rightly so; however, Harnack would have realized that the history of "Hellenization" or "Catholicization" of the Christian faith could not be told without it. And, as we have noted, the theme of an original purity, to which Christianity is to be recalled, is deeply rooted in Protestant theology and study of the early Church.

The concept of "purity" as it applies to early Christianity certainly needs further analysis, for New Testament writings recognize only Jesus as perfectly sinless; early Christian teachings were especially concerned to protect and elaborate the significance of his life and work, his sacrifice on the cross and resurrection. From the beginning the Christian church legitimately identified itself by defining the essential elements of faith in Jesus as Saviour. It did so through its earliest baptismal confessions, the canonization of New Testament writings and the development of creeds and doctrines; and such a process of self-identification was vital to its development as a true community.[76] The significance of the *regula fidei* for the early church can best be appreciated from this perspective.[77] New Testament writings like Paul's letters to the Corinthians, or the first chapters of Revelation indicate that from its beginning the early church was certainly not free of problems, controversy, and even deep division. Leaders of the stature of Paul and Barnabas could not get along, and had to part company. A romantic notion of these early Christian leaders needs correction. At the same time it becomes clear that use of the term "Hellenization" to characterize all these early problems would make the term virtually meaningless.

Historical investigation, clearly, will not provide the needed model, any more than it can answer the question of identity. The evidence does not support the assumption of an original condition of "pristine purity." Historical data are important for Christian faith, but are quite inadequate, as such, to answer questions of purity, contamination and subsequent need for repristination. To address the issue of identity we need to ask the methodological questions: how is true Christianity to be described? How is the Christian faith to be identified? Which elements of the faith are indispensable as the basis for true community? Which aspects of the faith allow room for disagreement, and at what point can one speak of denial or betrayal of the faith?

These are the critical issues; providing the solution is somewhat more complicated, for it is not only a matter of finding the correct answers. It is clear from history that Christians have had much difficulty in coming to agreement on such answers; it is by no means clear, either, that the answers were fully formulated, posited once and for all at some point in the early history of Christianity. Yet we should not for that reason conclude that Christians ever doubted that answers to such questions could be worked out; for the essential aspects of the faith had already been given, if in embryonic form.

It is, furthermore, also important to recognize that for Harnack Gnosticism and Hellenization did not present themselves primarily as external threats. He regarded them rather like a disease which does its deadly work of weakening the life of faith from within. This would appear to be the connotation of his reference to Hellenization as acute or chronic.[78] To remedy this condition it would be insufficient to isolate or separate the dangerous elements; surgery might give the more appropriate solution.

Metaphors of Change and Development
If one must use a metaphor, perhaps that of a seed and its growth is useful, and more helpful than that implied in Harnack's imagery of health and disease, or the Reformers' *ad fontes*.[79] It is evident from the New Testament writings themselves that early Christians like Paul kept going back to the Old Testament writings, as well as the events of the life and work of Jesus, to interpret these for the new Christian communities of the early church.[80] Yet it is also clear that in so doing Paul was challenged by the problems and misunderstandings which arose, whether problems of sexual ethics or the celebration of the Lord's supper, as in Corinth. It would thus appear that answers to the central questions of identity have had both an element of stability and fixity, because they go back to historical events which remain unchanged as such, and finished; yet they also have an element of flexibility because the need and a corresponding focus of interest does change from one generation to the next, as different problems arise and require new formulations of the faith to address them.

The metaphor of source and outflow, or of pure mountain spring issuing into a muddy stream, like that of health and disease, typically brings with it imagery of increasing pollution and impurity. In his paper on the use of water imagery J. Corbett has shown that exceptions could occur, as with the Thanksgiving hymn from Qumran which values the water from irrigation ditches, and the poetic popularization of the life of St. Martin of Tours by Paulinus of Périgueux, which he describes as a welcome cup of muddy water from the nearby stream. However Philo's elitism in praising the pure cold water from the distant mountain stream is far more typical in the ancient literature.[81] Unlike ancient theories of history, which usually regarded any change as a sign of deterioration, Christian beliefs are not invariably pessimistic.[82] The Christian faith looks forward at the same time as it returns to its origins. Thus, more like the seed and fully grown plant, both the elements of continuity with the root, and of growth in accordance with conditions of climate and environment, are vital for the healthy development of the mature plant.

The Significance of Creedal Formulations
From earliest New Testament writings, the Christian church reflected on the significance of Christ's suffering, death and resurrection, his deity and lordship. However, the formulation of central teachings regarding his deity and incarnation took shape particularly in the context of Greco-Roman views of deity. Because these were often characterized by docetism, i. e., questioning the reality of a fully divine person truly present on this earth as a human among humans, it became necessary to deal with the relationship of Christ's humanity and divinity.[83] The role of the creeds in this process of self-identity was indispensable, marking, in each case, wide-spread agreement on how best to answer challenges to the faith. These earliest challenges and the responses given were significant in setting the direction for discussions for many centuries to come. Yet in a real sense the actual date of creedal formulation is not the important issue. What is important is the broadly-based acceptance of these creeds for many centuries, as an expression of what the Christian church believes to be true, and confesses to be central biblical teachings.

We may conclude that it is certainly important for Christians to have a clear understanding of what they regard to be central Christian teachings, beliefs which constitute a *sine qua non*, and are vital for the Christian faith. However, such central teachings would not necessarily have been fully formulated *before* the faith was challenged by views which Christians considered incompatible. It is perhaps historically more likely that important teachings were formulated in the face of opposition, in the heat of debate, at a point when the respective parties were well aware of the significance of issues at stake in the confrontation.

Perhaps, then, Harnack's approach of understanding a dialectical development in the history of Christianity can be vindicated, if in a way rather different from his own application of the dialectic of Hellenization in the later contamination of the faith. While he focused on a "chronic" Hellenization of the faith in response to the "acute" Hellenization of Gnosticism, we may recognize a dialectic of Christianity expressing its identity in response to the challenges of various opposing views, using a process of creedal and dogmatic formulation to define for itself what it considered essential and indispensable for a meaningful community of faith. Accordingly we may understand the identity of the faith to be expressed in creeds and confessions reflecting a continuous process of self-identification in the face of opposition.

Religion and Culture

If it is useful to examine the identity of the Christian faith and corresponding questions of purity and contamination in terms of a dialectical process through which that identity is more clearly expressed in the face of opposition, the assumption of a dialectical process may also be helpful in examining an issue in the historical discussion of Judaism and Hellenization, the question of the interaction and mutual influence of religion and political environment, or culture.

Harnack's analysis of the Hellenization of Christianity assumed an intellectual/philosophical influence, with rational dogmatic formulation of belief contaminating the faith; for Harnack philosophical/cultural elements influenced religion negatively. It is important to note that his approach differs significantly from that of contemporary historians who regard Hellenization as a political and cultural force co-existing with, and providing the context in a supposedly non-threatening way for a variety of ethnic and religious groups. This raises the more general question of the relationship of religion and culture, an issue basic to our entire discussion and crucial for evaluating the role of Hellenization as it influenced Christianity in history.

Religion and Modern Pluralism
In this discussion it is important to remember that modern historians often regard religion as an expression of a particular culture; in so doing they typically restrict their definition of religion to outward forms: the festivals, rites and sacrifices of an ancient civilization, or the church buildings, liturgies, and processions of the contemporary scene. Marxists who viewed religion as an opiate have regarded it as a degenerate form of cultural power; a materialistic consumer mentality, likewise, relegates religion to items on the market. One's assessment of the place of religion, and of the relationship of religion and culture is evidently influenced by a more all-embracing attitude or worldview.

Contemporary secularization in Western countries for the most part excludes religion from the power structures of the public domain: parliamentary debates, stock markets or schools. Religion is relegated to the sidelines, the privatized sphere of home or church building. Still, as a private matter of conscience, freedom of religion is also considered a basic human right, and religious convictions are protected by legislation against state interference in many Western countries.

Religious freedom and pluralism is a fact of life in many countries; however, the separation of religion from public life which characterizes modern secularized society does pose problems for those who believe their faith should affect their lives more totally. For even today numerous religious groups insist that culture should be shaped, if not dominated by religion. Christianity, like Islam, is essentially a missionary religion. Christians are encouraged to be a leaven in society, to let their light shine and be a blessing to the nations in which they live.

If then one's faith is relevant for all of life, and religion a basic motivating factor in action, cultural expression will inevitably be affected.[84] Religion is not to be restricted to so-called private matters, to ethical or moral issues; it will have implications also for politics, justice and law, family life, psychology and philosophy or ideology.

In the attempt to understand Judaism and earliest Christianity it is likewise important to remember that the relationship between religion and politics within the Roman Empire was certainly not characterized by a neat separation of spheres. In antiquity the situation was markedly different from the contemporary state of affairs. In many ancient cultures the ruler had a special relationship to the gods of the people; accordingly, religion and political structures were usually closely intertwined. Although Alexander the Great assumed a divine lineage through the semi-divine Heracles, he also prided himself on his tolerant acceptance of various ethnic traditions and cultures. Yet religious freedom could not be assumed, as the Jews knew; they in turn also did not regard their religion as a private matter, but took pride in their sacred writings, especially the laws of Moses which governed their relationships as communities. Of course, the close relationship of politics and religion did not always work against the Jews, and in late antiquity, with Constantine, it worked in the favour of Christians as well. When historians assume the agreeable coexistence of Judaism (or Christianity), as a religion, within a culturally Hellenized context, they have clearly not told the full story.

Like the question of faith and reason, the issue of religion and culture has long been a subject of discussion dealing with two poles of approach within Christianity. From its history it is clear that the Christian faith can be practised in many different contexts. It can, as it were, accommodate itself to various ethnic, linguistic or political cultural patterns, in order to have a presence in different environments and thus be "all things to all" (1 Cor. 9:19-23). In this respect Christianity is at least as flexible as Judaism. Few Christians today would advocate return to a medieval model in which Christianity itself, with a well-developed hierarchy of ministries and orders, would constitute the superior cultural force. Within contemporary pluralism Christianity assumes a more modest role, yet continues to exert influence in many different linguistic and cultural contexts, among the numerous peoples who have accepted Christianity and whose cultures have rarely been unaffected by this acceptance.

Some environments are more hospitable than others, yet ironically even under overtly hostile regimes Christianity has been able to spread and flourish.

R. Niebuhr's Classification
The volume of essays based on the first "Christianity and the Classics" conference held at the Institute for Christian studies in 1984 focused on the relationship between religion and culture evidenced in the history of classical scholarship, and used the motifs from R. Niebuhr's *Christ and Culture*: separation, superiority, parallel status, identity and transformation. In a concluding contribution to that collection A.Wolters examined these five motifs as symbolic of the various ways in which the history of classical scholarship has intersected with the history of Christianity.[85] Wolters found Niebuhr's classification of the types of relationship useful as a tool for categorizing patterns in Christian use of the Greco-Roman classical heritage. Two patterns were found to be more prevalent than others: that of the superiority of the Christian faith over its cultural Greco-Roman background, the *praeparatio evangelica* motif, and that of transformation, identified as the *spoliatio* motif.

The present collection of essays continues the examination of these motifs by turning to an earlier and more formative period of Christianity, the first three centuries, before the Constantinian settlement. The investigation of the more prevalent motifs in this period takes one to earliest usage and allows for comparison, to determine whether later use was already foreshadowed at an earlier time.

The emergence of these motifs coincided with a time when both Judaism and Gnosticism had a strong impact on early Christianity. Although with Harnack one might be tempted to regard them as dialectically opposing wings of strong influences on the early Christian church, the body of scholarship which claims a close connection between Judaism and Gnosticism is not to be ignored. Today both are regarded as primarily religious movements, for both used revelatory documents as basic religious texts, and both acknow-

ledged the importance of human salvation through a redeemer, or
messiah. From the perspective of early Christians both had elitist
pretensions. In Romans 2:18-20 Paul speaks of the Jews who styled
themselves "a guide for the blind, a light for those who are in the
dark, an instructor for the foolish" because they regard the law as
source of all knowledge and truth.[86] Gnostics too styled themselves
as *pneumatikoi,* or "spiritual" because they had the key, *gnōsis,*
unlike others, the *psychikoi* and even worse, the *somatikoi* or
sarkikoi.[87]

It is certainly of interest as well that in current scholarship
dealing with early Christianity, both Judaism and Gnosticism vie for
a degree of recognition at the expense of a publicly discredited and
apparently outmoded Christianity. There is clearly a degree of
special pleading among scholars who seek to advance the cause of
Gnostic visionaries at the expense of "repressive" bishops who are
seen to infringe on the rights of popular causes. Since the holocaust
it has also been considered necessary or expedient to promote the
adherents of Judaism as survivors who have managed to maintain
their faith and religious identity in the midst of adverse conditions.
Nor is it easy in the current academic climate to peel away layers of
scholarly attitudes which are the more engrained as they are based
on contemporary historical realities.[88]

Historians today tend to recoil from Harnack's view of the
expansion of Christianity as an ultimately victorious faith, a vigorous
faith which triumphed in the Greco-Roman context in spite of strong
opposing forces.[89] Yet we have seen that his analysis of Hellenization in the history of dogma is not really triumphalistic; in fact the
dominant note seems to be one of pessimistic appraisal of what is
happening in early Christianity. Both Rowe and Henaut recognize
that he has, instead, anticipated rather well the later historiography
which regards early Christianity and "Catholicization," both before
and after the Constantinian settlement, in a rather ominous light:
cultural factors had invaded and corrupted the religious sphere. The
result was an unholy mix of religion and culture. What ought to have
been kept separate was mingled to the detriment of religious purity.

This was an unfortunate affair from both sides. Historians looking at the Constantinian agreement from the perspective of the medieval synthesis have also claimed that Christianity was given illegitimate political powers; Christian influence would inevitably create difficulties for groups characterized by differing religious convictions.

It is, thus, the perspective of modern pluralism which provides significant impetus for the present reconsideration of the issue of religion and culture. The motifs of Niebuhr will serve as a guide in examining the relationship with particular reference to early Christianity. The motif of separation or confrontation opens this discussion since one might expect this to provide a natural response to Harnack's assessment of contamination.

Religion and Culture Opposed
The theme of confrontation with dangerous cultural elements, denunciation, and withdrawal to avoid contamination has a respectable history within Christianity. The Israelites were called out from among the peoples of the Near East to be a separate people especially because of the dangers of paganizing through worship of agricultural deities like Baal and Astoreth. Cultural phenomena posed as religious dangers, as they frequently do, particularly when one part of the creation, whether the sky, or (human) sexuality and powers of reproduction would be deified. As D. Sly has indicated in her paper, the strong prohibition of intermarriage was aimed at avoiding an ever-present menace of idolatry.[90]

Indeed, evil is no mirage, as the Gnostics knew; we live in a fallen world. With his *City of God*, Augustine gave classic expression to the fundamental duality of direction, expressed in two loves, which make for two cities, the city of God and that of this world. The element of opposition is real, and tension arises as much from opposing claims as from pain and suffering which in turn results from evil and sin. Christians are called to oppose cultural phenomena which are incompatible with the Christian faith. Yet, even though cultural matters may be the bearers of evil, they may also be the unwitting objects of evil influences. It is important to recognize that the divide between good and evil does not fall between religion and culture as such; rather, the perspective of faith gives a criterion to distinguish between good and evil as these appear through or in cultural phenomena.

With the Calvinistic reformational approach in philosophy this basic opposition of religious directions has been identified as *antithesis*. Recognition of the antithesis follows closely on the Kuyperian thesis of Christ's lordship and claim upon the world. In this sense the antithesis and the accompanying radical choice, for or against Christ, is widely recognized by Christians. But how do Christians apply such a divergence of directions? Much less agreement will be found on implications of a religious antithesis for daily life, careers, associations, in short the cultural issues.

Acceptance of a basic religious antithesis, with an appreciation of the religious root of culture, has led to the further conclusion that all cultural forms are to be distinguished (in principle) as being for or against Christ. Scholarship is an important aspect of cultural expression; in fact reformational philosophy has been characterized by its inclusion of scholarly work among the areas of life which also must acknowledge Christ's claim, particularly by opposing views which do not recognize this claim.[91]

But this conclusion regarding a radical distinction, or division of cultural and scholarly efforts along the lines of religious divergence is not self-evident. Nor has it been as widely accepted. Christians are called to be an identifiable and holy people, a people freed from slavery to sin through the work of Jesus as Saviour (1 Pet. 2:9-10). However, this is not typically thought to imply that they live separate lives, geographically or even culturally isolating themselves from their environment, any more than it means that there is one great "blue-print" for how Christians have to live in this world. Christians are "in" but not "of" the world (John 17:13-18); "in" the world they continue their lives very much within an environment shared with those of different faiths, sharing language, race, clothing and shelter, transportation modes, careers and markets with non-Christians.

Isolationist movements have come and gone throughout history, whether as idealistic communes, or monastic orders. They continue to have a certain attraction. In some situations retreat may be useful. But historically separatist movements have not proven able to maintain their isolation and also succeed in their goal of maintaining a holy lifestyle. J. Klapwijk has identified various negative aspects of such isolationism: (1) it courts an unhealthy complacency; (2) a group which withdraws from communication (with friend or foe) tends to become irrelevant, and its faith privatized; and (3) such groups are not responsible in giving an account of their faith.[92]

Like isolationist movements, the organizational or social application of the antithesis also experiences its own moment in history. There are certainly occasions when it is expedient for a group to withdraw as an association, to draw strength from a community of like-minded people, and to work out a strategy to deal with opposing forces. Yet it is important to recognize that throughout history the "opposing forces" have been represented in a great variety of cultural phenomena; evil and sin take many different shapes, and are always changing. The point at which one particular culture, or religiously rooted cultural phenomenon, challenges the faith is likely to vary significantly from that of another culture, or another moment in time.

The significance of the opposition motif is therefore not primarily one of indicating tensions between religion and culture. The Christian faith, as we have noted, can be embodied in a variety of cultural contexts, under different political structures, among many different peoples. So the question remains: at what point does our acceptance of the "world" in which we live as our environment threaten our ability to bring renewal, hope or healing? At what point does contamination take place; when are identity and loyalty compromised? Culture does not invariably pose a threat. Yet it is to be opposed when a religiously motivated cultural phenomenon or program threatens the identity of the Christian faith.

The opposition motif is examined most closely in the paper on Tertullian; since Niebuhr used him as proponent of the "Christ against culture" position Tertullian has often been taken to epitomize oppositionism. But as this essay shows, "isolation" is not the last word even for Tertullian. Indeed, Fredouille has described Tertullian's approach as a transformation of ancient culture inasmuch as he made positive use of themes and stylistic features from contemporary philosophical schools in his theological argumentation.[93] Harnack regarded Tertullian as one for whom the faith was superior to culture.[94] W. Helleman's article shows that Tertullian's work does not lend itself to easy categorization, certainly not as an oppositionist; however it is clear that for Tertullian the *regula fidei* played a significant role in determining the borderline between what is and is not acceptable in defining the faith.

Synthesis
The remaining four motifs of Niebuhr assume a more positive view of culture. Niebuhr spoke of religion as "identified with," or given "parallel status" with culture. Again, religion could be regarded as a "perfection," or "transformation" of culture.

Of these four motifs, those indicating identity or parallel status between religion and the surrounding environment or culture are, as L. Frizzell has recognized, not well represented in the literature of early Christianity.[95] However, the aspect of identification with contemporary culture has historically been significant for Calvinistic reformational philosophy in categorizing patristic writers as representatives of *synthesis* thought. Much early Christian philosophizing has accordingly been regarded primarily as accommodation of basic Christian beliefs to current philosophical conceptions, compromising the faith with respect to the spirit of the age, whether or not this was intentional. Vollenhoven, as Klapwijk notes, regarded Tertullian not as an oppositionist but as a representative of synthesis.[96]

"Synthesis," clearly, is not a neutral term. In this context synthesis represents the philosophical counterpart of antithesis although it is not its precise opposite. Within reformational philosophy "synthesis" has a connotation analogous to that of "Hellenization" and "secularization" for Harnack; it expresses a process which is in principle illegitimate, perhaps even impermissible or impossible for true faith. In essence, "synthesis" refers to the combination of two elements, whether these occur in nature or as elements of thought, like themes or ideas. It indicates more than a juxtaposition, yet "synthesis" is not the appropriate term for a combination in which the original elements blend or harmonize so that they can no longer be distinguished, like the blending of green and yellow to give a blue color, or the harmonization of voices in which one can no longer distinguish individual sounds. In a synthesis the two component elements are essentially alien one to the other. When combined the mix is unfortunate and detrimental, particularly for the element which happens to be the more vulnerable of the two. It will suffer loss of characteristic identity, corruption or pollution.[97] From such an analysis it is clear that "synthesis" could not be the correct term for the mutual interaction of religion and culture as such, for we have noted that theoretically religion and culture are able to co-exist and interact without this necessarily having detrimental effect. As a negative interaction, "synthesis" can be identified particularly where a religiously motivated cultural phenomenon or political strategy threatens a position (or group) of different religious orientation, or when a religiously motivated philosophical position negatively affects a position of (Christian) faith. In such cases a pretence at harmony in effect masks a cacophony.

Herman Dooyeweerd spoke of synthesis in terms of an inappropriate interaction of basic religious motivating forces in culture, the *grond-motieven* which are either Christian or (like the form-matter motif of the Greeks) non-Christian. Inasmuch as these motifs are ultimately religious in orientation and expression, and thus inevitably in tension, "synthesis" is the appropriate term for such interaction.[98] His colleague Dirk Vollenhoven's approach was somewhat different, since he spoke of typical positions and currents in philosophy, noting the different ways in which basic themes reappear at different points in history and become variously (and inappropriately) intertwined with Christian positions.[99] In the analysis of patristic writers Justin's acceptance of the *logos* concept in his discussion of Christ, and Clement's reference to himself as a Christian Gnostic have typically been regarded as examples of synthesizing thought. Here evidently elements of Greek philosophical thought used in the interpretation of the faith had the ultimate effect of changing the basic character of the faith in an intellectualistic direction.[100]

As we have seen above, however, there is a real sense in which Christianity accepts and identifies itself with a culture; moreover, Christianity is compatible with many different cultural forms. There is, after all, much that Christians share with their cultural environment. W. Dyrness has affirmed this clearly: "Because of the intrinsic goodness of creation and the image of God in us and God's sustaining activity, we share basic features of our worldview with non-Christians in our culture. This makes possible a basic level of communication that relies on and grows out of our common experience. ... Christianity is inevitably expressed in terms of some culture, and culture results from human creativity within God-given structures."[101] Thus in some sense Christ is *in* culture. God's call comes to people through their own experience and history. "No culture is so fallen that the Good News cannot be communicated in its terms."[102] Although Christians experience tension, they also experience sufficient continuity with their world to allow for points of contact and communication. By focusing on communication in this way Dyrness approximates the emphasis also put on communication and contextualization by Klapwijk in his analysis of synthesis; for Klapwijk modifies significantly the traditional reformational approach of polarizing synthesis and antithesis in the remark, given in his discussion of early Christian philosophy, that inasmuch as these figures seek to be Christian, an antithetical aspect of their work can be recognized. "By the same token, because they respond to the questions and ideas of their times, something of a synthesizing intention can be distinguished as well."[103]

Philo's Synthesis of Faith and Philosophy
In the present collection this issue of synthesis is addressed most clearly in the paper of A. Wolters on Philo's understanding of the biblical portrayal of *creatio ex nihilo.* Wolters regards Philo's interpretation of Genesis as an integration of two inherently incompatible positions, for the role of the Creator in Genesis, who is to be sovereign over the matter from which he fashioned the world, is evidently interpreted according to the role assigned by Plato (in the *Timaeus*) to a demiurge who fashions pre-existent matter.[104]

With this discussion of Judaic and early Christian interpretation of the creation account in Genesis, Wolters deals with an important problem. The significance of this issue for conflicts with Gnostics who assigned an important role in creation to an inferior demiurge has been recognized in a number of other papers in this collection. Williams examines Marcion's rejection of the Genesis portrayal of creation and the response of heresiologists who affirm the importance of the Old Testament in terms of a *praeparatio evangelica*.[105] Tiessen also explores Irenaeus's appreciation of the positions of pagan Greek philosophers on divine providence and the goodness of creation as a *cosmos*, in his arguments with Gnostics on this issue.[106] The papers of Aune, Irwin, and Martens likewise recognize the importance of the *praeparatio* motif for Clement; like Irenaeus, Clement valued those philosophers who regarded the creator as a good and provident deity.[107] Thus Clement's well-known appreciation of the Greek philosophers is to be understood in terms of the polemical interchange with Gnostics who, as we know from Plotinus, were equally adept at claiming support from the philosophers for their views.

Wolters' discussion of *creatio ex nihilo* is significant also because it shows how deeply issues of religion, theology and philosophy could become intertwined. A biblical text crucial to the defense of the sovereignty and authority of God as *creator*, was interpreted with the aid of a philosophical view based on Plato's *Timaeus*. According to Wolters Philo compromised, or even betrayed his Judaic faith in Yahweh by introducing such philosophical terminology in his exegetical work on Genesis. Did Philo recognize how use of imagery from the *Timaeus* and its demiurgic god could undermine the ultimate sovereignty of God?

In his analysis Wolters implements the approach of Dooyeweerd; Philo's synthesis has attempted to integrate two religiously motivated positions. A fundamental religious antithesis has not been respected. The resulting portrayal of the creator as a demiurgic figure would eventually be seen to be unacceptable, or even ominous inasmuch as it may have contributed toward the Gnostic understanding of the demiurge.

The issue of "synthesis" as a question of philosophical influence on a religiously based position in the thought of Philo arises also in other papers. Aune has shown how deeply Philo was influenced by Middle Platonist positions on the passions.[108] Booth has also shown how, in his reference to Epicureans, Philo's views coalesced with attitudes prevalent among Platonists.[109] And Sly has illustrated how Philo's philosophically motivated judgments on the question of the passions affected his evaluation of the place and roles of women.[110] Jastram has specifically examined the occurrence of motifs of cultural adjustment in Philo's work. According to Jastram both *spoliatio* and *praeparatio* motifs, as used, reflect an inferiority of either contemporary Judaism or Hellenism with respect to a third cultural option, a cosmopolitan ideal as a "golden mean" between the others.[111] Quite unlike the judgment of Sly, who finds Philo "out of touch" with the lives of real people, particularly the women of his time, Jastram's analysis would put Philo in the vanguard of cultural progress and the advance of civilization in terms of a philosophical ideal in the Hellenistic time.

Philo's work presents us with a critical instance, if not a test case for the interaction of (the Judaic) faith and philosophy, of religion and culture in the Hellenistic world. We have seen that for contemporary historians Philo represents the Jew who did not think he was betraying his Judaic heritage when engaging fully in the Hellenized culture of his time; he regarded the allegorical approach in exegesis as an enrichment of the text, not a deformation of its intent. In light of Philo's own complaints regarding others, particularly among his own relatives, who betrayed their loyalty to the Judaic faith, one must make allowance for such a claim of remaining faithful, whatever the verdict of later reflection.[112]

The issue needs further exploration. In what sense is Philo to be characterized as an early representative of "synthesis" thinking? Later Judaism was profoundly uneasy about his enterprise, and it is always possible that from the perspective of later times weaknesses are revealed which may not have been so apparent to Philo himself. But the historian must ask whether Philo would himself have acknowledged that he was bringing about a "synthesis" of two incompatible ways of thought, one from the Old Testament with another from Plato's *Timaeus*, from Greek philosophy? If one recognizes pre-existent matter, for instance, is God still sovereign over his creation?

Further analysis of Philo's work will not necessarily provide the answers, although it may help settle the question whether sovereignty or ultimate authority was Philo's own concern in these discussions. On the basis of an exhaustive study of Philo's use of Plato, particularly the *Timaeus*, D. Runia has concluded that Philo would himself probably not have regarded faith and philosophy as two incompatible poles of thought. In other words, Philo himself would not have recognized the integration of religious and philosophical positions as an inherently illegitimate enterprise, one which would necessarily result in compromise of biblical views; accordingly, he is not to be regarded as the first important proponent of "synthesis."[113]

Such a conclusion is open to further question, but Runia's analysis is helpful in that it reflects the approach of contemporary historians who have correctly observed a degree of flexibility which characterized Judaism in adapting to many varied contexts within the ancient Near East and Greco-Roman world, particularly in the Hellenistic period. In a number of situations prominent Jews gave a public defense of Judaism in a manner appropriate to the religious and cultural environment.[114] An honest evaluation of Philo cannot ignore this aspect of his enterprise. Questions must still be asked, however, particularly because Runia's assessment appears to assume agreement on the acceptance, or acceptability of Judaism as Philo represented it in his exegetical work. Given the later history of appreciation of Philo, particularly within Judaism, such an assumption is surely not warranted.[115] It appears that we may have discovered a basic incongruity between the judgments of historians who seek to be fair to Philo on his own terms, and judgments based on a more systematic analysis of his work from the perspective of a later time.

With Harnack, Wolters in his analysis of Philo's work as a synthesis or (illegitimate) integration of incompatible religious positions, has recognized an instance in which a cultural element has been allowed to contaminate a religious position; philosophy has negatively influenced religion. Himself a proponent of the transformational approach in philosophy, Wolters makes his judgment of Philo on the assumption that ideally the situation ought to have been reversed; religious convictions ought, rather, to have influenced a philosophical position, whether to improve or actually change it.[116] However, if one is to make a correct assessment of change, or the extent of the influence which a Greek (Platonic) philosophical position may have exerted on Philo, it is important to begin by assessing the degree of (even unwitting) identification with current philosophical assumptions and sharing of positions common in his own time. This is an aspect of philosophical reflection, whether that of Philo or of early Christians, which has not always received adequate attention in studies of this period by Calvinistic reformational scholars when they characterize the work of Philo and other patristic thinkers in terms of a "synthesis." Philo would have been conscious of the need to speak the language and use the forms of his time in order to communicate clearly; acknowledging this is basic to making an accurate judgment regarding the impact he made in his own time, and also basic to a fair evaluation of his contribution for later history.

Praeparatio Evangelica and Spoliatio Motifs

Two motifs from Niebuhr's categorization are left, those which regard religion (1) as a "perfection," or (2) as a "transformation" of culture. With respect to the first of these the medieval theological construction relating the Christian faith to Aristotelian philosophy has provided the classic example.[117] It has traditionally been referred to as the *praeparatio evangelica* motif, since it regards the cultural heritage as a preparation for faith, while the faith itself functions to perfect or complete what is essentially good but not yet in finished condition in a culture.

We have seen from the above discussion of the *praeparatio* motif as it occurs in the papers of Williams, Martens, Tiessen and others (465), that early patristic use does not closely resemble its later use. This motif appears to have originated with a desire to affirm the validity of the Old Testament for Christian use and thought; this use was apparently expanded to affirm views of non-Christian thinkers who accepted divine providence and the goodness of creation and its creator god, in opposition to the Gnostics who only saw imperfection and evil in the world around them, and ascribed it to the malevolence or ignorant stupidity of the demiurge/creator.[118] Such use is best known from the work of Clement of Alexandria, who provided the groundwork for later development of this motif with Origen, Eusebius and Basil of Caesarea. In her discussion of Clement's instructions for the behaviour of women, Irwin illustrates how this motif operated in Clement's views on virtue. From Galatians 3:28 Clement recognized that men and women were basically equal, and that virtues of self-control and modesty applied equally for both. Nonetheless differences remained in dress, freedom of movement, and roles within the family. According to Irwin, Clement wished to protect the dignity of Christian women when he rejected misogynistic, ascetic and martyr roles as appropriate models. In this defense, however, Clement was deeply influenced by traditional Greek wisdom, and consciously accepted much from Platonic and Pythagorean views on the issue.[119] In the post-Constantinian period, the *praeparatio* motif became more closely associated with a hierarchical view of reality and values; for it could serve to vindicate the new role of Christians in society, and rationalize the corresponding stratification of power structures.

The last of Niebuhr's motifs, that of religion *transforming* culture, regards the faith as actively engaging with that culture to redirect it, to work for renewal and change. The motif has traditionally looked to the theme of *spoliatio*, based on the Exodus account of the Israelites taking "spoils" of clothing and precious metals from their neighbours as they leave Egypt.[120] In his discussion of this account Frizzell has examined Jewish embarrassment, and attempts to explain the acceptance of "spoils" as a return for years of slave labour.[121] From heresiologists we hear of Gnostic use of this passage to denigrate a god who would condone such unethical behaviour among his followers. Origen, in his use of the passage, first recognized potential dangers should such gifts be used for idolatrous purposes, and emphasized the importance of dedicating these cultural treasures in the service of God; he thus anticipated fourth century and later use of this motif to explain how Christians may use cultural gifts of non-Christian origin, if they do so with discernment.[122]

Since Niebuhr's discussion, this "transformation" motif has gained a high profile among Christians. P. Marshall has noted that many Christians in fact like to think of their own position as one of "transforming," while labelling others as belonging in less desirable categories. He gives the example of Anabaptist Mennonites whom many regard as "oppositionists" for advocating withdrawal in non-violent communities; yet the Mennonites themselves would disagree and claim that in their social stance they are in fact acting positively to change destructive patterns in society.[123]

This is also the motif on which J. Klapwijk has focused in his analysis of synthesis and antithesis in reformational philosophy.[124] Klapwijk is critical of an application of the Kuyperian thesis regarding Christ's lordship which rejects both those views which do not recognize this claim, as well as those characterized by an accommodation of Christian beliefs in "synthesis." In this way, according to Klapwijk, reformational scholarship has promoted an unhealthy systematic isolation of the Christian philosophical enterprise; it has been negligent in communicating with contemporary non-Christian work, and must take more seriously the call to give account and interact with those who share their culture but not their faith.[125]

Klapwijk proposes "transformational philosophy" as an alternative method characterized by "critical appropriation;" for such an approach he turns to Augustine's *De doctrina christiana* II,40,60, the presentation of the *spoliatio* motif. Klapwijk realizes, with Origen, that gifts may carry a high price, and ensnare the recipient in an unfortunate manner.[126] Critical appropriation, however allows for a positive model of transformation of cultural treasures as these are assimilated *into* a Christian position. On the other hand it is also possible that Christians adapt their own positions *to* such gifts; this may result in idolatry or other forms of contamination which Klapwijk identifies as "inverse transformation." As an example of inverse transformation Klapwijk refers to Tertullian's famous paradox, *credo quia ineptum*: the faith is believable because it is "foolish;" for with this slogan Tertullian indicated both his antithetical rejection of Greek philosophy as foolishness (*ineptum*) and his own place within that tradition, since the nature of foolishness would in turn be defined by that very same Greek philosophical tradition.[127]

Klapwijk has realized that the term "synthesis" does not do justice to the complexity of the factors at work in the thought of early Christians like Clement or Tertullian. "Synthesis" implies a reconciliation of that which is inherently incompatible and presupposes an opposition. With Runia we may observe that most early Christians too would not have assumed the implied antithesis *between* faith and philosophy as such, or have regarded their work in terms of a reconciliation of inherently incompatible themes. For Klapwijk the recognition of a "hidden conjunction of transformation and inverse transformation" as he found it in the thought of Tertullian was decisive for re-thinking the theme of "synthesis."[128] According to Klapwijk it is more useful to examine the *extent* to which Clement and others made efforts to reform Greek philosophy; the incorporation of elements from Middle Platonism or other Greek forms of thought should not be emphasized as much as the *manner* of so doing.[129]

The advantages of this new understanding of synthesis and antithesis, according to Klapwijk, may be seen in the way that it allows for dynamic and contextualized Christian philosophizing. As a model for Christian interaction with contemporary culture it allows for the full participation of Christians in the philosophical discussions of their time, and also for a response which can bring the message of Christ in a relevant manner.[130]

From the above discussion of Niebuhr's five motifs as they may be applied to a relationship between religion and culture, or faith and philosophy, particularly for early Christianity, it is evident that analysis is less straightforward, and categorization more difficult than for the later period of Christian history, when these issues had received more careful definition, and the "classical heritage" too had a clearer identity. When the latter formed part of a living cultural environment, a contemporary context within which the faith-community would live and grow, one could also expect the relationship between the faith community and its cultural context to be more fluid. Accordingly one would expect the motifs of interaction to function differently and be characterized by different emphases.

If the identification and analysis of motifs in this period was more complicated than for later times, our investigation also revealed some surprising twists and ironies of history. Both motifs turned up as elements in Gnostic and anti-Gnostic polemic, both with a somewhat rhetorical usage, and both with a primary reference which differed significantly from later use. The theme of *spoliatio* was originally the source of some embarrassment to Judaism, and became the occasion of Gnostic denigration of a god who would condone the unethical actions of despoiling one's friends and neighbours. The *praeparatio evangelica* theme appears to have originated with a Christian claim to the history and literature of Judaism as its own background and as a preparation for the coming of Messiah as the son of the supreme God, Yahweh.

In his discussion of the motifs Dyrness reminds the reader that even Niebuhr did not envision the various motifs operating in a mutually exclusive manner. In his conclusions Niebuhr recognized that one's particular status on the journey of faith, one's historical position as a Christian, whether individually or in community, and one's particular duties and obligations would determine the relative importance of the motifs.[131] Dyrness himself sees the motifs along a *continuum*, from an initial assumption of communication, namely that of Christ *in* culture, to a realization of tension between following the cultural norms and the demands of following Christ, thus placing Christ and culture *in paradox*, and finally recognizing Christ as the *transformer* of culture where there are opportunities for taking one's cultural environment captive for the kingdom of God. Only by recognizing where one belongs on this continuum can confusion regarding the significance of the motifs be avoided.[132]

This conclusion of Dyrness has validity and is helpful for our understanding of early Christianity. For it is difficult to make any meaningful evaluation of the patristic writers once they have all been categorized as "synthesizing" or "Hellenizing." To label them all as representatives of "transformation," however, does not advance our analysis significantly either. It would appear that for the early period of Christianity no one particular form of the relationship between "Christ and culture" can be chosen as significantly more important than another. Judgement on the motifs must proceed via discernment of a number of factors: the status of the faith of the writer (or group) under consideration, the historical circumstances, as well as the nature of the opposition encountered.

Discernment of historical factors must also include an evaluation of the cultural context. Cultures too are not monolithic. Different aspects of cultures demand varying response; some aspects need to be rejected, others can be accepted, while other aspects need transformation.[133] A degree of wisdom or discernment is required on the part of Christians, particularly when they act in community, as churches or associations for various purposes; they need to make judgments on what is incompatible with the faith, and what, given a particular historical situation, can most successfully be opposed. Both the means of Christian involvement with culture and its goals need to be examined. With Dyrness, Marshall has realized that the relationship between religious commitment and cultural form is neither straightforward or simple. But Marshall also affirms the underlying theme of the religious root of culture. Christ *does* transform culture. If faith shapes the totality of life, it will affect cultural expression as well. Faith, rightly understood, should present the more vital element; it is expected to take priority and extend its impact beyond questions of moral responsibility, to issues of politics and justice, family life, and philosophy. When this situation is reversed and cultural factors set the agenda for faith, or when religious issues are defined in terms of the "spirit of the age," Marshall recognizes the influence of what he calls "secularization." His definition of "secularization" thus is closely connected with his view of the role of religion. For him "secularization" is primarily evident in the privatization of religious commitment which characterizes pluralism in the modern state. In agreement with his basic position he also concludes that problems of religious pluralism will not be solved by restricting public expression of a diversity of religious views.[134]

Harnack also spoke of "secularization" in his discussion of the impact of "Hellenization;" for him the primary reference was intellectualization as evidence of a cultural element influencing the faith. He realized that cultural phcnomena posed the greatest danger not when these reveal a religious motivation clearly hostile and incompatible with Christianity, but when the faith as expressed and applied shows too comfortable an alliance with culturally dominant attitudes or themes. This is more typically the point at which faith is tempted to abandon its position of strength, idolatry threatens, and critical appropriation is numbed. Although Harnack identified the specific source of threat quite differently, he evidently would have agreed with proponents of Calvinistic reformational philosophy on the religious root of culture and the priority of religion in exerting a positive influence upon that world of culture.

Conclusions

Our study of early Christianity and the impact of Hellenization through Judaism and Gnosticism has raised many issues: questions of heresy and purity, religion and culture, philosophy, intellectualism and elitism, synthesis, syncretism, identity of faith, and dialectics of communication. We certainly do not pretend to have resolved them all. Our intention has been in part to show the continued influence of Harnack's magisterial formulation of the questions, and indicate how contemporary scholarship has built on these foundations. In many ways current thought has moved beyond Harnack in approaching such issues in the study of early Christianity, yet the lingering impact of his work has made our study a rewarding one.

The issues we have raised are old ones, issues which have a long history in Western thought. But it is worthwhile to return to them in search of new insight because of the persistence of misconception, misreading, and faulty understanding in contemporary discussion regarding early Christianity and its so-called Hellenic "baggage." These misconceptions arise not only from a desire to elevate the stature of Gnostics at the expense of the Christian church which rejected them, from the current re-evaluation of Judaism in the Roman Empire, or from impatience of those who wish to contextualize theology and find that early creeds and doctrinal statements add unnecessary complexity. Prominent adherents to the Calvinistic reformational approach in philosophy have also contributed to misunderstanding regarding the significant work of early Christians like Justin, Tertullian, or Clement, by categorizing their efforts in terms of "synthesis." The negative connotations of such a label made it virtually impossible to take seriously the discussions of these early Christian centuries, or to give a constructive analysis of the efforts of such thinkers. Calvinistic thinkers have evidently found Harnack's argumentation regarding the Hellenization of early Christianity congenial for their own analysis of this period.

Harnack's work is often regarded as the epitome of Protestant theology after the Enlightenment, in the tradition of Friedrich Schleiermacher, Albrecht Ritschl and Friedrich C. Baur. Martin Rumscheidt has characterized Harnack's work as "liberal theology at its height;"[135] and according to Stephen Neill, Harnack regarded the gospel as the "great declaration of the spiritual liberty of mankind."[136] Harnack's account of the expansion of Christianity was certainly not free of a triumphalist approach, as has been noted by J. G. Gager, but in the history of dogma Harnack was critical of the triumphalism of nineteenth century histories of dogmatic theology.[137] Subsequent generations have certainly learned to regard the history of early Christianity from this perspective, especially by questioning the Constantinian settlement as a true triumph for Christianity.

Much has happened during this century to change the focus of attention on early Christianity. We note only a few of the events of significance for our topic: the discovery of the Nag Hammadi documents and re-evaluation of Gnosticism in antiquity; the rise of feminism in theology, and the corresponding attractiveness of the Gnostic depiction of the feminine for numerous feminist scholars; "new age" spirituality which also finds an affinity with Gnostic focus on the spiritual dimension of life; the rise of Israel as a political state and thorough re-examination of the history of Judaism, particularly against the background of the holocaust; and, finally, the extensive re-examination of early Christianity resulting from contemporary efforts towards multilateral ecumenical dialogue. Critique of triumphalism from a modern post-liberal perspective recognizes that any optimism regarding the human situation must be tempered by sober reflection on the consequences of two major world wars, the holocaust, and political brinkmanship of decades of cold war.[138]

Ours is a post-liberal age in theology; but the prince of liberal theology has evidently not yet abdicated his position of power. Corresponding to profound shifts in approach to early Christianity, the essays of this study have noted extensive critique of Harnack's work: his historicizing approach, his negative evaluation of early

Catholicism and narrow definition of dogma, his romanticizing of a "pure" early Christianity, his misunderstanding of the role of Judaism with respect to early Christianity and also in relation to Gnosticism, his approach to Gnosticism as an intellectual and philosophical movement characterized by Hegelian "absolute knowing," and finally his programmatic analysis of Gnosticism as heresy.

Nonetheless, three enduring aspects of his argumentation may be singled out for re-examination: first, his focus on dogma as an intellectualizing of the faith with negative impact; second, his assumption regarding religion as the root of culture, evident in his use of the term "secularization;" and third, the importance of an element of dialectic in the history of Christianity. These assumptions evidently played a fundamental role in his thought. Because they point to positions taken within long-standing traditions, they continue to have significance long after more particular aspects of his work have been forgotten.

Dogma and Intellectualism
Analysis of the development of dogma as a rational or intellectual expression of the faith led Harnack to regard Hellenization as a contamination of Christianity. We have noted that such use of the "Hellenization" theme puts him squarely within a strong tradition in Protestant thought and Protestant-Catholic polemic. This obviously contributed to the impact of his views on dogmatic theology. Karl Barth and others have attempted to revive a more positive appreciation of creeds, dogma, and doctrine; their efforts have been well documented by P. Schrodt in his study of the question of dogma in recent theology. Yet for much of contemporary Christianity this is an anti-dogmatic age, where authoritative pronouncements are almost in principle considered suspect, and orthodoxy considered irrelevant.

It is somewhat ironic that also within circles of Calvinistic reformational philosophy Hellenization has been cited for the intellectualism which it introduced to early Christianity. Even J. Klapwijk, who is aware of the need for historical sensitivity in evaluating the work of Tertullian or Clement, continues in this vein when he remarks,

> Ancient thought left its mark on Christian theology; Christian theology subsequently determined ecclesiastical doctrines, and these ecclesiastical doctrines led on a grand scale either to an intellectualistic, dogmatic religious experience or else to hyper-spirituality, asceticism, and monasticism. The traces are still recognizable in the church today.[139]

Such reflection on intellectualism and dogmatic theology is ironic because among the branches of Protestantism Calvinists have made a substantial contribution in intellectual work, setting up universities and schools, or developing a philosophical arsenal for Christianity. Is suspicion of intellectualism a reflection of intimate acquaintance with its seductive nature? Intellectualism can easily turn into an elitism. There is indeed a point at which intellectualization of the faith becomes illegitimate. Some members of the Reformed family of churches even today regard purity of doctrine as a safeguard for the purity of the church. Harnack was certainly correct in showing that study of Christianity as the study of the development of doctrine or dogma needs correction from historical investigation; dogmatic theological works too often lose touch with the realities of history, so that crucial issues are misinterpreted and real motives in the history of Christianity misjudged.

It can be argued, however, that the opposite tendency which encourages anti-intellectualism presents at least as many problems for Christianity in our time. Harnack's romanticization of primitive Christianity and his anti-intellectual definition of true religion is not the solution, particularly if one values the church as an institutional expression of Christian ministry. A historically-oriented study can provide a useful corrective for accurate understanding of a period like that of the early church. Yet study on historical grounds alone cannot provide answers for important systematic, or methodological questions such as those of the identity of the faith. And this is precisely the point at which we value the disputes of the early Christian church. Through the major councils significant positions on questions regarding the life and work of Christ were agreed on and accepted by large segments of the church. Here we witness the church defining for itself its own identity. Harnack's narrow definition of "dogma" led him in misjudging its role for the history of Christianity. We have attempted to show that, in response to historicism, examination of the identity of the faith must not allow such an identity to be reduced to its historical dimension. Agreement on identity of necessity proceeds by way of common statement; and appreciation of rational expression should not be confused with either rationalism or intellectualism.

Religion and Culture
If religion is accepted as the arena of prior conviction and commitment, giving basic direction for life, Harnack was right in his assumption that religion ought to have the upper hand in the confrontation with cultural matters, particularly when culture comes in the form of philosophical positions which themselves bear religiously characterized worldviews. Such an assumption is evident in his discussion of Hellenization as a "secularization" of the gospel. With this term he betrays his view that the "world," or the "spirit of the age," may have taken a negative role in setting the agenda for faith. Not that religion should dominate as it did in the medieval period; for Harnack realized only too well the unhealthy character of that situation. Religion, properly understood, ought to have an impact for good; faith should shape one's life; Christ does transform culture.

The issue of secularization has not gone away, although intellectualization of the faith is no longer the important f actor. Today the priority of religious commitment is expressed in terms of a rejection of a pluralistic secularism which relegates faith and religion to the private sphere of life, well away from the public and political domain. Within the modern state various faiths need to co-exist in relative harmony. From the Christian perspective, however, political life cannot be considered a sphere which in principle is to be excluded from the redeeming work of Christ. A kingdom perspective on the role of the risen and ascended Christ in this world cannot accept such a position. Pluralism makes room for religion(s), but is uncomfortable when these assert a claim on public life beyond the so-called moral or private issues.

Because this modern position on religion and politics is at issue in historical re-evaluation of Judaism within the Hellenistic empires, we cannot avoid pursuing the implications. We have noted that also in antiquity religion and political affairs could not be neatly categorized as separate spheres of life. Judaism was never just a "religion." It had important ethnic and racial ties, a language and literature which it considered sacred, and "Torah" as a system of law which went far beyond a matter of personal life-style. Again, the Hellenistic rulers not only considered it their right to influence religious matters should these interfere with their ability to govern; these rulers were ready to assert divine pretension and demand obeisance at imperial shrines. In such a situation one could expect significant tension. The question of the relation of religion and culture appears even more complicated than for later periods. Not only is it more difficult to categorize positions according to Niebuhr's paradigms; in fact one may go so far as to conclude that such paradigms are not very useful in judging the situation for earliest Christianity and the Judaism of that period.

Nonetheless we have seen that if a religious commitment and its faith-expression are to have any meaning at all they must take priority in the making of decisions affecting cultural matters. If a religion cannot maintain itself as an instrument for good, for healing, and hope in society, one may well question its use. This is the reason why, even when we have questioned Harnack's analysis of dogma as an intellectualization of faith, and the adequacy of his portrayal of primitive Christianity in defining the identity of that faith, we can still value positively the normative role allowed for such an original condition. When compared with that of modern historians working with a pluralistic model, Harnack's approach on religion and culture can be appreciated for an appraisal of the role of religion which is both more realistic and better attuned to the situation in antiquity.

Dialectic in the History of Christianity
On several occasions we have noted the element of dialectical interaction in historical, philosophical and theological discussion. Harnack differed with F. C. Baur and the Tübingen school on the specific relationship of Jewish and Gentile Christianity, and on the historical process connecting Gnostics with German idealism. Nonetheless, the influence of Hegelian thought is evident both in use of terminology, as in the reference to *gnōsis* as "absolute knowledge," and in the recognition of dialectical interaction in historical developments, seen especially in his analysis of the impact of Gnosticism on the Christian church. Rowe has commented on the subtlety of Harnack's interpretation of the tension and debate between Gnostics and orthodox Christians. According to Harnack, Gnosticism affected Christianity particularly when the latter rejected it, when Christianity reacted to the threat of Gnostic positions, and responded with institutionalization and intellectualization.

It is ironic if precisely by defining the positions taken on creation or the divinity of Christ, to distinguish its own from Gnostic views on these matters, the Christian church took on some of the less desirable characteristics of Gnosticism, like intellectualism or elitism. Harnack was at least partly correct on this issue, for among the Church fathers one can observe a degree of "one-upmanship," with Gnostics and other Christians trying to outdo one another in their claims. One senses that orthodox leaders like Clement made efforts to demonstrate that "mainstream" Christianity was in no way inferior to the faith of those claiming to have superior insights, the elite challenging the rest of the Christian community. The church was influenced by elements of Gnosticism in spite of itself.

We have seen, however, that the process of self-definition in the church may also be understood as a dialectical process in which Christians achieved greater clarity on their own identity in the face of opposing views. From this perspective dialectical tension has a more positive aspect, in that challenging and being challenged can be regarded as an integral part of Christian life and a positive factor in the growth of Christian communities toward maturity.

In his analysis of early Christianity and the question of "synthesis," Klapwijk has also done much to recognize the dynamic element of dialectical tension even within the work of individual thinkers, for he has called attention to the "hidden conjunction of transformation and inverse transformation" in the work of Christians like Justin, or Clement. He has recognized that they were responding to the cultural issues of their own time, with the need of being relevant in communicating the message of the gospel; he sees a close connection between elements of tension and accommodation, polarity and adjustment. This allows him to appreciate Clement's self-reference as a "gnostic," for he comments that Clement may have both "intellectualized faith . . . and simultaneously reformed Greek thought. . . . In other words, transformation and its inverse can clash in the mind of a single person." Thus the *praeparatio evangelica* model of the subordination of culture to religion, as Clement embodied it, could simultaneously be recognized as a medium of reform and also an open door for "inverse transformation" in which a Christian position is adapted to and compromised by one that is not. For the latter process Klapwijk gives the example of "the 'Hellenization' of the Christian faith"![140] Such a comment indicates that although Klapwijk has done much to give a more nuanced answer on the relationship of religion and culture for early Christianity, he has not moved so very far from Harnack's own approach.

It is also clear that confrontation with a movement which challenges one's own religious positions will rarely proceed without mutual influence. This is important for any stage of the history of Christianity. And contamination, compromise, or syncretism is always a possible outcome. However, one can also approach the problem from another direction. In confrontation with the "spirit of the age," in dialogue with other religions, or in the process of contextualizing the gospel in an unfamiliar culture, it is extremely important that the group taking initiatives have a healthy sense of its own identity, and of the identity of the faith involved in such discussions. This sense of identity, as we have acknowledged, is not always a given from the start of interaction; indeed, such identity may well be further refined through struggle and interaction. The Christian faith has throughout its history been subject to such a process of refinement and clarification, and been strengthened in opposition with those who differed with and opposed it. One could go further and even claim that the faith is all the more vital and attractive as it goes out to challenge the spirits of the age, interacting with and confronting its opponents. In the midst of struggles the church receives its identity. The gospel must of necessity be communicated, if it is good news. The faith needs to be contextualized to answer the questions of the day. Christians have historically not been afraid to go out, to stand for their views, and even to suffer for them if need be.

It would appear from our study that both in the process of self-identification of faith within a given culture, and in the process of giving account and communicating the gospel where a culture acts as a threatening influence, positive appreciation of an element of dialectic can pay tribute to Harnack. It is of interest that such a dialectical element continues to be a relevant factor when understanding of early Christianity seeks to move beyond his positions. Indeed, throughout this study, as we have expressed appreciation for numerous aspects of his argumentation, like the question of the so-called "pure" essence of Christianity and the role of creeds and confessions for the identity of the faith, we have not been constrained by the particular forms in which he presented them.

Early Christianity was inescapably Hellenized, just as the Judaism from which it emerged was Hellenized. One might be tempted to think that "Hellenization" should have become a non-issue; after all, one's cultural and political context can not easily be ignored. For Harnack "Hellenization" was important for the intellectual element; linguistic and political considerations were secondary. For historical research the political aspect of Hellenization has dominated; modern historians have recognized the continued thriving of local cultures and religious communities, their identity apparently neither threatened nor compromised by interaction with

Hellenism. One must remember, however, that as a cultural process Hellenization presented a multiplicity of facets: linguistic, literary, athletic, aesthetic, or religious. It presented a corresponding variety of options for acceptance or rejection, whether for Jews or Christians. At present the extent to which early Christianity followed in the footsteps of Judaism in relating to its environment in the Hellenized world is widely recognized. Also in apologetics Christians often adopted patterns first used by Judaism, especially in the *diaspora*. For its part, Judaism was particularly concerned when cultural elements closely approximated religious issues, whether as a matter of ideology, philosophy or theology. Especially because religion and politics were not so widely separated in antiquity, secularization, accommodation and compromise were all the more a threat.

One may agree with Harnack and others that the Hellenic contribution to early Christianity was not an unmixed blessing. Yet as a cultural context for Christian religion it paralleled cultures of many other periods and places where Christianity has taken root. Like many other cultures it offered a philosophical and intellectual heritage which required a degree of critical appropriation, if not transformation.

As cultural context the Hellenistic world also played a very special role, because Christianity experienced its earliest developments and major disputes within the Hellenized Roman Empire. Indeed, the Greek language characterized not only the New Testament writings; most of the significant early debates also used the Greek language. Cultural connotations of Greek terms inevitably made their impact.

We cannot turn back the clock. This is the tradition in which we stand. We may bend and shape that tradition, but cannot simply abandon it. Since we cannot undo history, historical understanding supplies an important tool for evaluating early Christianity. Harnack has done Christianity a considerable service in providing that tool. Critique of his analysis of that period must go hand in hand with appreciation of his powerful vision for Christianity.

Notes

1. In the present century Marxism has given the significant impetus in forcing the church to reconsider its missiology, to be alert for paternalism, or imperialistic attitudes in theology and ecclesiology as well as missiology. The twin themes of contextualization and indigenization are clearly a response of the mission enterprise to indicate genuine interest in the local situations of emerging churches and abandon a domination which imposes modes and structures which may have worked well in Europe or North America, but are not necessarily as applicable in countries of the "two-thirds" world. Politically Marxism has received its death-blow; although in China Maoist communism has not yet disappeared, the rapids strides toward a money-driven market economy reveal the impending end of communism there. Western theological constructions are still widely based on liberation theology, emphasizing freedom, mutuality and empowerment. But such words may well have a hollow ring for spiritually starved peoples who survived the years of communist rule. Even in missions we discover that ethnicity is not the last word; around the globe peoples want to cling to their own way of life all the more because of the rapid internationalization of consumer products, global trade, rapid transportation with jet travel, the media, and the influence of the International Monetary Fund. The church is thus both local and international. Its problems are contemporary, but also reveal modes not unlike those experienced from the beginning. Problems with leadership are an example of this. Where the church grows rapidly, so do its offshoots, sects, cults, heresies. Can the church learn something from the past, to prevent some problems which need not be repeated? Emerging churches should not be encouraged to be a-historic. Through their connection with the West they are inevitably anchored in the history of early Christianity; history cannot be undone, and should not be forgotten either.

2. This argument was current some thirty years ago, and perhaps heard more often; today its appears that the case is closed. Over against the need for a living, vibrant faith we hear of dead dogmatism, "petrification," or scholasticism coming from the institutional church as it values the history of decisions from councils of the first centuries: Nicea, Constantinople, and Chalcedon. "De-Hellenization" is a term used by Leslie Dewart, *The Future of Belief* (New York: Herder and Herder, 1966), and *The Foundations of Belief* (New York: Herder and Herder, 1969); his intention is to provide "the conscious creation of the future of belief," (*Future*, 50). Dewart seeks an abandonment of a scholastic, i. e., Hellenic view of truth, one which equates intellect and reality (as intelligible), and equates faith with an actualization of intellect. Scholastic theory, according to Dewart, cannot take account of development; it does not note the changes in cultural context since early Christianity, or recognize the need for changes in the truth itself. Dewart wishes to relate truth more closely to consciousness and self-consciousness, which is necessarily changing, and constantly evolving. Through analysis of consciousness and knowledge he concludes that although the articles of faith have increased, for the scholastic model doctrinal development only makes explicit what is implicit in scripture. The body of revelation in scriptures is closed. By its nature novelty implies divergence or corruption of the original; *Future*, 80-93, and *Foundations*, 57-114.

In his analysis of this position in *The Problem of Dogma in Recent Theology* (Frankfurt am Main: P. Lang, 1978; 90-99) P. Schrodt points out the very narrow view of the development of dogma on which this discussion is based, and questions the dynamic conception of truth as excluding those who seek truth for its own sake. Relevant for our study is his discussion of the difficulty of creating new cultural forms or "re-conceptualization of Christian dogma" (*The Problem*, 96). Thought categories, according to Schrodt, are given with language. Greek was the language of the early disputes of Christian theology, and Greek-based theological terms will only be superseded when western culture as such no longer depends on the heritage of the Greek language. In fact, many words in English have a direct etymological relationship with the Greek, a percentage increased with scholarly, philosophical and theological language. Translation into other languages only shifts the problem somewhat, for many languages to which Christianity is new, like the Japanese or Chinese, are inadequate in providing equivalents for key terms of the Christian faith.

3. A recent discussion of the theme of "Hellenization" within Protestant Christianity may be found in J. Z. Smith *Drudgery Divine: On the Comparison of Early Christianities and the Religions of Late Antiquity* (London: School of Oriental and African Studies, U. of London, 1990). The first chapter opens with a reflection on the 1813 correspondence between J. Adams and T. Jefferson on the anti-trinitarian deism of J. Priestley; Jefferson hailed the deist call for simplicity, while Adams would sooner have found some way of confining Priestley to prevent him "spreading so many delusions" (2). According to Priestley, Platonists and priests had obscured the simple message of the evangelists and apostles (7). Examination of the language used turns up some interesting phrases: platonizing Christians had adapted (accommodated, borrowed, mixed, or substituted) ideas from Greek thought which corrupted (contaminated, or infected) the genuine (primitive, pure, simple, true) apostolic teaching, with the result of idolatry (confusion, corruption, deviation, error, innovation, taint, debasement) (9-12).

Of particular interest is his analysis (15-26) of the monograph of Walter Glawe, *Die hellenisierung des Christentums in der Geschichte der Theologie von Luther bis auf die Gegenwart* (Berlin, 1912; reprinted for Aalen: Scientia, 1973). To the list of those who ridiculed trinitarian theology as the product of foolish sophists and quibblers, Smith adds the work of M. Servetus with his *De Trinitaribus erroribus libri septem* (The Hague, 1531) and J. Biddle *A Confession of Faith Touching the Holy Trinity* (London, 1648), both of whom blamed Greek philosophy, particularly that of Plato, for these errors or pollutions. Language of the "corruption of a pure tradition" continued through the 18th and 19th centuries, much of it dealing very superficially with the issues, although a few like Souverain (1700) did give some attention to Justin Martyr's intent to combat the charge of Christianity as a religion of innovation; and

J. L. Mosheim (1753) also questioned whether there was more than superficial resemblance between Platonists and Gnostics.

4. J. Z. Smith, op. cit. 13, points to work done a century ago by M. Pattison, in his *Isaac Casaubon: 1559-1614* (2nd ed.; Oxford, 1892), where he reflects on the view of history at the time of the Reformation (a conception of history which in fact can be traced to classical antiquity): just as the fall of humanity was the key to human perversion, so the corruption of the church, as a steady deterioration from a splendid beginning, was the key to ecclesiastical history. For the reformers, according to Pattison, the real culprit was not tradition. Their perception of history, coloured by the degeneracy and corruption of their own time, motivated the appeal to the scriptures and the purity of early conditions (322). Progress only meant decay, increasing error. Cf. *Christianity and the Classics*, W. E. Helleman, ed. (Lanham, MD: University Press of America, 1990) 17-18.

5. For the present study, four of Harnack's works are of particular interest. First, the *Lehrbuch der Dogmengeschichte*, with four major editions, published by J. C. B. Mohr of Leipzig in the years 1886, 1890, 1894, and 1909; it was translated by Neil Buchanan as the *History of Dogma* (based on the third German edition) which appeared in 1900, and was republished substantially unaltered by Dover Publications of New York in 1961. *Die Mission und Ausbreitung des Christentums in der ersten drei Jahrhunderten*, also appearing in four editions between 1902 and 1924 was translated by James Moffatt as *The Mission and Expansion of Christianity in the first Three Centuries (1905). Das Wesen des Christentums* (1900), translated in 1902 by T. B. Saunders as *What is Christianity?* represents a much shorter presentation of Harnack's ideas for a popular audience. Fourth, his *Marcion, das Evangelium vom Fremden Gott*, first published in 1921, and revised in 1924.

6. Within theology the "post-liberal" school of thought, connected with writers like Brevard Childs and George Lindbeck, is well-known for its critique of the historical critical method, particularly as it has been used in Biblical studies. In his *The Bible in Human Transformation* (Philadelphia: Fortress, 1973) W. Wink indicates that the illusion of "objectivity," or scholarly detachment, linked with a suspense of judgment and personal involvement with the text, could no longer be maintained when over the past decades positions of scholars were seen to be linked with the reputations of particular academic institutions, if not with their personal interests, whether of sex, race or class; see the first chapter, "The Bankruptcy of the Biblical Critical Paradigm," especially 10-11. Such critique is more common at present; cf. A. C. Outler, "Towards a Postliberal Hermeneutics" *Theology Today* 42 (1985-86):281-91. See also *Paradigms and Progress in Theology*, J. Mouton, A. G. van Aarde, W. S. Vorster, eds. (S. Africa: Human Sciences Research Council, 1988).

7. K. S. Latourette, *A History of Christianity*, 2 vols. (New York: Harper & Row, 1975; 1st ed. 1953). The first volume, *The First Five Centuries*, of the corresponding multi-volume set, *A History of the Expansion of Christianity* was published by Harper in 1937. Cf. L. M. White, "Adolf Harnack and the 'Expansion' of Early Christianity: A Reappraisal of Social History," *The Second Century* 5 (1985/86): 97-127, particularly 98.

8. The title of Bk. I chapter IV of the *History of Dogma* is "The Attempts of the Gnostics to create an Apostolic Dogmatic, and a Christian Theology; or Acute Secularising of Christianity." The passage of interest is found under Section 2. "The Nature of Gnosticism" (227-28, Buchanan tr.).

> The Catholic Church afterwards claimed as her own those writers of the first century (60-160) who were content with turning speculation to account only as a means of spiritualising the Old Testament, without, however, attempting a systematic reconstruction of tradition. But all those who in the first century undertook to furnish Christian practice with the foundation of a complete systematic knowledge, she declared false Christians, Christians only in name. Historical enquiry cannot accept this judgment. On the contrary, it sees in Gnosticism a series of undertakings, which in a certain way is analogous to the Catholic embodiment of Christianity, in doctrine, morals, and worship. The great distinction here consists essentially in the

fact that the Gnostic systems represent the acute secularising or hellenising of Christianity, with the rejection of the Old Testament; while the Catholic system, on the other hand, represents a gradual process of the same kind with the conservation of the Old Testament.

The parallel passage from *What is Christianity?* is quoted by W. V. Rowe, "Adolf von Harnack," (in his n.26) in this volume, 96 .

9. M. Rumscheidt, ed., *Adolf von Harnack: Liberal Theology at its Height* (London: Collins, 1989) 11-12.

10. D. H. Williams, "Harnack, Marcion and the Argument of Antiquity" in this volume, 223-40.

11. At the beginning of Bk. I, ch. V of the *History of Dogma* (267-86, Buchanan trans.), in which Harnack deals with Marcion, he gives four reasons why Marcion is not "numbered among the Gnostics:" (1) soteriological, rather than speculative or apologetic interests guided him; (2) he emphasized faith rather than *gnōsis*; (3) he did not apply Semitic religious wisdom or Greek philosophy of religion in his exposition; and (4) he made no distinction between esoteric and exoteric religion.

12. Cf. L. L. Grabbe, *Judaism from Cyrus to Hadrian* in two volumes, Vol. 1: *The Persian and Greek Periods*; vol. 2: *The Roman Period* (Minneapolis: Fortress, 1991) 165 on the various aspects of Hellenization, and 247 on the complexity of "Hellenization" as a factor in the Maccabean revolt. Such complexity is generally not recognized in the Protestant-Catholic polemic referred to in notes 2, 3, and 4 above. The reason is not difficult to understand; the term "Hellenization" in this context is typically used with a secondary religious or philosophical reference, to which Rowe refers as the "concept of Hellenization," in his "Adolf von Harnack," in this volume 69f. It is, furthermore, often given a negative connotation when it is taken to represent an intellectualization, or intrusion of reason upon the territory of faith; in this sense it refers to a contamination, a pollution, or corruption of a pure, original New Testament religion. It should be noted, however, that the role of this secondary meaning is contingent on substantial consensus regarding

the primary meaning, if not also on further connotations of the term. Harnack could assume such consensus from the 19th century reaction within the church to Enlightenment exaltation of reason; cf. K. S. Latourette, op. cit. (1975, n.7 above), vol. II, 1120-30.

13. J. Z. Smith, op. cit. (n.3) 1-33. L. M. White (op. cit. [n.7] 99) also maintains Harnack's dependence on A. Ritschl's view of "early Catholicism;" on this issue see further S. Neill and T. Wright, *The Interpretation of the New Testament 1861-1961*, 2nd ed. (London: Oxford Univ. Press, 1988) 200-204, who observe that this prejudicial view, which characterizes mainly continental European Protestantism, has certainly contributed to the rather imaginative portrayal of an idealized early church.

14. The passage quoted in note 8 above shows clearly that from the perspective of history Harnack would qualify his judgment of the Gnostics as heretical. The parallel passage from *What is Christianity?*, T. B. Saunders, trans. (New York: Harper and Row, 1957) is similar: "While they (Gnostics) offer us a most magnificent historical spectacle, in the period itself they were a terrible danger" (205). It would appear that with this approach to Gnosticism it was Harnack's intention to argue for designating Catholics as inclined toward the same kind of heresy as has commonly been attributed to Gnostics. A contemporary reading might understand Harnack to overlook, or even exonerate heretical aspects of Gnostic teaching, but this would be to miss his true intention. Judgement of Gnostics as heretics is certainly out of fashion in current scholarship on early Christianity. The rise of the ecumenical movement may take some credit for the note of tolerance which informs these discussions. In his assessment of the contemporary stance P. Henry points to a number of contributing factors, particularly the impact of scholarly "objectivity" which has accompanied historical criticism; "Why is Contemporary Scholarship so Enamored of Ancient Heretics?", *Studia Patristica* XVII.I, E. A. Livingstone, ed. (Oxford: Pergamon Press, 1982):123-26. He notes that scholarship has now progressed to an advocacy stance in which those who "triumphed" in history are put on the defensive. He also recognizes a tendency to romanticize heretics as rebels with good cause, while a projection of contemporary political practice (and "dirty tricks") on the ancient situation adds to the scepticism regarding winners. As a result, anyone in a position of authority (including historical figures like the Fathers) comes under suspicion.

15. W. Rowe, "Adolf von Harnack" in this volume, 72f. On the universality of Hellenism, as distinguished from Jewish Christianity, see also Harnack's *History of Dogma*, chap. VI, "The heritage which Christianity took over from Judaism shews itself on Gentile Chistian soil, in fainter or distincter form, in proportion as the philosophic mode of thought already prevails, or recedes into the background" (Buchanan trans., 287); ". . . the term 'Jewish Christianity' is appropriate . . . to those Christians who really maintained in their whole extent, or in some measure, even if it were to a minimum degree, the national and political forms of Judaism and the observance of the Mosaic law in its literal sense, as essential to Christianity" (ibid., 289).

16. On the parochial character of classical Greek culture, see W. Rowe "Adolf von Harnack" in this volume, 71-72; cf. B. Henaut, "Alexandria or Athens" in this volume, 100.

17. On Harnack's positive evaluation of the identification of Jesus with the *logos*, see W. Rowe, "Adolf von Harnack" in this volume 78-81; cf. Harnack, *History of Dogma*, Buchanan trans., II.179-88; also, *What is Christianity?*, T. B. Saunders trans., 202-205, on the *logos*.

18. The German text of the crucial passage, cited in note 8 above, is given in the article of P. O'Cleirigh, "Symbol and Science" (endnote 29) in this volume 425-26.

19. When Harnack refers to the Gnostics as the *theologians* of the first century, he immediately follows this statement by referring to them as "the first to transform Christianity into a system of doctrines (dogmas). They were the first to work up a tradition systematically. They undertook to present Christianity as the absolute religion, and therefore placed it in definite opposition to the other religions, even to Judaism. But for them the absolute religion, viewed in its contents, was identical with the result of the philosophy of religion for which the support of a revelation was to be sought" (*History of Dogma*, Buchanan, trans., 228). From Harnack's footnote here it is clear that he is thinking of Heracleon, Basilides, Valentinus and Bardesanes (234-37).

20. T. Tiessen, "Gnosticism as Heresy" in this volume 346, where he quotes W. Loewe.

21. P. O'Cleirigh, "Symbol and Science," in this volume 418-20, the concluding remarks.

22. Harnack, *History of Dogma*, Buchanan trans., vol. I, 227-28; cf. above note 8.

23. Harnack, op. cit. I.224-25, 229; cf. 107-16. On Philo's philosophy of religion, which according to Harnack did not influence the first generation of believers, see 109-13. For Harnack's view of Judaism see above 433, and note 15; also below, the sections of this paper dealing with the origins of Gnosticism and the historical approach to Judaism. On Philo's philosophical Judaism see 465f.; on the issue of control of the passions cf. note 55 below.

24. D. H. Williams, "Harnack, Marcion" in this volume 228-30.

25. B. Henaut, "Alexandria or Athens" in this volume 103-104.

26. Harnack, *What is Christianity?*, Saunders trans., 197-99; cf. *History of Dogma*, Buchanan trans., I.224-25, quoted by Rowe, op. cit., 82.

27. Cf. W. Rowe, op. cit., on the importance of the goal of reforming Christianity for his concept of "Hellenization," in this vol. 85-88.

28. On the reception of these lectures, cf. S. Neill, op. cit. (n.13 above), 141.

29. L. M. White, op. cit. (n.7 above), 100-101, recounts the challenge of S. J. Case to Harnack that he be consistent in his historicizing of Christianity, i. e., that he not exclude its "essence" from historical analysis; other critics include G. Krüger and P. Wendland. Rowe, op. cit., in this volume 91-92, reflects on the importance of Harnack's desire to maintain an a-temporal "essence" of Christianity, unlike E. Troeltsch, his contemporary who was more consistent and thorough in applying the critical method, and thus went further than

Harnack in historicizing Christianity. Although Troeltsch may have corrected aspects of Harnack's work, his overall approach was not considered to be as attractive as that of Harnack. Bultmann's program to "de-mythologize" the New Testament may be considered a radicalization of Harnack's approach; however Bultmann also maintained the *kerygma* as the core of the gospel, and opposed his own approach to that of the more relativistic adherents of the "history-of-religions" school; cf. J. Z Smith, op. cit. (n.3 above), 41.

30. Rowe, op. cit., in this vol. 88-90.

31. Ibid., 91-92.

32. See above, note 6.

33. Cf. S. Carroll, "Gnosticism" in this volume 294. In the present volume the paper of Bos makes a strong case for regarding Gnostics as philosophically inclined, or at least heavily influenced by philosophical positions; most other treatments put less accent on the philosophical aspect of their writings. Carroll is basically sceptical of the philosophical pretensions of the Gnostics. However there is no unanimity on religious provenance with respect to Gnostic positions. Yamauchi has more to say *against* Gnostics as pre-Christian than *for* a positive affiliation. Tiessen on the other hand acknowledges views of Gnostics presented by heresiologists: they were "Christian," certainly in appearance, but held views fundamentally unacceptable to many Christian contemporaries. Tiessen does allow for limited philosophical influence on their views. Arnal and Halford argue for a link with Judaism through the wisdom tradition; while Brown would recognize Gnostic use of myth and symbol as a worthy alternative for religious expression, somewhat as Quispel has, alongside traditional Christianity with its accent on conscious articulation of beliefs in creed and doctrine. Recognizing Gnostic use of mythical language, O'Cleirigh acknowledges the intent of opposing traditional ("orthodox") appreciation of the creation as the product of a benevolent creator. Desjardins, Williams, and Schneider recognize how closely the threads of Judaism, Christianity and Gnosticism are intertwined in this early period.

34. Harnack acknowledged Bauer's views on Catholicism as the product (or synthesis) of the dialectical interaction of Jewish and Gentile Christianity in the *History of Dogma*, I.293. As we have seen above, 435, Harnack was certainly not oblivious to the Hellenization of Judaism; cf. references in n.23. But his view of Judaism as essentially national, ethnic, and exclusive (cf. 433 above, especially n.15) would not allow him to assign it a significant role in the later history of Christianity, as he argues repeatedly, especially 290-94. Nor did his view of Gnosticism allow him to integrate the two. For further discussion on the role of Judaism for Harnack's arguments see in this volume, Rowe, op. cit. 72-73; also Henaut, op. cit. 101-102; and 442f. On current views of Judaism and the origins of Gnosticism, in this volume see particularly Desjardins, "Judaism and Gnosticism" 309-21. A good discussion of the earlier positions of Grätz and Friedländer may be found in B. Pearson, *Gnosticism, Judaism, and Early Christianity* (Minneapolis: Fortress, 1990), particularly the first chapter, "Friedländer Revisited," 10-28. Numerous other essays in the present volume touch on the relationship between Judaism and Gnosticism in antiquity. These include the papers of A. P. Bos and W. Arnal, D. H. Williams, R. Halford, S. Carroll, W. E. Helleman, and L. Frizzell.

35. *History of Dogma* ch. IV, 228; cf. above note 19. The distinction between a primarily religious or philosophical designation is important for the exchange between Bos and Arnal in the present volume, and remains an undercurrent in other essays; this is a topic to which we will return below and in the concluding section of this paper. On Harnack's designation of *gnōsis* as "absolute knowledge" see below note 38.

36. For an introductory survey of positions of the "history-of-religions" school, particularly the work of O. Pfleiderer and R. Reitzenstein on early Christianity and Gnosticism see S. Neill, op. cit. (n.13), 168-74. The tendency to look to non-Hellenic religions for the origin of Gnosticism is still reflected in A. H. Armstrong, "Gnosis and Greek Philosophy," in B. Aland, ed., *Gnosis: Festschrift für Hans Jonas* (Göttingen, 1978), 87-124; here he attributes non-ra-

tional or pessimistic a-cosmic elements to an Oriental background, more specifically "Iranian dualism." Cf. A. P. Bos, op. cit. in this volume, 5. The history-of-religions school made its contribution in focusing on interrelationships among religions of the period, high-lighting the syncretistic nature of religious systems like Gnosticism.
37. Yamauchi, op. cit., in this volume 29-30.
38. Unlike discussions of the previous century, at present many scholars seem to take the primarily *religious* character of Gnosticism to be axiomatic (cf. above, notes 19, 33, and 35). This may be explained in part through actual observation of the Nag Hammadi documents which do not have very much of the "philosophic" character of documents known a century ago, or those known primarily through reports of ancient heresiologists. Another impor-tant factor is the demise of positivism, which has helped give the study of religion and religious texts a greater legitimacy within the universities. For our discussion it is important to distinguish between two types of knowledge, (1) that having a revelatory basis whether through vision, intuition or illumination and (2) knowledge based on the human faculty of reasoning and logical thought: rational, discursive knowledge as it is more typically connected with Greek philosophy. Such a distinction was operative already in the writings of ancient philosophers, and is particularly significant in the ex-change of Bos and Arnal. Bos refers to Aristotle's devaluation of the role of logic with respect to knowledge of ultimate principles (thesis 4, p. 6); Arnal in his response emphasizes the radically pessimistic views of the Gnostics, and points out that they abandon rational discourse for revelation as the basis of the knowledge required for salvation, 25-26). Discussion of the role of logic is picked up in the essay of Brown, who from a Jungian perspective expresses his appreciation for the kind of knowledge valued by Gnostics, as religious knowledge based on inner conviction, ex-perience and illumination, best expressed by myth and symbol, and regards such knowledge not only to be more universal, but also an appropriate balance for the rationalism accompanying doctrinal Christianity (Brown, 279-80, 284-87). The knowledge characteristic

of Gnostics is also discussed by O'Cleirigh, who shows that an appreciation of rational discursive knowledge by the orthodox gnostics like Clement of Alexandria went hand in hand with greater appreciation of the creation as the material realm created by a benevolent Maker. When Harnack refers to the Gnostics he designates their work as a philosophy of religion and a theology; they are scholars, and write works of a scholarly nature. Thus he would probably not have wished to make a sharp distinction between religious and philosophically qualified knowledge, as mutually exclusive alternatives, at least not for the Gnostics. This is clear from his discussion of the term *gnōsis*; he interprets it to represent "absolute knowledge." Cf. the *History of Dogma*, 232: "The name *Gnosis*, Gnostics, describes excellently the aims of Gnosticism, in so far as its adherents boasted of the absolute knowledge, and faith in the Gospel was transformed into a knowledge of God, nature and history." The term "absolute knowledge" is clearly reminiscent of Hegelian positions; cf. Rowe, "Hegel on Greek and Revealed Religion" in *Christianity and the Classics*, W. E. Helleman, ed. (Lanham, MD: University Press of America, 1990) 161-88.

39. On the school of Bultmann, cf. Desjardins, "Response" in this volume, 66; also his, "Bauer and Beyond: On Recent Scholarly Discussions of *Hairesis* in the Early Christian Era," *The Second Century* 8 (1991):65-82, especially 69. The significance of work done by followers of Bultmann like Koester and Robinson is attested in other essays of this volume, particularly those of Yamauchi, Henaut, and Halford. This school has played an important role in the translation and interpretation of the Nag Hammadi documents. Bultmann was himself influenced by existentialist thought, and this is evident particularly in the definition of Gnosticism typically given by such scholars; rather than focusing on dualism, such a definition typically focuses on human alienation in the cosmos, estrangement, and the need for "going back" to the Father. In the introduction to the English translation of the documents, J. M. Robinson also focuses on the element of estrangement: *The Nag Hammadi Library in English*, translated and introduced by Members of the Coptic

Gnostic Project of the Institute for Antiquity and Christianity, Claremont, California; J. M. Robinson, general editor (New York: Harper and Row, 1988), 1-10, especially 1. R. M. Grant and G. Quispel have been among the leaders in scholarly work looking at Judaism as a significant factor in the rise of Gnosticism; for other important contemporary representatives, see Desjardins, "Judaism" in this volume, 312-15.

40. In her article in this volume, 273-76, Halford concludes that Protennoia in the document *Trim.Prot.* is best understood as a parallel to Sophia in the gnosticized Jewish wisdom tradition.

41. Edwin M. Yamauchi, *Pre-Christian Gnosticism, a Survey of the Proposed Evidences*, 2nd edition (Grand Rapids: Baker, 1983; first edition 1973). The 1983 edition added chapter 12 and provided an update on new publications on Gnosticism.

42. Desjardins, "Response" in this volume 64.

43. W. Bauer, *Rechtgläubigkeit und Ketzerei im ältesten Christentum* (Tübingen: Mohr/Siebeck, 1934), was translated as *Orthodoxy and Heresy in Earliest Christianity*, R. Kraft, G. Krodel, eds. (Philadelphia: Fortress, 1971), based on the second German edition of 1964.

44. Yamauchi, "Gnosticism," in this volume 41-44. On the discussion of Bauer's thesis, particularly the critique of H. E. W. Turner, and later that of T. Robinson, cf. Desjardins, "Bauer and Beyond" (n.39), 71-72.

45. In reply to Desjardins' question regarding motivation, Yamauchi identified his approach as that of a conservative Christian; cf. the conclusions of Yamauchi, "Gnosticism" in this volume 44-47, and the observations of Desjardins in his "Response," in this volume 66-67. This position of Yamauchi is not necessarily connected with an anti-Catholic tradition, which in North America has never been as strong a motivation as in Europe; for Yamauchi acceptance of the authoritative nature of the scriptures would be a more crucial factor.

46. In his article "Cosmic and Meta-Cosmic" in this volume 1-2.9, Bos briefly mentions some of the traditional obstacles to accepting the position long associated with G. Quispel and R. M. Grant regarding Jewish origins for Gnosticism; he notes the questions of van Unnik and others. Desjardins' "Judaism" summarizes the important discussion carried on by Gruenwald, Pearson and Segal, among others, 310-15. Quispel has maintained the position argued over a number of decades; of interest is a recent exchange between profs. Bos and Quispel on Gnosticism, Nag Hammadi documents, Judaism and the current "new age" phenomenon. This was reported by K. van der Zwaag in *Beweging* 57 (1993):47-51, "Gnosis als roep in 'onzin' van deze wereld, Prof. G. Quispel en prof. A. P. Bos over de opleving van de gnostiek in de tijdperk van de New Age."

47. Cf. Desjardins, "Judaism," in this volume 309-21, especially 313-14. Quispel's approach with its strong appreciation of religious (mystic) experience is heavily influenced by Jungian psychology, and positively disposed toward the use of symbols, metaphors and mythologizing in the Gnostic documents. Such a positive evaluation of Gnostic myth and symbol is also reflected in the essay of S. Brown, as noted above (n.38). Brown concludes that the historic method is not appropriate for understanding Gnosticism; he uses the feminist questions as his example, "Gnōsis," in this volume 283-84; significance of female imagery necessarily eludes historical investigation.

48. In his conclusions Yamauchi ("Gnosticism," in this volume 44-47, especially 45) refers to B. Aland, M. Hengel, K.-W. Tröger, and Ugo Bianchi among those who have shifted their positions on this issue. On the heretical nature of Gnosticism, see above note 14, and also the discussions of Tiessen, Carroll and Helleman in this volume.

49. Yamauchi, "Gnosticism," in this volume 29; he makes a reference to A. H. Armstrong's article in the *Festschrift* for H. Jonas, "Gnosis and Greek Philosophy," also discussed by Bos, "Cosmic," in this volume, 5.

50. Carroll, "Gnosticism," in this volume 293-300.

51. On this, see above notes 36 and 49. Jonas regarded Gnostics, with Philo and Plotinus, as mystics; this Armstrong finds unacceptable. Contemporary scholarship emphasizing the mystical wing of Platonism is represented by scholars like A. Louth, *The Origin of the*

Christian Mystical Tradition, from Plato to Denys (Oxford: Clarendon, 1981). Plotinus is widely recognized as a mystic thinker; on Philo
as mystic, cf. D. Winston, *Logos and Mystical Theology in Philo of
Alexandria (Cincinnati: HUC Press, 1985).*
52. Carroll, "Gnosticism," in this vol. 295, refers to M. Smith's linking
Gnosticism with Platonism, particularly on the basis of his analysis
of *gnōsis*; in his endnote 9 Carroll refers to the dispute of Pétrement
with M. Smith on this issue in her *A Separate God*, 211, 486; on the
term *gnostikos*, see 359-62.
53. See in this volume, Bos, "Cosmic," particularly 4-13.
54. Bos quotes R. McL. Wilson at length in "Cosmic," 6. Other
key definitions, that given by U. Bianchi as a summary based on the
Messina colloquium, and that of K. Rudolph, are given in Bos's note
31; for Harnack's characterization of *gnosis*, see above note 38. Bos
has developed some of the implications of his own definition in his
note 31. As an important philosophical tool "abstraction" can be
traced back to the role of Parmenides; Bos has examined the issue
at greater length in his *In de Greep van de Titanen* (Amsterdam:
Buijten & Schipperheijn, 1991) 42f.
55. Schneider, *Acts of John*, in this volume 241-52, especially 244.
For the theme of impassibility Schneider refers the reader to the
important work of M. Williams, *The Immovable Race* (Leiden: Brill,
1985). The significance of this theme is highlighted in numerous
other papers in this collection, particularly that of Aune, and more
indirectly those of Sly and Booth. Not only Philo, but also the
document 4 Maccabees reflects a view of piety, or obedience to
Torah which must have been widely accepted in this period. It
explains acts of piety as occasions when "reason" exercises its
legitimate control over the passions, or sinful desires of the soul. This
occurs in such a manner that the soul cannot be moved or influenced
by these emotions. Aune points out that the New Testament does
not put such confidence in reason or in Torah, for Paul claims that
Torah cannot control the desires of the flesh, as in Rom. 7:4-25. Nor
is *apatheia* recognized as a virtue for earliest Christianity; cf. Aune,
"Mastery," in this volume 138-45. Sly continues on this theme,

indicating how Philo identifies the passions with the "feminine" and explaining the implications of such an identification for his view of women. Since the passions are to be ruled, as is appropriate for that which is weaker, Sly concludes that for Philo too women are to be controlled, and remain subservient to men; cf. Sly, "The Plight," in this volume 176-77. The danger of the voice of passion, or that of desire, is highlighted also in the contribution of Booth who examines the identification of the voice of desire with that of the serpent, the arch deceiver in the garden of Eden; cf. Booth, "The Voice," in this volume 159-68.

56. Schneider, op. cit. 247-51.

57. This is the essence of V. Unnik's argument mentioned by Bos, "Cosmic," in this volume, 9; it is of interest that Van Unnik presented his position in the *Festschrift* for Jonas, who also did not consider Judaism a likely origin for Gnosticism.

58. Cf. Desjardins, "Judaism," in this volume 311-14.

59. Rowe, "Adolf von Harnack," in this volume 71-74; Henaut, "Alexandria," 101-102 echoes and reinforces this point. Harnack was aware of the Hellenization of Judaism, but evidently did not wish to pursue a further connection with Hellenized Christianity. He may have been overly impressed by the exclusivism of the Jews, or by their "orthodox" positions on issues where the Gnostics went far beyond, or even directly contradicted traditional Jewish positions. His lead obviously has not stopped contemporary scholars from looking at Jewish roots for the Gnostics; yet the anti-Judaic nature and inversion of traditional Jewish interpretation of Biblical texts has been pointed out repeatedly, and Bos has called attention to the weakness of attributing to Judaism views, like those on the creator and demiurge, with which even today anyone who claims to be Jewish would feel quite uncomfortable; cf. the discussion with Quispel, reported in *Beweging* of 1993, mentioned in n.46 above.

60. Isaiah, passim, but especially chapters 49 and 56.

61. Acts 2:5-12.

62. Such Jewish distinctives are widely recognized; A. Mendelson deals with basic characteristics of Judaism in the Greco-Roman world, in his *Philo's Jewish Identity* (Atlanta: Scholars, 1988); cf. J. J. Collins, *Between Athens and Jerusalem, Jewish Identity in the Hellenistic Diaspora* (New York: Crossroads, 1983) particularly the introduction, 5f.

63. This passage comes from Isocrates' "Panegyricus" 48-50; cf. *Isocrates*, with Eng. trans. of G. Norlin, vol. I, in the Loeb Classical Library (Cambridge, Mass, 1958).

64. W. W. Tarn, and G. T. Griffith, *Hellenistic Civilization*, 3rd ed. (London: E. Arnold, 1952); this study stimulated renewed attention to the Hellenistic period as having an interest of its own. However it reflected a view which emphasized Greek influence in the older cultures of the Near East, at least partially as a result of Alexander's policy of intermarriage and racial mixture accompanied by new humanistic ideals which were also promulgated by Stoics, and in Rome by the Scipionic circle. Re-evaluation of these ideals and policies has followed on a more realistic appraisal of Alexander's generals and their implementation of such policies. For a summary of recent discussions, cf. L. L. Grabbe, *Judaism from Cyrus to Hadrian*, 2 vols., (Minneapolis: Fortress, 1992), vol. I, 164-68.

65. In his analysis of the "Hellenization" of Judaism, M. Hengel may be faulted for putting too much emphasis on educational institutions in his major publications, *Judaism and Hellenism* (1974), Jews, Greek and Barbarians: Aspects of the Hellenization of Judaism in the Pre-Christian Period (1980), and *The "Hellenization" of Judaea in the First Century after Christ* (1989); nonetheless, such institutions did provide the focus for cultural assimilation and cultural conflict. But our evidence for education in Palestine, especially for the pre-Maccabean period, is not extensive and much is left to the imagination of the scholar; cf. L. Grabbe, op. cit. (n.64), 153.

66. L. H. Feldman, in a lengthy (1977) review of Hengel's *Judaism and Hellenism* argues for a more conservative position on the extent of Hellenization, particularly the use of Greek language, and the influence of Greek literature and thought; L. H. Feldman, "Hengel's *Judaism and Hellenism* in Retrospect," *Journal of Biblical Literature* 96 (1977):371-82. Although he makes useful points in critique of the speed of the Hellenization in Palestine, he is faulted by Grabbe for the "assumptions that Hellenization means apostasy and intermarriage, and that those who are deeply religious could have been only minimally Hellenized. Neither of these assumptions would be accepted by many scholars; indeed they are clearly contradicted by the prime example of Philo;" Grabbe, op. cit., 151.

67. Grabbe, op. cit. (n.64), 156-58.

68. Ibid., 157, 161.

69. Ibid., 150-54, cf.163-64.

70. Ibid., 148-50.

71. Ibid., 163-64; 256-58. The particular issue of the Maccabean revolt, and implications of the contemporary approach for understanding this period of history in Palestine is much too complex for adequate treatment here. Older texts on the inter-testamentary period have a rather different approach on the policies of Antiochus; D. S. Russell, *Between the Testaments* (Philadelphia: Fortress, 1960) takes an approach more like that attributed to Feldman (cf. n.66 above) for whom Hellenization would be virtually equated with apostatizing. On the causes of the Maccabean uprising, cf. Grabbe, op. cit., 247; on the *political* nature of persecution, ibid., 250. Antiochus would certainly have realized the suicidal nature of trying to turn Jerusalem into a Greek *polis* without abundant local support; Bickerman in his analysis focused on Menelaus and the Tobiads as Hellenizers trying to reform Judaism, a thesis accepted by Hengel. Tcherikover assigned a strong role to the Hasidim who also overreacted. Was a "cult of Torah" the cause of trouble, and for that reason suppressed by the Syrians? Or did Menelaus introduce a Syrian cult which was supported by Antiochus? The issue is raised here mainly to indicate the range of contemporary approaches taken by historians on this issue, not to attempt a resolution. For further discussion, see 454f.

72. See, for example, David E. Aune, *The New Testament in its Literary Environment* (Cambridge, UK: James Clarke & Co., 1988) who begins his discussion by stating boldly: ". . . the Judaism from which Christianity emerged was already Hellenized. Early Judaism not only was diverse religiously but had undergone an increasing though uneven process of Hellenization since the late fourth century B.C. The Christianity reflected in Paul's letters is consciously rooted theologically in this Judaism and yet is struggling to discard the cultural markers of Jewish ethnic identity (e. g., circumcision, Sabbath observance, dietary restrictions, the wearing of religious paraphernalia)" (11-12). L. M. White, op. cit. (n.7), 107f., acknowledges the corrective influence of scholars like E. P. Sanders and J. Neusner on our understanding of Judaism of this period. On Feldman's critique of Hengel, see Grabbe, op. cit., 150-53 (referred to above, n.66).

73. Grabbe, op. cit., 165; cf. 247 on the Hellenists and Maccabees. Grabbe provides a useful summary of Hellenization, 164-70. For further discussion of Grabbe's characterization of Hellenization as primarily political or cultural in nature, see 454f. Note that current discussions of Philo, reflected by Grabbe, 151 (cf. n.66 above) assume the legitimacy of his "Hellenized Judaism," his particular understanding of Judaism as coloured or infected by Greek ways of thought; this reflects the more appreciative view of Philo which has developed in the past few decades; cf. D. T. Runia, *Philo of Alexandria and the Timaeus of Plato* (Leiden: Brill, 1986) 535f.

74. A useful summary discussion of these developments may be found in S. Neill and T. Wright, *The Interpretation of the New Testament* (n.13), 147f. They mention (147-50) the important early role of Edwin Hatch, best known for his work, with Redpath, on the *Concordance to the Septuagint*; it is interesting for the present study to note that his 1881 lectures *On the Organization of the Early Christian Churches* were translated into German by Harnack himself, and his 1889 lectures on *The Influence of Greek Ideas on Christianity* were translated into German by Preuschen, with additions by Harnack. The importance of Hatch is also evident from the comments of J. Z. Smith, op. cit.(n.3), 59-62.

75. On this, see above 436.

76. Rowe, "Adolf von Harnack" in this volume, 91, has a brief discussion of the role of the creeds. A more thorough treatment may be found in P. Schrodt, *The Problem of the Beginning of Dogma in Recent Theology* (Frankfurt am Main: P. Lang, 1978): see above n.2. Particularly helpful is the discussion of the formation of the confessions and creeds from New Testament times, and the role of Christological hymns, like those of Philippians 2:6-11, or Colossians 1:15-20, in his ch.6 "The Concrete Forms of the Developing Dogmatic Faith" (282-332). Schrodt signals the work of Jack T. Sanders in his 1971 publication, *The New Testament Christological Hymns* (Cambridge), giving formal analysis of literary structure, and highlighting liturgical elements which reflect an early emerging configuration of the redeemer or mediator figure (pre-existence, humiliation, exaltation), doctrinally consistent with much later confessions and creeds (321-29). According to Schrodt Harnack has given much too narrow a definition of "dogma" when he regards it as the work of the Greek spirit on the soil of the Gospel, and looks primarily for conceptually formulated teachings intended for apologetic and scholarly interaction; this has led him to ignore the emerging confessional formulae in the New Testament itself; see further, Rowe, op. cit., 79-81, 84-85, 88-91.

77. For discussion of the *regula fidei* see P. Schrodt, op. cit., 282-90, especially 286; also Helleman, "Tertullian" in this volume, 364, 370, 373.

78. The medical connotations were recognized by O'Cleirigh in (oral) discussion of the passage cited in his "Symbol and Science," n.29.

79. Above, 429-30.

80. Paul often returns to the Genesis account of Abraham as a giant of faith; a good example may be found in his discussion of law and faith as factors in the process of justification before God and release from the curse, Galatians 3:6-14. In 1 Corinthians 11:23-34 Paul clearly interprets a tradition handed down regarding Christ's last supper with the disciples, as he applies it for the Corinthian practice of sharing a commemorative meal.

81. See Corbett, "Muddying the Water," in this volume 206-15.

82. Cf. J. Z. Smith, *Drudgery Divine*, 13; see above 430 and n.4.

83. On docetism, see above 442; Schneider, "The *Acts of John*," in this volume 245-48 gives an example of the docetic representation of Christ. Cf. J. N. D. Kelly, *Early Christian Doctrines*, revised ed. (San Francisco: Harper and Row, 1978) 138-42 for a summary of docetism within early Christianity.

84. For my understanding of religion and culture see also the "Introduction" to *Christianity and the Classics* (1990), 16f. A more systematic treatment of religion than is possible here would need to differentiate carefully between religion in the broad sense, dealing with "heart-issues" and central commitments, and faith as a more narrowly defined aspect expressing such a commitment. The present study begins by assuming historical discussion of Christianity; accordingly the words "faith" for the most part represents the Christian faith, and "religion" too is used almost interchangeably with "faith" as one pole of the duo "religion and culture," or "faith and reason."

85. See Wolters, "A Typology of Attitudes" in *Christianity and the Classics* (1990), 189-203.

86. This text is often interpreted as a reflection of Jewish pride in their privileged status through possession of Torah; this led them to claim religious and cultural superiority especially when living in the midst of Gentiles in the *diaspora*; cf. F. F. Bruce, *Paul, Apostle of the Heart Set Free* (Grand Rapids: Eerdmans, 1977) 189.

87. See Tiessen, "Gnosticism as Heresy" in this volume, 342 on Irenaeus's understanding of these distinctions; Tiessen mentions the view of P. Perkins who has suggested that Gnostic teaching was essentially universalistic. E. Pagels has made similar objections to general understanding of the three-fold division of mankind. Her concern, however, is to challenge the approach taken by Clement, as well as Irenaeus and Origen in regarding Gnostic anthropology as deterministic in differentiating according to "nature;" see E. Pagels, *The Johannine Gospel in Gnostic Exegesis* (Atlanta: Scholars, 1989) 109-13. Cf. E. Clark, *Clement's Use of Aristotle. The Aristotelian Contribution to Clement of Alexandria's Refutation of Gnosticism* (New York: Mellen, 1977) 45-46.

88. On contemporary attitudes to heresy see P. Henry, op. cit. (above n.14); also, M. Desjardins, "Bauer and Beyond: On Recent Scholarly Discussions of *Hairesis* in the Early Christian Era," *The Second Century* 8 (1991):65-82.

89. See J. G. Gager, *Kingdom and Community* (New Jersey: Prentice Hall, 1975), 115-22, where he reflects particularly on Harnack's "triumphalist" approach in the *Mission and Expansion of Christianity*. Further analysis of Harnack's position as an embodiment of the *praeparatio evangelica* paradigm in understanding the history of Christianity along these lines may be found in the article of L. M. White, "Adolf Harnack and the 'Expansion' of Early Christianity: A Reappraisal of Social History" *The Second Century* 5 (1986): 97-127; on this paradigm see 469f. Nonetheless, on the basis of the analysis of *The History of Dogma*, both Rowe, "Adolf von Harnack" in this volume 87-88, and Henaut, "Alexandria," in this volume 101, have concluded that his views were basically more pessimistic.

90. See Sly, "The Plight of Woman" in this volume 180-82.

91. This reflects the formulation of J. Klapwijk, "Antithesis, Synthesis, and the Idea of Transformational Philosophy" *Philosophia Reformata* 51 (1986): 138-52; see 139f. for the argument that consistent application of the antithesis as A. Kuyper understood it implies the separate development of Christian scholarly work, as well as the formation of political and other cultural associations which separate Christians socially and organizationally from their opponents, i. e., those who do not recognize the all-embracing claim of Christ.

92. J. Klapwijk, "Epilogue," in *Bringing into Captivity every Thought*, J. Klapwijk et al., eds. (Lanham MD.: University Press of America, 1991) 247.

93. See the discussion of Fredouille in Helleman, "Tertullian" in this volume 365f.

94. Ibid. 369.

95. See Frizzell, "Spoils" in this volume 382-83.

96. Klapwijk, "Epilogue" (see n.92), 256.

97. S. Griffoen, "Het Synthesevraagstuk" in *Geloof en Filosofie*, J. Klapwijk et al., eds. (Amsterdam: Filosofisch Instituut, Vrije Universiteit, 1978) 91-98; also of interest is the account of the discussion which ensued, 99-109. The exchange with Prof. Smit (104f.) is particularly important for this analysis of "synthesis." See also the discussion of Klapwijk, "Antithesis" (above n.91), 140-41.

98. S. Griffioen, op. cit. (n.97), 94f. A. Wolters has given some useful observations on Dooyeweerd's terminology of *grond-motieven*, with his article "Ground-Motive," *Anakainosis* 6 (1983):1-4.

99. An excellent introductory discussion of Vollenhoven's approach may be found in a recent commemorative issue of *Beweging*; see especially A. Tol, "Vollenhoven als systematicus," *Beweging* 56 (1992):91-96. It is impossible to do justice to the work of Dooyeweerd and Vollenhoven within the scope of the present treatment, and we will not attempt to do so; in a future volume we hope to return to their views on classical antiquity and the systematic philosophical approach utilized by them.

100. Intellectualism is often mentioned as a source of danger for the Christian church; cf. Rowe, "Adolf von Harnack" in this volume 79-80, 84-85. Even Klapwijk still uses this language in his article, "Antithesis (n.91) 145-46, on which see my concluding observations, 477-79. In such discussions Justin Martyr and Clement of Alexandria are often singled out; cf. J. Z. Smith, op. cit., 16-20.

101. W. A. Dyrness, "Beyond Niebuhr: The Gospel and Culture," *The Reformed Journal* 38 (1988):12. Dyrness's reference to the communication levels made possible by such sharing is significant also for Klapwijk's approach which focuses on dialectical interchange between Christian and non-Christian philosophers; see 471-72.

102. Dyrness, loc. cit.

103. Klapwijk, "Antithesis" (n.91), 144.

104. Wolters, *"Creatio ex nihilo"* in this volume 107-21; see particularly his concluding observations, 120-21.

105. D. H. Williams, "Harnack," in this volume 224-35.

106. T. Tiessen, "Gnosticism," in this volume 340-41, 344, 347-53.

107. D. Aune, "Mastery," in this volume 142-45; J. Martens, *"Nomos Empsychos,"* in this volume 331-33; M. E. Irwin, "Clement of

Alexandria," in this volume 395-403. For a recent discussion of Clement's anti-gnostic arguments, see E. Clark, *Clement's Use of Aristotle. The Aristotelian Contribution to Clement of Alexandria's Refutation of Gnosticism*; see particularly ch. 5, "God and the Logos" (87-85) on Clement's use of Aristotelian themes regarding the ultimate deity (as mind). Clement affirmed the instrumental or causal role of the Logos (i. e., Christ, the Word) in creation; he did this in part to protect the immutability of God the Father, and remove grounds for the anthropomorphism of simple believers. But in this he echoed positions of Apologists like Justin Martyr and church fathers like Irenaeus (on whom see also above, n.106), who likewise emphasized that God made everything *through the Word*, thus positing close associations between Old and New Testament themes; cf. Clark, op. cit., 73-78.

108. Aune, "Mastery," in this volume 125-34.

109. Booth, "The Voice," in this volume 160-63, 167-68.

110. Sly, "The Plight," in this volume 176f.

111. Jastram, "The *Praeparatio*," in this volume 189-90, 193-95, 198-99.

112. Jastram, op. cit., 190-91.

113. D. T. Runia, *Philo of Alexandria and the Timaeus of Plato* (Leiden: Brill, 1986) 543; cf. Runia's review of Wolfson's *magnum opus* on Philo, "History of Philosophy in the Grand Manner: the Achievement of H. A. Wolfson," *Philosophia Reformata* 49 (1984): 112-33, especially 125-26. See on this also Klapwijk, "Epilogue" (n.92), 253.

114. On Jewish apologetic literature see J. Gager, op. cit. (n.89), 128; Gager's *Moses in Greco-Roman Paganism* (Nashville: Abingdon Press, 1972) provides a valuable discussion of acquaintance with Moses in non-Jewish literature and other sources. See also A. Momigliano, *Alien Wisdom, The Limits of Hellenization* (Cambridge, UK: Cambridge University Press, 1971) 74-122. Although Runia recognizes the apologetic aspect of Philo's work, he does not appreciate numerous conclusions regarding his work which have been based on this premise; cf. his *Philo of Alexandria* (n.113), 542-43.

115. J. Gager, op. cit. (n.89) 127, makes the telling remark when he discusses Christian appropriation of literature from Hellenistic, or *diaspora* Judaism: "Apart from a single passage in Josephus, Philo's immense corpus of exegetical and apologetic works passes without the slightest mention in subsequent centuries of Jewish history. With the disappearance of Alexandrian Judaism in the second century C.E., Philo's works seem to have been preserved and copied by Christian hands. In any case, his influence was felt exclusively in Christian circles among such figures as Clement of Alexandria, Origen, and Eusebius." See also the introductory chapter, "Philo's Logos Doctrine Against its Platonic Background," of D. Winston, *Logos and Mystical Theology in Philo of Alexandria* (Cincinnati: HUC Press, 1985) 9f. Although in his 1984 review of Wolfson's work (n.113 above), Runia recognizes the unique approach of Alexandrian Judaism and its excessively intellectualistic nature (128-29), in his *Philo of Alexandria* he attributes later neglect among Jews to lack of qualifications (as well as inclination) to deal with it (551). See also his *Philo in Early Christian Literature. A Survey* (Assen: Van Gorcum, 1993), especially 12-16.

116. Wolters, "A Typology" (n.85 above), 201-203.

117. Ibid., 196-97.

118. See above 465.

119. Cf. Irwin, "Clement" in this volume 395-97, 402-403; also W. E. Helleman, "Basil's *Ad Adolescentes*: Guidelines for Reading the Classics" in *Christianity and the Classics*, W. E. Helleman, ed. (1990) 32, 42-46.

120. Wolters, "A Typology" (n.85 above), 198-99.

121. Frizzell, "Spoils" in this volume 383-85.

122. Ibid., 387-90.

123. P. Marshall, "Overview of Christ and Culture," the introductory essay of R. E. VanderVennen, ed., *Church and Canadian Culture* (Lanham, MD: University Press of America, 1991) 1-9.

124. Klapwijk recognizes "transformation" in two senses, a positive or normative, and a negative or "inverse transformation;" cf. his "Antithesis," (n.91), 144, and also the "Epilogue" (n.92), 248f.

Klapwijk does not acknowledge the work of Niebuhr, although his use of such terms is clearly reminiscent of Niebuhr's classic treatment of the theme; however, throughout the discussion Klapwijk maintains a focus on philosophical issues, and this accounts for his more specialized use of the term. For a critical examination of Klapwijk's use of the *Spoliatio* motif see A. P. Bos, "Transformation and Deformation in Philosophy," *Philosophia Reformata* 52 (1987): 135-38.

125. See above, 460-61. Klapwijk's response focuses on the need to give account (*apologia*) of the faith, to respond to the challenges of one's time, and communicate the message of the gospel in words which can be clearly heard and understood, "Epilogue" (n.92), 247.

126. "Faith can transform an intellectual tradition; such traditions, too, are able to reinterpret the implications of the Christian convictions;" Klapwijk, "Epilogue" (n.92), 251-52. Cf. his "Antithesis" (n.91), 144-49. Also, Frizzell, op. cit., 387-90.

127. Klapwijk, "Epilogue," 256-57.

128. Ibid., 253.

129. Ibid., 254-55.

130. Loc. cit.

131. W. Dyrness, op. cit. (n.101), 12.

132. Loc. cit.

133. See P. Marshall, op. cit. (n.123), 3.

134. Ibid., 5-7.

135. Rumscheidt, op. cit. (n.9). He elaborates on the title on 33-35; cf. the final quotation on 41.

136. S. Neill, op. cit. (n.13), 143.

137. Carroll, "Gnosticism," in this volume 294; cf. J. G. Gager, op. cit. (n.89), 115-22.

138. J. G. Gager, loc. cit.

139. Klapwijk, "Antithesis" (n.91), 145-46.

140. Klapwijk, "Epilogue" (n.92), 254-55.

Bibliography

General Works and Collected Essays

D. L. Balch, E. Ferguson, W. A. Meeks, *Greeks, Romans and Christians, Essays in Honor of Abraham J. Malherbe* (Minneapolis: Fortress, 1990)

S. Benko, J. O'Rourke, eds., *The Catacombs and the Colosseum, The Roman Empire as the Setting of Primitive Christianity* (Valley Forge: Judson Press, 1971)

R. vanden Broek, J. Vermaseren, eds., *Studies in Gnosticism and Hellenistic Religion, Presented to G. Quispel* (Leiden: Brill, 1981)

J. H. Charlesworth, ed., *The Old Testament Pseudepigrapha*, 2 vols. (Garden City, NJ: Doubleday, 1985)

J. E. Goehring, C. W. Hedrick, J. T. Sanders, H. D. Betz, eds., *Gnosticism and the Early Christian World*; Essays in honor of J. M. Robinson (Soloma, Calif.: Polebridge Press, 1990)

W. E. Helleman, ed., *Christianity and the Classics, The Acceptance of a Heritage* (Lanham MD: University Press of America, 1990)

J. Klapwijk et al., eds., *Bringing into Captivity every Thought* (Lanham MD: Univ. Press of America, 1991)

A. H. Logan and A. J. M. Wedderburn, eds., *The New Testament and Gnosis: Essays in Honour of Robert McL. Wilson* (Edinburgh: T & T Clark, 1983)

J. Neusner, ed., *Religions in Antiquity, Essays in Memory of E. R. Goodenough* (Leiden: Brill, 1968)

J. Neusner et al., eds., *The Social World of Formative Christianity and Judaism, Essays in Tribute to Howard Clark Kee* (Philadelphia: Fortress, 1988)

A. D. Nock, *Essays on Religion and the Ancient World*, 2 vols. (Oxford: Clarendon, 1972)

B. A. Pearson, J. E. Goehring, eds., *The Roots of Egyptian Christianity* (Philadelphia: Fortress, 1986)

J. Ries et al., eds., *Gnosticisme et monde Hellénistique*; Actes du Colloque de Louvain La Neuve (Louvain, 1982)

D. T. Runia, ed., *Plotinus amid Gnostics and Christians* (Amsterdam: Vrije Universiteit Uitg., 1984)

E. P. Sanders et al., eds., *Jewish and Christian Self-Definition*, 3 vols. (Philadelphia: Fortress, 1980-82)

J. T. Sanders, C. Hedrick, H. D. Betz, eds., *Essays on Antiquity and Christianity, in Honor of J. M. Robinson* (Sonoma, CA: Polebridge, 1989)

W. R. Schoedel, R. L. Wilken, *Early Christian Literature and the Classical Intellectual Tradition, In Honorem Robert M. Grant* (Paris: Editions Beauchesne, 1979)

H. Thesleff, *The Pythagorean Texts of the Hellenistic Period*, Acta Academiae Aboensis, Ser. A: Humaniora, v.30, no. 1 (Abo: Abo Akademie, 1961)

General Interest

R. Boon, *Antiquitas Graeco-Roman et Dignitas Israelitica, De controverse 'Athene,' 'Rome,' 'Jerusalem' als fundamentele factor in het westeuropese secularisatie-proces* (Amsterdam: Vrije Univ., 1989)

H. Chadwick, *Early Christian Thought and the Classical Tradition* (Oxford, 1966)

S. L. Davies, *Revolt of the Widows: The Social World of the Apocryphal Acts* (Carbondale: South Illinois Univ., 1980)

D. Dawson, *Allegorical Readers and Cultural Revision in ancient Alexandria* (Berkeley: Univ. of Calif., 1992)

J. G. Gager, *Kingdom and Community* (New Jersey: Prentice Hall, 1975)

R. M. Grant, *Gnosticism and Early Christianity* (New York: Harper & Row, 1966 rev.)

R. M. Grant, *Gods and the One God* (Philadelphia: Westminster, 1986)

M. Hadas, *Hellenistic Culture, Fusion and Diffusion* (New York: Columbia, 1959)

A. von Harnack, *The Expansion of Christianity in the First Three Centuries*, vol. I (New York: Norgate and Williams, Putnam's, 1904)

A. von Harnack, *History of Dogma*, trans. of 3rd German ed., by N. Buchanan (New York: Dover, 1961)

A. von Harnack, *Marcion: The Gospel of the Alien God*, trans. from the 2nd German ed. of 1924, by J. E. Steely, L. D. Bierma (Durham, NC: Labyrinth, 1990)

A. von Harnack, *Outlines of the History of Dogma*, trans. E. K. Mitchell (Boston: Beacon, 1957)

A. von Harnack, *What is Christianity?*, trans. Th. Bailey Saunder, (Harper and Row, 1957)

P. Henry, "Why is Contemporary Scholarship so Enamored of Ancient Heretics?" *Studia Patristica*, E. A. Livingstone ed., 27.1 (Oxford: Pergamon Press, 1982):123-26.

J. Klapwijk, "Antithesis, Synthesis and the Idea of Transformational Philosophy" *Philosophia Reformata* 51 (1986):138-52.

K. S. Latourette, *A History of Christianity*, 2 vols. (New York: Harper & Row, 1975; first ed. 1953)

E. P. Meijering, *Die Hellenisierung des Christentums im Urteil Adolf von Harnacks*, Verhandelingen der Koninklijke Nederlandse Akademie van Wetenschappen, Afd. Letterkunde, Nieuwe Reeks, deel 128 (Amsterdam: North-Holland Publishing, 1985)

A. Momigliano, *Alien Wisdom, The Limits of Hellenization* (Cambridge: Cambridge UP, 1990)

S. Neill and N. T. Wright, *The Interpretation of the New Testament, 1861-1961*, 2nd edition (London: Oxford UP, 1988)

H. R. Niebuhr, *Christ and Culture* (New York: Harper and Row, 1951)

B. A. Pearson, *Gnosticism, Judaism, and Egyptian Christianity*: Studies in Antiquity and Christianity (Minneapolis: Fortress, 1990)

J. Pelikan, *Christianity and Classical Culture, The Metamorphosis of Natural Theology in the Christian Encounter with Hellenism* (New Haven: Yale University Press, 1993)

K. J. Popma, "Patristic Evaluation of Culture," *Philosophia Reformata* 38 (1973):97-113.

W. V. Rowe, "A Critical Study of E. P. Meijering's *Die Hellenisierung des Christentum im Urteil Adolf von Harnacks*" *Philosophia Reformata* 57 (1992):78-85.

M. Rumscheidt, ed., *Adolf von Harnack, Liberal Theology at its Height* (London: Collins, 1989)

D. T. Runia, *Philo in Early Christian Literature. A Survey* (Assen: Van Gorcum, 1993)

P. Schrodt, *The Problem of the Beginning of Dogma in Recent Theology* (Frankfurt am Main: P. Lang, 1978)

J. Z. Smith, *Drudgery Divine, On the Comparison of Early Christianities and the Religions of Late Antiquity* (London: School of Oriental and African Studies, U. of London, 1990)

J. Snyder, *The Woman and the Lyre, Women Writers in Classical Greece and Rome* (Carbondale: South Illinois Univ., 1989)

E. G. Weltin, *Athens and Jerusalem: An Interpretive Essay on Christianity and Classical Culture,* AAR Studies in Religion 49 (Atlanta, GA: Scholars, 1987)

L. M. White, "Adolf Harnack and the 'Expansion' of Early Christianity: A Reappraisal of Social History" *The Second Century* 5 (1985/6): 97-127.

R. L. Wilken, ed., *Aspects of Wisdom in Judaism and Early Christianity* (Notre Dame U., 1975)

Greek Philosophical Background

A. H. Armstrong, *An Introduction to Ancient Philosophy* (London: Methuen, 1965)

R. M. Berchman, *From Philo to Origen, Middle Platonism in Transition*; Brown Judaic Studies 69 (Chico, Calif.: Scholars Press, 1984)

A. P. Bos, *Cosmic and Meta-Cosmic Theology in Aristotle's Lost Dialogues* (Leiden: Brill, 1989)

E. A. Clark, *Clement's Use of Aristotle: The Aristotelian Contribution to Clement's Refutation of Gnosticism* (New York: E. Mellen, 1977)

A. A. Long, D. N. Sedley, *The Hellenistic Philosophers* (Cambridge UK: Cambridge UP, 1987)

W. Jaeger, *Early Christianity and Greek Paideia* (London: Oxford UP, 1961)

Hellenistic Judaism

J. Bartlett, *Jews in the Hellenistic World* (Cambridge, UK: Cambridge UP, 1985)

E. J. Bickerman, *The Jews in the Greek Age* (Cambridge, MA: Harvard UP, 1988)

B. B. Bokser, "Recent Developments in the Study of Judaism, 70-200 CE" *The Second Century* 3 (1983): 1-68.

J. J. Collins, *Between Athens and Jerusalem, Jewish Identity in the Hellenistic Diaspora* (New York: Crossroads, 1983)

D. Daube, *The New Testament and Rabbinic Judaism* (London: Athlone Press, 1956)

L. W. D. Davies, L. Finkelstein, eds., *The Cambridge History of Judaism*, 2 vols. (Cambridge, UK: Cambridge UP, 1984-1989)

L. Feldman, *Josephus and Modern Scholarship, 1937-1980* (Berlin: de Gruyter, 1984)

L. Feldman, *Josephus, a Supplementary Bibliography* (New York: Gardens Pub., 1986)

H. Fischel, ed., *Essays in Greco-Roman and Related Talmudic Literature* (New York: Ktav, 1977)

H. Fischel, *Rabbinic Literature and Greco-Roman Philosophy: A Study of Epicurea and Rhetorica in Early Midrashic Writing* (Leiden: Brill, 1973)

L. L. Grabbe, *Judaism from Cyrus to Hadrian*; vol. I, *The Persian and Greek Periods*; vol. II, *The Roman Period* (Minneapolis: Fortress, 1992)

I. Gruenwald, *From Apocalypticism to Gnosticism, Studies in Apocalypticism, Merkavah Mysticism and Gnosticism* (Frankfurt am Main: P. Lang, 1988)

M. Hengel, *The Hellenization of Judaea in the First Century after Christ* (London: SCM, 1989)

M. Hengel, *Jews, Greeks, and Barbarians, Aspects of the Hellenization of Judaism in the Pre-Christian Period* (Philadelphia: Fortress, 1980)

M. Hengel, *Judaism and Hellenism, Studies in Their Encounter in Palestine during the Early Hellenistic Period*, 2 vols., J. Bowden trans. (Philadelphia: Fortress, 1974)

R. A. Kraft, G. W. E. Nickelburg, *Early Judaism and its Modern Interpreters* (Philadelphia: Fortress, 1986)

S. Lieberman, *Hellenism in Jewish Palestine, Studies in the Literary Transmission, Beliefs and Manners of Palestine in the I Century B.C.E. - IV Century C.E.* (New York: Jewish Theological Seminary, 1962)

S. Mason, *Flavius Josephus on the Pharisees, A Compositional-Critical Study* (Leiden: Brill, 1991)

J. Neusner, *From Politics to Piety, the Emergence of Pharisaic Judaism* (Englewood Cliffs, NJ: Prentice Hall, 1973)

Yehuda T. Radday, "The Spoils of Egypt," *Annual of the Swedish Theological Institute* 12 (1983): 127-47

R. Reuther, *Faith and Fratricide, The Theological Roots of Anti-Semitism* (New York: Seabury, 1979)

P. Richardson, D. Granskou, eds., *Anti-Judaism in Early Christianity*, vol. I, *Paul and the Gospels;* (Waterloo, Wilfrid Laurier Press, 1986); S. Wilson, ed., vol. II, *Separation and Polemics* (Waterloo, Wilfrid Laurier Press, 1986)

E. P. Sanders, *Paul and Palestinian Judaism* (Philadelphia: Fortress, 1977)

E. Schnabel, *Law and Wisdom from Ben Sira to Paul* (Tübingen, 1985)

G. Scholem, *Jewish Gnosticism, Merkabah Mysticism and Talmudic Tradition* (New York: Jewish Theological Seminary, 1965)

E.Schürer, *The History of the Jewish People in the Age of Jesus Christ (175 B.C.- A.D.135)*, rev. and ed. by G. Vermes and F. Millar, 3 vols in 4 (Edinburgh: Clark, 1973-87)

A. F. Segal, *The Other Judaisms of Late Antiquity* (Atlanta, Georgia: Scholars, 1987)

A. F. Segal, *Rebecca's Children: Judaism and Christianity in the Roman World* (Cambridge, MA: Harvard UP, 1986)

A. F. Segal, *Two Powers in Heaven, Early Rabbinic Reports about Christianity and Gnosticism* (Leiden: Brill, 1977)

M. Simon, *Verus Israel, a Study of the Relations of Christians and Jews in the Roman Empire, 135-425 AD* (Oxford: Oxford UP, 1986)

E. M. Smallwood, *The Jews under Roman Rule, from Pompey to Diocletian* (Leiden: Brill, 1976)

V. Tcherikover, *Hellenistic Civilization and the Jews*, tr. S. Applebaum (New York: Atheneum, 1970)

G. Vermes, *The Dead Sea Scrolls in English*, 2nd ed. (Penguin, 1975)

R. D. Young, "The 'Woman with the soul of Abraham': Traditions about the Mother of the Maccabean Martyrs" in *"Women Like This": New Perspectives on Jewish Women in the Greco-Roman World*, A.-J. Levine, ed. (Atlanta: Scholars, 1991):67-81.

Philo

Y. Amir, *Die Hellenistische Gestalt und des Judentums bei Philon von Alexandrien* (Neukirchener Verlag, 1983)

P. Borgen, "Philo: Survey of Research since WWII" *ANRW* II 21.1:98-154.

F. H. Colson, G. H. Whitaker, *Philo, with an English translation* (Cambridge MA: Harvard UP, 1958-1962)

A. Mendelson, *Philo's Jewish Identity* (Atlanta, Georgia: Scholar's, 1988)

A. Mendelson, *Secular Education in Philo of Alexandria* (Cincinatti: Hebrew Union College Press, 1982)

R. Radice and D. T. Runia *Philo of Alexandria: An Annotated Bibliography 1937-1986* (Leiden: Brill, 1986)

D. T. Runia, *Philo of Alexandria and the Timaeus of Plato* (Leiden: Brill, 1986)

S. Sandmel, *Philo of Alexandria, an Introduction* (Oxford: Oxford UP, 1979)

R. Williamson, *Jews in the Hellenistic World: Philo* (Cambridge: Cambridge UP, 1989)

D. Winston, *Logos and Mystical Theology in Philo of Alexandria* (New York: HUC Press, 1985)

H. A. Wolfson, *Philo, Foundations of Religious Philosophy in Judaism, Christianity and Islam*, 2 vols. (Cambridge MA: Harvard UP, 1947)

Gnosticism

B. Aland, ed., *Gnosis, Festschrift für Hans Jonas* (Göttingen: VandenHoeck & Ruprecht, 1978)

U. Bianchi, ed., *Le origini dello Gnosticismo* (Leiden: Brill, 1967)

I. P. Couliano, *The Tree of Gnosis: Gnostic Mythology from Early Christianity to Modern Nihilism*, H. S. Wiesner, I. P. Couliano, trans., (San Francisco: Harper, 1992)

M. R. Desjardins, *Sin in Valentinianism* (Atlanta, Georgia: Scholars, 1990)

J. Doresse, *The Secret Books of the Egyptian Gnostics* (London: Hollis and Carter, 1960)

M. J. Edwards, "Gnostics and Valentinians in the Church Fathers" *Journal of Theological Studies* ns. 40 (1989):26-47.

M. J. Edwards, "Neglected Texts in the Study of Gnosticism" *Journal of Theological Studies* 41 (1990):26-50.

G. Filoramo, *A History of Gnosticism* (Oxford: Basil Blackwell, 1990)

R. M. Grant, *Gnosticism and Early Christianity*, revised ed. (New York: Harper and Row, 1966)

H. A. Green, *The Economic and Social Origins of Gnosticism* SBL Dissertation Ser. 77 (Atlanta: Scholars, 1985)

C. W. Hedrick, R. Hodgson Jr., eds., *Nag Hammadi, Gnosticism and Early Christianity* (Peabody MA: Hendrickson, 1986)

H. Jonas, *The Gnostic Religion, The Message of the Alien God and the Beginnings of Christianity*, 2nd ed. (Boston: Beacon Press, 1963)

K. L. King, ed., *Images of the Feminine in Gnosticism* (Philadelphia: Fortress, 1988)

J. Kloppenborg, "Isis and Sophia in the Book of Wisdom" *Harvard Theological Review* 75 (1982): 57-84.

B. Layton, *The Gnostic Scriptures, A New Translation with Annotations and Introduction* (Garden City NY: Doubleday, 1987)

B. Layton, ed., *The Rediscovery of Gnosticism. Proceedings of the International Conference on Gnosticism at Yale, 1978*; vol. I: *The School of Valentinus*; vol. II: *Sethian Gnosticism* (Leiden: Brill, 1980, 1981)

G. P. Luttikhuizen, "The Jewish Factor in the Development of the Gnostic Myth of Origins" in *Text and Testimony, Essays in Honour of A. F. Klijn*, T. Baarda, et al., eds. (Kampen: Kok, 1988)

Geo. W. Macrae, "The Jewish Background of the Gnostic Sophia Myth," *Novum Testamentum* 12 (1970): 86-101.

R. A. Norris, "Irenaeus and Plotinus Answer the Gnostics: A Note on the Relation between Christian Thought and Platonism" *Union Seminary Quarterly Review* 36 (1980): 13-24.

E. Pagels, *Adam, Eve, and the Serpent* (New York: Random, 1988)

E. Pagels, *The Gnostic Gospels* (New York: Vintage Books, 1981)

B. Pearson, "Early Christianity and Gnosticism: a Review Essay" *Religious Studies Review* 13 (1987): 1-8.

P. Perkins, *The Gnostic Dialogue: The Early Church and the Crisis of Gnosticism* (New York: Paulist Press, 1980)

S. Pétrement, *A Separate God, The Christian Origins of Gnosticism*, trans. C. Harrison (San Francisco: Harper, 1990); originally published as *Le Dieu séparé: Les origines du gnosticisme* (Paris: Cerf, 1984)

G. Quispel, *Gnostic Studies* (Istanbul: Ned. Hist.-Arch. Inst. in het Nabije Oosten, 1974)

J. M. Robinson, *The Nag Hammadi Library* 3rd ed. (San Francisco: Harper and Row, 1990)

K. Rudolph, *Gnosis, The Nature and History of Gnosticism* (San Francisco: Harper and Row, 1983); a translation by R. McL. Wilson, of the 1977 German edition.

D. M. Scholer, *Nag Hammadi Bibliography, 1948-69* (Leiden: Brill, 1971)

G. A. G. Stroumsa *Another Seed: Studies in Gnostic Mythology* (Leiden: Brill, 1984)

W. C. van Unnik, *Newly Discovered Gnostic Writings, A Preliminary Survey of the Nag Hammadi Find* (London: SCM, 1960)

G. Vallée, *A Study in Anti-Gnostic Polemics*; Studies in Christianity and Judaism (Waterloo: Wilfrid Laurier Press, 1981)

M. A. Williams, *The Immovable Race, A Gnostic Designation and the Theme of Stability in Late Antiquity* (Leiden: Brill, 1985)

R. McL. Wilson, *Gnosis and the New Testament* (Oxford: Basil Blackwell, 1968)

R. McL. Wilson, *The Gnostic Problem* (London: Mowbray, 1958)

E. Yamauchi, *Pre-Christian Gnosticism, A Survey of the Proposed Evidences*, 2nd ed. (Grand Rapids, MI: Baker, 1983)

Early Christianity

T. D. Barnes, *Tertullian* (Oxford: Clarendon, 1971)

W. Bauer, *Orthodoxy and Heresy in Earliest Christianity*, translated from the second German ed. by a team from the Philadelphia Seminar on Christian Origins and edited by R. A. Kraft and G. Krodel (Philadelphia: Fortress, 1971)

R. E. Brown, J. P. Meier, *Antioch and Rome, New Testament Cradles of Catholic Christianity* (New York: Paulist Press, 1983)

E. Castelli, "Women's Sexuality in Early Christianity" *Journal of Feminist Studies in Religion* 2 (1986): 61-88

J.Daniélou, *A History of Early Christian Doctrine before the Council of Nicea*; vol. I, *The Theology of Jewish Christianity*; vol. II, *Gospel Message and Hellenistic Culture* (London: Darton, Longman & Todd, 1964, 1973)

J. Davison, "Structural Similarities and Dissimilarities in the Thought of Clement of Alexandria and the Valentinians" *The Second Century* 3 (1983): 201-17.

M. Desjardins, "Bauer and Beyond: On Recent Scholarly Discussions of *Hairesis* in the Early Christian Era" *The Second Century* 8 (1991): 65-82.

C. H. Dodd, *The Interpretation of the Fourth Gospel* (Cambridge UK: University Press, 1953)

J.-C. Fredouille, *Tertullien et la conversion de la culture antique* (Paris: Etudes Augustiniennes, 1972)

A. van den Hoek, *Clement of Alexandria and his Use of Philo in the Stromateis, An Early Christian Reshaping of a Jewish model* (Leiden: Brill, 1988)

S. R. C. Lilla, *Clement of Alexandria, a Study in Christian Platonism and Gnosticism* (Oxford: Oxford UP, 1971)

E. Osborn, "Clement of Alexandria: A Review of Research, 1958-82" *The Second Century* 3 (1983): 219-44.

E. F. Osborn, "Reason and the Rule of Faith in the Second Century AD" in W. Rowan Williams, ed., *The Making of Orthodoxy* (Cambridge, UK: Cambridge UP, 1989)

J. M. Robinson and H. Koester, *Trajectories Through Early Christianity* (Philadelphia: Fortress, 1971)

R. D. Sider, *Ancient Rhetoric and the Art of Tertullian* (Oxford: Oxford UP, 1971)

R. D. Sider, "Approaches to Tertullian: A Study of Recent Scholarship" *The Second Century* 2 (1982): 228-59.

Index

Abraham 130, 137, 192, 194, 244, 443
abstraction xv, 14 (n.6), 18 (n.31), 413-14, 441
abyssos 116
Academy 90, 363, 399
accommodation xiii, 110, 341, 348, 361, 449-50, 456, 462, 482, 484, 487 (n.3)
Achamoth 411
Acts of Thomas 31
Acts of Andrew 242
Acts (Bible book of) 443
Acts of Peter 257 (n.16)
Acts of John xvii, 241-52, 442
Adam 163, 176, 311
Aeons 40, 341-42, 347, 351
Aland, B. 39, 45
Albinus 344
Alexander Lysimachus 191
Alexander the Great 99-102, 432, 444, 456
Alexandria 40, 46, 97 (n.31), 99-100, 179, 182-83, 190, 198, 200 (n.6), 242, 314-15, 320 (n.25), 344, 389, 395, 403
alien God 227-28, 232
alienation 5, 17 (n.29), 440
allegorize xvi, xix, 82
allegory 160-63, 166-67, 174-78, 194, 226, 235, 335 (n.9), 389-90, 413, 420 (n.2), 435, 466
Allogenes (Foreigner) 296-97

Ambrose 145
Amelius Gentilianus 297
analogy 174-75, 413
androgyny 283, 396
Andronicus 242
angels 233
anthropology xv, 44, 178, 342
anthropomorphism 39, 161-62
anthrōpos 396-97
anti-baptismal 32
anti-Epicurean 165
anti-gnostic 294, 417
anti-Greek 446
anti-Judaic 442
anti-Platonist 344
anti-semitic 385
Antioch 39, 42
antiquity 230-32, 372
antithesis 460-61, 464, 466, 470-72
apatheia xvi, 125, 127-30, 134, 136, 138, 144
Apelles 39, 233
Apocalypse of Peter 40, 340
Apocalypse of Adam 31-32, 45
apocalyptic 26, 32, 34, 82, 310, 312, 314, 316 (n.4)
apocryphal Acts 398
Apocryphon of John 31, 41, 250-51, 311, 340
Apollos 242
apologetes 95 (n.19), 417-18
apologetic 78, 102, 234-35, 340, 429, 433 484

apologists 232, 285, 332
apostasis 91
apostasy 163, 180
apostle 244
apostolic 346-47, 364
appropriation xix, 190-91, 383, 389
archetype 330
archon 10, 23
Archytus 324, 334 (n.3)
aretalogical 271-75
arete 89-90, 398
Aristotle 1-11, 26, 70, 88-89, 191-92,
    195, 366, 414, 441, 469
    —*De philosophia* 3-5, 10-11
    —dialogues 9
    —lost dialogues 24
    —*Eudemus* 4-5, 10-13, 23
    —*Protrepticus* 4-5, 10
    —*De Anima* 13
    —"*De Mundo*" 3-4, 10-11
    —*Metaphysics* 1
Armstrong, A. H. xv, 5-6, 295, 440
arrogance 279, 299, 440
ascend 414
ascetic 128, 235, 312, 402-403, 469
asceticism 35, 47, 345
Asia Minor 42, 241
Asatic 37
askesis 131-34, 138-44
assimilation 190
astral deities 19 (n.36)
atheism 166
Athens 71, 99-106, 361-65, 368-73
atomism 162, 167
Augustine 90, 390, 418
    —*De doctrina Christiana* 471
    —*City of God* 459
authoritarian 286
Babylon 398, 438
Babylonian 241, 442-43
Baer, R. 175, 177, 184 (n.3)
Balaam 180

baptism 234, 242, 251, 254 (n.5)
baptismal sect 32
Bar Kochba war 35, 321 (n.32)
Barbelognostic 41
Bardesanes 42
Baron, S. W. 182-83
Barth, Karl, 477
Basil of Caesarea 469
Basil 387
Basilides 39-40, 64, 434
bathing 401-402
Bauer, Walter 41-44, 46, 64, 439
Baur, F. C. 294-95, 437, 476, 481
Beer 208
betrayal 446, 449-51
Bianchi, Ugo 45, 420 (n.1)
bishop 38, 42, 282, 346, 353, 364, 435,
    458
Böhling, A. 32
Boon, R. 362, 370-73
Bréhier, E. 112
Bultmann, Rudolph 30, 45, 66, 104,
    282, 438
Burke, Gary 44
Burkert, W. 330
Cain 165, 245
Caligula 191, 198
Callimachus 243
Calvinistic philosophy 460, 462-64,
    466, 468, 470, 474-75, 477-78
Canaanites 180
canon 343, 347, 450
Cappadocian fathers 145, 387
Carpocratian 35, 345
catholic 73, 76-77, 83, 233-35, 430
Catholicism 87, 225-27, 235, 418
Catholicization 450, 458
cave (Plato) 12
Celsus 44, 93 (n.13), 233-34
Cerdo 228
Cerinthus 37

charioteer 126, 129
Charlesworth, J. H. 31
chastity 132
choic 41
Christ xvii-xviii, 231, 245-47, 327-29;
    see also Jesus
Christian 243-45
Christian religion 75
Christianity xiii, xvi-xix
Christianization 272, 323
christology 245-49, 251, 275-76
church 346-47, 435-46, 455
Cicero 3-4, 10, 172 (n.23), 230, 325,
    365
circumcision 177, 227, 443
Claremont (1985 conference) 283
classical culture xiii, 433
classical tradition 293-301
classical heritage 472
classical culture 339
classical scholarship 451
classicism 70
classics 373, 382-83, 390
Clement of Alexandria xviii-xix, 36,
    142-44, 168, 323-33, 348, 352,
    361, 386-89, 395-403, 409, 412-
    14, 418, 434-35, 464-65, 469, 471
    —*Miscellanies* 193
    —*Paidogōgos* (*Educator*) 144,
    395-402
Cleopatra 243-45, 248-49
clothing 397-401
Collingwood, R. G. 103-104
Cologne Mani Codex 30
"colonial" power 446
Colpe, C. 112, 272
communication 429, 461, 464, 468,
    471, 473, 482-83
community 451, 456
comparative 29
compromise 465

Comte, A. 8
concept 76
conceptual 410, 418
confrontation 459
Constantine 456-59, 476
contamination xiii, 208, 373, 448-54,
    459, 461, 468, 471, 477, 482, 487
    (n.3)
contemplation 133
contextualization 429, 464, 472, 482-
    83, 485 (n.1)
conversion 242-43, 247, 251, 263
    (n.36), 365-67, 379 (n.20), 410
convictions 455, 459, 479
Coptic codices 30
Corneen, F. V. 111-12
corruption 371, 448-50, 463, 487
    (n.3), 488 (n.4)
Corwin, V. 38
cosmic theology 4
cosmic gods 9, 11, 248, 252, 440
cosmic religion 3-4
cosmo-psychology xvi
cosmogony 17 (n.31), 233
cosmological dualism xv, 29
cosmological 44, 78, 225, 227-28, 271,
    427 (n.38), 431, 434
cosmopolitan xvii, 187-90, 195, 198-
    99, 466
cosmos 111, 311, 342, 344, 465
Couliano, I. P. 313
courtesan 181
covenant 209, 442
    —new covenant 209
creatio ex nihilo 107-124, 465
creation xviii, 107-24, 159, 273-74,
    300, 310, 349-53, 453, 464
creativity 159
creator (see also demiurge) 10, 39,
    120-21, 231-32, 234, 281, 342,
    344, 351, 353, 441, 465, 469

creed 91, 363, 429-30, 436, 450-54, 475, 477-79, 483, 505 (n.76)
critical appropriation 471
cross 247, 251-52
cultural (factors) 449
culture 189-91, 194-98, 225, 339, 361, 365-66, 373, 432, 446
curiositas 365-66
curriculum 415
Cynic 99, 136, 142
Cyril of Jerusalem 234
Damascus 209-11, 279
Daniélou, J. 9, 442
Daube, D. 384
Dead Sea scrolls 312
deliverance 441
demiurge (creator) xvi, 6-8, 23, 25, 39, 41, 45, 115, 118, 279, 281, 310-11, 320 (n.26), 342, 351-52, 410-11, 440-41, 465-66, 469
Democritus 171 (n.20)
Descent of Ishtar 34
desire 126-27, 140
Desjardins, M. 35, 41
Deuteronomy 389
development 3, 19 (n.34)
dialectical xx, 227, 363, 367, 413, 434, 454, 477, 481-83
diaspora 102, 183, 190, 443-47, 484
Dinah 181
Diogenes 137
Dionysus 399
disciplines 389
discursive thought 410, 416
disease 126, 129, 141, 451
divine reason 126
docetic 38, 48 (n.4), 442
doctrines 86, 279, 282-86, 419, 436, 450, 475-79
dogma xvi, xx, 79-81, 84, 86, 89-91, 95 (n.23), 100-101, 223, 225, 286,

343, 367, 431, 433, 436-38, 448, 454, 458, 477, 485 (n.2), 505 (n.75)
dogmatism 4, 448
Donglas, M. 175
Dooyeweerd, H. 463, 466
Doresse, J. 65
double theology 8-9, 13, 25-26
doxa 89
doxic 91
Drijvers, H. J. W. 31, 42
Drower, E. S. 30
Drusiana 242-43
dualism xv, 4-5, 17 (n.31), 31, 39, 44, 99, 167, 179, 225, 310, 341-42, 497 (n.39)
dualism (Iranian) 5, 17, (n.30)
Dynamis 40
Dyrness, W. 464, 473-74
Ecclesiastes 415
ecclesiastical 285, 294
Ecphantus 324, 330, 334 (n.3)
ecumenical 476
education xvii, 366-67, 370, 395
Edwards, M. S. 296, 340
effeminate 166-67
Egypt 383-90
Egypt 31, 39, 42-44, 46, 241, 246, 309, 313, 315, 383-90, 444, 470
Eleatic Stranger 328
Eleazar (4 Macc) 136, 138
elite 47, 213-15, 420 (n.1)
elitism xvii, 282, 452, 478
emanationist 341-42
emotions 135-36
encyclia xvii, 193-94
Encyclopedia Britannica 111, 113
enkrateia 140, 143
Enlightenment 286, 294, 370-73, 476
Enneads (Plotinus) 295-300
enthusiasm 436, 450

Epiphanius 36
ephebate 444, 447
Epicureanism xvi, 160-68, 344, 363, 377 (n.12)
Epinomis 3
eschatology 17 (n.31)
esoteric 249
essence 92, 437, 494 (n.29)
Essenes 128, 132, 194, 274, 442
ethics 195-96, 416
Ethiopian 349
ethnicity 432-33, 443
eucharist 246, 249, 263 (n.36)
euergetēs 324
Eurysos 339-31
Eusebius of Caesarea 234, 469
evangelical 436
Evans, C. 271
Eve 26, 162-63, 176, 179, 311, 403
evil 310, 347, 461, 469
evil 39, 159-61, 459
excision 129
exclusive (Judaism) xiv
exclusive 347, 433, 443-44
exegesis 205-15, 313, 389
exegetical work xvii, 229, 435, 465
existentialist 497 (n.39)
Exodus xix, 383-88, 470
exoterikoi logoi (Aristotle) 9
experience 280, 285, 436, 450
faith 349, 369, 434-46, 449-53, 455, 461-62
fall 163, 225, 298, 441
Father (God) 247, 273, 281, 349, 351, 353
Feldman, L. 111
female 175, 180, 283, 396
feminine xvii, 166, 174-76, 397, 47
feminism 283, 476
Festugière, A. J. 2-6
Ficino, M. 383

fifth element 11
Foerster, W. 41
footgear 399-400
Fortunatus 242-43, 249
Fossum, J. E. 32, 37
fount/font 206-207, 430, 452
fragrances 401
Fredouille, J. C. xviii, 362, 365-70, 372-73, 462
freedom 104, 398, 455-56
Friedlander, M. 437
Gaiser, K. 5
gender distinctions xvii, 174-76
Genesis xvi, 26, 61, 311, 330-31, 383, 385-86, 439, 443, 465
gentile 101
Gilson, Etienne 110
gnōsis xiv-xv, xviii, 1, 6, 8, 24, 29, 34, 41, 46, 79, 82-83, 90, 226, 248, 267 (n.49), 268 (n.50), 279-87, 311, 409-20
—as "absolute knowledge" 437, 477, 481, 497 (n.38)
—definition 420 (n.1)
Gnosticism xiii-xx, 4, 224, 228, 234, 249, 431-42, 448-54
—definition xiv-xv, 279, 287 (n.2)
Gnostics 329, 332, 385-86
God (unknown) 225, 231, 441
Goethe 371
golden calf 384, 388
"good" 396
Goodenough, E. R. 330
gospel 74, 87, 225-30, 232, 332, 352, 382
Gospel of Egyptians 251, 272
Gospel of Philip 41, 249-50, 412
Gospel of Truth 41, 340, 412
grace 229, 233, 247, 328
grace/nature 281, 383

Grant, R. M. 2, 24, 27, 27 (n.3), 28 (n.16), 34, 40, 313
Grätz, H. 310, 437-48
Greek language 444-47, 486 (n.2)
—Greek New Testament (*koine*) 447
Green, H. 315, 345, 347
Gregory Thaumaturgus 387, 389
—*Address of Thanksgiving* 415-16
Gregory of Nazianzen 387
Gregory of Nyssa 390
Grenfell, B. P. 447
grond-motieven 463
Gruenwald, I. 310
Gunkel, Hermann 45
gymnasium 191, 401, 444-47
Gymnosophists 194
Haenchen, E. 36
Hagar 179, 194
Halakah 211
harlots 179-82
harmonia 324-25
Harnack, Adolf von xiii-xx, 29, 39, 69-98, 99-106, 223-35, 241-42, 251-52, 282, 285, 294-95, 302 (n.6), 369, 409, 418-20, 430-40, 443, 448-54, 457-58, 462, 475-84
—and Hellenization 85-88
—*History of Dogma* 77, 431
Hebrew 72, 101-102, 371, 383-88
hedone 126-27, 134
Hedrick, C. 276
Hegel 112, 294, 437, 477, 481
Helen 34
Hellas 371
Hellenic learning 388
Hellenism 108, 189-90, 226
Hellenism 71, 224, 362
Hellenistic culture xvii, 1, 4
hellenismos 70

Hellenization 99-106, 224-27, 235, 285, 418-20, 429-37, 442-51
—acute xiii, xix, 29, 82-84, 96 (n.26), 225, 241, 282, 294, 418, 431, 434, 452, 454
—chronic 418, 434, 452, 454
—definition xiv, 70-72, 99-100, 432
—motives 72-74
—nature 74-76
—negative 81-85
—radicality 76-77
—positive 78-81
Hengel, Martin 45, 445-46
Henrichs, A. 30
Heracleitus 192
Heracleon 40
Heracles (choice) 398, 444, 456
Herder 371
heresies 377 (n.11), 433, 440, 477, 485 (n.1)
heresiologists 287, 294, 296, 440, 465, 470
heresy xv, xix, 36, 38, 42, 91, 168, 241, 281-83, 288 (n.12), 294, 309, 314-15, 339-53, 362-63, 450, 477
—as *hairesis* 91, 362-63
heretical 366, 388-89, 430, 491 (n.14)
Hermetic Corpus 2-3, 5, 16 (n.28), 23, 25, 29, 31, 43
Herodian dynasty 190
heroic 403
heterodox 438, 442
hexis 89-90
hierarchy 9
high priest 445
Hippolytus 36, 39, 40, 347
historians 468, 483
historical 91-92, 279-87, 478
historical-critical method 430-31, 437, 449-51, 484, 488 (n.6)
historicism 92, 372, 479

historicizing 92, 476, 493 (n.29)

history 283-84, 316 (n.8), 436-37, 446

history, theories of 452

History of Religions School 29, 45, 295, 438, 494 (n.29)

Hochban, J. 349

Hodayot (thanksgiving hymns) 212

Hoffmann, J. 39

holocaust 312, 372, 458, 476

Homer 371

homologies 207

homosexuality 36

Horus 246

human nature 1, 13

humanity 41

Hunt, A. S. 447

hylics 352

"Hymn of the Pearl" 31

hypercosmic god 3

hypostasis 9, 274, 297-98, 311

Idealism (German) 294, 437

Idealism (Platonic) 241

idealization 371, 436, 450

Ideas (Plato) 3-4, 10, 89

identification 462, 468

identity 434, 449-52, 479, 482-83

idolatry 459, 470, 474

Ignatius 38, 42

illumination xix, 19 (n.36), 352-53, 386, 410, 496 (n.38)

illuminator 32

imagery 206, 214, 272-75, 452

imagination xviii, 283

imitation 324

immovable 265 (n.42)

immovable (unwavering) 244, 250-52, 256 (n.13)

immutability xvii, 256 (n.13), 509 (n.107)

impassability 442

inscriptions 447

institution 85, 282, 284, 435, 478, 481

intellect (*nous*) 11, 298, 414, 486 (n.2)

intellectual 73, 80, 89, 215, 226, 279, 418, 431, 435-36

intellectualism 84-85, 429, 435, 448, 464, 474, 477-79, 481, 490 (n.12)

intelligence 90

intelligible 116, 299, 417

intermarriage 459

interpolation 241, 248, 250-52, 272-73

interpretation 311

Interpretation of Knowledge 41

intuition 441

Iran 30, 241, 309, 313, 438

Iranian redeemer myth 30

Iraq 30

Irenaeus 31, 39-40, 47, 168, 231, 282, 294, 339-53, 385-86, 410-11, 434, 440, 465

ironic 82, 84, 343

irrational 140, 215

irrigation 205, 211-15

Isaac 129-30, 136-37, 214

Isaiah 210, 443

Ischomachus 401

Islam 455

Isocrates 444

isolation 461-62, 471

Israel (and Israelites) 73, 310, 383-37, 459, 470, 476

Jacob 137, 214

Jaeger, W. 4, 7-9, 24, 70, 441

Jamblichus 419

Janssens, Y. 272

Jeroboam 388

Jerome 139, 145

Jerusalem 361-65, 368-73, 398

Jesus Christ 32, 37-38, 40, 73, 230-31, 247, 275, 341, 436, 450

Jethro 387

jewellery 397-99, 400
Jewish 2, 34, 73-76, 110, 126, 134, 272, 294
Johannism 33
John (Apostle) 43, 241-52
Jonas, H. 5, 9, 39, 65, 227, 313, 440, 442
Joseph 386
Judaism xiv, 442
Judaism xiii-xx, 38, 72-76, 82, 101-102, 108, 159, 189-09, 224-25, 230-31, 247, 309-15, 370, 438-39, 456, 467-68
Jung, C. xv, 279-80, 284-86
Junod, Eric 246
Justin Martyr 36, 47, 168, 230, 234, 332, 348, 352, 361, 464
—*Second Apology* 36
Kaestli, J.-D. 246
Kerygma 104, 223, 494 (n.29)
kindred 248-52
kingdom 72
kingship 324-33, 334 (n.4)
Klapwijk, J. 461-62, 464, 470-72, 477, 482
"Know Thyself" 412
knowledge 1, 7-8, 26, 79, 279-83, 311, 340, 342, 348, 350-53, 363, 410-19, 437
Koenen, L. 30
Koester, H. 32, 34, 39, 42-44, 46, 64, 66, 282, 438-39
Kraemer, H. J. 5
Kronos 25, 441
Kuyper, A. (and Kuyperian) 460, 470, 507 (n.91)
Lacedaemonia 327
lady (*aste*) 182-83
language 446, 450, 468, 484, 486 (n.2)
Latourette, K. 431
law/gospel 224, 227-30, 435

law (Mosaic) 135, 138-44, 180, 191-92, 210, 353, 395
lawgiver 327
Layton, B. 40, 272-73
Lazarus 398
Leah 178
Leipzig 431
Levites 36, 180
liberation 13, 226, 384
libertinism 47, 345
light 413
liturgy 234, 455
Living Law (*nomos empsychos*) xviii, 323-33
Loewe, W. 346
logos xvi, 7, 25, 40, 78-80, 89, 94 (n.16), 111, 133, 143-44, 247-48, 285, 323-27, 329-31, 352, 414, 417, 433, 448
logos spermatikos 348, 464
Lot's wife 179
Lüdemann, G. 36
Luke (apostle) 38, 232
Luther, Martin 86, 224, 229, 431
Luttikhuizen, G. P. 34, 313
luxuries 396, 398-99
Lycomedes 243-45, 257 (n.16)
Maccabean 432, 445-46, 430 (n.71), 449 (n.12)
Maccabees (4 Maccabees) xvi, 109, 125, 134-41, 144, 442
MacRae, George 26, 33, 273-75
Macuch, R. 30
Maenads 399
magi 194
magic 2, 30, 387
magical 35
male 160, 180, 396, 398
Malef 37
Malina, B. 178
Malsbary, G. 207

Mandaean 30-34
Mandaeism 33, 64
Mani 30
Manichaean 30-31
Marcion xvii, 38, 64, 168, 223-35, 344, 347, 431
Marcionites 31, 38, 42, 349
marry 165, 177-78, 402
Marsanes 411
Marshall, P. 470, 474
Martin (Bp. Tours) 206-208, 452
martyr xix, 137-40, 234, 402-403, 452
Marxists 455
masculine 166, 174-77
masculinity 397
mastery 127
material xv, 8, 18 (n.31), 225, 298, 342, 352, 417, 441
matter 25, 111-13, 297, 411
matter 25, 111-13, 297, 411
May, Gerard 109
McCue, J. F. 44
McIntire, Thomas 104
mean (golden) 195, 466
mediator 315
Mediterranean 205, 214-15, 382
Méhat, A. 347
Memar Marqah 37
men/women 396-403
Menander 39
Mennonites 470
Menoceus 164
Messiah 9
Messina (1966 intl. conference) xiv, 17 (n.31), 283, 420 (n.1), 440
metacosmic (god) 13, 23
metanoia 77, 367
metaphor 205-15, 342, 362, 367, 382, 413, 416, 452
metaphysical 4, 8, 82, 226, 294, 436

methodology (historical) 287, 449-52, 478
metriopatheia 127, 129
Middle Platonism 7, 24, 299-300, 344, 441, 446
midrash 208-12, 311, 313
mimēmata 115-18
mind 163, 166
Minucius Felix 230
miracle 242
misogynists xix, 402-403, 469
missiology 429, 485 (n.1)
Mithraic 32
Moabites 179-80
modesty (*aidōs*) 396
monastic 133, 139, 461
Mondésert, C. 413
monogenes theos 33
monotheism (Jewish) 7, 26
Montanists 345, 366
moral perfection 131-32
Morard, Françoise 32
Moses xviii, 120, 128-29, 159-60, 164, 167, 192-93, 198, 214, 230-31, 234, 244, 323-32, 349, 386-87, 390, 456
mother 136-38, 163, 273, 342
motifs xiii, xviii-xix, 142, 159, 189-99, 201 (n.9), 313, 361-62, 365, 372-73, 382-83, 432, 457, 459, 461, 463, 466, 469, 472-72; see also *praeparatio evangelica*, *spoliatio*, and R. Niebuhr
muddy cups (and mud) 206-208, 213-15, 452
Musonius Rufus 325
mystery (rite) 248-49, 264 (n. 40), 416, 418, 430
mystical 285-86, 310, 312, 314
mystics 442

myth xv, 6, 34, 39, 104, 282-86, 316 (n.8), 346, 411, 438, 441-42
mythologizing 434, 439
mythology 25, 103, 297-301
Naasenes 36
Nag Hammadi 16 (n.24), 29, 31, 33, 40, 45, 63-64, 271, 276, 283-84, 293, 295, 297, 302 (n.7), 312, 345, 340, 411, 439-40, 476
natural law 349-50
natural revelation 348-53
Nature 126-27, 344, 415-16
Neill, S. 476
neo-Hellenist 371-73
neoclassicism 370
Neoplatonists 296-300, 418
New Testament 29, 39, 45, 64-66, 85, 140-42, 164, 247, 395, 452-53
Nicholas of Flüe 286
Niebuhr, H. R. xiii, 456, 459, 462, 469-73
Noah 193
nomos empsychos xviii, 323-33; see also "Living Law"
non-rational passions 82
Norea 283, 311
Norris, F. W. 42, 46
nous 10-12, 23, 40, 90, 298
Novella 332
Numbers (Old Testament) 208-209, 213-14
Numenius 307 (n.25)
numinous 281
Octavius 230
"Odes of Solomon" 31
oikoumēnē 71
Old Testament xvii, 6, 39, 46-47, 73, 81-82, 165, 224-35, 348, 385, 431, 433, 435, 439, 465, 469
"On the Origin of the World" 25
Onan 166

Ophite 41
opposites 160-61, 175-76, 396-97
oppositionist motif xviii, 361, 373, 459-62, 470
optimistic 3-5
Oqdoad 40
orator 365
Orbe, A. 352
Origen xix, 41, 44, 143, 145, 231, 233, 248, 387-90, 414-18, 434-35, 469-71
  —*Commentary on the Song of Songs* 415
  —*Contra Celsum (Reply to Celsus)* 44, 259 (n.24), 416
  —*On First Principles* 414
original 437, 450
origins xv, xviii, 1, 6, 29, 63, 312, 440-41
Orphic 13
orthodox xix, 45, 87, 281-84
orthodoxy 42, 107, 110, 336 (n.17), 341, 343, 345, 439, 477
Pachomian 31
pagan 339, 347-48, 351, 382-83
Pagels, Elaine 42
paideia 193-95
Palestine 432, 443, 445-46
Pantaenus 389
papyri 447
paradigm 383, 390
paradise 275, 414
paradox 471, 473
Paraphrase of Shem 32
parasite 77, 196
parasitic 29, 313, 440
parasitism 76
parochial 492 (n.16)
Parrott, D. 32
passions xvi-xvii, 125-58, 162, 173, 176-77, 244, 250, 264 (n.37), 268

(n.50), 410-11, 435, 466; see also
pathē
—Pythagorean xviii-xix, 17 (n.30),
323-34, 330-32, 334 (n.3), 337
(n.20), 396, 399, 402
Passover 9
pathē (see also passions) 125, 135-36,
139-40
patriarchs 209, 325-26, 350, 383
patristic 293-96, 438, 464, 469, 473
Paul (apostle) xv, 65, 101, 141-42,
227-29, 279, 283, 348, 363, 368,
431, 436, 447, 451-52
Paulinus of Périgueux 206-208, 212-
15, 452
Pearson, B. 39, 46, 310, 313, 412, 439
perfection 144, 369, 469
Perictione 399
Perkins, Pheme 341-42, 344
Perpetua 403
persecutions 234, 266 (n.45)
Persian 11, 30, 49 (n.7), 194, 442
pessimistic 3-5, 7, 25, 440
Peter (apostle) 139
Pétrement, S. 33, 37, 40-41, 45, 283,
295, 440
Pharaoh 214, 387
Pharisees 198
Phibionites 35
Philip (The Evangelist) 349
Philo xvi-xviii, 3-5, 29, 34, 107-28,
214-15, 230, 244-47, 314, 323-33,
344, 385-86, 389, 435, 442, 446,
452, 465-68
—*On the Confusion of Tongues*
117
—*On the Creation* 115
—*On Husbandry* 131
—*On the Sacrifice of Abel and
Cain* 28
—*Special Laws* 180

Philocalia (see also Cappadocians)
387-88
philosophers 437
philosophical 25, 343, 430, 433-48,
465
philosophize (*philosophein*) 79, 396
philosophy (Greek) xv-xix, 2-7, 18
(n.31), 19 (n.36), 79-80, 85, 88, 94
(n.14), 134, 137, 159, 194-95,
285, 297, 299, 344, 347, 353, 363-
64, 367, 369, 395-96, 434, 463
—of history 104
—of religion 419, 434
—philosopher's cloak 403
—philosopher-king 11
—physical 410
Phineas 180
phoenix 281
physics 415-16
pietistic 87
piety 126, 132, 135, 137, 196-98
pilgrimage 443
Pindar 327
pious 141-42
Pistus Sophia 35
plagiarism 298
planetary gods 9
Plato 2-7, 11-13, 88, 118, 120, 139,
182, 192, 241, 247, 251, 297, 344,
351, 363, 469
—*Laws* 3
—*Phaedo* 5, 13, 89
—*Phaedrus* 298
—*Politicus* 10
—*Republic* 29, 89, 302 (n.7), 440
—*Seventh Letter* 416
—*Timaeus* xvi, 3-4, 10, 115, 119,
159, 289-99, 465-67 Platonic
psychology 126
Platonic 89

Platonism xvi, xix, 18 (n.31), 88, 136, 140, 145, 161, 194, 295-96, 300, 412, 414, 430-33, 440, 466; see also Middle Platonism and Neoplatonism

pleasure xvi, 126-27, 133-35, 160-67, 398; see also *hedone*

pleroma 40, 172 (n.20), 264 (n.37), 342

Plotinus 41, 293-300, 383, 440

pluralism xx, 348, 455-56, 459, 474, 479-80

Plutarch 12, 24, 325, 344

pneumatic 41, 342, 353

poet 211-12

Poirier, P. H. 31, 271

polarization 443, 446

poleis 71

political 432-33, 446, 454, 459, 479, 484

pollution 452

Polycarp 42

polymorphic 245-51

polytheism 167

Porphyry 296-97

Posidonius 136

positivism 8, 372, 437

post-liberal 476, 488 (n.6)

Potiphar's wife 179

praeparatio evangelica motif xiii, xviii-xix, 142-44, 159, 189-90, 193-94, 232, 235, 332, 382-83, 395, 435, 457, 465-66, 469-70, 472, 482

praescriptio 362, 375 (n.3)

pre-Christian baptismal sect 32

pre-Christian 32-33, 45

pre-Christian Alexandrian Gnosticism 34

pre-Christian Gnosticism 31, 45, 50 (n.26), 63-64, 438-39

privatized 455-56

Proclus 419

Prodicus of Ceos 398

progress (*prokopē*) 415-16, 419

prokopē 367; see also progress

prokoptōn 129, 131, 134, 138

Prologue 32

propaideia 142, 193-94

prophets 342

prophets 231, 233, 235

prostitute 398, 401

Protennoia 271-76

Protestantism 86, 224, 430, 439, 450, 477

providence xviii, 11, 166-67, 344, 347, 350-54, 465, 469

pseudo-Aristotelian 325

psyche (see also soul) 12

psychic 41, 342, 352

psychology xv, 279-81, 284, 287, 413

Ptolemaeans 349

Ptolemaeus 340, 409, 411-12;
—*Letter to Flora* 412

Ptolemy 40, 352, 432, 445

pure 66, 141, 206-207, 213-15, 371, 429, 431, 449, 477, 483, 487 (n.3), 488 (n.4)

purist 223-24, 373, 430, 439

purity 449-52, 454, 458-58, 478

purple dye 397-99

Pythagoras 192, 469

Quispel, G 2, 9, 34, 411, 439

Qumran xvii, 209-14, 314, 452

rabbinic (exegesis) 219 (n.20), 314, 347

Radday, Y. T. 384

rainfall 205-207, 212-15

Ramsay, W. 447

ratio 7, 351

rational xix, 25, 82, 126, 281, 286, 346, 352, 409-19, 435, 454, 479, 496 (n.38)

—rationalism 2, 294, 438
—rational principal 433
Reale, G. 5, 113
reason xvi, 13, 82, 130, 133, 135, 137, 141, 143, 284, 329, 331-32, 343, 351, 371, 415, 417, 435; see also *ratio* and rational
Rebecca 179
Rebecca's children 314
receptacle 115, 118
redaction 271-72, 276
redeemer xvii, 26, 32, 274-76, 458
redemption 226, 283
reform 227, 436, 471
Reformation (Protestant) 85, 87, 224, 286
reformational philosophy 460, 462-64, 466, 468, 470, 474
Reformed churches 478
regula fidei 364, 370, 451, 462
reincarnation 40, 268 (n.50)
Reitzenstein, R. 30, 438
relativism 437
religion xv, xx, 2, 9, 79, 226, 228, 285, 418, 438, 446, 45758, 478, 480
—and culture xix, 432, 449, 454-75, 479-80
—and culture opposed 459-62
—Judaic 9
—and modern pluralism 455-57
—Oriental 418
—Philo's synthesis of religion and philosophy 464-68
—and *praeparatio* and *spoliatio* motifs 469-75
—R. Niebuhr's classification 457-59
—synthesis religion 462-64
religion-and-politics 449, 456, 480
religious 458, 463, 474, 496 (n.38)
religionsgeschichtliche Schule 438
religious philosophy 294

religious autonomy 445
repristination 70, 286, 451
reproduction 175-76, 459
resurrection 242-51, 255 (n.11), 265 (n.40), 269 (n.51) 442
revealer 26, 353
revelation xv, 26, 39, 41, 81, 225, 231, 281, 332, 348-53, 387, 398, 418, 439, 451, 496 (n.38)
rhetoric 367, 402, 472
rhetorical 343, 364, 366
righteousness 210, 230, 328, 349
rites 445
Ritschl, A. 476
Roberge, Michel 32
Roberts, A. 351
Roberts, Colin 43
Robinson, James M. 33, 45, 275-76, 282, 438
Robinson, T. A. 42-43, 66
Robinson, Ges. Schenke 271
Roman 369
Romanticism 108, 370-72, 430, 436, 450, 477-78
Rome 295, 371
royalty 326, 328
Rudolf, K. 27, 30, 32, 37, 271, 273, 438
rule 126
"rule of faith" (see also *regula fidei*) xix, 345, 362-64, 370
Rule (Damascus Rule) 209-10
Rumscheidt, M. 476
Runia, David 119, 467-68, 471
sabbath 443
sacrament 248-48, 264 (n.40), 442
sacrifices 227
sage (see also wise men) 142, 209, 244, 249, 326-31, 387
saints 140
Sakla 273

salvation xv, 24, 26, 40, 48 (n.4), 225, 246-48, 311, 332, 347-48, 418, 442; see also soteriology
Samaria (and Samaritan) 36-37, 309, 314
Sandmel, Samuel 111
sapiential 275-76
Sarah 179
Saturninus 39
savior 246, 250
Schenke, H.-M. 438
schisms 285
Schleiermacher, F. 476
Schoedel, W. R. 38
Scholastic 486 (n.2)
Scholem, G. 310, 312
school 414
Schrodt, P. 477
Schürer, Emil 111-12
science (*wissenschaft*) 434
science 409, 413, 420 (n.2)
"scratcher" 209
Second Apocalypse of James 41
Second Treatise of the Great Seth 40
secret 342-43, 347-48, 353
sectarians (*hairetikoi*) 296, 313, 437-39, 442
secularization 434, 449-50, 455, 463, 474, 477, 479
secularizing 241, 362, 370
seed 452-53
Segal, A. 314-15
Seleucids 432, 444-45
self-control (*sōphrosyne*) 396
self-definition xx, 481
self-identification 450, 453-54, 483
self-knowledge 24
self-restraint 133, 142
Semonides 402
sense-perceptible 412

senses 163, 166
separatist 461
Septuagint 116, 190, 447
serpent xvi, 127, 161-68
Seth 311
Sethian 41, 249-51, 266 (nn. 46, 47,), 272-73, 297
sex, sexuality 175-83, 265 (n.44), 283, 459
Shelton, J. C. 31
Shepherd of Hermas 142
sickness 138
Sider, R. 364
Siegfried, Carl 112
silence 40
Silenus 12-13
Silranus 276
Simon (and Simonian) 34-37, 41, 64, 309, 345
simplicity 286, 431
sin, sinfulness 143, 325, 398
skēnē 33
skeptical 25, 90
Skeptics 192
slaves 384-85, 387
sleep 255 (n.11), 441
Smith, J. Z. (*Drudgery Divine*) 66
Smith, Morton 36, 295
socio-economic 52 (n.43)
socio-political 345
sociological 34
Socrates 400
Sodomites 166-67, 193
Solomon 387
Son 273
Sophia xvii, 9, 13, 26, 40-41, 264 (n.37), 273-76, 283, 410-11 — fall of 34, 411
Sophists 191
soteriology xv-xvi, 17 (n.31), 44, 228, 275, 316 (n.4), 342, 490 (n.11)

soul xvii, 12-13, 40, 126-27, 133-34, 182, 215, 298, 414-16, 435
—tripartite soul 136, 139, 161, 163; see also *psyche*
sovereignty 162-64, 176, 466-67
sovereignty of God 110, 120
space 115-17
sparks 6, 311, 441
Spartan 331, 371, 398
Spinoza 109
spirit 75-76, 79, 89, 91, 93 (n.12), 225, 227, 247
spiritual xv, 8, 183, 248-49, 251-52, 284, 386, 441, 476
spiritualizing 82-83
spoils 383-90
spoliatio motif xiii, xix, 159, 189-93, 201 (n.11), 382-91, 457, 466, 469-72
stability 243
stages 76, 144
Stauros-Hores 264 (n.37)
stave/staff 209-12
Stoa 3-4, 419
Stobaeus 324-25, 330
Stoic 331, 344, 351-53, 363
Stoicism 24, 99, 125-26, 136-37, 140-41, 145, 161, 329, 331, 367
stratigraphy 271-73, 275-76
Stroumsa, G. 310
subtle 84
Sulpicius Severus 206-207
superior 373, 456, 462, 481
supernatural (knowledge) xv, 18 (n.31), 248, 251, 441
surgery 129
symbol xv, xvii, xix, 91, 104, 210, 214, 284, 409-20, 434
synagogue 74, 183, 443
syncretism 190-91, 223, 235, 309, 341, 348, 430, 439, 444, 449, 482

synthesis xiii, xvi, 81, 120, 126, 332, 361, 368, 432, 450, 459, 462-68, 475
Syria 42
tabernacle 384, 386
targum 208-209, 311
Tcherikover, V. 445
teacher 210-12, 218 (n.19)
tensions 121
Tertullian xviii, 12, 47, 168, 231-32, 347, 349, 361-73, 403, 440, 462, 471
Tertullian's *De Praescriptionibus* 361-65, 368, 370, 372
Tertullian's *Apology* 368, 370
testimonia 441
tetrachord 126
Thanksgiving hymns (*Hodayot*) xviii, 211-14, 452
Theano 399
Thecla 405
theologians 492 (n.19)
theological 432-37, 441, 447
theological xix-xx
theology, liberal 476
theology, dogmatic 476
theology, double xvi
Theophilus of Antioch 230-31
Theophrastus 70
theoria 90
Therapeutae 128, 132, 139, 179, 194
thought 103
thought (*epinoia*) 36
Three Steles of Seth 37
Thunder 34-35, 273
Tiberius Julius Alexander 191
Titans 13
Torah xvi, 9, 126-27, 135, 138, 141, 193-94, 197-98, 208-13, 274
Torah 310-12, 442, 480
torture 135, 137

Tröger, Karl-Wolfgang 45, 313
tradition 230-32, 235, 294, 313, 346-48, 382, 397, 430
Trajan 35, 38
trajectory 276
transcendent xv, 4-5, 8, 10, 12-13, 19 (n.36), 26, 40, 298, 311, 409, 441
transcending 163, 194
transfiguration 247, 249
transform 225, 232
transformation xviii, 107-108, 190, 249-50, 269 (n.50), 365, 373, 462, 468, 469-73, 482
—inverse 471, 482; see also motifs: *spoliatio*
translatio 207-208, 215, 216 (n.6)
transmigration 76-77
Trimorphic Protennoia xvii, 323, 271-76, 438
Tripartate Tractate 44, 412
triumphalism 294, 458, 476
Tübingen School 294, 437, 481
Turner, J. 271
typology 346, 375 (n.2), 382, 386
universal 72, 101, 104, 224, 344, 430
universalistic 341, 444
universality xiv, 74, 433
unknown god 8
Unknown Gospel 43
unmoved mover 4, 5
Unnik, V. W. C. 9, 313
Vallée, G. 342, 345
Valentinian Exposition 41
Valentinianism 29, 35, 168, 249
Valentinians 35, 40-42, 250-51, 264 (n.37), 344, 352, 364, 409-12, 414, 417-19
Valentinus xix, 40-41, 64, 340, 434
Verweltlichung 420, 434
vice 398
virgins 132, 177-79, 186 (n.13)

virtue (see also *aretē*) xvii, xix, 89, 129, 131-32, 135, 137, 142, 160, 166, 396, 398-99, 402, 416, 469
Vollenhoven, D. 462-63
Voltaire 370
Vorlage 33
vulnerability 396
war 315
Waszink, J. H. 12
water xvii, 205-15, 452
well 208-11, 214
Whig 101
whiggish 87
white 397-98
whore 398
Widengren, G. 30
Wilson, S. G. 224, 315
Wilson, R. McL. xv, 6, 24, 36, 65, 441
Winston, David 109, 112-19
wisdom 9, 26, 79, 132, 166, 178, 214, 227, 271-76, 311, 327, 331, 361, 364, 382-82, 388-89, 415-17, 469
Wisdom of Solomon 111
wise men 402
Wisse, F. 343
wives 164, 178
Wolfson, H. A. 109, 112-19, 121, 174
women xvii, xix, 60 (n.122), 132, 138, 163, 166, 173-83, 283, 395-403, 466, 469
Word 353
world-flight 382
world-soul 7, 11, 298, 410, 441
worship 446
Xenocrates 12
Xenophon's *Oeconomicus* 401
Yahweh 310-11
Zeller, E. 112
Zeno 192
Zoroaster 296-97
Zostrianos 296-97